LEGITIMACY AND CRIMINAL JUSTICE

LEGITIMACY AND CRIMINAL JUSTICE

International Perspectives

Tom R. Tyler
editor

Russell Sage Foundation
New York

The Russell Sage Foundation

Library of Congress Cataloging-in-Publication Data

Legitimacy and criminal justice : international perspectives / edited by Tom R. Tyler.
　　p. cm.
　Includes bibliographical references and index.
　ISBN 978-0-87154-876-4 (alk. paper)
　1. Criminal justice, Administration of. 2. Social policy. 3. Law enforcement. I. Tyler, Tom R.
　　HV7419.L45 2008
　　364—dc22

2007010929

Text design by Suzanne Nichols.

RUSSELL SAGE FOUNDATION
112 East 64th Street, New York, New York 10021
10 9 8 7 6 5 4 3 2 1

TABLE OF CONTENTS

About the Authors   ix

PART I   INTRODUCTION   1

Chapter 1   Preface   3
                Michael Tonry

Chapter 2   Legitimacy and Criminal Justice:
                International Perspectives   9
                Tom R. Tyler, Anthony Braga, Jeffrey Fagan,
                Tracey Meares, Robert Sampson,
                and Chris Winship

Chapter 3   The Foundations of Legitimacy   30
                David J. Smith

PART II   THE ROLE OF LEGITIMACY IN POLICING   59

Chapter 4   Introduction   61

Chapter 5   Policing, New Public Management,
                and Legitimacy in Britain   63
                Mike Hough

Chapter 6   Rebuilding Legitimacy and Police
                Professionalism in an Emerging Democracy:
                The Slovenian Experience   84
                Gorazd Meško and Goran Klemenčič

Chapter 7   Police Legitimacy in Chile   115
                 Hugo Frühling

Chapter 8   Building Legitimacy Through
                 Restorative Justice   146
                 John Braithwaite

PART III   FORMAL AND COMMUNITY-BASED
                 ROUTES TO LEGITIMACY   163

Chapter 9   Introduction   165

Chapter 10   When the Poor Police Themselves: Public
                 Insecurity and Extralegal Criminal-Justice
                 Administration in Mexico   167
                 Jennifer L. Johnson

Chapter 11   Between Damage Reduction and Community
                 Policing: The Case of Pavão-Pavãozinho-
                 Cantagalo in Rio de Janeiro's Favelas   186
                 Graziella Moraes D. da Silva and Ignacio Cano

Chapter 12   Popular Justice in the New South Africa:
                 Policing the Boundaries of Freedom   215
                 John Comaroff and Jean Comaroff

PART IV   LEGITIMACY AND MINORITY-GROUP
                 RELATIONS   239

Chapter 13   Introduction   241

Chapter 14   Police, Justice, and Youth Violence in France   243
                 Sophie Body-Gendrot

Chapter 15   Ethnic Minorities and Confidence in
                 the Dutch Criminal-Justice System   277
                 *Catrien Bijleveld, Heike Goudriaan,
                 and Marijke Malsch*

Chapter 16   Legitimacy and Criminal Justice: Inequality
and Discrimination in the German
Criminal-Justice System   302
Hans-Jörg Albrecht

Chapter 17   Minorities, Fairness, and the Legitimacy of
the Criminal-Justice System in France   333
Sebastian Roché

Index   381

ABOUT THE AUTHORS

TOM R. TYLER is University Professor at New York University, where he teaches in the psychology department and the law school.

HANS-JÖRG ALBRECHT is director at the Max Planck Institute for Foreign and International Criminal Law in Freiburg, Germany.

CATRIEN BIJLEVELD is senior researcher at the Netherlands Institute for the Study of Crime and Law Enforcement (NSCR) and a professor in criminology at the Free University, Amsterdam.

SOPHIE BODY-GENDROT is a University Professor at Sorbonne-Paris IV and the Director of the Center of Urban Studies.

ANTHONY BRAGA is a senior research associate at the Kennedy School of Government, Harvard University, and at the Berkeley Center for Criminal Justice at the University of California, Berkeley.

JOHN BRAITHWAITE is an Australian Research Council Federation Fellow in the Regulatory Institutions Network (RegNet), College of Asia and the Pacific, Australian National University.

IGNACIO CANO is Professor of Research Methodology at the State University of Rio de Janeiro.

JEAN COMAROFF is Bernard E. and Ellen C. Sunny Distinguished Service Professor of Anthropology at the University of Chicago and director of the Chicago Center for Contemporary Theory.

JOHN COMAROFF is the Harold H. Swift Distinguished Professor of Anthropology at the University of Chicago and a Senior Research Fellow at the American Bar Foundation.

JEFFREY FAGAN is professor of law and public health at Columbia University, and director of the Center for Crime, Community and Law at Columbia Law School.

HUGO FRÜHLING is a professor and director of the Center for the Study of Public Safety at the Institute of Public Affairs of the University of Chile.

HEIKE GOUDRIAAN is assistant professor at the Faculty of Law, Department of Criminal Law and Criminology of Leiden University, The Netherlands.

MIKE HOUGH is professor of criminal policy at the School of Law, King's College London and the director of the Institute for Criminal Policy Research.

JENNIFER L. JOHNSON is assistant professor of sociology at Kenyon College.

GORAN KLEMENČIČ is a senior lecturer in criminal law and police powers at the Faculty of Criminal Justice, University of Maribor, Slovenia.

MARIJKE MALSCH is a senior researcher at the Netherlands Institute for the Study of Crime and Law Enforcement (NSCR) in Leiden, the Netherlands.

TRACEY MEARES is professor of law at Yale Law School.

GORAZD MEŠKO is an associate professor of criminology and dean at the Faculty of Criminal Justice, University of Maribor, Slovenia, an honorary visiting fellow at the Department of Criminology, University of Leicester, UK, and president of the Slovenian Association of Criminal Law and Criminology.

GRAZIELLA MORAES D. DA SILVA is currently a Ph.D. candidate at Harvard University.

SEBASTIAN ROCHÉ is a professor of political science, senior research fellow at the CNRS (National Center for Scientific Research) and at the Institute of Political Science, University of Grenoble, France, and also teaches at the National Academy of Police Commissioners (ENSP) in Lyon.

ROBERT SAMPSON is Henry Ford II Professor of the Social Sciences at Harvard University.

DAVID J. SMITH is Honorary Professor of Criminology at the University of Edinburgh, Scotland, co-director of the Edinburgh Study of Youth Transitions and Crime, and visiting professor at the London School of Economics.

MICHAEL TONRY is Sonosky Professor of Law and Public Policy, University of Minnesota, and senior fellow, Netherlands Institute for the Study of Crime and Law Enforcement, Leiden.

CHRIS WINSHIP is Diker-Tishman Professor of Sociology at Harvard University and also a member of the faculty of the Kennedy School of Government.

PART I

Introduction

Preface

Michael Tonry

This volume derives from an exploratory conference whose participants sought to learn about differences between the United States and other Western countries in how and what scholars, practitioners, offenders, and the general public think about legitimacy in the criminal-justice system. The papers initially commissioned for the conference dealt with European countries but were augmented by papers on a number of Latin American countries, South Africa, and Slovenia.

This speculative venture has had a valuable payoff. We have learned that systematic scholarly interest on legitimacy is mostly American; that not much systematic research or theory building has occurred elsewhere; that problems of legitimacy are important everywhere; and that a number of plausible, testable hypotheses can be formulated that can guide future inquiry. Put differently, the comparative and cross-national study of legitimacy is an important, policy-relevant subject in need of a research community to do the work.

The papers are centrally concerned with two questions: whether structural differences between countries' legal systems generate different levels of perceived legitimacy in the eyes of citizens generally and those accused of crimes particularly, and whether the views of majority and minority groups differ substantially.

Neither question can be answered with much confidence. There are no comparative or cross-national literatures. The best that can be done is to commission papers on individual countries and through them try to look across national boundaries.

The scholarly literatures on procedural justice and legitimacy are distinctly American. It would be an exaggeration to refer even to nascent literatures in other

English-speaking countries, continental Europe, or elsewhere. Why that is the case is a third important question.

My guess is that the answer centers on the United States' distinctive constitutional scheme premised on notions of limited powers of government and entrenched rights of citizens, compared with the étatist traditions of Europe, including Britain, and much of the rest of the world. Concepts of vested substantive rights against the state and procedural protections against state intrusion were probably predicates to the development of a theory of procedural justice and a research agenda aiming to understand the effects of alternative ways of implementing procedural protections. This American hegemony will not last because these differences between the United States and Europe are eroding. Within Europe, the application of the European Declaration of Human Rights and the decisions of the European Court of Human Rights are creating stronger substantive rights and procedural protections. That, however, is a work in progress and is unlikely yet to have fundamentally affected the sensibilities of practitioners or the agendas of researchers.

It is possible, however, to tease out from the essays in this volume and from related literatures some hypotheses relating to the two main questions. Before doing that, I need to bound the term "legitimacy" as I use it here. I am concerned with two conceptions: perceived legitimacy of state institutions and processes, particularly the courts and the police, in the eyes of the public at large; and the perceived legitimacy of courts and police in the eyes of people who have direct dealings with them.

The first of these, a "Caesar's wife's" notion, is the prevalent European conception of legitimacy and results in emphases on transparency of process, accountability of decisionmakers, and complete separation of justice-system processes from political influence.

The second, the prevalent American conception, is more particularist and focuses on how people's experiences in the criminal-justice system affect their perceptions of it.

Whether people in general regard institutions and their operations as legitimate is germane to confidence in government, cooperation with government, and willingness to participate in public life. Whether suspects and defendants believe that police and courts are legitimate is germane to their general satisfaction with their criminal-justice experiences, their willingness to accept decisions adverse to their interests, and their willingness to cooperate with agents of the state. The literature tells us that the extent to which perceived legitimacy in either sense is higher or lower turns on such factors as whether rules are seen to be fairly and consistently applied, whether people are given opportunity to have their say, whether citizens' claims are given respectful consideration, and whether decisionmakers are seen to be fair and impartial.

A number of testable hypotheses emerge from the essays in this volume and relevant literatures:

First, perceived legitimacy of the police, public confidence in the police, and citizens' willingness to cooperate with police, especially among disadvantaged minority groups, are likely to be higher when police interact with citizens in ways that are respectful, unbiased, and nonviolent. As the essays in this volume on Argentina, France, Germany, Mexico, Slovenia, and South Africa attest, these conditions often are not met, especially in relation to minority groups.

Second, perceived legitimacy, public confidence, and willingness to cooperate may be higher among minority groups in the context of the courts than in that of the police. Although people in general express greater confidence in the police than in the courts, minority respondents express less confidence in the police and are much more likely to believe police to be brutal or dishonest. Research on courts also shows lower levels of minority satisfaction with them, but differences between blacks and whites are much less than the differences in levels of confidence of the two groups in the police.

Third, perceived legitimacy, public confidence, and citizens' willingness to cooperate in court proceedings are likely to be higher for all groups when prosecutors and judges are nonpartisan career civil servants than when they are partisan, politically elected or selected, and nonprofessional. The strongest evidence for this comes from Dutch studies, and the underlying logic should apply to other countries.

Fourth, hypotheses become harder to formulate after that. There are good a priori reasons to suppose that features of criminal courts in European civil law systems achieve greater legitimacy in the eyes of defendants than do equivalent features of Anglo-Saxon common law systems. The former are characterized by professional judges and prosecutors, traditions in most countries that a guilty plea is by itself an insufficient basis for a conviction and a requirement that every case be tried, requirements that judges explain sentences in writing in every case, automatic rights to appeal convictions with, in many countries, a right to a trial de novo on appeal. The latter are characterized by politically selected and attuned officials, assembly-line case processing, plea bargaining as the predominant form of case disposition, oral statements of reasons for sentences, and limited rights of appeal.

Each of the features listed for European justice systems is on its face more likely to imply fair consideration, even-handedness, and impartiality than are the features listed for Anglo-Saxon countries. But because there are significant differences between countries within broad civil law and common law categories, and because a system's formal structure and putative procedures and values do not necessarily predict how cases are handled, useful hypotheses are most likely to be available at national or subnational levels.

MINORITY GROUPS, THE POLICE, AND LEGITIMACY

Problems of police legitimacy are similar everywhere: interactions among police culture and structure, overrepresentation among offenders of members of some minority groups, young men's high levels of testosterone, and cultural differences appear to contribute to comparable conflicts arising between police and young minority men and to relatively low police legitimacy in the eyes of minority groups.

Survey evidence in the United States has for years shown that blacks have considerably less confidence in the police than do whites, have considerably lower confidence in police honesty, and are three times more likely to believe that police brutality is common. The evidence is less extensive in England, but there, too, Afro-Caribbeans have less confidence in the police than do whites, and are less likely to believe that police respect the rights of suspects.

The American literatures on legitimacy and procedural justice suggest that even-handedness, impartiality, respectfulness, and a chance to say one's piece are predicates of greater perceived legitimacy than when those characteristics are absent or not followed. If that is true, it would be astonishing if perceptions of police legitimacy held by some minority groups were not lower than those of majority populations. Disproportionately, many members of minority groups live disadvantaged lives; commit crimes; are stereotyped by others as deviant; are arrested, convicted, and imprisoned; and have emotionally charged encounters with the police. If police officers are as or more racially or ethnically biased as other members of their subgroups in their countries, as one would expect them to be, the prospects are high that minority suspects will be treated unfairly, or in ways they perceive as unfair. Many of the essays in this volume confirm these speculations. Police relations with minority groups in South America, France, and Slovenia are fraught with tension, stereotyping, imputed bad motives, and misunderstanding.

MINORITY GROUPS, THE COURTS, AND LEGITIMACY

It is likely that courts, by contrast, more often than the police behave in ways that are conducive to perceived legitimacy, though this no doubt varies widely from place to place, between countries, and within them. Most of the chapters in this volume focus on police issues. Only a few—those on Germany, France, and the Netherlands—touch on the judicial system experiences of minority suspects. The scant evidence they adduce does not suggest the existence of large disparities in court outcomes, even though higher minority arrest rates produce large disparities in imprisonment rates. Values of equal treatment characterize most Western judicial systems, and conditions giving rise to emotional confrontation are many fewer in the court system than with the police.

It would be surprising if perceptions of court illegitimacy were as great as those of police illegitimacy. The only European study on this point that I know of, done in England by Roger Hood and Stephen Shute (Shute, Hood, and Seemungal 2005), bears this out. Three-quarters of white suspects felt fairly treated by the English courts and slightly less than three-quarters of nonwhites felt this way. Though there was a difference of a couple of percentage points, the main message was that there was very little difference.

PARTISANSHIP, POLITICS, AND PROFESSIONALISM

Given these observations, there are plausible a priori reasons to suppose that continental civil-law systems achieve higher levels of perceived legitimacy in the eyes of suspects than do Anglo-Saxon common law systems. Comparatively speaking, though, the difference between court systems that are and are not directly linked to partisan politics may be more important—a series of ingenious studies by Jan de Keijser and in his colleagues in the Netherlands suggests just this (Eiffers and de Keijser 2006). Research in the English-speaking countries indicates that very large percentages of lay people believe that judges are too lenient, even though this belief is based on substantial underestimates of the severity of sentences judges imposed, and even though survey respondents often support sentences less harsh than judges impose.

De Keijser and his colleagues wanted to learn whether Dutch citizens thought judges too lenient (they did), whether citizens would impose harsher sentences than judges did (unlike in the English-speaking countries, they would), and whether judges knew their sentences were perceived as too lenient by citizens and were in fact less severe than citizens would impose—the answer to both questions was yes. Perhaps the most interesting question was whether laypeople believed that judges should pay more attention to their, the laypersons', punishment preferences and change the sentences they imposed accordingly. They did not. They wanted judges to exercise their own best judgment.

The best way to understand de Keijser's findings is that citizens have confidence in the integrity and independence of the judiciary and want judges to make the decisions, in individual cases, that they believe to be the most appropriate, irrespective of what the citizenry might think. This implies a high degree of trust in the judiciary. Dutch judges and prosecutors are not elected, nor are they selected on partisan political bases. Most are career officials. Most subscribe to the notion that they should be, and should be seen to be, virtuous, in the sense of being completely impartial and completely nonpolitical. Contrast this with the American system of partisan elections and media-cultivating officials, or the English system of criminal justice bureaucracies headed by partisan politicians who openly undertake to influence the outcomes of individual cases.

In most of continental Europe, judges and prosecutors are career civil servants who self-select into those career lines as university students and progress along career ladders in which they are socialized to hold the professional values of independence, impartiality, nonpartisanship, and professionalism. If de Keijser's findings generalize to other European countries, the implication is that continental legal systems may foster greater legitimacy in the eyes of citizens than do the United States' and England's. If true, this is ironic, because a primary rationale of American partisan selection methods, and England's recent descent into penal populism, is the assertion that public confidence will be greater if citizens believe officials are accountable to public opinion.

CIVIL-LAW AND COMMON-LAW COUNTRIES

Plausible hypotheses can be developed that various procedural features of continental civil-law systems should be perceived by suspects and defendants as more legitimate than corresponding features of common-law systems—for example, in civil law, the requirement that a trial take place in every case versus disposition of most cases by guilty pleas and plea bargains. Many features of American criminal court processes would probably shock most officials and citizens alike in Europe, for example, federal "real offense sentencing," in which defendants are punished for alleged crimes of which they were acquitted, or the common practice of conditioning a plea bargain on the defendant's agreement to waive rights to appeal questionable practices.

It is not easy to design genuinely cross-national comparative research to delve into these matters. It is somewhat easier to imagine laboratory research on narrow procedural differences. The difficulty, however, even if practicable projects can be undertaken, will be to disentangle the effects on perceived legitimacy of particular practices and procedures from the effects of differences in the independence and nonpoliticization of court systems.

Fortunately, we now have a volume that raises these questions. A European literature on legitimacy in relation to police and courts may be nascent, but genuinely comparative inquiry into the nature and effects of differences in legal systems is nonexistent, a reality that this project has exposed.

REFERENCES

Eiffers, Henk, and Jan W. de Keijser. 2006. "Different Perspectives, Different Gaps: Does the Public Demand a More Responsive Judge?" Leiden, Netherlands: Netherlands Institute for the Study of Crime and Law Enforcement.

Shute, Stephen, Roger Hood, and Florence Seemungal. 2005. *A Fair Hearing? Ethnic Minorities in the Criminal Courts.* Cullompton, Devon, England: Willan.

CHAPTER 2

Legitimacy and Criminal Justice: International Perspectives

Tom R. Tyler, Anthony Braga, Jeffrey Fagan, Tracey Meares, Robert Sampson, and Chris Winship

All societies create institutions and authorities whose purpose is to maintain social order. Two key institutions are the police and the courts, agencies that work cooperatively to create and enforce laws and regulations that shape public conduct in socially desirable ways. Societal viability is linked to the effectiveness of those authorities and institutions and societies cannot survive without being able to enforce their rules (Tyler and Huo 2002).

This need for a strategy of social-order maintenance is universal across societies, but the degree of variation in approaches to law enforcement is striking. Within the United States, for example, cities are the primary level at which policing occurs, and American cities differ markedly in their approaches to policing. Some cities, such as Boston and Chicago, have been characterized by cooperative styles of policing, which emphasize a partnership between the police and communities. Other cities, such as New York and Los Angeles, are characterized by a more distant, even antagonistic, relationship .between the police and the community. Furthermore, within all cities the police deal with many communities, and issues about the nature of policing are especially central to the relationships of the police with minority-dominated communities.

The Russell Sage Foundation working group on the criminal justice system focuses on an issue that is central to the effectiveness of legal authorities in all societies—their legitimacy among the people in the communities where they function. Although it is possible to imagine that legal authorities might control communities through the use of sanctions or rewards, both history and recent social science research argue that the effectiveness of legal authorities in maintaining social order benefits from, and may depend upon, their ability to motivate voluntary cooperation that is based upon a perception of their legitimacy (Tyler 2006a, 2006b). Legitimacy is of particular importance in societies such as the United States, in which there are political, social, and economic divisions among the members of different ethnic and cultural groups.

LEGITIMACY

The focus of this volume is on legitimacy in the context of the criminal-justice system. To examine this issue, we must first examine three larger conceptual questions. The first concerns the definition of legitimacy. The second concerns the reasons legitimacy is important within a social system. Finally, we need to explore what factors create and sustain legitimacy, that is, what forms of social organization or what dynamics of authority are viewed by the members of particular social groups as being appropriate and hence legitimate the exercise of authority.

What is legitimacy? When people are influenced by an authority or institution not by means of the use of power but because they believe that the decisions made and rules enacted by that authority or institution are in some way "right" or "proper" and ought to be followed (Zelditch 2001), then that authority is perceived as legitimate. In other words, subordinates "relate to the powerful as moral agents as well as self-interested actors; they are cooperative and obedient on grounds of legitimacy as well as reasons of prudence and advantage" (Beetham 1991, 27). In the context of law and legal authorities, having legitimacy means that those in the community being regulated believe that their authorities "deserve" to rule and make decisions that influence the outcomes of members of the community. The belief that some decision made or rule created by these authorities is "valid" in the sense that it is "entitled to be obeyed" by virtue of who made the decision or how it was made is central to the idea of legitimacy.

Why does legitimacy matter? The legitimacy of authorities is important because when authorities are viewed as legitimate, the decisions they make and the rules they create are to a greater extent deferred to voluntarily (Tyler 2006a, 2006b). Seeking to gain influence over others solely on the basis of possession of power is costly and inefficient. The use of power, particularly coercive power, requires a large expenditure of resources to obtain modest and limited amounts of influence over others. Further, people's behavior is only controlled in settings in which effective surveillance can be established, and the influence of coercion does not extend over time. People who comply as long as a police officer is present will cease to comply when that officer leaves. It is therefore valuable to have alternative bases upon which to bring people's behavior into line with the law.

Legitimacy is especially valuable as an alternative basis of authority because it links behavior to internal values. People become self-regulatory, in the sense that their behavior is shaped by their values, rather than by the contingencies of the external environment. As a consequence, they voluntarily defer to the law, doing so because they think it is right and proper to do so, rather than because they expect rewards or fear punishments for their behavior. Such deference, to the extent it occurs, makes it much easier for legal authorities to effectively establish and maintain social order.

What creates, sustains, or undermines legitimacy? In *Economy and Society,* the sociologist Max Weber's classic treatment of legitimacy (1922/1968), Weber (1864–1920) distinguishes among legitimacy based on deference to customs and values (traditional authority), legitimacy based on devotion to the actions or character of an authority (charismatic authority), and legitimacy linked to the process of rule creation and interpretation (rational authority). Weber's work makes clear that the legitimation of authority and institutions through "the rule of law," while widespread in "modern" societies, is only one of many ways in which social arrangements might potentially be justified. And, in fact, a wide variety of forms of legitimation are found through history and across societies and cultures (Tyler 2006b).

INTERNATIONAL PERSPECTIVES ON LEGITIMACY

The Russell Sage working group believed that American efforts to speak to the issue of legitimacy and its role in maintaining social order would be aided by information about how problems of social order have been managed in other societies, particularly societies that have ethnically or culturally diverse populations. For this reason, the members of the working group organized an international conference on legitimacy, diversity, and criminal justice around the globe (Paris, January 16 to 18, 2004). The conference brought together speakers from a number of European countries who addressed themselves to the issue of policing minority populations within their own societies. The working group subsequently recognized the importance of broadening the exploration of this issue beyond European societies. (Scholars working this issue within other societies were identified; this volume includes several chapters about policing in other areas of the world, in particular Latin America.)

Each section of this volume addresses one of the three conceptual questions outlined earlier, from an international perspective. Part II includes chapters whose focus is on the role of legitimacy in policing. The goal of the chapters is to define the role of legitimacy in the criminal-justice context. Part III focuses upon the question of whether the legitimacy of the legal system is central by considering societies in which the legal system is not the core framework within which social order is maintained. Finally, the chapters in Part IV present efforts to define legitimacy within diverse societies—societies in which there are variations in the perspectives taken by the members of different ethnic and cultural groups on the legitimacy of the legal system.

Part II begins with a chapter by Mike Hough, in which he examines the policing system in the United Kingdom. Legitimacy is conceptualized in very similar ways in England and the United States, and the legal system in England is experiencing some of the same forms of public discontent documented within American society. In contrast to American and England, Gorazd Meško and Goran Klemenčič, in chapter 6, consider policing in Slovenia, a society that is undergoing rapid transition from autocracy to democracy. In such a situation the issue is more directly focused upon understanding how to remold the police in a manner that will create legitimacy and in the process to manage the potentially unattainable expectations of the public for the rapid creation of a truly nonauthoritarian legal system. Chapter 7, by Hugo Frühling, discusses similar issues in the context of policing in Chile, a society that has emerged from a period of military dictatorship. Finally, John Braithwaite, in chapter 8, articulates a general critique of current conceptualizations of legitimacy by exploring the degree to which the appropriation by the state of the right to manage reactions to violations of the law is not viewed as legitimate among the populations of a number of societies, populations whose discontent is fueling an international movement for a shift in authority away from the traditional legal system and into alternative procedures loosely grouped under the umbrella term "restorative justice."

The question of whether legitimacy is integral to social order can be viewed from many directions. One way, reflected in the chapters in Part III, is to examine what happens when the legal system is not legitimate. In chapter 10, Jennifer Johnson considers the case of Mexico, a society in which the traditional police are viewed as incompetent and corrupt. In this setting an alternative volunteer extralegal force is created in communities to provide the basis for social order. In chapter 11, Graziella Moraes D. da Silva and Ignacio Cano also consider alternative community policing initiatives, in their case in Brazil. Finally, John Comaroff and Jean Comaroff consider the case of the transitional society of South Africa, a country in which an authoritarian police force lost its legitimacy during a regime transition.

In each of these cases, the legitimacy of the traditional legal system is weak and communities seek alternative mechanisms for maintaining social order. Their efforts to do so raise a number of questions addressed in this part, including "How do traditional and alternative agents of social control coexist?"; "Does the existence of one type of authority undermine the legitimacy of the other?"; "How do alternative authorities gain legitimacy?"; and "What are the dangers associated with relying upon informal (that is, unregulated) agents of social control?" More broadly, these chapters raise questions about the relationship between national-level authority and the interests of local constituencies. Are those interests convergent, so that there can be a consensus about how authority should be exercised, or do interests diverge, creating conflicts among local- and national-level institutions and authorities?

The chapters in Part IV consider the question of what creates and maintains legitimacy. The general question of what creates and maintains legitimacy calls for a broad cultural analysis of authority and authority relations within societies differing in their political, religious, and social histories and social dynamics. The chapters in Part IV are more modest in their ambition. In keeping with the theme of this volume, they consider the case of diverse societies and the problems they encounter in seeking to define a common meaning of legitimacy between agents of social control and diverse populations.

Those problems have most recently been manifested in France, and the case of France is examined by both Sophie Body-Gendrot and Sebastian Roché. France is an especially interesting society, from a legitimacy perspective, because the state has, by definition, denied the relevance of ethnicity to law. That definition of a single standard of law has clashed with the experiences and understanding of minority-group members, resulting in large-scale national riots. In chapter 16, Hans Jörg Albrecht shows that Germany has experienced many of the same types of tensions in its efforts to define a common model for the legitimacy of legal authorities in the midst of an increasingly diverse society. In chapter 15, Catrien Bijleveld, Heike Goudriaan, and Marijke Malsch consider the case of the Netherlands. In the Netherlands, unlike in France and Germany, there is positive evidence of the ability of a legal system to gain the trust and confidence of minorities by defining a model of legitimacy built around a broader view of appropriate policing.

A SOCIAL SCIENCE PERSPECTIVE ON LEGITIMACY

As we have noted, there are core conceptual issues underlying the experiences of all of the societies considered in this volume. All societies must manage social order. Furthermore, many societies must find ways to unite populations that are ethnically, culturally, politically, socially, and economically heterogeneous. The goal of this volume is to draw upon the experience of societies throughout the world to provide a rich set of insights about both common and unique problems, and about the viability of different solutions to problems of policing and the maintenance of social order.

LEGITIMACY AS A SOCIAL SCIENCE CONCEPT

As we have already indicated, legitimacy is a property of legal authorities that, when it exists, leads people to feel that the actions of the police and courts are appropriate, proper, and just and ought to be voluntarily deferred to and followed (Tyler 2006a). In contrast to compliance based upon the fear of sanctions or the promise of rewards, legitimacy-based deference is motivated by people's internal values, and occurs irrespective of the immediate presence of legal authorities (Tyler 2006a). In particular, people are motivated to follow legal rules and decisions outside of the range within which their behavior is under surveillance by legal authorities. Herbert C. Kelman and V. Lee Hamilton (1989) refer to legitimacy as "authorization" to reflect the idea that a person authorizes an authority to determine appropriate behavior within some situation, and then feels obligated to follow the directives or rules that authority establishes.

One straightforward and widely noted perspective on social regulation builds upon the basic set of human motivations that are instrumental or "rational" in character. That means that people want to minimize their personal costs and maximize their attainment of rewards. This image of the person underlies deterrence, sanctioning, or social control models of social regulation (Nagin 1998). To implement such deterrence strategies police officers carry guns and clubs, and can threaten citizens with physical injury, incapacitation, or financial penalties. Their goal is to establish their authority: "The uniform, badge, truncheon, and arms all may play a role in asserting authority" in the effort to "gain control of the situation" (Reiss 1971, 46). The police seek to control the individual's behavior "by manipulating an individual's calculus regarding whether 'crime pays' in the particular instance" (Meares 2000, 396). Judges similarly shape people's acceptance of their decisions by threatening fines or even jail time for failure to comply.

The importance of legitimacy to securing rule following and deference to the decisions of legal authorities has been increasingly recognized as the limits of deterrence-based approaches to order maintenance have become more evident (Fagan, West, and Holland 2003; Meares 2004; Meares, Katyal, and Kahan 2004; Meares and Skogan 2004; Tyler and Huo 2002). Those limits include the high cost of effective surveillance (Meares 2000), the large costs of maintaining an incarceration system to delivered sanctions (Fagan, West, and Holland 2003), and the damage that a sanction-based orientation toward the public does to the relationship between legal authorities and members of the public (Tyler 2003).

THE VALUE OF SELF-REGULATION

It has been widely argued that self-regulatory approaches that rely upon the encouragement of deference-based legitimacy are often more effective than is sanction-based compliance. Irrespective of whether the question is why people obey a judicial order or why they do what the police request, studies show that rule following, especially in the long term, depends upon creating and maintaining legitimacy.

In addition, legitimacy matters during particular personal experiences with legal authorities. When dealing with people police officers focus not only upon displays of force, but upon establishing their "legitimate right to intervene" in a particular situation (Reiss 1971, 46). When legitimacy is higher, people are more likely to voluntarily defer to officers (Tyler and Huo 2002). When legitimacy is low, the police are more likely to have to use physical force, introducing "the risk of injury to both the arrested person and the officer" (Reiss 1971, 60). Interestingly, Albert J. Reiss finds that 73 percent of injuries to officers occur when the officers are interfered with, and interference most typically comes from people other than the parties involved in the immediate situation—from bystanders or family members. "When such persons question the legitimacy of police intervention and a police officer reacts to control their behavior, more serious conflict may ensue as each party attempts to gain control of the situation. This results more often in injury to the officer" (Reiss 1971, 60).

Legitimacy is central to social stability because it promotes both general rule following and deference during personal encounters with legal authorities. It has been widely suggested that the ability of legal systems to function in democratic societies depends upon being able to gain such voluntary compliance with the law (Easton 1975; Engstrom and Giles 1972; Parsons 1967; Sarat 1977; Scheingold 1974). Whether such voluntary compliance is in fact necessary to the viability of social regulation, it is unquestionably true that legal authorities benefit when the public is generally motivated to follow the law, and are particularly aided when people do so because of their own internal ethical values. If many or most of the people within a society are voluntarily following the rules, authorities are freed to direct their coercive force against a smaller subset of community residents who do not hold supportive internal values.

WHAT DO WE WANT FROM MEMBERS OF THE PUBLIC?

The costs of sanction-based models of social order have always be an issue, one that has become more prominent as discussions of the police and courts have focused more heavily upon the need for voluntary cooperation from members of the community.

The importance of gaining active cooperation from the public in the effort to fight crime and disorder has also become more central to discussions of law and policing. It has been recognized that the police have great difficulty maintaining social order and managing crime without the active cooperation of people within the affected communities (Sampson and Bartusch 1998; Sampson, Raudenbush, and Earls 1997). This includes people acting as individuals, people who report crime, who work in neighborhood groups, and who attend neighborhood meetings. It also includes the involvement of important community groups such as churches, groups that represent the community and its members (Berrien and Winship 2003; Meares 2002).

As the centrality of order maintenance has become increasingly linked to effectiveness in developing and maintaining community cooperation, it has been recognized that it is important to understand why people within communities view the police, the courts, and the law as legitimate. It is also important to examine how and when such legitimacy shapes cooperation. Current research suggests that legitimacy shapes rule following among both adolescents (Fagan and Tyler 2005) and adults (Sunshine and Tyler 2003; Tyler 2006a; Tyler and Huo 2002).

And of course it is important to understand the factors that shape legitimacy. One central focus of past research has been the strategies used by the police to manage crime (see, for example, Braga 2001a, 2001b, 2002, 2005). However, studies consistently suggest that public views of the police and the law are not simple reflections of the crime rate. This has been found in the United States (Skogan and Frydl 2004), in England (see Mike Hough, chapter 5, this volume), and in Chile (Hugo Frühling, chapter 7, this volume).

Recent discussions of policing acknowledge the important role that policing strategies have in shaping crime, but argue that attention needs to be given to a larger framework within which the influence of police actions on police legitimacy in the eyes of the public is also studied (Skogan and Frydl 2004). Such concerns have fueled a series of reforms in the manner in which legal authorities act, including community policing and neighborhood courts (Fagan and Malkin 2003).

Research suggests that the public not only evaluates legal authorities in terms of the ability of the police to fight crime but also is sensitive to the way the police exercise their authority. As a consequence, the procedural justice of police actions is central to police legitimacy, and policies such as racial profiling, which are not evaluated to be just, undermine police legitimacy (Fagan 2002; Tyler and Wakslak 2004).

DIVERSE PERSPECTIVES ON LEGITIMACY

Concern with the level of legitimacy that exists within different communities has led to a focus on another key finding within the literature on order maintenance. It is consistently found within the United States that minority-group members evaluate the police, the courts, and the law as being markedly less legitimate than do whites (Garofolo 1977; Huang and Vaughn 1996; Schuman et al. 1997). This finding has been widely noted in discussions of low "trust and confidence" in the police, the courts, and the legal system among minority-group members. The discrepancy in trust and confidence observed is large and has been persistent over time. The lowest levels of legitimacy are expressed by African Americans and the highest levels by whites. Hispanics typically express intermediate levels of legitimacy (Lasley 1994).

These low levels of legitimacy make the issue of how to effectively police minority communities central to discussions of order maintenance. Understanding how to engage in effective order maintenance in minority communities is important not only because of evidence that trust and confidence in legal authorities is low among minority group members but also because those communities are most subject to high levels of crime and poverty. The members of minority communities are most in need of effective order maintenance and are least able to sustain such efforts through community-based means.

Concern about order maintenance within minority communities has led to a number of efforts to understand how legitimacy is understood among the members of minority groups, as well as to explore various strategies for effectively policing minority communities.

While addressing concerns about policing minority communities within the United States the working group recognized that the issue of managing social order within ethnically diverse societies was not unique to the United States. On the contrary, as has been demonstrated by recent riots in France, many countries throughout the world are struggling with the question of how to manage increasingly diverse populations. And, as is the case within the United States, ethnicity often coexists with poverty, unemployment, and high rates of criminal activity.

THE WORKING GROUP'S CONFERENCE IN PARIS

To gather information about how policing is done in other societies, the working group organized an international meeting on legitimacy, diversity, and criminal justice around the globe. Speakers from a number of European countries took up the issue of policing minority populations within their own society. The goal of the meeting was to explore how different societies approach the maintenance of social order, with a particular focus on their efforts to manage ethnic and cultural minorities.

Several key issues underlie the approaches that different societies have taken in their efforts to maintain social order in ethnically and culturally diverse societies. To begin with, it is important to recognize that diversity can occur for a wide variety of reasons. Some countries, such as Belgium or Switzerland, have a long history of stability built around the political union of different ethnic and cultural groups. These countries have diversity, but it is not linked to the influx of immigrants. Other countries, such as the United States, France, Germany, England, and the Netherlands, are diverse because they are incorporating new groups of immigrants into their societies. Hence, one issue is whether all forms of diversity have the same influence upon the existence of crime and disorder and on the best strategies for maintaining order.

Perhaps the most basic issue is how diversity influences crime and social-order maintenance. Within the United States the waves of immigration from Europe during the early twentieth century were associated with the development of disadvantaged minority communities and with increasing crime. However, research suggests that the current waves of immigration into the United States are having the opposite impact, with immigrants less likely to commit crimes than native-born Americans (Robert J. Sampson, "Open Doors Don't Invite Criminals," op-ed, *New York Times*, March 11, 2006, A15). If this is true, it suggests that the connection of diversity to problems of crime and social control may not be direct and may depend upon the conditions within a particular society. In other societies—Germany (see Hans-Jörg Albrecht, chapter 16, this volume) and France (Sebastian Roché, chapter 17, this volume)—studies suggest that recent waves of immigration have led to increases in crime.

Consistent with this hypothesis, chapters in this volume suggest a variety of types of relationship between the police, the law, and minority communities. Similar to the United States, studies in France suggest that the police generally lack legitimacy within minority communities (see Sophie Body-Gendrot, chapter 13, and Sebastian Roché, chapter 17 this volume). On the other hand, research in the Netherlands suggests that minority-group members have levels of trust in the police similar to those of long-term residents of Holland (see Bijleveld, Goudriaan, and Malsch, chapter 15, this volume).

Legitimacy is not only an issue among minority groups. Societies differ in the general level of police legitimacy. The legitimacy of the police is generally high among all groups within American society, although it is clearly lower among minorities. In Slovenia (see Gorazd Meško and Goran Klemenčič, chapter 6, this volume), Mexico (Jennifer Johnson, chapter 10, this volume), and Brazil (Graziella Moraes D. da Silva and Ignacio Cano, chapter 11, this volume) police legitimacy is generally low throughout the whole society.

STRATEGIES OF ORDER MAINTENANCE ACROSS SOCIETIES

One issue is the degree to which societies view it as being important to maintain a uniform set of political and social values that immigrant groups need to assimilate into, and the degree to which societies are open to varying forms of multicultural models. The French approach is striking for its articulation of a model in which ethnic diversity is not recognized as an issue. Rather, it is expected that those who immigrate into French society will adopt French values and lifestyle. This approach to managing immigrants has also been characteristic of the United States, where immigrants have been expected to assimilate into American values and into an American lifestyle. In the United States, critics ranging from philosophers (Rawls 1993) to social commentators (Schlesinger 1992) have suggested that such an assimilationist approach is the most viable, and perhaps the only viable, approach to managing ethnic and cultural diversity.

The approach taken to policing is related to the perspective that societies have on how to manage issues of diversity. One approach involves top-down policing (Mike Hough, chapter 5, this volume). Police officers are not drawn from local communities and do not reflect or even acknowledge local norms and values. They represent societies' dominant institutions and values, and they articulate and enforce those values in their dealings with the population.

National-level policing has several elements. One is the potential enforcement of a single set of norms and values through a society. In this case, the laws articulate a set of national priorities rather than reflecting local conditions. Further, police personnel are assigned to communities outside their home communities in which they do not share the values, norms, and lifestyles of the members of the community. Hence, their actions are not constrained by personal relationships with members of the local community or through adherence to local norms.

A contrasting approach is when the norms and values enforced by the police are negotiated between ethnic or culturally based communities and the dominant institutions of society. That negotiation often occurs through the mediating role of important institutions such as churches and mosques, whose leaders can speak for their communities. Such a mediating role has already been mentioned to have been important in the context of American cities such as Boston (Berrien and Winship 2003; Braga 2001a) and Chicago (Meares 2002).

An important issue within any community is not only the degree to which local concerns, norms, and values play a role in shaping strategies of social control but also how such norms are represented. For example, such norms can potentially be attended to and incorporated into the strategies of order maintenance enacted by the police and courts. Or those authorities can withdraw and allow the community to fill the vacuum by creating informal systems of order maintenance whose actions are tolerated by state authorities. One example is the effort of the Brazilian police to cooperate with communities to manage crime (da Silva and Cano, chapter 11, this volume). In a more extreme case, Jennifer Johnson describes, in chapter 10, how in particular regions of Mexico the community has created a private system of policing and corrections that exists outside the formal state. Similarly, alternative policing has become important within South Africa (see Comaroff and Comaroff, chapter 12, this volume).

An example of the effort of societies to balance community values against state control of the law is the worldwide development of the restorative-justice movement (See John Braithwaite, chapter 8, this volume). Braithwaite describes the development of professional policing and with it the gradual removal of conflict resolution from the hands of local communities. These social developments have led victims as well as members of the community more generally to feel excluded from efforts to punish wrongdoing appropriately and restore justice. The victim's rights movement is an example of an effort to restore a role for those directly involved in crimes in determining what should happen to restore justice. The restorative-justice movement builds on this impulse, bringing many members of the community, including the victim and the offender's family, into discussions about how to restore justice and status in the aftermath of wrongdoing. Braithwaite argues that the increasing importance of this more informal approach to justice is linked to the declining legitimacy of the formal state, a declining legitimacy that undermines the claims of the state to be the sole agent dispensing justice.

POLICE BEHAVIOR

Irrespective of whose norms the police enforce, the issue of police behavior is a separate, important issue. Studies in the United States emphasize that both whites and minority-group members focus on the way the police exercise their authority both when making general evaluations of the legitimacy of the police (Sunshine and Tyler 2003) and when reacting to personal experiences with the police (Tyler and Huo 2002).

Studies of the police and courts in other societies suggest that similar procedural considerations are important in shaping the legitimacy of the police, the courts, and the law across a variety of societies (Cohen and White 2000), including the Netherlands (see Bijleveld, Goudriaan, and Malsch, chapter 15, this volume; Wemmer, van der Leeden, and Steensma 1995); Germany (Haller and Machura 1995); the Soviet Union (Gibson 1996; Machura 2003), Japan (Ohbuchi et al. 1995; Sugawara and Huo 1994); and South Africa (Gibson 2002).

Although the link between procedural justice and legitimacy is widespread, it is also clear from studies of procedural justice that the link between the procedural justice of authorities and their legitimacy is not universal (Tyler, Lind, and Huo 2000). In particular, studies conducted in China suggest that there are other systems of order maintenance besides the Western model, which links deference to legitimacy and legitimacy to the just exercise of authority.

THE CHAPTERS IN THIS VOLUME

The core issue linking the chapters in this volume is a concern with how to effectively maintain social order in democracies and transitional societies. The chapters raise a series of core questions, each of which is answered differently within the broad range of societies examined by the authors represented. The goal of the volume is to bring together authors whose societies vary widely in the issues the police and other legal authorities confront and the approaches that have been taken to address these varying concerns.

Is legitimacy necessary to the maintenance of social order? One central concern underlying many of the efforts to examine the struggles with social order that have occurred across the world in recent decades is the question: Can societies effectively create and maintain social order in either the short or the long term on an instrumental basis? In other words, can the legal system be based solely or largely on coercion and the fear of punishment? Can that system be viable if it delivers the goods by effectively managing crime. Put another way, do authorities need to have legitimacy in some broader sense than through being viewed as competent to control crime or at least constitute a credible threat to anyone thinking of breaking the law? Do authorities need to be viewed as reasonable, appropriate or justified in some larger way if order is to be maintained? And, do they need to be able to draw upon public feelings of obligation to obey because the police are legitimate?

The answer to these questions depends in part on what legal authorities need from the populace. Research has documented the problems associated with sanction-based law enforcement, including the costliness of deploying a surveillance system that credibly presents sufficient risk of punishment to deter undesirable behavior, as well as the undermining effects of such an approach on relations with the public. Similarly, seeking to maintain order can be difficult, since the factors shaping crime and disorder are often linked to core structural features of societies and so are beyond the control of agents of law enforcement.

Perhaps the key issue shaping the centrality of legitimacy is the degree to which legal authorities need voluntary cooperation from the population. Within the American context research emphasizes the need for widespread deference to the law and the decisions of legal authorities, as well as the value of public willingness to work with the authorities to jointly maintain social order. Such cooperation facilitates the task of order maintenance and may be the only viable model in a society such as the United States, where the ability of the authorities to intrude into the lives of citizens is severely restricted both by law and by cultural norms.

It is clear from the chapters in this volume that a heavy reliance upon public cooperation is not a universal aspect of policing, although it is widely found. It is important to examine the degree to which other types of relationship between people and their agents of social control can also produce an effective and viable legal order. In other words, must there be active public support for legal authorities to produce a functioning legal system?

The reach of this volume is wide, but there are some important contexts not covered, one being China, where authorities are providing economic growth and social stability to their population but are not creating a society that has or relies upon legitimacy, at least legitimacy as conceived in Western terms, as a basis for ruling. Can societies maintain themselves over time by a strategy of coercion combined with the delivery of services?

The fall of the Soviet Union and the end of its control over Eastern European states was taken to illustrate the limits of coercion as a form of social control. Was that, however, an overgeneralization from the experience of one type of autocratic government? For example, should the failures of Soviet communism be linked to its inability to deliver desired services, such as the effective maintenance of order, rather than to any intrinsic concern over the more normative legitimacy of the state. Is dissatisfaction with the current Russian government a reflection of its difficulties maintaining order more than of a concern that it is not legitimate in Western terms?

Examination of the case of the Soviet Union highlights the distinction between colonial or alien rule and the norms or values of particular societies. The view of people within Eastern European societies about the importance of the legitimacy of rule imposed by the Soviet Union may have been very different than the legitimacy concerns of Russians. This distinction is related to the question of whether there is anything intrinsically psychological about authorities' desire for legitimacy beyond the desire to have effective social order. For example, do people have an innate sense of justice to which they expect authorities to conform? The issue of colonialism raises the question of how people feel about order, effective or not, that is imposed from outside.

The international scope of this volume highlights the shifting nature of political regimes, the extent of mass global immigration, and the complexities of managing social order in an era of terrorism. Issues of social order tend to become central to discussions about society during periods of transition and instability. After the Second World War, for example, the question of how to create viable societies occupied the attention of many theorists in international relations because societies were rapidly collapsing and re-forming. Such issues have subsequently faded from centrality in discussions about Western democracies because a generally stable social order has been created and maintained for almost fifty years. However, recent events suggest that we are in a new period of increasingly rapid and widespread social change that will undoubtedly rekindle discussions about how to build strong institutions and stable societies, about whether legitimacy as it has been conceived within Western democracies remains viable, and, further, about whether this model is exportable to the broader world.

Of particular concern in this analysis is the ability of new societies to emerge as viable entities that can attain and maintain stability. Advocates of legitimacy as a basis for governance acknowledge that one problem with this form of authority relations is that it requires time to develop. The state must demonstrate to the population that it merits legitimacy, a process that can only occur over time. In this sense societies that have been stable do not provide useful guidance to transitional and emergent nations that are facing the immediate problem of finding ways to maintain social order. For these societies a key issue is whether instrumentality, either in the form of coercion or effective service provision, can form the basis for short-term stability. A larger question is whether such short-term stability can be translated into legitimacy over the long term and, through that transformation, can create stability over time.

Of course, irrespective of whether legitimacy is needed, these chapters reinforce the evidence of American research that legitimacy facilitates trust and fairness and, as a consequence, effectiveness and stability in the operation of the criminal-justice system. Although authorities might be able to function while relying on coercion and their ability to provide security, those that can rely upon only these factors to shape public behavior must devote a lot of resources to their job and can expect little from their citizens during times of difficulty or crisis. It is often when societies most need help from their members that they are least able to provide immediate incentives to motivate this kind of behavior. Hence, legitimacy is of great value to social survival.

The chapters in this volume also make clear that the type of basic data that would allow societies to monitor the perceived legitimacy of their criminal-justice system are widely lacking and not being collected. Even within the United States, where the most data are available, national-level data are not systematically collected to monitor the changing views of the public regarding legal authorities, and many other societies collect little or no such data, either nationally or locally, as the chapters in this volume make clear. One obvious suggestion is to make the collection of such empirical data a more central part of future research efforts.

What is legitimacy? To the degree that a legal system is to rest upon legitimacy, societies face the issue of understanding how to create and sustain that legitimacy. In other words, they have to ask what type of justifications can be put forward for the exercise of authority that will be widely accepted among members of that society. Ever since Weber published *Economy and Society,* social scientists have recognized that there are multiple ways in which social order can be legitimized. Weber's distinction between rational-bureaucratic, traditional, and charismatic authority is one example of an effort to create a typology, but it is not clear whether it is adequate for understanding the multiplicity of forms of legitimacy discussed in this volume, which make it clear that societies justify the creation and use of institutionalized force in a wide variety of ways.

One recurring theme is whether social institutions can be defined by reference to shared cultural or religious values. A hallmark of industrialized Western states is pluralism, where the state does not take particular moral positions on issues of right and wrong, creating an arena of freedom in which people can differ in their moral values. Such an approach to social organization leads the institutions of government to seek legitimacy through the procedures and practices of the authorities, rather than by moral solidarity with the values of the population. In other words, the police in a society with a single unified moral code could justify their actions by reference to a commonly agreed-upon set of moral values, whereas the police in pluralistic societies have a more complex task.

This is not to say that there are not widely, if not universally, shared moral values. Murder is considered wrong in most societies. But pluralistic societies must constantly struggle over which actions are appropriate targets for law enforcement. The police court public opposition when they seek to enforce laws against lifestyle crimes, such as drug use and homosexual behavior. Police forces in Western countries have sought to avoid generating opposition by focusing on the delivery of services and avoiding the problems that might arise by enforcing rule-prohibiting behavior that is generally not viewed as immoral or inappropriate within the community.

On the other hand, legitimacy research suggests clear guidelines about how the police and the courts can create and maintain legitimacy, which should be cause for optimism on the part of legal authorities. If, for example, the police needed to control crime successfully to maintain legitimacy, they might find that task quite difficult. Fortunately, this is not necessary, for research consistently suggests that the factor that most decisively shapes the police's legitimacy is the way they and other legal authorities exercise their authority when enforcing the law. People engage in fairly sophisticated evaluations of the police that incorporate perceptions of the character and intentions of the police, their sensitivity to people in the community, and their professionalism.

Research findings indicate that the fairness of legal authorities' actions shapes perceptions of legitimacy. Four elements of such fairness consistently emerge from research. First, people want to have an opportunity to state their case to legal authorities. When the police stop people, citizens value the opportunity to provide an explanation. People want to be allowed to provide information that justifies their actions and expresses their views about what is appropriate in the situation. Interestingly, having provided the information they view as relevant to the authorities, people are typically accepting of procedures that leave final decisions in the hands of authorities.

Second, people react to evidence that the authorities with whom they are dealing are neutral. This quality of neutrality involves the police making decisions that are based on consistently applied legal principles and the facts of the case. Openness about how decisions are made facilitates the perception that decisionmaking procedures are neutral. So, for example, explaining how decisions are made about whom to stop and search mitigates imputations of racial profiling. Much of this idea of neutrality is captured in the concept of transparency: decisionmaking that can withstand open scrutiny.

Third, people are sensitive to whether they are treated with dignity and politeness and their rights as citizens are respected. Studies consistently suggest public sensitivity to respect for rights, both political rights and the right to be treated with inherent human dignity. The police gain public support by acknowledging those rights. In some studies of responses to police action, the police have been trained to give members of the public a card indicating that they have the right to complain and telling them how to do so. People have been found to view such efforts very favorably, accepting police intrusions much more willingly when they know that they have the right to complain and have been told how to do so. It is interesting that in such a situation, few people actually do complain.

Finally, people focus on cues that communicate information about the intentions and character of the legal authorities with whom they are dealing. People react favorably when they believe that the authorities are sincerely trying to do what is best for the people in their communities. Authorities communicate this type of concern when they listen to people's accounts and explain their actions in ways that show an awareness of and concern about people's needs and interests. Because of the power that law enforcement authorities have, and the fact that interactions with them are often tinged with fear on the part of the public, being reassured about the benevolence of police intentions is very important to public support.

These four factors shape how people react to the implementation of policing policies and practices. They suggest that legitimacy is shaped by how the police implement their policies. Research has demonstrated these effects repeatedly in the context of ordinary policing practices, both when personally experienced and on a community level.

DEALING WITH DIFFERENCES

The chapters in this volume further highlight the importance of the ways societies deal with differences of treatment experienced by the members of various groups. Pluralism implies that there are distinct groups within society, groups whose values, traditions, and interests need to be in some way recognized and acknowledged. Recognition, if not acknowledgment, seems inevitable in societies such at the United States that have a long tradition of assimilating new groups into society, and it may also be becoming more central to Western European societies as immigrant groups have come to form increasing proportions of their populations.

In the United States law enforcers must recognize group differences, because there are large and persistent differences in the relationship between the police and between majority and minority communities. The gap between the level of trust and confidence that whites and African Americans express in police, the courts, and the law is frequently noted to be one of the largest found in studies of public opinion, one that has remained fairly constant across several recent decades.

Race, of course, is intertwined with poverty. The result is that minority-group members are more likely to be the target of police attention and minority status can become a cue of potential dangerousness. The chapters in the final section of the book pose the question of how to deal with this linkage between race, poverty, and the law-enforcement experience. Societies are found to differ in the degree to which they make official ethnic group distinctions or focus on the issue of different treatment for different groups.

The example of France is very relevant here. Officially, the French ignore ethnicity. But the policy of not acknowledging ethnicity did not prevent the social problems associated with ethnicity from having serious social consequences—witness the recent riots throughout the country.

OVERVIEW

Throughout the history of social thought it has been recognized that people exercise influence over others by possessing the ability to shape the gains and losses of others by using force or threatening to do so to deter undesired behavior or reward or promote desired behavior. A core aspect of social dynamics is that legal and other authorities can exert power over others by virtue of their possession of the means to use force.

It has also been recognized that seeking to gain influence over others solely on the basis of possession of power and a monopoly on the potential use of force to threaten rule breakers is costly and inefficient. The use of force, particularly coercive power, requires a large expenditure of resources to obtain modest, limited influence over others. It is therefore important that people also believe that the decisions made and rules enacted by others are in some way right or proper and ought to be followed—that they perceive their rulers and authorities as possessing legitimacy. Thus, people also follow authorities because they feel that they are obligated to do so, not only out of fear of the consequences if they do not obey.

The classic argument of social theorists has been that for authorities to perform effectively, those in power must convince everyone else that they deserve to rule and make decisions that influence the quality of everyone's lives. Central to the idea of legitimacy is the belief that a decision made or rule created by these authorities is valid and is "entitled to be obeyed." Legitimacy in this sense is especially central to discussions of law and legal authority, since legal authorities are in the business of restricting and regulating by telling people what they are not allowed to do.

Some argue that it is impossible to regulate using only power, and others suggest that it is possible, but more difficult than when one has legitimacy, it is widely agreed that legal authorities benefit from having legitimacy, and find governance easier and more effective when a feeling that they are entitled to rule is widespread within the population. One question to be answered, then, is when is legitimacy more or less helpful and when is it not central? And when may alternative forms of authority, themselves legitimate in different terms, replace state legitimacy as a means for creating social order?

Thus, seeking to rule on the basis of possession of power alone requires enormous expenditures of resources, first, to create a credible system of surveillance through which to monitor public behavior and punish rule violators and, second, to provide incentives for rewarding desired behaviors, those that benefit the group. Recent empirical research suggests that these strategies of governance can be successful, for example, that deterrence strategies can shape crime-related behavior. However, the same research shows that such instrumental influences are small and come at high material costs. This leaves societies vulnerable, since disruptions in the control of resources brought on by periods of scarcity or conflict quickly lead to the collapse of effective social order. When the public views government as legitimate it has an alternative basis for support during difficult times. Further, when government can call upon the values of the population to encourage desired behaviors, the society has more flexibility in how it deploys its resources. In particular, it is better able to use collective resources to benefit the long-term interests of the group, since they are not required immediately for ensuring public order.

The roots of the modern approach to legitimacy lie in the writings of Max Weber. Like Sigmund Freud and Emile Durkheim, Weber argues that social norms and values become a part of people's internal motivational systems and guide their behavior independent of the influence of incentives and sanctions. As social norms and values are internalized and become part of the individual's own behavioral goals, external control is replaced by self-control. People who internalize social norms and values become self-regulating, taking on the obligations and responsibilities associated with those norms and values as aspects of their own motivation. One aspect of values—obligation—is a key element in the concept of legitimacy. It leads to voluntary deference to the directives of legitimate authorities and rules. Hence, unlike influence based upon the influencer's possession of power or resources, the influence motivated by legitimacy develops from within the person who is being influenced.

The chapters in this volume touch on policing and police practices in many societies throughout the world, but they also touch on core questions of social order that are central to the effort to effectively maintain societies by regulating the behavior of their members. That task, typically carried out by formal authorities and institutions associated with the legal system, is crucial to the viability of any group of people trying to work and live together. These efforts are organized around the development and maintenance of legitimacy.

REFERENCES

Beetham, David. 1991. *The Legitimation of Power.* Atlantic Highlands, N.J.: Humanities.

Berrien, Jenny, and Christopher Winship. 2003. "Should We Have Faith in the Churches? The Ten-Point Coalition's Effects on Boston's Youth Violence." In *Guns, Crime, and Punishment in America,* edited by Bernard Harcourt. New York: New York University Press.

Braga, Anthony A. 2001a. "The Effects of Hot Spots Policing on Crime." *Annals of the American Academy of Political and Social Sciences* 578: 104–25.

———. 2001b. "More Gun Laws or More Gun Law Enforcement?" *Journal of Policy Analysis and Management* 20(3): 545–9.

———. 2002. *Problem-Oriented Policing and Crime Prevention.* Monsey, N.Y.: Criminal Justice Press.

———. 2005. "Hot Spots Policing and Crime Prevention: A Systematic Review of Randomized Controlled Trials." *Journal of Experimental Criminology* 1(3): 317–42.

Cohen, Ellen S., and Susan O. White. 2000. *Legal Socialization: A Study of Norms and Values.* New York: Springer-Verlag.

Easton, David. 1975. "A Reassessment of the Concept of Political Support." *British Journal of Political Science* 5(4): 435–57.

Engstrom, Richard L., and Michael W. Giles. 1972. "Expectations and Images: A Note on Diffuse Support for Legal Institutions." *Law and Society Review* 6(4): 631–36.

Fagan, Jeffrey. 2002. "Law, Social Science and Racial Profiling." *Justice Research and Policy* 4(December): 104–29.

Fagan, Jeffrey, and V. Malkin. 2003 "Theorizing Community Justice Through Community Courts." *Fordham Urban Law Journal* 30(3): 897–953.

Fagan, Jeffrey, and Tom R. Tyler. 2005. "Legal Socialization of Children and Adolescents." *Social Justice Research* 18(3): 217–42.

Fagan, Jeffrey, Valerie West, and Jan Holland. 2003 "Reciprocal Effects of Crime and Incarceration in New York City Neighborhoods." *Fordham Urban Law Journal* 30(5): 1551–1602.

Garofolo, James. 1977. *Public Opinion About Crime.* Washington: Government Printing Office.

Gibson, James L. 1996. "A Mile Wide but an Inch Deep: The Structure of Democratic Commitments in the Former USSR." *American Journal of Political Science* 40(2): 396–420.

———. 2002. "Truth, Justice, and Reconciliation: Judging the Fairness of Amnesty in South Africa." *American Journal of Political Science* 46(3): 540–56.

Haller, Volkmar, and Stefan Machura. 1995. "Procedural Justice in German Courts as Seen by Defendants and Juvenile Prisoners." *Social Justice Research* 8(2): 197–215.

Huang, W. S. Wilson, and Michael S. Vaughn. 1996. "Support and Confidence: Public Attitudes Toward the Police." In *Americans View Crime and Justice,* edited by Timothy J. Flanagan and Dennis R. Longmire. Thousand Oaks, Calif.: Sage.

Kelman, Herbert C., and V. Lee Hamilton. 1989. *Crimes of Obedience.* New Haven, Conn.: Yale University Press.

Lasley, J. R. 1994. "The Impact of the Rodney King Incident on Citizen Attitudes Toward Police." *Policing and Society* 3(4): 245–55.

Machura, Stefan. 2003. "Fairness, Justice, and Legitimacy: Experience of People's Judges in South Russia." *Law and Policy* 25(2): 123–50.

Meares, Tracey. 2000. "Norms, Legitimacy, and Law Enforcement." *Oregon Law Review* 79(2): 391–415.

———. 2002. "Praying for Community Policing." *California Law Review* 90(5): 1593.

———. 2004. "Mass Incarceration: Who Pays the Price for Criminal Offending?" *Criminology and Public Policy* 3(2): 295.

Meares, Tracey, and Wesley Skogan. 2004. "Lawful Policing." *Annals of the American Academy of Political and Social Science* 66(18): 593

Meares, Tracey, Neal Katyal, and Dan Kahan. 2004. "Updating the Study of Punishment," *Stanford Law Review* 56(5): 1171.

Nagin, Daniel S. 1998. "Criminal Deterrence Research at the Outset of the Twenty-First Century." In *Crime and Justice: A Review of Research,* edited by Michael Tonry. Volume 23. Chicago, Ill.: University of Chicago Press.

Ohbuchi, Ken-ichi, Kazyhiko Teshigahaya, Kei-ichiro Imazai, and Ikuo Sugawara. 1995. "Procedural Justice and the Assessment of Civil Justice in Japan." *Law and Society Review* 39(4): 875–92.

Parsons, Talcott. 1967. "Some Reflections on the Place of Force in Social Process." In *Sociological Theory and Modern Society.* New York: Free Press.

Rawls, John. 1993. *Political Liberalism.* New York: Columbia University Press.

Reiss, Albert J. 1971. *The Police and the Public.* New Haven, Conn.: Yale University Press.

Sampson, Robert J., and Dawn Jeglum Bartusch. 1998. "Legal Cynicism and (Subcultural?) Tolerance of Deviance: The Neighborhood Context of Racial Differences." *Law and Society Review* 32(4): 777–804.

Sampson, Robert J., Stephen Raudenbush, and Felton Earls. 1997. "Neighborhoods and Violent Crime: A Multilevel Study of Collective Efficacy." *Science* 277(5328): 918–24.

Sarat, Austin. 1977. "Studying American Legal Culture." *Law and Society Review* 11(3): 427–88.

Scheingold, Stuart A. 1974. *The Politics of Rights*. New Haven, Conn.: Yale University Press.

Schlesinger, Arthur 1992. *The Disuniting of America*. New York: Norton.

Schuman, Howard, Charlotte Steeh, Lawrence Bobo, and Maria Krysan. 1997. *Racial Attitudes in America*. Cambridge: Cambridge University Press.

Skogan, Wesley, and Kathleen Frydl, editors. 2004. *Fairness and Effectiveness in Policing: The Evidence*. Washington: National Academy of Science.

Sugawara, Ikea, and Yuen J. Huo. 1994. "Disputes in Japan: A Cross-Cultural Test of the Procedural Justice Model." *Social Justice Research* 7(2): 129–44.

Sunshine, Jason, and Tom R. Tyler. 2003. "The Role of Procedural Justice and Legitimacy in Shaping Public Support for Policing." *Law and Society Review* 37(3): 555–89.

Tyler, Tom R. 2003. "Procedural Justice, Legitimacy, and the Effective Rule of Law." In *Crime and Justice: A Review of Research,* edited by Michael Tonry. Volume 30. Chicago, Ill.: University of Chicago Press.

———. 2006a. "Why People Obey the Law: Procedural Justice, Legitimacy, and Compliance." New Haven, Conn.: Yale University Press.

———. 2006b. "Legitimacy and Legitimation." *Annual Review of Psychology* 57: 375–400.

Tyler, Tom R., and Yuen J. Huo. 2002. *Trust in the Law: Encouraging Public Cooperation with the Police and Courts*. New York: Russell Sage Foundation.

Tyler, Tom R., and Cheryl Wakslak. 2004. "Profiling and the Legitimacy of the Police: Procedural Justice, Attributions of Motive, and the Acceptance of Social Authority." *Criminology* 42(2): 13–42.

Tyler, Tom R., E. Allan Lind, and Yuen J. Huo. 2000. "Cultural Values and Authority Relations." *Psychology, Public Policy, and Law* 6(4): 1138–63.

Weber, Max. 1922/1968. *Economy and Society*. Edited by Guenther Roth and Claus Wittich. Berkeley, Calif.: University of California Press.

Wemmer, Jo-Anne A., Rien van der Leeden, and Herman Steensma. 1995. "What Is Procedural Justice? Criteria Used by Dutch Victims to Assess the Fairness of Criminal Justice Procedures." *Social Justice Research* 8(4): 329–50.

Zelditch, Morris. 2001. "Processes of Legitimation: Recent Developments and New Directions." *Social Psychology Quarterly* 64(1): 4–17.

CHAPTER 3

The Foundations of Legitimacy

David J. Smith

The starting point for the enterprise reported in this volume—an enterprise that should be regarded as a work in progress—is the substantial American tradition of research on procedural justice as a key influence on the legitimacy of legal authority. This is a relatively new body of work that uses the concepts and tools of social psychology to tackle a very old set of problems. It was given its impetus in the late 1980s by Tom Tyler and his associates, and has gathered pace since then. The central problem, encapsulated in the title of Tyler's 1990 book, is to explain *Why People Obey the Law*. According to the usual formulation of the problem, people obey in the last analysis because they can be physically forced to comply—in the words of Mao Tse-Tung, recalled by Tyler (2006), "Political power grows out of the barrel of a gun." However, it would be cumbersome and expensive for rulers to use immediate physical force as the usual means of securing compliance. Instead, they encourage the majority to believe that their decisions and laws are right and proper and ought to be obeyed. In other words, social order depends on the widespread belief that the authorities, and their political and legal framework, are legitimate. As long as that belief is widespread, people will largely regulate their own behavior by reference to internalized values that correspond with the law and its underlying principles, and force need only occasionally be used when people get out of line.

From the viewpoint of those in positions of power, legitimacy looks like one of a number of resources that can be used to control behavior. Other methods of control, such as surveillance associated with the threat of punishment, or incentives that reward desired behavior, are apt to be more costly, so achieving legitimacy must be crucial for successful government of a state or management of an organization. The core finding of the recent tradition of research in the style of social psychology is that people are more likely to believe that authority is legitimate and to accept its rules and decisions if they experience the exercise of authority as being fair. The central implication for policy, according to Tyler (2006), is that the police and the courts should focus on following fair procedures rather than delivering outcomes such as punishment of offenders or crime control. By following fair procedures they will encourage people to believe that the system is legitimate, and if they believe the system is legitimate people will tend to regulate their own behavior.

Up to now this reasoning has been supported by studies that chart the way Americans evaluate the police and the courts in light of their personal encounters with them. Studies with cross-sectional designs have found that belief in the legitimacy of the police and courts is linked with favorable evaluations of the fairness of the procedures followed and of the behavior of the officials involved where individuals have had relevant personal experiences. More powerful panel studies have found that belief in the legitimacy of the police at a later time, after controlling for these beliefs at an earlier time, is linked to favorable evaluations of encounters with the police in the meantime. This has been interpreted as showing that experience of the police behaving fairly strengthens belief in the legitimacy of their authority. The relevant studies have shown that whether the police action was considered fair has more influence than whether the outcome favored the individual concerned.

These studies comparing the experiences and views of individual Americans, as they themselves report them, have been used to draw the far-reaching conclusion that the authorities gain cooperation not primarily by achieving outcomes that benefit the community, such as peace or lower levels of crime, nor through the fear of punishment, but by following procedures that are experienced as being fair in themselves (regardless of whether the outcomes of these procedures are fair to different sections of the community). The conclusion is based on research into the views and self-reported experiences of individuals in one society at one point in history, although, importantly, it is found to apply equally to men and women, to different age and ethnic groups, and to different social classes within that society. There is a strong temptation to move from that densely populated but restricted evidence base to the general conclusion that fair procedures are always and everywhere the main foundation of legitimacy. Instead, the present volume makes a start on broadening the base by bringing together studies of a number of different societies using a range of research techniques other than those of social psychology.

It is important to take a wider view of these issues, because the American procedural justice research, although powerful, is limited in scope. Obviously it applies to a particular society at a particular stage of development. It shows that within that society, differences between individuals in their views of the legitimacy of the police and courts and their willingness to comply with decisions made by the police and courts are linked with perceptions of the fairness of the procedures followed. It does not follow that procedural fairness is the sole or central foundation of legitimacy in all societies at all stages of development. It is worth spelling out these limitations in more detail:

1. The strength of the procedural justice studies is that they clearly focus on a small number of factors in order to show clearly that personal experience of fair process is more influential than a favorable outcome. This means, however, that a wide range of other factors not covered by the studies could also have an important influence on beliefs about the legitimacy of the police and courts.

2. The studies deal with legitimacy at the individual but not at the collective level. They seek to explain why this person has a stronger belief in legitimacy than that person, and why beliefs change within the same individual. However, police legitimacy is a collective phenomenon that amounts to something more than the sum of individuals' beliefs.

3. Closely linked with the second point, the causes or explanations of legitimacy may not be the same at the individual and collective levels; consequently the explanations for secular change in police legitimacy in a society from one epoch to another may be different from the explanations for intra-individual change in legitimacy beliefs. To cite a different example, level of education and training explains much of the difference between individuals in the likelihood of un-employment, and people who improve their education and acquire new skills improve their chances of getting employment, yet changes in the education and skills of the population do nothing to explain the rise in the unemployment rate in Britain from 3 per cent in 1970 to 12 per cent in 1980, a period when educa-tion and training rapidly improved. Similarly, differences in height between British twenty-year-olds in 1960 were largely explained by genetic inheritance, but the average height of twenty-year-olds had steadily increased over the pre-ceding century not because of a change in the genetic pool but because of improvements in diet. Of course, both diet and genetic inheritance influence height, but one or other factor becomes dominant depending on whether the focus is on individual differences or on change in the collectivity over time.

4. The procedural justice studies focus on direct personal experience of the police and courts, as perceived by the individual concerned. However, there is exten-sive evidence that most learning is vicarious: from observing the behavior of others and its consequences, from fashion, from the media, and—especially important for the views of minority groups about authority figures—by word of mouth (Bandura 1986). Large sections of the population have little or no contact with the police or courts in any case.

5. This research tradition studies interactions with the authorities as described and evaluated by the members of the public involved, so "fair procedures" are ones they consider to be fair. This means that the measure of whether procedures

were fair in a particular instance is colored by general views about the legitimacy of the police or courts, so there is some overlap between the explanation (procedures experienced as fair) and what is to be explained (belief in legitimacy, compliance). The strongest designs use powerful strategies to overcome this problem, and succeed in showing that prior beliefs about legitimacy influence the evaluation of encounters with the police, which in turn influence subsequent beliefs about their legitimacy. This should tend to set up causal spirals in which legitimacy is either repeatedly reinforced or repeatedly eroded. However, the research provides no information from a neutral viewpoint about the police-public encounters in question. It seems to leave open the possibility, therefore, that prior beliefs in police legitimacy (or illegitimacy) are the powerful factor, whereas particular experiences of the police are shaped by those beliefs, or interpreted and perceived to fit with them.

6. The studies are of course restricted to a particular society at a particular stage of development. Would the conclusions apply to the Wild West in 1865, to Northern Ireland in 1980, or to Egypt today? The question seems particularly hard to answer for societies where there are competing sources of authority (as in Northern Ireland) or where legitimate authority, as in the Wild West, is inchoate or nascent. Yet this weakness is crucial, since it is precisely in such situations that the question of how to establish legitimate authority becomes most urgent.

Given these limitations, the varied studies collected in the present volume build on and extend the findings of the procedural justice studies in important ways. They cover a range of contemporary societies with political systems and social and economic conditions that stand in marked contrast to those existing in the United States. In several cases they capture societies and neighborhoods at a moment when order is precarious and the struggle to establish legitimate authority may be close to a tipping point at which it may either fragment or be rapidly consolidated. They adopt methods from political science, sociology, and anthropology that give some insight into how law enforcement institutions work within the wider social structure, and how this has changed in recent history. Several chapters provide case studies of specific initiatives that have had some success in building the legitimacy of the law enforcement authorities. These materials provide a starting point for comparative research on the foundations of legitimacy in contrasting political systems and social conditions, and they help to place the findings from the tightly specified procedural justice research in a much broader perspective.

Whereas the procedural justice research sets out to explain why individuals believe in the legitimacy of the police or the courts, the chapters in this volume shift the emphasis to the dynamics of change in the system as a whole. The central question that they raise is how the legitimacy of the police and courts comes to be established where there was disorder before, and how it may be eroded. The following pages do not attempt to review or synthesize the findings of these diverse studies. Instead, they pick out and discuss a few of the themes that arise, with emphasis on those that are connected with the dynamics of change.

INSTITUTIONAL AND POLITICAL FRAMEWORK

Historians and sociologists have generally assumed that the way people regard the police is part and parcel of the way they regard the whole political and social order and its institutional framework. Maintaining order by force if necessary is usually seen as the core function that defines the modern state, and following Egon Bittner (1970) the police are seen as the specialist arm of the state with responsibility for performing that function. The way people evaluate personal experiences, stories, and symbols relating to the police must therefore depend on where the police sit within a wider political and institutional framework, and also on where this political and social order is coming from, and in which direction it is heading. The point is richly illustrated by the stories of policing in various countries that are told in this volume.

Britain is rightly thought of as a country where the police over much of the last hundred years have enjoyed a very high level of legitimacy. Yet it is worth recalling that when the modern police were first established in Britain, during the first half of the nineteenth century, they met with strong opposition and hostility from various sections of society. Robert Reiner has argued in his study *The Politics of the Police* (2000) that trust in the modern police is something that has been hard won not only through the pattern and practice of policing but also through associated political strategies, and through wider social changes. More specifically, Reiner (51–59) detailed eight policies and practices that helped to legitimate the police in the century from 1850 to 1950:

- Establishing a disciplined organization with clear standards and lines of responsibility

- Allowing the police to be subject to the rule of law, or at least creating the appearance that they were

- Following the strategy of minimal force, and propagating an image and ideology of the British police associated with that

- Remaining aloof from politics and (increasingly, in the first half of the twentieth century) insulated from direct political control

- Cultivating the idea that the police were accountable to the courts and in a mystical way to the British people rather than to the state

- Emphasizing the service role in order to secure acceptance for coercive actions

- Emphasizing the primacy of prevention rather than detection
- Cultivating at least the appearance of effectiveness in controlling crime and maintaining order

Although initial hostility to the police came from all sections of society, the police had been created to control the working class, and the pattern and practice of policing concentrated on working-class haunts, pursuits, and pleasures. Consequently, in the long run hostility to the police was bound to come mainly from the lower part of the working class, and difficulties in establishing police legitimacy were largely a reflection of class struggles and divisions. As Reiner has also pointed out (2000, 58) probably the most important condition for the legitimation of the police was the incorporation of the working class "gradually, unevenly and incompletely" into political and social institutions.

In this account of the struggle to achieve police legitimacy in Britain, efforts to achieve procedural justice are lent significance by the wider political and social context. It was not just the behavior of the police that was important, as it filtered into consciousness through personal experiences, but equally the stories that were told about the police force, and the accompanying social changes and political ideology. Many of the chapters in this volume illustrate the same close linkage between policing and its social and political setting in societies where police legitimacy is still relatively fragile. In chapter 6, Gorazd Meško and Goran Klemenčič vividly illustrate how a form of policing—in this case "community policing"—can take on a completely different significance because of its "historical resonance."

> "Community policing" existed in Slovenia prior to 1991. Its underlying principle was however as much or more about social and political control in all spheres of community as about safety, security and problem solving. It was an endeavor of "big brothers and sisters" controlling "little brothers and sisters." Because of this experience, contemporary community policing is not perhaps as popular as it could and should be; coupled with the historical experience it can even produce negative results.

This comment goes right to the heart of the question. It shows that the same policing behavior can have an entirely different meaning depending on the political context. This highlights the point that legitimacy, as understood by Max Weber (Gerth and Wright Mills 1948) and more recently by Tyler (2006), is a positive concept: in other words, the authorities are legitimate if people generally believe that they ought to be obeyed. This makes it possible to say that a political system, such as Nazi Germany, or a sociolegal system, such as slavery in the British colonies and the American South, though clearly evil, can still be legitimate. A closely connected point is that practices such as torture of suspects may be regarded as entirely normal and fair within one legitimate political system, but as abnormal and unfair within another. This point is acknowledged but seldom pursued in depth within the American procedural justice literature (for an exception, see MacCoun 2005). Although this does seem the most coherent way of analyzing the problem, a consequence is that the linkages between fairness and legitimacy are self-referential within a particular social, political, and moral system. As long as we remain within a particular system, fairness helps to explain and support legitimacy, and the legitimate authority helps to define fairness. However, if we are concerned with dynamic processes that bring about change from one social and political system to another, with accompanying changes in the pattern and practice of policing and the law, then fairness of procedures is inadequate as a way of describing or explaining what is happening. This is because the whole configuration is changing: for example, not only is police behavior changing, but so is the social and political structure that gives it meaning.

The example from Slovenia is of changes in the political system that create a double vision that shifts between two ways of seeing a police practice, like the shift in the gestalt psychology experiment between seeing a drawing as a duck or a rabbit. A similar effect may be produced when people migrate from one country to another with a very different culture. In chapter 15, Catrien Bijleveld, Heike Goudriaan, and Marijke Malsch cite an example from a Dutch study of a nonwhite juvenile "who states that of course the employee of the 'HALT' bureau [dispensing diversionary juvenile justice] has embezzled his fine" and that Moroccan parents "tend to view the Child Welfare Council as the enemy." As these authors put it, "One way to understand this is to realize that many non-Western migrants come . . . from countries where the government is viewed as an entity to distrust a priori." What is important, on this interpretation, is not so much how these youngsters are actually treated by the Dutch authorities but, more, the spectacles the young people have brought with them from their country of origin through which they view this treatment. Although Bijleveld, Goudriaan, and Malsch add that more experience of the Dutch system may change these subjects' view, the problem is that this experience, too, could be interpreted in a similar way until something happens to make them change their way of seeing the world.

Weber's idea that the state has a monopoly of the legitimate use of force is no longer widely accepted, nor is the idea that the public police alone make use of this monopoly (see, for example, Johnston 2007; Shearing 2007). The idea that all sources of order are concentrated in the state can better be understood as a core element of the ideology developed to legitimate the state, an ideology that reached its high point in the mid-twentieth century. Similarly, the public police may have to claim a monopoly of the legitimate use of force in order to maintain their position (Crawford 2007), but they never actually had such a monopoly in Western countries. John Comaroff and Jean Comaroff in chapter 12 and Jennifer Johnson in chapter 10 of this volume argue that developments associated with "neoliberalism" have in recent years encouraged the growth of ambiguously legitimate centers of power outside the direct control of the state. In many countries, strategies of privatization have been applied to a range of public services such as education, health, transport, housing, and, of course, criminal justice. It has further been argued (Garland 1996, 2001) that in responding to crime, governments have followed a strategy of "responsibilization," which means implementing a crime prevention policy through nongovernmental organizations and individuals, thus seeking to avoid as far as possible taking direct responsibility for failure. According to Comaroff and Comaroff and to Johnson, such developments lend legitimacy to organizations that dispense "informal justice" with some degree of more or less ambiguous toleration by the formal criminal justice system. As Johnson puts it, taking the law into one's own hands is an insurgent form of privatization. The growth of such competing centers of legitimacy in the field of law enforcement in South Africa and Mexico is clearly of the first importance from a theoretical as well as a practical viewpoint, because it means that the dynamics of legitimacy in these countries cannot possibly be explained through concepts of fair procedure within either the official or informal justice systems.

In Britain, the process of legitimizing the police in the nineteenth century, as described by Reiner (2000), was driven from within the country, although this was quickly followed by an evangelizing phase in which an alternative version of British practices and values was exported to the colonies (Mulcahy 2005). By contrast, in several of the countries covered in this volume, the process of legitimation was partly driven by international law and by international bodies that were sources of standards and practices from outside. For example, in chapter 6 Meško and Kemenčič make it clear that reports by the UN Committee against Torture, the European Commission for the Prevention of Torture, and the European Commission Against Racism and Intolerance, together with judgments by the European Court of Human Rights, have had an important influence on the evolution of the police forces in Slovenia over the period of transition to democracy. A contrary example is provided by France, as described by Sophie Body-Gendrot in chapter 14. The Committee for the Prevention of Torture, established by the European Court of Human Rights, has twice found the French police responsible for mistreatment and has pointed to a significant risk of mistreatment in French police stations. However, the French government, perhaps seeing France as the "fons et origo" of human rights, has responded defensively without setting in motion any process of reform. What this contrast perhaps indicates is that pressures from international bodies are likely to have an influence on countries in transition that are seeking to join the club of democratic nations, but less likely to have an influence on a country that sees itself as the oldest established member.

The example of Slovenia shows that international bodies can have an influence on the development of the criminal justice system in a country in transition to democracy. Johnson's study also shows that an informal justice system in Guerrero, Mexico, was connected with international human rights organizations and with a political demand for self-help stimulated by Zapatista groups at home.

Both national and international links became a source of legitimacy in defense against the Guerrero state government.

The examples of different countries show that different legitimating myths are possible, and that all may work independently to some extent of the pattern and practice of policing or people's experience of it. In Britain, the myth, as described by Reiner (2000), involves an almost mystical identification between the police and the British people, bypassing the government at a symbolic level. In France, by contrast, the police are seen as the direct expression of the power and authority of the state, which itself retains very high prestige and legitimacy (much higher than in Britain or in countries influenced by British political culture). According to Body-Gendrot, this myth of legitimation works so well that the French system could continue to avoid openness and scrutiny in a variety of ways (refusal to introduce an effective system for the investigation of complaints against the police, denial of the findings of the European Committee for the Prevention of Torture) while continuing until recently to enjoy a high level of confidence and support. A paternalistic policy of this kind, like the Catholic church's policy of turning a blind eye to child abuse by the clergy, may work very well for a long time, until a real point of crisis is reached. Similarly, the analysis by Bijleveld, Goudriaan, and Malsch suggests that in the Netherlands most people were until recently content with the workings of the police and criminal justice system, even though its workings were extremely distant and they could not possibly understand court proceedings or participate in the criminal justice process in any way. Presumably the explanation for this acceptance must be that the legitimacy of the state has been established by other means, and people tend to accept criminal justice processes as an aspect of the state's functions. There is possibly a third kind of myth of legitimation in the United States, where the police are seen as the instrument of a local elected administration, so that their policies, even if unjust, can always be defended on the grounds that they are what people voted for ("he's a monster, but he's our monster").

CLASS AND INEQUALITY

Durkheim saw criminal justice as a source of solidarity as people joined together in a "passionate response" against crime; the procedural justice research follows in the Durkheimian tradition in arguing that common values of fairness are ones around which everyone can unite in support of the law enforcement system. Marx emphasized instead the class-based nature of law. Although, unlike later writers in the Marxist tradition, he never put forward the crude argument that law is simply an instrument through which the ruling class maintains its dominance, he did argue that the law tends to reflect the underlying power structure and therefore to express the interests of the ruling class. From that perspective, the legitimacy of the law, the police, and the courts is an aspect of what Gramsci called hegemony—the organizing principle whereby the rulers maintain the allegiance of the population both through reforms and compromises that take account of different interests and also through influencing the way people think. In chapter 16, Hans-Jörg Albrecht explains how German sociology of law has shifted back and forth between the Durkheimian and Marxist traditions, and there has been a similar interplay between these traditions in other European countries and in North America. It emerges very clearly from several chapters in this collection that an account of the divisions between classes is indispensable to an understanding of the process of building legitimacy, and that an undiluted Durkheimian view would be grossly inadequate. In this respect, contemporary research on societies in transition fully supports David Garland's (1990) analysis of theories and historical materials.

In chapter 11, Graziella Moraes D. da Silva and Ignacio Cano explain the background to the development of a new policing initiative in the favela of Pavão-Pavãozinho-Cantagalo in Rio de Janeiro, later extended to another three communities nearby. This background is the extreme contrast between rich and poor which is vividly expressed in the geography of the city. The rich live in comfortable, safe, and tranquil neighborhoods, whereas the poorest live in favelas, shantytowns built on steep hills consisting of temporary buildings largely without basic facilities such as running water, sewage, and electricity. The favelas are characterized by very high rates of violent crime and widespread drug dealing. Many of them are controlled by organized groups of drug dealers, who prevent people from moving freely through the neighborhood. From day to day there is little law enforcement and police protection in the favelas. Policing is seen as a way of protecting the rest of the city from the residents of the favelas. From time to time, in response to incidents caused by residents of a favela, the police enter it and shoot at will, treating it like a war zone. Police officers are rarely if ever disciplined for killing innocent people, and in fact there was for some years a scheme for rewarding police officers for the number of people they killed. An essential part of the context for the launching of the new police initiative, according to da Silva, was that this particular favela is close to the wealthy district of Copacabana and therefore poses a threat. When five young men from Cantagalo, accused of being drug dealers, were shot dead by the police, residents from the favela came down into the wealthy district and began destroying property. That was the trigger for introducing a far more progressive form of policing which seems to have resulted in a substantial reduction of violence. In part, the initiative involved major improvements in standards of police conduct, and in that way it fitted the procedural justice model. The most basic change, however, was that now for the first time the favela was being policed, rather than being attacked from time to time in the style of a military campaign. The threat posed by the proximity between the favela and the wealthy neighborhood had been enough to induce an accommodation between starkly conflicting class interests, and in the event it seems that the outcome benefited both sides in the class conflict.

Class divisions are also the background to the development of an informal justice movement in Guerrero, southwestern Mexico, as described by Johnson in chapter 10.

This is the poorest rural part of the country, occupied by indigenous coffee farmers at a time when relentless competition has driven down the price of coffee. Initial conditions for the development of the movement were the growth of the drug trade and underfunding by the central government of local law enforcement, so that very poor people with strong communal ties and economic networks formed through coffee-producer cooperatives saw their fields and villages running out of control and prey to gangs of criminals. It was in those circumstances that people with very little power sought to make the law their own, and that appropriation of the law was clearly a move in a battle between classes.

In chapter 7, Hugo Frühling shows that views of the police in Chile are sharply divided along social-class lines. Debate on policing tends to be framed as a contest between harsh enforcement and human rights, on the assumption that harsh enforcement reduces crime, and, contrary to the procedural justice school, that fair treatment gets in the way of effective enforcement. Some, and especially members of the middle classes, vote for parties that supported the military regime, and unquestioning support for the police goes along with that.

DRAMA, STORIES, SYMBOLS

In chapter 8, John Braithwaite develops the idea that people use stories to make sense of their experience of being wronged, and find a way of rebuilding their lives through telling a new story of survival and renewal. In one aspect, stories are a way of finding pattern and meaning in personal experience, but in another they are a way of communicating and multiplying that patterned, interpreted experience so that it becomes the common property of a whole group of people and resounds and reverberates through their exchanges and relationships. The procedural justice model focuses mainly on personal experience evaluated as being fair (within the rules) or not, and the influence of this experience and personal evaluation on general views about the police and criminal justice system. This model may need to be adapted to take account of the way people use a few nuggets of experience, spun into stories, to make sense of the lives of a whole group. These stories are told in the first person, giving a unique and essentially one-sided perspective on conflict. Drama provides an alternative mode of representation in which the viewpoints of different actors can be given equal weight. The meaning of stories and dramas, and their narrative or dramatic structures, depend on attaching symbolic values to actions and events. The social world is extremely complex, so that we could not possibly learn everything that we need to know about it from direct experience. Most of our social knowledge comes through vicarious experience filtered and refracted through stories and drama, and symbolically represented.

Particular stories may often be used to illustrate a "grand narrative" about "our own people" and the police. The point is illustrated by Stephen Small's (1983) study of a group of young African Caribbeans living in a self-help hostel for the unemployed in South London. Small, a British-born African Caribbean, was 23 years old at the time of the research. He acted as a voluntary worker in the hostel where nobody knew or suspected he was carrying out research until it was later explained to them. This was participant observation in the fullest sense. All members of the group were extremely hostile to the police, and this hostility was so uniform that it could not possibly be explained by their personal experience, which was varied. These young people believed that the police were corrupt, that they singled out African Caribbeans for abuse, and that they frequently fabricated evidence against them. They would often spontaneously tell stories to illustrate these themes, drawing the materials from their own experiences, from the accounts of acquaintances and relatives, from television, and from newspapers (especially the ethnic minority press). The main point of reference was a strong identification with African Caribbean culture (five out of fifteen members of the group were Rastafarians) and a strong sense of black identity. In one aspect, this identity was an important source of self-respect, and was built on specific features of African Caribbean youth culture, such as reggae music, the Rastafari movement, and an emphasized version of West Indian patois, a very distinct variety of English that is hard for most Londoners to understand. In another aspect, this ethnic identity was defined in opposition to the dominant white culture, and the police were seen as the obvious symbol of an oppressive white authority. Consequently, refreshing the group's hostility to the police was a source of group solidarity and ethnic pride. There was in fact plenty of evidence at this time of racial discrimination in Britain, and evidence of racial prejudice within the police force and of unfair and oppressive treatment by the police of African Caribbean people. Also, quite apart from their identity as African Caribbeans, these young people belonged to a group (young, male, unemployed, often out late at night) who would be much more likely than most to be picked up by the police. Hence there was no shortage of personal experiences that could provide the raw material for stories of police oppression. At the same time, it was clear that all such experiences were interpreted to fit with the grand narrative, and Small found it impossible to persuade group members to reinterpret these stories in ways that would not fit with it. Thus, for members of this group, stories from personal experiences and also those from friends, people at clubs, and the media were crucial as a point of reference in interpreting their relationship with the police, but the grand narrative was much larger, and could not possibly be understood or explained solely by reference to those personal experiences.

In chapter 5, Mike Hough argues that confidence in the police has declined in Britain because the new public management methods have caused the police to focus on activities and problems that people don't notice, and to give less attention to things they care about. In this view, people care about certain problems that may seem unimportant from the viewpoint of a rational bureaucracy but that have symbolic value. He develops this argument with reference to the "signal crimes perspective" of Martin Innes and Nigel Fielding (2002), which suggests that specific forms of crime and disorder have special significance as symbols that things are getting out of control. This idea of course has something in common with the "broken windows" theory of James Q. Wilson and George Kelling (1982), but instead of proposing a single symbol of disorder and decline, Innes and Fielding (2002) propose a method for identifying a number of specific crimes and signs of disorder that have exceptional symbolic power. The argument is that the police can boost their legitimacy by demonstrating that they are tackling these symbolically important problems. If this is true, it implies that the police communicate messages that can influence legitimacy beliefs through actions and gestures that have symbolic value as well as through implementing fair procedures. Similarly, I argued (Smith 1991) that the police in London could only shift the paradigm used by young African Caribbeans to interpret their relations with them by making "grand symbolic gestures."

In France, the Muslim head-scarf issue, as described by Body-Gendrot in chapter 14, provides a striking example of the power of a symbol as a threat to the ideology that constitutes the foundation of the state. The principle of "laïcité," enshrined in a law dating from 1905, provides that education in state schools should be entirely secular, so that schools may be seen as the expression of a unitary state that includes everyone and makes no distinction between people on the basis of their beliefs or origins. When Muslim girls insist on wearing a head scarf at school, this is not only a claim to a specific identity (in combination with the identity of being French) but also a knowing and deliberate affront to the symbolism of oneness in the public sphere that legitimates the French state.

THE DIRTY HARRY PROBLEM

A deep problem for the procedural justice model as for any other model of police legitimacy is the moral ambiguity that underlies policing and our attitudes to it. Carl B. Klockars (1980) analyzed this problem as it was dramatized in the 1971 Warner Brothers film *Dirty Harry*. Harry confronts Scorpio, a psychopathic killer who has already struck twice, and who has now kidnapped a fourteen-year-old girl, demanding a ransom of $200,000 for her release. Scorpio has already confessed to the kidnapping at an earlier time when there was to be a ransom exchange, and has sent one of her teeth and a description of her clothing, leaving no doubt that his victim exists. He already has the money and has not produced the girl; there seems to be no way of finding out where the girl is except from him, yet he has no reason to disclose this information. In the crucial scene, Harry shoots Scorpio in the leg as he is trying to escape and demands to know where the girl is held, and when Scorpio refuses to disclose her location stands on Scorpio's bullet-mangled leg to torture a confession of the girl's location out of him. "As it turns out, the girl is already dead and Scorpio must be set free. Neither the gun found in the illegal search, nor the confession Harry extorted, nor any of its fruits—including the girl's body—would be admissible in court." Klockars volunteers that he would want Harry to act as he did—to torture the information out of Scorpio—in these circumstances, and considers the implications. He argues that Harry faces a genuine and inescapable moral dilemma—"a situation from which one cannot emerge innocent no matter what one does" (33). He argues, further, that in order to ensure that dirty means are not used "too readily or too crudely," we must punish the individuals who use them and the agencies that endorse them, even while accepting that there are a few situations, such as the one encountered by Dirty Harry, in which we actually want individuals, following their inner moral compass, to use such dirty means.

In line with Klockars's analysis, we found in our observational research, published in *Police and People in London* (Smith and Gray 1983), that the "working rules" of police officers—the guiding principles of their conduct—although influenced by the law, could often diverge from it and that there are also "presentational rules" that exist to give an acceptable appearance to the way police work is carried out, but are not adhered to. The systematic ambiguity created by this partly formal and partly informal rule system is the way the police organization deals with the conflicting demands that the Dirty Harry problem crystallizes. Along with it goes a typically distant, authoritarian, and ineffective style of management, with very little observation or direct supervision of police work on the ground by middle or senior managers (as also detailed in our London study). This has the merit of accommodating the police's on-the-ground solution to the Dirty Harry problem by ensuring, for the most part, that managers do not have direct, specific knowledge about rule breaking. The organization can therefore proclaim the formal rules while leaving space for police officers to follow working rules that diverge from them. It can be argued that this systematic ambiguity, at the level of rule systems and organizational structure, perfectly meets the demands and expectations of the public. As the British criminologist Tank Waddington has often pointed out, where they are the suspect, people want Dixon of Dock Green (an avuncular community policeman in a British television series of the 1960s) to be the police officer knocking on their door, but where they are the victim, they want Dirty Harry to be knocking on the door of the offender. In other words, at least in some circumstances, breaking the rules as they are defined by law reinforces police legitimacy. Hence the police officers who brought about three notorious miscarriages of justice in Britain in 1974 and 1975, all of them involving treatment of Irishmen suspected of committing acts of terrorism—police beat suspects and fabricated evidence— could plausibly justify their behavior to themselves on the basis of their belief that they had tacit public support for their actions.

Moreover, the public is in the happy position of not having to actively collude with Harry's dirty behavior. As Reiner (2000, 81, n. 3) has put it, "Seeing an authority (like the police) as legitimate does not necessarily imply agreement with the concrete content of rules or their specific enforcement. It only means acceptance on some minimal basis of the authority's right to make or enforce rules." Our attitude can be that Harry must exercise his judgment on how best to behave, that we recognize his right to do so on our behalf, and that if he chooses when faced with an inescapable dilemma to do something dirty, we may not approve, but it may strengthen our belief in the legitimacy of the police if he follows that course.

BOTTOM-UP VERSUS TOP-DOWN JUSTICE

Three contrasting examples are described, in this volume, of law enforcement or popular justice initiatives that either started at a local level or reflected an effort made to respond to local needs. In chapter 10 Johnson traces the history of a popular-justice movement, called CSSJAR (Community System for Security, Justice Administration, and Re-education) in the extremely poor rural coffee-growing region of Guerrero, Mexico, which grew up at a local level out of associations between coffee farmers despite the resistance and sometimes outright opposition of the state government. This movement, run by unpaid volunteers, acts as police, court, and penal system. At crucial moments in its history it has used consultative or directly democratic procedures to make key decisions. It appears to operate entirely outside or beyond the norms of the formal legal system, yet, in the estimation of participants, in a broadly principled way. It is branded as illegal by the Guerrero state government, yet continues to act in parallel with the state police. A major confrontation occurred in 2002, when state police officers arrested five ex-commanders of extralegal brigades on kidnapping charges, but massive demonstrations of popular support forced the state government to back down. Today the movement continues to grow in the face of renewed opposition from the state. Whereas vigilante groups are typically responsible for brutal executions and lynchings, CSSJAR "has elaborated sentencing guidelines that reject retribution and prioritize reintegration." It imposes sentences of manual work that involve building infrastructure in villages, and villagers feed the prisoners. There are also supposed to be efforts at reeducation through talks by villagers and discussions with them, although it is conceded that these seldom take place.

In chapter 12, Comaroff and Comaroff list a wide variety of alternative justice movements in South Africa, but describe the organization Mapogo in some detail. Mapogo—the biggest alternative justice movement in South Africa by a wide margin—is the creation of a charismatic moral entrepreneur named Monhle John Magolego. It mobilizes chiefly black people in rural areas who have a stake in society—typically, small businessmen—to protect themselves and their businesses against crimes that are mostly committed by young unemployed men, in regions where there is a lack of work and the rate of unemployment among young men is very high. The movement has many thousands of members, although not the sixty thousand it claims. It uses highly visible and symbolic demonstrations of strength and authority in villages to establish its credentials and attract attention. Its mode of operation when a crime is committed is to question the victims, then quickly identify the supposed culprits, and beat and in some cases kill them. The official authorities in the two provinces where Mapogo operates have responded differently to the organization. Police officials in the Northern Province arranged to meet the movement's leadership, although this has yet to produce a framework for cooperation, whereas those in Mpumalanga Province took a strong anti-vigilante stance. Nevertheless, despite unsuccessful efforts to prosecute members of Mapogo, the movement has not been outlawed, and the police do not interfere very much in its operations.

In a formal sense, both CSSJAR and Mapogo are outside the law. The official authorities are opposed to CSSJAR but their key attempts to suppress it rebounded and only succeeded in strengthening its legitimacy among local people. Another reason for its survival is its links to national and international organizations. The attitude of the authorities to Mapogo is ambivalent and varies from one province to another, but in any case there has been no serious attempt to suppress it.

The comparison shows some similarities and some striking differences between these two alternative justice movements. The obvious similarity is that both spring from the widespread perception—richly justified in the eyes of an outside observer—of a gross failure by the state's criminal justice system to control crime and disorder. In circumstances where law enforcement is extremely weak in their own area and in ways that directly affect their own lives, there is a chance that people will "take the law into their own hands." The success of both movements is connected with the widespread perception that they have made a difference: that they have controlled crime and restored order where the official system had failed. There is also some similarity in the ambiguous mixture of hostility and tolerance to the alternative justice movements that is shown by the official authorities. In detaining, judging, and punishing alleged offenders, both movements engage in acts of justice in their own eyes that are clearly criminal acts in the eyes of the law, although the law for the most part has prudently averted its gaze. There the similarities end. CSSJAR grew out of an association of very poor farmers who were all essentially equal, and is based on democratic, communitarian principles, whereas Mapogo has an authoritarian structure dependent on the charismatic leadership of one man. CSSJAR has a nonpunitive penal philosophy broadly based on restorative-justice ideas, with a strong ethic of reintegration of transgressors into the community, whereas Mapogo delivers brutal retribution. We are not told much about methods of investigation and trial used by CSSJAR, but there are hints that procedures are orderly and objective. In the case of Mapogo, it seems clear that they are not much concerned with evidence or trial but proceed directly to punish the suspects named by victims.

Both of these movements in their different ways have achieved a high level of legitimacy among the local population. Faced with dynamic change, as described in these case studies, it is hard to see how the procedural justice model can help to explain this legitimacy. Once each movement was established, local people seem to have regarded its procedures as fair, although what counts as fair is entirely different in the two cases. If we define fairness as a positive concept, as the procedural justice model does, then of course the legitimacy of the two movements is associated with the fairness of their procedures (defined in terms of the way they are perceived by local people). However, this looks like a trivial, almost tautologous, statement that does nothing to explain the dynamic through which the movements achieved legitimacy. If instead we define fairness as a normative concept (appealing to values above and beyond the two societies in question), then the procedures are probably fair in the case of CSSJAR but are clearly unfair in the case of Mapogo, so fair procedures cannot explain the legitimacy of both movements.

In one of its aspects, the idea of justice is abstract and universal, and this fits well with the hegemonic project of legitimating a strong, centralized state which takes direct responsibility for the law and the criminal justice system. However, as explained by Braithwaite in chapter 8, the hegemony of universal justice is always in tension with the needs of local people and particular ethnic and interest groups, and to maintain its legitimacy the state's justice system may need to accommodate these needs. The case studies in South Africa and Mexico describe circumstances in which the tension between local needs and nationally sponsored justice has become so great that the link has snapped and official justice has largely been replaced by alternative justice at a local level. The case study in Rio de Janeiro describes a different resolution of the conflict. Here in the special circumstance where a favela threatens a wealthy neighborhood nearby, the police have abandoned their usual policy of leaving the favelas to their own devices except for occasional military incursions and have instead set out to establish something like a normal pattern of policing that responds to local needs. All the indications are that the drastic reduction in police violence entailed by this policy has led to a major reduction in violence by members of the community. Here the new style of policing has a high level of legitimacy among residents of the favelas in question because the police are no longer shooting at them, there is a general reduction in violence, and the police show signs of listening to the views of local people. However, the problem is that in a society marked by extreme divisions between rich and poor, these policies will often not have legitimacy outside the neighborhoods immediately affected by them. Paradoxically, therefore, the state and its criminal justice system need to have a high level of legitimacy at the national level in order to back up local variations in the way that law enforcement and justice are delivered.

As mentioned earlier, several of the studies in this volume connect alternative justice movements with the growth of private security and risk management outside the direct control of the state, and with the more general trend toward privatization and neoliberal philosophies. In this world, the idea that the state can retain a complete monopoly of criminal justice will be increasingly hard to sustain. This can be illustrated by drawing a contrast between a monist and pluralist conception of the state. At one extreme, French republican ideals are a kind of secular mono-theism, and France still sees itself as a kind of atheistic yet theocratic state, where part of the state religion is unbelief in any God except for the state itself. Within this framework, the criminal justice system sees itself as abstract and universal, the expression of a single, central, historically monarchical power. At the other, plu-ralist extreme, the criminal justice system can see itself as a set of relationships between a number of actors, including victims, offenders, prosecution, defense, judge, local communities, and national public. Each draws on a common fund of law, although each may interpret it differently, yet each has distinctive goals, expec-tations, assumptions, satisfactions. In late modern conditions, it seems likely that the French republican ideal is doomed, because there is such a lively growth of groups outside the state that take action in the field of justice, not only business organizations but also voluntary groups concerned with victims, rape, child abuse, and so on. Some version of a pluralist approach is inevitable, as argued by Braith-waite in chapter 8. In such a system, the law, the police, and the courts still con-stitute an overarching framework, yet at many points they are also competing with the other games in town. For example, the store can use its security guards to eject shoplifters instead of calling the police. A pluralist system has to work well enough for everyone that most of the time they want to go on playing the game within the overarching framework: the danger is that someone will get really upset and take away the ball, which is what has happened in different ways in South Africa and Mexico. Without some method of accommodation, this threatens the fragmenta-tion of the state and the loss of all of the gains in terms of order and justice that had earlier been achieved by state-building.

ETHNIC IDENTITY AND LEGITIMACY

The countries covered in this volume either have a dominant majority group along with substantial ethnic minorities, or, like Brazil and South Africa, a more complex patchwork of ethnicities. In the case of South Africa and the South American coun-tries, we do not at present have the materials that would allow us to distinguish between the influence of ethnic identities and structural factors such as poverty and inequality on the perception of the legitimacy of the criminal justice system. But in the case of the four European countries examined—France, Germany, the Netherlands and Britain—discussions about the legitimacy of the police and crim-inal justice system in recent years have been closely connected with discussions about the place of ethnic minorities within the polity. In the case of Britain, there were serious antipolice riots in Brixton (South London) and in five other cities in 1981, and several more similar events during the 1980s. These disturbances hap-pened in areas having substantial populations of African Caribbeans, who accounted for a majority of the participants. Official reports and social research found that they were for the most part an expression of African Caribbean hostility to the police. In

France (see chapters 14 and 17), disturbances broke out in November 2005 in the Parisian suburb of Clichy-sous-Bois and eventually spread to more than three hundred municipalities. The participants were mainly young, and mainly French citizens of North African origin. The disturbances mainly took the form of destroying property, but there is little doubt that the symbolic targets were the police. In France and Britain, therefore, it is clear that there have been severe problems in relations between the police and certain specific minority groups. In the Netherlands, too, police relations with ethnic minorities became a political issue following the murder of Theo van Gogh, an outspoken critic of Islam, by a Moroccan migrant in November 2004. Even before that, as reported by Bijleveld, Goudriaan, and Malsch in chapter 15, a number of municipal officials had spoken out about crime and disorder caused by groups of ethnic minority youths. Nevertheless, there have been no disturbances in the Netherlands nor in Germany on the pattern of those in France and, much earlier, in Britain.

It is clear that friction in relationships between the police and ethnic minorities are not just a function of structural factors such as poverty, inequality, and a concentration of minorities in decaying neighborhoods. In Britain, for example, the 1981 disturbances did not spread to areas of Bangladeshi and Pakistani settlement, even though these groups suffered greater deprivation on all available indices than did African Caribbeans. Some years later there were disturbances in Bradford, in the North of England, by Muslims originating from the Indian subcontinent in response to the publication of Salman Rushdie's novel *The Satanic Verses,* which was said to slander the prophet Mohammed. These did not involve African Caribbeans. The sequence neatly demonstrates that structural factors can be only a part of the explanation.

To the extent that there are deficits in police legitimacy that are specific to certain ethnic minority groups, this raises important questions about the foundations of legitimacy. One question is how far these deficits can be explained by the procedural justice model—by a pattern and practice of policing ethnic minority groups that they find to be unfair. To the extent that the procedural justice model fails, this leaves the field open to other possible explanations. Two will be considered here. The first is that the state's policy of multiculturalism versus assimilation may somehow be related to the hostility of ethnic minorities toward representatives of state authority. The second is that deprived groups may find a source of identity by defining themselves in opposition to the state.

Regarding the actual treatment of ethnic minority groups by the police and criminal justice system, the information available for the four European countries covered in this volume is both fragmentary and highly complex, so that it is very hard to summarize. In the case of Britain, I have concluded that there is evidence for biased treatment of ethnic minorities by the police and at several stages of the criminal justice system, and of widespread racial prejudice within the police force (Smith 2005). In the case of Germany, Albrecht in chapter 16 concludes that there is no clear evidence of bias, except for a systematic tendency (springing from the law) for foreigners and especially asylum seekers to be held in pretrial custody more often than people of German nationality. This is not to deny that many specific abuses against members of ethnic minorities may occur. In the case of France, Sebastian Roché shows, in chapter 17, that people originating from countries outside France are overrepresented within the criminal justice system, but this can probably be explained by higher levels of (self-reported) offending. There are very high levels of imprisonment of foreigners in France, a country that "stands out of the crowd" in this respect, but Roché considers that this is probably explained by pretrial detention of migrants (especially asylum seekers) rather than imprisonment of people from abroad who are settled in France. Although the evidence is incomplete, it suggests little or no bias against ethnic minorities as people move from one stage of the criminal process to the next, for example, in disposals before trial or sentence following a finding of guilt. In the case of the Netherlands, Bijleveld, Goudriaan, and Malsch (chapter 15) find that ethnic minorities are heavily overrepresented in the statistics of registered offenders, and that their representation increases substantially from the police stage to the prison stage. There is no "conclusive" evidence as to whether this pattern is caused by bias at various stages of the system, although some Dutch writers have suggested that it may be.

What is crucial to the debate is the perceptions of the fairness of the system among ethnic minorities. In Britain, the survey evidence shows that African Caribbeans are considerably more critical of the police and hostile to them than white people (FitzGerald et al. 2002). The differences remain after controlling for area of residence and social background factors. Extensive qualitative research shows that, at least among certain groups of young African Caribbeans, antipolice attitudes are an important element of their view of themselves and their place in the world. For Germany, Albrecht (chapter 16) concludes that in general, differences between ethnic groups' levels of trust in the police are not marked, although there are particularly low levels of trust among certain specific groups in specific places, especially Turks in Berlin. For France, Roché has generated survey evidence showing that young people of North African origin are much more critical of the police and judiciary than people of French origin, and that they are especially critical of police violence. Body-Gendrot refers to a considerable body of qualitative and anecdotal evidence that supports this conclusion. For the Netherlands, the analysis by Bijleveld, Goudriaan, and Malsch of several surveys shows that there is no evidence of weaker belief in the legitimacy of the police among ethnic minorities than among people of Dutch origin, a finding that is remarkable in light of the elevated rates of offending and criminalization of these ethnic minorities. Qualitative studies suggest a major culture and knowledge gap affecting how minorities view the Dutch criminal justice system, and at times these findings seem to conflict with the survey evidence, but this is probably because the samples for the qualitative studies were unrepresentative.

It is worth repeating that these conclusions are based on fragmentary evidence, but even more brutal summary seems to show the following:

- In Britain there is evidence of bias against certain ethnic minorities by the police and at various stages of the criminal justice process, and African Caribbeans clearly have lower trust in the police than do other ethnic groups.

- In Germany there is no clear evidence either of bias or of low trust among ethnic minorities.

- In France there is no evidence of bias in the criminal justice process, but there is evidence of the possible targeting of ethnic minorities by the police, and there are complaints of police violence directed at minorities. There is clear evidence of low trust in the police and judiciary among ethnic minorities.

- In the Netherlands there is evidence suggestive of bias in the criminal justice process, but levels of trust in the police and criminal justice system are similar among minorities and people of Dutch origin.

On the whole, this pattern is hard to interpret in terms of the procedural justice model. Notably, distrust among ethnic minorities in France is not explained by what is known about bias in the system (but perhaps it could be explained by aggressive, sometimes violent, behavior by police officers, about which there is no systematic evidence); and normal levels of trust in the police among minorities in the Netherlands are surprising in view of the minorities' high levels of offending and criminalization and the suggestive evidence of bias in the criminal justice process.

These summaries are, of course, far too extreme, but the point of the exercise is to show that the available evidence is far from fitting neatly with the theory that low levels of trust among ethnic minorities can be wholly explained by the way they are treated. It certainly leaves the field open to other possible explanations for patterns of trust among ethnic minorities. One possibility is that the response of ethnic minorities depends on the wider social and political context of criminal justice. In France a widely shared political ideology emphasizes a beneficent centralized state having a direct relationship with individuals. As both Roché and Body-Gendrot point out, this ideology explicitly denies legitimacy to intermediate groups, including ethnic minority groups, and rejects a model of the polity as an accommodation between interest groups. These principles clearly imply that ethnic minorities should assimilate to French practices and norms, at least in the public sphere. In all three of the other countries, by contrast, the state is seen as an accommodation between the interests of preexisting groups, although this is explicit only in the case of the Netherlands. In line with this general orientation, both Britain and the Netherlands have followed explicitly multicultural policies that emphasize the positive value of the cultures of ethnic minorities and encourage dialogue and accommodation between minority and majority traditions. In the Netherlands, this trend of policy has reversed in recent years, but there is still a notable contrast with France. In Germany, the dominant political philosophies are compatible with multiculturalism, although this has not been pursued as strongly as in Britain. What stands out from this comparison is that the two countries that have had major problems in relations between ethnic minorities and the police—France and Britain—are those that provide the clearest contrast between multiculturalism and assimilationist policies. Even though the evidence is fragmentary, it does support Roché's conclusion that these broad ideologies may have little effect on real lives or the way that people think.

As mentioned earlier, there is evidence in Britain that African Caribbeans can take pride in defining themselves as a group that is oppressed by the state and is in conflict with it. In that worldview, the police are the most obvious symbol of an oppressive white authority. It is not clear from the available evidence whether the same pattern of thought underlies the disturbances in France. If so, this would suggest that minorities can define themselves in opposition to the state regardless of the dominant state ideology.

POLICE LEGITIMACY AND RESULTS

A central finding of the procedural justice research is that beliefs in legitimacy are influenced much more by process than by results. In this context, "results" covers a wide range of outcomes. It can mean the outcome of a particular case as it affects the individuals concerned. For example, was the accused found guilty or not guilty? Did the victim have the satisfaction of seeing the offender punished? It can also mean the overall results of policy and practice. For example, do people think the police or alternative justice movements are more successful in controlling crime? According to the procedural justice model, neither favorable outcomes for the individual nor effectiveness in controlling crime is important as an influence on legitimacy beliefs, when compared with the fairness of procedures followed (Sunshine and Tyler 2003). Some of the case studies included in this volume throw some further light on this question.

According to Johnson (chapter 10), a widespread perception that the criminal justice system was ineffective in controlling crime provided the initial impetus for the formation of an alternative justice movement in Guerrero, Mexico. Also, the perceived effectiveness of the CSSJAR where the official system had failed was one of the chief sources of its legitimacy. Effectiveness in this context means primarily controlling crime, but a secondary element is seeing known offenders punished. The CSSJAR initially collaborated with the justice system of Guerrero state, for example by handing over suspects, but the participants became disillusioned when suspects who had been caught in the act were later released, and this helped to persuade them to deal with the whole process themselves. From the account of Comaroff and Comaroff in chapter 12, the perceived ineffectiveness of the official justice system again provided the impetus for the growth of Mapogo, the vigilante-style alternative justice movement in South Africa, although in this case a talented moral entrepreneur exploited and perhaps magnified feelings that the system was not working. The movement later gained legitimacy by showing that wrongdoers were being punished, although it is difficult to say whether this counts as effectiveness, given that procedures were so summary that the people punished may well not have been guilty. In any case, people seem to believe in the legitimacy of the movement partly because they think it is controlling crime through punishing known offenders. These two case studies seem to raise a serious doubt about the claims made on behalf of the procedural justice model. Focusing on social dynamics, on the way a new movement gathers strength, they seem to show that demonstrating or appearing to demonstrate effectiveness is central to the process of legitimation.

At the same time, Johnson points to the paradox that the "resounding success" of CSSJAR in "cracking down on crime" is one of the forces working toward its dissolution. Local officials believe that the movement has reduced theft, cattle rustling, armed robbery, and drug-related activities by between 90 and 95 percent, but because the threat of crime has receded, levels of participation in some villages have decreased. This double-sided character of evaluation by results is often striking in political and professional discourse about policing. On the one hand, politicians and senior police officers want to maintain that crime is rising, so that more resources need to be devoted to the police. On the other hand they want to maintain that the police have been successful in controlling crime, otherwise there would be little point in spending more money on them. This does show that the relationship between success and legitimation is not entirely straightforward. A moral panic about failure to control crime can be used to legitimate law enforcement, as can the argument that law enforcement methods are showing good results.

Da Silva's account of the GPAE (Grupamento Policial em Areas Especiais) policing initiative in Rio de Janeiro shows that the definition of "success" or "results" can be problematic. Although statistics are not available for the area covered by the initiative, it seems that it dramatically reduced the level of violence there. Residents were aware of the change, and it seems likely that this strengthened the legitimacy of the local police in their eyes. It is much less clear, however, that this change legitimized the police in the eyes of residents of Copacabana nearby. Their focus is on the safety of their own area, which had been threatened by the favela nearby, and they expect the police to protect residents in middle-class areas by repressing those in the favelas. To residents of Copacabana, the reduced violence in the nearby favela may be evidence that the police are not shooting the gang leaders there, as they should do. In a sharply divided society, what counts as success among the poor may count as failure among the rich.

Of course, the police leaders in charge of the GPAE initiative would reply that the new style of policing in the favela provides better protection to residents of Copacabana than the former punitive incursions, and indeed, da Silva argues that it was adopted precisely to avert the threat to the wealthy neighborhood nearby. No information is provided about the actual views of residents of Copacabana, but two possibilities present themselves. One is that their trust in the police is restored by a softly-softly policing style in the favela nearby as long as it prevents their own neighborhood from again coming under attack. The other is that they disapprove of the policy of tolerating low-level drug dealing in the favela, and regard military-style punitive expeditions as effective in themselves in that they successfully punish wrongdoers on the spot. This shows that what counts as effective policing is problematic in several ways. In a divided society, there is the question, effective for whom? Furthermore, some may consider immediate retribution to be satisfying and effective in itself, whereas others may place a higher priority on preserving the peace and controlling crime in the long run. After making these qualifications, da Silva's account implies that judgments about the legitimacy of the new-style police in the favela were closely bound up with judgments about their effectiveness in some sense or other.

In chapter 5, Mike Hough shows that in Britain over the past ten years, rising concern about crime and declining trust in the police have been combined with decreases in the actual level of crime. He argues that this is partly a consequence of populist politics in which law and order has become a central issue in the competition between the two main parties. He also argues, however, that a second factor is the use of "new police management" methods, and associated measures of police performance. These measures focus on the outputs of policing, such as the number of burglars arrested, and the outcomes, such as changes in the rate of burglary. In Hough's view, this focus on outputs and outcomes—broadly, on "results"—has tended to erode police legitimacy. On one interpretation, this can be explained in terms of the procedural justice model. New police management leads to a focus on effects rather than process, on what police achieve rather than the way they do the job, but people care about how they do the job more than about what they achieve. On another interpretation, the problem is that new police management leads to a focus on the wrong objectives. People have not noticed the reduction in burglary and car theft, but they have noticed the increase in small symbols of disorder, which the police now neglect. Hough does not argue that the consequences or results of policing have no importance for policy, nor that they have no influence on people's trust in the police. He does argue for a rebalancing of the politics of the police and of police management to place more emphasis on the craft—on how the job is done—and to take account of consequences at longer intervals, in a more measured way.

It may just be possible to reconcile the various findings in this volume on legitimacy and results. The dynamics of alternative justice movements seem to be closely bound up with perceptions of the ineffectiveness of the official justice system and of the effectiveness of the alternative, yet the very success of these movements may undermine them, because once crime is controlled the need for them recedes. The British example shows that trust in the police and concern about crime are interconnected and tend to follow the same trend, but that they are not related to actual crime trends. This could be because in a developed, basically peaceful society, people do not notice trends in crimes such as burglary and car theft, which are relatively rare events in people's lives. In those circumstances, it is hard for people to evaluate the results of policing, they are easily influenced by political grandstanding, and they start to notice small signs of disorder in the neighborhood.

CONCLUSION: LEGITIMACY, TRUST, AND PROFESSIONAL STANDARDS

The extensive research on procedural justice has certainly shown that people care deeply about fairness of procedures. How satisfied people are with the way a conflict was resolved depends not only on whether they get the outcome they wanted but also on whether they consider that the procedure was fair (MacCoun 2005). However, the chapters in this volume, which extend the field of research well beyond the American psychological studies considered by Robert J. MacCoun (2005), raise new questions about the capacity of the procedural justice model to explain why systems become more or less legitimate, or why alternative justice movements spring up and sustain themselves. There is also an older line of research on links between experience and views of the police which demonstrates that fair procedures do not build legitimacy from the ground up. In our study of policing in London, carried out in the early 1980s, we found that experiences of adversarial contact with the police (stops, searches, and arrests) were strongly related to holding critical views of the police. Perhaps more surprising, the number of experiences of crime victimization was also consistently and strongly related to critical views, where there was no obvious connection between the substance of the views and the experience. For example, the more dealings people had had with the police as victims of crime, the more likely they were to believe that police officers fabricate evidence and beat up prisoners in the cells. Finally, a measure of all contacts with the police, whether in a service or adversarial context, was also strongly related to critical views (Smith 1983, 274–301).

The analysis can be taken one step further by considering how people evaluated their contacts with the police. Although the information is available in the early London survey, the relevant analyses have not been published.[1] However, Wesley Skogan (2006) has recently conducted a thorough study using primarily data from Chicago, but with comparative results for Seattle; Washington, D.C.; St. Petersburg, Florida; New York; Indianapolis; and urban parts of England and Wales. The main purpose of the analysis was to show whether experience of being well treated by the police (as perceived by the individual member of the public) is associated with having good opinions of the quality of policing, and experience of being badly treated is associated with having poor opinions. Analysis of the Chicago survey showed that experience of negatively evaluated encounters (both those initiated by the citizen and those initiated by the police) was strongly related to lower general opinions of the police, whereas experience of positively evaluated encounters was not significantly related to general opinions. A similar pattern of findings was produced for each of the other cities. These findings are entirely consistent with the earlier London findings, but also help to explain them. They suggest that the police can easily lower people's opinions of them by treating them badly, but cannot improve people's opinions by treating them well. This means that the procedural justice model is important for explaining how trust is eroded, but does not explain the origins of trust.

At the deepest level, these origins lie in the basic conditions of social life. There are benefits from living in a society in which most people trust the police, and benefits from cooperating with the police in resolving conflicts. That kind of society is likely to guarantee our security in the long run, even if a particular conflict is not resolved in our favor. Hence some level of trust in the authorities, and in the police in particular, is a basic condition of our social life. However, our trust might be misplaced, in which case we could lose badly from unfair or discriminatory treatment, so we need to be vigilant. In that context, it is not surprising that our satisfaction with our treatment is closely bound up with our evaluation of its fairness.

On this model, trust in the authorities does not originate from our experience of being fairly treated. Instead, we trust the police because we want to believe, if possible, that we live in a society where most people trust the police, because a society in which most people trust the police will be far more secure than any other. Gorazd Meško and Goran Klemenčič put the point eloquently (chapter 6):

> The main issue is trust; people have an internal need to view authorities as benevolent and caring and to trust them. This view is directly tested during a personal encounter with those authorities, and people's views are powerfully shaped by whether they in fact do receive the behavior they expect from the police and the criminal-justice system as a whole.

So the origin of trust is a leap of faith (see Smith 2007 for a fuller discussion). If enough people can make that leap of faith, there will be benefits for all. The procedural justice theory, as presented by Tyler and his colleagues, is an inductive theory that holds that belief in the legitimacy of the system arises from observing a large number of instances where the police successfully resolve conflicts, behave fairly, act in a firm but polite manner, refuse to accept bribes, use the minimum of force, and so on. From this large number of particular instances, people move to the general proposition that the police exercise their authority legitimately, and deserve to be obeyed.

The most obvious problem with an inductive theory of this kind is that many people believe in police legitimacy without having had much experience with the police at all, and in fact the less experience they have had, the more likely they are to believe the police are legitimate. This can be explained if we assume that instead of gradually building general views from particular experiences, people leap to the bold hypothesis that the police are worthy of trust and ought to be obeyed. They then retreat from that hypothesis only if it is falsified by their experience.[2]

This shift of emphasis helps to accommodate some of the findings of the preceding chapters. Although, as Meško and Klemenčič argue, people have a deep need to believe that the authorities are worthy of trust, they certainly will not make the leap of faith in all circumstances. There are a number of factors in the social and political context that influence whether they are ready to jump, such as whether the regime is stable enough to provide benefits, and whether they are at the bottom of the heap in a sharply unequal class system. Myths, symbols, and stories can influence whether they are ready to adopt the bold hypothesis.

This way of putting the matter overstates the point, because clearly, beliefs in the fairness of procedures had some constructive role, for example, in building the legitimacy of the modern British police and of the alternative justice movement in Guerrero, Mexico. More precisely, the argument is that legitimacy is established by a number of factors in various combinations, including, among many others, fair procedures, but failures of procedural justice have the most decisive role in eroding it.

The proposed shift of emphasis has the merit of highlighting the difficult question of what counts as falsification. People will lose faith in the police if they consider their procedures unfair, but the procedural justice model has too little to say about what counts as an unfair procedure. The problem is that once they have made the leap of faith, people will try to see the procedures as being fair, especially where someone else is the loser, and will often condone actions by the authorities that are morally and legally against the rules.

It remains true that the police and the criminal justice system can be effective only to the extent that people trust them. Even if, as argued here, procedural justice is but one among many factors that create the conditions in which people can make the decision to trust, it remains the key factor in maintaining trust within an established system. It follows that the appropriate model for evaluating and managing policing is one of professional standards and good practice. The appeal of the police should be for a leap of faith based on a virtue ethic, on a notion of the kind of people police officers are or should be, not one based on an instrumental ethic concerning the results they promise to achieve. The bottom line is that maintaining police legitimacy means actively cultivating the values and ethic of policing as a profession.

NOTES

1. Unpublished analyses fit with results from later studies described here.
2. This is analogous to Karl Popper's (1959) view that scientific theories, and all empirical statements, are conjectures open to falsification rather than generalizations from particular instances.

REFERENCES

Bandura, Albert. 1986. *Social Foundations of Thought and Action: A Social Cognitive Theory.* Englewood Cliffs, N.J.: Prentice-Hall.

Bittner, Egon. 1970. *The Functions of Police in Modern Society.* Chevy Chase, Md.: National Institute of Mental Health.

Crawford, Andrew. 2007. "Reassurance Policing: Feeling Is Believing." In *Transformations of Policing,* edited by Alistair Henry and David J. Smith. Aldershot, England: Ashgate.

FitzGerald, Marian, Mike Hough, Ian Joseph, and Tariq Qureshi. 2002. *Policing for London.* Cullompton, England: Willan Publishing.

Garland, David. 1990. *Punishment and Modern Society: A Study in Social Theory.* Oxford: Clarendon Press.

———. 1996. "The Limits of the Sovereign State: Strategies of Crime Control in Contemporary Society." *British Journal of Criminology* 36(4): 445–71.

———. 2001. *The Culture of Control.* Oxford: Oxford University Press.

Gerth, H. H. and C. Wright Mills, editors. (1948). *From Max Weber: Essays in Sociology.* London: Routledge and Kegan Paul.

Innes, Martin, and Nigel Fielding. 2002. "From Community to Communicative Policing." *Sociological Research Online,* 7(2). Accessed at http://www.socresonline.org.uk.

Johnston, Les. 2007. "The Trajectory of 'Private Policing.'" In *Transformations of Policing,* edited by Alistair Henry and David J. Smith. Aldershot, England: Ashgate.

Klockars, Carl B. 1980. "The Dirty Harry Problem." *Annals of the American Academy of Political and Social Science* 452: 33–47.

MacCoun, R. J. 2005. "Voice, Control and Belonging: The Double-Edged Sword of Procedural Fairness." *Annual Review of Law and Social Science* 1: 171–201.

Mulcahy, Aogán. 2005. "The 'Other' Lessons from Ireland? Policing, Political Violence, and Policy Transfer." *European Journal of Criminology,* 2(2): 185–210.

Popper, Karl. 1959. *The Logic of Scientific Discovery.* London: Hutchinson.

Reiner, Robert. 2000. *The Politics of the Police.* 3rd edition. Oxford: Oxford University Press.

Shearing, Clifford. 2007. "Policing Our Future." In *Transformations of Policing,* edited by Alistair Henry and David J. Smith. Aldershot, England: Ashgate.

Skogan, Wesley. 2006. "Asymmetry in the Impact of Encounters with Police." *Policing and Society* 16(2): 99–126.

Small, Stephen. 1983. *Police and People in London: Volume 2, A Group of Young Black People.* London: Policy Studies Institute.

Smith, David J. 1983. *Police and People in London: Volume 1: A Survey of Londoners.* London: Policy Studies Institute.

———. 1991. "The Origins of Black Hostility to the Police." *Policing and Society* 2(1): 1–15.

————. 2005. "Ethnic Differences in Intergenerational Crime Patterns." In *Crime and Justice: A Review of Research,* edited by Mike Tonry. Volume 32. Chicago, Ill.: University of Chicago Press.

————. 2007. "New Challenges to Police Legitimacy." In *Transformations of Policing,* edited by Alistair Henry and David J. Smith. Aldershot, England: Ashgate.

Smith, David J., and Jeremy Gray. 1983. *Police and People in London: Volume 4, The Police in Action.* London: Policy Studies Institute.

Sunshine, Jason, and Tom R. Tyler. 2003. "The Role of Procedural Justice and Legitimacy in Shaping Public Support for Policing." *Law and Society Review* 37(3): 513–47.

Tyler, Tom R. 1990. *Why People Obey the Law.* New Haven, Conn.: Yale University Press.

————. 2006. "Psychological Perspectives on Legitimacy and Legitimation." *Annual Review of Psychology* 57: 375–400.

Wilson, James Q., and George Kelling. 1982. "Broken Windows: The Police and Neighborhood Safety." *Atlantic Monthly,* March 29.

PART II

The Role of Legitimacy in Policing

CHAPTER 4

Introduction

The concept of legitimacy has been extensively studied within the American context, as both the introduction and the overview by David Smith make clear. The chapters in this section of the book broaden the discussion by examining whether and how legitimacy might matter within other political and social settings. England and Wales, examined by Mike Hough, share many features with the United States, including long-term stability, and provide a comparison to the American experience. In contrast, Slovenia, which is the focus of the chapter by Gorazd Meško and Goran Klemenčič, is a society in rapid transition; the policing that occurs in such societies provides a contrast to the American and British policing experiences. Chile, discussed by Hugo Frühling, has a history of military dictatorship. Finally, John Braithwaite discusses a major movement toward change in the criminal-justice system that seeks to restore legitimacy and bring the system into line with public views about what is appropriate and just following wrongdoing.

The chapter by Hough considers questions policing and police community relations within a British context. His treatment of public perceptions of the police separates public views from crime rates. Traditionally, one of the central tasks of police management in Britain was seen as keeping a sensible balance between crime control and order maintenance. Recently, however, politicians' attempts to "modernize" the police have resulted in a greater focus on crime control. Whilst there have been falls in crime since the mid-1990s, these have gone largely unnoticed by the public; and indeed, the narrowing of police function resulting from "modernization" appears to have damaged public satisfaction with and confidence in, the police.

Chapter 6 focuses on a post-Communist state, Slovenia. Change is again the focus, but in this case the issue is one of political change, as Slovenia moves toward democracy. Meško and Klemenčič consider the challenges of transforming the police in the midst of broader political change. Difficulties in that transformation, they argue, have led over time to diminished trust and confidence in the police.

Turning to Chile, Frühling describes that country's national militarized police force and examines why such a force seems to enjoy high legitimacy in Chile, at least among the country's better-off citizens. Several perspectives are presented to help readers understand this popularity, including the viewpoint that the police are seen as necessary to maintain order and that national-level policing plays a valuable role in lowering lower-level corruption.

Finally, John Braithwaite discusses the restorative-justice movement. This movement is an effort to confront problems of illegitimacy in the legal system by creating new legal procedures that meet people's need for justice better than that delivered by the traditional criminal-justice system. Restorative-justice procedures allow the parties to a dispute to involve themselves more directly in proceedings that shape how the offender is treated. Unlike criminal-justice procedures, in which the state takes over control of the process for adjudicating a response to alleged wrongdoing, in a restorative-justice system the community plays a central role. Rather than focusing on punishment, the procedures seek to bring offenders back into the community by causing them to feel shame at their actions; this helps them reestablish relationships with people in the community and to the norms that bind the community together.

CHAPTER 5

Policing, New Public Management, and Legitimacy in Britain

Mike Hough

This chapter is an attempt to unravel two puzzles in British policing.[1] The first is that crime is falling; government efforts to further reform policing continue; and yet public ratings of the police show little response to these. The second is that public, political, and—to an extent—academic debate about policing has become locked within a self-evidently crude instrumentalist model of crime control, which has largely ignored issues to do with fairness and legitimacy. I shall suggest that the puzzles can be solved with the same key. I shall trace the fairly complex linkages between the government's "modernization" agenda for the police, the quality of police service, and public ratings. In essence, I argue that attempts to modernize the British police have narrowed police function in a way that has damaged public satisfaction with and confidence in the police. Senior police picked up on this before central-government politicians and their civil servants, and initiated a new "Reassurance Policing" policy to counteract the trend. I conclude by suggesting that the new policy (or in some senses the reversion to an old policy) serves as a means to revivify police legitimacy—although there are various reasons why political and police debate is at best oblique in its recognition of this.

LEGITIMACY AND CRIMINAL JUSTICE

Max Weber's analysis of power, authority, and compliance has become so embedded in our political thinking that it has become paradoxically invisible. Any thoughtful political analyst takes for granted that power relations achieve stability only if naked power is transformed into authority by processes of legitimation. And as we now live beyond the reach of both traditional and charismatic authority,[2] it is the processes by which rational authority is legitimated that are now of interest to political analysts. Power is legitimate, and is thus transformed into authority when its use follows rules that are regarded as fair by both the dominant and subordinate, and when the latter confer their consent to the use of this power. The value of Weber's insights to the Machiavellian politician is that compliance derived from authority is more stable, and much less painfully bought, than that which is tightly linked to the deployment of brute force. Few would take issue with these basic principles when they are spelled out in this way—yet British debate about criminal policy has been largely deaf to these issues over the last fifteen years.

Certainly the idea of policing by consent has a long history; its origins can be traced to the establishment of the Metropolitan Police in 1829, and the stress laid by its founders on the importance of securing public cooperation.[3] And community policing principles, articulated by various senior officers over the postwar period consistently emphasized policing by consent (see, for example, Alderson 1979, 1984). The judicial inquiry chaired by Lord Scarman into the urban riots that occurred in 1981 also attached great importance to the improvement of "police community relations," and its recommendations did much to shape policing practice over the following decade (Scarman 1981).

These riots, notably the one in Brixton, South London, had a racialized quality to them: many of the rioters were black, and the trigger for the events were often grievances about the quality of policing among minority ethnic groups. Lord Scarman identified the immediate problems underlying the Brixton riots as an interaction between intense levels of social deprivation and a history of unlawful policing methods, racially prejudiced police conduct. and lack of community consultation. However, he also recognized the wider dilemmas facing the police in striking a balance between enforcing the law in a high-crime area and the risk of alienating sections of the community who tended to find themselves disproportionately targeted.

With benefit of hindsight, some of the Scarman analysis seems weak. The inquiry located failings at the individual rather than organizational level, and it shied away from concepts of institutional racism. More important for our purposes, the idea that the Metropolitan Police had through its policing style jeopardized its legitimacy among black Londoners was at best submerged or implicit. This can been seen as the consequence of the focus on failings of individual officers at the expense of focusing on systemic problems.

Since then, the relationships between policing style and public compliance have remained resolutely undertheorized, and empirical research on the subject has been minimal. At best, there has been a loosely articulated assumption that good relations between police and public will yield cooperation and compliance with the law. However, even this somewhat truistic principle of reciprocation has become increasingly less visible in public and political debate throughout the 1990s and into the twenty-first century.

Reflecting this, there has been very little academic engagement in Britain with the American "procedural-justice" literature whose origins can be traced to John Thibaut and Laurens Walker (1975) and whose development is closely associated with Tom Tyler and colleagues (see, for example, Lind and Tyler 1988; Tyler and Huo 2002; Tyler 2003; Tyler and Fagan 2005; see MacCoun 2005 for a review). Discussions of legitimacy have been largely absent from British criminology and from government research since 1990, the notable exceptions being Robert Reiner's (1992) analysis of the politics of the police and work by Richard Sparks (1994) and by Sparks, Anthony E. Bottoms, and Will Hay (1996), who used legitimacy as an organizing concept in their analysis of prison regimes' capacity to maintain order.[4] Only very recently has the concept of legitimacy resurfaced explicitly in analysis of mainland British policing (see, for example Crawford 2007; Smith 2007)—although it has been quite widely applied in analyses of policing in Northern Ireland.[5]

One can only speculate why the United States should have taken up issues of procedural justice so vigorously in the late 1980s and 1990s at a time when Britain was turning its back on the concept of policing by consent. Perhaps it is unsurprising that American commentators should be more preoccupied about the relationships between deploying legitimate authority and—often lethal—force, given their much greater reliance on the latter. The tensions between police and minority ethnic groups have also been more evident in many American cities than in Britain, although the latter could hardly claim to be free of problems in this area. Taking into account not only the American experience but also that of Northern Ireland, however, it seems a fairly uncontroversial conclusion that concerns about police legitimacy surface most often in jurisdictions where consent to police authority is most precarious.

Relations between the British police and poor urban communities have undoubtedly been much calmer over the last decade and a half than in the 1980s, which has reduced pressure on the police and policing academics to scrutinize the quality of consent to policing among the public. Certainly there have been riots over this period, and some of these reflected conflict between ethnic groups. However, in contrast to the 1980s, policing was not the focus of urban discontent. However, the thesis that lack of interest in issues of police legitimacy in Britain reflects a relative lack of problems related to legitimacy is hardly persuasive. Relations between police and public remain poor for some groups, including those minority ethnic groups who are at above-average risk of social exclusion. They remain particularly poor for young men from these groups (see, for example, FitzGerald et al. 2002). Only the most complacent of commentators would argue that Britain now faces no risk of the sort of rioting that occurred in the Paris suburbs in the summer of 2005.

In short, other explanations are needed for the lack of engagement in Britain with ideas about police legitimacy and public compliance, and for the retreat from ideas about policing by consent that were commonplace in the 1970s and 1980s. The main theme of this paper is that debate about policing was drawn away from these issues by the combined effect of the New Public Management (NPM) reforms of the British police, which can be dated to around 1990, and the related emergence at the same time of a crude political populism in relation to law and order. These interacted in such a way that political questions about criminal justice in general, and policing in particular, began to be cast more simplistically than previously. Political debate started to take for granted a narrowly instrumental model of crime control. Politicians across the spectrum tended to assume that the role of the police is to control crime, and that the criminal-justice system achieves its purpose largely through the deployment of credible deterrent threat. More subtle conceptions of policing appear to have disappeared from political debate.

NEW PUBLIC MANAGEMENT IN BRITAIN

Over the last two decades of the twentieth century and the first years of the twenty-first, Conservative and Labour governments in Britain have shared a "modernization" agenda for public services.[6] From 1979 onward the Conservative government aimed to get better "value for money" out of the public sector, through a mixture of "modern" management methods and downward pressure on budgets. The favored solutions included budgetary cuts, applying private-sector management methods to the public sector, the introduction of purchaser-provider splits (or quasi-markets) within bureaucracies, and the introduction of new providers, usually from the private sector, to compete with existing ones. These were intended to yield both efficiencies and greater responsiveness to the consumers of public services.

Many aspects of this approach were retained—indeed developed and extended—by New Labour from 1997 onward. Reform of public services is now a key government priority, and one associated closely with the current prime minister, Tony Blair. Like the Conservative administration, New Labour's basic approach has been to secure greater accountability through performance-management regimes that rely on quantitative performance indicators and target setting. The concept of competition as a lever on performance has been retained, though the language of "privatization" and "market testing" has now been replaced by that of "contestability."[7]

This new form of public-sector governance—dubbed "New Public Management," or NPM—emerged in the late twentieth century in many developed countries (see McLaughlin, Muncie, and Hughes 2001 for an account of its development within criminal justice in Britain).[8] NPM is associated first with a consumerist orientation to the delivery of public service: the public is to be treated as a private-sector organization would treat its customers. Under some administrations, this has been accompanied by a strong ideological commitment to paring down the public sector, which can be traced to neoliberal political philosophies about the virtues of small government (see, for example, Wilson 1990). Others have judged pragmatically that the best way to drive up public-sector performance is for central government to set broad objectives and for local agencies to have the freedom to choose how best they should set about achieving the nationally set objectives. In other words, there is tight central control over the ends to be pursued by public services, but local control over the means by which the ends are achieved.

One of the defining metaphors of modernization was introduced by the management theorists David Osborne and Ted Gaebler (1992), who are associated with the emergence of New Public Management in the United States. They suggested that the job of government is not to row but to steer. In other words, government should ensure that public services are provided, but should not necessarily aim to provide these services directly itself. The metaphor was taken up with enthusiasm by central-government politicians and administrators in Britain but was appreciated less by their local-government counterparts, who were usually cast in the role of rowers. This model of governance is often supported by reference to private-sector organizations whose success is built on radically decentralized decisionmaking to local managers, within a central framework of simple performance targets.[9]

If the key feature of NPM is the centralized definition of ends and the decentralization of decisions about means, various further features emerge as a consequence. NPM's logic points inevitably to a particular emphasis on processes of prioritization. It is hard to quarrel with the basic principle that organizations should identify their key priorities and focus their energies on them. The risk is that systematic and focused action against misidentified or poorly identified priorities can have worse consequences than poorly marshaled and ineptly implemented action against well-specified priorities. I shall aim to show that British policing fell prey to this precise risk.

NPM AND POLICING IN BRITAIN

Policing in Britain is organized locally. There is no single national police force; instead there are forty-three local forces, historically enjoying a great deal of independence from central government.[10] Traditionally, chief constables have been accountable primarily to their local police authorities—county-level bodies—and only indirectly, through these authorities, to central-government politicians. Police forces operated until the recent past under the doctrine of "operational independence," whereby neither local- nor central-government politicians could direct chief constables to deploy their officers to tackle specific problems.[11]

Partly as a result of the way that they were structured, the police managed to escape the reforming attention of the Thatcher administration for the first ten years of the latter's life. Throughout the 1980s the Labour opposition failed to offer any plausible challenge to the Conservatives on "law and order" and there was little political capital to be made from "taking on" the police—even though crime was rising quite steeply over this period. However, in the early 1990s, New Labour, still in opposition, began to promote policies that promised to be "tough on crime, tough on the causes of crime." Ever since then, criminal-justice politics have been characterized by intense political competition, with the two main parties aiming to prove themselves tougher than their opponents at every opportunity. Political debate about crime has been marked—or marred—by intense populism (see Roberts and Hough 2002; Roberts et al. 2003). Politicians have wanted to see politically marketable results from the police, and as a consequence, the latter have fallen increasingly under the NPM spotlight. The key changes since the early 1990s have been changes in legislation designed to provide central government with greater powers to "steer" the "rowers" at local police-force level and also to push the development of quantitative performance-management systems designed to enable the steerers to give the rowers their direction. In other words, there has been a considerable shift in power from the local government—as represented by chief constables and their police authorities—to central government, in the shape of the home secretary.

The first major step in "modernizing" the police was to introduce legislation under the Conservative administration shifting the balance of power away from local police authorities toward the home secretary, who gained new powers under the Police Act of 1996 to set national policing objectives, supported by measurable performance indicators. The legislation also required more explicit articulation of local policing plans, with local objective setting. Modernization has continued apace under New Labour. Key changes have included new requirements on police authorities to publish their policing plans; new powers for the home secretary to dismiss underperforming chief constables; and the establishment of a centralized Police Standards Unit, tasked with monitoring the performance of local police forces against their targets. The establishment of internal markets[12] (with purchaser-provider splits) has not yet been a feature of police modernization nor has there to date been any significant threat of exposing police to competition from the private sector—although this is beginning to happen at the margins of police function.

The targets set for the police by their local police authorities and by the home secretary have, at least until very recently, been very largely to do with crime. This has led to a marked simplification of public statements about policing. The police have had to formalize their organizational aims and objectives, and to state them publicly in a way that allows quantitative targets to be set. This has led to an emphasis on crime-fighting goals. These have the appearance, at least, of being readily quantifiable. At the same time they are also capable of commanding public assent because they are simple and comprehensible, and appear to offer the public protection from specific, identifiable threats. The fact that these pressures were at work until the mid-1990s against a backdrop of rising crime and the increasingly populist political debate about "law and order" also limited senior officers' room to maneuver in proposing a more subtle balance of policing goals. Now that the use of national and local targets has become institutionalized, it is increasingly hard for senior officers to challenge the system. They are also subject to a system of performance-related pay linked to target achievement, adding a further disincentive to challenge the rationale or integrity of the targets. As of 2005, chief officers were collectively charged with reducing crime by 15 percent over a three-year period.

I shall discuss later in this chapter how at the turn of the twenty-first century senior police in Britain have reacted against this narrowing of policing function, and have encouraged the government to adopt a more balanced approach. However, some policing initiatives have compounded the effects of NPM. In particular, the National Intelligence Model (NIM) has been developed by senior police officers and implemented in a way that has compounded rather than mitigated the impact of NPM. NIM is a set of "business processes" for identifying policing priorities, and police strategies and tactics for responding to these processes. As its name suggests, NIM requires formal analysis of information and intelligence, to establish a version of the classic management process of iteratively identifying problems, responses to problems, the impact of the responses, and the need for readjustment of response (for a description, see http://www.ncis.co.uk/nim.asp). Arguably, NIM has locked the police more tightly into crime-fighting goals, because the only information collected in any detail by police at the local level relates to crime.

TRENDS IN CRIME AND PUBLIC PERCEPTIONS

Trends in crime in Britain can be simply described. With minor fluctuations most categories of crime increased, year on year, from 1950 until the mid 1990s. Since then, with some exceptions, crime has fallen. This broad picture can be derived both from recorded crime statistics and from the British Crime Survey (BCS), though the interpretation of recorded crime statistics since 1998 has been complicated by successive changes to procedures for compiling the statistics (for a discussion of recording changes, see, for example, Nicholas et al 2005). The decade from 1995 to 2005 shows a steep overall decline of 44 percent, as measured by the BCS.

Some—numerically small—crime categories have not followed this trend. Mugging showed some growth in the late 1990s, according to the BCS, and a steeper growth according to police statistics—probably reflecting the increasing ownership of cell phones among teenagers, who were the both the main offenders and the victims for this offense.[13] There are also indications that stranger violence is on the rise, most probably fueled by increasing consumption of alcohol among young people (Hough, Mirrlees-Black, and Dale 2005). Gun crime is also rising rapidly, though it still represents a very small proportion of the totality of violent crime, and a tiny proportion of overall crime.[14]

The reasons for these decreases in the major crime categories are unclear, and hard to establish convincingly. It would be surprising if the narrowing of police focus to crime-fighting was without impact. In seems probable that the sharp falls in burglary and vehicle crime reflected in part the activities of specialist police squads established to tackle these crimes, and the growing sophistication of policing

FIGURE 5.1   TRENDS IN PERCEPTIONS OF CRIME TRENDS IN BRITAIN,
1996 TO 2004

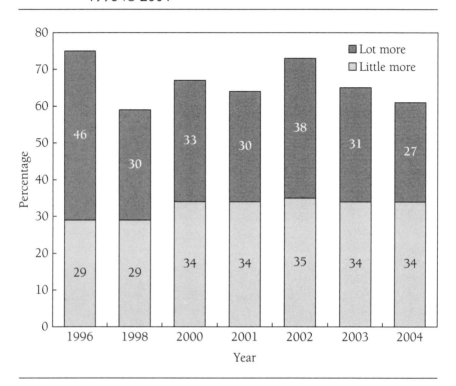

Source: British Crime Survey (see Nicholas et al. 2005).
Note: Question asked: "I would like to ask whether you think that the level of crime in the country as a whole has changed over the past TWO YEARS. Would you say there is more crime, less crime or about the same amount since two years ago?"

strategies designed to tackle persistent offenders. At the same time, Britain has been exposed to the same factors that have resulted in falling crime in other developed Western economies. Improved household and vehicle security is clearly implicated. So, too, is the collapse in the price (and thus black market price) of the audio equipment and other electronic goods that were traditionally targeted in burglary and vehicle crime. The prison population has also nearly doubled since 1992 (Hough, Jacobson, and Millie 2003), and it is implausible that there have been no incapacitative benefits from the increase.[15] Whatever the case, it is clear that people in Britain have not been sensitive to the trend. For some years the BCS has asked people whether they think crime has risen over the last years. Figure 5.1 shows the trend from 1996. In every year apart from 1998, over 60 percent of the respon-

FIGURE 5.2   TRENDS IN RATINGS OF THE POLICE LOCALLY, 1982 TO 2002

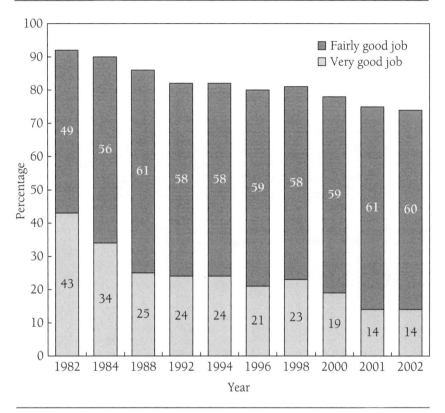

Source: British Crime Survey (see Nicholas et al. 2005).
Note: Question asked: "Taking everything into account, would you say the police in this area do a good job or a poor job?"

dents thought that crime had risen, despite the fact that it had been consistently falling.

Equally or more worrying from the viewpoint of senior police managers, trends in ratings of police performance have continued to decline over time. Figure 5.2 shows trends from 1982 in the proportion of Britons thinking that their local police did "a very good job." (They were asked about the police "in this area." The term "area" was left undefined, but it was implicitly at a more local level than force or county level. In interpreting this figure, it makes sense to focus on the trend for "very good job" as in this context "fairly good job" is equivalent to "don't know" or "undecided.")[16] Clearly there is a long-run downward trend. The proportion of people who thought the police did a very good job in 2002 and 2003 was a third of the figure in 1982.

The marked decline in ratings until 1996 is not especially surprising. After all, crime was actually rising over this period until 1995, and as mentioned earlier, the 1980s saw some of the worst riots that had ever occurred in British cities, some of which were linked to tensions between the police and the public. But the continued, and steep, declines in approval ratings thereafter were puzzling, because for the first time in half a century, the underlying trend in crime had actually reversed.

Clearly one should guard against overinterpreting a single trend-line, but other survey data were pointing in the same direction. For example, the BCS also asks a more general question about police performance; this also showed a fall, from 64 percent thinking the police did a "good or excellent job" in 1996 to 47 percent in 2001 (Nicholas and Walker 2004). That the trend should mirror ratings of police performance in the respondents' local area is unsurprising. More noteworthy is that other criminal-justice agencies (except the Prison Service) showed trend-lines that were steady rather than falling. So there were grounds for thinking that there were specific explanations for the police trend.

THE "REASSURANCE GAP"

Perhaps equally important, the survey data chimed with senior police officers' own perceptions that the police were rapidly losing ground in terms of public approval. Senior officers associated with the reforming wing of the Association of Chief Police Officers (ACPO) were beginning to talk about the "reassurance gap" as a way of referring to the divergence of trends in crime as perceived by the public and as measured by statistics. The ACPO analysis of the reasons for this gap focused on trends in public perceptions of incivility and antisocial behavior, for example as measured by the BCS. This showed that the proportion of the population who regarded drug dealing as a problem in their area more than doubled, from 14 percent in 1992 to 33 percent in 2000. Similarly, the proportion regarding "teenagers hanging around on the streets" as a problem rose over this period from 20 percent to 32 percent, and for vandalism the figures rose from 26 percent to 32 percent (see Nicholas et al. 2005 for the most recent trends). As one chief constable expressed it (O'Connor 2001):

Why has this [reassurance] gap arisen? Research suggests that it is because the incivilities that the public experiences in town centres and on housing estates belie the soothing message of criminal statistics. The police have become increasingly less visible and the public are sceptical about alternatives.

The ACPO argument, in essence, was that reductions in crime had been bought at the expense of a retreat from the policing of less serious, but more visible, forms of disorder. Within it there was a submerged critique of the government's NPM approach to modernizing the police—that the prioritization of specific "volume crimes" such as burglary and car theft had necessarily deprioritized other important police functions such as the policing of low-level disorder.

There are, of course, competing explanations for the reassurance gap. The role of the British tabloid media is clearly implicated. Reporting of crime tends to the sensational, and right-of-center newspapers are especially attached to the idea that Britain is a country in a state of spiraling moral decline. There were also imbalances between workloads and resources in some forces that could account for public dissatisfaction. The fact that there has been a policy of progressively more inclusive recording of crime has given them ample scope for running alarmist stories—even if the increases in crime are very largely illusory.

Falling police ratings may also reflect broader social shifts. For example, throughout the postwar period there has been a progressive decline in deference to authority, reflected for example in the rapidly falling popularity of the royal family and growing skepticism about the British Broadcasting Corporation. The long-run decline in ratings of the police seem likely to reflect generational differences, rather than a reaction to falls in the quality of policing. However, it should be stressed that the steepest falls in ratings of the police occurred over a five-year period from the mid-1990s—at precisely the time when NPM "modernization" reforms were having their most marked impact.

THE UNINTENDED EFFECTS OF NPM TARGET SETTING

Despite the existence of broader societal factors, ample support for the ACPO analysis is provided by the Policing for London Study (PFLS) that I mounted with colleagues from 2000 to 2002. It also renders explicit a series of unintended effects of NPM target setting in a way that was politically difficult for police chiefs to voice (FitzGerald et al. 2002). PFLS found that these unintended consequences were a significant factor in falling public confidence in the Metropolitan Police. The study involved a large-scale sample of Londoners and analysis of administrative records, as well as extensive qualitative interviews and focus groups with members of the public and with police officers.

Britain's public administration is now highly centralized, and there has been plenty of experience of centrally set NPM targets—and their unintended or perverse effects—in other public services. Targets to reduce hospital waiting lists have distorted access to treatment, favoring patients whose operations can be done quickly over those who are in greatest need. This was certainly unintended by central government, and arguably perverse, in that the reforms were never intended to operate at the expense of those in greatest need. Similarly, measuring schools' performance by the number of pupils getting a specified number of exams at a specified level has focused effort on those of middling ability whose performance can be raised across that critical threshold; to meet the target there is no need to put effort into the high performers and no point in bothering with those of limited ability. This form of educational triage was certainly not foreseen by central government, and served to undermine their intention, which was to achieve improvements across the board in educational achievement.

In other words, the bluntness of central-government controls means that they often fail to work as intended. The assumption behind setting such relatively crude targets is that agencies will tailor their work to the intention behind the target. The reality is that when individuals' rewards and organizations' resources are at stake, organizations adopt a contractual approach to meeting targets, achieving them with scant regard to the unintended consequences of doing so.

The PFLS suggests that this is just as true of policing as it is of other public services. A recurrent phrase in our interviews with police officers was "What can't be measured doesn't count and what doesn't count doesn't get done." As has been discussed, successive home secretaries set quantitative performance targets that gave primacy to crime-fighting objectives at the expense of order maintenance. Especially in the 1990s they also imposed the same priorities across widely differing areas, regardless of variations in crime problems. This limited the capacity of local police to prioritize according to local need.

The crime-fighting focus also brought growing specialization, at least within London, with the establishment of teams to tackle burglary, robbery, drugs, vehicle crimes, and hate crimes. Specialized units can work well on their own terms, but there is also a risk that they may be set up in a way that strips the uniformed patrol strength of its officers, and erodes their job satisfaction and skills. The PFLS suggests that this happened.

The highly centralized management system with a heavy emphasis on compliance with numerical targets also appears to have disempowered middle managers and demoralized their staff. The targets that local managers had to meet did not match with the workforce's understanding of what the job was actually about. This compounded the cynicism about management that is in any case inherent in "cop culture," and undermined the workforce's sense of purpose. As one senior manager put it, "Everything that can be valued can't necessarily be measured, but we're now a police service that subscribes to the philosophy that what gets counted gets done."

Concerns about staff management and staff development were numerous. There is some reason to believe that "it was ever thus"—many studies of the police have found this, including the Policy Studies Institute study entitled *Police and People in London: A Survey of Londoners* (Smith 1983), of which the PFLS was the sequel. Cynicism about management has been an enduring feature of the police occupational culture. In the PFLS study, however, disaffection with managers was very explicitly linked with the current performance-management regime. These problems were compounded by the rapid turnover of senior staff at borough level, which made it hard to ensure sufficient continuity to provide for effective leadership. Senior staff also felt that their ability to provide this leadership was hampered by the plethora of demands relating to performance management and by other demands on their time. Cumulatively these factors appeared to have a serious impact on the morale of the staff who carried the main burden of responsibility for day-to-day contact with the public.

REASSURANCE POLICING AND NEIGHBOURHOOD POLICING

From 2000 ACPO began to develop what it called a Reassurance Policing Strategy to respond constructively to the "reassurance gap," and plans for a pilot of the concept surfaced in 2001. Reassurance Policing drew on the Signal Crimes Perspective (SCP) developed by Martin Innes, Nigel Fielding and Sophie Langan (2002). SCP suggests that particular acts of crime and disorder, and particular forms of social control, have a disproportionate impact upon how individuals and communities experience and construct their beliefs about crime, disorder, and control. The theoretical framework focuses upon the ways in which different forms of crime and disorder, and different forms of policing, signify meanings about the wider conditions of social order.

SCP's implications for policing—if policing is constructed as the production of a public sense of security—is that the police should be as systematic as possible in identifying signal crimes and signal disorders, and in committing effort to tackling these in proportion to the impact they have on public perceptions of crime. Incivilities and antisocial behavior are more common and more visible than the crimes the government's NPM target regime focuses on. Innes and colleagues found that specific subsets of incivilities tended to function as what they termed "signal disorders," some of these being alcohol-related problems, drug-related problems and signs of drug use, young people loitering, aggressive begging, and graffiti and vandalism. These findings go some way to explain the resilience of public concern about security and order, even if BCS measures of anxiety about the crime types that have shown the largest declines, burglary and vehicle crime, show a fall commensurate with the crime trends.

ACPO secured—initially lukewarm—government support for the Reassurance Policing Strategy pilot. Resources followed, and the pilot started in 2002. Originally planned for two police forces, the Metropolitan Police Service and Surrey Police, it soon extended to several other forces. In practical terms it involved assigning small policing teams full-time to clearly defined neighborhoods. They were tasked with auditing their area for signal crimes, and mounting appropriate problem-solving responses. There was also an emphasis on establishing a visible police presence, on responsiveness to public concerns, and on policing styles that would engender public trust and confidence. The intellectual underpinnings of Reassurance Policing were thus rather more subtle than those on which NPM in the 1990s drew. The latter presupposed that the task of the police is simply the control of crime, and that the police should concentrate their efforts on those crimes that deserve highest priority. By contrast, reassurance policing recognized that public perceptions of crime and of policing played a part in processes of social control. Reassurance Policing did, however, adopt one dimension of the NPM agenda: a consumerist focus, in its very explicit orientation toward reducing citizens' sense of insecurity.

In practical terms Reassurance Policing had much in common with the community policing experiments that were tried in the 1970s and 1980s. An important difference, for our purposes, is that the idea of policing by consent was much less visible in Reassurance Policing. In other words, public security, rather than compliance with the law, was the primary police product of Reassurance Policing. The majority of the public were not to be policed, but to be protected. Reassuring the public and tackling crime were regarded as interdependent, of course, but the public's compliance of the law was taken as unproblematic—with the exception, of course, of the minority of people engaged in criminality. Good relations between police and public were seen as supporting efforts to tackle crime by increasing the flow of intelligence, but not as a means of legitimating police authority and thus securing greater compliance with the law. Although I have no evidence for suggesting this, it always appeared to me that the concepts of police legitimacy and legitimating authority infused the thinking behind Reassurance Policing, but that these were purposefully never rendered explicit—a point to which I shall return at the end of the paper.

After a positive Home Office evaluation (Tuffin, Morris, and Poole 2006) the Reassurance Policing pilots have been judged a success, and the program has been reshaped into a much larger Neighbourhood Policing Programme, launched in April 2005. This aims to achieve national coverage of neighborhood policing teams in local areas by 2008. The teams are small, and their composition is intended to be tailored to local circumstances. For example, the teams in London typically comprise a sergeant, two or three constables, and two or three police community support officers, who as their name suggests are police ancillaries who operate without full police powers. Teams elsewhere may include wardens or youth workers. Much of the thinking behind the Reassurance Policing pilots has been retained—in particular, the responsiveness to local needs and priorities and the emphasis on close links between police and community, although the terminology of reassurance has been dropped.

In parallel with the Reassurance Policing pilots, the Home Office has developed its own antisocial-behavior strategy, in the form of the TOGETHER campaign (http://www.together.gov.uk). It is significant that this strategy is labeled a campaign, involving emotive appeals to the moral majority to take a stand against loutishness and declining standards. Although it shared in common with the Reassurance Policing work an attempt to respond to public concerns about antisocial behavior, its designers failed to recognize, in contrast to the ACPO work, that what was required was a restoration of the balance between order maintenance and crime control that the government's NPM agenda had actually upset (see Millie et al. 2005, for a fuller discussion).

CONCLUSIONS—TIME FOR A NEW APPROACH TO PERFORMANCE MANAGEMENT?

Though the Home Office evaluation of the Reassurance Policing Strategy was positive, it is still too early to say what impact the change in direction of policing policy will achieve. One can only welcome the move away from the simplistic conception of crime control that was embedded in NPM thinking in the 1990s. The performance-management regime that the Home Office is developing for the police is becoming more multidimensional, and includes measures that relate to the policing of antisocial behavior. There are some signs that public concern about low-level disorder peaked in the first part of this decade, and that it is now declining (see Nicholas et al. 2005, table 2e).

The questions that I posed at the start of the chapter were why substantial falls in crime have not been reflected in public perceptions and why public and political debate about policing has locked itself into a reductionist model of crime control. The answers to both questions are to be found in the government's attempts to "modernize" the police through a target-setting regime associated with the New Public Management. The answer that I have offered to the first question is that the targets selected for the police in the 1990s narrowed police function, and squeezed out the capacity or motivation of the police to respond to problems of low-level disorder. This retreat from the policing of disorder was noticed by the public, but the decreases in crime were not. The result has been a fall in public ratings of the police. Whether one views the public as consumers of public protection services or as citizens whose consent to police authority is required, the downward trend in perceptions is obviously undesirable.

The answer to the second question, about the crudity of political debate about policing, is more complex. One hypothesis is that the pace of centralization that occurred in the process of modernization was not accompanied by an equivalent growth within central government in understanding of the institutions to be "modernized." In other words, those who controlled police performance management simply lacked a subtle understanding of the nature of policing.

This is probably itself too simple a reading of what happened. A more plausible variant of the argument is that the nature of the current political process is such that politicians find themselves trapped in "commonsense" discourse even in situations where more subtlety of thought and action might be preferable. Over the last two decades, the British media have increasingly constrained politicians' room to maneuver when it comes to criminal-justice issues; this has occurred in parallel with the development of the modernization agenda. The press can define the terms of political debate, and they can force politicians to respond within the terms they set. Thus, however subtle a grasp there may be in central government of the nature of policing, politicians' public pronouncements, including the targets that they pursue, have been forced into a simple mold (see Roberts et al. 2003 for a fuller discussion).

A different explanation altogether is that government lacks skills and knowledge not in relation to the institutions it aims to control but of the processes of control themselves. Thus the tools for performance management that are available to New Public Management modernizers are too crude for their ambitions. Experience of the modernization agenda to date suggests that this has occurred in several public services. There are ample examples of the perverse effects of target setting and of statistical performance management not only in criminal justice but in education, health, and transport.

The point at issue here is not whether historically such perverse effects have occurred in the past—for they clearly have—but whether they are an inevitable consequence of the NPM approach to performance management. Those charged with police performance management within government would probably accept that early efforts resulted in some loss of public confidence in the police, but would assert that these reflected teething problems. They would argue that they have done a great deal to strike a better balance between competing police functions; they might point to new policing targets relating to public confidence and perceptions of disorder. Time will quite rapidly tell whether the perverse and unintended consequences of NPM control mechanisms will simply be designed out, as experience in using them grows. I remain pessimistic, for reasons to be discussed presently.

There is a final possible explanation of the crudity with which policing has been conceptualized by NPM modernizers. The institutions of the criminal-justice system evolved in Victorian times into a shape that is still recognizable today, and many are struggling. The difficulty in finding any effective solutions is that there is no coherent political discourse about approaches to institution building and about strategies for achieving institutional legitimacy that will work in the twenty-first century. The NPM modernization agenda has very largely framed the issues in ways that ignore the central requirements of institutions as they relate to legitimacy. Its concerns have to do with efficiency, effectiveness, and consumer satisfaction—none of which manage to encapsulate the subtleties of institutions' legitimacy.

Why British scholars of policing have taken such little account of the United States' procedural-justice literature is a puzzle that cannot be answered here. It could simply reflect the vagaries of academic fashion and of academic networks. A more interesting question is whether, assuming they do engage with this body of work, they will inject its ideas into the thinking of those responsible for British police policy and management. One can see many possible benefits. If neighborhood policing finds its feet, then there will be a need for clearer answers to questions about the purposes of engagement with and responsiveness to the public. Is the strategy simply designed to maximize cooperation and information flow? Or are there more fundamental underlying issues, about legitimizing police authority and securing public compliance. If so, how is this best approached? The procedural-justice literature provides a valuable set of concepts and a growing body of empirical research to help answer these questions.

It is possible, of course, that British debate on policing could be forced back to issues of legitimacy and consent by a deterioration in relations between police and public. The more the police are forced to adopt a narrow crime-fighting role, the more likely such a deterioration becomes. It would take only a single riot resembling those in Paris in 2005 to remind us that if socially marginal groups withdraw their consent to being policed, the consequences can be catastrophic.

The more a procedural justice perspective is adopted in thinking about police performance, the greater will be the need to reengineer the existing performance management framework. One of the central tenets of New Public Management is that conventional bureaucracies lose sight of outcomes in their obsession with process and that performance management systems should retain a clear outcome focus (see Osborne and Gaebler 1992). Home Office managers would probably admit to the crudity of outcome measures applied before their own tenure, but in fact, for many years now there has been a rumbling of dissent amongst police professionals and scholars about performance measures based on outcomes (see, for example, Joint Consultative Committee 1990; Horton and Smith 1988; Neyroud and Beckley 2001).

A common theme in these critiques is the need to improve performance by developing professional standards and focusing the efforts of managers on ensuring that their staff maintain these professional standards. Christine Horton and David Smith (1988) argue for the development of good practice standards; Peter Neyroud and Alan Beckley (2001) advocate development of a "professional model" of police practice that gives the individual officer greater personal responsibility within an ethical framework. American commentators such as George L. Kelling (1999) have also argued for the development of good-practice guidelines. The relationship between establishing professional and ethical standards and the legitimation of police authority is self-evident.

These writers have conceptualized performance management as a two-stage process. Managers need to identify ways of working that achieve policing goals—to develop best practice. Best practice should be defined not simply in narrow instrumental terms but rather in terms of behavior that consolidates and supports police authority. Then managers need to ensure that their staff meet best-practice goals. What they should not do is expect a close-coupled relationship between delivering best practice and reducing crime. According to these perspectives, performance monitoring is not about the setting of targets for goal achievement (or outcome achievement) but about monitoring policing practice against professional and ethical standards. While policing needs to remain outcome-focused, it does not make sense to deny the complexity of the policing environment and to expect to see a simple relationship between policing effort and the achievement of crime targets. The police, and their local partners, cannot be held directly responsible for the level of crime, and politicians should stop trying to do so.

By way of conclusion, I should draw attention to some worrisome features of police legitimation strategies. This paper is a cri de coeur against the narrow instrumentality of government by NPM performance management. My hope is that if politicians accord more importance to the legitimacy of institutions of social control, these institutions will treat citizens with more respect and dignity than they do when they pursue the narrower remit of crime control. But there is a risk that the pursuit of public compliance through legitimation strategies could itself be transformed into a form of narrow instrumentality. People accord institutions legitimacy because they believe that these are infused with legitimating values, such as a respect for procedural justice and for fair outcomes. If they suspect that these values are only skin-deep—instrumental in the way of the well-drilled politeness of supermarket assistants, waitpersons, and call-center staff, the costs in terms of institutional legitimacy could be very high indeed. Considerations of this sort may have disinclined politicians and senior police to talk about policing legitimacy.

NOTES

1. This chapter is almost entirely about policing in England and Wales. The Scottish and Northern Irish systems are separate and different. With apologies to the latter, I refer to "British" policing simply in the interests of brevity.
2. Those who take issue with this claim can treat it as an aspiration rather than a description.
3. See, for example, the fourth of Charles Rowan and Richard Mayne's nine principles of policing (as cited in Reith 1956), "To recognise always that the extent to which the co-operation of the public can be secured diminishes proportionately to the necessity of the use of physical force and compulsion for achieving police objectives."
4. For example, a search of all abstracts of the British Journal of Criminology shows that the term "legitimacy" appears twelve times in total; only three of these abstracts relate to policing, one of which was by American academics. The term "procedural justice" appears once, in the same article by American academics. It is striking that a hundred-page Home Office systematic review of research on "reassurance policing" (Dalgleish and Myhill 2004) made no reference at all to "legitimacy" or to "procedural justice" and included only one reference to Tyler, under a list of unobtainable publications.

    Concerning the politics of the police, for the purposes of my argument it is worth noting that Reiner's (1992) work was the second edition of a book originally published in 1984, at a time when the concepts of legitimation and organizational legitimacy had greater political currency in Britain.
5. Though the concept has had more obvious relevance to policing in Northern Ireland, it would be hard to offer an analysis of the (now disbanded) Royal Ulster Constabulary without reference to its problems of legitimacy. See the Patten Report (1999) and Aogán Mulcahy and Graham Ellison (2001).

6. Some, especially within New Labour, would take issue with the idea that moderniza-tion is a variant of NPM, precisely because of the latter's identification with "small gov-ernment," in contrast to modernization's commitment to social justice. However, the means to achieve these different ends look remarkably similar. There is something in the argument that NPM was exported from Thatcherite Britain to the United States, whence it was reimported to Britain by Tony Blair during the Clinton administration.

7. Privatization refers to the transfer of services from the public sector to the private sector, as has happened with British public utilities. "Market testing" was the term used under the Conservative administration for arrangements whereby public bodies tendered in competition with the private sector for contracts covering the work over which they pre-viously enjoyed a monopoly. Thus the Prison Service has for some time competed against private security companies for contracts to run prisons, and has often won these contracts. The Labour Government's preferred term for the same process is "market test-ing." See, for example, Lord Patrick Carter's (2003) review of the correctional services.

8. The term "New Public Management" was coined by Christopher Hood (1991). See Eugene McLaughlin, John Muncie, and Gordon Hughes (2001) for an account of its development within criminal justice in Britain.

9. For example, some companies let local managers have extensive freedom over their operations, provided that they meet a single target specified in terms of growth of profits.

10. However, at the time of writing there were proposals for a series of large-scale amalga-mations, some of which had already been announced, the expectation being that over time the number of forces would fall from the present forty-three to around a dozen.

11. The boundary between policy issues and operational issues was always opaque, how-ever, and it was probably in the interests of chief constables to keep it so.

12. Internal markets involve the commissioning by one part of an organization of services from another part of the same organization, for a specified price.

13. Teenagers' experience of crime is poorly captured by the BCS, and this probably explains a large part of the discrepancy. Only those aged sixteen or over are included in the sam-ple, and nonresponse rates are in any case high for teenagers and young adults.

14. In total there were 10,340 recorded firearms offenses in 2003 and 2004, or 0.9 per-cent of the total of 1.1 million recorded violent crimes; 440 of these were firearms offenses involving serious injury and 1,860—0.2 percent of the total—were firearms offenses involving slight injury.

15. Though this benefit will certainly be smaller than has been claimed by Conservative politicians (see Bottoms, Rex, and Robinson 2005, chapter 3).

16. The alternative response in the middle ground was "fairly poor job"—a much less bland statement than "fairly good job," at least in English as spoken in England.

REFERENCES

Alderson, John. 1979. *Policing Freedom*. Plymouth, England: McDonald & Evans.
———. 1984. *Law and Disorder*. London: Hamish Hamilton.
Bottoms, Anthony, Sue Rex, and Gwen Robinson. 2005. *Alternatives to Prison: Options for an Insecure Society*. Cullompton, England: Willan Publishing.

Carter, Lord Patrick. 2003. *Managing Offenders, Reducing Crime.* London: Prime Minister's Strategy Unit.

Crawford, Adam. 2007. "Reassurance Policing: Feeling Is Believing." In *Transformations in Policing,* edited by Alistair Henry and David Smith. Aldershot, England: Ashgate Publishing.

Dalgleish, David, and Andy Myhill. 2004. "Reassuring the Public: A Review of International Policing Interventions." Home Office Research Study 284. London: Home Office.

FitzGerald, Marian, Mike Hough, Ian Joseph, and Tarek Qureshi. 2002. *Policing for London.* Cullompton, England: Willan Publishing.

Hood, Christopher. 1991. "A Public Management for All Seasons." *Public Administration* 69(1): 3–19.

Horton, Christine, and David Smith. 1988. *Evaluating Police Work.* London: Policy Studies Institute.

Hough, Mike, Jessica Jacobson, and Andrew Millie. 2003. *The Decision to Imprison: Sentencing and the Prison Population.* London: Prison Reform Trust.

Hough, Mike, Catriona Mirrlees-Black, and Michael Dale. 2005. "Trends in Violent Crime Since 1999/2000." London: King's College, School of Law, Institute for Criminal Policy Research. Accessed at http://www.kcl.ac.uk/depsta/law/research/icpr/publications/ViolenceReport.pdf.

Innes, Martin, Nigel Fielding, and Sophie Langan. 2002. "Signal Crimes and Control Signals: Towards an Evidence-Based Conceptual Framework for Reassurance Policing." A report for the Surrey Police. Guildford, England: University of Surrey.

Joint Consultative Committee. 1990. "Operational Policing Review." Report. London: Association of Chief Police Officers, Superintendents' Association, and Police Federation.

Kelling, George L. 1999. " 'Broken Windows' and Police Discretion." Research report NCJ 178259. Washington: National Institute of Justice. Accessed at http://www.ncjrs.gov/pdffiles1/nij/178259.pdf.

Lind, E. Allan, and Tom Tyler. 1988. *The Social Psychology of Procedural Justice.* New York: Plenum Press.

MacCoun, Robert. 2005. "Voice, Control and Belonging: The Double-Edged Sword of Procedural Justice." *Annual Review of Law and Social Science* 1: 171–201. Accessed at http://repositories.cdlib/csls/fwp/30.

McLaughlin, E., J. Muncie, and G. Hughes. 2001. "The Permanent Revolution: New Labour, New Public Management and the Modernisation of Criminal Justice." *Criminal Justice* 1(3): 301–17.

Millie, Andrew, Jessica Jacobson, Eraina McDonald, and Mike Hough. 2005. *Anti-Social Behaviour Strategies: Finding a Balance.* York, England: Joseph Rowntree Foundation.

Mulcahy, Aogán, and Graham Ellison. 2001. "The Language of Policing and the Struggle for Legitimacy in Northern Ireland." *Policing and Society* 1(2). Accessed at http://www.bbc.co.uk/northernireland/learning/history/stateapart/agreement/policing/support/pj1_c031.shtml.

Neyroud, P., and A. Beckley. 2001. *Policing, Ethics and Human Rights.* Cullompton, England: Willan Publishing.

Nicholas, Sian, and Alison Walker. 2004. "Crime in England and Wales 2002/03. Supplementary Volume 2, Crime, Disorder, and the Criminal Justice System—Public Attitudes and Perceptions." Online report 02/04. London: Home Office. Accessed at http://www.homeoffice.gov.uk/rds/pdfs2/hosb0204.pdf.

Nicholas, Sian, David Povey, Alison Walker, and Chris Kershaw. 2005. "Crime in England and Wales, 2004/2005." Home Office Statistical Bulletin 11/05. London: Home Office.

O'Connor, Denis. 2001. "Civility First: The Reassurance Policing Concept." *Criminal Justice Management* July: 26–27.

Osborne, David, and Ted Gaebler. 1992. *Reinventing Government: How the Entrepreneurial Spirit Is Transforming the Public Sector.* Reading, Mass.: Addison-Wesley.

Patten Report. 1999. *A New Beginning: Policing in Northern Ireland.* Belfast, Northern Ireland: Independent Commission on Policing in Northern Ireland. Accessed at http://www. belfast.org.uk/report/fullreport.pdf.

Reiner, Robert. 1992. *The Politics of the Police.* 2nd ed. London: Wheatsheaf Harvester.

Reith, Charles. 1956. *A New Study of Police History.* London: Oliver & Boyd.

Roberts, Julian V., and Mike Hough, editors. 2002. *Changing Attitudes to Punishment: Public Opinion, Crime and Justice.* Cullompton, England: Willan Publishing.

Roberts, Julian V., Loretta Stalans, David Indermaur, and Mike Hough. 2003. *Penal Populism and Public Opinion.* Oxford: Oxford University Press.

Scarman, Lord. 1981. *The Brixton Disorders: Report of an Inquiry by the Rt. Hon. Lord Scarman OBE.* London: HMSO.

Smith, David J. 1983. *Police and People in London: Vol. 1, A Survey of Londoners.* London: Policy Studies Institute.

———. 2007. "New Challenges to Police Legitimacy." In *Transformations in Policing,* edited by Alistair Henry and David Smith. Aldershot, England: Ashgate Publishing.

Sparks, Richard. 1994. "Can Prisons be Legitimate? Penal Politics, Privatisation and the Timeliness of an Old Idea." *British Journal of Criminology* 4(special Issue): 14–28.

Sparks, Richard, Anthony E. Bottoms, and Will Hay. 1996. *Prison and the Problem of Order.* Oxford: Clarendon Press.

Thibaut, John, and Laurens Walker. 1975. *Procedural Justice.* Hillsdale, N.J.: Erlbaum.

Tuffin, Rachel, Julia Morris, and Alexis Poole. 2006. "An Evaluation of the Impact of the National Reassurance Policing Programme." Home Office Research Study 296. London: Home Office.

Tyler, Tom R. 2003. "Procedural Justice, Legitimacy and the Effective Rule of Law." In *Crime and Justice: A Review of Research,* edited by Michael Tonry. Volume 30. Chicago, Ill.: University of Chicago Press.

Tyler, Tom R., and Jeffrey Fagan. 2005. "Legitimacy and Cooperation: Why Do People Help the Police Fight Crime in Their Communities?" (Fall 2005). Columbia Public Law Research Paper No. 06-99. Accessed at SSRN, http://ssrn.com/abstract=887737.

Tyler, Tom R., and Yuen J. Huo. 2002. *Trust in the Law: Encouraging Public Cooperation with the Police and the Courts.* New York: Russell Sage Foundation.

Wilson, James Q. 1990. *Bureaucracy: What Government Agencies Do and Why They Do It.* New York: Basic Books.

CHAPTER 6

Rebuilding Legitimacy and Police Professionalism in an Emerging Democracy: The Slovenian Experience

Gorazd Meško and Goran Klemenčič

Efforts to develop a more professional, legitimate, accountable, and efficient police service are present in all societies. There are few, if any, countries that can be fully satisfied with the level of professionalism of its police service, its level of legitimacy within the society—especially among different ethnic, socioeconomic, or other minorities—and with the outcomes the police deliver in terms of security while respecting the rule of law and individual liberties. However, the challenges posed to the police organization are incomparably greater in an emerging democracy or a post-conflict state; Slovenia was such a state in the early 1990s, and is today a modern parliamentary democracy. In between there has been a period marked by dramatic changes in the sociopolitical, economic, and legal system, as Slovenia underwent a transformation from being a constituent part of the Federal Socialist Republic of Yugoslavia, a semi-authoritarian one-party state, to becoming an independent country governed by the rule of law and a member of the European Community. Clearly, dramatic changes during the transitional period and the rapid pace of these changes in itself, as well as the proximity of armed conflicts in the Balkans, resulted in uncertainty in crime-control policies, strategies, and operations. The impact on the Slovenian police, as an organization, on individual police officers and on the way the police is perceived by the public was remarkable. Furthermore, the process of democratization of the political system went hand in hand with the process of gaining independence from Yugoslavia, a process in which the Slovenian police played a prominent part in 1991 as an armed opposition to the Yugoslav army.

The problems of the criminal-justice system in Central and Eastern Europe (including a widespread belief that crime pays, perception that police are not successful in crime fighting, the leniency of judges, a backlog of unprocessed cases, problems of formal social control, huge turnover in the police forces, problems with training), as discussed by Matti Joutsen (1995), has also been part of social reality in Slovenia. Such problems influence the quality of policing in a transitional society. Solving such problems is a huge challenge for politicians, policymakers, police management, and police officers as well as society in general.

Slovenian policing after 1991 has been characterized by several attempts at police reform in order to move closer to Western-style policing. Despite organizational and professional cultural obstacles, some notable changes have been achieved. Although it would be an overstatement to say the reform of the Slovenian police was a success story, we can claim reasonable optimism and characterize the Slovenian police as a relatively modern and professional law enforcement service far closer to its Western counterparts than to the Communist-area "militia"; its present orientation is based on the motto "to protect and serve" and community policing is at the heart of its announced strategy. This transformation has been a result of a complex set of processes that has not always delivered promised results. Even though community policing, professionalism, protection of human rights, and the restraints on the arbitrary use of force top the official agenda, the understanding of the underlying principles of problem-oriented policing and its practical implementation remains weak, and human rights monitoring entities continue to voice their concerns over the inadequate system of accountability of police officers for ill treatment of civilians.

The goal of this chapter is to present and discuss some of these processes, explain changes in Slovenia in general and the transformation of its police in particular, share the lessons learned, and highlight key obstacles and challenges that still lie in the path to a greater police professionalism and accountability and consequently of a higher level of legitimacy of the Slovenian police within the community it polices.

THE TRANSITION

The process of transition of Slovenian police from a Communist-era "militia" to a democratic law enforcement service cannot be evaluated without outlining the specific historical background and the environment in which the transition took place—the violent breakdown of the former Socialist Republic of Yugoslavia, the independence process, rapid changes in the sociopolitical, economic, and legal systems, all leading to the full accession to the European Union in 2004. More specifically, during this process the police organization has endured significant reforms of its institutional framework (separating police organization from secret and intelligence services and redefining its relationship with the rest of the executive branch of government), legal framework governing its powers and duties (adoption of a new Constitution and new laws in the field of criminal justice, strengthening judicial and citizens' oversight and becoming subject to monitoring from European and international human rights bodies), and fundamentally reforming its recruitment and training policies and practices.

Background Information

In order to better understand the present state of policing in Slovenia we need first to put the country and its police organization in a broader geopolitical perspective. The Republic of Slovenia is an Eastern European country of 2 million people situated between Italy, Austria, Hungary, Croatia, and the Adriatic Sea. Formerly the more northerly of the six republics of the former Socialist Federal Republic of Yugoslavia, now it is one of the newborn European states. In late eighties, when it was still a constituent part of Yugoslavia, it started on the path of democratization, holding its first free multiparty elections after World War Two in 1990, followed by a plebiscite at which more than 88 percent of the electorate voted for the country's independence from Yugoslavia. The Declaration of Independence on June 25, 1991, triggered a violent intervention by the Yugoslav federal authorities. After a brief armed conflict between the Yugoslav army on one side and Slovenian police and territorial guards on the other, a political agreement was reached under the auspices of the European Union to withdraw the Yugoslav army from Slovenia. Thus, the country was spared the tragic developments that followed in Croatia, Bosnia, and Herzegovina. In December 1991 a new constitution with an extensive bill of rights was proclaimed; the following year Slovenia became a member of the United Nations and, in 1993, of the Council of Europe by ratification of the European Convention on Human Rights. In 2003 Slovenia joined NATO and it became a member of the European Union in 2004.

As for the Slovenian police, its organizational beginnings reach back to the Austro-Hungarian monarchy, to the year 1849, when the Gendarmerie Corps was founded. During 1945 and 1991 it was part of Yugoslav police force that was—as in many other Communist countries—called the "milica" (militia). Initially a centralized police force, the Yugoslav police had gradually become more decentralized, transferring a lot of responsibilities to the individual republics. At the outset of the democratization process, Slovenia—then a republic of former Yugoslavia—had a rather independent police structure subordinated to the Slovenian Secretariat of Interior; it was also decentralized (police chiefs were appointed by local authorities and approved by the secretary of the interior). In contrast with the Security Service, the uniformed and criminal police was by and large not associated with political oppression. This fact and the role of the police in the struggle for independence from Yugoslavia contributed to an interesting phenomenon when compared to experiences from other transitional countries, namely, that the public "approval rating" of the Slovenian police, as indicated through public surveys, was unusually high at the beginning of the transition period; afterward it decreased until 2001, when the trend stabilized.[1] Regretfully there has been no in-depth research conducted into this phenomenon. One possible explanation of the seemingly paradoxical indicator is the passive, if not supportive, role of the police in the process leading toward democratization and independence, along with the relatively low crime rates. In the first years of transition, Slovenia did not experience an increase of violent predatory crime, which did characterize the breakdown of order in other post-Communist countries. In addition, the surveys likely registered overall positive views, and general public excitement with emerging democracy, of the larger political change, which indirectly contributed to a positive evaluation of the police. Consequently, during the most turbulent period of change in the political system, the police was not perceived as a repressive bastion of the Communist regime but rather as a partner in securing the independence of and democracy in the new Slovenia. This view is anchored in fact, for it was the police together with the Territorial Guard that confronted the Yugoslav army after the Declaration of Independence.

Reform of the Institutional Framework

The very first reforms introduced were symbolic, but important: renaming the "milica" the "police" and changing the insignias. The next challenge was to make a clear separation between law enforcement bodies and the security and intelligence services. Already in 1991 security and intelligence services were removed from the Ministry of the Interior (known until 1991 as the Secretariat of the Interior) and stripped of law enforcement powers. The Slovenian Security and Intelligence Agency (SOVA), which in the past (also under a different name) used to be part of the Ministry of the Interior and in possession of extensive powers with little or no judicial oversight, has been reorganized, its powers of covert surveillance and interception of communications curtailed and put under judicial supervision; parliamentary oversight of the security and intelligence services was introduced. The constitution of 1991 also expressly prohibited members of the police and the armed forces to belong to a political party (article 42). As yet no specific research exists in Slovenian on this particular topic, but it can be argued that this prohibition alone contributed to operational police officers in Slovenia rarely being perceived as instruments of different political forces (the same, as we shall explain, cannot be said for top-level management).

Furthermore, a landmark institutional reform of the police occurred in 1998 with the adoption of the new Police Act, which created a General Police Directorate as an autonomous body within the Ministry of the Interior. This new status of the police organization changed the relationship between the police and the Ministry of the Interior dramatically, but, more important, it also positively impacted the perception of the police organization by the public. Whereas previously the police was just one of the services under the Ministry of the Interior and the minister was at the top of the police chain of command, directly supervising its operations, this person was now replaced in this position by a newly created post, that of director general of the police, which was filled by a government appointment to a five-year term. Thus, this post has therefore become—at least in theory—a professional and not a political position, subject to transparent appointment procedures and safe-guarded from political pressures or removal. This change of status has reflected positively in the public perception of the police in general; since 1998 the public and the media have started seeing the police as an independent professional body, and not as an "organ" of the Ministry of the Interior. Similarly, police officers started identifying themselves more as members of the police organization and not as (privileged) employees of a ministry. A professional, the director general of the police, rather than a political appointee, the minister, became the visible voice of the service. With this also came a clearer accountability and responsibility of top police management. However, this divorce of the police and the politics has not been all smooth; since 1999 the public has witnessed ongoing jurisdictional clashes between the director general and the minister, at one point resulting in the director general's challenging the oversight powers of the minister before the Constitutional Court.

Institutional reforms were closely linked to the process of the centralization of the police organization in Slovenia. This was partially a by-product of a separate reform of the local government, but was also driven by the notion that in-depth reform of the police requires a clear hierarchy and a central command. Under the Socialist system, the Slovenian police organization was quite decentralized (Pagon 2004b; Meško 2004; Meško and Lobnikar 2005). Before 1991, all police stations in the country were considered community-level units. Commanders of local and regional stations were appointed by local authorities, after such appointments were approved by the secretary of the interior. Today the police organization in Slovenia is highly centralized, with only one national, state-funded police force (numbering just over ten thousand officers), leaving local authorities with almost no influence in that area. All police stations are state-level units, but they only operate at the local level. The local government has no say in their operation or in the appointment of their commanders. While such centralization arguably eased the management of reforms, it soon conflicted with the new policing strategy that the police wanted to adopt—community policing. The next section will shed more light on these issues.

Reform of the Legal Framework

As the changes in the political system were driven by demands for democratization and respect for human rights, societal changes brought about significant changes in the criminal-justice system in general and in policing in particular.

First, the 1991 constitution put a strong emphasis on the protection of human rights and fundamental liberties (and included a number of rights directly relevant for the police practices: Miranda rights, strong limitations on pretrial detention and search and seizure powers, habeas corpus, protection of privacy, and fundamental rights in criminal procedures—the right to counsel, the right to cross-examine hostile witness, and so forth).

Second, the new constitution led to the creation of two institutions, the Constitutional Court and the ombudsman, which had an important influence on police practices in Slovenia. The Constitutional Court has during the 1990s ruled unconstitutional a number of laws and regulations governing different police powers and practices, especially in the areas of detention, covert surveillance, access to a lawyer, use of physical force, stop-and-frisk, and identity checks (Zupančič et al. 2002). These rulings have further limited police powers and strengthened the principles of legality and proportionality as fundamental conditions for the use of force. The ombudsman has unrestricted access to detention centers and persons in custody as well as to all official documents, regardless of the level of confidentiality, and has led to significant improvement in the legal and material conditions relating to police custody (Klemenčič, Kečanović, and Žaberl 2002).

Third, new legislation on criminal procedures, in particular on the pretrial investigation, adopted in 1995, introduced adversarial elements into the pretrial and the trial stage of judicial processes. It granted the judiciary greater control over the police by mandating the exclusion of illegally obtained evidence and strict search warrant requirements. A telling and, in comparison to other countries, a rather unique example of this change is revealed by statistics on the need for a search warrant to search premises: in the 1980s, on average over 8 percent of all searches of premises were conducted without a warrant, under the "exigent circumstances" rule, whereas during 2001 and 2004 only 1 percent of all searches were without a warrant (Grilc and Klemenčič 2006).[2]

Fourth, when Slovenia in 1993 became a member of the Council of Europe and ratified the European Convention on Human Rights, the country became subject to the jurisdiction of the European Court and later to the oversight of the European Committee for the Prevention of Torture, which among other things has the power to conduct on-site inspection of places of police custody.

Fifth, the new Police Act of 1998 significantly changed basic police powers, limiting the powers of stop-and-frisk and abolishing preventive identification checks and preventive detentions as well as significantly raising the threshold for the use of coercive measures.

Sixth, in 2001 the criminal police was put under more effective control of public prosecutors in the process of investigating crimes; in fact, the criminal police, while remaining within the institutional framework of the police organization, has become operationally fully subordinated to the prosecution service. Given the nonpolitical and independent nature of the Prosecution Service, this move—apart from contributing to the efficiency of criminal investigations—has arguably also symbolically strengthened the independence, professional status, and nonpolitical nature of the criminal police. However, this change also had a broader negative consequence: part of the accountability and responsibility has been shifted to the Prosecution Service. An overview of media reports discovers that following this new relationship between the police and prosecutors when the former is asked to explain their actions in a particular case, the police rarely comments and refers all questions to the prosecutor's office.

Seventh, the new Police Act introduced civilian oversight in the resolution of complaints against mistreatment by the police, an experiment that will be discussed further.

A plethora of legal changes, not followed by adequate in-service training, resulted in uncertainty on the part of police officers about the scope and conditions of their coercive and investigative powers. A survey conducted in 1999 indicated an alarmingly low level of knowledge among ordinary police officers of the legal requirements for the use of specific police powers. Similarly, sometimes evidence was excluded in court as illegal, not because the police intentionally violated the rights of the suspect but because in conducting their investigations they were ignorant of recent or minor changes in the law that affected the use of the information collected. Furthermore, a rash of legislative changes limiting police powers accompanied by proactive institutional oversight mechanisms (the ombudsman, courts, civil society) have to some extent resulted in a situation, particularly notable between 1998 and 2000, in which failure by the police to intervene and use its powers were as big a problem as the excessive use of force (Klemenčič, Kečanović, and Žaberl 2002).

Reform of Police Recruitment and Training

The basic training of police officers in the former Yugoslavia was of a military character, which reinforced the military aspects of the police organization. At the heart of the system was the Police Cadet School. Boys entered this school at the very young age of fourteen or fifteen—right out of primary school—and the training lasted four years, after which they became police officers. In addition to the police cadet system, an abbreviated police training was also offered to adult men who had already undergone military training and wanted to join the police force. Specific criminal police units could also recruit people with college degrees in the law, economics, and certain other areas. This system was abolished in the mid-1990s; in its stead recruits now attend the police academy, which offers an eighteen-month course to candidates who have finished high school and are at least eighteen years old. The system was also opened to female candidates. (Until the mid-1990s the Slovenian police had just a few female officers—almost exclusively working with the criminal police in the area of sexual crimes and juvenile delinquency.)

A study conducted in 1976 (Skalar 1976) offers valuable insight into police officers' characteristics in the mid-seventies and eighties. The high-quality study is worth examining in detail because of its intriguing findings during the time when socialism held sway and Slovenia was a republic of the Socialist Republic of Yugoslavia. Thus, in comparison to the research conducted after 1991, it presents valuable information on the change in the police characteristics. The study shows positive and negative aspects of police cadet training and socialization into a professional police culture. The first principal finding was a positive correlation between the physical ability of police officers and their efficiency at work. The more physically able police officers were the more their superiors valued their performance. The social origin of the police officers was quite typical, with the majority of those in the study being working-class people and people from rural areas (Skalar 1976).

Motivation for joining the police force was an issue of special interest to the researchers. Joining the police force was related to the following factors: prestige and social power, feelings of inferiority, romantic view of policing, material and social expectations about police profession, family tradition, and parental motivation. The results showed that 14.3 percent of the police officers joined the police force because they wished to work in a prestigious public organization, have the opportunity to exert power over other people, and give orders to other people. Another motive was related to a wish for an opportunity to intimidate bad (criminal) people (17.8 percent). A third group of motives for joining the police force was related to feelings of inferiority (respondents' perception of inferiority in comparison to other citizens), the understanding of the police profession as a source of social security, and a need for the tough policing of deviants (21 percent). Forty-four percent of the respondents confirmed all three statements; 21.3 percent joined the police force because they were convinced of the superiority and sophistication of the equipment available to the police for crime investigation and traffic control (tuned-up motorbikes, police cars, and so forth). About one fifth of the police officers joined the police force because they wanted to become detectives in the criminal police. The idea of social security (a good salary) and not too demanding training was a motive for 14.7 percent of the police officers. A family tradition and decision to join the police force because of a police friend was mentioned by one-quarter of police officers. Just over seventeen percent (17.3 percent) said that parents had forced them to enroll in the police cadet school to learn discipline and the same percentage said that the police cadet school was their best chance for a career (Skalar 1976).

Twenty-three years later, in rather sharp contrast to these findings, a study of male and female police trainees at the Police Academy (Pagon and Lobnikar 1999) revealed that the two dominant reasons for joining the police were the diverse nature of work and the opportunity to help people, and the opportunity to interact with people was very important, ranking third in the female and fourth in the male sample. A general attitude toward the police (respect for police officers, reputation, the image portrayed in movies and other media) contributed little to the reasons for police trainees' decisions to become police officers. In fact, the respondents believed that the police in Slovenia were more disrespected than respected and more bureaucratic than nonbureaucratic, but they were inclined to believe that the Slovenian police were effective, responsive, helpful, approachable, and professional. In addition, they perceived police work as responsible, exciting, physically and intellectually challenging, and flexible (Pagon and Lobnikar 1999). Comparing the results of the two studies tellingly reflects the effects of the democratization process in general and, more specifically, changes of the role of the police in society from the perspective of young police recruits. Such a comparison also, however, gives evidence of the "clash of generations' values" common in transition societies. There were indications of a professional cultural conflict between former police cadets (four-year police training) and new police recruits (eighteen-month police training) who had their basic training in the Police Academy.

Impact of Reforms on Attitudes and Values of Police Officers

The scope and pace of the reforms after 1990 could not but have an impact on the values and attitudes of police officers who joined the police in the "old" system. Immediately after 1991, just a small number of top-ranking officers retired, meaning that there was a small turnover of staff in the uniformed police; there was also no systematic "lustration" (literally, "purification") process in which "old cadre" would be removed. From the perspective of staff, the system (which as we explained above enjoyed a rather high level of legitimacy) remained fairly untouched and the turnover of staff remained low during the 1990s. (Notable exceptions were highly educated inspectors of the criminal police, such as those who worked in the economic crime divisions, who frequently left for better-paid jobs in the private sector.) The Police Act adopted in 1998, apart from introducing significant organizational changes—as well as changes in the scope of police powers and conditions for their use—included provisions enabling police officers to retire at a relatively early age. To the surprise of the general public and the government, 504 senior police officers used this opportunity and retired within a year of the adoption of the new Police Act. In the Slovenian context this was not an insignificant number and indicated the price the reforms exacted on mid- and top-level police management. Studies of the reasons for the early retirement (Lobnikar, Gorenak, and Prša 1999) showed that the main reasons for deciding to retire early were bad relationships between employees and employers, feelings of uselessness, and fear of disadvantageous future changes in the Slovenian retirement system. Further studies of the impact of the reform process (Dvoršek, Meško, and Viltužnik 1998) highlighted that the problem of the motivation for work is related to trust between police of officers, lack of special skills, prevalence of behavior that undermined the workplace, lack of "sound competition," organization of work on all three levels of police organization, and a low level of professional ethics.

The study emphasizes the need for a serious reassessment of the values of the police as an organization and of the role of the police in Slovenian society. The study results furthermore suggested that police chiefs should receive extra training in strategic management if they are to take over positions on the regional and state level. The latter finding gains additional relevance from the perspective of evaluating the transition processes. Namely, some models offered for organizational change have been forced on the police, who were either not interested in a specific reform or lacked the funding to implement it. The study showed that police chiefs working at regional and state levels shared too many functions with local police chiefs, such as setting priorities in solving local problems, assessment of local public safety and crime problems, understanding of a local police officer's duties, tools and skills for performing everyday policing. This may be a positive, since it implies that regional- and state-level police chiefs are aware of local police problems; on the other hand, such a local mentality maintained at regional and state levels implies a lack of strategic management and decisionmaking skills.

Finally, we would also like to point out to the results of a cross-cultural study conducted by Gorazd Meško, James Houston, Peter Umek, and Joanne Ziembo-Vogl (2000) on the moral values of Slovenian and American criminal-justice students, police, and prison officers. The study implied that Slovenian attitudes vary consistently from those found in West Michigan, gravitating toward greater leniency and tolerance. Unlike the West Michigan respondents, who view morally debatable variables in strict black and white terms, the Slovenian sample views these same variables with a greater tolerance for the "gray" aspects of human behavior. Explaining this more liberal attitude is difficult, but may be rooted in the history of the past decade, when Slovenes enjoyed the intensive experience of gaining political autonomy and personal freedom. Thus, the feeling may be that absolutes are difficult to come by and an attitude has arisen to live and let live so long as the behavior does not threaten group cohesion. This may be especially so in a country that, although small, has long been known for its strong sense of national identity and that has fiercely maintained a sense of independence in spite of a history of political oppression (Meško, Houston, Umek, Ziembo-Vogl 2000).

THE CHALLENGES OF CONTEMPORARY POLICING IN SLOVENIA

One of the modern trends of policing in a democratic society long advocated by police scholars is professionalization of the police. As Paul H. Hahn (1998), Stephen J. Vicchio (1997), Edwin J. Delattre (1996), and Louis W. Fry and Leslie J. Berkes (1983) point out, aspirations by the police to become professionalized either create, or at least place renewed emphasis on, several requirements such as a wide latitude for discretion, higher educational requirements, higher standards of professional conduct, and self-regulation.

Professionalism, Ethics, and Police Deviance

A sense of professionalism, in the widest sense, means that the police have accepted the need for balancing effectiveness and justice, that they have acquired the skills to reconcile both demands in the varying conditions of their work, and that they apply such skill consistently. In practice, balancing justice and effectiveness requires the capacity to make reasoned judgments. Professional police should not engage in the arbitrary (in other words, discriminatory), sporadic, corrupt, or abusive exercise of their powers. The (limited) autonomy granted to the police is based on the trust by society that the police will have internalized a set of values, a code of ethics, and professional conduct that embodies a democratic balance. The public then trusts the police to exercise self-control. Professionalism also refers to particular values, skills, occupational orientation, and policies of a police service (Caparini and Marenin 2004, 6–7).

Issues related to professionalism, legitimacy, ethics, deviance, and respect for human rights by the Slovenian police have been a focus of intensive research since 1993. This research identified some notable obstacles to a higher level of professionalism of the Slovenian police service that future reforms will need to take into consideration.

The paramilitary philosophy of policing with roots in the Communist era remains strong within the Slovenian police, and one of the consequences of this tradition is an undervaluing of the need for police ethics (Pagon 2000). According to the paramilitary philosophy, police officers must execute the orders from their supervisors as if they were in a military chain of command. Police officers are not supposed to question orders, so there is not much need for moral deliberation or personal ethics. Within this framework the basic virtue of police officers is absolute obedience. Police leadership, on the other hand, is either not accountable to anybody (since they are setting their own goals and can always tailor the statistics to fit their needs) or they are accountable only to the political party in power, with which they have been in a symbiotic relationship. It is not surprising that police ethics do not thrive in such a context. Police officers are often misled to believe that as long as they perform their work strictly according to the law, there is no need for police ethics. Proponents of this view also deny police officers the right of discretion. Unfortunately, when one is faced with a moral or ethical dilemma, the laws prove themselves to be of little use. As L. H. Newton puts it ("Doing Good and Avoiding Evil," accessed at http://funrsc.fairfield.edu/~cnaser/dgea/good-evil.html), "Our first job . . . in all fields of practice, is to distinguish, in every context, between the demands of law and the demands of ethics—between the danger of being sued, prosecuted, jailed or defrocked, and the much subtler, but more pervasive danger of being systematically and cruelly wrong. One of our first lessons was that we must think beyond the law and teach nervous professionals to do the same" (cited in Pagon 2000). Further problems identified in the recent research (Meško 2000; Meško and Lobnikar 2005) point to another, related, problem that arises from a lack of ethics and independent thinking: a lack of flexibility in solving problems in complicated situations, rigidity and a legalistic mentality in the majority of police officers.

Although courses on police ethics and human rights have been introduced in basic police training and different in-service training, police ethics in Slovenia is still at the beginning of its development (Pagon 2000). A number of courses on "police ethics" deal mainly with philosophical ethics, and the word "police" in the name simply means that police officers or students of police studies are the target group of the course. Following the postulates of applied ethics, the described development should be achieved by the joint efforts of police scholars (theoreticians) and police practitioners. According to Milan Pagon (2000) this development should take place in three interrelated directions: applying the principles of applied ethics to police profession; establishing standards of ethical conduct in policing; and defining the means and content of education and training in police ethics. To further the genuine professionalization of police work, this development must parallel other efforts for implementing contemporary philosophy and other forms of policing, including the increased educational requirements for the further professionalization of police work (Pagon 2000). From our perspective Pagon's reflection implies new challenges for the police, especially with reference to a changing society and the application of ethics in procedures that involve people from different social groups with a special focus on the marginalized and a good knowledge about the current clients of police services.

According to the research on police deviance (Meško 1994, 1998), the following factors are typical for Slovenian police officers' personality and attitudes: real self (emotional instability, anxiety, neuroticism, and femininity); pro-social orientation (extroversion and sociability); professional self (toughness, rigidity, physical power, and self-control); attitudes toward deviants (feelings of inability, "respecting" criminals and belief that crime pays, belief that criminal-justice system is inefficient and that too few police powers are available to police officers); and cynicism (bitterness, spontaneous aggressiveness, distrust toward police chiefs, "them and us" mentality).

One of the most intriguing findings of these studies is the existence of police officers' positive attitudes toward criminals and negative ones toward victims of crime. These findings call for the reconsideration of police professionalism and their policing role in society. Another significant finding of the study concerned police officers' reactions in cases of conflict: avoidance strategies on the one hand and potential aggressiveness on the other. These findings indicate questionable police professionalism in Slovenia.

Furthermore, the code of silence, well documented in police literature and present in the police services worldwide, remains strong in the Slovenian police. A study conducted in 2000 (Pagon and Lobnikar 2000) revealed that even in cases involving serious cases of police deviance, such as police brutality, bribery, and theft, 8 percent of line officers said that they would not report any of the cases described in the questionnaire. In six out of eleven cases, the majority of line officers said that they would not report a fellow police officer who engaged in a particular type of violation. Even on the level of supervisors, at least one out of ten supervisors said that they would not report a police officer who engaged in the described violation, with the exception of the three most serious cases. Accordingly, police reformers should also focus their efforts both on changing the occupational culture of police organizations (police subculture) and on increasing the police supervisors' awareness of the actual extent of the code of silence in their organization.

In addition to the issues discussed above, arguably the key obstacle on the path to police professionalism in Slovenia is police cynicism. Both workplace and organizational cynicism have a strong presence in the Slovenian police.[3] Organizational cynicism is directed against the methods of managing the organization, and against the procedures, rules, and regulations used by police leadership. This workplace cynicism is exhibited as a contemptuous distrust toward law enforcement and the services for the community where officers do their work. It can be described as the loss of respect and pride for the police profession (Pagon 1993). Four dimensions of police cynicism were identified in the Slovenian police through different studies (Pagon 1993; Meško 1998; Lobnikar and Pagon 2004):

- Cynicism toward police leadership
- Cynicism toward norms and laws governing the behavior of officers while on duty
- Cynicism toward the legal system, which governs police activities
- Cynicism concerning the respect the public feels for officers

Similar dimensions of police cynicism are also revealed: cynical attitude towards the public, cynical attitude towards the organization; cynicism is reflected also by officers' attitude towards their work, towards the solidarity with the community, and by a cynical attitude towards the education and training for the police profession (Pagon 1993). A typical career development of Slovenian police officers is characterized (Meško 1998) as follows: idealism, realism, cynicism, and resignation.

The presence of marked police cynicism in the Slovenian police can partially be attributed to the reforms of the institutional and legal framework discussed earlier. If cynicism exceeds a certain level, it is unhealthy and can be a barrier to change that needs to be overcome. The Slovenian police might be at this point today, and it is a challenge of police management and leadership to cope with that. First, though, Slovenian police management needs to fully recognize and acknowledge the problem, and they do not seem to be doing this today.[4]

A culture of blame and of generalized cynicism are significant characteristics of Slovene police officers. One can assert that cynicism is a problem not only of the Slovene police but is a characteristic known to all contemporary police forces; that may well be, but it is, in our opinion, the greatest obstacle in the path of police professionalism. It is also the case that police officers on the streets are not always professionally supported by their superiors. Accordingly, when something goes wrong, the main response of superiors is to find a scapegoat and blame or sacrifice police officers who occupy the bottom rungs of the police hierarchy. This causes a great deal of mistrust in police officer towards their superiors, which leads to an ongoing unprofessional attitude, one that often manifests as dependent behavior (such as asking a chief for his opinion before exercising any task). It in fact symbolizes the transference of responsibility from police officers to their superiors. These examples are not typical just for the Slovene police but can be found in any police force worldwide. Police respect of "communities" starts with a mutual respect of police officers within the police organization.

New Policing Strategies—Community Policing

A changing society requires changes in the police and in their practices. Countries emerging from an authoritarian system of governance, in an effort to reform their law enforcement institutions in a short period of time, rush (or, as is often the case, are rushed by the international and donor community) to embrace "Western" models of policing without a complete comprehension of the underlying philosophy and requirements of such models. In this respect Slovenia in 1991 was no different from other emerging democracies. Two distinct new policing strategies were on the rise in many Western police organizations: community policing and covert policing (the latter is not discussed in this chapter). Officially, the Slovenian police promptly embraced both and announced a fundamental change in its policing strategies and its intention to approximate the Western style of policing. As with all things, so with law enforcement: the "new" is never completely new and the old never really goes away. Aspects of "new policing" existed in the past and the "old" strategies continue into the present. There have been informers and undercover agents since history began and much of the rhetoric surrounding the introduction of community policing harks back to the idealized world of law enforcement past, or, in the case of former authoritarian regimes, to the omnipresent social control in everyday life (Squires and Klemenčič 1998). Thus, our description of the shift in Slovenian law enforcement strategies seems clearer and starker than the intricacy of the real world—which is inevitable with any descriptions of complex historical transformations.

Slovenia, like many other post-Communist countries, at first officially embraced community policing, as practiced in the United States and the United Kingdom.[5] However, the implementation of the concept was less than satisfactory. Research

(Beck 2004; Meško and Lobnikar 2005) has indicated numerous obstacles and dilemmas in its implementation. Some of the problems were similar to those identified in other countries in transition who took over a foreign model of community policing as they found it, without carefully adapting and changing the model to fit local legal and cultural conditions (Beck 2004; Meško and Lobnikar 2005). Some problems stemmed from the fact that community policing remains a modern catchphrase of police reformers without a solid and agreed definition of its essential features. Some problems were related to the obstacles to professional policing already discussed in this chapter.

Nevertheless, community policing currently remains the official framework within which the Slovene police carry out their strategic aims and directives. Simultaneously, it continues the process of transformation from a mechanism of constraint into a community service. Among other things, this approach to the performance of police activities requires an organizational division of tasks into the fields of prevention, discovery, and investigation of crime. In doing this the specialized services at the state and regional levels deal with serious forms of crime, whereas local police services, in partnership with the community, deal with less serious crimes and with the issues of public safety and order in the community. Community policing imposes the incorporation of other services and organizations into the performance of police activities and the decentralization of its work. It demands new approaches to the measurement and evaluation of its success and efficiency. It also means that the members of the police need to acquire higher levels of knowledge and skill to perform their work (Meško and Lobnikar 2005). The challenging goals of the Slovene police are praiseworthy, but in reality there exist many obstacles to achieving the stated goals of contemporary Slovene (community) policing.

The organizational structure envisioned by community policing entails power being decentralized, shifted away from police chiefs and toward lower-ranking officers working within communities and toward cooperation with civilian organizations within the communities themselves. On both counts Slovenia faces significant problems. As already discussed, in the 1990s the police organization in Slovenia was highly centralized, leaving little room for local community involvement. Realizing the existence of this gap, the police started in the late 1990s appointing individual police officers as "community-level" police officers with no reactive duties, only preventative ones. In addition it supported the establishment of local safety councils so as to start developing partnerships in local crime prevention and local partnership-based provision of safety. In addition to the idea of working together with citizens, local safety councils are meant to be a place where communities, police, and other agency representatives meet and try to find common solutions for solving local safety and security problems. However, this partnership—while a step in the right direction—has not yet not produced optimal results. One of the problems lies in the fact that members of the police are seen to be universal "solvers" of societal and social problems. A study of public perceptions of responsibility for solving local safety, security, and crime problems (Meško and Lobnikar 2005) revealed the following ranking of problem solvers: the police, social-care institutions, prosecutor's office, courts, other law enforcement agencies, NGOs, and educational institutions. The study further showed that a low level of responsibility, lack of coordination, training, knowledge, and so forth are the main obstacles to developing common efforts in local community safety and crime prevention efforts. Citizens' suggestions for the better policing of their communities tend to more police officers on the beat, greater visibility and approachability of police officers, better cooperation and communication between the police and local people, adequate police training in communication and social skills, as well as some knowledge on cultural diversity. In the view of the respondents, in order to promote "community policing" it is first necessary to pay more attention to professional policing, learning skills for solving problems, the development of a sense of belonging to the community, and solving social problems. These research results furthermore indicated that the most significant obstacles to local safety endeavors are unclear roles of institutions and representatives of civil society in such activities; diverse understanding and conceptualization of safety problems; diverse understanding of partnership; vertical relations among partners; mere discussion of diverse problems but a lack of executive powers; lack of political will and departmentalism; police officers' questionable willingness to listen to those who do not share the same view of the problem; feeling that such local councils are an extended police arm (in all cases the police initiated the establishment of such councils); ignorance and apathy on the part of local citizens (crime prevention is not an attractive and "profitable" activity); centralized arrangements and local problem solving (no firm legal background); "informal for the purpose of formal"—cooperation was only based on the goodwill of the representatives of state and local institutions, local administration, and civil society without any responsibility or firm legal framework. In contrast, the advantages of such councils are democratization of formal social control; cooperation of (responsible) citizens and getting to know each other; development of more active cooperation between all local key persons; facilitating of "safety consciousness" and discussions of local problems and "communities that care" mentality.

Another important obstacle for community policing was that none of several reforms initiated since 1990s successfully changed the mentality of street police officers, especially officers who joined the police before the 1990s. Thus we observe here a common gap between strategies and official regulations, between announcing and implementing a new strategy on a sustained basis. Assessment of reforms must go beyond rhetoric to actual changes where it counts, in the behavior of police leaders, mid-level managers, and street cops. Two corollary points follow from this observation. First, police reform must be based on a clear understanding of the police and their work; second, the basic goal of reforms is a police culture that incorporates democratic values. Without such a culture as a foundation, there will be nice plans, well-designed policies, and soothing rhetorical flourishes—but little actual implementation on the street. A study of the attitudes toward community policing (Pagon and Lobnikar 2000) conducted on a sample of ninety-five police officers and seventy-five citizens in Slovenia revealed that both the police and the public favored community policing over the previous traditional, paramilitary style of policing. The only two observed differences were that the public emphasized crime prevention whereas the police emphasized crime investigation and that the public emphasized centralization of public relations to a lesser degree than the police did. The study's authors observed that the mainly positive attitudes of police officers were still, to some extent, plagued with traditional police thinking. The perception of an overall public willingness to cooperate with the police was significantly stronger in the public than in the police. Specifically, the public perceived themselves as more cooperative than did the police in the following areas: crime prevention, evaluating police effectiveness, maintaining public order, dealing with youth offenders, defining the goals of the police, and dealing with juvenile delinquency.

Another obstacle to a more successful implementation of community policing in Slovenia lies in the historical resonance of some of its strategies. "Community policing" existed in Slovenia prior to 1991, but its underlying principle was more about social and political control in all spheres of community than about safety, security, and problem solving. It came down to "big brothers and sisters" controlling "little brothers and sisters." Because of this experience, the contemporary concept of community policing is perhaps not as popular as it could and should be; coupled with the historical experience it can even produce negative results—community policing involves engagement in a world of inequity. If the police get involved in actions that are futile attempts to solve problems deriving from social inequity—such as "solving" of the Roma family problem in 2007, where the police played a prominent role and caused a bitter criticism of their methods (Nicholas Wood, "Roma family's move raises rights questions," *International Herald Tribune,* November 6, 2006, http://www.iht.com/articles/2006/11/06/news/gypsy.php)—they may end up acting in a discriminatory or partisan fashion. Given many police officers' training and personal values and attitude, many are not a good or easy fit with the new, Western philosophy of community policing. Broadening the police mandate to include community policing without providing a clear conceptual base may result in the partisan exercise of authority (Meško and Lobnikar 2005).

Community policing in Slovenia is perceived by citizens and the police as just another technique within the framework of traditional policing, rather than as a completely new, organization-wide philosophy of policing (Pagon 2004a). Despite its mission and vision statements, the Slovenian police are still characterized, at least to some extent, by bureaucratic, centralized, and paramilitary organization. Police officers in such an organization are likely to be rewarded for producing desirable statistics and reinforced for exhibiting obedience and conformity; meanwhile the paramilitary organizational structure encourages an authoritarian leadership approach. Instead of just claiming that community policing is the prevailing way of policing, Pagon suggests examining in detail the following aspects of policing: understanding of the philosophy of community policing; police priorities; the police subculture; police recruiting, selection, and promotion; training of police officers; training of police management; mechanisms for dealing with police misconduct and deviance; and establishing the moral climate within the police (Pagon 2004a, 124–25).

To sum up our conclusions on community policing in Slovenia, the main problems facing the Slovenian police are related to different understandings of community policing on different levels of the police organization, particularly concerning decentralization and accountability issues. Community policing means more than announcing cooperation with citizens henceforth, but requires proactive measures to develop local security networks and encourage more freedom, more responsibility, and greater accountability of community policing officers. The Slovenian police are challenged by two goals: organizational (adaptation of organization to the community policing model) and communal (reestablishment of police-citizen cooperation) (Meško 2004; Meško and Lobnikar 2005). Community policing as it is understood in decentralized Western governmental arrangements is not what is happening in Slovenia. Community policing as largely understood and practiced in Slovenia is carried out within the centralized chain of command and is often little more than a phrase paid lip service in the political rhetoric.

Further study is needed that compares community policing strategies in post-socialist countries with Western community policing.

Policing and Minority Communities

In the UN Committee Against Torture's "Conclusions and Recommendations: Slovenia" (2003), the committee expressed concern regarding allegations of excessive use of force by the police, especially against members of ethnic minorities. Also in 2002, police use of excessive force against minorities—Roma (Gypsies) and foreigners—was highlighted in the second report on Slovenia by the European Commission Against Racism and Intolerance (2002). The commission suggested that Slovenia establish an agency independent of the police with the power to investigate any future incidents and conflicts between the police and minorities (European Commission Against Racism and Intolerance 2002, paragraph 42). Even before the two reports, nongovernmental organizations and academic researchers had been voicing concerns in this area. In 2000 an extensive study of police officers' attitudes toward different social groups and of intra-police attitudes stemming from officers' ethnic origins was conducted in Slovenia (Umek, Meško, and Abutović 2000). The results of this study echoed those of many other similar studies on police prejudice (Ainsworth and Pease 1987), revealing negative attitudes and prejudice of police officers against ethnic minorities and socially marginalized groups. Slovene public opinion polls on national conscience and ethnic relations suggest two main findings: first, Slovenes express a strong consciousness of national and ethnic identity, and second, it is evident that phenomena such as xenophobia and ethnocentrism are increasing

(Toš 1994). The Slovenes also express a high level of social distance toward such socially marginalized groups as drug users, alcoholics, homosexuals, and AIDS victims. The Slovene population also expresses extremely negative attitudes toward Muslims, Jews, and Roma (Gypsies).[6] According to empirical research, the attitudes of Slovenian police officers are even more extreme than the representative sample of the Slovenian population. In seeking an explanation for such attitudes we can point to the so-called police personality, but the authors doubt the existence of such a personality. One of the central characteristics of the hypothetical so-called "police personality" is fanaticism, which can be recognized by extreme (positive or negative) attitudes and prejudice. This explanation implies the assumption that police officers reflect the characteristics of their environments and society. Prejudice against former Yugoslav ethnic groups could be attributed to police officers' experience in high-crime areas in Slovenia and more frequent contacts with the deviant members of such immigrant groups and the political changes that have taken place over the last ten years (Slovenia's breaking away from the former Yugoslavia in 1991 and its subsequent independence).

Such attitudes can be a serious problem, and as the above mentioned reports from international monitoring entities attest—they are indeed a problem in Slovenia. In addition, the efforts to recognize and deal with this problem on the level of top police management have been less than optimal. It should be a top priority to include such topics as ethnic tolerance and intercultural skills in police basic education, at both basic and advanced training levels. Recruitment of more police officers from vulnerable ethnic groups is a worthy goal, but it is unlikely to happen anytime soon—over the last thirty years Slovenian police had only one Roma police officer. As in some other countries, police officers from minority groups could effectively deal with the problems of their specific community. This approach has two advantages: First, such police officers understand the problems and needs of such communities and deviant individuals. Second, they influence and diminish negative attitudes and prejudices held by their police colleagues. But this can be a problematic approach because of the marginalization of the marginalized. In other words, the de facto separation between mainstream and minority becomes institutionalized. Therefore, we recommended the teaching of respect for diversity among all officers, regardless of their ethnic background, rather than further exacerbating the schism between groups by hiring officers of a particular ethnic group to deal with the citizens of that ethnicity. Working together and mixing of ethnic groups is a potential solution.

Accountability for Mistreatment

Certainly, an important factor related to police legitimacy and professionalism is performance in the area of respect for human rights and civil liberties and accountability for abuse. What follows is a summary of some of the findings of national and international monitoring mechanisms in the area of human rights that highlighted an uneasy gap between the proclaimed democratic goals and standards of the Slovenian police toward respecting human rights and the persistent inadequacies in the system of police accountability for ill treatment and the excessive use of force. The reports on Slovenia highlight a clear systemic deficiency in the response of Slovenian authorities to the allegations of abuse of police powers resulting in ill treatment of individuals: the failure of the police, prosecutors, and judicial authorities to react to the allegations with a prompt, independent, and efficient investigation. What makes those reports relevant beyond Slovenian borders is that similar, if not identical, conclusions have been reached in reports on many other Western European and, even more so, Eastern European countries.

The ombudsman and nongovernmental organizations such as Amnesty International have on a number of occasions voiced their concern over the failure of Slovenian police and judicial authorities to ensure thorough and prompt investigation into allegations of the mistreatment of individuals by the police, and in implementing adequate measures against the perpetrators of these violations (Amnesty International 2003, 2004). Similarly, international organizations such as the UN Committee Against Torture, the European Committee for the Prevention of Torture, and the European Commission Against Racism and Intolerance stressed in their reports on Slovenia that insufficient investigation of alleged police brutality remain a serious problem in the country (2002). For example, in its conclusions and recommendations, published after its hearing of Slovenia's second periodic report in year 2003, they expressed concern regarding allegations of excessive use of force by the police, especially against members of ethnic minorities. It also noted the lack of an independent system to investigate complaints and allegations of ill treatment promptly and impartially (UN Committee Against Torture 2003). The UN Committee Against Torture recommended that Slovenia "take measures to establish an efficient, reliable and independent complaints mechanism to undertake prompt and impartial investigations into allegations of ill treatment or torture by police and other public officials and to punish the offenders" (Rec. 6(c)). The committee stressed, further, that Slovenia should strengthen existing efforts to reduce occurrences of police brutality (in particular when it is ethnically motivated), and devise modalities for collecting data and monitoring the occurrence of such acts in order to handle the issue more efficiently (UN Committee Against Torture 2003, Rec. 6(d)). The use of excessive police force against minorities and foreigners was also highlighted in the second report on Slovenia by the European Commission Against Racism and Intolerance in 2003. The commission suggested that Slovenia establish an agency independent of the police with the power to investigate circumstances that could lead to future incidents and conflicts between the police and minorities (European Commission against Racism and Intolerance 2002). In both its 1996 and 2002 reports on Slovenia the Committee for the Prevention of Torture stressed that one of the most effective ways of preventing police brutality is effective investigation into complaints and, where appropriate, establishing adequate disciplinary and criminal sanctions (European Committee for the Prevention of Torture 2002, item 18; European Committee for the Prevention of Torture 1995, item 16). According to the committee, the effectiveness of the investigation process is significantly influenced by its impartiality and independence (European Committee for the Prevention of Torture 2002, item 17).

Finally, Slovenia was found responsible for violation of article 3 of the European Convention on Human Rights, which prohibits torture and ill treatment, before the European Court of Human Rights (2000) in Strasbourg in the case of *Rehbock v. Slovenia* because of inhuman treatment of a suspect in the course of his arrest by the Slovenian police. The court pointed out that the Slovenian investigation of Mr. Rehbock's allegations of ill treatment by the police had been conducted by the same police administrative unit whose employees had allegedly ill-treated him and that the domestic investigation had been ordered a full five months after the incident took place (paragraph 74). In late 2006 the European Court of Human Rights issued another ruling against Slovenia for violation of article 3 in *Matko v. Slovenia* (European Court of Human Rights 2006), whose circumstances were similar to those in *Rehbock:* a suspect was mistreated by the officers of a special unit during an action against organized crime and the prosecution service and the courts failed to properly investigate the victim's allegations of ill treatment. Preceding the decision in *Matko* by three months, the Slovenian Constitutional Court had ruled in a landmark decision (Up-555/3, Up-827/04) that the Slovenian legal system lacked a procedure to undertake an effective independent investigation into alleged police misconduct (the case involved a suspect who died during a house search, allegedly of an asthma attack).

The problem identified in Slovenia by domestic and international human rights and judicial institutions was not primarily the reported scope of the use of excessive police force, the high occurrence of ill treatment, nor even torture, but the lack of accountability and effective legal remedy when such incidents occurred. It should be noted that Slovenia is not the only European country being criticized by international human rights groups, the courts, and academic researchers for the ineffective investigation of alleged ill treatment. Indeed, insufficient investigation into police misconduct remains a problem throughout Europe, even in established democracies (Moore and O'Rawe 1997).

The failure to provide adequate accountability measures for police brutality can to a great extent be attributed to the continuous reliance on internal oversight and complaint-resolution mechanisms. There are numerous causes of inadequate internal control mechanisms in relation to human rights, related to specificities of police powers, organization, and subculture, which often directly or indirectly lead to impunity of law enforcement officials for violations of human rights. This approach has historical foundations in the way Slovenia viewed police organizations: as centralized quasi-military organizations that subscribe to classical organizational principles as detailed by classical theorists such as Max Weber (Weber 1947). From this perspective, it is logical to think that the control mechanisms that ensure discipline within the rank and file can only come from within the organization (Terrill 1996). This mind-set is exaggerated in postauthoritarian countries that have also emerged from a socialist political system that was predominantly centralized, bureaucratic, and nontransparent.

In most continental European countries, complaints against the police are still processed by the police themselves and within the criminal-justice system. Three decades ago, however, the United States, the United Kingdom, Canada, Australia, and other common law countries started emphasizing the active role of citizens in the oversight of serious police misconduct. They experimented with special external oversight bodies (special commissions, committees, agencies) that are not a part of the police organization or the competent ministry (such as the Ministry of Interior, Ministry of Justice). This process was closely linked to the problems of legitimacy of the police within society, especially as perceived by various minorities. Indeed, allegations of discrimination linked to excessive use of force by police against different minorities and a perceived lack of accountability for such conduct has been a leading impetus in the search for external oversight mechanisms. Of course, the differences between common law and civil law systems cannot be removed from the historical, cultural, legal, and political context, which resulted in quite distinct models of policing. The development of civilian oversight over complaints procedures in common law jurisdictions was frequently the result of society's dissatisfaction with and resistance to police treatment of minorities. Civilian oversight became the "right" of the society to monitor the implementation of powers given to the police by the constitution and the law.

Modeled on these practices in common law countries, Slovenia introduced in 1998 limited public participation in the process of resolution of complaints against the police, by adopting a so-called "civilian in-house mode" (Goldsmith 1988). To our knowledge this was a first in Central and Eastern Europe. The complaints procedure remained internal, within the police force (further changes moved the procedure out of the police to the Ministry of Interior), and included citizens in the determination of complaints, all with the purpose of ensuring objectivity and impartiality, similar to a jury.

This experiment was driven by the goal of promoting openness of the police organization to the community, but the new entity did not really solve the problems it aimed to solve: It failed to fully live up to the benchmarks set by the European Court of Human Rights; it does not provide for independent investigation; it does not ensure ex-officio investigation; it does not have oversight of the work of the public prosecutor and plays no role in the detection, investigation, and prosecution of criminal offenses committed by police officers. It only provides a sort of customer service and has proved to have a very limited impact on ensuring the accountability for police abuse. Its creation did, however, reveal a number of problems: concerning the selection of citizens to sit on the panels, distrust of the citizens toward the efficiency of the panels, the lack of general awareness that citizens in fact do have a possibility of playing an active role in the oversight of the police, and so forth (Zidar and Klemenčič 2004).[7]

Providing an efficient system of accountability for police abuse by means of effective independent investigation into allegations of abuse is a clear international standard. Furthermore, it is directly linked to legitimacy of the police in a given society and the standards of democratic policing. The basic requirement is police accountability; professional behavior and accountability sustain legitimacy; accountability helps professionalize the police; legitimacy grants the police a necessary degree of professional autonomy (Caparini and Marenin 2004, 5).

Slovenia still falls short of standards set by the European Court of Human Rights in the area of investigating allegations of police brutality. Furthermore, in many instances the court has ruled that consistent reliance on internal oversight mechanisms, even with limited public participation, will not solve the problem. Slovenia is thus under pressure to find alternatives in external oversight mechanisms. Human rights organizations are vocal advocates of the civilian oversight model as introduced in many common law jurisdictions. However, we believe that the historical circumstances of the civil law system, along the socialist legal system, and the resultant models of police organization and criminal-justice administration present serious obstacles to the establishment of citizens oversight schemes that could meet the standards of the European Court.

Significant opportunity to secure a greater level of accountability for police abuse is, we believe, represented by public prosecutors and their specialization in the field of investigation of prosecution of police abuse. In the last two decades, many European countries have acknowledged that effective investigation and prosecution of specific forms of criminality requires specialized autonomous prosecution bodies, free from undue outside pressures and interests, which are given adequate powers and resources. Consequently, specialized prosecution services with exclusive jurisdictions over money laundering, corruption, economic crime, trafficking human beings, cyber crime, and other forms of serious and organized crime are being put in place throughout Europe.[8] Special units have yet to be established in the area of human rights violations conducted by law enforcement officials, but the trend suggests that such a model might work for the creation of a specialized department (or the designation of individual prosecutors) having exclusive jurisdiction over the cases involving allegations of police ill treatment.

In Slovenia, moves have been made in this direction. Following the rulings by the European Court and the Constitutional Court in 2006, the Slovenian government in early 2007 proposed to the parliament a new law creating a special prosecutorial department within the General Prosecutors Office that would have exclusive powers to investigate and prosecute criminal offenses (including alleged police brutality) of police and other law enforcement powers. In addition to prosecutors the department would employ a number of investigators with police powers to enable efficient and independent investigations into violations of human rights by the police. This, for the Slovenian legal environment, quite dramatic, institutional proposal will likely be approved by the parliament, but its future impact can only be speculated. And the academic community has raised some concerns in regard to some of its provisions.

Further prospects in developing effective investigation mechanisms into alleged police brutality in Slovenia should focus on strengthening the supervisory and investigative function of the public prosecutors, possibly through specialized departments. This is not to say that civilian oversight is not a viable option in Slovenia. Civilian oversight over the police can contribute to greater accountability of police officers to respect human rights in police procedures; of police leadership and competent state bodies responsible for ensuring the qualifications and working conditions that enable professional and lawful police work; and of competent bodies to investigate complaints in accordance with national law and international standards. However, external or internal complaints authority with participation of civilians cannot in itself provide accountability for violations by the police because it lacks power to investigate and prosecute. Regardless of that it can, through its published reports, inform the public about police violations and the reasons behind them, such as inadequate training, and the success of investigations into alleged violations. This information gives citizens democratic mechanisms to call the state to account.

To sum up, "police investigating police" always raises doubts about the effectiveness of such investigation. This paradox will have to be resolved, either by providing mechanisms for independent investigation or at least by providing strong supervision and participation by independent authorities such as a public prosecutor or civilian oversight bodies.

CONCLUSION

Common traits of democratic policing are supposed to include nonpartisanship (political neutrality); representative composition of personnel that reflects the ethnic makeup of society; integrity; fairness; accountability; sensitivity; moral consensus; civilian control; public-service orientation; obedience or commitment to the rule of law; concern for human rights; responsiveness to civic society; impartiality; minimal, last-resort use of force; accessibility; separation from military forces and cultures; ability to keep the general order (Caparini and Marenin 2004, 7). If we compare past and present, we can see significant progress in many aspects of the democratization of policing in Slovenia. We also see that the main impediments to this democratization have roots in the past, mainly (Pagon 2005): police subculture; a heritage of paramilitary structure and philosophy of policing; centralization of the police service; existing sporadic political pressures and political criteria in the selection of top management; insufficient emphasis on management skills of top-level police managers; lack of clear strategy concerning police education and in-service training, especially in the areas of adapting to changes in the legal environment and developing intercultural skills for policing multicultural societies; almost a total absence of special training for tasks, especially communication skills and negotiation skills (Rejc and Kečanović 2005).

Regardless of all efforts of the Slovenian police to become more professional, legitimate, and accountable, several challenges must still be met. Public cooperation with the police is needed for the creation of a law-abiding environment, in which the authority of the law and of law enforcers is respected and there is belief in values that society must protect. This issue is related to the use of police force as well as so-called voluntary compliance to norms.

We conclude our reflections with two ideas: people's compliance with the law and police compliance with the law. It is an arena where police and (potential) law breakers meet and laws are enforced (Tyler 2004; Skogan and Meares 2004).

Police legitimacy is closely related to people's belief that the police serve the people honestly and impartially. Indicators of increased police effectiveness are related to increasing professionalism in policing, including declining rates of complaints against the police and lower levels of excessive police use of force against citizens. A key antecedent of legitimacy is procedural justice, so society's general opinion on the fair treatment of people by the police and in the criminal-justice system is significant. The main elements of procedural justice are participation, neutrality, treating people with dignity and respect, and feeling by people that they have been treated more fairly than they anticipated. The main issue is trust; people have an internal need to view authorities as benevolent and caring and to trust them. This view is directly tested during a personal encounter with those authorities, and people's views are powerfully shaped by whether they in fact do receive the behavior they expect from the police and the criminal-justice system as a whole. The important role played by legitimacy in shaping people's law-related behavior suggests the possibility of contributing to creating a law-abiding society in which citizens internalize values that lead to voluntary obedience to the law and to the decisions of law enforcement authorities such as the police. Increasing the legitimacy of the police and other criminal-justice institutions can lead to a more law-abiding society. This cannot be accomplished overnight simply through changes in the allocation of resources and the redefinition of goals within government agencies. It requires the inculcation of appropriate social and moral values among children and the enhancement of those values among adults. Where people are found to comply with the law and support the police and courts as institutions, they believe that those institutions exercise authority fairly (Tyler 2004, 95).

Many of the encounters police officers have occur under potentially troublesome circumstances. Most police officers are honest and stay out of trouble for their entire careers. Most citizens who come into contact with the police are satisfied with the experience, even when they are on the receiving end of an investigation. However, police are what the British call "the sharp end of the stick" when it comes to regulating the social and economic relations in society (Skogan and Meares 2004: 68).

The police force in transition is most likely to commit transgressions in the context of interrogations, search and seizure procedures, use of (lethal) force, engagement in corrupt practices, and racial profiling (Zidar and Klemenčič 2004). How to minimize the risks is a long-standing question asked by many police scholars and practitioners. Wesley Skogan and Tracey L. Meares (2004, 78–81) suggest some answers that are relevant also to the Slovenian context. First, the effectiveness of strategies to secure officer compliance with department policies should be measured by the quantified reduction in police deviance from those directives and especially reduction in corruption. Second, internal control and police control process is to be reviewed as well as the prevailing patterns of police deviance studies to build a proper response to police deviance, especially in the fields of internal accountability, training, internal inspection, and willingness to challenge informal practices and peer tolerance. Third, officers should be rewarded for good performance, and more emphasis should be placed on reinforcing positive behavior than on punishing deviant behavior.

In Slovenia, as in other democratic countries, people expect the police to enforce the law; promote safety; reduce crime, victimization, and the fear of crime; and redress wrongs. However, they do not believe that the police should have unlimited power to prevent, reduce, or deter crime. Furthermore, the majority of police officers exercise their duties within the boundaries set by the law, with respect for personal dignity and civil liberties, and with the aim of serving the citizens and communities they police. Dilemmas and obstacles described in this chapter that are experienced by the Slovenian police as they strive to improve the quality of service should be viewed from a historic and developmental perspective.

NOTES

1. This assessment is based on the results of wide-ranging opinion surveys conducted regularly by the Centre for Public opinion Research at the Faculty of Social Sciences, University of Ljubljana. Surveys included questions such as "How much do you trust the police?" and "How satisfied are you with the performance of the police?" (Toš 1999, 2004; see also "Dokumenti SJM," accessed at http://cjm.si/edokumenti).

2. This reduction is attributed to a provision of article 36 of the Slovenian constitution that limits warrantless searches of premises to situations of immediate and serious danger to life, health, or property and to the apprehension of a suspect caught in flagrante and being chased. The constitution prevents warrantless searches when there is only a danger that evidence will be destroyed prior to obtaining a warrant. Searches of premises by consent, while not prohibited by the constitution, are not regulated in the law and consequently are not undertaken by the police.

3. We can define police cynicism (see Pagon 1993, which builds on Niederhoffer 1967, a classic work) as an attitude characterized by three elements: feelings of hatred, envy and

distrust; inability to express these feelings openly toward the individuals and structures that provoke them; and a continuous experience of anger arising from a feeling of impotence and continuous adversity. Milan Pagon (1993) also follows Brian O'Connell, Herbert Horman, and Barry R. Armandi's (1986) definition of police cynicism as contempt and distrust toward the employing organization. Contempt means that officers do not respect their organization, and distrust refers to doubts that the police organization is efficient and trustworthy. Although in the beginning the researchers studied police cynicism as an integral and undivided concept, but they later established that it should be broken down into organizational and workplace cynicism.

4.   Wallace Graves ("Police Cynicism: Causes and Cures," http://www.fbi.gov/publications/leb/1996/june964.txt) describes some measures managers can take to deal with police cynicism. He stresses the role of police leadership. Police leaders must demonstrate their commitment to the ideals of honesty, fairness, justice, courage, integrity, loyalty, and compassion. Leaders who fail to prove themselves trustworthy help sow the seeds of cynicism. By explaining the intent of rules and providing comprehensive and continuous training, police managers can help police officers feel confident and empowered in the legal area so that a police officer can develop trust in the judicial system. Graves also emphasizes that police leaders need to build a culture of integrity within their agencies so that officers have something to believe in when all else seems to fail. Branko Lobnikar and Milan Pagon (2004) are in complete agreement with these measures.

5.   Mike Brogden (1999) states that policing is bedeviled by definitional problems. Given the different legal, cultural, and organizational origins of police forces internationally, the prospects of reaching an agreed definition of "the police" results in little more than a description such as "Policing is what people in blue (or whatever color), uniforms do." Varying legal codes govern and determine police duties—restrictive in the Napoleonic Code, permissive in common law—and this is one source of confusion. Culture, from the generalities of national tradition to the specifics of canteen culture (where it exists) of the police, has inspired different police styles and conventions. The development of community policing in different national and local contexts reflects the tensions between legal, cultural, and organizational structures of policing. The complexity of that mix—law, culture, and organization—makes it difficult to transplant practices from one setting to another, whether it be from smalltown America to an urban ghettos or from Newport News to downtown Antwerp or from a small American city to Ljubljana. Conversely, the absence of community policing models in Austria, Belgium, and many Eastern European countries needs to be understood within the specifics of historically derived law, culture, and organization. Community policing as popularized from its North American roots, is an American cherry pie. It is not a model that can be culturally transplanted to domains with different structures and traditions. The "failure" of community policing in much of Western Europe, as in the cities of North America, is partly one of implementation. But the larger impediment is its alien legal, cultural and organizational history. It seems that community policing is the best-selling and the least thoroughly scientifically tested product of American criminology. Who would not like to live in a community without problems, without risks, in the place where everybody is kind of "happy," and where social cohesion is the main characteristic of the community? Reality is a little bit different. Tim Hope (1994) discusses a dimension of crime

prevention, "authoritarian communitarianism," which could be understood in some parts of our society with its post-socialist, post-Communist culture as a revival of communist idea of total control.

6. This is particularly interesting in light of the fact that the mentioned ethnic groups represent a negligible part of the Slovenian population. According to the census of 2002, Muslims form 0.53 percent, Roma 0.17 percent, and Jews less than 0.01 percent of the population (Statistical Office of the Republic of Slovenia, http://www.stat.si/eng/team_demografsko_prebivalstvo.asp.).

7. For an in-depth analysis of the pros and cons of the Slovenian reform model of the complaints-resolution procedure, see Zidar (2004).

8. Examples are Italy (National Anti-Mafia Prosecution Office), Spain (Special Prosecutor's Office for the Repression of Economic Offences Related to Corruption), the U.K., Romania (Prosecutor's National Anti-Corruption Directorate), Croatia (Prosecution Office for the Suppression of Corruption and Organized Crime), Slovenia (Group of State Prosecutors for Special Matters), Lithuania (Department of Organized Crime and Corruption within the Prosecutor General's Office), Norway (National Authority for Investigation and Prosecution of Economic and Environmental Crime), Sweden (National Economic Crimes Bureau within the Prosecution Service), and others (see Klemenčič, Stušek, and Gaika 2006).

REFERENCES

Ainsworth, Peter B., and Ken Pease. 1987. *Police Work*. London: Methuen and British Psychological Society.

Amnesty International. 2003. "Republic of Slovenia Before the Committee Against Torture." Report, April. AI Index: EUR 68/001/2003. Accessed at http://news.amnesty.org/library/Index/ENGEUR680032003?open&of=ENG-352.

———. 2004. "Slovenia." Report of Amnesty International–Slovenia. Accessed at http://www.amnesty.si/datoteka.php?md5ime=1eee2a9c15ba72017fa125940794eee4.

Beck, Adrian. 2004. "Understanding the Criticality of Context in Developing Community Policing: A Post Soviet Case Study." In *Policing in Central and Eastern Europe: Dilemmas of Contemporary Criminal Justice*, edited by Gorazd Meško, Milan Pagon, and Bojan Dobovšek. Ljubljana, Slovenia: University of Ljubljana, Faculty of Criminal Justice.

Brogden, Mike. 1999. "Community Policing as Cherry Pie." In *Policing Across the World: Issues for the Twenty-first Century*, edited by Rob I. Mawby. London: UCL Press.

Caparini, Marina, and Otwin Marenin. 2004. "Police Transformation in Central and Eastern Europe: The Challenge of Change." In *Transforming Police in Central and Eastern Europe: Process and Progress*, edited by Marina Caparini and Otwin Marenin. Geneva, Switzerland: Geneva Centre for the Democratic Control of Armed Forces.

Delattre, Edwin J. 1996. *Character and Cops: Ethics in Policing*. 3rd ed. Washington: American Enterprise Institute Press.

Dvoršek, Anton, Gorazd Meško, and Rafael Viltužnik. 1998. "New Police Organisation: The Way to Success?" In *Policing in Central and Eastern Europe: Organization, Managerial, and Human Resource Aspects*, edited by Milan Pagon. Ljubljana, Slovenia: College of Police and Security Studies.

European Commission Against Racism and Intolerance. 2002. "Second Report on Slovenia." Report no. CRI(2003)39. Accessed at http://www.coe.int/t/e/human-rights/ecri.

European Committee for the Prevention of Torture. 1995. "Report to the Slovenian Government Regarding the Visit to Slovenia That Took Place Between February 19 and 28, 1995." Report no. CPT/Inf (96) 18. Accessed at http://www.cpt.coe.int/en/states/svn/htmls.

———. 2002. "Report to the Slovenian Government on the Visit to Slovenia Carried Out by the European Committee for the Prevention of Torture and Degrading Treatment or Punishment, from 16 to 27 September 2001 (CPT)." Report no. CPT/Inf(2002)36. Accessed at http://www.cpt.coe.int/documents/svn/2002-36-inf-eng.htm.

European Court of Human Rights. 2000. *Rehbock v. Slovenia*. Case no. 29462/95, November 28, 2000.

———. 2006. *Matko v. Slovenia*. Case no. 43393/98, November 2, 2006.

Fry, Louis W., and Leslie J. Berkes. 1983. "The Paramilitary Police Model: An Organizational Misfit." *Human Organization* 42(3): 225–34.

Goldsmith, A. J. 1988. "New Directions in Police Complaints Procedures: Some Conceptual and Cooperative Departures." *Police Studies* 11(1): 60–71.

Grilc, Jure, and Goran Klemenčič. 2006. "Preiskava stanovanja in drugih prostorov—analiza prakse in odprta vprašanja" ["Search of premises: analysis of practice and outstanding legal issues"]. Unpublished paper. Ljubljana, Slovenia: University of Ljubljana, Faculty of Criminal Justice and Security Studies.

Hahn, Paul H. 1998. *Emerging Criminal Justice: Three Pillars for a Proactive Justice System*. Thousand Oaks, Calif.: Sage Publications.

Hope, Tim. 1994. "Community Crime Prevention." In *Building a Safer Society: Strategic Approaches to Crime Prevention*, edited by Michael Tonry and David P. Farringron. Chicago, Ill.: University of Chicago Press.

Joutsen, Matti. 1995. "Crime Trends in Central and Eastern Europe: Crime Policies and the Rule of Law—Problems of Transition" [In Slovene]. Ljubljana, Slovenia: University of Ljubljana, Institute of Criminology.

Klemenčič, Goran, Bečir Kečanović, and Miroslav Žaberl. 2002. *Vaše pravice v polilcijskih postopkeh* [*Citizens' rights in police proceedings*]. Ljubljana, Slovenia: Pasadena Publishing.

Klemenčič, Gorazd, Janusz Stušek, and Inese Gaika. 2006. *Specialised Anti-Corruption Institutions: Review of Models*. Paris: Organisation for Economic Co-Operation and Development.

Lobnikar, Branko, Vinko Gorenak, and Jože Prša. 1999. "Vzroki predčasnego upokojevanja delevcev Ministrstva za Notranje Zadeve in policije" ["Reasons for Early Retirement among the Employees of the Ministry of the Interior and the Police"]. *Varstvoslovje* 2: 9–17.

Lobnikar, Branko, and Milan Pagon. 2004. "The Prevalence and the Nature of Police Cynicism in Slovenia." In *Policing in Central and Eastern Europe: Dilemmas of Contemporary Criminal Justice*, edited by Gorazd Meško, Milan Pagon, and B. Dobovšek [In Slovene]. Ljubljana, Slovenia: University of Ljubljana, Faculty of Criminal Justice.

Meško, Gorazd. 1994. "Policijska subkultura" ["Police Subculture"]. *Revija za Kriminalistiko in Kriminologijo* 2(00): 143–9.

———. 1998. "Strukturalna Analiza stališč med policisti in nepolicisti" ["Police Officers' Personality Characteristics and their Attitudes toward Marginal Social Groups"]. Ph.D. dissertation, University of Ljubljana.

———. 2000. "Storilci kaznivih dejanj, storilci Prekrškov in Žrtve kaznivih dejanj v Očeh Slovenskih policistov" ["Criminals, Public Disorder Offenders, and Victims of Crime in the Eyes of Slovenian Police Officers"]. *Varstvoslovje* 3: 64–273.

———. 2004. "Local Safety Councils in Slovenia." In *Urban Safety,* edited by Von der Kijver Kees. Enschede, Netherlands: IPIT.

Meško, Gorazd, James Houston, Peter Umek, and Joanne Ziembo-Vogl. 2000. "Comparing Moral Values of Slovenian and American Criminal Justice Students, Police Officers and Jail Officers." In *Policing in Central and Eastern Europe: Ethics, Integrity and Human Rights,* edited by Milan Pagon. Ljubljana, Slovenia: College of Police and Security Studies.

Meško, Gorazd, and B. Lobnikar. 2005. "The Contribution of Local Safety Councils to Local Responsibility in Crime Prevention and Provision of Safety." *Policing: An International Journal of Police Strategies and Management* 28(2): 353–73.

Ministry of the Interior. 1999. *1998 Report on the work of the police* [In Slovene]. Ljubljana, Slovenia: Ministry of the Interior.

Moore, L., and M. O'Rawe. 1997. *Human Rights on Duty.* Belfast: Committee on the Administration of Justice.

Murphy, P. V. 1996. Foreword to *Character and Cops: Ethics in Policing,* by E. J. Delattre. 3rd ed. Washington: American Enterprise Institute Press.

Niederhoffer, Arthur. 1967. *Behind the Shield: The Police in Urban Society.* New York: Doubleday.

O'Connell, Brian, Herbert Horman, and Barry R. Armandi. 1986. "Police Cynicism and the Modes of Adaptation." *Journal of Police Science and Administration* 14(4) 307–13.

Pagon, Milan. 1993. "Policijski cinizem: vzroki, Značilnosti in posledice" ["Police Cynicism: The Causes, Characteristics, and Consequences"]. *Revija Policija* 4–5: 389–403.

———. 2000. "Police Ethics and Integrity." In *Policing in Central and Eastern Europe: Ethics, Integrity and Human Rights,* edited by Milan Pagon. Ljubljana, Slovenia: College of Police and Security Studies.

———. 2004a. "Ethics, Education and Integrity." In *Policing a Safe, Just and Tolerant Society,* edited by Peter Viliers and Rob Adlam. Winchester, England: Waterside Press.

———. 2004b. "A Study of Police Reform in Slovenia." In *Transforming Police in Central and Eastern Europe: Process and Progress,* edited by Marina Caparini and Otwin Marenin. Geneva, Switzerland: Geneva Centre for the Democratic Control of Armed Forces.

———. 2005. "Opportunities and Impediments to Police Reform in Eastern Europe." In *Police Reform and Human Rights: Opportunities and Impediments in Post-Communist Societies,* edited by Niels Uildriks. Oxford: Intersentia.

Pagon, Milan, and Branko Lobnikar. 1999. "Reasons for Joining and Beliefs about the Police and Police Work Among Slovenian Female Police Rookies." *Police Science and Management* 2(3): 252–66.

———. 2000. "Comparing Supervisor and Line Officer Opinions About the Code of Silence: The Case of Slovenia." In *Policing in Central and Eastern Europe: Ethics, Integrity, and Human Rights,* edited by Milan Pagon. Ljubljana, Slovenia: College of Police and Security Studies.

———. 2004. "Police Integrity in Slovenia." In *The Contours of Police Integrity,* edited by C. B. Klockars, Sanja Kutnjak-Ivkovi, and M. R. Haberfeld. London: Sage Publications.

Rejc, Adriana, and Bečir Kečanović. 2005. "Modeli strateške kontrole vzrokov za Odškodninske zahtevke" ["Models of Strategic Control of Causes of Complaints Against Public Servants"]. In *Odgovornost države, lokalnih skupnosti in drugih nosilcev javnih pooblastil za ravnanje svojih organov in uslužbencev* [The State and Local Government Responsibility for the Misconduct of their Employees], edited by N. Toš. Ljubljana: Pravna Fakulteta.

Skalar, V. 1976. *Izbor, usposabljanje in delovna uspeanost MiliNikov Kadetov* [*Selection, Training, and Efficiency of Police Officers who Finished the Police Cadet School*]. Ljubljana, Slovenia: University of Ljubljana, Institute of Criminology.

Skogan, Wesley, and Tracey Meares. 2004. "Lawful Policing." *Annals of the American Academy of Political and Social Science* 593(1): 66–83.

Squires, Dan, and Gorazd Klemenčič. 1998. "The Law and the 'New' Law Enforcers." In *Policing in Central and Eastern Europe: Organisational, Managerial and Human Resources Aspects,* edited by Milan Pagon. Ljubljana, Slovenia: College of Police and Security Studies.

Terrill, Richard J. 1996. "Citizens Oversight of Police: Development in the West." In *Comparing First-Hand Knowledge with Experience from the West,* edited by Milan Pagon. Ljubljana, Slovenia: College of Police and Security Studies.

Toš, Niko. 1994. "O nacionalni identiteti in etnonacionalizmih. Slovensko javno mnenje 1992–1993" ["On National Identity and Ethnocentrisms. Slovenian Public Opinion 1992–1993"]. Report. Ljubljana, Slovenia: University of Ljubljana, Faculty of Social Sciences.

———, editor. 1999. "Vrednote v prehodu II: Slovensko javno mnenje 1990–1998" ["Values in Transition II: Slovenian Public Opinion 1990–1998"]. Report. Ljubljana, Slovenia: University of Ljubljana, Faculty of Social Sciences.

———, editor. 2004. "Vrednote v prehodu III: Slovensko javno mnenje 1999–2004" ["Values in Transition III: Slovenian Public Opinion 1999–2004"]. Report. Ljubljana, Slovenia: University of Ljubljana, Faculty of Social Sciences.

Tyler, Tom R. 2004. "Enhancing Police Legitimacy." *Annals of the American Academy of Political and Social Science* 593(1): 84–99.

Umek, Peter, Gorazd Meško, and Rado Abutovič. 2000. "All Different All Equal: A Fairy Tale About Police Impartiality." In *Policing in Central and Eastern Europe: Ethics, Integrity and Human Rights,* edited by Milan Pagon. Ljubljana, Slovenia: College of Police and Security Studies.

UN Committee Against Torture. 2003. "Concluding Observations/Comments." In "Conclusions and Recommendations: Slovenia." Report no. CAT/C/CR/30/4.

Vicchio, Stephen J. 1997. "Ethics and Police Integrity." Keynote address, National Institute of Justice, National Symposium on Police Integrity. Washington, D.C. (July 14–16). Accessed at http://www.fbi.gov/publications/leb/july972.htm.

Weber, Max. 1947. *The Theory of Social and Economic Organization.* New York: Free Press.

Zidar, Katrina. 2004. "Civilian Oversight of Police—Lessons for Slovenia." Ljubljana, Slovenia: Amnesty International. Accessed at http://www.amnesty.si/datoteka.php?md5ime= 1eee2a9c15ba72017fa125940794eee4.

Zidar, Katrina, and Goran Klemenčič. 2004. "Confronting a Phenomenon of Impunity and Denial: Contemporary European Trends in Dealing with Allegations of Ill Treatment by Law Enforcement Officials." In *Policing in Central and Eastern Europe: Dilemmas of Contemporary Criminal Justice,* edited by Gorazd Meško, Milan Pagon, and B. Dobovšek. Ljubljana, Slovenia: University of Ljubljana, Faculty of Criminal Justice.

Zupančič, Bostjan M., Goran Klemenčič, Peter Pavlin, Aleš Mihael Jeklič, Petja Toškan, Boštjan Rejc, Saša Sever, Andrej Auersperger Matić, Nina Peršak, Mitja Jelenič Novak, Andraž Zidar, Anže Erbežnik, Boštjan Makarovič, Petra Mahnič, and Matevž Pezdirc. 2000. Ustavno *kazensko procesno pravo* [*Constitutional Criminal Procedure*]. Ljubljana, Slovenia: Pasadena Publishing.

CHAPTER 7

Police Legitimacy in Chile

Hugo Frühling

Crime rates in Chile have experienced a sustained increase since the return to a democratic system of government in 1990. In recent years incidents of theft reported to the police increased from 714.1 per one hundred thousand inhabitants in 2001 to 971.4 per one hundred thousand inhabitants in 2004. Robberies with violence or intimidation reported to the police also increased, from 189.4 per one hundred thousand inhabitants in 2001 to 298.1 per one hundred thousand inhabitants in 2004. This rise in crime has been confirmed by two surveys, both undertaken in 2003, which also revealed high levels of feelings of insecurity among the population and significant rates of victimization, especially with regard to crimes against property. According to the "National Urban Survey on Citizen Security" (Chile, Ministry of the Interior, National Institute of Statistics 2003), 30.3 percent of the respondents in a 2003 victimization survey stated that they had suffered at least one of the following crimes: car theft; theft of objects from a vehicle; burglary; pickpocketing; robbery with violence; theft; assault resulting in injury; economic crimes; or corruption. Nevertheless, this perception of insecurity does not translate into a criticism of the country's two police forces, which continue to receive important levels of support from the population. This is especially the case of the Carabineros de Chile, one of the two police forces that exist in the country.[1] The Carabineros is a national militarized police force responsible mainly for public order and security; it dedicates only a minor proportion of its resources to the investigation of crimes. Public support for the Carabineros and for the much smaller Investigative Police (Policía de Investigaciones de Chile), in charge of criminal investigations, is notoriously higher than that received by other components of the criminal-justice system, such as the courts.

Surprisingly, this favorable opinion continues to hold fast despite the constant increase in reported crimes, and is a tremendous contrast with the poor image that affects police forces in most other Latin American countries. At a time when a significant portion of the police in the region have undertaken processes of structural reform to increase their efficiency and to respond to negative perceptions on the part of the public at large, Chilean police have had to undertake only gradual changes during the democratization period.

This chapter examines the reasons behind the public support for the police in Chile, based on the concept of police legitimacy. Police legitimacy is understood here as a concept that comprises two aspects: public support for the legal structure and the functions of the police within the state, and significant levels of voluntary public cooperation with the police (Vagg 1996).

Our analysis describes the organizational changes undertaken by various police forces in Latin America as the result of the processes of democratization, which began twenty years ago, and the need to improve their efficiency and control over police abuses and corruption. A second section examines political transformations in Chile during the past few decades, as well as the situation faced by Chile's two police forces during the period that began with the transition to democracy in 1990 and the changes that have been made in the police in order to foster a closer relationship with the public. Finally, we examine the results of the two surveys cited earlier in order to draw some conclusions regarding the challenges that Chilean law enforcement must confront in the future. The survey results indicate considerable support for the police, as the public understands that they are not responsible for the increase in crime and can play an important role in reducing its incidence. Support for the police seems to be in line with information coming from other surveys that reveal considerable support in Chile for law-and-order policies to deal with social disorder. The "Latinobarómetro," an international survey that covers eighteen Latin American countries, reported that in 2004 45 percent of Chileans preferred to live in an orderly society, even though some freedoms had to be restricted. This percentage is considerably lower than that of Honduras, where 69 percent of respondents expressed this opinion, but it is much higher than that of Uruguay, where only 32 percent of those interviewed preferred order to freedom (Latinobarómetro 2004, 14). However, and despite the support for the police they show, the two surveys do reveal a series of challenges: respondents from lower socioeconomic backgrounds tend to have a much less favorable image of the police than those in higher income brackets. Poorer respondents also were more critical of the police with regard to their efficiency in dealing with problems that most affect them, such as drug trafficking in their neighborhoods. The survey also shows that problems of concern to considerable segments of the population are precisely those in which they deem the police the least effective. In light of this reality, it seems unlikely that the reforms undertaken to date in Chile will be sufficient to provide security for a society that is moving toward economic modernization, but where social differences persist.

POLICE REFORM IN LATIN AMERICA

During the decade of the 1990s, crime and violence became two of the most pressing social and political problems in Latin America. According to data compiled by the Inter-American Development Bank, around 140,000 homicides were committed in Latin America and the Caribbean during 1996 (Londoño and Guerrero 1999, 3). Partly in response to this sharp increase in crime and partly to reduce public mistrust regarding the honesty of the police, the democratic governments that took office in Central and South America during the 1980s and 1990s implemented a number of initiatives for police reform. At the beginning, many of the reforms aimed to create civil police that were autonomous from the armed forces. Such is the case of the new police forces in El Salvador, Guatemala, Honduras, and Panama. For example, police reform in El Salvador managed to integrate combatants from both sides of the country's civil war. The institutional design established a General Inspectorate of Police (Inspectoría General de la Policía) responsible for investigating legal infractions committed by the police and independent of the chief of police (director general de la policía). In addition, the Police Academy, which recruits and trains police, was separated from the police forces in order to ensure academic independence (Neild 2002; Costa 1999). In 2001, as crime (particularly gang-related crimes) continued to increase, the law regulating the National Police was changed, and the inspector general was placed under the supervision of the chief of police. More recently, a police officer was named director of the Police Academy, which demonstrates a loss of independence with regard to the police forces (FESPAD and CEPES 2004).

The cases of Guatemala, Honduras, and Panama are even less successful than that of El Salvador. The police in these three Central American countries confront serious problems in the functioning of their police academies, control over police corruption and abuse falls short, and adequate equipment is lacking (MINUGUA 2003; Ungar 2004). On average, these police forces have a scant ten-year history, and they have a long way to go in terms of the institutional development required to confront the recent waves of violent crime.

With the objective of controlling the militarization of the police, the law regulating the National Police of the Dominican Republic was modified to prevent active members of the armed forces from joining law enforcement.[2] In the case of the provincial police of Mendoza, Argentina, the legislation that approved both the provisional system of public security of the province of Mendoza and the law of the police of the province of Mendoza came into force in 1999. The new legislation subordinated the police to the Ministry of Justice and Security, which assumed the directorship of the institution. This law decentralized the structure of the police, establishing district police and an Inspectorate General of Security (Inspección General de Seguridad) responsible for investigating complaints against the police within the ministry and headed by civilian representatives of various political parties. The University Institute of Public Security also was created to oversee the training of police and was placed under the leadership of civilian instructors, not police officers. In February 2005, a new program was implemented to bring the police closer to the community, with the hope of improving the public image of the police.

Various countries have undertaken community police programs in order to improve law enforcement's relationship with the public and thus contribute to police efficiency. The population has supported these programs, but they have not lasted over time due to the constant political changes that often result in an emphasis of hard-line policies in direct contradiction to the ideals and aims of the community policing programs (Frühling 2003, 2004).

A number of countries have reformed their police force's internal disciplinary systems because of the key role they play in preventing abuse and corruption. These disciplinary systems most commonly face four problems: they tend to focus on breaches of internal discipline rather than incidents of police abuse (Neild 2002, 4); they sometimes delay making any decision on crimes committed by police until the judiciary rules on the issue, which might take a long time; the internal discipline is preserved through punitive rather than preventive measures, which might be counterproductive in terms of ensuring voluntary adherence to the law by police officers (Eijkman 2006); and procedures are secret and offer little access to complainants. Offices of professional responsibility in charge of investigating these cases usually are located only in the capital cities and are not truly accessible to the public at large. All these features usually present serious difficulties for evaluating whether police misconduct incidents are diminishing and whether the efficiency of the system is improving.

These transformations in the police forces have fostered more democratic institutions. Nonetheless, public opinion still demonstrates a widespread mistrust of police throughout the region, with the exception of isolated cases, such as Chile's two police forces and the National Police of Colombia and of El Salvador. Public mistrust of the courts is also extremely high. The Latinobarómetro has revealed that in 2003, 62 percent of the population surveyed expressed trust in the Catholic church, 29 percent in the police, and 20 percent in the judiciary (Latinobarómetro 2004, 34). Latinobarómetro figures for 2004 indicate that 65 percent of those surveyed in Mexico, 58 percent in Paraguay, and 57 percent in Argentina believe that it is possible to bribe the police in their country. The lowest percentage of affirmative responses to this question came from Colombia (30 percent), Chile (22 percent), and El Salvador (20 percent) (Latinobarómetro 2004, 54). Thus, 78 percent of the population in Chile believe their police to be honest. As we will see in more detail later, victimization surveys reveal lower levels of police corruption than in some other countries. According to the victimization survey that we will examine, only 1.2 percent of the respondents said that a civil servant had requested or demanded payment of a bribe from them or some member of their household. In 21.7 percent of these cases, the civil servant in question was a Carabinero. In a study carried out in Buenos Aires during 2003, 5.7 percent of the respondents said that they had been asked for bribes in the past twelve months, in 72.2 percent of these cases by a police officer.

THE POLICE AND THEIR ROLE IN CHILE

The territory occupied by Chile is located in the southern part of the American continent. From Copiapo south to the Bio Bio River, Spanish conquerors took the land from a variety of indigenous peoples in the sixteenth century. That territory was extended as a result of the War of the Pacific, in which the Chilean armed forces defeated those of Peru and Bolivia (1879 to 1883).

The country has 15,600,000 inhabitants. Historically, Chile distinguished itself from some other Latin American countries through its stable political system. Political independence from Spain, in 1818, was followed by more than a decade of political disorder and anarchy. In 1830, however, the military triumph of one coalition of forces inaugurated a new political order in which an authoritarian government controlled the armed forces and asserted civilian authority. Consolidation of authoritarian government after 1830 gave Chile a national political system with administrative capabilities. During the second part of the nineteenth century, the country gradually moved toward legislative checks on the presidency. In fact, as Arturo Valenzuela states, "From 1830 until 1973, all Chilean presidents were followed in office by their duly elected successors. Deviations to this pattern occurred only in 1891, in the aftermath of a brief civil war, and in the turbulent period between 1924 and 1932, when four chief executives felt pressured to resign in an atmosphere of political and social unrest and military involvement in politics" (Valenzuela 1989, 160).

In 1970, Salvador Allende, a Socialist Party member, was elected to the presidency and initiated a series of policies aimed at transforming the economy and society of the country. Three years later, amid growing ideological polarization and increasing civil violence, the armed forces intervened, provoking the breakdown of Chilean democracy. The Allende administration was deposed in a violent coup d'état in September 11, 1973. At first, it seemed as if the rule of government would be jointly shared by the commanders of all the branches of the armed forces and of Carabineros. Very soon, however, General Pinochet took over as president of the Republic. Between 1973 and 1990, he presided over a very repressive regime that received the continuous support of the business community, who perceived democracy as a system that had permitted the electoral triumph of the left. Pinochet promoted free-market policies, which meant the transfer of huge public assets to the private sector.

The military regime established in 1973 was characterized by its stability and by the fact that power was accumulated in the person of the commander-in-chief of the Army. The fact that the regime was very repressive and that it was able to ensure the support of the armed forces and powerful sectors of Chilean society such as the business community helps explain this stability.

On March 11, 1990, a civilian government presided over by Patricio Aylwin took office after wining the first presidential elections since 1990. He was supported by the left-of-center political alliance, the Concertación de Partidos por la Democracia, formed by political parties that had opposed the military dictatorship.

During the following sixteen years, three more presidential elections took place, and each one of them has been won by the candidate of the Concertación. Chilean politics has kept many of its historical traits, such as a stable system of government, a vigorous party system, and stable electoral alignments. However, polarization has been greatly reduced, and there is strong consensus across the political spectrum on economic and social policies. The economy of the country has grown and experienced modernization during the democratization period. While some corruption scandals have erupted in recent years, Chileans as well as foreigners tend to view Chilean public administration as more honest than that of many other Latin American countries.

The Chilean Police

The Chilean constitution assigns the task of law enforcement to the Carabineros de Chile and the Investigative Police. The first institution was formed in 1927 with the definitive unification of the state and municipal police and the army's corps of Carabineros (Maldonado 1990; Frühling 1998). The second institution was created in 1933 as a civil institution responsible for criminal investigation.

From this period on, both police forces were to report to the Ministry of the Interior, which was responsible for preserving the public order. Under the military regime of Augusto Pinochet (1973 to 1990), the Carabineros underwent considerable transformation, as the institution's general-in-chief functioned as a member of the military junta. During this time, the Carabineros adopted institutional regulations that guaranteed the institution greater autonomy from the ministries of state and that simultaneously reinforced the military characteristics of this police force. Second, the Carabineros was permeated by the process of ideologization that occurred in the armed forces. The emphasis on the imposition of public order and the hostile attitudes toward the Communist Party and leftist parties in general became increasingly widespread, as was evident from the institution's policies and discourse (Frühling 1998). In 1974, both the Carabineros and the Investigative Police were placed under the Ministry of Defense. Law decree number 444 (published in the *Diario Oficial* (official government newspaper), May 4, 1974) established this change under the rationale that ensuring the chain of command for the Carabineros required that the police force not be required to report to a minister of state primarily concerned with politics, which would hamper the technical efficiency of the police. Indeed, this institutional change ensured a relatively high degree of operational autonomy, since the Ministry of Defense was not involved in the preservation of public order or citizen security.

Today, the military nature of the Carabineros is evident in the institution's discipline and training. Like the army, the Carabineros has separate schools for commissioned and noncommissioned officers, and the personnel of this institution fall under the jurisdiction of the military courts for violations of the law committed in the course of their service.[3] The role of the Carabineros traditionally has been that of security police, including the preservation of public order and control and regulation of vehicular traffic. In recent years, this role has evolved and now has a tendency to overlap with that of the Investigative Police. Under the new oral and adversarial criminal procedure system, the prosecutor decides whether the Carabineros or the Investigative Police will be responsible for an investigation. Today, the Carabineros de Chile has 36,777 officers.

The Investigative Police is a much smaller, civil institution, with just 6,514 posts, of which 3,444 are detectives. The principal function of the Investigative Police is the investigation of crime. In the period preceding the military regime, the Investigative Police also controlled activities that could pose a threat to the stability of the political regime. With the exception of the current democratic period, the director of this institution always has been an individual close to the president of the republic and has not himself been a member of the Investigative Police.[4] As the result of both of these factors, the Investigative Police are perceived as closer to the government in power than the Carabineros.

Following the transition to democracy, the first democratic governments maintained closer relations with the Investigative Police than with the Carabineros, owing to the perception that the officers of the latter were in ideological lockstep with the military regime. Nonetheless, the prestige the Carabineros enjoyed throughout Latin America—as a result of the professional competence and disciplined structure of this institution—helped mitigate this mistrust.[5] Another factor was the increasing concern of the population with the crime rate, which led them to welcome the presence of the Carabineros in their neighborhoods. By the late 1990s the prestige of the institution within Chile had been restored.

Increase in Crime in Chile

Since the early 1990s there has been a widespread perception in Chile that crime has reached uncontrollable levels. Surveys undertaken by the Center of Public Studies-ADIMARK (1992 and 1993) and by the Center of Public Studies (1995 to 1999) have consistently identified crime as one of the three problems that the government should make a greater effort to resolve (information available at http://www.cepchile.cl). If the definition of crime is taken to include drug-related issues—from the use of illegal substances to drug trafficking—crime is the second most important social problem, behind only poverty, in the eyes of the general citizenry, according to the 2003 "National Urban Survey on Citizen Security" (Chile, Ministry of the Interior, National Institute of Statistics 2003). Drug trafficking is seen as a problem that is particularly relevant for the poorest sectors polled in the victimization survey.

In this survey, 80.5 percent of the respondents stated that they believed that crime had increased nationwide, even though only 44.6 percent felt that crime had increased in their own neighborhoods. These findings seem to be evidence of the gap between perceptions of reality and actual experience, which normally is reflected in surveys of this sort. At the same time, past experiences of victimization strongly influence the impression that crime has increased, to the extent that a greater percentage of individuals who were victims of crime in the previous year stated that crime had increased.

The extent of the increase in crime throughout the country only can be measured on the basis of the crimes reported to both police forces, since there is no published series of national victimization surveys that would allow such a comparison. Figures of reported crimes as registered by Chile's Ministry of the Interior indicate that there has indeed been a significant increase in crime since 1999 (see figure 7.1).

This increase is particularly relevant in the case of robbery involving violence or intimidation. Violent robbery has increased constantly, with a greater proportional increase in cases of robbery with assault (direct violence against the victims) than in cases in which the victims are merely threatened. This increase in robberies with violence or intimidation has been picked up by the mass media and in political debate as proof of the rise in crime. Nonetheless, only a minority—albeit a growing one—of robberies with violence or intimidation actually lead to an assault on the victim that resulted in injury (Goldstein Braunfeld 2003).

Nearly one-third (30.3 percent) of the respondents in the 2003 victimization survey stated that they had suffered at least one of the following crimes: car theft; theft of objects from a vehicle; burglary; pickpocketing; robbery with violence; theft; assault resulting in injury; economic crimes; or corruption (Chile, Ministry of the Interior, National Institute of Statistics 2003). A higher percentage of victims report crimes in Chile than is the case in many provinces of Argentina, which indicates greater trust in the Chilean police. Thus, in the Chilean case, 47.5 percent of the respondents who had been victims of robbery in their homes reported the crime. A similar survey undertaken by the Ministry of Justice in the city of Buenos Aires in 2003 found that only 38.4 percent reported the crime, and a victimization study carried out in 2003 in Greater Buenos Aires found that only 28.6 percent reported the crime.[6] In the case of theft, 26.5 percent of the victims in Chile reported the crime, while in the Greater Buenos Aires area only 16.9 percent did so.

The increase in crime is not distributed uniformly in terms of geography nor does it affect all social sectors equally. Recent qualitative studies reveal that in the past fifteen years, drug-trafficking rings have consolidated in poor urban sectors

FIGURE 7.1   CHANGES IN THE RATE OF REPORTED CRIMES OF GREATER SOCIAL
SIGNIFICANCE BY QUARTER, 1999 TO 2003

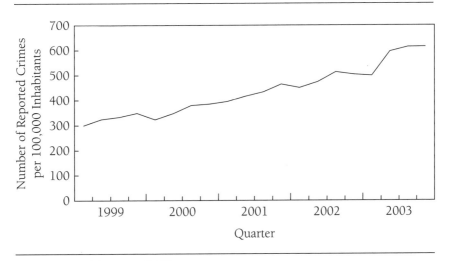

Source: Ministry of the Interior (2003).

(Lunecke and Eissmann 2005). This phenomenon has been especially noteworthy in certain neighborhoods with higher levels of poverty and greater numbers of drug traffickers. An unpublished study in Santiago examined three different types of neighborhoods: those under the control of traffickers, those classified as "in transition," and those termed "disorganized" (Candina et al. 2003).

The first set of neighborhoods is characterized by major drug-trafficking rings that rely on the constant participation of small-time dealers. They are centers of drug distribution with a strong trafficker presence. The traffickers themselves ensure security in public spaces so that the sale of drugs to those who come in from other sectors of the city to do business is not negatively affected by security. In this sort of neighborhood, police are not trusted, and the courts and police are suspected of being in collusion with the heads of the trafficking rings.

The neighborhoods defined as being "in transition" have a strong presence of mostly local, small-time dealers. Nonetheless, there are no trafficking rings established in these areas and therefore no formal or informal control of violence, which results in a greater incidence of street crime.

Finally, in the "disorganized" neighborhoods there is drug use and small-time drug dealing, but without any organization. In these neighborhoods there are high levels of insecurity and violence in the public spaces, in addition to very low levels of social organization (Candina et al. 2003).

Citizens' concern with levels of crime has resulted in the appearance of new actors that strive to ensure citizen security and in various efforts on the part of police forces to participate in this new social scenario.

Policy on Citizen Security in Chile

Increasing insecurity has led to the emergence of new actors and to several changes within the police force.

New Actors Take the Stage   As in other countries, the increased perception of risk combined with certain changes in the administration of public spaces have led to the appearance of other actors that provide services of citizen security either in competition with or as a complement to the central government and the police forces. A leading example is the private security industry, which has enjoyed a boom in recent years.

Currently these companies report over 80,000 employees engaged in security work, 62,000 of whom are "security guards." Eighty-four percent of these security businesses were established after 1990, and from 2002 to 2003, the industry grew at a rate of 16.67 percent (Abelson 2006).

The municipalities are a second group of actors in this new crime prevention scenario. The democratic election of mayors and city council members—which occurred for the first time in 1992—resulted in the emergence of local authorities with a vested interest in the development of programs in citizen security, sometimes in direct competition with those developed by the central government and even the police themselves.

In recent years, some municipalities have organized a range of activities with the intent of promoting crime prevention at the local level. The researcher Luis Sandoval has classified the measures in the following categories: those that seek to prevent by dissuasion, including contributing resources to Carabineros, hiring municipal guards, and establishing municipal law offices who bring charges if serious crimes occur that affect residents of the municipality; measures that seek to diminish the opportunities for criminal activity, including closing cul-de-sacs, installing lighting in these areas, and installing community alarms; and finally, measures such as programs of alcohol and drug abuse prevention whose aim is to control factors that contribute to crime, as well as efforts to eradicate undesirable activities, such as prostitution or street vendors, among others (Sandoval 2001).

In Chile, the emergence of municipal crime prevention programs has not led to the creation of municipal police, even though on various occasions certain mayors have proclaimed the need to establish municipal law enforcement services, which indeed has occurred in many Latin American cities. But the opposition of the Carabineros (with the support of the government) has prevented such initiatives from amounting to anything. This clearly indicates the influence of the Carabineros in the debate on public security in Chile, and it also confirms that the public feels that the Carabineros is capable of responding to increasing public insecurity. Indeed, the general citizenry sees Carabineros and, to a lesser extent, the government as those primarily responsible for citizen security.[7]

Changes in the Police Forces   During the past decade, both the Investigative Police and the Carabineros have adopted some reforms in order to adapt to the new conditions of the democratic regime. During the early 1990s, the Investigative Police made an effort to improve ethical standards among its personnel. A significant number of detectives were fired; important changes were made in the training curricula, incorporating human rights courses; and a special department, the Departamento Quinto—Department Five—was established to investigate incidents of corruption or abuse of the rights of individuals (Candina and Lunecke 2004). At this time there is insufficient information to allow the accurate evaluation of the improvements resulting from the police's internal control system.

The Carabineros have made more gradual changes since the beginning of the transition, preserving for several years a fair degree of autonomy vis-à-vis the political authorities. In part this is the direct result of the military nature of the institution. At the same time, the director general was granted broad powers by the law that regulates the institution, which came into force four days before the return to democracy. Article 10 of this law states that, just as in the armed forces, promotion and dismissal of officers would occur via a presidential decree and at the request of the director general. Until 2005 this regulation prevented the president of the Republic from dismissing or promoting an officer of the Carabineros without the blessing of the general-in-chief. In addition, both forces fall under the purview of the Ministry of Defense, which serves to increase the autonomy of the Carabineros in particular, since they do not have to report to the Ministry of the Interior, which is responsible for maintaining citizen security.

Democratic governments after 1990 considered this structure to be antidemocratic and have attempted to modify the laws in order to increase the powers of the president to include the power to dismiss officers of the armed forces and the Carabineros and to place Carabineros and the Investigative Police under the purview of the Ministry of the Interior.[8] Nonetheless, the primary political parties' criticism of the legal structure of the Carabineros and the relatively high autonomy of the institution's hierarchy does not appear to have had a significant impact on the public's support of the institution.[9]

With regard to the increase in citizen insecurity, in the late 1990s the Carabineros undertook a restructuring process to increase the number of operative personnel—which suggested that the institution had ceased to perform twenty-four of the sixty-seven tasks assigned to it by law.[10] In March 1999, the General Inspectorate of Police announced that the institution would soon begin the periodic evaluation of all personnel, using new performance indicators currently under development.[11] In addition, after the democratic government took power, the

Carabineros began to incorporate the notion of community participation in the institution's discourse, in keeping with that of the government and the municipalities.

One result of this was that in 1999 the Plan Cuadrante, the Quadrant Plan, was put into action. "Quadrant" refers to a portion of the city. One primary objective of this program was to increase the presence of police on the street. The area under supervision by each police station, a police force under the command of a major, was divided up into small sectors called "quadrants." Vehicles and human resources were portioned out according to the specific needs of each quadrant.

According to the official information of the Carabineros, responsibility for the management of each quadrant is assigned to police officers who bear the title of "delegado," delegate, or the lower-ranking "subdelegado," subdelegate. These officers are to attend to and resolve the problems brought to them by the citizens in their quadrant. The Carabineros also has adopted the practice of public accountability by sharing statistical information on police activities with community leaders and public officials from the quadrants (Frühling 2003). Although there is no external public evaluation of the results of the plan, it is clear that the Carabineros has made efforts to strengthen its links with the population.

Despite the changes introduced by the two police forces, reports of police abuse continue. A study by Claudio A. Fuentes on cases heard by the military courts reveals that charges of unnecessary violence brought against Carabineros personnel have increased during the 1990s, even though cases of homicide, attempted homicide, and shootings decreased since 1992. However, deaths of prisoners in the custody of the Carabineros also have increased: between 1990 and 1994, sixteen such deaths were reported, and between 1995 and 2000 this number grew to thirty-six (Fuentes 2001).

Fuentes asks why police violence is not an issue of public debate in Chile, a country in which the defense of human rights played a relevant role under the military regime. Among other explanations, he mentions the lack of effective external control over the Carabineros, the weakness of human rights organizations, and the focus of public concern on crime rather than on the defense of rights (Fuentes 2001).

But one might have to dig deeper to find the reasons for this lack of public debate on police violence. The experience of past polarization and violence has left many Chileans appreciative of stability and social order. A significant portion of the electorate has consistently voted for parties that supported the military regime. Moreover, the Carabineros as well as the armed forces have come to be seen as permanent institutions of the state whose members may have committed serious crimes during the military dictatorship but who since then have rejoined the democratic polity.

Latinobarómetro's 2004 report shows that Chilean society is equally divided between those who favor order over freedom and those who believe that the enjoyment of human rights should never be restrained in order to achieve an orderly society (Latinobarómetro 2004, 14). As cited earlier, 45 percent of Chileans stated that they preferred to live in an orderly society even though some freedoms had to be restricted. This percentage is considerably lower than that of Honduras, where 69 percent of respondents expressed the same opinion, but it is much higher than that of Uruguay, where only 32 percent of those interviewed preferred order to freedom. On the contrary, 50 percent of Chileans expressed a preference for rights, even if it affected the social order. In the same survey, 75 percent of those interviewed in Chile agreed that some harsh treatment by the government might be justified ("un poco de mano dura del gobierno no viene mal"—"there's nothing wrong with a little rough treatment"). On the other end of the spectrum are the citizens of Uruguay, who consistently showed strong support for human and democratic rights, and authoritarian attitudes received little support. Only 32 percent of Uruguayans felt that some harsh treatment by the government might be justified. The Chileans' inclination toward order might partly explain why they respect their police.

However, this respect also is based on the belief that, for the most part, the legal system works in Chile and that the police play a role in attaining compliance with the law. In the same Latinobarómetro report, Chile ranks second to Colombia in positive responses to the question "On a scale of one to ten, do you believe that in your country the state manages to make people obey the law? A ranking of ten would mean that all laws are obeyed, while one means than no laws are followed." Where Chile obtains a 5.37, Argentina get only 4.05 (Latinobarómetro 2004, 19).

Thus, it can be said that some general attitudes of Chileans are consistent with their appreciation of their police over some other institutions in the country.

A Brief Comparison with Argentina   Police-reform efforts have taken place in several Argentinean provinces in recent years. The most radical effort took place in Buenos Aires province and targeted public security. In 1997, two events contributed to the decision to intervene in the operation of the police force in that province. First, there was a marked increase in citizens' concerns about crime. Second, it was proved that members of the Buenos Aires police had participated in the 1994 attack on the Jewish community headquarters, and in the assassination of José Luis Cabezas, a photojournalist working on a story about police corruption (Sain 1998, 70).

In December 1997, Governor Eduardo Duhalde launched an intervention in the Buenos Aires police; he created a Ministry of Justice and Security that would be responsible for dismantling the Buenos Aires force as it then existed. The entire upper command was dismissed, and more than three hundred superintendents and senior officers were removed. The plan, implemented by León Arslanián, who later became minister of justice and security, was put together entirely by civilians.

In the event, the major obstacle to the reform effort was that it failed to have visible effects on citizens' sense of insecurity. It was probably unreasonable to expect immediate success; nevertheless, as the electoral campaign approached, Carlos Ruckauf, the Peronist candidate for governor, criticized the management of Minister Arslanián and expressed his opposition to the police reform initiated in 1997, claiming it was too protective of human rights. When Ruckauf was elected, he partially reversed the reform effort.

Police-reform efforts such as this one are clearly distinguishable from changes in the police that have taken place in Chile. In many Argentinean provinces, the police are considered to be abusive, corrupt, and inefficient. Argentineans distrust their institutions and political leaders, given the many social and economic problems they have faced in the post-dictatorship period. Reform efforts have been initiated as a consequence of the eruption of scandals or incidents that reveal police inefficiency. The reform plans have been formulated entirely by civilians and opposed in many instances by the police. Thus, levels of support for the police in Argentina tend to be lower than in Chile, the reforms are less gradual and more radical, and they are not promoted by the police itself (Sain 2002).

PUBLIC PERCEPTION OF CRIME AND THE POLICE

Naturally, the police in Chile have been questioned regarding the increased crime rates in Chile. And the elected governments in the country also have criticized the regulations that until recently allowed the excessive autonomy of the armed forces and the Carabineros from the president. But despite this situation, police legitimacy, in particular that of the Carabineros, is not questioned.

Two surveys carried out by the Chilean government in 2003 cast light on this phenomenon. The first was undertaken by the Ministry of the Interior and the National Institute of Statistics (Instituto Nacional de Estadísticas, or INE). The "National Urban Survey on Citizen Security" was the first nationwide victimization survey in which participants responded in person to the questionnaire and the results were made public. A total of 16,289 respondents age fifteen and older were interviewed during September and November 2003. The sample was representative of the national urban environs, the regional urban areas, and the urban areas of the country's seventy-seven most populace municipalities. The second survey, the "Study on Perceptions and Evaluation of Carabineros," polled the Metropolitan Region and the Fifth and Eighth Regions in October 2003.

As these two surveys polled very different populations, their results are not strictly comparable. Thus, the findings of this combined analysis should be taken as hypotheses.

Especially Significant Results
The two surveys focus on diverse aspects of the public perception of the police.

Perception of the Police Role in Crime Control   Crime and drug trafficking are two major issues of concern for the survey respondents. In the victimization survey, respondents were of divided opinion when they were asked to explain the reasons for the levels of crime in Chile. One group strongly believed that crime is due to a lack of employment opportunities and other social circumstances; the other group emphasizes the shortcomings of the police or the criminal-justice system, such as the lack of police presence on the streets or the courts' giving weak sentences. The lack of visible police patrols is identified as one of the leading causes of crime. When questioned about the causes of the levels of crime, this lack of police patrolling ranks fourth, following the lack of job opportunities, the courts' giving weak sentences for criminals, and drug use. When this same question is asked specifically with regard to the neighborhood in which the respondent lives, the lack of police patrolling takes second place, after the lack of job opportunities. These responses reveal that the public views the police as playing a very important role in crime control, so they are extremely supportive of the police in their efforts to fulfill this role, regardless of any criticism they may have of law enforcement. A closer look at the answers focusing in particular on the lack of police patrolling and the courts' application of weak sentences, disaggregated by socioeconomic group, clearly reveals that the residents of the lower-income sectors attribute greater importance to the lack of police patrolling, whereas those from upper- and middle-income brackets place greater weight on weak sentences of the justice system. These findings reveal that the poorer neighborhoods perceive police patrolling as playing a very important role in crime control, but at the same time, these sectors express greater dissatisfaction with the protection they receive from the police than the residents of wealthier neighborhoods, who support more severe sentences.

The importance of the police's role in reducing levels of crime, as perceived by all social sectors in Chile, is corroborated by the fact that only 1.4 percent of the survey respondents feel that the lack of community organization is the reason for the levels of crime in their neighborhoods. In Chile, regardless of socioeconomic status, people seem to believe that only the state and, more specifically, the police, can ensure lower crime rates. The importance of police action to which we refer is confirmed by the victimization survey: 32.5 percent of the respondents stated that the Carabineros bears the primary responsibility for citizen security, followed by the government as the most responsible (26.1 percent) and the courts (20.8 percent). In summary, the general population places great importance on the police in crime control, which explains the strong demand for a visible police presence. The following section examines why the significant increase in crime has not damaged the institution's sterling image.

Confidence in the Police and Police Legitimacy   The two surveys reveal different results regarding the public's level of confidence in the two police forces. In the survey of public perception of the Carabineros, 82 percent of the respondents stated that they had confidence in this police force, while only 35 percent stated that they had confidence in judges and 31 percent, in members of parliament. While this percentage is quite high overall, the percentages decrease with the respondents' income levels.

Nonetheless, when the respondents were asked by the victimization survey to identify their level of confidence or trust regarding various authorities, 32.6 percent stated that they had great confidence in the Carabineros, 50.4 percent said that they had little confidence in the institution, and 15.5 percent had none whatsoever. While these figures are none too favorable, they are quite a bit better than the respondents' answers regarding ministers of the Supreme Court, senators, or the minister of the interior. In other words, although the levels of confidence may be different in the two surveys, in both surveys the Carabineros are held in higher esteem than other public officials. In the case of the Investigative Police, 30.4 percent of the respondents stated that they had great confidence in this institution, while 18.3 percent stated that they had no confidence in this police force at all.

As evidenced by other studies, the levels of confidence in the Carabineros are influenced by the age and socioeconomic level of the respondent as well as by whether the respondent has been a victim of crime in the past twelve months. While 25.50 percent of respondents aged nineteen to twenty-four express great confidence in Carabineros, 44.61 percent of the respondents aged sixty or older espoused this view. On the other hand, 41.37 percent of the respondents from higher income brackets stated that they had great confidence in the Carabineros, but only 30.27 percent of the poorest sector shares this view. Among respondents who had been victims of crime in the past twelve months, 29.7 percent had great confidence in the Carabineros but among those who had not experienced crime in this same period of time, 35 percent shared this opinion.

Confidence in the police can be rooted in various factors. Their work in the realm of citizen security may be perceived as efficient. Of all the institutions mentioned in the victimization survey, the Carabineros ranks third among those most highly respected by the respondents for their efforts in the area of citizen security, following the National Children's Service (Servicio Nacional de Menores) and the National Women's Service (Servicio Nacional de la Mujer). The Investigative Police follow the Carabineros in this ranking. Though these figures are only mildly positive, they are much better than the evaluations of other political institutions.

In the survey on the perceptions of the Carabineros, the institution receives an even more positive appraisal. Only the National Women's Service ranks higher in the esteem of the respondents, and 50 percent report a positive or very positive evaluation of this police force. Yet again, a difference can be noted in the opinions expressed by different socioeconomic sectors: while 70 percent of the highest income sector (ABC1) evaluated the Carabineros positively, only 38 percent of the lowest income sector (E) share this view. Nonetheless, sectors C2, C3, and D give the Carabineros a mostly favorable review.

This primarily positive evaluation of the Carabineros seems to indicate that this police force enjoys a high degree of institutional legitimacy. As stated earlier, one manifestation of this institutional legitimacy is citizens' willingness to collaborate voluntarily with the police. The only indicator that we have in this respect comes from the national victimization survey, which makes reference to the percentage of crimes reported by the victims. The overwhelming majority of such reports are made to Carabineros, since this institution has a presence throughout the entire country.

The percentages of reported crimes expressed here are significant. In some cases, such as robbery with violence or intimidation, the percentages are similar to those in industrialized countries, whereas in other cases—car theft or theft of objects from vehicles or residential robbery, for example—the percentages of reported crimes are much lower. A comparison of data from a victimization survey carried out in the city of Buenos Aires in 2003 reveals a higher percentage of crime reports in the case of Chile.[12] In Chile, 47.5 percent of the victims had reported residential robbery, whereas in Buenos Aires, 38.4 percent of the victims reported this crime. Robbery with violence or intimidation was reported by 46.1 percent of the victims in Chile, whereas in Buenos Aires only 33.9 percent of the victims reported this crime. In Chile, 26.5 percent of the victims who suffered theft of personal items reported the crime compared to 18.1 percent of such victims in Buenos Aires. A civil servant's attempt to extort a bribe was reported by 10.8 percent of the victims of this crime in Chile, whereas none the victims of attempted bribery filed a police report in Buenos Aires.

The Carabineros' positive image is also evident when respondents are asked whether they feel that the institution has taken adequate steps to confront the problems of crime. The public perception in this regard is overwhelmingly positive. This finding reveals that most citizens feel that the Carabineros are willing to take appropriate action with regard to crime, even though the results may be less successful than intended, judging by the increase in crime rates.

This significant support for the police does not spring from the community-relations initiatives being developed by the institution in the context of the Quadrant Plan. In fact, most of the population has no knowledge of the Quadrant Plan, as the responses to a question from the victimization survey demonstrate, and the poorer sectors of the population are even less likely to know about this plan.

The survey on perceptions of the Carabineros asks respondents whether they have heard about the sessions of public accountability that the Carabineros started three years ago; 95 percent of the respondents answered no, with only 4 percent acknowledging that they had heard about this initiative. Only 9 percent of those who responded in the affirmative actually had attended one of these public meetings. At least three conclusions can be drawn from these responses: that public opinion grants the police a central role in crime control; second, that it does not place equal importance on the institution's public accountability; and third, that neither the Quadrant Plan nor the public meetings have been adequately publicized or implemented by the Carabineros.

Confidence or trust in the police also depends on the perception that the police act with probity and not for personal gain. The survey on the perception of the Carabineros asks very forthrightly whether in the past twelve months the respondent

FIGURE 7.2   PERCENTAGE OF PEOPLE WHO KNOW ABOUT THE QUADRANT
PLAN, BY SOCIOECONOMIC GROUP

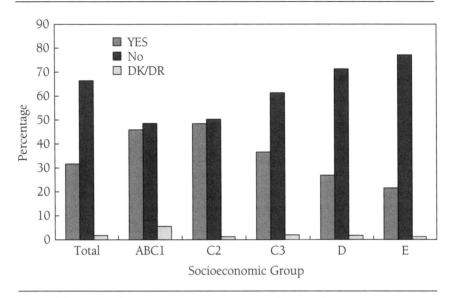

Source: Chile, Ministry of the Interior, and National Institute of Statistics (2003).

has been the victim of or witness to a Carabinero using his or her post for personal gain. Eighty-eight percent of the respondents said they had been neither victim of nor witness to such an act. Only 6 percent had witnessed a Carabinero acting for personal gain, and 2 percent had been the victim of such an abuse. This perception of comparatively low levels of police corruption—in relation with those of other Latin American countries—also are reflected in the national victimization survey, in which only 1.2 percent of the respondents maintain that a civil servant requested or demanded payment of a bribe from themselves or some member of their household. In 21.7 percent of these cases, the civil servant in question was a Carabinero. In a study carried out in Buenos Aires during 2003, 5.7 percent of the respondents said that they had been asked for bribes in the past twelve months, in 72.2 percent of these cases by a police officer.

Perceptions of the Quality of Police Service   A fundamental dimension with regard to the fulfillment of citizens' expectations of the police is related to the quality of services the latter provide. The victimization survey asked those who had visited a police station in the past twelve months how they would evaluate the treatment they had received from the Carabineros: 69 percent evaluated it as good or very good.

Those who visited a station of the Investigative Police in the past twelve months gave this police force a similarly respectable evaluation.

A positive perception of an institution depends primarily on the positive perception of its individual members. The victimization survey lists a series of statements regarding officers of the Carabineros and asks the respondents whether they agree with the statements.

The statements that received more positive responses were: Carabineros are responsive (78.9 percent); Carabineros are disciplined (73.9 percent); Carabineros are efficient (66.2 percent); Carabineros have good manners (65.1 percent); and Carabineros treat people well (63.2 percent). Affirmations are much less common in response to the statement, "Carabineros are corrupt"—39.3 percent of the respondents agree and 38.8 percent disagree.[13] At the same time, in the responses to the questions as to whether Carabineros are corrupt or whether they treat people well, there are notorious differences in the opinions of respondents from the highest income bracket (ABC1) and the lowest (E).

The statements that receive a higher percentage of positive responses seem to be associated with a military ethos or culture, which emphasizes discipline, responsiveness in serving the public in those matters in which the police play a social role, Carabineros' good manners and their considerate treatment of civilians, and a certain general efficiency probably associated with military organization.

Nonetheless, there are greater levels of disagreement with each statement among the lower-income sectors. Thus, with respect to the statement, "The Carabineros have good manners," only 15.3 percent of the group ABC1 respondents disagree, while 34.3 percent of group E disagree. With regard to the statement, "Carabineros are corrupt," 60.1 percent of the group ABC1 respondents disagree, while only 35.5 percent of the group E respondents share this opinion. The most impressive difference is evident with regard to the statement, "The Carabineros treat people well." Only 10 percent of the respondents in the ABC1 group disagree but 34.9 percent of group E disagree.

Two reasons may account for the poorer sectors' more negative perceptions of the police. First, these socioeconomic groups are more likely to be the targets of police control. Second, the police responsible for taking action in the most troubled areas of the cities are those who receive the worst evaluations.

The lowest income sectors' perception that police action is not completely impartial is echoed in the responses of the general population to the questions from the survey on perceptions of the Carabineros, which evaluate a range of police actions. Fifty-nine percent of the respondents agree that the Carabineros enforces the law, 57 percent feel that these police are committed to their job, and 52 percent give this police force the highest marks for honesty. However, a lower percentage (48 percent) of respondents expressed a positive evaluation of the Carabineros' impartiality, and 13 percent of the respondents felt that these police were not impartial. Even more surprising is the fact that a significant percentage of those

TABLE 7.1   RESPONSES TO STATEMENTS ABOUT CARABINEROS,
             BY SOCIOECONOMIC GROUP

Statement	Total	ABC1[a]	C2[a]	C3[a]	D[a]	E[a]
Carabineros are corrupt						
Total	100.0	100.0	100.0	100.0	100.0	100.0
Agree	39.3	29.2	23.0	35.1	44.3	44.6
Disagree	38.8	60.1	54.3	43.5	32.9	35.5
Don't know or didn't respond	21.9	10.7	22.7	21.4	22.8	19.9
Carabineros treat people well.						
Total	100.0	100.0	100.0	100.0	100.0	100.0
Agree	63.2	83.8	73.5	65.3	60.6	57.9
Disagree	29.5	10.0	21.2	27.7	31.5	34.9
Don't know or didn't respond	7.3	6.2	5.3	7.0	7.9	7.2

Source: Chile, Ministry of the Interior, National Institute of Statistics (2003).
[a] ABC1 = Highest socioeconomic level, represents 7.7 percent of the population
   C2 = Second level in income and education, represents 15.4 percent of the population.
   C3 = Third level in income and education, represents 22.4 percent of the population.
   D = Fourth level in income and education, represents 34.8 percent of the population.
   E = Poorest and least educated level, represents 20.3 percent of the population.

who feel that Carabineros are biased based this opinion on law enforcement's unchecked recourse to the use of force (forty-one percent of the sample said they had seen Carabineros using unnecessary force).

This survey also reveals a very positive evaluation of the Carabineros' efforts in terms of public service, but a notoriously lower evaluation with regard to crime control. In the national victimization survey, 78.9 percent of the respondents rate the Carabineros' efforts with regard to assistance and rescue operations during natural disasters good or very good. Assistance for household emergencies (being locked out, gas leaks, and similar problems) receives positive evaluations from 57.3 percent of respondents. Traffic control also is evaluated highly by 60.7 percent of respondents. However, the police duties considered most pressing by the general population receive the worst evaluations: fighting drug trafficking and use receives 32.6 percent approval, and crime control, as stated earlier, is evaluated positively by only 33.8 percent of the respondents.

To return to the original question, why is it that despite Chileans' belief that the Carabineros bears the primary responsibility for citizen security, the increase in crime has not affected their legitimacy? The first reason might be that, given Chileans' favorable attitude toward order and legality, they tend to believe the police are doing their best to control crime and that other components of the criminal-justice system, such as the courts, are failing in that respect. Chileans' positive view of the Carabineros is further strengthened by the perception that the police act with probity and not for personal gain.

Chileans have a positive view of police officers. They are seen as responsive, disciplined, and efficient. Finally, the institution is well evaluated in terms of public service, but it receives a notoriously lower evaluation with regard to crime control.

The survey also asks respondents to evaluate the efforts by the Investigative Police. Since the public has less contact with this police force and because many of the questions demand a level of knowledge that the public probably lacks, we have not analyzed the responses regarding this police force.

The Public's Demands of the Police   Several questions were included in the survey on perceptions of the Carabineros to determine the specific demands that the public makes on the force and to evaluate the quality of the actions taken by the police to meet these needs. The goal was to establish the gap between the expectations regarding police action and the perception of the quality of police procedures.

This type of study is useful because it identifies the public's specific demands of the Carabineros, which do not always dovetail with general perceptions regarding the population's most pressing needs

The organization of these demands in the order of their priority should lead to changes in the posting of police as well as in their priorities for action. In addition, this sort of analysis can help to establish the kinds of action that the public identifies as meeting their needs and provides an evaluation of these actions.

The first question from the survey on the perceptions of Carabineros that is useful for this sort of analysis asked the respondents to list, in order of importance, the problems in their neighborhood that most require action by Carabineros (see table 7.2). The sale of illegal drugs was the leading issue of concern followed by consumption of alcohol in public areas and by minors in local establishments; robbery and assault of homes, businesses and other establishments; traffic accidents; gangs; and assault and muggings of passers-by in public areas.

These answers reveal the serious damage that the sale of illegal drugs causes to social networks and daily life, especially in poor urban areas. The second area of concern is a problem that is not strictly criminal in nature but that relates to the lack of effective controls to prevent the sale of alcohol to minors. Robbery and assault of homes, businesses, and other establishments, an issue that receives so much attention in the press, ranks just third in order of importance to the public.

The order of importance of demands also varies considerably by socioeconomic group in the regions surveyed. This strongly suggests a need to decentralize police priority setting and action in order to respond to this range of demands. The increased presence of illegal drugs is a much more serious problem for poorer sectors (groups D and E), and consumption of alcohol by minors is a greater concern

TABLE 7.2   PERCEPTIONS OF THE MOST SERIOUS PROBLEMS REQUIRING ACTION
BY CARABINEROS, BY SOCIOECONOMIC GROUP (PERCENTAGE)

Problem	Total	ABC1	C2	C3	D	E
Sale of illegal drugs	38	10	27	31	50	51
Consumption of alcohol in public areas and by minors in local establishments	19	17	24	21	16	12
Robbery and assault of homes, businesses and other establishments	13	13	13	19	7	14
Traffic accidents	9	21	10	8	8	8
Gangs	7	5	7	7	7	7
Assault and muggings of passers-by in public areas	6	14	10	5	5	5
Car theft or theft of objects from vehicles	4	19	6	4	2	1
Domestic violence	2	0	1	2	3	1
Fighting in public areas	1	0	1	2	2	1
Prostitution in public areas	1	1	1	1	0	0
Extortion of "tolls" from passers-by in public areas	0	0	0	0	0	0
Total	100	100	100	100	100	100

Source: Chile, Ministry of the Interior—Carabineros (2003).

for the middle class (C2 and C3), whereas the upper income group (ABC1) is most worried about traffic accidents.

The respondents were then asked whether they perceived any concrete action by the Carabineros on the concerns that they had just identified as being priority problems for their neighborhood. Table 7.3 presents the answers to this question. Notably, only two concerns are given a primarily positive evaluation: traffic accidents and robbery and assault of homes, businesses, and other establishments. All the other responses are primarily negative. The greater percentages of negative responses are concentrated in the evaluation of the Carabineros' response to sales of illegal drugs, gangs, and the consumption of alcohol by minors.

Table 7.4 compares the population's demands on Carabineros, in order of importance, with the population's perception of concrete action by this police force on each problem. The hierarchical order of the perception of concrete action by Carabineros was determined by subtracting the negative from the positive responses.

TABLE 7.3 PERCEPTIONS OF CONCRETE ACTIONS TAKEN BY CARABINEROS, BY SOCIOECONOMIC GROUP (PERCENTAGE)[a]

	Total		ABC1		C2		C3		D		E	
	Yes	No	Yes	No	Yes	No	Yes	No	Yes	No	Yes	No
Traffic accidents	60.30	29.70	78.90	14.20	57.40	29.90	65.90	24.70	57.30	32.00	46.50	47.20
Robbery and assault of homes, businesses and other establishments	45.50	56.80	30.20	42.00	31.50	52.60	31.70	54.30	29.50	60.60	29.80	67.00
Car theft or theft of objects from vehicles	38.60	52.80	38.60	49.00	40.00	47.00	39.50	51.10	36.60	53.60	27.30	68.40
Assault and muggings of passers-by in public areas	37.40	53.70	39.70	44.50	37.80	46.60	37.10	50.80	29.80	58.30	33.20	62.70
Consumption of alcohol in public areas and by minors in local establishments	37.30	46.30	51.80	27.30	43.10	41.40	42.10	42.90	33.10	51.10	33.70	59.20
Fighting in public areas	35.70	44.20	70.20	22.70	49.50	38.30	49.50	39.50	38.30	51.20	39.00	54.80
Gangs	34.20	51.10	64.80	24.30	39.10	45.70	43.50	46.10	28.70	58.60	33.00	63.10
Domestic violence	31.90	44.50	28.20	38.20	23.30	38.20	34.40	40.70	33.80	47.90	33.40	57.80
Sale of illegal drugs	30.60	46.30	24.90	43.00	31.50	43.10	42.00	40.40	35.00	49.60	33.30	59.20
Prostitution in public areas	22.40	45.30	26.20	31.30	18.20	40.00	22.60	44.30	22.70	47.40	25.60	58.40
Extortion of "tolls" from passers-by in public areas	19.10	45.40	9.20	29.70	18.20	33.00	21.30	45.80	18.30	50.90	23.80	53.80

Source: Chile, Ministry of the Interior—Carabineros (2003).

[a] Question asked: "Do you perceive concrete action taken by Carabineros on these problems in your neighborhood?"

TABLE 7.4   RANKING OF PROBLEMS AND CARABINEROS' RESPONSE

Problem	Importance	Ranking	Action	Ranking
Sale of illegal drugs	38	1	−15.7	7
Consumption of alcohol in public areas and by minors in local establishments	19	2	−9.0	3
Robbery and assault of homes, businesses and other establishments	13	3	−11.3	4
Traffic accidents	9	4	30.6	1
Gangs	7	5	−16.9	9
Assault and muggings of passers-by in public areas	6	6	−16.3	8
Car theft or theft of objects from vehicles	4	7	−14.2	6
Domestic violence	2	8	−12.6	5
Fighting in public areas	1	9	−8.5	2
Prostitution in public areas	1	10	−22.9	10
Extortion of "tolls" from passers-by in public areas	0	11	−26.3	11

Source: Chile, Ministry of the Interior—Carabineros (2003).

The control of the sale of illegal drugs is the issue that evidences the greatest discrepancy between the demand's level of priority and the public's perception of Carabineros' action. This concern primarily affects lower-income areas.

The next question in the survey on the perceptions of Carabineros relates to the importance of different actions by the police to meet the previously identified needs. The respondents were asked to evaluate the actions by Carabineros as very important or important, of average importance, of little importance or unimportant.

Table 7.5 lists, in order, the net opinions of the respondents, calculated by subtracting the percentage of those declaring the action of little importance or unimportant from those who found the action to be important or very important in their neighborhood.

The survey on the public's perceptions of Carabineros then asks for reactions to a number of actions by this police force, which include those mentioned previously, as well as several others. A net evaluation—derived from the difference between the percentages of positive and negative responses (those who considered the Carabineros successful in carrying out these actions versus those who saw them as falling short)—reveals findings that coincide in many aspects with the findings

TABLE 7.5   IMPORTANCE ATTRIBUTED TO ACTIONS BY CARABINEROS

Action	Percentage Finding Important
Visible patrolling of the streets, especially at night	95.2
Rapid dispatch of vehicles in response to emergency calls	94.7
Apprehension of criminals	94.2
Undertaking operations against drug traffickers	91.9
Apprehension of people who consume alcohol or drugs in public areas	90.9
Protection of crime victims	90.6
Controlling the sale of alcohol to minors in bars and liquor stores	90.5
Respect for individuals' rights	89.2
Provision of useful information to prevent mugging of residents and business owners	88.3
Community relations	83.7
Working with neighborhood groups toward solutions	82.4
Enforcement of traffic laws and direct traffic	82.0
Checking identification of suspicious individuals	81.8
Holding regular public hearings to which neighborhood residents are invited	79.0
Apprehension of those practicing prostitution in public areas	76.1
Taking action against the extortion of "tolls"	72.1

Source: Chile, Ministry of the Interior—Carabineros (2003).

from the national victimization survey. The more positive evaluations are concentrated in the areas of public assistance and not in actions related to crime control.

Once again, the Carabineros receive better evaluations in the provision of public assistance and rescue operations during natural disasters, in assistance and rescue during traffic accidents, in maintaining public order in large-scale events, and in assistance in the case of household emergencies. They receive lower marks for actions that have been quite highly ranked in terms of significance in other questions from the survey, such as the protection of crime victims or operations against drug traffickers.

CONCLUSIONS

Both the Carabineros and the Investigative Police clearly receive greater public support than the police of other Latin American countries. This esteem for the police

TABLE 7.6   EVALUATION OF CARABINEROS' ACTIONS
(PERCENTAGE OF THOSE SURVEYED)

Action	Negative (Bad/ Very Bad)	Positive (Good/ Very Good)	Net Evaluation (Positive- Negative)
Assistance and rescue during traffic accidents	3.8	69.2	65.4
Assistance and rescue during natural disasters	4.3	69.5	65.2
Enforcement of traffic laws and directing traffic	7.6	62.9	55.3
Search for missing persons	5.4	58.2	52.8
Assistance in household emergencies	6.3	58.2	51.9
Preservation of the public order during large-scale events	9.5	58.8	49.3
Border control	4.1	50.2	46.1
Control and provision of security in public marches or protests	10.8	55.3	44.5
Apprehension of criminals	14.0	51.1	37.1
Stopping acts of vandalism	10.6	47.6	37.0
Respect for individuals' rights	15.6	45.3	29.7
Dealing with cases of domestic violence	13.0	42.2	29.2
Patrolling main streets on foot	22.4	46.1	23.7
Protection of crime victims	18.3	39.4	21.1
Visible patrolling of the streets, especially at night	24.1	42.3	18.2
Community relations	20.0	37.0	17.0
Investigation of crimes	16.0	32.3	16.3
Investigation of economic crimes	15.0	30.9	15.9
Checking the identification of suspicious individuals	19.7	32.4	12.7
Undertaking operations against drug traffickers	24.1	35.9	11.8
Apprehension of people who consume alcohol or drugs in public areas	25.9	35.4	9.5

(continued)

TABLE 7.6   EVALUATION OF CARABINEROS' ACTIONS
             (PERCENTAGE OF THOSE SURVEYED) (CONTINUED)

Action	Negative (Bad/ Very Bad)	Positive (Good/ Very Good)	Net Evaluation (Positive- Negative)
Apprehension of prostitutes soliciting in public	21.0	28.9	7.9
Rapid dispatch of vehicles in response to emergency calls	28.2	35.3	7.1
Work in the area of drug-use prevention	29.6	32.4	2.8
Control of the sale of alcohol to minors in bars and liquor stores	29.4	30.5	1.1
Taking action against the extortion of "tolls"	24.0	22.9	−1.1
Provision of useful information to prevent mugging of residents and business owners	29.6	28.3	−1.3
Working with neighborhood groups to resolve problems	39.3	22.1	−17.2
Holding regular public meetings to which the residents of the area are invited	37.5	20.2	−17.3

Source: Chile, Ministry of the Interior—Carabineros (2003).

forces is partly the result of a general appreciation for order and legality among Chileans. They have a positive attitude toward their gradual transition to democracy and a certain tendency to view both the police and the armed forces as permanent national institutions. The population places great importance on the role of the police in crime control. In times of rising crime, this high level of public appreciation has helped the police gain financial and political support for its policies. Efforts carried out by both police forces to improve relations with local governments and the public have helped them to fully insert themselves into the democratic system and enjoy high levels of legitimacy, despite the fact that their legal structures and organizational autonomy from the elected government has been the subject of debate for years.

This legitimacy can also be ascribed to citizens' positive evaluation of the attention they receive from the police, and the public appreciates certain characteristics of members of the Carabineros related to discipline, education, and public service.

Thus, it can be said that Chileans are moved to support the police given their general attitudes toward the values the police represents, as well as because they appreciate the public social role the police performs as the most visible state institution in emergencies.

Nonetheless, residents of lower income sectors have a more negative opinion of the Carabineros with regard to all of these aspects, including the institution's impartiality. In these sectors, there is a lack of confidence in the police as well as a feeling that the institution provides less protection. This feeling is supported by additional data that reveal a significant increase in private security that benefits the wealthiest sectors.

The findings also lay bare a number of important challenges, particularly for the Carabineros. For instance, there is an overwhelming lack of awareness regarding the institution's plans for outreach to the community, although actions in this sense are not a priority for the respondents. Another concern is the gap between the problems perceived as priorities in the respondents' neighborhoods and the perception of the quality of the Carabineros' actions to resolve them. The surveys also reveal different social sectors make different demands, which indicates the need to decentralize police action. Thus, in order to maintain present levels of support the Carabineros will have to become more responsive toward vulnerable populations, both in terms of showing more impartiality toward the poor and increasing decisionmaking decentralization to deal with different social demands. This will probably affect the centralization of power within the institution, and will call for more innovation and personal initiative in an organization characterized by its militarized structure.

NOTES

1. Our analysis focuses mainly in two surveys undertaken in 2003 in Chile (see Chile, Ministry of the Interior, National Institute of Statistics 2003, and Chile, Ministry of the Interior, Carabineros 2003).
2. Laws of the Dominican Republic, Institutional Law of the National Police, no. 96-04, article 39, paragraph II.
3. The military jurisdiction of the Carabineros covers not only crimes committed by police, but also crimes committed by civilians against members of the Carabineros.
4. During the military regime (1973 to 1990), the directors of the Investigative Police were retired army generals. Since 1992, the directors have come from the police ranks.
5. Throughout Latin America, the Carabineros is considered to have high professional standards. Between 1996 and 2003, 481 officers from 21 nations received scholarships from the Chilean government to study in academies of the Carabineros.
6. See Ministry of Justice, Safety and Human Rights of Argentina, National Directorate of Criminal Policy Research Department, "Victimization Studies, City of Buenos Aires, 1997 to 2001, Buenos Aires, October 2002," available at http://www.polcrim.jus.gov.ar/ Victimizacion/Evolution%20study%20City%20of%20Buenos%20Aires%201997-2001.pdf.

7. The national victimization survey asked what persons or institutions bore the main responsibility for ensuring citizen security: 32.5 percent of the respondents named the Carabineros; 26.1 percent mentioned the government; 20.8 percent, the courts; 9.1 percent named citizens themselves; only 4.9 percent, the municipalities; and just 2.0 percent, the Investigative Police (Chile, Ministry of the Interior, National Institute of Statistics 2003).

8. On May 19, 2004, a unanimous agreement was reached by the Senate Committee of Constitutional Affairs, which stated that both police forces were to report to a future minister or vice minister of security (*El Mercurio*, May 20, 2004, A1). The constitution was finally amended in 2005 to state that until this ministry is created, the Carabineros will continue to report to the Ministry of Defense.

9. In a National Public Opinion Survey carried out by the Center of Public Studies in December 2002, 41 percent of the respondents considered the Carabineros to be the most trustworthy institution in Chile, second only to the universities (57 percent), and the churches (46 percent). Only 19 percent of the respondents voted for the courts.

10. See "Plan antidelictivo: Carabineros Deja de Cumplir Funciones Extra Policiales" ["Anti-crime Plan. Carabineros Will No Longer Carry Out Non-police Tasks"], *El Mercurio*, January 12, 1999, A1, 10.

11. "Por Primera Vez los Carabineros Serán Evaluados a Diario por Su Desempeño." ["For the First Time Carabineros Will Be Evaluated for Their Performance"], *La Segunda*, March 24, 2000, 19.

12. See note 6.

13. The two surveys are not strictly comparable. However, they could be consistently compared in terms of citizens' perceptions of police corruption. Our hypothesis is that the percentage of persons personally affected by acts of corruption is relatively small, but perception that members of the Carabineros are corrupt is higher, especially among the poor.

REFERENCES

Abelson, Adam. 2006. "Private Security in Chile: An Agenda for the Public Security Ministry." Security and Citizenship Program Bulletin No. 6. Santiago, Chile: FLACSO.

Adimark. 2004. "Modelo estimativo del Nivel Socio-económico en los hogares de Chile" ["Estimated Model of the Socioeconomic Level of Chilean Households"]. Accessed at http://www.Adimark.cl/medios/estudios/Mapa_Socioeconomico_de_Chile.pdf.

Candina, Azun, and Alejandra Lunecke. 2004. "Formación en Derechos Humanos y Control Institucional. Los Cambios en la Policía de Investigaciones de Chile (1992–2002)" ["Training in Human Rights and Institutional Control: Changes in the Investigative Police of Chile 1992–2002"]. In *Participación Ciudadana y Reformas a la Policía en América del Sur* [*Citizen Participation and Police Reform in South America*], edited by Hugo Frühling and Azun Candina. Santiago: Centro de Estudios del Desarrollo.

Candina, Azun, Tamara Cerda, José Garcia, and Marco Ensignia. 2003. "Los Barrios Vulnerables de Santiago" ["The Vulnerable Neighborhoods of Santiago"]. Unpublished manuscript. On file at Division of Public Security Ministry of the Interior, Chile.

Center of Public Studies. "Surveys of the Center of Public Studies. Information Available." Accessed at http://www.Cepchile.cl.

Chile, Ministry of the Interior, National Institute of Statistics. 1999–2003. Reports on Crime Statistics. Accessed at http://www.Seguridadpublica.gov.cl/estadisticas.html.

————. 2003. "National Urban Survey on Citizen Security." Santiago, Chile: Ministry of the Interior and the National Institute of Statistics.

Chile, Ministry of the Interior, Carabineros. 2003. "Study on the Perceptions and Evaluation of Carabineros." Santiago, Chile.

Costa, Gino. 1999. *La Policía Nacional Civil de El Salvador (1990–1997)* [*The National Civil Police of El Salvador, 1990–1997*]. San Salvador, El Salvador: UCA Editores.

Eijkman, Quirine. 2006. "To Be Held Accountable: Police Accountability in Costa Rica." *Police Practice and Research* 7(5): 414.

FESPAD and CEPES [Fundación de Estudios para la Aplicación del Derecho and Centro de Estudios Penales de El Salvador]. 2004. "Estado de la Seguridad Pública y la Justicia Penal en El Salvador, Julio 2002–Diciembre 2003" ["Public Security Conditions and Criminal Justice in El Salvador, July 2002-December 2003"]. Report. San Salvador, El Salvador: FESPAD and CEPES.

Frühling, Hugo. 1998. "Carabineros y Consolidación Democrática en Chile" ["The Carabineros and Democratic Consolidation in Chile"]. *Pena y Estado* 3(3): 81–116.

————. 2003. "Policía Comunitaria y Reforma Policial en América Latina. ¿Cuál es el Impacto?" ["Community Policing and Police Reform in Latin America: What Is the Impact?"]. Serie Documentos del Centro de Estudios en Seguridad Ciudadana. Santiago, Chile: Universidad de Chile.

————, editor. 2004. *Justicia en la Calle: Estudios sobre Policía Comunitaria en América Latina* [*Justice in the Streets: Studies on Community Policing in Latin America*]. Washington: Inter-American Development Bank.

Fuentes, Claudio A. 2001. "Denuncias por Actos de Violencia Policial" ["Reports of Police Violence"]. Santiago, Chile: FLACSO-Chile.

Goldstein Braunfeld, Eduardo. 2003. "Los Robos con Violencia en el Gran Santiago. Magnitudes y Características" ["Armed Robbery in Greater Santiago: Magnitudes and Characteristics"]. Serie Estudios CESC. Santiago, Chile: Universidad de Chile, Instituto de Asuntos Públicos.

Latinobarómetro. 2004. "Summary Report, Latinobarómetro 2004: A Decade of Measurements." Santiago, Chile: Corporación Latinobarómetro. Accessed at http://www.latinobarometro.org/uploads/media/2004_01.pdf.

Londoño, J. L., and Rodrigo Guerrero. 1999. "Violencia en América Latina. Epidemiología y Costos" ["Violence in Latin America: Epidemiology and Costs"]. Working Papers Series R-375. Washington: IDB.

Lunecke, Alejandra, and Ignacio Eissmann. 2005. "Violencia en Barrios Vulnerables: Una Aproximación desde la Exclusión Social" ["Violence in Vulnerable Neighborhoods: A Social Exclusion Approach"]. *Persona y Sociedad* 19(1): 73–100.

Maldonado Prieto, Carlos. 1990. "Los Carabineros de Chile: Historia de una Policía Militarizada" ["The Carabineros of Chile: History of a Militarized Police"]. *Ibero-Americana. Nordic Journal of Latin American Studies* 20(3): 3–31.

MINUGUA [The United Nations Verification Mission in Guatemala]. 2003. "Policía Nacional Civil. Tres Aspectos Estratégicos: Formación, Capacidad de Investigación y Presupuesto" ["National Civil Police, Three Strategic Aspects: Training, Investigative Capacity, and Budget"]. Report. Guatemala City, Guatemala: MINUGUA.

Neild, Rachel. 2002. "Sosteniendo la Reforma: Policía Democrática en América Central" ["Sustaining Reform: Democratic Police Forces in Central America"]. Washington: WOLA.

Sain, Marcelo. 1998. "Democracia, Seguridad Pública y Policía" ["Democracy, Public Security, and the Police"]. In *CELS Documentos de Trabajo del Seminario Las Reformas Policiales en Argentina [CELS, Working Documents from the Seminar on Police Reform in Argentina]*. Buenos Aires, Argentina: Proyecto Policía y Sociedad Democrática.

———. 2002. *Seguridad, Democracia y Reforma del Sistema Policial en la Argentina [Security, Democracy, and Reform of the Police System in Argentina]*. Buenos Aires, Argentina: Fondo de Cultura Económica.

Sandoval, Luis. 2001. "Prevención de la Delincuencia en Santiago de Chile" ["Crime Prevention in Santiago, Chile"]. In *Policía, Sociedad y Estado: Modernización y Reforma Policial en América Del Sur [Police, Society, and the State: Police Modernization and Reform in South America]*, edited by Hugo Frühling and Azun Candina. Santiago, Chile: Centro de Estudios del Desarrollo.

Ungar, Mark. 2004. "La Mano Dura: Current Dilemmas in Latin American Police Reform." Mimeograph. On file at Library Institute of Public Affairs, Universidad de Chile.

Vagg, Jon. 1996. "The Legitimation of Policing in Hong Kong: A Non-Democratic Perspective." In *Policing Change, Changing Police*, edited by Orwin Marenin. New York and London: Garlang.

Valenzuela, Arturo. 1989. "Chile: Origins, Consolidation, and Breakdown of a Democratic Regime." In *Democracy in Developing Countries: Latin America*, edited by Larry Diamond, Juan Linz, and Seymour Martin Lipset. Volume 4. Denver, Colo.: Lynne Rienner.

CHAPTER 8

Building Legitimacy Through Restorative Justice

John Braithwaite

Until the nineteenth century, criminal justice in the most developed nations such as Britain and United States was mostly a victim-initiated process.

SANITIZING THE VICTIM

Two centuries ago, if a case went to court it was not a result of arrest by professional police and prosecution by a state prosecutor. The victim might enlist the help of others to apprehend the felon by hiring private investigators or by enrolling a posse of volunteers. The prosecution would also be a private prosecution, by victims, thief takers, or bounty hunters seeking a reward. There were certainly village constables, mostly volunteers, who in various ways steered and refereed the private enforcement. We have all seen elements of this world in the genre of the Hollywood Western. Much private justice comes down to a blood feud, a life for a life. Sometimes the sheriff oversees fair play in gunfights to end blood feuds; sometimes he intercedes to substitute negotiated settlement for a shoot-out; when he is the only one strong enough to stand up to bad guys who terrorize the town, he might gun them down himself. More rarely the felon is captured and taken before a rowdy, participatory community trial, convened in a makeshift locale such as a saloon.

The spread of professional police after Prime Minister Robert Peel established the influential model of the London Metropolitan Police in 1829 was rapid in Anglophone nations, then globally. Every significant city in the world today has a professional paramilitary police. The professionalization of prosecution was less rapid, more institutionally variegated, but no less inexorable in its "publicization" of the private. It is difficult to resist the conclusion that this public takeover of justice was a good thing—among other things, it protected offender rights and reduced the violence associated with private justice. Data from many nations show that crime and violence fell dramatically and, with some hiccups, mostly continuously for a century or more after 1829—in many places right through to the 1950s or '60s (Warner 1934; Ferdinand 1967; Lane 1967, 1979, 1980; Graham 1969; Richardson 1970; Gatrell and Hadden 1972; Skogan 1975; Gurr, Grabosky, and Hula 1977; Gatrell 1980; Gurr 1981; Mukherjee 1981; Monkkonen 1981, 1982; Hewitt and Hoover 1982; Wilson and Herrnstein 1985). The abuses of bounty hunters—those who set up innocent people up so they could collect a reward—also ended. These developments were overwhelmingly positive, yet the project of the professionalization of justice went too far. Victims, the central stakeholders in crimes, were progressively almost totally disempowered. This undermined the legitimacy of criminal-justice institutions. Some European nations such as Germany and Austria managed this crisis with more finesse while maintaining low crime and imprisonment rates compared to Anglophone nations. Some of the institutional adaptation to manage the crisis has nevertheless been radical—such as rape trials in Germany, where there are two prosecution tables in the courtroom, one for the public prosecutor, the other for the (publicly funded) private prosecutor who sits with the alleged rape victim and her family (Frey 2004).

MOVEMENTS TO REINSTATE THE VICTIM

The professional capture of criminal justice has proved more total in Anglophone nations than in many non-Anglophone nations; in the former, criminal justice has also proved less adaptive and more resistant to popular reengagement. But all national criminal-justice systems have been forced to engage with two big movements for change. The first was a retributive movement that rose in the 1970s. The vanguard of this movement was punitive victim advocacy. Its ideology was that "nothing works": the rehabilitation professionals were mollycoddling criminals; there should be a return to long, certain sentences and to capital punishment. From 1976 an influential group of criminal lawyers and criminologists latched on to the anti-rehabilitation, anti–indeterminate sentences, anti–early release (for good behavior), "truth-in-sentencing" part of this program (see, for example, Von Hirsch 1976). A certain kind of legal professionalism was actually further entrenched by this uneasy alliance between liberal legalists and a punitive victim-rights movement. We see the uneasy settlement between them in reforms of the 1980s to allow victim impact statements. These allow victims to seek to influence proceedings with an address before sentencing, which most judges manage to resist in their determination to defend the integrity of consistent sentencing, just as judges continue to silence victims during the trial proper, continuing to limit their role to the supply of evidentiary cannon fodder for the lawyers.

In the 1990s a second movement to reempower victims grew on the embers of that crumbling settlement. It was restorative justice. It sought to engage the victims movement with a more radical program that gave victims a direct voice in the course of proceedings as opposed to voice only through legal mouthpieces. Its ideology was that the lawyers had "stolen" people's conflicts (Christie 1977). It sought to persuade the victims movement that getting a sincere apology and offers of reparation from the offender was of more tangible and emotional benefit to them than a longer prison term. Using their voice to craft solutions that helped prevent the same thing from happening to other victims could help their recovery. It could even reduce post-traumatic stress (Angel 2005). Indeed, forgiveness, though only if they were ready for it, also tended to be good for peoples' emotional well-being (Park and Enright 1997; Enright and Fitzgibbons 2000; Enright and Kittle 2000; Taft 2000, Petrucci 2002, Regehr and Gutheil 2002).

Restorative justice is a process that takes values such as healing, apology, and forgiveness seriously, as well as practical prevention of recurrence, as it seeks to restore victims, restore offenders, and restore communities. It is a process where all the stakeholders in a crime have the opportunity to discuss what harm has been done and what needs to be done to repair that harm, prevent it from happening again, and meet the needs of the stakeholders. Often, both victims and offenders are supported by loved ones who assist them to identify their hurts, their needs, and the remedies they are able to offer. Later, we will discuss restorative justice that occurs over minor assaults in school playgrounds without being referred to the police, police-diverted, or prosecutor-diverted restorative justice, restorative justice ordered by courts (say between a finding of guilt and passing of sentence), and restorative justice in corrections.

The first just-deserts movement failed to restore legitimacy to the criminal-justice system (see the declining levels of trust in Sherman 1999). The reason is that retributivism is an ideology that chases its own tail. When sentences get longer, the reaction is that they are still not long enough. Until the suffering of the offender equals the accumulated suffering of perhaps many victims, revenge cannot be sweet. When the sadistic murderer is hung, this seems too good for him; perhaps he should have been boiled in oil? Revenge feeds on itself until a more conciliatory mentality displaces it. This is why law and order politics is not as smart for politicians as the opinion polls suggest. The effect of the law-and-order politician's locking up criminals for longer is to create more voracious demands to lock them up for even longer. When the law-and-order politician calls a halt so there is some money available for other programs to get her reelected beyond building more prisons, she is viewed as selling out her law-and-order constituency. Law-and-order auctions—to win elections—have big losers, including the legitimacy of the justice system, but they do not have big political winners.

In this chapter, I argue that the second antiprofessional movement, restorative justice, holds more promise of rebuilding legitimacy and restoring victim rights.

Moreover, there are grounds for hope that it might be able to accomplish this while preserving the historical gains that professionalization delivered. Although the early reactions to this reform movement from both legalists (Sandor 1993; Brown 1994) and rehabilitationists (Levrant et al. 1999) was to shudder at its populism, partly in response to the antilegalist, antitherapeutic discourse of the reformers, the twenty-first century has seen considerable rapprochement among these camps. Lord chief justices of England and Wales and other jurisdictions began to give speeches about the virtues of restorative justice, appellate courts gave it explicit recognition in their decisions (Thorburn 2005), rehabilitationists began to see that because restorative justice builds stronger popular commitment to implement preventive decisions that emanate from the criminal process (Latimer, Dowden, and Muise 2001; Bonta et al. 2006), a restorative-justice circle can be a superior delivery vehicle for rehabilitative interventions that work than orders made in a traditional criminal trial (Braithwaite 2002, 95–102). In a Canadian Department of Justice meta-analysis of eight evaluations of restorative-justice programs with control-group comparisons, compliance with agreements and orders was 33 percent higher in the cases that went to restorative justice (Latimer, Dowden, and Muise 2001, 17).

This professional rapprochement with both the legalists and the rehabilitationists has reversed some of the early delegitimation of restorative justice by justice professionals who were influential with the public. The rapprochement was partly driven by the fact that repeatedly the professionals noticed that restorative justice was perceived as just and satisfying by victims, offenders, police and other participants in the process from the community (Braithwaite 2002, chapter 3). Even the worst run restorative justice programs secured outcomes of 80 percent or 90 percent of participants being satisfied with the process and the outcome, something the most well-run, well-resourced courts were not achieving. Once thousands of people in a city had participated in a restorative-justice conference (say, five hundred conferences with an average attendance of seven citizens (500 × 7 = 3,500), a significant constituency for restorative justice beyond the hard-core reformers was being created. Once those reformers had the self-confidence to engage with the victims'-rights movement, to invite their leaders to sit in on restorative-justice conferences, to invite conservative politicians to do so, even to invite television film crews in, the greater satisfaction of citizens with the justice they were getting began to become apparent to potential recruits to the punitive politics of law and order.

JUSTICE OF THE PEOPLE, JUSTICE OF THE LAW

A legitimacy ideal that has been articulated for restorative justice is that it would assist the justice of the law to filter down into the justice of the people and the justice of the people to bubble up into the justice of the law (Parker 1999; Braithwaite and Parker 1999). The role of restorative-justice circles as bridge-building institutions to enable this is part of a wider story about republican governance where pluralized mutual checking of power is institutionalized (Braithwaite 1997). So the bubbling up, filtering down metaphor is about power from above (that is, legal rights) checking abuse of power from below. Equally it is about power from below (the restorative-justice circle calling to account excessive police violence during arrest) checking abuse of power from above. For example, the hope is that the story of reconciliation being retold following a restorative-justice conference over an egregious act of discrimination against a female assistant professor in a university might have dual effects on the rippling of justice. On the one hand, it becomes an occasion to filter down the justice of university equal employment opportunity policies into the warp and woof of departmental politics. On the other, the story of how the injustice was inadequately dealt with by a lip-service EEO regime becomes an occasion for a university-wide, or even wider, politics of transformation on gender justice. That is the model of restorative storytelling as a fulcrum for checking abuses of power from above and from below. Crucial to this possibility is the insight that culturally resonant narratives can do what mute EEO policies cannot on those occasions when a big enough splash is created at one node of governance to cause ripples to spread across the whole pond of an organization or a society.

Declan Roche (2003, 214) and Kathleen Daly (2004, 506) have challenged John Braithwaite and Christine Parker's (1999) "bubbling up" conception of restorative justice as a vehicle of democratic impulses. Roche argues that "the real instrument of change of formal law is formal law itself . . . [because] the law works as a self-referential system of communication." First, Braithwaite and Parker's (1999) normative push is precisely about rendering formal law less self-referential. Second, the contested empirical idea of autopoiesis (Teubner 1987), that law is overwhelmingly self-referential, is simply less true in the contemporary "age of statutes" (Calabresi 1983), when less law is made by judges reading old legal texts and more by reading new statutes. The legal content of many of those new statutes does come from democratic impulses from below. Third, we will argue a little later that democratic impulses to change policies of executive governments are often more important than those that change formal law. But first we consider more fully the second point, that the normative push for statutory reform could come from below more often, more democratically, and more deliberatively via the vehicle of restorative justice. This is the point, for example, of Braithwaite and Parker's (1999) illustration of how Australian insurance law and policy changed following a press conference to publicize the outcome of a series of restorative conferences concerning exploitation of rural indigenous consumers by major insurance companies (see also Parker 2004).

Another example comes from Braithwaite, Toni Makkai, and Valerie Braithwaite's (2007) study of nursing home regulation in three nations. They found exit conferences at the end of nursing home inspections in the 1980s in the United States to be quite restorative and multipartite. The participants in these exit conferences— generally fifteen to twenty staff, residents, relatives, management, proprietors, church representatives for church-run homes, advocacy groups, inspectors, and sometimes other kinds of participants—would sit down together to discuss the problems detected in the inspection and movement toward a "plan of correction." Two decades on, exit conferences are much less restorative, having succumbed to "adversarial legalism" (Kagan 1991). Particularly important during the 1980s was the role of advocates in these processes. A September 1991 survey of five hundred twenty facilities in forty states found representatives of the state ombudsman to be present at a quarter of exit conferences, residents of the facility were present in half, and attorneys were present in only 2.5 percent (American Association of Homes for the Aging 1991). Most of the ombudsmen were trained community volunteers and some of the state and local-area ombudsman programs were contracted to advocacy organizations, such as Citizens for Better Care in Michigan, that were prominent in national nursing home politics.

When I interviewed leaders of the Oklahoma ombudsman program, I was told that the two hundred fifty volunteer advocates' training included the understanding that "part of the ombudsman's role is to monitor development of the law." This meant both Oklahoma and federal law, and concrete examples of ombudsmen's influencing both were provided. A facilitating linkage of volunteer ombudsmen (many of them retirees) in Oklahoma was to the Silver Haired Legislature, convened from time to time by the American Association of Retired Persons, to define an elderly-issues agenda for legislators that sometimes touched on nursing home law. "Bubbling up" was facilitated by linkage of a volunteer ombudsman in a remote rural community in Oklahoma to networking meetings of the state ombudsman program, and in turn linkage of state ombudsman programs to the National Association of State Long Term Care Ombudsman Programs and the National Citizens' Coalition for Nursing Home Reform (NCCNHR). Braithwaite, Makkai, and Braithwaite (2007) show that the latter organization, partly in collaboration with the former, led the transformation of United States nursing home law in the 1980s and '90s (1987). This law reform had some big effects, including the reduction of chemical and physical restraint in nursing homes (the rate of physical restraint went from 42 percent of nursing home residents across the United States at the end of the 1980s to 4 percent today). State ombudsmen counted among many of the leading activists of the NCCNHR. The high-water mark of its influence was April 24, 1987, National Nursing Home Residents' Day, when NCCNHR convened most of the major nursing home interest groups, including some industry groups, to discuss and settle which of a wide-ranging raft of law reforms each interest group would sign on to as a consensus position. This long list of consensus reforms then became the blueprint for the most sweeping set of national nursing home law reforms in United States history.

Let us now consider how democratic impulses to change policies of executive governments are often more important than those that change formal law. I recently challenged British advocates on restorative justice in schools with our failure to define the institutional mechanisms whereby private troubles can bubble up to become public issues. Belinda Hopkins, the author of *Just Schools: A Whole School Approach to*

Restorative Justice (2004), replied that restorative justice advocates were seeking, not very successfully to date, to seduce British educational policy to an explicit way of bubbling up specific personal narratives into national policy. This approach was the constant revision of National Practice Guidelines on Restorative Justice in Schools (Restorative Justice Consortium 2005b) adapted for restorative justice in school settings in light of bottom-up experience.[1] She explained that in conferences, workshops, and around the table in drawing up these Guidelines and Principles, "Personal narratives from professional experiences are shared and help to make the strong case for policy review and change." Her claim was that ordinary people's stories do "inform the debate and influence decision making." It was mainly the lack of punitive response to "bad news" stories'—for example, those involving domestic violence or school bullying—and bad outcomes' befalling victims (even suicide, in one influential school bullying case) that had actually limited the roll-out of restorative justice in a democratically responsive way. My own experience as a member of a committee that debated and drafted the 2004 Australian Capital Territory Restorative Justice Act was that aspects of that law were drafted in response to specific stories of real cases in the experience of those around the table.

This emphasis on personal stories could of course be taken further. General principles in something like the British National Practice Guidelines document could be illustrated by personal stories of ordinary citizens that have shaped their drafting. This indeed is an interesting translation of the old idea that corporate cultures can be a storybook more than a rule book (Shearing and Ericson 1991) into the more democratically ambitious idea that the networked governance of national institutions can be guided by a storybook. Many leading corporations, such as 3-M, have come to the conclusion that an excess of abstraction in corporate policies is a problem. So policies and plans are brought to life by stories intended to create the desired kinds of sensibilities among employees (Shaw, Brown, and Bromiley 1998):

> Stories are central to human intelligence and memory. Cognitive scientist William Calvin describes how we gradually acquire the ability to formulate plans through the stories we hear in childhood. From stories, a child learns to "imagine a course of action, imagine its effects on others, and decide whether or not to do it." . . . Cognitive scientists have established that lists, in contrast, are remarkably hard to remember.

Iris Young has been an influential thinker about the link between narrative and justice. Storytelling for Young can be "an important bridge between the mute experience of being wronged and political arguments about justice" (Young 2000, 72). Human beings tend to make sense of their experience of injustice through an architecture of narrative. Just as psychotherapy can be a form of narrative repair when people cannot construct an adaptive story about their worries, restorative justice can be about restorying lives in disarray because of a crime. Then they are renar-rated as the lives of people who have survived, transcended or repaired injustice (Zehr 2000; Pranis 2001; Neimeyer and Tschudi 2003). As a general matter, the nonnarrative processing of human experience might be somewhat exceptional (Neimeyer and Levitt 2001). Courtrooms and law books can undermine real worlds of justice because they too ruthlessly crush narratives about new injustices with old abstractions. Narratives are meaning making; in addition to giving meaning to personal identities such as "reformed drug abuser" or "rape survivor," they can give new meaning to justice itself.

A restorative institution such as a truth and reconciliation commission (there have been twenty-five now worldwide) makes it easier to understand how a jus-tice institution can turn the private troubles of victims into public issues (but see Stanley 2005 on the suppressed recognition of women's truth in the East Timor Commission, for example). Public commission hearings in which victims confront perpetrators attract more attention than the average court case. The stature of a leader such as Nelson Mandela resides in his legacy of restorying South Africa as a nation that has transcended an unjust institution. Whatever their race, all South Africans begin to share the identity that they have all been victims of Apartheid, all impoverished by it to become something less human.

Let us try to better understand what is democratically at issue in our bubbling up, filtering down of legitimacy by sticking with the school example. Whole-school programs with a restorative ideology are taking hold in education systems of the Anglophone world much more rapidly than restorative justice is taking hold in criminal-justice systems. These school programs first seek to filter the justice of rights down into the justice of the school community. Classroom by classroom, whole-school programs initiate conversations among administrators, teachers, stu-dents, parents, and other community members such a janitors and counselors about what is acceptable and what is not. This engenders a rights culture intended to secure the rights of children and staff alike to be safe against, for instance, bullying. Democratic deliberation in local sites such as classrooms teaches and affirms com-mitment to rights enshrined in the law and builds commitment to intervene in, say, playground bullying when these rights are threatened. Systemwide education poli-cies to nurture and resource whole-school restorative programs systemically foster filtering down of the justice of the law into a popular culture of rights in schools.

That is the filtering-down side. The bubbling-up side at the microlevel of the school has been documented in cases in the literature of, for example, school con-ferences dealing with minor incidents of sexual harassment or sexual assault. One case describes the reversal from blaming the victim as a girl who was "asking for it" in the antirights culture of an Australian school (Braithwaite and Daly 1994; Braithwaite 2002, 66–70). In the outcome of that conference, the responsible boy and his friends agreed to go out into the school to spread the message that this girl was not responsible for what happened to her. The boys were responsible, and the boys attending the conference accepted an obligation to confront and change the patriarchal culture of that school, which was disrespecting of girls' bodies. On my account, what is happening here is that justice impulses from below, from dominated teenage girls, bubble up through the agency of remorseful boys to transform the private justice system of one school.

The next step is to constitute justice storybooks, as in my conversation with Hopkins on national guidelines for restorative justice in schools, that create a path for local stories to bubble up to influence systemwide justice. These can be stories more oriented to learning how to secure victim rights or the rights of alleged perpetrators, children's rights or those of parents or teachers.

JUSTICE IN MANY ROOMS

Legalists will of course say that school justice systems or corporate justice systems (as at 3-M) are a far cry from state legal systems. The restorative-justice theorist finds that an overstated reaction at three levels. First, there is the legal pluralist response that justice occurs in many rooms (Galanter 1981), where courtrooms in a sense do best by justice through overseeing (checking and balancing) the justice making that occurs in those many rooms. Second, the restorative-justice theorist says we are not born just; we are not born democratic. We have to learn to be democratic citizens who will do justice well in courtrooms and other rooms later in life as complainants, witnesses, jurors, lawyers, journalists reporting the case, and in other roles. Enriching justice experiences in school are important to our learning to be just, in particular, to learning to make human rights active cultural accomplishments as opposed to passive legal restraints.

Third, state justice is itself not mainly transacted in courtrooms. It is lawyerly myopia to see it that way. The empirical evidence is that "the process is the punishment," that police and prosecutors exact more punishment outside courtrooms than inside them (Feeley 1979). So when (as in cases discussed by Roche 2003) a mother complains about excessive use of force against her son during arrest, or discrimination against her son because he was arrested whereas the police treated other perpetrators more leniently, this is not a marginal issue. It is a story at the heart of how we would want the justice of the people to bubble up into the justice of law enforcement.

In my experience as a commissioner with Australia's national competition and consumer protection regulator, I chaired conferences that discussed allegedly illegal conduct by major corporations in which they complained about the unfairness of how we as the regulator treated them in our enforcement work. I would take these concerns back to meetings of the full commission to discuss whether the complaints justified a need to revise our policies and procedures. There were other cases where such complaints about unfair process through such channels were ignored and were revisited by the corporation attacking us in the media. Such bubbling up of checks and balances about pretrial justice is absolutely fundamental to the quality of a justice system and therefore its legitimacy in the eyes of citizens. Not post-trial but, rather, intra-trial, we should also look forward to the day when a judge sends a case to a restorative-justice conference not only for a recommendation on sentence but also for information on any injustices that should be repaired in the context of this trial. We should look forward to the day when such a conference returns to the judge with some advice on how she might have handled the case with more propriety or sensitivity, or why an apology from her to a witness might be in order.

Two centuries ago, in Jeffersonian America, democracy was close to the people. Electors may never have met the governor or the president, but most knew the mayor or a local legislator they elected to vote in the capital. Today the debates that matter most—whether to go to war, increase taxes, make a key appointment—take place in the executive offices of the capital. Deliberation on the floor of chambers that are open to citizens—legislatures, town meetings—count less and less as decision-making nodes. Nevertheless, disputes over specific injustices that affect citizens continue to be heard in chambers that are no less open to ordinary citizens than they used to be. Restorative justice is partly about reconceiving the judicial branch of governance more than the legislative branch as a site where deliberative democracy can be reinvigorated, where ordinary stakeholders can be given a more genuine say. When people have been a victim of injustice, whether as a victim of crime, of a consumer rip-off, or of school bullying, there is more edge to their desire for participation than there is to participate in neighborhood watch or consumer or school policymaking. The restorative-justice circle in a school to confront a playground assault thus becomes an opportunity for young citizens to acquire a taste for becoming deliberatively democratic.

So far my argument has been that democracy can be made more legitimate by more effectively allowing the justice of the law to filter down into the justice of the people and the justice of the people to bubble up into both the justice of the law and the justice of state enforcement. In the next section, we argue that legitimacy requires much more than making the legal order legitimate. A bigger question is the social order.

THE LEGITIMACY OF THE SOCIAL ORDERS OF THE STATE AND THE STREET

Trust in the government of the United States and other Western governments started a big, long decline in the 1960s (Putnam 2000). Trust in Washington was over 70 percent at the beginning of the 1960s, and below 30 percent in the early 1990s (Nye and Zelikow 1997). Gary LaFree (1998) summarized evidence across time and space suggesting that where governmental legitimacy was low, crime was higher. Income inequality was also implicated in this picture, being associated with both higher levels of crime and perceptions that the system is unfair. Elijah Anderson

(1999, 130) found in his ethnography of black urban offenders that "many feel wronged by the system, and thus its rules do not seem to them to be legitimate." In other words, the illegitimacy of the social order is one of the things that creates the illegitimacy of the legal order.

Many subcultures of the street are consequently about rejecting one's rejectors (Cohen 1955). Participants in minority street cultures feel rejected by mainstream society. When police and white officials enter such streets purveying crime prevention programs, they tend to be seen as quintessentially worthy of rejection. This renders these officials incapable of changing the culture of street crime. One innovative attempt to re-theorize this dilemma has come from the LIFERS Public Safety Initiative Steering Committee of the Graterford State Penitentiary in Pennsylvania (LIFERS 2004). These long-term prisoners contend that arresting gang members takes only those individuals off the street, their place to be taken by new recruits to the gang (Reiss 1980). Even when those arrested are rehabilitated in prison, crime is not reduced because their illicit niche on the street has been filled by another.

This is one reason the Graterford LIFERS advocate transformation rather than rehabilitation. They conceive rehabilitation as being about change in the way a person behaves, whereas transformation involves a fundamental change in personal philosophy whereby the process of transformation is not complete until manifest in "personal efforts to transform others ensnared in the street crime lifestyle" (LIFERS 2004, 64S). Shadd Maruna (2001) found that one predictor of serious offenders' "making good" was involvement in helping others to make good.

The more practice one has, the greater the likelihood that one will perfect the desired changes in personality. Therefore, artists become great artists not by attending discussion groups about great art but by practicing. Writers become accomplished writers not by talking to professional writers but by writing. Prisoners desiring to learn more socially productive behaviors do so not by sitting through endless hours of therapeutic group sessions but by returning to their communities and practicing the socially productive behaviors that they seek to make part of their lives (LIFERS 2004, 64S).

Their most important point is that "society should begin to use the experience, knowledge, insight, and expertise of transformed ex-offenders to do the work that members of the community and those in positions of authority are not equipped to do" (LIFERS 2004, 65S). The idea is to change a sequence of

conviction → rehabilitation → replacement on the street

to

conviction → personal transformation → transformation
of the culture of street crime.

When long-term prisoners are given a chance to return to their street to deploy their street cred to transform a culture they know, that chance is given to someone who might have legitimacy on the street. Authority figures do not enjoy legitimacy on the street precisely because they do enjoy legitimacy in the mainstream.

There are many ways released offenders can transform their street. One is by brokering terms of peace agreements between gangs that include the renunciation of armed violence, as we have seen the Alliance of Concerned Men do in Washington, D.C. (Marcia Slacum Greene, "Feuding Gang Factions Report a Truce in SE: Slaying of Boy, 12, Spurs Effort to End Violence," *Washington Post,* January, 30, 1997). The day delegates from the 2005 World Congress of Criminology visited Graterford in 2005, Tyrone Parker, from the Alliance of Concerned Men, said to me that changing the law in states like Pennsylvania to allow the early release of lifers from a transformative group is important because there is a "shortage of strong black men who are role models who can show how the street can be transformed for the better." Pre-release restorative-justice conferences could be one vehicle for negotiating conditions for graduated release to the street of inmates to work on transforming the culture of street crime on their old block. Earlier release of long-term prisoners with street legitimacy would also be a step toward a more legitimate social order that holds out a better future for minorities who run afoul of the law than a life of perpetual incarceration. Early release to participate in crime-prevention programs that hold out a prospect of saving a future generation of victims, where the decision to release gives the offender's original victim a say in a restorative-justice circle about whether release should happen, might secure the legitimacy of the early-release program.

The other important feature of the LIFERS program is that it empowers prisoners as generators of criminological theory. We criminologists can lend legitimacy to them by the simple gesture of listening to their ideas. Simultaneously criminology can also become more legitimate when some influential ideas in its repertoire come from below. This is what made the Graterford event for the 2005 World Congress of Criminology so special.

RESTORATIVE JUSTICE AND LEGITIMACY: CONCLUSION

It has been argued that professionals sidelining of victims over the past two centuries has undercut the legitimacy of the criminal-justice system. Restorative justice can reinstate victims' voices while averting violence as a means of private revenge and preserving the rights focus that less privatized justice has delivered. Indeed, restorative justice can be a vehicle for rights that are more active cultural accomplishments, enlivened by participatory storytelling processes, than the passive rights of legal texts.

Narratives of restorative justice might also better bubble up the justice of the people into the justice of the state. Law-making dialogue could be better informed by stories from below if restorative-justice programs institutionalized a channel for communicating personal stories that should be made political. Advocacy NGOs that are funded to monitor outcomes of restorative-justice programs could play that role. For example, children's-law centers can watch for stories of abuse of children as victims or offenders in restorative-justice processes and feed those stories into deliberation over policy change and into policy documents. Environmental NGOs can do that for restorative environmental-justice programs, Aboriginal rights NGOs for Aboriginal-justice programs, women's rights NGOs for abuses of the rights of women in restorative-justice programs, unions for abuses of workers' rights, and so on.

A social order that enabled higher-quality justice in many rooms would enjoy more legitimacy than one where justice could only be obtained by paying lawyers to take cases to court (thus a justice that is mostly only available to the rich). Policies and guidelines for enacting justice in different chambers of private and public governance (schoolrooms, corporate towers, police stations, offices of universities) might be transformed from rule books to storybooks, where the stories are channeled up through restorative-justice programs.

The criminal-justice system will become more legitimate as it becomes more effective at preventing crime and helping victims. The restorative-justice idea is that these two objectives can be brought together in various ways (see Braithwaite 2002 for a range of them). A promising new way bubbled up from below, from Graterford Penitentiary, is engaging victims with early-release restorative justice conferences for transformed long-term offenders, then sending those offenders back to their block to transform the culture of street crime. The Graterford LIFERS argue that their members have the street legitimacy for doing work such as negotiating gang truces to reduce violence. These ideas are but illustrative sketches of the possibility that street legitimacy, the legitimacy of a just social order and a just legal system, might be bound together in an integrated strategy for building democratic legitimacy. Justice that occurs in many rooms can empower more meaningfully than justice that occurs in very big chambers on Capitol Hill. We can tell how much power a person has by how many listen to his or her stories. It follows that restorative strategies for institutionalizing listening to the stories of little people in little rooms are simple strategies of empowerment. When the people have more power through such practical strategies and feel that they do, legitimacy grows.

NOTES

1. The U.K. also has more general principles (Restorative Justice Consortium 2005a) that were also developed collaboratively by practitioners, partly on a foundation of sharing crime narratives.

REFERENCES

American Association of Homes for the Aging. 1991. "ANHA Questionnaire on OBRA Surveys." Washington: American Association of Homes for the Aging.

Anderson, Elijah. 1999. *The Code of the Streets.* New York: Norton.

Angel, Caroline. 2005. "Crime Victims Meet Their Offenders: Testing the Impact of Restorative Justice Conferences on Victims' Post-Traumatic Stress Symptoms." Ph.D. dissertation, University of Pennsylvania.

Bonta, James, Rebecca Jesseman, Tanya Rugge, and Robert Cormier. 2006. "Restorative Justice and Recidivism: Promises Made, Promises Kept?" In *Handbook of Restorative Justice: A Global Perspective,* edited by Dennis Sullivan and Larry Tifft. London: Routledge.

Braithwaite, John. 1997. "On Speaking Softly and Carrying Sticks: Neglected Dimensions of Republican Separation of Powers." *University of Toronto Law Journal* 47(1): 1–57.

———. 2002. *Restorative Justice and Responsive Regulation.* New York: Oxford University Press.

Braithwaite, John, Toni Makkai, and Valerie Braithwaite. 2007. *Regulating Aged Care: Ritualism and the New Pyramid.* Cheltenham, England: Edward Elgar.

Braithwaite, John, and Kathleen Daly. 1994. "Masculinities, Violence and Communitarian Control." In *Just Boys Doing Business?: Men, Masculinities, and Crime,* edited by Tim Newburn and Elizabeth A. Stanko. London and New York: Routledge.

Braithwaite, John, and Christine Parker 1999. "Restorative Justice Is Republican Justice." In *Restoring Juvenile Justice: An Exploration of the Restorative Justice Paradigm for Reforming Juvenile Justice,* edited by Lode Walgrave and Gordon Bazemore. Monsey, N.Y.: Criminal Justice Press.

Brown, Jennifer Gerada. 1994. "The Use of Mediation to Resolve Criminal Cases: A Procedural Critique." *Emory Law Journal* 43(4): 1247–1309.

Calabresi, Guido 1983. *A Common Law for the Age of Statutes.* Cambridge, Mass.: Harvard University Press.

Christie, Nils. 1977. "Conflicts as Property." *British Journal of Criminology* 17(1): 1–16.

Cohen, Albert K. 1955. *Delinquent Boys: The Culture of the Gang.* Glencoe, Ill.: Free Press.

Daly, Kathleen. 2004. "Pile It On: More Texts on Restorative Justice." *Theoretical Criminology* 8(4): 499–507.

Enright, Robert D., and Richard P. Fitzgibbons. 2000. *Helping Clients Forgive: An Empirical Guide for Resolving Anger and Restoring Hope.* Washington: American Psychological Association.

Enright, Robert D., and Bruce A. Kittle. 2000. "Forgiveness in Psychology and Law: The Meeting of Moral Development and Restorative Justice." *Fordham Urban Law Journal* 27(00): 1621–31.

Feeley, Malcolm M. 1979. *The Process Is the Punishment: Handling Cases in a Lower Criminal Court.* New York: Russell Sage Foundation.

Ferdinand, Theodore N. 1967. "The Criminal Patterns of Boston Since 1849." *American Journal of Criminology* 73(1): 688–98.

Frey, Sylvia. 2004. "Victim Protection in Criminal Proceedings: The Victim's Rights to Information, Participation and Protection in Criminal Proceedings." Work Product of the 123rd International Senior Seminar of the United Nations Asian and Far East Institute for the Prevention of Crime. Fuchu, Tokyo, 2004.

Galanter, Marc. 1981. "Justice in Many Rooms." In *Access to Justice and the Welfare State*, edited by Mauro Cappelletti. Alphen aan den Rijn, Netherlands: Sijthoff.

Gatrell, V. A. C. 1980. "The Decline of Theft and Violence in Victorian and Edwardian England." In *Crime and Law Since 1850*, edited by V. A. C. Gatrell, Bruce P. Lenman, and Geoffrey Parker. London: Europa.

Gatrell, V. A. C., and Tom B. Hadden. 1972. "Criminal Statistics and their Interpretation." In *Nineteenth Century Society*, edited by E. A. Wrigley. Cambridge: Cambridge University Press.

Graham, Fred P. 1969. "A Contemporary History of American Crime." In *Violence in America: Historical and Comparative Perspectives: A Report to the National Commission on the Causes and Prevention of Violence*, edited by Hugh Davis Graham and Ted Robert Gurr. New York: Praeger.

Gurr, Ted Robert 1981. "Historical Trends in Violent Crime: A Critical Review of the Evidence." In *Crime and Justice: An Annual Review of Research*, edited by Michael Tonry and Norval Morris. Volume 3. Chicago, Ill.: University of Chicago Press.

Gurr, Ted Robert, Peter N. Grabosky, and Richard C. Hula. 1977. *The Politics of Crime and Conflict: A Comparative History of Four Cities*. Beverly Hills, Calif.: Sage.

Hewitt, John D., and Dwight W. Hoover. 1982. "Local Modernization and Crime: The Effects of Modernization on Crime in Middletown, 1845–1910." *Law and Human Behavior* 6(3/4): 313–25.

Hopkins, Belinda. 2004. *Just Schools: A Whole School Approach to Restorative Justice*. London: Jessica Kingsley.

Kagan, Robert A. 1991. "Adversarial Legalism and American Government." *Journal of Policy Analysis and Management* 10(3): 369–406.

LaFree, Gary. 1998. *Losing Legitimacy: Street Crime and the Decline of Social Institutions in America*. Boulder, Colo.: Westview Press.

Lane, R. 1967. *Policing the City: Boston, 1822–1885*. Cambridge, Mass.: Harvard University Press.

———. 1979. *Violent Death in the City: Suicide, Accident and Murder in 19th Century Philadelphia*. Cambridge, Mass.: Harvard University Press.

———. 1980. "Urban Police and Crime in Nineteenth-Century America." In *Crime and Justice: An Annual Review of Research*, edited by Michael Tonry and Norval Morris. Volume 2. Chicago, Ill.: University of Chicago Press.

Latimer, Jeff, Craig Dowden, and Danielle Muise. 2001. *The Effectiveness of Restorative Justice Practices: A Meta-Analysis*. Ottawa, Ontario: Department of Justice, Canada.

Levrant, Sharon, Francis T. Cullen, Betsy Fulton, and John F. Wozniak. 1999. "Reconsidering Restorative Justice: The Corruption of Benevolence Revisited?" *Crime and Delinquency* 45(1): 3–27.

LIFERS Public Safety Steering Committee of the State Correctional Institution at Graterford, Pennsylvania. 2004. "Ending the Culture of Street Crime." *Prison Journal* 84(4): 48–68.

Maruna, Shadd 2001. *Making Good: How Ex-Convicts Reform and Rebuild Their Lives*. Washington: American Psychological Association.

Monkkonen, Eric H. 1981. "A Disorderly People? Urban Order in the Nineteenth and Twentieth Centuries." *Journal of American History* 68(3): 536–59.

———. 1982. "From Cop History to Social History: The Significance of the Police in American History." *Journal of Social History* 15(4): 573–91.

Mukherjee, Satyanshu Kumar. 1981. *Crime Trends in Twentieth-Century Australia.* Sydney: Allen & Unwin.

National Citizens' Coalition for Nursing Home Reform. 1987. *Campaign for Quality Care in Nursing Homes.* Washington: National Citizens' Coalition for Nursing Home Reform.

Neimeyer, Robert A., and Heidi Levitt. 2001. "Coping and Coherence: A Narrative Perspective on Resilience." In *Coping With Stress: Effective People and Processes,* edited by C. R. Snyder. New York: Oxford University Press.

Neimeyer, Robert A., and Finn Tschudi 2003. "Community and Coherence: Narrative Contributions to the Psychology of Conflict and Loss." In *Narrative and Consciousness: Literature, Psychology, and the Brain,* edited by Gary D. Fireman, Ted E. McVay, and Owen J. Flanagan. New York: Oxford University Press.

Nye, Joseph S., Jr., and Philip D. Zelikow. 1997. "Conclusion: Reflections, Conjectures and Puzzles." In *Why People Don't Trust Government,* Joseph S. Nye, Jr., Philip D. Zelikow and David C. King. Cambridge, Mass.: Harvard University Press.

Pranis, Kay. 2001. "Democratizing Social Control: Restorative Justice, Social Justice, and the Empowerment of Marginalized Populations." In *Restorative Community Justice,* edited by S. Gordon Bazemore, Mara Schiff, and Gordon Bazemore. Cincinnati, Oh.: Anderson.

Park, Younghee Oh, and Robert D. Enright. 1997. "The Development of Forgiveness in the Context of Adolescent Friendship Conflict in Korea." *Journal of Adolescence* 20: 393–402.

Parker, Christine. 1999. *Just Lawyers.* Oxford: Oxford University Press.

———. 2004. "Restorative Justice in Business Regulation? The Australian Competition and Consumer Commission's use of Enforceable Undertakings." *Modern Law Review* 67(2): 209–46.

Petrucci, Carrie J. 2002. "Apology in the Criminal Justice Setting: Evidence for Including Apology as an Additional Component in the Legal System." *Behavioral Sciences and the Law* 20: 337–62.

Putnam, Robert D. 2000. *Bowling Alone: The Collapse and Revival of American Community.* New York: Simon & Schuster.

Reiss, Albert J., Jr. 1980. "Understanding Changes in Crime Rates." In *Indicators of Crime and Criminal Justice: Quantitative Studies,* edited by Stephen E. Fienberg and Albert J. Reiss, Jr. Washington: US Government Printing Office.

Restorative Justice Consortium 2005a. *National Practice Guidelines for Restorative Practitioners.* London: Home Office.

———. 2005b. *Statement of Restorative Justice Principles as Applied in a School Setting.* London: Restorative Justice Consortium.

Richardson, James F. 1970. *The New York Police: Colonial Times to 1901.* New York: Oxford University press.

Roche, Declan. 2003. *Accountability in Restorative Justice.* Oxford: Oxford University Press.

Regehr, Cheryl, and Thomas Gutheil. 2002. "Apology, Justice and Trauma Recovery." *Journal of American Academy of Psychiatry and the Law* 30(3):425–30.

Sandor, Danny. 1993. "Juvenile Justice: The Thickening Blue Wedge." *Alternative Law Journal* 18(3): 104–8.

Shaw, Gordon, Robert Brown, and Phillip Bromiley. 1998. "Strategic Stories: How 3M Is Rewriting Business Planning." *Harvard Business Review* (May–June): 41–54.

Shearing, Clifford, and Richard V. Ericson. 1991. "Towards a Figurative Conception of Action." *British Journal of Sociology* 42(4): 481–506.

Sherman, Lawrence W. 1999. "Trust and Confidence in Criminal Justice: A Background Paper." Philadelphia, Pa.: University of Pennsylvania, Fels Center of Government.

Skogan, Wesley. G. 1975. *Chicago Since 1840: A Time-Series Data Handbook.* Urbana, Ill.: Institute of Government and Public Affairs, University of Illinois.

Stanley, Elizabeth. 2005. "Truth Commissions and the Recognition of State Crime." *British Journal of Criminology* 45(6): 582–97.

Taft, Lee. 2000. "Apology Subverted: The Commodification of Apology." *Yale Law Journal* 109(5): 1135–60.

Teubner, Günther. 1987. "Juridification: Concepts, Aspects, Limits, Solutions." In *Juridification of Social Spheres: A Comparative Analysis of the Areas of Labor, Corporate, Antitrust and Social Welfare Law,* edited by Günther Teubner. Berlin: Walter de Gruyter.

Thorburn, Stan A. 2005. "Observing the Application of Restorative Justice in Courts of New Zealand." Paper presented at the International Symposium on Latest Developments in International Criminal Justice Reform. Shenzhen City, Peoples Republic of China, August 19–20, 2005.

Von Hirsch, Andrew. 1976. *Doing Justice: The Choice of Punishments.* New York: Hill & Wang.

Warner, Sam Bass. 1934. *Crime and Criminal Statistics in Boston.* Cambridge, Mass.: Harvard University Press.

Wilson, James Q., and Richard Herrnstein. 1985. *Crime and Human Nature.* New York: Simon & Schuster.

Young, Iris Marion. 2000. *Inclusion and Democracy.* Oxford: Oxford University Press.

Zehr, Howard. 2000. "Journey of Belonging." Paper presented at the Fourth International Conference on Restorative Justice for Juveniles. Tübingen, Germany.

PART III

Formal and Community-Based Routes to Legitimacy

CHAPTER 9

Introduction

From an American perspective, policing is a formal and centralized process, conducted by institutions and authorities connected to the state. The chapters in this section make clear that this is only one of a variety of approaches that can be taken to creating and maintaining social order. In particular, when the formal state lacks legitimacy, communities may create alternative mechanisms for maintaining social order, mechanisms that resemble the informal policing authorities found in the history of many societies that now have formal and professionalized police forces.

Jennifer Johnson (chapter 10) touches on this theme in the case of Mexico, arguing that volunteer extralegal mechanisms for policing arose because the police were regarded as incompetent and corrupt. However, the development of this more popular system of informal justice is viewed as a threat to the state, and, as Johnson notes, it is not clear whether a state can tolerate the widespread existence of alternative bases of authority and maintain its own legitimacy. If the state claims the monopoly on the use of force, its legitimacy is undermined when other institutions arise that take over the function.

Graziella Moraes D. da Silva and Ignacio Cano (chapter 11) also examine community policing initiatives, in Brazil. Again, the question posed is how this informal mechanism arose in response to crisis conditions and, once existing, how it related to the traditional police. Does this mechanism enhance the legitimacy of the traditional police, or does it undermine that legitimacy?

Finally, John Comaroff and Jean Comaroff (chapter 12) focus on South Africa in the period after the fall of the Afrikaner regime. In this situation, they argue, the police lacked legitimacy, being viewed as neither competent nor moral, and people turned widely to various forms of private justice, including private police forces and community-based groups. These police forces were created and used to resolve social and intergenerational tensions that emerged in the wake of the end of the Afrikaner era.

In all of these cases alternative forms of policing arise in response to a failed state. Either the police are unable to maintain social order, or they are corrupt and distrusted, or both. In such cases, people create informal or alternative mechanisms to maintain social order. The creation of private forces raises a number of issues. Perhaps most important is whether these forces act as agents of particular parties within the society, serving more as a militia than as a police force. One of the reasons that the state tries to claim a monopoly on the use of force is so that the state can create some types of mechanisms through which force is applied justly, following due processes of law. Of course, as noted, it is when such mechanisms have failed that private ordering occurs. Nonetheless, it is still important to examine whether such private ordering, when it occurs, is able to achieve the ends of justice.

Further, it is important to ask whether private ordering is viable in the long run. As noted in the chapters, one reason that private ordering can arise is that there is a perceived crisis. Under such conditions, people may be willing to make the private maintenance of order a high priority. However, it is unclear whether these efforts can be sustained. In emergencies, for example, people often are willing to put aside their private agendas to pitch in and help others. However, without an institutional framework for the long term it is difficult to sustain such efforts. There need to be mechanisms for training and funding agents of social control, as well as ways to regulate and direct their behavior. Who decides, for example, the targets and range of action for the police?

Finally, the development of an alternative police force can create conflict between this new force and the traditional forces of social order. The issue of concern in the future is gaining an understanding how such conflicts are managed. Do the police withdraw, as the police have in some American ghettos, and allow informal police "gangs" or "vigilantes" to maintain their own form of social order? Or, do the police seek to co-opt or undermine these informal forces?

CHAPTER 10

When the Poor Police Themselves: Public Insecurity and Extralegal Criminal-Justice Administration in Mexico

Jennifer L. Johnson

In the face of dramatic increases in violent crime in the 1990s in Latin America and the inadequacy of top-down police reform to stem this tide, citizens throughout the region have intensified efforts to protect themselves. As the current boom in the private security industry evidences, a growing number of such citizens have turned to the free market to procure protection (Davis 2003; Davis et al. 2003; Regalado Santillán 2002; Smulovitz 2003). Through the consumption of gated residences, private security personnel, high-tech alarm systems, and even armored cars, these members of the Latin American elite and upper middle classes self-provision the protection that the public sector has failed to supply. But how do members of society who lack the purchasing power to acquire this kind of private protection—clearly, the vast majority of Latin Americans—endeavor to protect themselves?

This chapter examines a collective self-help policing and penal justice initiative that emerged in contemporary rural Mexico to protect local citizens from common criminals and to compensate for the state's incapacity to bring offenders to justice through legal channels. The movement originated in 1996, when forty-two farming communities in the southern state of Guerrero mobilized volunteer policing brigades to patrol the roadways and footpaths that crisscross an isolated mountain region the size of the state of Delaware. Comprising more than five hundred armed individuals, these brigades initially detained criminal suspects and turned them over to the state judicial system for prosecution. In 1998, however, these patrols ceased to operate in tandem with mainstream legal institutions and began adjudicating cases locally. By the end of the following year, this extralegal criminal justice system had sentenced sixty-one convicts to forced labor on local public works projects for terms ranging from two weeks to five years. At the time this observation was made, more than half of the convicts sentenced since adjudication had begun had completed their sentences and been released (Martínez Sifuentes 2001).

Condemned by the Guerrero state government and the National Human Rights Commission as illegal and in egregious violation of basic legal norms and protections, this movement has nonetheless grown in size and popular support. Local observers claim that in its ten years of existence, this extralegal system of policing, adjudication, and correction has eliminated between 90 and 95 percent of all crime in the six contiguous counties that it currently covers (Rojas 2005a).[1] Federal troops and state police have attempted to disband the movement by forcibly disarming its police brigades and by imprisoning its commanders, but these moves have been thwarted by mass protest. As of November 2005, this movement held thirteen convicts in custody (Rojas 2005c) and continued to patrol sixteen hundred square miles of national territory in spite of staunch opposition from the federal and state governments.

Although unique in some respects, this initiative—called the Sistema Comunitario de Seguridad, Impartición de Justicia y Reducación (SCSIJR)—Community System for Security, Justice Administration, and Reeducation (CSSJAR)—by participants and the press—reveals common themes that link diverse popular responses to the current crisis of public security in Mexico. For one, the formation and tenacity of the CSSJAR in rural Guerrero highlights the extraordinary reticence of Mexicans of all classes to turn to the police to redress criminal victimization. By regional standards, victimization rates in Mexico are not unusually high, but rates of nonreporting stand as a stark indictment of the capacity of the Mexican system to bring offenders to justice. According to the United Nations International Crime Victimization Survey, carried out in Mexico for the first time in 2004, a full 75 percent of all crimes committed between 1999 and 2003 went unreported (Instituto Ciudadano de Estudios Sobre la Inseguridad [ICESI] 2004). In Mexico City, residents reported to the police only one in every eleven alleged crimes committed; in Guerrero state, this figure dropped to one in thirteen.

In part, this reluctance stems from the widespread belief that the Mexican law enforcement and judicial system is incompetent. A survey conducted by the Mexican Health Foundation in 1999, for instance, indicated that the most frequently cited reason for not reporting crimes to police was that respondents considered it "pointless" to do so (Mexican Health Foundation Survey 1999, cited in John Bailey and Jorge Chabat 2002, 47-8n9). This public perception of inefficacy has persisted in spite of (or perhaps because of) the highly touted but largely unsuccessful efforts to crack down on crime of former President Vicente Fox and former Mexico City Mayor Manuel López Obrador.

Coupled with this sense of futility, however, is a deepening distrust of the fundamental integrity of this system fueled by the proliferation of a new form of criminality in contemporary Mexico: the victimization of ordinary individuals by highly organized crime rings sustained by renegade elements of the military and the police. Many observers note that one of the greatest challenges to the legitimacy of the Mexican criminal justice system is the exponential growth of organized crime and the burgeoning involvement of Mexican officials in illicit activities ranging from petty thieving operations to massive drug and arms cartels (Benítez Manaut 2000; Davis 2002, 2003; Davis and Alvarado 1999; Gómez-Céspedes 1999; Llopart 2003; López-Montiel 2000; Shelley 2001; Zamora Jiménez 2003). Not coincidentally, this nexus between state agents and organized crime has evolved hand in hand with Mexico's transition to democracy. As Diane E. Davis elucidates, this is so because political liberalization has attenuated the ties that bind traditional security forces to the centralized political actors precisely at a time when lucrative opportunities for extralegal counterallegiances have materialized (Davis 2002, 2003). The upshot of these trends is that ordinary Mexicans continue to fear victimization by common criminals but in addition, and increasingly, violence perpetrated by the very agents of the state charged with ensuring their safety.

Thus, the self-help policing initiative analyzed here forms part of the same pragmatic search for alternatives to reliance on the Mexican criminal justice system that has prompted the nation's upper and middle classes to demand private security services. Although exceptional in its degree of institutionalization and its nonviolent nature, the CSSJAR popular justice movement also forms part and parcel of a disturbing trend that became perceptible in Latin America in the course of the 1990s: the heightened proclivity of the poor to take the law into their own hands. Since the late 1980s, vigilante violence or lynching in urban slums and impoverished rural settlements throughout the region has been on the rise (Castillo Claudett 2000; Goldstein 2003; Huggins 1991; Snodgrass Godoy 2004; Vilas 2001a, 2001b). In Mexico, vigilantism and its relationship to public insecurity became the center of public debate in November 2004, when national television aired live footage of an angry crowd lynching three undercover federal police officers on the outskirts of Mexico City (Lloyd 2004; Ramírez Cuevas 2004). The brutality of the incident, its widespread media coverage, and the blatant failure of backup police to prevent the deaths of two of these agents resulted in the dismissal of Mexico City's chief of police and raised to unprecedented levels the fear that vigilantism had reached epidemic proportions.

Already in the mid-1990s, however, similar events had provoked public intellectuals to decry lynching as one of the most serious problems afflicting contemporary Mexico (Monsiváis 1996; Marotta 1998). In the wake of atrocities committed in Puebla state by vigilantes who paid an amateur cameraman to film them, these scathing critiques roundly rebuked the appalling indifference of state officials and the Catholic church to vigilante acts of violence. Tacitly legitimating "taking the law into one's own hands," this apathy permitted first-degree murderers to evade the legal and moral consequences of homicide by taking refuge under the cover of "the will of the people." Denouncing vigilantism as "crime in the name of popular justice," these accounts thus construed the rise of vigilante violence in Mexico as fundamentally an increase in crimes of opportunity abetted by the laxity of state and social institutions (Monsiváis 1996).

The scholarly literature on vigilantism in Latin America suggests another plausible interpretation. As neoliberal economic reform has polarized Latin American societies and pushed the poor further toward the social margins, vigilante violence constitutes a symbolically charged means of expressing the depths of despair and disaffection experienced by urban neighborhoods and rural communities rendered most vulnerable by privatization. From this perspective—more than irrational mob violence or rationally calculated criminality—vigilantism can be construed as an act of radical protest that mocks the state's inefficacy even as it asserts a powerful if perverse form of communal agency (Goldstein 2003). Indeed, taking the law into one's own hands collectively and violently can be considered an insurgent form of privatization that permits the poor to exert agency over and against the emasculating forces of neoliberalism (Snodgrass Godoy 2004).

Like the wave of vigilante violence sweeping urban slums and remote villages throughout the country, the case of extralegal policing and justice administration examined here represents a profound indictment of the Mexican criminal justice system. Moreover, notwithstanding crucial differences, these phenomena both give witness to an extraordinary disposition among the poor to collectively bring criminals to justice when the state has proved unwilling or unable to do so. In contrast to vigilante violence, however, the CSSJAR movement in Guerrero has garnered widespread if at times tacit acceptance from a number of key actors in Mexican society and beyond. This chapter documents how and from whom the CSSJAR has gained support, and what the remarkable resilience of this movement implies about legitimacy and criminal justice in Mexico.

Drawing on ethnographic and interview data gathered by the author as well as other primary and secondary sources, the case study presented here traces the trajectory of this movement from its origins as a supplement to official law enforcement through its transformation into an exceedingly effective but highly contested alternative justice system. Ironically, although the CSSJAR today directly challenges state authority in the region, the movement emerged in response to ad hoc government attempts to involve local citizens in a fight on crime that had strained existing law enforcement far beyond capacity. Indeed, as the following section elucidates, the willingness of state agents to relax an already ambiguous boundary between official and unofficial law enforcement consistent with the spirit of privatization and decentralization served as a crucial condition for the rise of institutionalized extralegal policing and justice administration in Guerrero's Costa Chica Montaña region.

THE ORIGINS OF EXTRALEGAL JUSTICE ADMINISTRATION IN GUERRERO, MEXICO

The Costa Chica-Montaña region in Guerrero, Mexico, provides excellent empirical terrain for examining the relationship between neoliberal transformation, public insecurity, and popular justice administration in its various forms. Ranked one of the poorest microregions in the world, according to the 2004 Human Development Report on Mexico (Programa de las Naciones Unidas para el Desarrollo 2005, 10), this pocket of coffee-growing communities in the Sierra Madre del Sur suffered immediate and far-reaching consequences when international coffee prices plunged in the early 1990s as a result of market deregulation (Bartra 2001; García 2000; Wasserman 2002). Against the backdrop of deepening economic crisis and social instability, violent crime in the region spiked, especially along rural roadways. By mid-decade, armed assault on vehicles transporting money, goods, and passengers had become commonplace and had become the occasion for multiple incidents of rape and homicide (Barrera Hernández 2001; Cano 1996).

Some evidence suggests that the expansion of the illicit drug trade in Guerrero contributed significantly if indirectly to this crime wave. Since at least the 1970s, the isolation and inaccessibility of Guerrero's mountain region had facilitated the covert cultivation of heroin-grade poppies and marijuana. The economic crisis of the 1980s and 1990s enabled drug operations to recruit and arm an unprecedented number of local residents. According to reports compiled by a local nongovernmental organization, victimization in the region during this time occurred primarily at the hands of petty-theft rings engaged in highway robbery and livestock rustling (Barrera Hernández 2001). Although official crime statistics cannot corroborate this hypothesis, multiple narrative accounts attribute this phenomenon to the proliferation of robber bands—"bandas de delincuentes"—that had spun off from or worked loosely under the auspices of locally-entrenched drug and arms cartels (Barrera Hernández 2001; Martínez Sifuentes 2001; Rojas 2005c).

To break up these criminal enterprises required a degree of familiarity with the region's topography and social organization that only local police corps possessed, but decades of underfunding by state government had left these bodies grossly unprepared to address criminal activity at this scale and level of organization. In 1983, constitutional reforms aimed at decentralization assigned formal responsibility for guaranteeing public safety to the municipality, the functional Mexican equivalent of a United States county (Rodríguez 1997). With a negligible tax base and limited state funds, however, few if any of the extremely resource-poor municipalities in rural Guerrero had succeeded in equipping, training, and maintaining an effective municipal police force in the 1990s.

Moreover, state government disinterest in the development of this remote indigenous region had permitted a plethora of diverse and largely informal law enforcement norms and practices to flourish over time at both the municipal and village levels. In the absence of external guidelines and oversight, for instance, methods of selecting, remunerating, and deploying municipal police varied widely from one contiguous county to the next (Dehouve 2001; Rowland 2006). This lack of standardization hampered the regional coordination necessary to catch and prosecute highly mobile robber bands. Arguably, from the perspective of those directly involved in policing these municipalities, the weak presence of state government in law enforcement also made the difference between official and unofficial, formal and informal, social control increasingly difficult to discern.

Given the municipalities' inability to reestablish the rule of law in the region, some villagers resorted to taking the law into their own hands violently. The most notorious—though by no means the only—incident of vigilante violence to occur in the Costa Chica-Montaña region in the 1990s took place in December 1993, when individuals from the Tlapanec community of Zapotitlán de Tablas lynched seven men suspected of belonging to a local thieving ring that had allegedly victimized neighboring communities repeatedly. Among Mexicans, the people of Guerrero, or "guerrerenses," are known as fiercely independent and extremely quick to settle disputes violently without the intervention of the state police or judiciary. Whether fact or fiction, gruesome media images of the "strange fruits" of Zapotitlán de Tablas reinforced this mystique of guerrerenses as "ungovernable," and brought unwanted international attention and embarrassment to the federal government in the throes of negotiating the NAFTA accords (Vilas 2001b). Coupled with growing international concern over drug production and trafficking, this turn of events set into motion a dramatic buildup of security forces that by the end of the decade would transform Guerrero into the most heavily militarized state in Mexico second only to Chiapas (Díaz and Corro 1996; Yaworsky 2002).

With the onset of the Chiapas debacle in January of 1994, the pace of militarization quickened. In Guerrero's Costa Chica-Montaña region, the presence of federal troops intensified dramatically and intervention of the military in civilian activities including law enforcement expanded significantly. Paralleling a national trend spurred by fear that public security writ large had spiraled out of control, civilian government increasingly relied on federal troops to fight drug trafficking, contain guerrilla activities, provide disaster relief, and build roads, bridges, air landing strips and military barracks (Benítez Manaut 2000; López-Montiel 2000).

In spite of the strong tangible presence of state security forces, high rates of violent crime persisted. Partly in response to the intractability of this crisis of public security in the Costa Chica-Montaña and elsewhere in Guerrero, in 1995 the state executive branch initiated two sets of reforms designed to improve police performance (Dehouve 2001; Rowland 2006). First, the state government moved to standardize and finance the municipal police forces across the seventy-six municipalities that make up Guerrero. In the remote coffee-growing counties where the CSSJAR would crystallize, this meant that for the first time within memory, municipal policemen would earn a regular (though meager) salary, and the size of and rules regulating these police forces would become uniform. Although personnel would continue to be recruited from local villages, the intention of these reforms was to make the municipal police a more professionalized and dependable vehicle of law enforcement (Rowland 2006).

Second, the government created a new state police force to shore up the power of the municipal police. Called "la motorizada" or motorized police to connote its statewide jurisdiction and special mobility enabled by the use of motor vehicles (as opposed to foot patrols), this force was expected to collaborate more effectively than the notoriously corrupt and abusive state judicial police (Dehouve 2001). In the Costa Chica-Montaña region, local village councils were permitted to name or elect a dozen or so individuals to be incorporated into this entity. Though the precise motives for encouraging local representation in this presumably highly professionalized law enforcement agency remain obscure, participants and the villages that had named them widely interpreted this gesture as an official invitation to become more active in the policing of their own region (Cano 1996).

The broader point here is that this spate of government-initiated police reform blurred a historically ill-defined boundary between who should and could collectively enforce the law and who could not, precisely at a time when the government's incapacity to police the region had become glaringly apparent and the need for police protection in the region had become critical. Under these circumstances, reforms that encouraged greater local participation in state-sponsored police widened the gray space between legal and extralegal and laid the groundwork for the CSSJAR by lending credibility to the notion of organized self-help policing as a supplement to official law enforcement. Tellingly, this logic came to make sense not only to villagers desperate to contain violent crime at the local level but also, and most remarkably, to key actors within the state and federal government.

At the grassroots, this understanding of the need for a pragmatic partnership between official law enforcement and community-based police patrols began to crystallize in 1995, when representatives from more than forty villages located in five contiguous counties convened to collectively discuss the extent of lawlessness in their region and to propose potential solutions. Following months of similar assemblies, in 1996 these villages mobilized extralegal policing brigades with the explicit purpose of aiding official law enforcement. Five hundred men strong, these volunteer brigades patrolled the desolate roads and footpaths that connected disparate villages to each other and the region as a whole to the Pacific coast. Familiar with the territory and with a direct interest in ridding it of crime, these brigades proved extraordinarily effective at detaining criminal suspects and delivering them to the appropriate legal authorities. Far from condemning these armed brigades as illegal or a threat to state security, the governor of Guerrero donated a truck and twenty low-caliber firearms to this collective effort. Moreover, with the state government's approval, federal troops stationed in the Costa Chica-Montaña trained this police force in the proper use of these weapons. Over time, these brigades came to be known as "la comunitaria," or "the community police," to distinguish them from official municipal, state, or federal police forces.

The distinctiveness of the community police, however, stemmed as much from its origins in indigenous forms of self-governance as from its extra-official status. To date, the vast majority of indigenous communities in Guerrero's Costa Chica-Montaña regulate village affairs by drawing on concepts and practices evolved from a religious-civil cargo system[2] dating to Mexico's colonial period. Although the specifics vary by ethnic group—villages of Amuzgo, Mixtec, Nahuatl, and Tla-panec descent coexist in the region—and within ethnic group by locality, these governance structures typically incorporate the tradition of naming authorities ("nombrando autoridades") in a distinct fashion and with different functions than local leaders appointed according to contemporary administrative and electoral law (Nicasio González 2005). These individuals, in many cases chosen by consensus during community assemblies, constitute the ultimate locus of legitimate authority within their villages and in interactions with government officials and other outsiders.

In essence, the assemblies of indigenous authorities ("asambleas de autoridades indígenas") convened in 1995 and 1996 represented the extension of this mode of collective decisionmaking to the regional level. The intractability and increasing brutality of crime had provided an impetus for this scaling up, and the receptivity of state government had afforded opportunity. A further factor was that overlapping organizational networks and infrastructure established by regional coffee producer cooperatives presented an additional, crucial, means for this consolidation.

Since the 1970s, populist economic policies in Mexico had encouraged small-scale coffee farmers to market and process their harvests collectively. By the mid-1990s, however, the liberalization of international coffee markets and domestic neoliberal reforms had crippled many Mexican coffee farmers, but two regional cooperatives persisted in Guerrero's Costa-Chica Montaña region. Active since 1985, the larger of the two retained nearly one thousand members and access to credit and market niches long after these had evaporated for most producers (García 2000; Ravelo Lecuona and Avila Arévalo 1994). As long-standing economic enterprises subsidized by the state, both cooperatives had garnered material resources such as vehicles, telephones and fax machines, and centrally located offices and warehouses that they put at the disposal of the CSSJAR (Johnson 2001, 2005).

Moreover, for the better part of a decade these organizations had promoted a democratic culture that hinged on monthly assemblies of community representatives and on the disposition of villages to supply volunteer labor on a rotating basis. At the village level, this tradition of community service sustained the elaborate hierarchy of civil and religious duties that defined community membership for all able-bodied adult males. Though weakened by out-migration and the penetration of partisan politics and competing religious influences in area villages, the custom of fulfilling this obligation to community—referred to as "prestando servicio," literally, "lending service"—remained embedded in the organization of regional coffee collectives and ultimately constituted the operational model for the community police.

Thus, a mutually reinforcing combination of local governance structures, regional organizational resources, and political opportunity empowered the rural poor in Guerrero's Costa Chica-Montaña region to collectively collaborate with the state's justice system in order to protect themselves. Within two years of the movement's inception, however, participants had become deeply disillusioned with the judicial branch's repeated failure to prosecute detainees, and openly criticized the district attorney's office for releasing criminal suspects even when they had been caught in the act by community policing brigades. In the context of growing frustration with government corruption and fear of retribution at the hands of former detainees, the movement resolved to keep captives in its own custody and to adjudicate and correct them locally.

The section below analyzes this transformation from pragmatic partnership with state agencies to alternative justice system through the analytical lens of the movement's shifting and broadening bases of legitimacy. Perhaps predictably, the movement's initiative to administer justice extralegally met with stiff resistance from within Guerrero's state judiciary. This opposition precipitated a series of arms sweeps through villages actively involved in the movement and the issuance of warrants for the arrest of community policing commanders (Johnson 2005). These veiled and not-so-veiled threats to shut down community policing in the region prompted one of the earliest indicators of the breadth and depth of the legitimacy that the movement had achieved to date.

BROADENING BASES OF LEGITIMACY: LEGITIMATE FOR WHOM?

On the afternoon of February 11, 2002, the wife of a local resident convicted of attempted homicide by the community police and sentenced to forced labor in its custody accompanied state judicial police to CSSJAR headquarters in the county seat of San Luis Acatlán. Eyewitnesses quoted in a reputable national news outlet reported that these police officers burst into a well-attended meeting, shouted insults and threatened violence, then disarmed and detained five ex-commanders of the extralegal brigades on kidnapping charges, without showing proper warrants for their arrest. The following day, nearly one thousand protesters from sixty or more outlying hamlets gathered at the state penitentiary in San Luis Acatlán to demand the release of these prisoners (López Bárcenas 2002; Rojas 2002a). The title of one newspaper account that thoroughly documented this incident read "Detention of Five Community Policemen in the Montaña and Costa Chica Inflames Guerrerenses" (Rojas 2002b).

The angry popular response to these arrests provides a rough measure of the degree of legitimacy that inhabitants of Guerrero's Costa Chica-Montaña region afforded the extralegal criminal justice system that had taken root in the region. Four years after the movement had begun to adjudicate criminal cases and "re-educate" convicted offenders, the detention of respected CSSJAR participants in broad daylight struck a nerve among villagers who had come to perceive this extralegal alternative as their only true means to safety and integrity. Some residents continued to report crimes and press charges through official channels, but increasingly, victims of crimes perpetrated locally demanded the intervention of the CSSJAR, even when municipal police patrols had detained the pertinent suspect. Such was the reach of the CSSJAR's popularity and its acceptance by local government that, at the behest of victims seeking to proceed through the alternative system, municipal police frequently transferred prisoners to CSSJAR custody with the tacit understanding that the movement would follow through with adjudication and correction if appropriate. Not surprisingly, therefore, the public humiliation of CSSJAR leaders—interpreted as a calculated and highly symbolic assault on the movement—touched off discontent and exposed the extent of the movement's local legitimacy in its breach.

Clearly, by 2002, dissension at the grassroots existed and the February incident reveals the contours of these fault lines as well. The most visible source of contention quickly materialized among individuals who claimed that family members had been kidnapped by the CSSJAR and successfully located powerful allies in state agencies to back these claims. In March 2000, for instance, the detention of an alleged cattle rustler believed to be in cahoots with high-level government officials provoked the intervention of the municipal president of San Luis Acatlán, the director of a state-funded agricultural school, the assistant district attorney of the Costa Chica region, and troops from the Forty-ninth Infantry Battalion on his behalf. The accused ultimately regained his freedom, though the circumstances surrounding his discharge remain ambiguous. Whereas one written account contended that the CSSJAR released this prisoner on its own initiative (Barrera Hernández 2001), another stated that he had escaped (Rojas 2005b).

In some respects, the February 2002 standoff between judicial police and hundreds of incensed villagers represented the culmination of tensions between the state and the extralegal justice movement that had been building since 1998. During this time, complaints lodged by locals had provided periodic opportunities for the state judiciary to discredit and debilitate the CSSJAR. This piecemeal strategy had failed, and by 2002 opponents of community policing had mobilized sufficient support within Guerrero state's executive branch to launch a frontal attack against the movement. The state district attorney acceded to immediate popular pressure and freed the five detainees in short order, but within weeks, Guerrero's secretary of public security pronounced the CSSJAR to be in explicit violation of the law and ordered the movement to cease and desist by March 26, 2002.

To date—more than four years after this ultimatum was issued—the CSSJAR persists in its efforts to police the region, and the regional assembly that oversees it continues to adjudicate and reeducate criminal offenders. It has weathered unprecedented changes in partisan leadership at the state level—Guerrero elected its first opposition party governor ever in February 2005—and in the municipalities, and has earned the reputation for impartiality in partisan politics. In a Mexican state torn by postelectoral violence throughout the 1990s and into the new millennium, this is no mean feat. Finally, and perhaps most remarkably, this movement has not only persisted but expanded both in size and diversity, even as the Guerrero state government continues to brand it illegal. From forty-two, the number of villages integrated into the CSSJAR system has grown to over sixty in six counties, and the latest tally of armed and active community policemen is 612 (Rojas 2005a). Significantly, the villages to most recently join the CSSJAR include human settlements populated primarily by mestizos and families of Afro-Caribbean descent (Avendaño 2003). That is, extralegal policing and justice administration in Guerrero, Mexico, is no longer the exclusive domain of indigenous coffee farmers but rather has begun to appeal to a more representative subset of the nation's rural poor. What explains this extraordinary capacity to thrive in the face of condemnation by state authorities?

The resilience of the CSSJAR stems in part from its efficacy at ridding the region of crime and its moral authority over and against a conventional criminal justice system perceived as exceedingly corrupt. Contrasting the virtues of the community police with the vices of "the other police," one municipal commissioner interviewed in 2003 favored the extralegal alternative because "the other police only lived to extort money from the people" (Avendaño 2003). Indeed, compelled by a history of victimization at the hands of the state agents entrusted to protect them, the architects of the CSSJAR have gone to great lengths to eliminate all forms of commercial exchange from the process of administering justice. On the grounds that money corrupts, the CSSJAR collects no fees, fines, or bail and, with very few exceptions, pays no salaries. All personnel serve to fulfill obligations to their villages of origin and receive in-kind support in the form of food, shelter, uniforms, and basic weaponry.

The CSSJAR also differs from its official counterpart in its penal philosophy and sentencing practices. Premised on the assumption that the erosion of community attachments is the root cause of criminality, the CSSJAR has elaborated sentencing guidelines that reject retribution and prioritize reintegration. To "reeducate" offenders into community norms, the CSSJAR imposes penalties of manual labor that vary in length from two weeks for a minor offense such as the theft of a chicken to five years in the case of homicide. One observer reported that small groups of convicts guarded by community police work fifteen days at a time in a given village to build or repair bridges, roads, schools, churches, and even basketball courts (Martínez Sifuentes 2001). Villagers in these communities assume the cost of and prepare meals for these prisoners. In principle, reeducation also entails orientation or lectures from elders in these villages, but participants concede that these talks seldom take place.

This communitarian and nonpunitive approach has engendered an acute sense of ownership over justice administration locally that has minimized division within the movement, maximized grassroots support in the region, and blunted the impact of scandal when it occurs. In the late 1990s, one such scandal erupted when villagers victimized by a regional cattle-rustling ring nearly stoned to death an alleged perpetrator apprehended by and in the custody of a community policing brigade from that village. This attempted lynching triggered intense criticism from outsiders, but it also set in motion a process of critical reflection within the CSSJAR that prompted movement leaders to request guidance, training, and informal oversight from regional human rights advocates. Far from fissuring the movement, this crisis activated a local consensus affirming its legitimacy that impelled the CSSJAR to forge alliances with other institutional actors. In the long run, these relationships with regional, national, and even international rights organizations have played a crucial role buffering extralegal justice administration in Guerrero, Mexico, from state repression and retaliation.

This observation highlights another key source of movement legitimacy. In the crucible of the Chiapas conflict beginning in 1994, the impressive efforts of indigenous coffee farmers in Guerrero to collectively police themselves attracted the attention of a burgeoning national activist network hoping to craft civil society consensus around the Zapatista agenda for indigenous autonomy. It is likely that among the leaders of Guerrero's coffee cooperatives, an awareness of and degree of sympathy toward the Zapatista cause predated the emergence of the CSSJAR (Hébert 2002). In 1998, however, a team of talented human rights lawyers and popular educators active in a Zapatista solidarity group in Mexico City began explicit collaboration with the movement. Accompanied by groups of middle-class Mexican college students eager to learn more about the struggles of indigenous peoples in their country, the organization gave a series of workshops in the Costa Chica-Montaña region geared toward members of the community police. These three-day consciousness-raising events expounded the rights of Mexican indigenous peoples to land, education in their native languages, and self-governance, and their legal guarantees under international and national law (Cruz Rueda 2000; Johnson 2005).

This initial nexus between extralocal rights activism and Guerrero's CSSJAR paved the way for a more intimate association between extralegal policing and indigenous autonomy. In public forums, CSSJAR spokespersons began to refer to extralegal justice administration in the Costa Chica-Montaña region as an expression of the inherent rights of indigenous peoples to govern themselves. In 2001, this interpretation took on a more palpable political form when the CSSJAR joined other grassroots organizations composed of indigenous peoples to occupy Guerrero's congressional building to protest legislative reforms that excluded constitutional guarantees for indigenous self-governance (Méndez 2001a, 2001b). Internet-accessible media coverage of this event increased the exposure of the CSSJAR to potential allies, and by 2002 its extralegal justice system had acquired explicit recognition from a handful of international advocates in both indigenous rights and peace and justice movements.

Thus, when Guerrero state government mounted a full-fledged offensive against the CSSJAR in February 2002, it unwittingly violated more than the integrity of an isolated campaign for public security. In May, the Brussels-based Peace Brigades International published a blow-by-blow account of these hostilities against the CSSJAR in its Mexico Project Report and posted this document to the World Wide Web (Brigadas Internacionales de Paz 2002). By September, the Chicago-based Chiapas Media Project had produced a video documentary of the CSSJAR entitled *Reclaiming Justice* and had appealed to university and church-based sponsors throughout the United States to screen it as part of a larger rights campaign in solidarity with indigenous peoples in Mexico (Chiapas Media Project 2002). These transcendent ties and the international spotlight they have trained on the Costa Chica-Montaña region have broadened the CSSJAR's bases of legitimacy in ways that help explain the state's unusual reticence to eliminate extralegal justice administration through force. In the language of resource mobilization theory, the tenacity of the CSSJAR owes as much to its national and transnational conscience constituents as it does to the loyalty of its local participants.

Although authorities have to date abstained from applying brute force to disband the CSSJAR, there are clearly strong pressures working against the CSSJAR from both without and within. The state maintains its stance that the movement operates illegally and continues to wage low-intensity warfare of sorts against it by means of arrest warrants for village-level elected officials ("comisarios municipales") who cooperate with the movement. In the first nine months of 2005 alone, the state prosecutor issued six such warrants (Rojas 2005a). This persistent harassment belies the surface impression—in the absence of open confrontation—that state authorities have come to accept the CSSJAR as a legitimate alternative to the official criminal justice system.

Another force working toward the dissolution of the CSSJAR is—ironically—its resounding success in cracking down on crime. According to a recent press account, local elected officials in the Costa Chica-Montaña region believe that in its ten years of operation (1995 to 2005), the CSSJAR has reduced theft, cattle rustling, armed robbery, kidnapping, and drug-related activities ("siembra de enervantes") by 90 to 95 percent. Minus the imminent threat of victimization, participation levels in some villages have decreased (Rojas 2005a).

Moreover, in the context of this newfound peace and security, heightened economic need has induced some participants to question the long-term viability and equity of the movement's nonmonetary nature. Chronically depressed international prices for coffee have rendered growing numbers of small-scale farmers in Guerrero's Costa Chica-Montaña region unable to make a living locally and have spurred unprecedented levels of out-migration to urban areas and the United States. As the search for regular employment becomes more imperative, newer recruits to the CSSJAR have pressed to convert policing as community service into a system based on full-time, year-round salaried positions (Rojas 2005b). This proposal has gained additional momentum from villages that have borne the brunt of the risks associated with citizens policing themselves. In the course of the movement's decade-long trajectory, seven members have lost their lives in the line of duty and countless others have sustained injuries (Rojas 2005a). Also, in many cases community policing has irreparably ruptured social relations between participants and offenders from the same or neighboring villages. As the toll that these fiduciary, physical, and social costs take on individuals and communities becomes more apparent, the grassroots consensus around policing and justice administration as a right and duty of community membership may begin to unravel. Indeed, some local residents have voiced the opinion that given the hardships that participants endure, "the government" should pay the community police for their service (Rojas 2005b). Arguably, this statement is a strong indication that the nature of self-help policing as initially conceived among the rural poor in Guerrero's Costa Chica-Montaña region is in flux, if not on the verge of decline.

In light of these factors, the greatest threat to the movement's continuation and independent existence is likely to be the state government's long-standing proposition to fold community policing back into the municipal system. A recent study suggests that administrations in the municipalities where the CSSJAR operates already support the movement financially by passing on a portion of federal transfers for public security. In part, this contribution pays for the salaries of thirty-five full-time employees working out of the CSSJAR's central office in San Luis Acatlán (Rowland 2006). As the boundaries between government and self-help law enforcement, between salaried and service-driven participation, blur, the gray space between official and unofficial that allowed the movement to emerge in the first place appears to be shrinking.

Thus, even as the CSSJAR has become a legitimate and desirable alternative for an ever greater number of citizens, the exigencies of institutionalization delineated by social movement theorists foreshadow the absorption of the entire movement into the official system or a split between "co-opted" elements and a more radical wing (Koopmans 1993; Piven and Cloward 1979; Tarrow 1989, 1994). Regardless of the outcome, however, the fact remains that for the better part of a decade, a sizable subset of Mexico's rural poor have policed themselves and collectively administered a brand of justice at odds with the official criminal justice system. Indeed, whether it endures or not, this movement's extraordinary resonance well beyond the borders of the Mexican nation-state suggests that it is not an accident of history but rather a barometer of ideological and cultural shifts occurring on a broader scale.

CONCLUSION

Any discussion of legitimacy and the criminal justice system necessarily begs the question of legitimacy for whom, but this caveat is especially pertinent in highly class and race-stratified societies such as contemporary Mexico. This chapter has examined issues of public confidence in Mexico's criminal justice system from the perspective of the rural poor and, in particular, those of indigenous descent. Doubly disadvantaged by their status as peasants and Indians, individuals classified as such have occupied the very bottom rungs of Mexico's social, economic and political hierarchy for much of modern history.

The wave of public insecurity that swept Mexico in the 1990s and into the new millennium has affected all Mexicans irrespective of class or racial status, but the collective and individual responses to this crisis have varied considerably. At the highest echelons of Mexican society, the urban upper and upper-middle classes have quietly committed to protecting themselves by purchasing safety and security through the private sector. At the opposite extreme, Mexicans who lack the material means to absorb this burden have turned increasingly to vigilante violence to guarantee the security of their own communities and to obtain retribution. Strange bedfellows at first blush, these disparate responses reflect a common cultural undercurrent with implications for the study of penal justice in Mexico and elsewhere: the growing acceptance—legitimacy, even—of the state's absence from the realm of law enforcement and justice administration.

Stripped of the buffer that economic resources afford, the strategies that poor people craft to confront criminality under these crisis conditions expose the logic of this underlying cultural shift with particular clarity. As recent literature on contemporary Latin America suggests, one discourse that has come to envelop and legitimate acts of vigilante violence is that of privatization. Pervasive and extremely adaptable, the neoliberal ideology of private sphere and individual efficacy tacitly infuses self-help measures for law enforcement and justice administration with a certain moral authority. Grounded in the notion that private enterprise and self-interested citizens impart justice more efficiently than corrupt government, "taking the law into one's own hands"—no matter the atrocities entailed—has become a desirable alternative to reliance on the official criminal justice system for a broad swathe of Mexican society.

Like the collective acts of other Mexicans who have "taken the law into their own hands," the formation of Guerrero's Community System for Security, Justice Administration and Re-Education by the rural, indigenous poor reflects this subtle change. In contrast to the spontaneous and frequently ephemeral nature of other collective acts, however, the CSSJAR has evolved into a sustained and codified expression of the legitimacy of self-help and extralegal justice administration. That this effort requires ongoing sacrifices from hundreds of ordinary citizens on a daily basis and that it has garnered material and moral support from a wide range of advocates regionally, nationally, and internationally suggests the depth and breadth of this new conception of legitimate authority and pushes the boundaries of dominant frameworks for understanding vigilantism.

ACKNOWLEDGMENTS

The author would like to thank the Department of Sociology at Kenyon College for supporting this project and Emily MacClean Burns for her invaluable research assistance.

NOTES

1. These are the counties of San Luis Acatlán, Malinaltepec, Marquelia, Copanatoyac, Metlatónoc, and Altamajalcingo del Monte.
2. Anthropologists of Meso-America define the cargo system as "a series of ranked offices . . . that male members assume" (Friedlander 1980, 132) to fulfill communal obligations and obtain social status. In this context, the term "cargo" refers to something that must be taken upon one's shoulders, such as a load or burden.

REFERENCES

Avendaño, Elia. 2003. "Sistemas legales de pueblos indígenas: ejemplos, experiencias, y medidas gubernamentales, administrativas y judiciales para vincular el derecho consuetudinario en los sistemas nacionales de justicia" ["Indigenous Legal Systems: Examples, Experiences, and Governmental, Administrative and Judicial Measures for Linking Customary Law to National Justice Systems"]. Paper presented to the United Nations Seminar on Indigenous Peoples and Justice Administration. Madrid, November 12 to 14, 2003.

Bailey, John, and Jorge Chabat. 2002. "Transnational Crime and Public Security: Trends and Issues." In *Transnational Crime and Public Security: Challenges to Mexico and the United States,* edited by John Bailey and Jorge Chabat. La Jolla, Calif.: University of California, San Diego, Center for U.S.-Mexican Studies.

Barrera Hernández, Abel. 2001. "Cuando la justicia se hace pueblo" ["When Justice Encounters the People"]. Tlapa de Comonfort, Mexico: Centro de Derechos Humanos de la Montaña "Tlachinollan, A.C."

Bartra, Armando. 2001. "Un cafecito para el plan Puebla-Panamá" ["The Puebla-Panama Plan over Coffee"]. *La Jornada* (Mexico), July 31, 2001.

Benítez Manaut, Raúl. 2000. "Containing Armed Groups, Drug Trafficking, and Organized Crime in Mexico: The Role of the Military." In *Organized Crime and Democratic Governability: Mexico and the U.S.-Mexican Borderlands,* edited by John Bailey and Roy Godson. Pittsburgh, Pa.: University of Pittsburgh Press.

Brigadas Internacionales de Paz. 2002. "Policía Comunitaria Indígena en el estado de Guerrero" ["Indigenous Community Police in Guerrero State"]. *Boletín Informativo del Proyecto, Número IX*: 4.

Cano, Arturo. 1996. "Guerrero: La Mano Blanca" ["Guerrero: The White Hand"]. *Reforma* (Mexico), January 14, 1996.

Castillo Claudett, Eduardo. 2000. "La justicia en tiempos de la ira: Linchamientos populares urbanos en América Latina" ["Justice in the Time of Wrath: Popular Urban Lynching in Latin America"]. *Ecuador Debate* 51: 207–26.

Chiapas Media Project. 2002. *Reclaiming Justice: Guerrero's Indigenous Community Police.* Distributed by Chiapas Media Project, Chicago, Ill.

Cruz Rueda, Elisa. 2000. "Sistema de seguridad pública indígena comunitaria" ["Indigenous Community Policing"]. In *Análisis Interdisciplinario del Convenio 169 de la OIT [Interdisciplinary Analysis of ILO Convention 169]*, edited by José Emilio Rolando Ordóñez Cifuentes. Mexico City: Universidad Nacional Autónoma de México.

Davis, Diane E. 2002. "From Democracy to Rule of Law?: Police Impunity in Contemporary Latin America." *Revista: Harvard Review of Latin America* (Fall): 21–25.

———. 2003. "Law Enforcement in Mexico City: Not Yet Under Control." *NACLA Report on the Americas* 37(2): 17–24.

Davis, Diane E., and Arturo Alvarado. 1999. "Descent into Chaos? Liberalization, Public Insecurity and Deteriorating Rule of Law in Mexico City." *Working Papers in Local Governance and Democracy* 99(1): 95–107.

Davis, Robert C., Christopher W. Ortiz, Sarah Dadush, Jenny Irish, Arturo Alvarado, and Diane E. Davis. 2003. "The Public Accountability of Private Police: Lessons from New York, Johannesburg, and Mexico City." *Policing and Society* 13(2): 197–210.

Dehouve, Daniele. 2001. *Geopolítica Indígena: Los Municipios Tlapanecos* [*Indigenous Geopolitics: The Tlapenec Counties*]. Mexico City: CIESAS.

Díaz, Gloria Leticia, and Salvador Corro. 1996. "En Guerrero en los pasados dos años, más soldados, más patrullajes y más violencia" ["In Guerrero in the Past Two Years, More Soldiers, More Patrols, and More Violence"]. *Proceso* (Mexico) June 29, 1996: 1024.

Friedlander, Judith. 1980. "The Secularization of the Cargo System: An Example from Postrevolutionary Central Mexico." *Latin American Research Review* 16(2): 132–43.

García, Carlos. 2000. "De la Costa a la Montaña" ["From the Coast to the Mountains"]. In *Crónicas del sur: utopías campesinas en Guerrero* [*The Chronicles of the South: Peasant Utopias in Guerrero*], edited by Armando Bartra. Mexico City: Era.

Goldstein, Daniel M. 2003. " 'In Our Own Hands'?: Lynching, Justice and the Law in Bolivia." *American Ethnologist* 30(1): 22–43.

Gómez-Céspedes, Alejandra. 1999. "The Federal Law Enforcement Agencies: An Obstacle in the Fight Against Organized Crime in Mexico." *Journal of Contemporary Criminal Justice* 15(4): 352–69.

Hébert, Martin. 2002. "Politico-Cultural Contacts Between Mexican Indigenous Groups." *Social Justice: Anthropology, Peace and Human Rights* 2(2–3): 113–39.

Huggins, Martha K., editor. 1991. *Vigilantism and the State in Modern Latin America: Essays on Extralegal Violence.* New York: Praeger.

Instituto Ciudadano de Estudios Sobre la Inseguridad (ICESI). 2004. "Encuesta internacional sobre criminalidad y victimización" ["International Survey on Criminality and Victimization"]. Accessed at http://www.icesi.org.mx/index.cfm?Nid=431.

Johnson, Jennifer L. 2001. "What's Globalization Got to Do With It? Political Action and Peasant Producers in Guerrero, Mexico." *Canadian Journal of Latin American and Caribbean Studies* 26(52): 267–83.

———. 2005. "Appropriating Citizenship: Resources, Discourses and Political Mobilization in Contemporary Rural Mexico." Ph.D. dissertation, University of Chicago.

Koopmans, Ruud. 1993. "The Dynamics of Protest Waves: West Germany, 1965–1989." *American Sociological Review* 58(5): 637–58.

Llopart, Jordi Pius. 2003. "Robocop in Mexico City." *NACLA Report on the Americas* 37(2): 22–23.

Lloyd, Marion. 2004. "After Lynchings, Mexico Looks Inward, Justice System, Police Criticized." *Boston Globe,* December 12, 2004: A51.

López Bárcenas, Francisco. 2002. "Autoridades 'delincuentes' " [" 'Delinquent' Authorities"]. *La Jornada* (Mexico), February 16, 2002.

López-Montiel, Angel Gustavo. 2000. "The Military, Political Power and Police Relations in Mexico City." *Latin American Perspectives* 27(2): 79–94.

Marotta, Rosanna. 1998. "Carlos Monsiváis en torno a la redención de Caín: 'La violencia es un Estado paralelo' " ["Carlos Monsiváis on the Redemption of Cain: 'Violence is a Parallel State"]. *Diálogo Iberoamericano* 16(July–August): 10–16.

Martínez Sifuentes, Esteban. 2001. *La policía comunitaria: un sistema de seguridad pública indígena en el estado de Guerrero* [*The Community Police: An Indigenous Public Security System in Guerrero State*]. Mexico City: Instituto Nacional Indigenista.

Méndez, Enrique. 2001a. "Segundo día de bloqueo al congreso de Guerrero; la procuraduría estatal investiga a ocho dirigentes" ["Second Day of Blockade of Guerrero's Congress: State's Attorney General Investigates Eight Leaders"]. *La Jornada* (Mexico), June 13, 2001.

———. 2001b. "Consultará el congreso de Guerrero con cuatro etnias la reforma indígena" ["Guerrero's Congress Will Consult Four Ethnic Groups on Indigenous Reform"]. *La Jornada* (Mexico), June 14, 2001.

Monsiváis, Carlos. 1996. "Los linchamientos: El crimen a nombre de la justicia popular" ["Lynchings: Crime in the Name of Popular Justice"]. *Proceso* 1037(September 15): 38–42.

Nicasio González, Maribel. 2005. "Nombramiento de autoridades y participación en un municipio pluriétnico de la Montaña de Guerrero" ["The Designation of Authorities and Participation in a Pluri-ethnic County in Guerrero's Mountain Region"]. Paper presented to the Fifth Congress of Mexican Rural Studies Association. Oaxaca, Mexico, May 25–28, 2005.

Piven, Francis Fox, and Richard A. Cloward. 1979. *Poor People's Movements: Why They Succeed, How They Fail.* New York: Vintage Books.

Programa de las Naciones Unidas para el Desarrollo. 2005. Informe sobre Desarrollo Humano Mexico 2004. [Human Development Report, Mexico 2004]. Mexico City: Grupo Mundi-Prensa.

Ramírez Cuevas, Jesús. 2004. "Linchamientos: la injusticia popular" ["Lynching: Popular Injustice"]. *Masiosare* (Mexico), November 28, 2004: 8–9.

Ravelo Lecuona, Renato, and José O. Avila Arévalo. 1994. *Luz de la Montaña: una historia viva* [*Luz de la Montaña: A Living Testimony*]. Mexico City: Instituto Nacional Indigenista.

Regalado Santillán, Jorge. 2002. "Public Security Versus Private Security?" In *Transnational Crime and Public Security: Challenges to Mexico and the United States,* edited by John Bailey and Jorge Chabat. La Jolla, Calif.: University of California, San Diego, Center for U.S. Mexican Studies.

Rodríguez, Victoria E. 1997. *Decentralization in Mexico: From Reforma Municipal to Solidaridad to Nuevo Federalismo.* Boulder: Westview Press.

Rojas, Rosa. 2002a. "Ultimatum to Guerrero Police, March 10." Accessed at http://www.eco.utexas.edu/~archive/chiapas95/2002.03/msg00289.html. Originally published as "Algunos dicen que la defenderán hasta las últimas consecuencias" ["Some Say They Will Defend the Community Police to the Bitter End"]. *La Jornada* (Mexico), March 10, 2002.

———. 2002b. "Enardece a guerrerenses de la Montaña y Costa Chica la detención de cinco Policías comunitarios" [Detention of Five Community Policemen in the Montaña and Costa Chica Inflames guerrerenses]. *La Jornada* (Mexico), February 13, 2002.

———. 2005a. "Reducen hasta 95% la delincuencia en seis municipios de Guerrero" ["The Community Police Reduce Crime by up to 95% in Six Counties in Guerrero"]. *La Jornada* (Mexico), September 27, 2005.

———. 2005b. "La calma uno de los riesgos para la continuidad de la policía comunitaria" ["Tranquility is One of the Risks to the Community Police's Continuity"]. *La Jornada* (Mexico), September 28, 2005.

———. 2005c. "La policía comunitaria ha sido mejor que todas las demás: ex-comandante" ["The Community Police Have Been Better than All the Rest, Says Ex-commander"]. *La Jornada* (Mexico), September 29, 2005.

Rowland, Allison M. 2006. "Local Responses to Public Insecurity in Mexico: The Policía Comunitaria of the Costa Chica and the Montaña de Guerrero." In *Public Security and Police Reform in the Americas*, edited by John Bailey and Lucía Dammert. Pittsburgh, Pa.: University of Pittsburgh Press.

Shelley, Louise. 2001. "Corruption and Organized Crime in Mexico in the Post-PRI Transition." *Journal of Contemporary Criminal Justice* 17(3): 213–31.

Smulovitz, Catalina. 2003. "Citizen Insecurity and Fear: Public and Private Responses in Argentina." In *Crime and Violence in Latin America: Citizen Security, Democracy, and the State*, edited by Hugo Frühling and Joseph S. Tulchin. Baltimore, Md.: Johns Hopkins University Press.

Snodgrass Godoy, Angelina. 2004. "When 'Justice' is Criminal: Lynchings in Contemporary Latin America." *Theory and Society* 33(6): 621–51.

Tarrow, Sydney. 1989. *Democracy and Disorder: Protest and Politics in Italy, 1965–1975.* Oxford: Polity Press.

———1994. *Power in Movement: Social Movements, Collective Action and Politics.* New York: Cambridge University Press.

Vilas, Carlos M. 2001a. "(In)justicia por mano propia: linchamientos en el México contemporáneo" ["Taking (In)Justice in One's Own Hands: Lynching in Contemporary Mexico"]. *Revista Mexicana de Sociología* 1(1): 131–60.

———. 2001b. "Tristezas de Zapotitlán: violencia e inseguridad en el mundo de la subalternidad" ["The Misery of Zapotitlán: Violence and Insecurity in the Subaltern World"]. *Bajo el Volcán* 2(3): 123–42.

Wasserman, Miriam. 2002. "Trouble in Coffee Lands." *Regional Review Quarter* 2: 4–13.

Yaworsky, William Raymond. 2002. "Nongovernmental Organizations in the Highlands of Guerrero, Mexico." Ph.D. dissertation, University of Oklahoma.

Zamora Jiménez, Arturo. 2003. "Criminal Justice and the Law in Mexico." *Crime, Law and Social Change* 40: 33–36.

CHAPTER 11

Between Damage Reduction and Community Policing: The Case of Pavão-Pavãozinho-Cantagalo in Rio de Janeiro's Favelas

Graziella Moraes D. da Silva and Ignacio Cano

The strongest worry of a favela is what it does not want to see: the deaths, especially those of innocents. So, residents of favelas think like this: "It is good that the policeman and the dealer are talking. At least tomorrow there will be no shooting." What he [the resident] does not want is his door full of bullets, is to be unable to take his son to school, is to be unable to go back home from work or from school.
    —Member of focus group in Pavão-Pavãozinho-Cantagalo,
    carried out by "Viva Rio" (2004)
    (Grupamento Policial em Areas Especiais)

When will the police win the daily fight with drug dealers? Only when it understands that we are in a war against these criminals, which needs to be summarily executed, by capturing these criminals and keeping them in high-security prisons. The other option of elimination would be direct confrontations with a better-armed police, ready to face the last consequences. In this latter case, any complaint by human right activists should be disregarded, since in reality they only defend the human rights of criminals.
    —Letter to Jornal O Globo, August 31, 2005

The other [police] units do not like us here. . . . This culture is something very strong in the police. . . . So when you do not kill people, they think you are not working. . . . I don't know. . . . It is a cultural thing here, and it will take a while to change it.

—GPAE military policeman, July 2005

With an average homicide rate of fifty to sixty per hundred thousand residents, Rio de Janeiro is one of the most violent cities in the world. Violence is concentrated in poor neighborhoods, especially in favelas (shantytowns). A significant portion of these homicides occurs in violent confrontations with policemen who "invade" these communities in "arrest and apprehend" operations.[1] As an attempt to stop this violent dynamic, a program called GPAE, for Grupamento Policial em Areas Especiais—literally, Police Group in Special Areas—was implemented in one of these favelas, Pavão-Pavãozinho-Cantagalo, in 2000. In one year GPAE succeeded in eliminating police casualties and reducing homicides in this community. However, since 2003, the program has experienced a series of crises and has even been discontinued for several moments.

This chapter explores the reasons why such initiative—a success, according to the police officers who led it—did not become a mainstream policing strategy in Rio's favelas. We contend that although GPAE was successful as a strategy of damage control and also as a way to improve the relationship between poor communities and the police, it is in contradiction with the prevailing policing paradigm of the "war on crime." On the one hand, tensions between three very different goals—protect the upper and middle classes, reduce violence in poor neighborhoods, and reduce overall crime and drug dealing—created this contradiction and undermined the program. On the other hand, changes in government and in the leadership of the program directly affected its development, since there was not enough institutional support for it within the military police.

It is not possible to understand policing without knowing the context in which it is carried out. Therefore, before discussing GPAE, we present a political and historical background for Brazil, Rio de Janeiro, and the favelas, with a special focus on Pavão-Pavãozinho-Cantagalo. In the second part of the chapter, we discuss the creation of GPAE and the inherent tensions in the development of the program. We conclude with a general evaluation, in which we try to understand why its initial success did not guarantee its stability.[2]

BACKGROUND: SOCIAL EXCLUSION, POLITICAL TURMOIL, AND POLICE VIOLENCE IN BRAZIL

Brazilian society is one of the most unequal in the world. Despite periods of strong economic growth, such as during the so-called economic miracle of the 1970s, in the past fifty years Brazil's Gini coefficient has remained stable at approximately

TABLE 11.1   POLICE ORGANIZATIONS IN BRAZIL AND THEIR RESPECTIVE ROLES

Type	Administration Level	Main Roles	Uniformed	Size
Federal	Federal	Border control and specific federal crimes	No	Small
Civil	State	Investigation of crimes	No	Medium
Military	State	Patrolling, crime prevention, and the maintenance of order	Yes	Large

Source: Authors' compilation.

0.6. There are many possible and complementary reasons for such a stark pattern of social exclusion: a long history of slavery, abolished only in 1888; long periods of dictatorship in the twentieth century (1937 to 1945, 1964 to 1984); lack of public services in poor neighborhoods; low levels of schooling; and high levels of corruption in the public and private sectors.

Brazil's population is concentrated in urban areas, which are among the most violent in the world, with homicide rates similar to or even higher than those of countries undergoing civil war. Using states or municipalities as units of analysis, the degree of urbanization turns out to be the most powerful factor associated with homicide rates in Brazil (Cano and Santos 2001). Yet when we compare rates between different neighborhoods inside the cities, poverty is by far the largest predictor of violence (CEDEC 1996; Soares 2000). Correlation coefficients between violence and poverty reach 0.6 in the case of Rio de Janeiro (Cano 1998).

The traditional answer of the Brazilian states to violence in these poor neighborhoods has been rather violent itself.[3] Some analysts argue that rather than help solve the problem, state action has contributed to it. Indeed, police forces in Brazil are mostly conceived as a government tool, rather than as an independent actor controlled by law and civil society. They have historically played a repressive role vis-à-vis the lower classes. The original mission of the police was to keep slaves and recently freed men under control, usually through violent means (Bretas 1997; Holloway 1997). After the republic was declared and slavery abolished, police remained as an organization used against poor people and against political enemies in periods of dictatorship (1930 to 1945; 1964 to 1984).

Present-day Brazilian police forces are divided into three main groups: federal, state civil, and state military. Table 11.1 specifies the function of each organization. Owing to their higher numbers and to the nature of their work, military policemen are most often involved in violent actions and are the focus of this paper.

Human rights concerns were almost absent from Brazilian public debate until the 1980s. As a result, police in Brazil are generally violent. Figure 11.1 (from Cano 1997), compares victims of police confrontations in Rio de Janeiro and São Paulo

FIGURE 11.1   PERSONS KILLED AND INJURED IN CONFRONTATIONS WITH POLICE

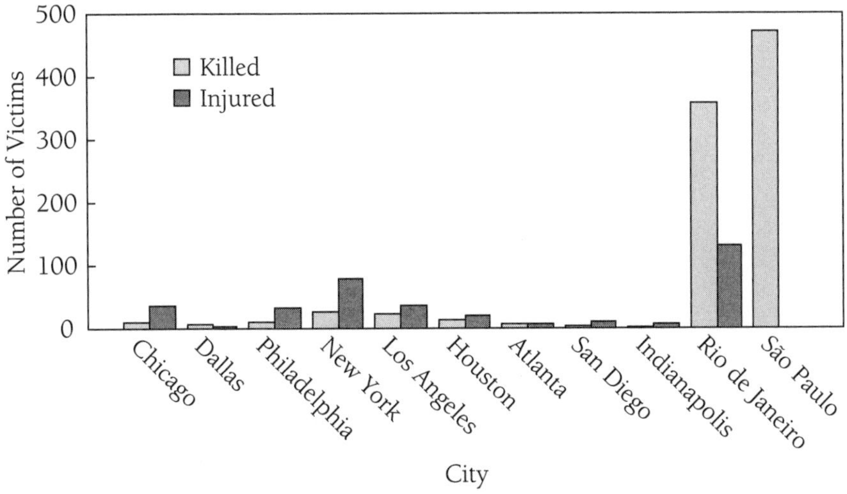

Source: Geller & Scott (1992); Cano (1997).

with various American cities. It shows a huge gap between the countries, despite the fact that American police forces have also been accused of excessive use of force in comparison to those of other developed countries. Rio de Janeiro's police— together with São Paulo—are among the most violent in Brazil (Lemgruber, Musumeci, and Cano 2003; Cano 2003; Justiça Global 2004). Further, the trend in the number of victims of police violence in Rio has been upward. In 2003, for instance, police in the state of Rio de Janeiro registered killing 1,194 people in armed confrontations, a record and a figure that is higher than the overall number of homicides in many countries with similar population size.

Rio de Janeiro: Violence, Favelas, and Policing

The city of Rio de Janeiro is internationally known not only for its natural beauty and its Carnival, but also for its favelas and its violence.[4] Rio de Janeiro became the symbol of violence in the country, and its favelas became the image associated with the inability of the Brazilian state to maintain a monopoly on violence.[5] Since the 1980s, high rates of homicide and other crimes made violence the most-debated political issue in Rio de Janeiro. The three quotes at the beginning of this chapter illustrate how heated and controversial this debate can be.

Traditionally, lethal violence has been high in Rio de Janeiro, but it experienced a dramatic increase in the 1980s. Figure 11.2 illustrates the strong growth of overall

FIGURE 11.2   EVOLUTION OF HOMICIDE RATE PER 100,000 RESIDENTS
IN THE CITY OF RIO DE JANEIRO

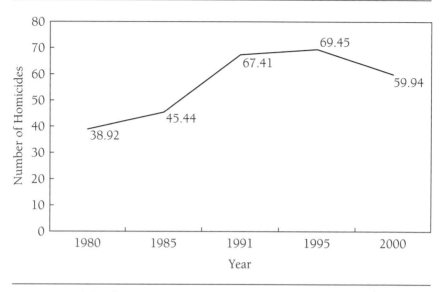

Source: Cano et al. (2004).

homicide rates in the city during the eighties and nineties (Cano et al. 2004). There was a decline during the 1990s, but the rates never receded to the levels of 1980. According to the same source, guns were used in 83 percent of the estimated 3,276 victims of homicide in the city of Rio in 2001.

As for other crimes, the trend in the last decades has also been upward. Figure 11.3, based on police records, portrays the evolution of various crimes in the city of Rio de Janeiro during the 1990s. It shows that criminality is high and has been on the increase, for the most part, during the last fifteen years. As expected, victimization surveys (CPDOC/FGV-ISER 1996; OPS/ISER 1997; PIAPS 2002) indicate much higher figures. Robbery rates, for instance, are approximately ten times those obtained through police figures. Underreporting is a universal phenomenon, but the immense differential between police and victimization data in Rio is also an index of the lack of trust in the police and the criminal justice system.

Although the feeling of insecurity is widespread throughout the city, violence is not equally distributed among neighborhoods and demographic groups. During the 1980s and 1990s, homicide rates for young males between twenty and twenty-four years of age rose to astounding levels—above three hundred per hundred thousand residents. Blacks and browns are overrepresented among the victims—their rate is

FIGURE 11.3   NUMBER OF CRIMES PER 100,000 RESIDENTS IN RIO DE JANEIRO, 1991 TO 2003

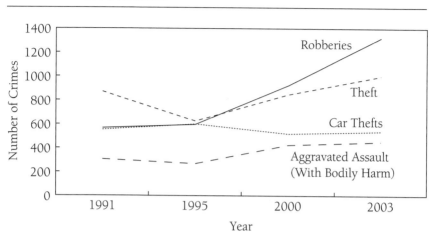

Source: Cano et al. (2004).

more than twice as high as that of whites (84.7 per 100,000 black residents in the state of Rio de Janeiro; 72 for browns; and 32 for whites).[6] However, socioeconomic status and, particularly, place of residence yield the strongest correlations with homicide rates. This is the case not just in Rio but also in all metropolitan areas in the country. Despite the fact that class and race are highly correlated in Brazil, studies have shown that socioeconomic residential segregation is much stronger than racial segregation in Brazilian metropolitan areas (Telles 2004) and homicides are largely concentrated in poor neighborhoods, especially in shantytowns, known as favelas (Cano 1998).

Favelas: History, Policies, and Policing

Favelas have traditionally served as a cheap housing alternative for recent migrants and low-income workers. Formally, they can be defined as irregular housing settings, which first emerged in Rio de Janeiro in the beginning of the twentieth century (Zaluar and Alvito 1998). Favelas were initially located on steep hills in the center of the city or in the most privileged neighborhoods—both areas with strong demand for low-wage labor. According to the National Household Sample Survey (Pesquisa Nacional de Amostra Domiciliar/Instituto Brasileiro de Geografia e Estatística (PNAD/IBGE)), in 2000 there were 516 favelas in the city of Rio de Janeiro, with more than one million residents. Today, levels of poverty vary between the different favelas (Urani 2002), but their social indicators are consistently lower

TABLE 11.2   TRENDS IN RIO DE JANEIRO AND ITS FAVELAS, 1950 TO 2000

Year	Favela Population	Rio Population	Favelas as Percentage of Rio Population	Growth Rate, Favelas	Growth Rate, Rio Population
1950	169,305	2,337,451	7.24%	—	—
1960	337,412	3,307,163	10.20%	99.3%	41.5%
1970	563,970	4,251,918	13.26%	67.1%	28.6%
1980	628,170	5,093,232	12.33%	11.4%	19.8%
1991	882,483	5,480,778	16.10%	40.5%	7.6%
2000	1,092,958	5,857,879	18.66%	23.9%	6.9%

Source: Cano et al. (2004).

than those of the rest of the city. Population growth in these areas has been consistently faster than average (see table 11.2).

Through the decades, favelas have been portrayed in Brazilian literature and arts as romantic places with dense community networks and a special connection with symbols of Brazilian culture such as samba music and Carnival. Yet they have also been portrayed as violent areas, in which there is no law or public order (Lins 2002). There is some truth in both portraits, but the policy-relevant fact is that governments have not traditionally invested much in those areas. Favela residents typically do not pay real estate taxes, since they do not have official property titles, and they are generally treated as second-class citizens.

During the 1970s, the residents of a few favelas, especially those located in the richest areas of the city, were forcefully removed to public housing projects in distant and precarious suburbs (Perlman 1976). The threat of removal contributed to the low investment in infrastructure, both public and private. After the redemocratization of the country in the late 1980s, the forced removal of favelas and their residents became unfeasible for political and economic reasons (Lins 2002; Perlman 2003).[7] But most favelas had no access to running water, sewage, or electricity until very recently. Since the 1990s, governments have invested in infrastructure through widely known programs such as Favela-Bairro.[8] However, urban services such as electricity, water, and, particularly, sewage are not universal, and are usually acquired informally.

Urban improvements, modest though they may be, have not ended the strong stigma associated with these places. The common use of the word "favelado" to refer to favela residents is overwhelmingly associated with poverty and—for many—with crime or moral degradation. The increasing power of drug dealers in these areas has created a violent environment that has led to serious infringements on basic rights, such as the right to come and go freely and even the right to wear clothes of colors associated with enemy groups. Thus, violence has increased the segregation of communities traditionally seen by the middle class as no-go areas.

For many years—and today, still, in many communities—policemen have been the only representatives of the state in favelas. However, their presence tends to be occasional rather than permanent, for the purpose of pursuing criminals and confiscating drugs and weapons. In Rio de Janeiro in particular, police strategies in favelas mirror military strategies and consist in periodical occupations and interventions against the "enemy." This produces frequent shoot-outs between police and drug dealers and provokes deep feelings of insecurity among residents—as illustrated by the first quotation in the beginning of this chapter.

Analyses of police shoot-outs in favelas reveal excessive use of force and the frequent occurrence of summary executions (Cano 1997). More opponents are killed than injured in these confrontations and there are several cases of shooting at point-blank range. The number of people killed by police was higher in favelas than in the rest of the city, and the ratio between the numbers of opponents killed and the number of opponents wounded was twice as high in favelas (3.6) than in other parts of town (1.6).[9] These analyses provide strong evidence of the police's intent to kill in their actions in the poorer areas of the city, legitimized by the ideology of the "war on crime." Further studies have shown that the legal inquiries into these events produced no disciplinary consequences for the military policemen involved, even in the cases when there was clear evidence of summary executions (Cano 1999).

As a predictable result, relationships between poor communities and police in Rio have always been very tense, and allegations of police abuse and corruption are common in the context of this "war on crime." Policemen break into houses, and residents are often shot in the crossfire. Young residents of poor communities tend to view police officers as their enemy, and this perception tends to be reciprocated by a significant number of policemen who work in the area, who see the local youth as potential criminals. The increasing power and heavy weaponry of drug dealers in favelas has further encouraged the use of military tactics and the disrespect of residents' basic human rights by police. Favelas' residents are left in a situation in which they fear police as much or more than they fear drug dealers (Perlman 2003).

This chapter focuses on a group of favelas located within three of the richest neighborhoods of the city: Ipanema, Copacabana, and Lagoa. The favelas of Pavão and Pavãozinho, close to Copacabana, and that of Cantagalo, close to Ipanema, form an urban continuum on the same hill overlooking some of the most famous beaches in the world. The first residents of this area settled in Cantagalo in approximately 1907. For the most part, they were former slaves, migrants from the inner state of Rio de Janeiro, from Bahia, and from Minas Gerais. The communities of Pavão and Pavãozinho were created during the 1930s by migrants from the northeast of Brazil, the poorest region of the country. Today 75 percent of the residents from Pavão and Pavãozinho are originally from the Northeast, and most residents of Cantagalo, Pavão, and Pavãozinho are nonwhite: blacks and browns, according to Brazilian official race categories (Blanco 2002).[10]

With a current population estimated to be around twenty thousand residents in 2000—eight thousand in Cantagalo and twelve thousand in Pavão-Pavãozinho— these communities are probably among the most "prosperous" groups of favelas in the city of Rio de Janeiro.[11] Yet despite their relative affluence when compared to other shantytowns, many of the communities' households have no sewage, and most of them are located on the slopes of steep hills separated by narrow alleys inaccessible by car. More important, all residents of these communities share with other favelas the stigma of violence and crime.

The proximity to wealthy neighborhoods bring about the feeling of relative poverty and inequality among these residents, but it also seems to bring certain benefits, such as the large number of social initiatives in these communities when compared to other favelas in Rio. NGOs, international organizations such as Unicef, and a large number of daycare centers, schools, and churches (especially evangelical) compete for the affiliation of residents. This proximity to rich neighborhoods was also a powerful reason why these communities were chosen for the pioneer policing initiative of GPAE.

GPAE: A NEW STRATEGY FOR DAMAGE CONTROL

As favelas grew in size and violence increased, the traditional strategy of Rio de Janeiro's military police in favelas was (and mostly still is) that of carrying out incursions in order to arrest and apprehend. In reality, favelas have never been policed for the maintenance of law and order. Rather, interventions in favelas were meant to control crime and violence in the rest of town. In other words, policing in favelas was not intended as a way to protect the people who lived there but as a way of protecting the city from the favelas themselves.[12]

Since the harsh and militarized approach to public security dramatically failed to control crime and violence, the debate over public security has intensified in recent decades. On the one hand, some social actors argue that this strategy failed precisely because it is not tough enough; hence, they propose an intensification of this war on crime—as exemplified by the second quotation in the beginning of this chapter.[13] On the other hand, critics of this militarized approach expose the failure of this traditional paradigm to fulfill its promises of security and highlight the abuses committed in its name. As an alternative, they suggest new strategies where crime control and respect for human rights not only could coexist but also could benefit each other and create a better relationship between the police and the community. In this paper we focus on one of these strategies—the GPAE.

The Origins of GPAE as a Crisis-Control Mechanism

GPAE was triggered by a widely publicized public security crisis. In May 2000, five young men accused of being drug dealers were shot dead by the police in

Pavão-Pavãozinho-Cantagalo (from now-on referred to as Cantagalo). Typically, the victims of fatal shootings that occur as a result of police interventions in favelas are said to have been involved in drug dealing—especially when they are young and male—whether the police action is legitimate or not. In this case, the community claimed that they were innocent and that there was no shoot-out, labeling the episode a summary execution. In an act of revolt, residents of the community came down into the wealthy neighborhood of Copacabana and destroyed cars, stores, and buses.

These events were widely reported in the media. In fact, violence that occurs in rich areas of Rio de Janeiro always makes waves in the media and exerts a strong influence on public security policies. From the point of view of public authorities, this event could be described as a worst-case scenario, since one can argue that security policies were historically devised precisely to preserve order in middle-class areas. Further, the extension of violence to well-off areas triggers the overall perception—something similar to a moral panic—that insecurity is rampant and out of control (Ben-Yehuda 1986). As a result, the government was pressed to come up with a solution that could balance the social demand for a tough war on crime and the rage of the community concerning the abuses committed while waging that "war."

The answer of the government of Rio was to create a new special police unit for Cantagalo, somewhat inspired by the ideas of community policing. The main purpose was to signal to the community the desire to decrease police violence and corruption, so as to avoid further revolts, while signaling to the middle classes the continuing commitment to fight against crime. The unit was to be called Grupamento Policial em Áreas Especiais—GPAE (literally, "police grouping in special areas").[14]

In short, the creation of GPAE was not a carefully planned project of community policing, but rather a crisis-control mechanism used in an attempt to manage tensions between the police and poor communities living in rich neighborhoods. In this way, it mirrored previous short-lived experiences of community-oriented policing in Rio, which had been prompted by similar episodes.

The most well known of these previous community-oriented initiatives was called Grupo de Aplicaçao Prático-Escolar (GAPE)—literally, Grouping for Applied Practice. Despite its short existence and poor documentation, GAPE is considered the first hallmark of community policing projects in Rio. In the early 1980s, Colonel Carlos Nazareth Cerqueira, a progressive commander of the military police in Rio, designed GAPE in the favela of Providência in the central area of the city. As in the case of GPAE, the initiative was triggered by a crisis of police corruption and violence in the favela related to drug dealing. Cerqueira planned for GAPE to be implemented in four steps. First, there was a massive police occupation of the favela by special forces and other units in order to drive the drug dealers away from the community and break their control of the area. Second, the new policing project was presented to the community, and the police attempted to build a closer relationship with residents, particularly local leaders. Third, special units and other forces left the favela, and the new permanent policing project took over. Naturally, this involved a difficult transition, particularly after massive police operations in the community. Finally, there was an expectation at the time that this police occupation would be followed by "social occupation," thus altering the focus from repression to social prevention. This meant initiating various projects and services that improved the life of the community and offered young people a better chance of social inclusion. However, these social investments never occurred, and the project ended abruptly for political reasons. Another shortcoming, specific to the GAPE, was that its personnel were recruits in training who were replaced periodically and did not stay long enough to foster deeper knowledge of and contact with the community.

Interviews we conducted with police officers about the Providência project show a strong institutional resistance against community-policing approaches, revealing the resistance and uneasiness of the police vis-à-vis an experimental form of policing that contradicted the traditional understanding of what being a policeman means. Many policemen evaluated this experience as second-rate policing, and believed that they were being asked to perform tasks that were not part of their duties.[15]

Successful Implementation: Leadership and Individual Initiative

As in the case of the GAPE, the institutional attention and resources granted to GPAE were not in line with its potential significance. Other than the government decrees creating the force, there were no official documents or guidelines. Neither was there a plan for data collection that would permit a specific evaluation of the intervention. The lack of proper documentation is a constant in these alternative policing programs in Rio. These experiences are executed as a crisis-management strategy, but without proper institutional reflection and with very little attention given to planning or evaluation. It could be argued that governments and police entered these processes halfheartedly, knowing they were not meant to last long. Hence, regardless of their intrinsic value, several new models are doomed to fail due to the lack of consistency in their application.

The advantage of this lack of planning and institutional support, however, is the space for individual creative action. In the case of GPAE, it was the leadership of Major Antonio Carballo Blanco that was decisive in defining the initial success of the program. Major Carballo Blanco had been the director of community affairs for the secretary of public security and had worked closely with the previous reformist secretary, Luiz Eduardo Soares, for several years.[16] He did not have the usual profile of a military policeman: in 2000 Carballo Blanco was completing a degree in sociology, and had visited Boston, together with the NGO Viva Rio, in order to learn about the results of the Boston Ceasefire project in reducing violent crime and improving community-police relationships (Winship and Braga 2006). Because of the lack of institutional support, Carballo Blanco had plenty of freedom to design GPAE according to his own criteria and to develop partnerships with other organizations.

However, in designing the project Carballo Blanco did not have nearly as many resources as he needed and had been promised. The official size of the unit was one hundred fifty men, but only around one hundred policemen were placed under the orders of Major Carballo Blanco. Contrary to his intentions, most of them had not volunteered for this special duty but were officers transferred from other battalions, many of them because of discipline problems or some other problem that prompted their commanders to transfer them.

Training of these policemen lasted for two weeks, during which Carballo Blanco tried to transmit the spirit of the initiative to his men. He divided the training into two sections: the first was more theoretical and focused on interpersonal relationships, managing conflicts, histories of popular communities, the community-policing approach, human rights, models of appropriate use of force, problem-solving methodologies, and prevention strategies. The second part was more technical and focused on use of arms and ammunition. At the end of the training, policemen were required to sign a letter of commitment to what Carballo Blanco defined as GPAE's three core principles: no guns in the community, no children in criminal activities, and no police abuse of residents.

GPAE officially debuted in September 22, 2000. As in the case of GAPE, it was preceded by an action by special forces to disperse drug dealers and to reestablish state control over the area. Right after this force's action, the police convened a community assembly where they handed out to residents leaflets that explained the project. Major Carballo Blanco publicly presented to the community GPAE's core principles and policing priorities: to confiscate guns, particularly those openly carried in public; to prevent children and minors from being used in criminal activities; and to prevent police abuses and corruption. Aside from policing strategies, Major Carballo also made clear that GPAE would try to help the community attract social projects and investment.

Furthermore, he openly said that although the police would arrest anybody who was seen breaking the law, he knew that criminal activities, notably drug trafficking, would probably continue to exist in the community. But policing would be centered on the above-mentioned priorities. This was meant to calm the community so residents would not have to fear drug-searching aggressive operations, which are the usual strategy of the military police in many favelas and often trigger armed confrontations and police abuses.

At the same time, this message deliberately targeted drug dealers, who were warned that they would have to keep a lower profile and take a less violent approach if they did not want to become a police priority again. A paradoxical effect was that although the police presence was obviously detrimental to the dealers' business, since it would drive customers away, it also entailed a protective factor for them, since rivals would be discouraged from trying to attack local dealers and take over the community.

In the beginning, GPAE faced significant resistance, both within the community and within police ranks. It is important to note that GPAE was a top-down initiative, not a community demand, and residents were distrustful of any police presence, particularly one that seemed to want to intervene in their daily affairs by being permanently stationed in their midst. After all, police were traditionally used to watch them, not to protect them. They particularly feared that police would press citizens to denounce the local drug dealers. Interviewees mentioned that after the previous experience of community policing that had ended abruptly (such as GAPE), individuals who had developed a close relationship with the police suffered reprisals.

As for the policemen, most of them had been sent into the favelas against their will. Furthermore, they considered the assignment to be second-class policing, a social intervention that placed policemen in nontraditional roles. Social prejudice also played a role, for, as one interviewee put it, some colleagues asked, "Why serve people who are poorer than us?"

Major Carballo Blanco overcame the resistance of the community and police almost single-handedly by making an example of his own attitude. He made an effort to be available to citizens, walked door to door to introduce himself, and circulated through the alleys alone and unarmed. The simple gesture of giving community leaders his cell-phone number—asking them to call if there was any problem—had an overwhelming impact. Community leaders did call and often complained of police abuses and corruption. For the first time, the voice of the community was heeded by police, and citizens felt empowered to get rid of policemen who were not up to reasonable standards.

Major Carballo Blanco made a point of dealing with these issues himself, promptly investigating all accusations. If some kind of irregularity was detected, the offending policeman was immediately transferred out of GPAE while the disciplinary inquiry proceeded at its usual—slow—pace. This meant that, for the first time, impunity for police abuses could not be taken for granted. In fact, more than 70 percent of the original agents were replaced during the first year of the program— mainly due to drug addiction and criminal activities (corruption, extortion, and similar abuses). As a result, the remaining agents enjoyed a new kind of legitimacy among the citizenry. This change of climate between police and the community was arguably the most outstanding impact of the whole experience.

Aside from Major Carballo Blanco's strong leadership in fighting police misconduct, there is broad agreement that a permanent presence of the same officers in the community also helps inhibit abuses. Policemen were known by the community, sometimes by name, and this established mutual social control mechanisms. An officer who encountered the same citizens every day would think twice before committing an abuse. On the other hand, policemen learned who was who in the community and, hence, started to treat people according to their individual nature rather than on the basis of broad-brush stereotypes or suspicions.

From an operational point of view, GPAE policemen devoted their time to the following tasks:

Crime prevention, mostly patrolling

Following-up complaints and tips, which they called "qualified repression"

Arresting people who were caught in criminal activities

Answering calls for assistance and other activities[17]

Community contacts

Supporting community demands made to other institutions

In contrast to previous community policing in Rio, community development was an important element behind GPAE. Carballo Blanco stressed the need to address wider social needs of the community, in particular the effort to obtain social projects that could create socioeconomic opportunities for the youngsters. This need fits in with the belief, both on the part of police officers involved in GPAE and on the part of community leaders, that social prevention is essential for crime control.

Partnership with other state agencies and NGOs was essential for this social intervention. In all, forty-two institutions created partnerships with GPAE. Viva Rio, a powerful local NGO with which Major Carballo Blanco had close ties, was particularly involved in the project. It attracted other social interventions in the community, and undertook an evaluation of GPAE in 2004. The most important Brazilian news organization, Rede Globo, and international organizations such as Unicef also funded local social projects.

The contribution of government programs was also essential, particularly in the area of income and job creation. There were many different training and income transference programs, but the most significant one was Jovens pela Paz (Youngsters for Peace). It paid minimum wages to young people in poor areas in return for their attending certain courses and carrying out certain community activities. The idea of the program was that this income transference, small though it may be, might make drug dealing less attractive to some youngsters. Major Carballo Blanco negotiated grants for 180 "Jovens pela Paz" within the community. Such community programs were not new in Rio; the great novelty was the mediation of a police officer to access these resources.

The success of these social partnerships, however, was based not on the institutional profile of GPAE itself but on two other factors: first, Major Carballo Blanco's personal profile and his ability to articulate support for the community in government and in private circles; second, Cantagalo's proximity to rich neighborhoods gives it much more visibility and attention than favelas in working-class areas could ever get. As a result, it is difficult to generalize the success of GPAE to other officers and to other favelas in lower-income areas where social attention is virtually nonexistent.

By 2002, GPAE was established in Cantagalo and had revealed its potential. First and foremost, shoot-outs and the open display of weapons diminished dramatically, promoting a perception of relative security in the community. Residents could come back home at any time of the day or night without the constant fear of entering a war zone. An important part of this deescalation was the fact that the police did not enter the community shooting in special operations—rather, they were stationed there. GPAE did not promote armed confrontations. In fact, one of the self-professed principles of GPAE is the preservation of life, the priority of reducing lethal violence. After all, policemen spent a good deal of their time in the community, and they had an interest in keeping it quiet and peaceful.

During all these months since GPAE had been introduced, not a single resident and not a single policemen had been killed in police interventions. In the few incidents with the police that involved shooting, there were no fatal victims, and these confrontations tended to fade away with time. This does not mean that lethal violence had simply ended in the community, and in fact, several incidents were reported during that period.[18] Unfortunately, it is impossible to know the exact impact of GPAE, as no separate criminal data for Cantagalo was collected—police lump Cantagalo data in with that of the surrounding rich neighborhoods. The lack of criminal data specifically related to the community prevents a more detailed evaluation of the decrease in the number of homicides, let alone other violent crimes, but the increased feeling of security and the dropoff in shoot-outs were confirmed by all available sources. The absence of records to evaluate GPAE, however, underlines the hastiness with which it was implemented and a lack of vision on the part of police authorities regarding the experiment's potential as a model for a less violent policing strategy in favelas.

In short, during its first years, GPAE performed fairly well its task as a damage-control strategy, rather than as a solution for crime. Obviously, the drug trade did not end, nor was it the aim of the intervention to end the drug trade, but it continued in a more discreet manner. Security improved in Cantagalo, and the community was pleased with the absence of shoot-outs. The government was freed of the political embarrassment of favela residents rioting and invading rich areas of town. The attention of the press was not focused on crime or violence in the area, and the innovative experience even brought some positive attention from the media.

Changes in Command and the First Crisis: Weak Institutionalization and the Paradigm of Police Productivity

In March 2002, Major Carballo Blanco was transferred to another post within the military police. Major José Augusto de Oliveira Junior replaced him. Major Augusto had been Major Carballo Blanco's second-in-command since the beginning of GPAE, which ensured the continuity of the project. His evangelical background brought him closer to the evangelical churches inside the community, in whose religious activities he participated. José Augusto remained as commander of GPAE for approximately one year.

However, by 2003 external factors started putting pressure on GPAE, and the failure to institutionalize it placed the project at risk. First, Sebastião Teodoro, a local community leader who had been deeply involved in the project—died in a car accident. He had been a valuable player in maintaining dialogue between the community and the police and his presence would be missed. Community leaders play the role of bridging the gap between residents, including dealers, and institutions, notably the police, thus helping to strike a balance. With his death, the community association lost an effective leader. Second, social projects started to decline and the promises of achieving social inclusion for all the young people in the community never materialized.

On the other hand, and this may be the most important factor, drug trade had turned even more volatile in 2003 in the city at large. Invasions of favelas by rival gangs became more common, particularly in the South Zone of the city, adding to the insecurity of the communities in this zone, including Cantagalo. The arrival of new gang members intensified armed incidents in the favelas. Furthermore, the risk of an invasion of Cantagalo by other groups increased, since Cantagalo is strategically located for drug business, because of the middle class drug consumers in nearby neighborhoods. In this new scenario, pressure within police ranks to show more "productivity"—to increase the number of arrests and apprehensions— mounted. The third quotation at the beginning of this chapter illustrates this common understanding of police "productivity."

Major Marco Aurélio Santos, who had not participated previously in GPAE, was appointed local commander in 2003. The choice was intended to bring GPAE closer to more traditional police tactics and to increase "productivity."[19] As a result, new officers replaced many of the policemen who had been working in Cantagalo for some time. The outcome was predictable. Under Marco Aurélio, the relationship between GPAE and local leaders became more distant and more strained. Soon enough, old practices such as special search and arrest operations, corruption, and blackmail haunted the community again. Under Major Aurélio, frequent gun battles again took place. Allegations of police misconduct were not acted upon. Suddenly, GPAE looked like any other police unit.

A single incident brought the GPAE story full circle. In March 2004, police killed three local residents in an alleged shoot-out, accusing them of being drug dealers, and literally dragged their bodies down the favela. Once again, the community claimed that the victims were innocent and labeled the episode a summary execution. Once again, the streets of Copacabana witnessed fire and destruction provoked by an angry mob that came down the hill in protest, repeating the past with astonishing fidelity. Riot police were called in, and the papers and TV stations covered the story intensely. It would be hard to call the actions of the rioting residents irrational or to condemn them, for they had learned over time that only after riots does the state take action. The subsequent official enquiry acknowledged that at least one of the three victims was not a drug dealer and uncovered the fact that these supposedly community-oriented police agents had been using ski masks to disguise their identities. The whole situation had returned to square one.

The state government convened a meeting with local leaders in which they demanded that Carballo Blanco be reinstated as local commander. The government offered Major Augusto, who had been second in command during Carballo Blanco's term, instead. In August 2004, Major Augusto became GPAE commander for the second time and remained in this post until 2006, the period in which we conducted the interviews. When he returned, he had to revisit most of the accomplishments that had been achieved over the first few months of the project. He transferred troublesome policemen, called back some of his old men, and mended the relationship with local leaders.

Incidentally, for all the initial resistance, some of the old policemen actually wanted to go back and work in Cantagalo, revealing that they had adapted well to that kind of policing. Two of the alleged advantages mentioned were that GPAE is supposed to be less risky than other areas where shoot-outs are common, and that the community climate vis-à-vis the police is more agreeable. As a result of these measures, the spirit of the project was reestablished, and a relative peace ensued once again.

GPAE Today: Limitations and Expansion

Since the return of Major Augusto the original spirit of community policing has been reinstated in Cantagalo, but today GPAE is a smaller and even more under-resourced project. In 2006, it had only fifty-four policemen, about half the original force. This partially reflects a general downward trend in the size of police units, but the scale of the reduction in Cantagalo reveals, once again, the lack of institutional support for the program within the military police.

The usual pattern with Rio police is that policemen work twenty-four-hour shifts and then have forty-eight hours free; in practice, officers are allowed to perform other jobs between their shifts. GPAE is no exception to this rule. GPAE officers work in groups of eight, and the police routine involves three types of activities:

- Patrols around the community according to various schedules so as not to create a predictable routine. Patrolling is carried out both by car and on foot. At night, only the main streets are patrolled and always by car, so as not to provoke armed confrontations.

- Community and assistance activities, such as helping residents who are sick, and other emergencies. Some demands are referred to other public institutions.

One officer is in charge of community relations, and he maintains daily contacts with community leaders and organizations.

• Administrative duties, such as answering the phone, ammunition control, gathering data on GPAE activities, and other bureaucratic tasks.[20] Each day six policemen are charged with performing these administrative tasks.

A few interesting innovations have also been introduced. For example, as a way to reinforce the idea that gun control is a priority, policemen who confiscate guns earn days off. Additionally, the state of Rio has implemented a bonus to each police officer, regardless of the unit, as a bounty for any confiscated weapon.

Up to the moment when the research was carried out, not one single fatality had resulted from a GPAE intervention in Cantagalo. In other words, not one local resident and not one policeman lost his or her life in a shoot-out involving GPAE agents, with the obvious exception of the period under Major Marco Aurélio. Community residents seem to acknowledge these benefits, though both residents and police also frankly acknowledge the fact that drug dealers have not disappeared.

At the time of our study, the streets of Cantagalo were free of the sight of drug dealers walking around with machine guns—a common sight in other favelas. Unlike in other communities, where they can sell drugs in fixed locations (as they used to in Cantagalo), now they must do so walking around the community, generally at night. Thus, they cannot claim to control the area, at least not in the way they do in most favelas. In Cantagalo, unlike in the vast majority of favelas, anyone can walk around without taking special precautions and without fear of being stopped or harassed by policemen or drug dealers. Some claim that this is the case only in the main streets of Cantagalo, and that in the higher, more hidden, and more isolated sections, GPAE officers still walk around strongly armed and in a state of tension and fear (Cardoso 2002). Even when it comes to armed confrontations, however, GPAE officers act differently. A police officer declared that in the armed confrontations they have with local dealers, "Dealers do not shoot to kill policemen, they shoot in the air," since they know that "we will not execute them" if we catch them. This sentence perfectly embodies the idea that deescalation is possible even in very conflict-laden situations.

In 2002, GPAE was extended to three other communities: the favelas of Formiga, Chácara do Céu, and Casa Branca, in the neighborhood of Tijuca; the community of Vila Cruzeiro, in the neighborhood of Penha; and the favela of Cavalão, in Niterói, a different municipality within the metropolitan area of Rio.[21] In general, the context of the creation of these units was very similar to that of Cantagalo: there was a crisis between police and the community, usually triggered by police violence, and the initiation of the project was preceded by the intervention of special forces.

These projects are still in place and seem to have been successful in reducing police violence. Nevertheless, the decrease of lethal violence is not equally striking in all communities. In the case of Vila Cruzeiro, for example, the results have been quite disappointing.[22] One of the main differences between Cantagalo and the other communities was precisely that the latter do not command the same degree of public attention by society, the media, or the authorities. They are located in middle- to lower-middle-class neighborhoods, and, as a result, the level of investment in social projects has not reached that achieved by Carballo Blanco in Cantagalo.

In October 2004, the military police decided to set up a structure that would integrate all these different GPAE initiatives. The newly created CPAE (Comando de Policiamento em Áreas Especiais) is an effort to institutionalize GPAE. CPAE is the central organ to which each individual GPAE has to report. Colonel Ubiratan Angelo, an officer with experience in community relations, was appointed as the head CPAE. The commanding officers of each of the GPAEs were now given the title of "commander" to highlight that they were at the same level as commanders of normal battalions, rather than subordinated to them. GPAEs continued to be linked to the battalions of their areas, but they report to them only from an administrative standpoint, not from an operational or doctrinal perspective. In fact, policemen from conventional battalions in the area are not supposed to enter GPAE communities, unless in hot pursuit or while giving support to an operation coordinated by GPAE. Different interviewees admitted that the coordination with other battalions had been, and still is, a source of conflict.

The creation of the CPAE should serve to coordinate and standardize the GPAEs, as well as way to provide a forum where experiences could be exchanged in search of better performance. Indeed, CPAE has organized meetings that bring together officers and community leaders in all the communities where the project is now established. CPAE has also centralized training, which was extended from two to four, or sometimes eight, weeks, still too short a time to expect anything other than an introduction. A serious attempt to achieve significant learning, let alone attitude change, on the part of the trainee officers, would take far longer.

When the leaders of CPAE are asked why, if GPAE is considered successful, it is not widely applied in favelas as the new paradigm of policing, they respond by saying that it is a very expensive type of policing model in terms of the number of officers involved. With the overall police contingent dwindling, they argue, it is very difficult to expand the program. This position may contain a kernel of truth, but it certainly cannot hide the weight of the ambiguity that the police feel toward their role and their model. Indeed, they acknowledge that there is considerable resistance among many policemen to the initiative. CPAE's leaders need to use the GPAE units' positive but little-publicized arrest and apprehension statistics to convince both an external and internal audience that GPAE is, after all, real policing.[23]

Positive Results and Shortcomings

Depending on the approach one takes, GPAE can be considered a success or a failure. If we focus on the community and human rights outcomes, one can point to a considerable degree of success: it has contributed to a better relationship of residents with police, reduced police violence, and improved the perception of security, at least among some groups of residents. If, however, we focus on the organizational level, there are obvious problems with the internal organization and the institutional incorporation of GPAE within the military police. Overall, we argue that, provided some basic conditions are met, GPAE can work successfully as a violence-deescalation and damage-control strategy and become a more reliable alternative to the "war on crime" mainstream police approaches in Rio.[24]

In the eyes of the police officers who manage the program, the relationship with the communities is positive, though not always smooth. For instance, a "work accident"—as the policemen call the collateral damage of shoot-outs—happened in the favela of Formiga: an innocent person died in the crossfire between police and drug dealers. In spite of the terrible nature of the incident and the apparent euphemism involved in the term "work accident," the fact that police consider this as a problem, rather than as a routine incident, is undoubtedly a step forward.

However, the long history of tense relationships between police and favela residents and the instability of public policies in these low-income communities make citizens somewhat skeptical of the project. Youngsters especially—the main target and victims of police abuse—seem to be particularly dubious. In a study in which researchers interviewed one hundred young residents of Cantagalo in September 2001 (one year after GPAE's implementation), Regina Novaes (2003) found that 83 percent of the interviewees identified a reduction in verbal and physical abuse and in the policy of "shoot to kill" inside the community. One third of the interviewees acknowledged that there were fewer shooting incidents and fewer homicides in the community (including those between police and dealers, and between dealers themselves). However, most youngsters see no difference between GPAE and military police in the level of officers' disrespect for the youths in the favelas, such as approaching and questioning for no good reason. And at least 17 percent of the youngsters perceive GPAE and military policy as very similar in all aspects, which suggests strong skepticism.[25]

There is a general acknowledgment among residents and policemen, however, that there had been a decrease in both police lethal violence, in particular, and violent crime, in general, and that the environment in the communities had become less tense. Occasional demands by other communities to implement GPAE, usually after crises triggered by police interventions, are cited as evidence of success. In addition, the fact that after the incidents in 2004, the residents of Cantagalo demanded the return of Major Carballo Blanco (perceived as the representation of the original spirit of GPAE) shows that the community might be feeling a certain commitment to the project. This stance might in turn strengthen the network of support for the project, making GPAE stronger (Winship and Braga 2006).[26]

Decreases in the number of incidents of lethal violence and of police corruption are the most recognized benefits of GPAE. It seems to be consensual that the communities with GPAE have less armed confrontations involving policemen, but it is hard to assess whether violence among drug dealers or residents has also decreased. Similarly, community leaders and CPAE commanders claim that police corruption is under control in GPAE units, as opposed to the widespread corruption of other units. Yet there are reports of incidents of corruption (mentioned in the evaluation by Viva Rio; see Caruso 2004). In any case, only a serious evaluation of the project would allow us to test these claims. The lack of an internal evaluation reflects problems regarding the internal organization within the police.

On the organizational level, the most striking feature of the experience of GPAE in Cantagalo is the stark dependence on the figure of the local commander. GPAE would not exist without Major Carballo Blanco, and it can be easily undermined by the appointment of a commander who does not fully believe in the program— as in the case of Major Marco Aurelio. This is because it is the commander who ultimately determines which other policemen will work in the project, through transfers. However, individual leaders alone cannot bring about sustainable structural and systemic change. Their influence is short-lived, and old institutional and social patterns, unless similarly transformed, linger on. Only strong institutional support can guarantee a degree of continuity.

The lack of institutional support is evident in the understaffed and undertrained contingents of policemen working in GPAE. As a rule, GPAE units do not have the full complement of officers that they were designed to have. As already mentioned, this is a general trend in Rio's police over the last few years, but it could have far greater consequences in this particular context. If there were a sizable body of officers trained on this community-based, damage-reduction strategy who incorporate GPAE spirit as their own, new commanders could choose their men from among this trained group, which would enhance the stability of the project. However, training is given only to those who have already been chosen to be part of the project, putting the cart before the horse. In addition, the working conditions are also very precarious. For instance, the GPAE office in Cantagalo is located in a public school, with no adequate facilities for policemen who are working on twenty-four-hour shifts.

Interviewees in the GPAE also complained about the lack of a specific activity of data collection in the community, beyond the usual intelligence obtained in community-oriented policing. Information appears to be critical for the success of such an intervention. A proper impact evaluation of the project is simply not possible, for relevant data have not been collected. The simple analysis of whether deaths and crimes decreased after GPAE was implemented can only be carried out from an impressionistic point of view, since police records in the district do not separate out events that occurred in the target communities from those of nearby areas. This is an immense lost opportunity that can be attributed to traditional deficiencies in data management in police institutions in Brazil, but can also be linked to the lack of consciousness of the potential of the project. Demonstrating a quantifiable decline in lethal violence would be crucial to generating wider support for the program.

There are also problems in the relationship between GPAE and the military police units in nearby neighborhoods. A police shoot-out that occurred in Cantagalo in 2003 illustrates these problems. It was triggered by the attempt of policemen of another unit to abuse local residents just outside the community. It ended up inciting community protests and provoking an attempt by "outside police" to occupy the community, which triggered an armed response by drug dealers. GPAE officers had to intervene to protect the other policemen, but nobody was killed. This episode highlights several elements: the lack of coordination and the difficult relation between GPAE and other police units; the fragility of the GPAE with respect to other police units and initiatives; and the role of police corruption in promoting violence.

CPAE managers recognize most of these problems, such as the insufficient number of volunteers among the police force, which means that many officers are only reluctant participants, the limitations of infrastructure and staff, and the overwhelming dependence of the whole initiative on the figure of the local commander. They would like to have a salary bonus for GPAE policemen, to increase interest among the ranks and morale among those already participating, but have failed to guarantee the necessary resources. They also point out that, as drug dealing adapts to the presence of GPAE by becoming more fragmented and dispersed, the GPAE should create more advanced posts inside the community to disrupt and head off the drug trade. However, more men and more resources would obviously be needed in order to do this.

Predictably, conservative sectors have started to criticize GPAE by claiming that police were turning a blind eye toward the drug trade, despite the little-publicized police records that showed a regular number of arrests and apprehensions by GPAE officers that are said to compare favorably with those of other units. The mayor of Rio, the main political opponent of the governor, accused the experiment of being a way in which "the police was used to give protection to dealers' selling spots." However, this interpretation misses the point that the goal of GPAE was not to eliminate drug dealers but to put a lid on violence, guns, and children used as workers in the drug trade. If GPAE policemen are confronted with people in other illegal activities, the legal procedures are to be carried out according to the law: apprehension and arrest. In addition, these critics do not mention the fact that the traditional approach favored by them—guided more by the ideologies of zero-tolerance and the "war on crime"—failed to stop the drug trade and produced many victims and intense insecurity in the favelas.

Despite being active for more than six years, GPAE is still considered a pilot project and is often treated as something that is "not really police" by other sectors of the military police. In our interviews, GPAE policemen expressed some resentment vis-à-vis the rest of the police force, who see officers in GPAE as of lower status. As mentioned before, this perception is still shared by some GPAE policemen, especially those who did not volunteer for the assignment. Many have a fuzzy understanding of their role, which they often perceive as something between a policeman and a social worker.

Indeed, GPAE is still an odd experiment in an otherwise very different paradigm of public security. Many of the difficulties it faces can be attributed to this contradiction between GPAE and the rest of the military police. GPAE was not conceived as a strategy to modify policing in the city but rather as a short-term mechanism to respond to crises between police and poor communities. It must be evaluated with respect to these limited objectives. If the outcome is considered positive, it might help induce wider changes in police institutions. However, in the current tense security atmosphere in Rio de Janeiro—in which several communities are at risk of suffering armed attacks from rival gangs expanding their territories—GPAE commanders fear for the future of the project.

CONCLUSION

Overall, one can conclude that GPAE achieved a significant degree of success in terms of the modest objectives it set itself, especially considering the context and the limited means with which it had to work. As a damage-reduction strategy, it significantly reduced lethal violence in poor communities by simply changing police tactics and attitudes. This reduction caused a considerable improvement in the relationship between police forces and the favelas in which the program was implemented. This underlines the importance of the role of state agents in Brazil as actors that can be used to either stimulate or deflate general levels of lethal violence.

In the case of GPAE, the illusory goal of defeating crime or eliminating drug dealing was traded for the more realistic one of reducing shoot-outs in the community and promoting a safer environment. These are exactly the needs of residents in poor communities. Indeed, despite several serious shortcomings—the application of the program was not smooth, mistrust still exists on both sides, and there have been some incidents of deaths in crossfire and of police corruption—the present situation tends to be clearly better for local citizens than the traditional paradigm. Further, even if GPAE has been unable to expel dealers and eliminate their role in the community, it has certainly made gains in disrupting the local control of drug dealers over the territory than the traditional strategy of periodical violent incursions. This traditional strategy results in many more victims and, except for very short periods of time, left the community completely at the hands of the dealers.

As a damage-control intervention, GPAE also served well the political purpose of avoiding community unrest. Communities with GPAE have, with a few exceptions, stopped being a headache for the government in terms of providing negative media exposure. The acute crisis in Cantagalo in 2004, after the initial spirit of the project gave in to the traditional approaches, should serve as a lesson to stay the course. The community demand for the return of Major Carballo Blanco also illustrates the success of the initiative among residents.

For all its potential, state authorities implemented GPAE with very limited resources and, with the initial exception of Cantagalo, without the social investments that were supposed to confer sustainability to the experiment. The military police as a whole still have reservations about this community approach. The lack of resources and absence of proper evaluation reveal that they never intended it to be a model that the institution should move toward emulating more generally. The strange nature of this experiment is reflected in the difficulties in the relationship of GPAE with the rest of the organization.

Thus, GPAE is a very fragile model, very sensitive to the political climate and to changes of command. Nevertheless, results so far, feeble though they may be because of the lack of quantifiable data, might point the way toward new forms of policing that can bring relative peace to poor communities and bridge the abyss between them and the police, while still fighting crime. From the perspective of Cantagalo's residents, this change means having the right to come and go, a basic right that was lost, as suggested by the lyrics of a popular funk song:

"Eu so quero e ser feliz, andar tranquilamente na favela onde eu nasci, e poder me orgulhar e ter a consciencia que o pobre tem seu lugar."

"I just want to be happy, walk around with no worries in the favela in which I was born, and be proud and conscious that poor people have their place."[27]

AFTERWORD

In January 2007, Colonel Ubiratan Angelo, who was the head of CPAE at the time we conducted our study, was appointed general commander of the military police of Rio de Janeiro. This opens up new possibilities for community policing in Rio's favelas in the future.

NOTES

1. These operations are often carried out without an arrest warrant or any specific information on drugs/arms deliveries, simply in order to "occupy" the territory and expel the dealers during short periods.

2. Our analysis of GPAE is based on the following materials: official information obtained from GPAE's website (www.policiamilitar.rj.gov.br/ac_gpae.htm); the graduation thesis written by the first commander, Antonio Carballo Blanco (2002), which summarizes his experiences during the first years; an evaluation carried out by the NGO Viva Rio, which collaborates with the GPAE project; interviews conducted with civilians and policemen

from both high and low ranks; and several secondary sources for contextual and background information. Seven interviews with community leaders, NGO members, and police officers were conducted from July to September 2005.

3. Brazil is a federal state, and policing is mostly a state rather than a federal responsibility.

4. Rio de Janeiro is the name of both the city and the state. When we refer to Rio de Janeiro (or simply Rio), we mean the city, not the state. To refer to the state we say the state of Rio de Janeiro or the state of Rio.

5. Despite being the focus of public attention, Rio de Janeiro's homicide statistics are not the worst in the country. In fact, data published by Unesco (Waiselfisz 2004) reveal that in 2002 the Metropolitan Area of Rio de Janeiro had only the third highest homicide rate in the country, after Vitória (Espirito Santo) and Recife (Pernambuco).

6. According to the 2000 census, Brazil's population is mostly white (54 percent), and the second-largest group is racially mixed, the so-called browns ("pardos," 40 percent). Six percent of the population self-classify themselves as black. Blacks and browns are overrepresented among the poor in Brazil, even though poverty affects all racial groups.

7. The lack of resources to build public housing projects, and the failure of this model— are shown in *Cidade de deus* (*City of God*), a book by Paulo Lins (2002) that became a blockbuster movie.

8. The main urban development program for favelas started in the nineties under the name "favela-bairro" (favela-neighborhood), which embodies the stated intention to integrate these irregular settings into normal neighborhoods. The program is divided in three phases. First, there is a focus on basic infrastructure (especially sewage, electricity, paving streets, and access routes). Second, the houses are painted. Third, the streets are given names and zip codes, and residents receive a property title.

9. As argued by Paul Chevigny (1991) in his comparison of police violence in Brazil, Argentina, and Jamaica, "If the police kill more than they injure or if the precision of their shots begins to increase suddenly, this suggests that the shots may be fired deliberately" (Chevigny 2001, 9). Cano refers to this ratio as the "lethality index" and uses it as a strong indication of excessive use of force (Cano 1997).

10. The impact of these initial differences can still be felt today: whereas 95 percent of Cantagalo residents declare themselves to be homeowners, only about 40 percent are homeowners in Pavão and Pavãozinho. This may be related to the fact that residents in Cantagalo appear to be more involved politically in community organizations in order to press for improvements for their community.

11. These figures were provided by the residents' associations. Today, Pavão and Pavãozinho share a residents' association, whereas Cantagalo has a separate one. There are talks of merging them into a single association, but unsolved differences have delayed the integration process so far.

12. Aside from these incursions, there were so-called Departments of Ostensible Policing and Posts of Community Policing, small police posts inside the favelas. They were thought of mainly as watch posts without any specific community approach.

13. The most extreme example of this approach, which effectively became public policy, was a plan of "bravery awards" and promotions to be awarded by the secretary of public security of Rio de Janeiro to policemen involved in lethal shoot-outs. This program introduced a bonus of 50 percent, 75 percent, and up to 150 percent on top of the

basic salary and was targeted specifically to policemen who participated in shoot-outs where opponents were killed. Rather unsurprisingly, the number of people killed by police doubled after the program was introduced, and, perhaps more interesting, the ratio of the number of opponents killed to the number of opponents wounded also doubled (Cano 1997). This controversial program lasted from 1995 to 1998, when it was abolished by the state assembly. However, policemen who obtained the award during that period continue to receive the pay bonus up until this day.

14. The first idea was to call it Police Grouping in Areas of Risk, but it was thought that the word "risk" could further stigmatize the communities.

15. Interviewees also mentioned other pilot experiences in the eighties, in the favela of Maré and in the favela of Acari, the latter carried out by the Civil Police. However, it was difficult to gauge the extent of these projects' effectiveness, since we found no documentation. In 1994, there was another experiment in community policing, this time named as such, in the neighborhood of Copacabana. It involved the whole neighborhood, which includes a number of favelas, but was not focused on them, so it is not such a relevant precedent for GPAE. Despite the fact that citizens apparently welcomed the new model, the experiment in Copacabana did not last long.

16. Soares, a social scientist, had been the coordinator of public security and had tried to initiate a reform program in this area, but he had recently left the government in a bitter conflict, accusing the governor of being too soft on police corruption.

17. These social services are commonplace in routine police activity but allegedly became more common after the relationship with the community improved.

18. During this period the news media covered a few cases in Cantagalo: one resident was killed at the entrance of the community by another police unit. Local dealers, in separate incidents, killed another two residents who were believed to be somehow involved with drugs, and their remains were left on display in public places in Copacabana to scare the enemy. Other incidents were reported, where dealers pushed their victims over the cliff at the top of the hill or disposed of their bodies by burying them in secret locations.

19. In March 2003, Major José Augusto was removed, and Major Roberto took over for a few months. He was also close to Carballo Blanco and José Augusto and their ideas. He did not last for long, and the incident that prompted his removal was very revealing of the new approach to community-police relationships. His participation in a popular traditional June festival in the community was said to have infuriated police commanders, who believed his connection with local residents had gone too far and he had "gone native."

20. The GPAE is based in a state school in Cantagalo—where it also stores ammunition in case of attack—and four small outposts within the community.

21. This expansion took place during the interim state government of the Partido dos Trabalhadores in the second semester of 2002 because the governor at the time decided to give up his mandate to run for president. Luiz Eduardo Soares—a supporter of community-policing approach who was a strong influence on Carballo Blanco—became state secretary of security and pushed the project forward.

22. Vila Cruzeiro is the community in which Tim Lopes, a reporter of the most important news organization in the country, Rebe Globo, was executed by local drug leaders when he was trying to film drug sales. Predictably, this event received enormous publicity and created the pressure for intervention.

23. There are occasional demands for GPAE to be introduced in other communities, and the possibility of such expansion was said to be under consideration. The managers named two criteria for introducing the program to a community: it has to be a violent and conflict-torn area, and it must be a small or medium-size community, with clear boundaries. CPAE claims that clear boundaries are needed so the police can define the area and its residents and so they can isolate it from external elements. In fact, the program administrators recognized that Vila Cruzeiro does not meet this second condition, resulting in some of the problems the program has been facing in that community.

24. As already mentioned, the NGO Viva Rio carried out an evaluation of GPAE, based mainly on interviews and focus groups with researchers, policemen, and local residents of three of the four communities where GPAE was implemented (Caruso 2004). Its conclusions also point out the reduction in the homicide rate and in the open carrying of arms as the main advances. Nevertheless, the Viva Rio report strongly criticizes the lack of institutionalization, the tepid support shown by the local population, and the lack of application of the other components of the model beyond police activity. They mention nine points as evidence of the lack of institutionalization: 1. insufficient staffing; 2. poor training; 3. the ambiguous image that policemen have regarding their own role; 4. a perception by the rest of the police force that agents in GPAE are of lower status; 5. precarious working conditions; 6. the use of the model as a crisis strategy for conflicts rather than as a sustainable program; 7. the isolation of the police component from the other, social, components, where they exist; 8. the difficulties in the interdiction of drug trafficking, whose practices could not be stopped; and 9. the existence, still today, of cases of police corruption by local drug dealers.

25. The interviewees were asked to identify three positive and three negative aspects of GPAE and the military police as a whole: 17 percent said that there was no difference between the two.

26. However, one interviewee criticized the symbolic impact of GPAE as a special unit, which focuses on policing favelas. He argued that this might create even more isolation and segregation, since favela residents are always seen as the objects of a different approach.

27. Funk is the most popular music style in Rio de Janeiro's favelas. This one is called "Rap da Felicidade" (Happiness Rap) and was composed in 1995 by Cidinho and Doca, two favela residents.

REFERENCES

Ben-Yehuda, Nachman. 1986. "The Sociology of Moral Panics: Toward a New Synthesis." *Sociological Quarterly* 27: 495.

Blanco, Antonio Carballo. 2002. "Grupamento de Policiamento em Áreas Especiais: Uma Experiência—Piloto" ["Police Grouping in Special Areas: An Experience"]. Thesis. Requisite to obtain the degree of Social Science at the University of the State of Rio de Janeiro.

Bretas, Marcos. 1997. *Ordem na cidade. O exercício cotidiano da autoridade policial no Rio de Janeiro: 1907–1930* [*Order in the City: The Daily Exercise of Police Authority in Rio de Janeiro: 1907–1930*]. Rio de Janeiro: Rocco.

Cano, Ignacio. 1997. *Letalidade da ação policial no Rio de Janeiro* [*Lethality of Police Action in Rio de Janeiro*]. Rio de Janeiro: Istituto Superior de Estudos da Religão (ISER).

————. 1998. "Análise espacial da violência no município do Rio de Janeiro" ["Spatial Analyses of Violence in the Municipality of Rio de Janeiro"]. In *Saúde e espaço: estudos metodológicos e técnicas de análise* [*Health and Space: Methodological Studies and Analytical Techniques*], edited by A. L. Najar and E. Marques. Rio de Janeiro: Editora da FIOCRUZ.

————. 1999. *Letalidade da ação policial no Rio de Janeiro: a atuação da justiça militar* [*Lethality of Police Action in Rio de Janeiro: The Action of Military Justice*]. Rio de Janeiro: Istituto Superior de Estudos da Religão (ISER).

————. 2003. "Uso da força letal: vitimização letal pelos policiais e contra os policiais no Brasil" ["Use of Lethal Force By and Against Policemen in Brazil"]. Unpublished paper (mimeographed). Rio de Janeiro: Secretaria Nacional de Segurança Pública.

Cano, Ignacio, and Nilton Santos. 2001. *Violência letal, renda e desigualdade social no Brasil* [*Lethal Violence, Income, and Social Inequality in Brazil*]. Rio de Janeiro: 7 Letras.

Cano, Ignacio, João Trajano Sento-Sé, Eduardo Ribeiro, and Fernanda Fernandes Souza. 2004. *O impacto da violência no Rio de Janeiro* [*The Impact of Violence in Rio de Janeiro*]. Unpublished research report. Rio de Janeiro: Laboratório de Analise da Violência, Universidade Estadual do Rio de Janeiro (UERJ).

Cardoso, Marcus. 2002. *Eu finjo que não te vejo e você finge que não me vê* [*I Pretend I Don't See You, and You Pretend You Don't See Me*]. Ph.D. dissertation, University of the State of Rio de Janeiro.

Caruso, Haydée, editor. 2004. *Relatório de avaliação do GPAE* [*GPAE Evaluation Report*]. Rio de Janeiro: Viva Rio.

Centro de Estudos de Cultura Contemporânea. 1996. *Mapa de risco da violência: cidade do Rio de Janeiro* [*Violence Risk Map: City of Rio de Janeiro*]. São Paulo: University of São Paulo, Centro de Estudos de Cultura Contemporânea.

Centro de Pesquisa e Documentação História, Fundação Getúlio Vargas, and the Institute for the Study of Religion. 1996. *Pesquisa de vitimização no município do Rio de Janeiro* [*Survey of Victimization in the City of Rio de Janeiro*]. Rio de Janeiro: CPDOC, FGV, and ISER.

Chevigny, Paul. 1991. "Police Deadly Force as Social Control: Jamaica, Brazil and Argentina." *Série Dossiê Nucleo de Estudos Violencia*, no. 2, 1991. São Paulo: Núcleo de Estudos da Violência, University of São Paulo.

Geller, William, and Michael Scott. 1992. *Deadly Force—What We Know: A Practitioner's Reference on Police-Involved Shooting*. Washington: Police Executive Research Forum.

Holloway, Thomas. 1997. *Polícia no Rio de Janeiro: repressão e resistência numa cidade do século XIX* [*Police in Rio de Janeiro: Repression and Resistance in a Nineteenth Century City*]. Rio de Janeiro: Editora Fundação Getúlio Vargas.

ISER. 2003. "O galo e o pavão" ["The Cock and the Peacock"]. *Cadernos do ISER* 58(22): 128.

Justiça Global. 2004. In *Relatório anual do centro de justiça global* [*Human Rights in Brazil: 2003: Global Justice Center Annual Report*], edited by Sandra Carvalho. Rio de Janeiro: Justiça Global.

Lemgruber, Julita, Leonarada Musumeci, and Ignacio Cano. 2003. *Quem vigia os vigias?* [*Who Guards the Guards?*]. Rio de Janeiro: Editora Record.

Lins, Paulo. 2002. *Cidade de Deus* [*City of God*]. Sao Paulo: Companhia de Letras.

Novaes, Regina. 2003. "Policia, policias: as percepções dos jovens" ["One Policeman, Many Police: Youngsters' Perceptions"]. In "O Galo e o Pavão" ["The Cock and the Peacock"]. *Cadernos do ISER* 58(22): 128.

OPS and ISER. 1997. *Pesquisa de vitimização* [*Victimization Survey*]. Rio de Janeiro: OPS and ISER.

Perlman, Janice. 1976. *The Myth of Marginality: Urban Poverty and Politics in Rio de Janeiro.* Berkeley, Calif.: University of California Press.

————. 2003. "The Metamorphosis of Marginality in Rio de Janeiro." *Latin American Research Review* 39(1): 189–92.

PIAPS. 2002. *Pesquisa de vitimização no Brasil 2002* [*Research on Victimization in Brazil*]. Brasília: Secretaria de Segurança Publica.

Soares, Glaucio Adilon. 2000. "Homicídios no Brasil: vários factóides em busca de uma teoria" ["Homicides in Brazil: Various Facts in Search of a Theory"]. Paper presented at the annual meeting of the Latin American Studies Association (LASA). Miami, Fla., March 27–29, 2000.

Telles, Edward Eric. 2004. *Race in Another America: The Significance of Skin Color in Brazil.* Princeton, N.J.: Princeton University Press.

Urani, André. 2002. "Principais resultados do estudo em 51 favelas na região metropolitano do Rio de Janeiro" ["The Main Results of a Study on 51 Favelas in the Metropolitan Area of Rio de Janeiro"]. Paper presented at Instituto de Estudos do Trabalho (IETS) Conference. Fundação da Industria do Rio de Janeiro (FIRJAN), Rio de Janeiro, July 15, 2002.

Waiselfisz, Julio Jacob. 2004. *Mapa da violência IV: os jovens do Brasil* [*Map of Violence IV: Youngsters in Brazil*]. Brasília: UNESCO Brasil.

Winship, Christopher, and Anthony Braga. 2006. "Partnership, Accountability, and Innovation: Clarifying Boston's Experience with Pulling Levers." In *Police Innovation: Contrasting Experiences,* edited by David Weisburd and Anthony Braga. Cambridge: Cambridge University Press.

Zaluar, Alba, and Marcos Alvito, editors. 1998. *Cem anos de favela Rio de Janeiro* [*One Hundred Years of Favelas in Rio de Janeiro*]. Rio de Janeiro: Fundação Getúlio Vargas.

CHAPTER 12

Popular Justice in the New South Africa: Policing the Boundaries of Freedom

John Comaroff and Jean Comaroff

The irony of freedom is that its boundaries must be carefully policed. If the state does not police these boundaries, then people will do it themselves. And that is a great and sad irony: to see people who fought for freedom take it away on their own initiative.

—Steffan Riebe, veteran East German police commander
(Steinberg 1999b)

For all the hope stirred by the end of apartheid, the transition to democracy in South Africa, beginning in 1994, opened up a social and moral vacuum—not to mention a huge wealth-gap—in which violence and disorder, real and imagined, became commonplace. By the late 1990s, a police service regarded as incompetent, toothless, and overzealously committed to human rights was struggling to cope with rising rates of murder, rape, robbery, and carjacking. Frightened citizens, irrespective of race, class, geography, or gender, came to believe that the inability of government to guarantee their safety mocked their newfound freedoms. It also persuaded them that alternative modes of enforcement were desirable and necessary. Wealthy South Africans, who saw themselves as imprisoned in their heavily secured homes, neighborhoods, and workplaces, had long subscribed to this notion, but the residents of poor, largely black areas, which had far less police coverage, soon began to share it.

To many of the latter, community justice appeared—in the words of the charismatic founder of Mapogo a Mathamaga, the nation's largest indigenous vendor of private policing—as an "African way of stopping crime." Counterviolence, ran the rationale, was a pragmatic way to "take back the streets." And to restore order in a world run amok, a world increasingly in thrall to angry young men.[1] This was ironic, of course, in a country that had so proudly just rid itself of the trappings of a police state with the active help of those very "young lions."

The appeal of "cultural" policing and "community" enforcement gave rise to a bewildering array of security, investigative, and quasi-judicial services offered by private companies, local associations, NGOs, religious fraternities, tribal authorities, and vigilante organizations—each with its own distinctive approach to crime. Alternative justice was not new here. Black townships had a checkered history of *mabangalala,* the vernacular term for vigilantes, and of *makgotla,* the Sotho-Tswana term for informal courts. Likewise, the white suburbs had long bought their own protection: "armed response," they called it. But the dramatically heightened turn to these things in face of doubts about the capacity of the state to control violence brought into sharp focus the anxieties about disorder that saturate life in this post-colony.

From the first, alternative policing was justified on pragmatic grounds: as a way of dealing with a failure of governance. At a deeper level, however, it reflected a subtle yet profound re-conception of the public sphere and the nature of the state. In the "new" South Africa, a neoliberal democracy that deferred to the private sector and the primacy of the market, law and order came to be perceived as more contingent, more fragile than it had previously been. It could no longer be taken for granted as the product of state regulation or moral community. The corollary? A growing sense of anxiety about the prospect of political and social breakdown, of ethical entropy and generational strife. In the upshot, many South Africans harbored an unspoken fear that civil society was impossible—that, given changes in the nature of the public sphere, only a mix of individual initiative, communal action, and dispersed economic forces, all under the increasingly minimalist mediation of the managerial state, could guarantee a habitable social world. It was out of this collective shift that the metaphysic of disorder first arose, serving to rationalize counterviolence as an appropriate means of dealing with criminality.

We do not suggest that the threat of violence and disorder was, or is, purely imaginary. Reports of murderers at large, prisoners escaping custody, massive numbers of unsolved dockets, uninvestigated sexual assaults, and police malfeasance flooded the media daily. They still do. Indeed, as a growing body of studies indicate, elevated crime rates are endemic to the social reality constructed by neoliberalism almost everywhere; they are said to arise from a stark polarization of the worlds of the rich and the poor, one fed by a rapidly changing labor market and the loss of regular employment for a large sector of the population—above all, for young black men.[2] The effects and imperatives of neoliberalism are not our main concern here, though. We bring them up to make the point that the way in which South Africans have framed and addressed the problem of disorder has been driven by ideological considerations as much as by instrumentalities. It is, after all, a tenet of neoliberal faith that many of the functions of government ought to be outsourced; this despite evidence that, in measures of efficiency and profitability, the private sector does not necessarily outperform public institutions. How governance in South Africa came to be privatized is a complicated story. For now, though, it is enough to note that a great deal of security and enforcement has been franchised out to commercial licensees—which in turn has legitimated claims by others to fight crime "informally" in the interest of "the community."

No form of alternative policing epitomizes this shift in social authority more comprehensively than Monhle John Magolego and his anticrime movement, Mapogo a Mathamaga. Magolego's brand of rough justice is rooted in rural areas, but it has evolved into a major private enterprise in South Africa. It owes its success in part to its appeal to "traditional" African law—or an imagined version of it—and to a willingness to inflict highly theatrical counterviolence in defiance of the state. In its early days, the organization entered the beleaguered, crime-saturated communities of the new South Africa like a sovereign, redemptive force, albeit one that arrived in a reinforced BMW and sent out press releases. Its effective marketing, its invocation of local culture, and its play on the fears of ordinary citizens only go so far to explain its success, however. Mapogo also has white members, for instance, with whose legacy of frontier justice it also resonates. To grasp its success fully, Mapogo must be seen in the context of the outsourcing of government and, more generally, of the ideological drift in South Africa toward moral and executive deregulation. Thus, before analyzing its operations, let us look briefly into the various elements on which the movement is built. We begin with the efforts of the South African constabulary itself to disperse policing, or some of its functions, into the private sector. These efforts say a good deal about law and order in neoliberal times—and about the ground in which alternative enforcement has spread its roots.

THE FALL AND FALL OF COMMUNITY POLICING

North American models of policing, which have had a profound impact on the world, have undergone three successive phases (Martin 2000). The first stressed order; the second, law enforcement; and the third, service, as exemplified by community policing. In South Africa, the last phase dawned after apartheid ended and was marked by a series of lexical shifts: the South African Police Force became the South African Police Services, or SAPS; police stations became "community service centers." Community policing was not meant to replace the earlier models, but, to cite a refrain of SAPS itself, to build upon existing methods of law enforcement.

As we indicated, community policing is typically defended as a matter of practical necessity. For example, a November 20, 1998, article in the South African newspaper *Business Day*, about the brutal difficulties of rural law enforcement, quoted Antoinette

Louw of the Institute for Security Studies as saying that, in the countryside, SAPS had no choice but to rely on this model. Without it, she implied, few would be arrested or convicted, even for serious crimes. Which, almost certainly, is true. As Steffan Riebe, the former German police official and organic intellectual quoted at the beginning of this piece, observed, the efficacy of detection has always been proportional to intimate local social knowledge (Steinberg 1999b).[3] But the precise meaning of "community" in "community policing" is left undefined. Moreover this autonomic stress on the pragmatic leaves unsaid something deeper and equally significant.

The invocation of the concept of community—or, more precisely, "the community"—has had a resoundingly ambivalent history since the 1980s. Once used without critical reflection in sociology and anthropology, the term now calls forth almost universal suspicion. Nevertheless, and in inverse ratio to this scholarly skepticism, the notion of community has become a panacea of government everywhere. Institutions—the clinic, the prison, the school, the bureaucracy—were, as Michel Foucault famously observed, modernity's hallmark, the disciplinary tools with which it upheld the natural order of things. Now, it appears, postmodernity, under the hegemony of neoliberalism, is de-institutionalizing the capillary mechanisms of the body politic and turning "the community," a cipher with no intrinsic substance, into the signifier of the private sphere collectivized. An abstraction, it is reified into a responsible public space in order to make the claim that "stakeholders"— not to be confused with "the people"—ought to take the initiative for effecting social ends. Thus it was that the last Conservative British government could speak of "releasing" mentally ill patients from a contracting national health service into "the community" for care, as if there were something—or as they say in Sotho-Tswana, *somebodies*—out there to look after those people.

Community policing in South Africa drew upon a spotty but nationwide network of so-called community police forums, or CPFs. Its members were supposed to meet regularly with representatives of the SAPS to discuss strategies for combating crime and problems of enforcement—and to be persuaded to volunteer the information needed to prevent felonies and arrest felons. CPFs were not created to apprehend suspects or actively patrol neighborhoods. At the Lomanyaneng Police Station (this "community center" is still called a station by everyone) in the North West, we met Inspector Irene Lefenyo, who revels in her crime prevention work.[4] The inspector, a bright and energetic young woman, visits surrounding villages and urges their inhabitants to establish CPFs, with a view, eventually, to regulating their own communities. She targets schools, which are prime sites of drug dealing, rape, violence, and gang activity, encouraging them to "adopt a cop." But, she lamented to us, "People do not seem . . . interested. They are not ready to take us as friends." Scheduled meetings of the "community policing committee" at the station go unattended. Joe Leteane, a local Tswana royal said to know everything and everybody, was blunt about the whole business: a forum existed in Mafikeng, he said, but he "knew nothing of it"—his way of being dismissive—except that no one took it seriously.[5] Those associated with it, he added, were *bampimpi,* informers, a very bad and dangerous thing to be. Not long ago, a suspected *mpimpi* (singular) was likely to be killed by necklacing.

Captain Patrick Asaneng, a SAPS community liaison officer, understood perfectly well why people shun the CPFs. In South Africa, he said, nobody cooperates easily with the police. The memories and nightmares of apartheid have not been laid to rest. "For myself," said Asaneng, "I don't think that I would go to a forum after I take off this uniform." Mind you, Inspector Lefenyo tells of a time when two men from Lomanyaneng did approach her to form a CPF. They called a meeting of the local residents to discuss their anxieties about crime and the inefficiency of the police. SAPS officers were invited. By the time they arrived, however, the crowd was angry and vocal. Residents said they wanted to "take care of themselves" and asked permission to establish a forum to do so. Sensing that sanction was being sought for a vigilante organization, the officers tried to convince those present of the advisability of a partnership between "concerned citizens" and the SAPS. They failed.

In the North West, as in many parts of the country, community policing remains central to the state. It is invoked as both a panacea and a prescription in a disordered, violent world. But Joe Leteane and Patrick Asaneng, citizen and policeman, respectively, are correct: it has little purchase on the hard-edged realities of the new South Africa. Closer to the pulse was the demand, by the people in Lomanyaneng, to be allowed to "take care of themselves."

PRIVATE JUSTICE IN PUBLIC

The efforts of South Africans in predominantly black urban and rural areas to "take care of themselves" grew palpably from 1995 to 2000. It was in these areas that alternative justice grew apace—and mutated into several different forms. (The white zones, as we shall see, could largely buy over-the-counter services to prevent crime and leave "justice" to others.) Reports surfaced almost daily of "criminals" being "dealt with" (read: "killed") by their "communities." This land may lack a death penalty, but the penalty of death is meted out more and more by "ordinary people," under the signs of civility, morality, decency, and, above all, order.

The degree of organizational and procedural elaboration involved in informal justice, however, varies widely. In South Africa, we may distinguish six broad types.

Lone Rangers

At one extreme are urban lone rangers: individuals who patrol tough streets as guardian angels of the vulnerable. One such man, Tutu Mgulwa, provided an escort service for abused young women. Mgulwa claimed to have begun his anticrime crusade after a friend was sexually assaulted by a policeman (Mathiane 1999; Molwedi 2000). Dubbed the "sex vigilante" by the press, Mgulwa specialized in tracking down and seeking to convict rapists; he founded the South African Stop Child Abuse organization, although it seems to have been chiefly an umbrella for his solo activities. In 1998, he paraded a youth accused of rape naked through the streets of Atteridgeville, a large township outside Pretoria. Such carnivalesque marketing of his services led women to seek his help, and Mgulwa often landed in court with his clients as a prosecution witness—or on charges of having assaulted the suspects. Mgulwa was seen as a saint by "the community" and regarded by SAPS as a violent, habitual felon. His career was derailed in 2000 when he was jailed. For what? Rape, of course. Mgulwa cried conspiracy by certain corrupt officers whom he had exposed in his heroic civilian work. The judge decided otherwise. But if there was a covert effort to neutralize this lone ranger, it showed a fine symbolic sense, showcasing as it did the ever-present ironies in the cyclic neighborhood dramaturgy of cops and criminals.

Women of Vision

There are many instances of groups of people coming together, spontaneously or on a regular basis, to "take care of themselves." In 2000, three young women from Khayelitsha, Cape Town, having confessed to multiple thefts, were undressed and beaten by a mob of angry residents; their lives were saved not by the police but by local officials of the South African National Civics Organization, who, again in the name of "the community," resolved the trouble (Dlakavu 2001).[6] In Bredasdorp, on the southeast coast of the Cape Province, a crowd "went on a rampage" in November 1999, attacking a gang allegedly involved in drugs, terror, and abalone smuggling. When the police tried to remove the corpses of two youths who were killed, they met fierce resistance from community members who wanted to set the bodies on fire, according to *The Citizen*, a South African tabloid (1999). And in the village of Madibogo, in the North West, fifty residents armed with sticks, whips, knives, and guns killed a forty-five-year-old "youth" (an unemployed black male), who was said to have stolen "stock belonging to the community." The mother of the dead man, Sarah Kali, blamed a local church pastor for leading the assault; his followers, she alleged, were members of the local community police forum who had taken the law into their hands. Which brings us back to that meeting at Lomanyaneng, at which residents demanded the right to "take care of themselves."

Such actions sometimes congeal into organizations, as exemplified by two remarkable women's groups. One formed in the colored township of Westbury, in Johannesburg, where employment was scarce and criminal violence a part of everyday life. Two women created Women of Vision after a spate of sexual attacks on elderly females in 1999. Its first act was to march on the home of a suspected rapist, apprehend him, and turn him over to the police (Magardie 2000a).

The other group is more prone to violence. The traumatized older women who formed it in Soweto in 2000 were reported to sleep with *pangas* (large machetes) under their pillows. Shalo Mbatha, a reporter for the *Sunday Independent* (Johannesburg) who interviewed them in March 2001, said the women claimed to know well who were the miscreants in their midst—and spoke of killing suspected robbers as if it were commonplace. The group lacked a formal name, but its actions followed a pattern: the victim was dragged into the open and laid into by everyone present with whatever came to hand.

Such rituals of violent justice have "a festive mood," combining "ultimate deterrence" and "payback time," one participant was quoted as saying. "It [feels] good to strike back." The woman added that the police "seemed relieved that one of the thugs was dead when they arrived." Another participant said that the police had been invited to a forum to discuss local anxieties about crime. "But they never came," this woman said. "They really do not care" (Mbatha 2001).

Kangaroo Courts and Tribal Police

Informal community justice is often organized around people's tribunals, or, as the media like to refer to them, "kangaroo courts." So ignominious was the history of people's tribunals in the late apartheid era (Haysom 1986; Kane-Berman 1977) that many were disbanded altogether after 1994, and if not, they were sometimes renamed "anticrime committees" (Minnaar 1995). The extent of these courts' respect for due process varied. In the nightmare version, self-appointed court functionaries arraigned a suspect on a complaint made by some member of the community, a summary "trial" was held—with scant attention to the quality of evidence or the rights of the accused—ending in a guilty verdict, followed by the swift execution of an inevitably harsh sentence, varying from a brutal lashing to death. If the police tried to intervene, the size and frenzy of the crowd often prevented them. Some policemen who tangled with the tribunals were known to face severe reprisals (Ngobeni et al. 2000).

The tribunals appealed to a populist "African" form of justice; they laid claim, albeit in a limited way, to the mantle of so-called "tribal courts" and their customary authority to discipline "trouble makers" (Haysom 1986). In parts of the post-colonial countryside, this circle has turned. The "tribal police," recognized by the government under the rubric of traditional law, began to mimic the "community" justice of the townships. Thus, for example, in 1999, Chief Setumo of the Tshidi-Rolong in Mafikeng ordered the tribal police to "clean and rid our village of all unwanted elements, including rapists, thieves, murderers, car hijackers and women and child abusers"; troublesome youth were to be singled out (*The Mail* 1999a).[7] Tshidi-Rolong in the region can now appeal to those police, for a fee, to punish anyone causing them trouble if compelling reasons can be given.

Which is why Josephine Seleko went to them on March 22, 2000. She had developed shingles. A *ngaka,* or seer, whom she consulted told her to sacrifice a chicken and gave her a medicinal unction, to no avail. Her employer, a lecturer at the local university, told her that shingles is often caused by stress. "Yes," she replied, "we are troubled. My younger brother [kleinbroer] is harassing my mother and me. He is beating us and stealing." The thirty-one-year-old unemployed brother—Josephine called him Lightie, slang for "little boy"—was tormenting the two of them at night, demanding money. He was said to be especially aggressive when the old woman's pension was paid. After going to the police produced no response, a neighbor told Josephine to seek out the tribal police at the local capital, who, in exchange for fifty rand (then about eight dollars), would pick up and deal with the culprit. Go, she said, "to the people who hit them on the back." This appealed to Josephine. Having suffered theft, verbal abuse, and physical assault, she seemed afraid for her life. Another neighbor also pointed to the kgotla, or chiefly court. "They will thrash him thoroughly," she said. "They do it outside, and make the criminal walk home [in pain and embarrassment]. Those who do it are from the chief." Josephine added, "The tribal policemen, they will give him a chance to make a statement. Then they will punish him, right there."

Interestingly, this approach combines elements of conventional policing, in that it is done by people who hold a degree of recognized authority, but by irregular means; customary law, in that it involves "tribal" punishment, but without a full trial; community justice, in that the response to crime is "informal" but not carried out by a "mob"; and private protection, in that it is a fee-for-service response to attacks on persons or property. In the end, the tribal police never did deal with Lightie. Josephine was unable to get to the capital with the necessary money. Sadly, the problem resolved itself. She died of a stroke, suddenly, a few weeks later.[8]

Praying and Slaying: Religion as Law Enforcer

Religion has also made its presence felt in informal policing and people's justice. In its Christian manifestation, this has included efforts to bolster the moral infrastructure and thus to combat crime by means of conscience. As a hedge bet, divine intervention has also been sought. Thus in Atteridgeville, Pretoria, the Concerned Residents Association held an "Anticrime Prayer Day" in June 2000 (Hlahla 2000); the Mafikeng Development Forum had organized an interdenominational "Crime Prevention Through Prayer" campaign in 1997 (The Mail 1997a, 1997b); and the "Spiritual Services Division" of SAPS had held a National Day of Prayer Against Crime a few years earlier. In the North West Province, the premier, Popo Molefe, urged churches to involve themselves actively in support of community policing forums and to persuade congregants to provide information to SAPS.[9]

A more proactive, violent approach was taken by a Muslim organization, People Against Gangsterism and Drugs, or PAGAD, formed in 1995 on the Cape Flats in Cape Town. It came to national attention in 1996 by virtue of a gruesome murder broadcast live on prime-time television. Rashaad Staggie, an infamous local gang leader, was doused with petrol, set alight, and shot. The burning recalled the killing of informers and witches; the shooting, the summary assassinations of street justice. An African National Congress news briefing later observed, "PAGAD was initially welcomed by ordinary citizens, but . . . opinion has turned firmly against it after police linked it to ongoing urban terrorism that has seen a spate of bombings, drive-by shootings and assassinations of policemen" (ANC 1999b). This seems a fair assessment. It has been argued that the organization's crime-fighting goals folded into militant Islamicist politics, the tactics of which generated much crime and urban terror. A 1999 study found that PAGAD, in its first forty-two months, was linked to almost seven hundred acts of violence, including assassinations of gangsters, drive-by shootings, and bombings (Premdev and Chetty 1999). Since the millennium, and after some high profile arrests, its activities have ceased.

Despite its record of violence, the state was careful in its dealings with the organization. PAGAD might have evoked public antipathy, but groups like it that use the metaphysic of disorder to justify informal policing and community justice address a local need, a populist desire for strong, self-motivated collective action, and a fervent belief in the capacity of counterviolence to, well, counter violence. All in the name of "the community." All justified by the absence of the state. All rationalized by the need to take initiative for making a world at once safe, morally founded, and spiritually clean.

The Respectable Face of Alternative Justice

The summary character of counterviolence and its lack of authorized due process have led to the entry of a number of NGOs—those missionaries of the neoliberal age—onto the terrain of alternative policing and community justice. One, to be found in Westbury, the same colored township that produced Women of Vision, is Conquest for Life. With funding from the Open Society Foundation and the British High Commission, it established the Victim Offender Conference Pilot Project, the lofty goal of which is to lead the way to "alternative justice" in South Africa (Magardie 2000b). To this end, the project established in Gauteng Province forums at which crime victims and perpetrators meet voluntarily for purposes of mediation, the admission of guilt, and restitution—in the form of money, service, or an apology. Successful outcomes, it was hoped, might remove the need for a trial. As this suggests, Conquest for Life seeks to "introduce a more restorative, as opposed to retributive, approach to justice," in part—note this—by calling on the model of the *lekgotla,* the customary court. In short, unknown to each other, experiments in urban community justice and the rural criminal-justice system are beginning to establish a middle ground, in spirit, judicial principle, and due process, between two antithetical traditions.

A second project concentrates more on alternative policing than on mediation. Called the Peace Corps in Gauteng and the Peace and Development Project Western Cape in Cape Town, it has been funded by Danish, German, and American sources; the Cape chapter is run by a German NGO. Its recruits, known as "community peace workers," must be eighteen, have no prison record, be politically independent, and have ten years of schooling. After a four-week training course, they patrol the streets by day, unarmed, in fairly large groups, gaining information about criminal activities in "the community," intervening in unarmed conflicts and family disputes, monitoring pension pay-outs and other potential sites of violence, administering first aid, helping lost people or those under the influence of drugs and alcohol, and so on. Twice a month, on payday, when people carry home their wages, they also do night patrols. Like Conquest for Life, this one claims to have had considerable success—if, in nothing else, as a model for community self-regulation. Certainly the one we observed, in Crossroads, took the work very earnestly. At the same time, its cadres were well aware, as they confessed to us, that their impact on the troubled cityscapes of Cape Town remained small indeed. Would it grow? Yes, we were told, if somewhat hesitantly. But more important to those working long daily shifts was the fact that this was a new, inspirational—and legal—way of actually doing alternative policing.

NGOs dedicated to combating crime have their tragicomic side, too. One, the Ithutheng ("Student") Trust—or at least its coordinator, Jackie Maarohanye—organized a ritual. One Sunday in 1999, some 2,500 "juvenile delinquents" (mainly schoolchildren) were persuaded to throw their illegal weapons, for the most part firearms, into the Klip River in Soweto during an uplifting ceremony that included singing and, oddly, the sound of gunshots. The next day, police divers searched the river and found a handful of knives, axes, and spears—but nothing capable of shooting a bullet. They had disappeared. A local newspaper photographed one man searching in the water; another confessed happily that he was about to fetch a large magnet to catch himself a pistol. What started out as an effort to rid the town of the means of violence turned out to be an elaborate exercise in redistributing them.[10]

Private Plans: Home Protection and Business Watch

Alongside alternative justice, which is associated primarily with black communities, there is, finally, the burgeoning private security industry. Its objective is more crime prevention and protection than the apprehension of felons. One manifestation is Business Watch, which, in some towns and cities, has brought entire commercial centers under video surveillance and frequently deploys special enforcement officers paid by the corporate sector. In some Johannesburg neighborhoods, these officers, renamed "street managers," were for a time "security guards registered and trained as police reservists, kitted out in police uniform and supplied with state firearms"[11] (Ngobeni 2000a). The other manifestation of this industry focuses on home protection; it is epitomized by the likes of Baywatch, a well-known security firm in Cape Town. Firms of this kind provide "rapid" armed response for the private sphere. By and large, Business Watch and Baywatch, which operate in the spaces of insecurity opened up by the perception of inadequate police cover, have been confined to middle-class white zones. But their analogues are to be found across the invisible borders of class and race that still cut deeply across the social terrain of the post-colony.

MAPOGO: LEOPARDS, "AFRICAN JUSTICE," AND VIGILANTES

Which returns us to Mapogo a Mathamaga, or Business Shield, South Africa's biggest, most colorful, and most controversial self-policing operation. A force to be reckoned with north, east, and west of Johannesburg, Mapogo subsumes all the modalities of alternative policing and informal justice discussed earlier; it even mimics aspects of private security companies, community policing forums, and NGOs. In short, Mapogo offers a living summation of our arguments about all these phenomena. It is the creation of Monhle John Magolego, a charismatic postal-worker-turned-entrepreneur who founded it in 1996 when he was about fifty years old. Magolego is a veteran of the post-apartheid conflicts between unemployed youths and older black businessmen-turned-vigilantes in Sekhukhuneland, Limpopo Province (Delius 1996).

Clearly, he is also a skilled self-publicist. "My movement is a response to a real need," he told us solemnly, to "the failure of democratization to ensure a 'better life for all,' and to protect the property of honest, hardworking citizens."[12] But the "need" Mapogo fills surpasses mere protection, as Magolego concedes. "We are sick to death of the soft-handed techniques of democracy," he told members of the Afrikaans press in their own tongue, literally and figuratively. "Crime knows no color. If they won't listen, their arses must burn" (Bothma 2000).

Magolego prefers to call his mode of justice "the African way of stopping crime." He rejects the term "vigilante," but the same logic holds: Mapogo presents itself as a justifiable and necessary response by ordinary people entitled to enjoy the fruits of their labors and to restore order in a society run amok.

Magolego understands well the angst of South Africa's petty bourgeoisie, which cuts across lines of race and color. He originally set out to serve one hundred black small-businessmen in Limpopo Province, but Mapogo spread like wildfire, drawing shopkeepers of all races and even isolated white farmers, who posted Mapogo's logo—a snarling, double-headed beast, part tiger and part leopard—on their gates (Watkin 1999). Magolego, who remains in control of the organization despite challenges to his leadership,[13] took credit in 2000 for having ninety branches and as many as sixty thousand members; the police are dubious, but agree that the number of members runs to many thousands.[14] Although it remains predominantly a rural phenomenon, Mapogo has begun expanding into the urban areas. It has an office in the central business district of Pretoria, only three hundred yards from police headquarters.

A Self-Proclaimed Evangel of Justice

Mapogo opens new branches with an elaborate ritual, which unfolds untrammeled by state intervention. Thus, the founding of the predominantly white chapter in

Nelspruit, in Mpumalanga Province (formerly Eastern Transvaal), was held at the local civic center and conducted almost entirely in Afrikaans (Morobi 2000). We were invited to witness Mapogo's triumphal entry into a large village near the Mozambique border; our observations accord well with other accounts of parallel events (Soggot and Ngobeni 1999; Steinberg 1999a).

The symbolism at these rituals opens a window onto Mapogo's political sociology. Magolego heads these forays himself, traveling in a large, well-maintained BMW. He is flanked by loyal supporters—sometimes including white farmers—clad in Mapogo T-shirts, some of whom wield *sjamboks,* a weapon associated with rough, racist discipline on Afrikaner farms. Trailing a truck with a huge banner, the procession makes its way, horns blaring, to the house of the local chief—who, according to Magolego, has typically requested his presence there. The long audience that follows leaves no doubt that the convoy bears the royal imprimatur; its presence promises a return to "traditional discipline" of times past.

At the opening in Nelspruit, a cross-section of the village had gathered at a local motel from a brace of middle-aged businessmen with cell phones in hand to a couple of elderly churchwomen garbed in blankets and piously intoning Methodist hymns. As Magolego's assistants set up a stall to sell bumper stickers, placards, and shirts, a crew of local workers prepared meat donated by grateful residents. After some time, Magolego himself, attired in a stylish suit, swept into the room accompanied by armed bodyguards and a video technician.[15] All subsequent proceedings—the prayer, Magolego's address, the enrolling of new members, even our interview—were captured on video.

Mapogo comes to town, then, like a tent revival. Even government officials are wont to describe it in supernatural terms: a "legendary organization that finds criminals like magic," one called it in an article in *Business Day,* a respected Johannesburg daily, on August 25, 1999. And Magolego, who cultivates an image of piety, is the revival's main preacher. He always carries a gun, a cell phone and a bible, and sometimes employs the latter to describe his mission. Like the great "fisher of men" in Luke, Magolego has been enjoined—by God, he has said—to "fish people" through his movement. He claims to be an active Catholic and defends rural Catholic establishments free of charge; a week after the Nelspruit event, he was to visit a Catholic mission in Bronkhorstspruit that needed help with repeated theft and vandalism. Here, as always, religion's presence has been accompanied by signs. Two, in fact, were observed by a reporter in March 2000 near White River, outside an Afrikaans Christian camp. "Jesus Christ is our Lord," one notice-board proclaimed confidently. The other was a flat apocrypha: "This property is protected by Mapogo a Mathamaga."

Magolego also describes his founding of Mapogo as a conversion experience. The crime attending the birth of the "new" South Africa, especially the killing of businessmen, "dissatisfied" him deeply. "What we were suffering was not merely theft," he said. "It was war." In August 1996, an incident involving an elderly shopkeeper in Jane Furse, near Pietersburg, made a deep impression. Taken from his shop one night, the victim was found dead in the morning under a bridge, naked and bereft of his private parts. To Magolego, this was "the last straw." Enough was enough. The killing had to be stopped. He and colleagues called a meeting of almost one hundred black businessmen from that part of Sekhukhuneland to be held August 25. It was here that Mapogo was born. Magolego addressed the gathering; all present, he told us, felt motivated to "engage in the struggle" on behalf of the nation. Note the appropriation of liberation movement lingo; note also that the atrocity that had finally moved Magolego to action had the hallmarks not only of a robbery, but of a ritual killing of a man of venerable age.

Magolego emerged as the new movement's leader and founding visionary. He also suggested its name, choosing a moniker that would convey its meaning unambiguously across cultural boundaries but would also be culturally idiomatic. The word *mapogo* alludes to a Sesotho saying: "Ge ole nkwe nna ke lepogo ka mo ka ne mathamaga"—"If you are a leopard, remember I am a tiger; we are both of the same color." Magolego claims that it was used in Sotho parlance to warn people inclined to violence that they "are not the most powerful beings on earth." It says to them: Your force will be met by my like force. Mapogo a Mathamaga literally means "brown-spotted leopards," but the phrase carries a message captured clearly by the group's logo showing the back-to-back heads of a snarling leopard and a tiger.

Magolego has a more personal version of his summons as well. It was on August 18, 1996, that he announced his call for the meeting to consider founding Mapogo. Four days later, likely as a consequence, he was attacked. Magolego was driving home in a Mercedes when he suddenly decided to visit a friend. Outside her house he was confronted by armed youth, who took his bible, his bag, and his keys, but withdrew, leaving a cache of liquor untouched on the back seat. Clearly, this was a warning shot. Magolego said that the event's "uncanny" timing produced a "trauma" in him. He had never been robbed before. But he went ahead with the launch of the organization and now calls this experience a kind of "baptism." He said that he has never been attacked since then.

Mapogo's Modus Operandi

Mapogo spokespeople claim to have kept in communication with government and the police from the start. Within one month, the group said it informed public safety officials in Limpopo Province as to why it had organized but did not receive a reply. In the meantime, it set about its business of apprehending those who stole the property of its members. (Mapogo deals mostly with property crimes, but on occasion it gets involved in murders and assaults.) Cadres volunteer for specific "operations" and provide much of the physical force that Mapogo deploys. In urban areas, "reaction units" are drawn from the unemployed, who are appropriately "rewarded."[16]

When attacks occur, units visit the victim and the victim's family, gather information, and then find the "right people," as Magolego puts it. The police are skeptical. One reporter quoted Seth Nthai, then a safety and security official for Limpopo Province, as saying, "The notion that Mapogo has a sophisticated intelligence network is nonsense. If a crime is committed [they] will not try to get to the bottom of it. They will go to a known criminal and beat him up" (Steinberg 1999a).

Magolego denies this and counters that policemen will never get the help they seek. People simply deny all knowledge and avoid testifying in court against offenders. Community policing is an abject failure for this reason. But Mapogo protects its members if they stand in the witness box. And they draw on deep-seated local knowledge in countering crime. "We rely on community knowledge to do this," Magolego told us. "People used to be afraid to provide information. But they were not once they joined Mapogo," he said. They could "punish the boy next door without fear" because they had the organization behind them.

Deterrence is crucial to Mapogo's strategy. Women, who may join Mapogo but not participate in the action, appear to regard merely displaying the Mapogo logo as having a prophylactic effect on the chance of being raped and physical abused. Units are instructed to warn offenders before taking any action, reminding them of the consequences if they persist. Given the fearsome name of Mapogo, this is often enough to ensure that no further trouble ensues.

How exactly did Mapogo establish its awesome reputation? Effective marketing is one answer. As soon as it was established, the movement set about making its intentions known. As a result, when it attacked known criminals with *sjamboks,* "Television, radio, and newspaper reporters rushed to the hospitals to take pictures, showing the entire country the backsides of [our] victims." This established a popular perception of the organization's punch. And perception is what counts. Once, in Nelspruit, Mapogo members were accused of taking a man suspected of concealing evidence to a dam filled with crocodiles and of plunging him in. "I asked my local members if it was true, and they denied it," Magolego later said. But, he added, "it's wonderful that people think that it happened; that's exactly what we want."[17]

Mapogo members are reported to have administered electric shocks to the genitals of suspects and to have dragged other suspects behind vehicles, another method beloved of lynch mobs under apartheid. Clearly, these unorthodox techniques cannot merely be explained as means to an end, although they are clearly very effective means indeed; the choice of method also reenacts a visceral memory of violence past. Clearly, also, local operatives have considerable license in inventing their methods of doing business.

It is this that has been at the center of the censure of Mapogo by the media and the police. Jonny Steinberg (1999a) quotes critics who found the organization "no better than a gang of common criminals," whose "jungle justice" substitutes rumor for evidence and produces terror by inflicting public violence on scapegoats. Lieutenant Hannie Kriek, who monitors the group for SAPS, conceded to a different reporter that Mapogo is "very effective." But he added, "you can't fight crime with crime. They're scaring people like hell" (Watkin 1999).

Accounts of mutilation and death resulting from Mapogo's disciplinary procedures fill the news media and, as we shall see, have led to mostly failed efforts to prosecute its leaders. Mapogo does not aim to kill anyone, insists Magolego, who has apologized to bereaved families and offered to pay for funerals. But he adds that, even in a hospital, patients sometimes die (Soggot and Ngobeni 1999).

Fears of a Backlash

Police worry that Mapogo "has encouraged a racist-backlash among white right-wingers."[18] It has given them "a legitimate discourse," says Seth Nthai, Limpopo Province safety and security official. "They can now call [all] blacks criminals and feel they have reason to beat people." It is true that Mapogo's rough justice appeals to pistol-packing farmers in strongholds of the white right. Mapogo's use of the *sjambok* in its policing recalls methods favored on Afrikaans farms in the heyday of apartheid. Informal justice also encourages resort to the dreaded "kangaroo courts" that flourished as alternative courts under the apartheid regime (see above).[19] But Nthai raises an even more profound concern: the movement has come to mean so many different things to different people that Mapogo's "legendary" powers have evolved into an ideology with a momentum of its own, beyond the control of Magolego. So much so that, when an incident occurs in the organization's name, it is not always clear whether its leadership even knew about it. The state has shown decided ambivalence toward Mapogo. It has, after all, curbed crime in areas where law enforcement is lacking or ineffectual. One former policeman in the Limpopo Province town of Dendron put it thus: "The police come here only to pick up girls. The people like what they've seen of Mapogo. If they find a man breaking into a house they [will] hit him or kill him, anything but taking [sic] him to the police. I'll join the beating because I'll be helping my brother" (McGreal 1999).

The official opposition alliance in South Africa at the time, the United Democratic Movement, was also sympathetic and courted Magolego to run for office. He came close to winning a seat in the provincial legislature in 1999 (ANC 1999a; Watkin 1999). The party leader in Limpopo Province called on the government to stop "victimizing" groups like Mapogo. Such organizations play a constructive role in rural communities, he said, where it was often the only law enforcement agency at work. Instead of fighting them, the authorities should recruit their members as police reservists or as community constables. "The community" again.

To bolster this image of respectability, Magolego announced in June 2000 that Mapogo was "going mainstream"; he had started a "professional security firm" in Limpopo Province that refrained from flogging suspects, used marked patrol vehicles, and was registered with the national Security Officers' Board (Ngobeni 2000b).

The African National Congress remains unimpressed, however. A few months earlier, it had directed any members who had joined Mapogo to withdraw (Makgotho 2000). Magolego countered by observing how ineffective the ANC, and the government, had been in dealing with disorder: "Mapogo would cease to exist if the government was tough on crime," he declared, and vowed that his followers would arrest corrupt police in Limpopo Province. They promptly "disciplined" a constable in Groblersdal suspected of theft (Premdev and Chetty 1999).

THE BOUNDARIES OF FREEDOM

Informal justice of the kinds meted out by Mapogo boldly usurps the powers of the state and raises the prospect of lawlessness, of an irresponsible public sphere, of "the dark side of freedom" (Steinberg 1999a). No wonder the government has responded with ambivalence that borders on incoherence. In 1998, the two provinces most affected by Magolego's activities took diametrically opposed approaches to them. In Mpumalanga, police officials adopted a firm "antivigilante" stance; Premier Matthews Phosa insisted that Mapogo was no better than "a gang of common criminals" and asserted that no group that rivaled official law enforcement agencies would be recognized, negotiated with, or tolerated. His counterparts in Limpopo Province, by contrast, arranged to meet with the movement's leadership. It is true that this has yet to produce a framework for cooperation, but province officials insisted that "the bona fides of Mapogo's leadership" were not in question.[20]

Although there have been efforts to prosecute members of Mapogo on charges of murder, kidnapping, assault, and torture, the movement remains legal (Swindells 1999). Nor does it appear that police interfere with its operations very much. "We [tell] them to bugger off," a white steelworker and Mapogo member from Tsaneen is reported to have said. Apparently, "they" comply (Soggot and Ngobeni 1999).

Nevertheless, police harassment looms large in Mapogo's discourse. In Limpopo Province, Magolego points out, a special detachment within the Serious Violent Crime Unit was formed specifically to concentrate on the movement: "[They] regard us as criminals. But we are stopping crime, and assisting the police, and hence the entire government of South Africa." In the new South Africa, Magolego continued, there is nothing like the right of "citizen's arrest." Quite the opposite: police are hampered by the need for search warrants to follow up leads and criminals have excessive rights. In order to get evidence, he chuckled, one sometimes had to apply pressure—"If you need water out of a sponge, you squeeze it a little." Magolego became agitated as he mentioned a Limpopo Province police report that found a total of two hundred twenty cases pending against people identified with the movement. And yet many policemen also belong to his organization, he said. They shake his hand when they meet him, urge him to keep up his campaign, and pledge their silent support.

Mapogo's success invites questions about police legitimacy. The premier of Mpumalanga expressed the view that predominated before the public sphere was reconfigured in South Africa in the 1990s; recall his refusal to acknowledge any "rivals" to "official law enforcement agencies." In this view, the state alone confers the authority to police citizens. But Mapogo *was* taken seriously as a policing operation; by marketing and branding itself skillfully, and by manipulating its news media coverage, it established its presence as a powerful agency of enforcement in the public perception. This reflects its mastery of the ways and means of neoliberalism, which created the opening for Mapogo in the first place.

In spite of seeing himself as under siege, or perhaps because of this, John Magolego has always had grand ambitions. Two controversial and failed efforts by the state to prosecute him for murder seem not have dislodged these ambitions.[21] Magolego is searching out anticrime groups elsewhere in the world in hopes of convening a summit and leveraging funds. He is acutely aware that his movement is part of a global phenomenon. He is right. Although it vests its operations in distinctive regional idioms and patterns of social relationship, Mapogo does seem to be the result of current exigencies of worldwide scale. Like alternative policing elsewhere, it seems to be an ideologically motivated response to the effect that neoliberal conditions have on the ability of states, especially post-totalitarian states, to maintain law and order. To wit, Magolego and Mapogo are living embodiments of the argument we made at the beginning. They have been able to appeal to notions of "traditional" African justice and simultaneously to the frontier enforcement of the white right; signs, here, of the rise of "authoritarian populism," a refraction of the "responsible public sphere" asserting an underside that cuts across old divisions of race and culture (Steinberg 1999a). More generally, though, what might all this tell us about the political economy of law and order in South Africa and elsewhere in the world at present?

One explanation of Mapogo is essentially economic: that for the rural white and black petty bourgeoisie it is an affordable and populist version of more expensive security services, such as Baywatch. But this does not account for Mapogo's complex form, for the principles that unite its members, or for the common views they appear to hold on a range of social issues that give shape to perceptions of disorder. One such issue involves the uncivil war between generations in South Africa. It is notable how frequently Magolego stressed the youthfulness of the criminals who were the sworn opponents of his movement. And how he characterized the way Mapogo empowers citizens, permitting them to "take care of the boy next door" without fear. One Mapogo member, speaking to a reporter, said the point of such discipline was to "take someone young and unemployed, someone with no wife, someone who may well put food in his mouth by stealing from someone like me, and make him beg for mercy" (Steinberg 1999a). Also notable is the way Magolego also expressed his concern for "businessmen," a term connoting not merely affluence but social seniority as well. The only concerted opposition to the organization in rural communities has come from young men, who have boycotted shops owned by members of Mapogo. Who exactly *are* the criminals in this pitched battle between generations? In its effort to impose order from below, is Mapogo also criminalizing youth? Is the organization a gerontocracy striking back in a drama in which age has become tantamount to class? How might this conflict relate to the broader historical conditions behind the rise of informal policing, such as the growing privatization of the means of producing social order or the problematic reification of "the community"?

As noted earlier, Magolego himself was a veteran of longer-standing conflicts in Sekhukhuneland that pitted young people against senior black men of means. These were battles that had their analogue across the country during the 1980s, when, after the Soweto uprising, black youths declared war on their parents for having acquiesced to, or even profited from, the forces of domination. Violent clashes of this sort were common in villages in Sekhukhuneland at the time, as young men waving homemade ANC and South African Communist Party flags engaged in "mass action" against so-called "sell-outs"—traditional authorities and mature men of business such as Magolego, who hired "vigilantes" to counter them. Times have changed. The revolution has come and gone. But the youths are still on the margins. Some rural areas in the North West Province today have unemployment rates of more than 60 percent. Now "traditional authority" is nostalgically revived, and black businessmen are celebrated as the organic agents of another revolution, the coming of the Age of Neoliberalism. Now the youthful comrades of the heroic past threaten law and order, the Magolegos of the new world piously oppose them in the name of "community" and civility, and the youths "fight back with blind rage" (Steinberg 1999a).

The struggle for social order in the countryside, then, is rooted not merely in post-colonial conditions but also in a transformation that predated the end of apartheid and was the conditions for its demise: the triumph of neoliberal capitalism on a global scale, itself best viewed as a set of material, social, technological, and moral processes that play themselves out in locally grounded dialectics. One such dialectic is the growing salience of generation as a principle of social determination, both in respect of the distribution of power and resources, and of popular perceptions of conflict and disorder.

CONCLUSION

The South African writer John Coetzee once asked us whether we thought it possible to classify human societies according to the manner in which they "managed the problem of youth." It was a profound question that displayed Coetzee's customary capacity to get beneath the surface reality of things, thus to probe the horizons of history. And it challenges us to think about why it is that, not only in South Africa, the troubled face of the young manifests so graphically the disquieting implications of our "new world order."

Elsewhere we have argued that youths, from the ghettos of Chicago and Los Angeles to the *backveld* of Limpopo and the North West provinces, have tended to assume the status of a new underclass as the effects of neoliberalism have disproportionately disadvantaged young men in formerly working-class communities (Comaroff and Comaroff 2000). This was especially so after South Africa's transition to democracy, which was undermined by increasing unemployment; not coincidentally, there was, at the time, an upsurge of witch hunting in which the witches were mostly old and the hunters mostly youths. The post-apartheid state found itself challenged by precisely the liminal violence previously courted by the ANC among adolescents to destabilize the illegitimate Afrikaner regime. It was these "veterans" who suffered most acutely the effects of a society seeking to reconcile liberation with (neo)liberalization. The collapse of the old system of labor-intensive industrial production, based as it was on migrant labor, had its most brutal impact in rural areas like Sekhukhuneland, eroding the infrastructure of peasant-proletarian life, the male career, and the means of reproducing communal worlds (Comaroff and Comaroff 1999; Delius 1996). At the same time, new appetites and expectations emerged, propelled by expanded educational access and by global media directed at the young. The frustration of thwarted desire was goaded by the visible wealth of those with established footholds in the economy, those who had been able to capitalize on the entrepreneurial opportunities opened up by privatization, those who seemed to accumulate wealth while their kin and neighbors struggled. Young men, claiming to act in the communal interest, turned their wrath on people who benefited from this new wealth; and it is from their victims, and other propertied citizens preyed upon by crime, that Mapogo draws its impetus and continuing support. In the process, youth are criminalized. They become the nightmare anticitizens who must be disciplined if order is to be restored.

Issues of generation are thus central to struggles in the name of justice and order in the South African countryside. They are also part of the more encompassing historical shifts of which we spoke at the outset: the increasing tendency to privatize the means of security as old norms disintegrate and the center cannot hold. Here the metaphysics of disorder are depicted, graphically, in age-based images of violence, images that justify the various forms of counterviolence we have discussed. That counterviolence is the product of a historical moment in which the very notions of community, civility, citizenship, and order are in deep dispute. In this moment the state no longer has sole monopoly over the means of force, nor the capacity to secure the peace. It is these conditions, as much as the exigencies of violent crime per se, that call forth the host of complexly wrought enforcement enterprises we have discussed. Despite their manifest imperfections, these belong to a larger effort, not merely to confront disorder, but to establish new visions of moral being and social responsibility, to conjure community from the ashes.

NOTES

This chapter is an abridged version of a lecture delivered as part of the Jensen Memorial Lectures in June 2001 at Goethe-Universität, in Frankfurt am Main, Germany. Written in Cape Town and Frankfurt, it is based on research undertaken in 1999 and 2000.

1. A survey of 2,486 households conducted by Nielsen Market Research Africa in late 1999 confirms this. It found that nearly half of South Africans support local vigilante groups. The support was higher among the poor and blacks, who live in less policed areas, than it was in richer white communities (Goko 1999).

2. Numerous studies and reports, both empirical and analytical, have traced the social and material impact of neoliberalism on post-colonial societies around the world. *Report on the World Social Situation 2005: The Inequality Predicament* (United Nations 2005) is a recent and comprehensive example; see also Joseph Stiglitz (2002) and, for a more general discussion of the downsides of market fundamentalism, John Gray (1998). On the way in which neoliberal policies have changed economic and social conditions in South Africa in particular, see, among many other studies, Patrick Bond (2003); Adam Habib and Vishnu Padayachee (2000); David A. McDonald and John Pape (2002); and John S. Sharp (1998).

3. Riebe was a police commander in East Berlin during the late Cold War years.

4. We came to know Inspector Lefenyo well and had many conversations with her. These comments are from an interview conducted at Lomanyaneng Police Station on February 24, 2000.

5. Joe Leteane, in a conversation with the authors at his home in Mafikeng on August 8, 2000.

6. The role of the South African National Civics Organization in community life can, however, be ambiguous. In Mdantsane in the Eastern Cape Province, the local chapter has been accused of being behind vigilante activity (Premdev and Chetty 1999).

7. Before his death in 2000, Chief Setumo told us how determined he was to prove that his realm could be "cleaned out" of miscreants.

8. This account is based on several conversations with Josephine Seleko, her mother, her employer, and members of the Tshidi-Barolong royal kgotla (chiefly court), from March 14 to June 9, 2000.

9. His address to the "Believers' Summit on Religion and Crime" was reported in "Crime, Violence and Religion," *The Mail*, May 29, 1998. A similar plea was made, before the same audience, by Mduduzi Mashiyane, of the Institute for Democracy in South Africa (*The Mail* 1999b).

10. For two reports, somewhat conflicting, see Gill Gifford (2000) and Selby Bokaba (2000). The first of these reports refers to the Ithutheng Trust as the Student Trust, established by Nelson Mandela, whose director, Jackie Maarohanye, claims that she organized the event after the former president asked her to tackle the crime problem in schools.

11. In putting a stop to the practice, the police commissioner at the time, George Fivaz, "issued a circular that police reservists are not allowed to perform police work on a private basis." According to our police sources, though, many officers do work privately, although not in uniform. In one Johannesburg neighborhood, it appears that six reservists continued for some time to serve as "street managers," without uniform or guns, using cell phones to communicate with the SAPS in the event of trouble.

12. Interview with John Monhle Magolego in Acornhoek, March 11, 2000.

13. In 1998, there were reports of a split in the organization over its violent methods and the question of whether to abandon them. Although some senior members favored abiding by the law, Magolego believed that "criminals should get a taste of their own medicine." He prevailed. In 2000, there were rumors that a white member, a building contractor named Pieter Oosthuizen, was "restructuring and even computerizing" Mapogo's activities and taking over its financial management, leaving Magolego to concentrate on "being the leader." Magolego denied this. He repudiated Oosthuizen's claim to authority and implied that some Afrikaner cadres had tried to exert unwarranted control (Morobi 2000; Steinberg 1998b).

14. In the interview of March 11, 2000, Magolego sought to impress on us the difficulty of assessing the size of Mapogo's membership.

15. On such occasions, Magolego sometimes dons a ceremonial blazer with gold tassels and leopard-skin epaulets and pockets (Soggot and Ngobeni 1999).

16. Magolego insists that the organization is not lucrative. Members are assessed an annual fee, based on what they can afford; the average is between the equivalent of about eight and sixteen U.S. dollars. Businesses pay a hefty amount to join and are charged on a monthly basis, according to size; the range seems to be from about sixty to one hundred sixty dollars. Much of Mapogo's income goes toward legal costs, as members have often been brought before the courts.

17. Magolego has obviously told this story before (Soggot and Ngobeni 1999). But there is evidence that such events have occurred: two members of Mapogo were charged with murder and accused of having fed a man to crocodiles in the Kruger National Park in January 2001 (*Mail and Guardian* 2001).

18. Magolego has drawn vocal support from some highly visible right-wingers, such as Gaye Derby-Lewis, who was handed down a life sentence for plotting the murder of the South African Communist Party leader Chris Hani in 1993. Derby-Lewis, whose husband, Clive, is a former member of parliament, claims to have helped found the Pretoria branch of Mapogo and to have signed up new members in the city (Gilmore 1999).

19. Informal courts are alleged to have been convened by Mapogo in order to deal with suspected criminals. In one reported case, a Mamelodi housewife appealed to the Pretoria High Court for protection against having to appear in one such "court," having been fingered by a diviner as a thief (*The Star* 2000).

20. A Limpopo Province spokesman stated in October 1998 that the leaders of the organization had earlier signed an agreement pledging not to inflict instant justice on apprehended felons. It had not been honored, however (Steinberg 1998a).

21. In Limpopo Province, Magolego and eleven other Mapogo cadres were charged in 2000 with the murder of a young male shop burglar. The charges were dropped in August of that year because reliable witnesses could not be found. In October 2001, Magolego was again indicted for homicide, in this instance in connection with the 1999 death in Greater Phalaborwa of Motlatsi Mafisa, a Mapogo leader who was alleged to have embezzled its funds. This case, too, eventually collapsed.

REFERENCES

African National Congress (ANC). 1999a. ANC Daily News Briefing, June 24, 1999.
——. 1999b. "Vigilante Groups on March with Whips, Guns and Petrol Cans." ANC Daily News Briefing, July 23, 1999.

Bokaba, Selby. 2000. "Ditched Weapons Sink Without Trace." *The Star* (Gauteng Province, South Africa), March 14, 2000.

Bond, Patrick. 2003. *Against Global Apartheid: South Africa Meets the World Bank, IMF and International Finance.* New York: Zed Books.

Bothma, Peet. 2000. "Mapogo—Refleksie Op Polisie" ["Mapogo—Reflection on Police"]. *Die Beeld* (Johannesburg), November 26, 2000.

The Citizen. 1999. "Residents in Bloody Vigilante Gang Spree." November 22, 1999.

Comaroff, Jean, and John L. Comaroff. 1999. "Réflexions sur la jeunesse: Du passé à la post-colonie" ["Reflections on Youth: From the Past to the Postcolony"]. *Politique Africaine* 80 (December): 90–110.

———. 2000. "Occult Economies and the Violence of Abstraction: Notes from the South African Postcolony." *American Ethnologist* 26(3): 279–301.

Delius, Peter. 1996. *A Lion Amongst the Cattle: Reconstruction and Resistance in the Northern Transvaal.* Portsmouth, N.H.: Heinemann.

Dlakavu, Monde. 2001. "Three Thieves Saved from Street Flogging." *Cape Argus* (Cape Town, South Africa), January 8, 2001.

Gifford, Gill. 2000. "Emotional Scenes as Soweto Youths Throw Their Weapons Away." *The Star* (Gauteng Province, South Africa), March 13, 2000.

Gilmore, Inigo. 1999. "Derby-Lewis Joins Mapogo." *Sunday World* (Johannesburg), July 4, 1999.

Goko, Jetho. 1999. "Two Out of Three Have No Faith in Police, Says Survey." *Business Day,* November 15, 1999.

Gray, John. 1998. *False Dawn: The Delusions of Global Capitalism.* London: Granta.

Habib, Adam, and Vishnu Padayachee. 2000. "Economic Policy and Power Relations in South Africa's Transition to Democracy." *World Development* 28(2): 245–63.

Haysom, Nicholas. 1986. "Mabangalala: The Rise of Right-Wing Vigilantes in South Africa." Occasional paper no. 10. Johannesburg: University of the Witwatersrand, Centre for Legal Studies.

Hlahla, Patrick. 2000. "Churches Urged to Fight Crime." *Pretoria News,* June 30, 2000.

Kane-Berman, John. 1977. *Soweto: Black Revolt White Reaction.* Johannesburg: South African Institute of Race Relations.

Magardie, Khadija. 2000a. "Westbury Women Do For Themselves." *Mail & Guardian* (Johannesburg), February 11–17, 2000.

———. 2000b. "Alternative Justice Settles Disputes." *Mail & Guardian* (Johannesburg), March 31-April 6, 2000.

The Mail (Mafikeng, South Africa). 1997a. "MDF's Prayers Against Crime." March 21, 1997.

———. 1997b. "Prayers vs. Crime." April 4, 1997.

———. 1998. "Crime, Violence and Religion." May 29, 1998.

———. 1999a. "Dept., School and Barolong to Take Fight to Criminals." November 5, 1999.

———. 1999b. "Community Policing: Role of the Church." May 29, 1999.

Mail & Guardian (Johannesburg). 2001. "Charged with Murder." January 19–25, 2001.

Makgotho, Selby. 2000. "Vigilantes Threaten to 'Arrest' Corrupt Police." *City Press* (Johannesburg), February 27, 2000.

Martin, Jeffrey T. 2000. "Social Orders and Their Guardians: Policing, Ritual and Tradition in Contemporary Taiwan." Ph.D. dissertation, University of Chicago.

Mathiane, Nomavenda. 1999. "To Some This Man Is a Saint—To Others Just a Vigilante." *Business Day,* June 25, 1999.

Mbatha, Shalo. 2001. "Striking Back and Feeling Good About It." *The Sunday Independent* (Johannesburg). March 4, 2001.

McDonald, David A., and John Pape, editors. 2002. *Cost Recovery and the Crisis of Service Delivery in South Africa.* Pretoria, South Africa: Human Sciences Research Council Publishers, and London: Zed Books.

McGreal, Chris. 1999. "We Fight Crime the African Way." *Guardian Unlimited* (London), May 12, 1999.

Minnaar, Anthony. 1995. "Desperate Justice. Crime and Conflict." *Indicator South Africa* no. 2. Durban, South Africa: University of Natal, Centre for Social and Development Studies.

Molwedi, Phomello. 2000. "Sex Vigilante Guilty of Rape." *The Star* (Gauteng Province, South Africa), July 28, 2000.

Morobi, Phillip. 2000. "Mapogo's Sharp Claws Attract White Members." *City Press* (Johannesburg), March 5, 2000.

Ngobeni, Evidence wa ka. 2000a. "Red Tape Snags 'Bobbies on the Beat' Plan." *Mail & Guardian* (Johannesburg), March 3–9, 2000.

———. 2000b. "Mapogo Goes Mainstream." *Mail & Guardian* (Johannesburg), June 15–22, 2000.

Ngobeni, Evidence wa ka, Pule waga Mabe, and Ntuthuko Maphumulo. 2000. "Law Breaks Down in Mamelodi." *Mail & Guardian* (Johannesburg), August 11–17, 2000.

Premdev, Sharlene, and Kuben Chetty. 1999. "The Brutal Hand of Vigilante Justice." *Democracy Watch* 7: 2–3.

Sharp, John S. 1998. " 'Non-Racialism' and Its Discontents: A Post-Apartheid Paradox." *International Social Science Journal* 50(156): 243–52.

Soggot, Mungo, and Evidence wa ka Ngobeni. 1999. " 'We Must Work on Their Buttocks.' " In *The Mail & Guardian Bedside Book, 1999,* edited by D. Macfarlane. Auckland Park, South Africa: Mail & Guardian.

The Star (Gauteng Province, South Africa). 2000. "Wife Gets Protection from Vigilantes." February 4, 2000.

Steinberg, Jonny. 1998a. "Provinces Adopt Conflicting Stances on Mapogo." *Business Day,* October 6, 1998.

———. 1998b. "Vigilante Group Splits Over Illegal Methods." *Business Day,* October 8, 1998.

———. 1999a. "Guilt Is Not the Point for Vigilante Group," *Business Day,* August 25, 1999.

———. 1999b. "Freedom Breeds Crime: Grist for Authoritarian Mill." *Business Day,* September 15, 1999. Online edition. Accessed at http://www.bday.co.za/99/0915/comment/e8.htm, January 10, 2001.

Stiglitz, Joseph E. 2002. *Globalization and Its Discontents.* New York: Norton.

Swindells, Steven. 1999. "Mapogo Leader Defends Street Justice." *Woza* (online journal), November 26, 1999. Accessed January 10, 2001 at www.aegis.com/news/woza.

United Nations. 2005. *Report on the World Social Situation 2005: The Inequality Predicament.* New York: Department of Economic and Social Affairs, Division for Social Policy and Development. Accessed May 17, 2006 at http://www.un.org/esa/socdev/rwss/media%2005/cd-docs/media.htm.

Watkin, Daniel. 1999. "Vigilantes Push Limits of Justice in South Africa." *Detroit (Mich.) News,* July 18, 1999.

PART IV

Legitimacy and
Minority-Group Relations

CHAPTER 13

Introduction

The issue of minority-group relations can be approached in a variety of ways. One approach involves focusing on social dynamics and examines the way that societies manage the problems of having distinct social groups within a common social and legal system. These issues are confounded with questions of poverty and social marginality, since both recent immigrants and the members of stigmatized groups are likely to be poorer and less well educated, and to live in areas that suffer from a variety of social problems, including high levels of crime and incivility. Irrespective of whether the defining framework is ethnicity, religion, or social class, the problem of maintaining social order becomes more complex when societies have to deal with social groups that are more socially marginal and, hence, more likely to be involved in and victimized by criminal activity.

America is an example of a society that has a long and troubled history of difficulty in the relationship between legal authorities and the minority community. The stormy relationship between the police and the African American community is one example. Studies of trust and confidence in the police, the courts, and the law have found strikingly lower ratings among African Americans than among whites for decades. And, as the chapters in this section make clear, there are similar ethnic tensions in European societies. Hans-Jörg Albrecht, for example, details the differential experiences of minority and nonminority residents of Germany with the legal system, and Catrien Bijleveld, Heike Goudriaan, and Marijke Malsch examine how increasing diversity is being managed in the Netherlands.

It is also possible to address issues involving minority groups by looking at the statistics involving minority-group involvement in the criminal-justice system. If a substantial difference is found, say, in the proportion of people in different groups who are arrested, incarcerated, and so forth, this suggests a problem within the system. Authors of chapters in this section of the volume also point to such evidence of differential outcomes, raising questions about the actual effectiveness and fairness of criminal-justice systems.

And, finally, the chapters raise issues concerning how societies deal with questions of diversity. France provides one clear model, since the French choose not to collect ethnicity-based data or to address policy issues in terms of ethnic groups, basing their model upon a "color-blind" form of Republicanism in which everyone is considered by definition to be an equal member of civil society. Roché outlines this policy and examines its impact upon the criminal-justice system in France. It is difficult to form a clear sense of how minority-group members are treated in the criminal-justice system, as well as how they view their experiences with legal authorities. One clear hint about such feelings is provided by the wave of riots that has recently occurred in France. These riots and their social implications are addressed by Sophie Body-Gendrot in chapter 14.

Overall, these chapters point to the multiplicity of ways that societies can deal with the ethnic, religious, historical, or other subgroups that exist within them. They can ignore such groups, focusing on only the national or superordinate group. They can acknowledge the various groups, but encourage loyalty only to one superordinate group. In the United States, for example, people are encouraged to assimilate into one dominant culture. Only one language is viewed as official, and everyone is encouraged to speak it. Finally, countries can embrace diversity and try to celebrate the unique aspects of their many cultures. In Canada, for example, differences in language (at least, French and English) are acknowledged, and given official status.

The manner in which a society seeks to deal with difference shapes the way it manages social order. It influences whether group-based differences are recognized and viewed as potentially problematic. It has implications for whether the police view policing minority communities as problematic, and whether they adopt particular strategies of policing based upon ethnicity. The manner chosen, conversely, also shapes whether the members of a society think of their own experience in group-based terms, viewing their disparate treatment as linked to their membership in particular groups. And, it shapes whether and why people break social rules and, even, rise up against the state, either as individuals committing crimes or as groups taking collective action.

CHAPTER 14

Police, Justice, and Youth Violence in France

Sophie Body-Gendrot

On November 12, 2005, a caption under a picture of burned cars at Clichy-sous-Bois, published by the *New York Times*, read: "Disorders in immigrant enclaves in France remind many of the 1960s in the U.S. or the riots in Los Angeles." The media, using words such as *disorders, riots, disturbances, unrest, rebellion, confrontation, lawlessness,* and many more in an indistinguishable fashion, make all events look alike. By using blanket words, such as "riots," in this case, they combine in one category phenomena that are in fact distinct from one country, one city, one month, one year to another. What they have in common is to evoke an unbearable threat to social order. But then while the Anglo-American media emphasized "the ethnicity of the rioters, the clash of civilizations, the fury of Muslims of North African descent, the role of French Arabs and of French Africans" (Smith 2005), the French media focused on the social causes of the rebellion and on the consequences of globalization for post-Fordist, marginalized, working-class areas.

The reason why I do not use the term "riot" for these forms of violence is because they are not a "prelude to negotiation" (Hobsbawn 1959), they do not lead to further social integration via their transformations into conflicts. What is striking is that these youths ask nothing. They probably are aware that there are no structures, there is no social proposal elaborated to engage in a dialogue with them. On the contrary, disorders erupt and will erupt again, as a consequence of the powerlessness of the state and of society's general indifference to what takes place at its margins. The nature, the futility, the contagion of the events and their questioning of the state mark a major difference with those of the United States.

There are similarities, however. First, the relegation of 8 percent of the French population (4.6 million of 63 million) to "sensitive urban zones" (ZUS) (Délégation Interministérielle à la Ville 2004; see also Roché, chapter 17, this volume). The average unemployment rate in France has been around 10 percent for about twenty years, but in these neighborhoods, the rate averages 20 percent; it may be as high as 40 percent of the working-age population in certain areas and be even 15 percent higher for youths and for immigrants. In the United States, according to studies by Gary Orfield (2004) and Ronald Mincy (2004), half of black men in their twenties were jobless in 2004, up from 46 percent in 2000; the rate was 72 percent for black high-school-dropout males, compared with 34 percent of white dropouts and 19 percent of Hispanic dropouts (Eckholm 2006, 2). In French problem areas, 27 percent of the population is poor, three times as many as elsewhere. The concentration of ethnic and racial minorities, with heavy social handicaps, either because they have just arrived or are single-parent families with numerous young children or suffer various types of dislocations, is another convergence with conditions in American ghettos. Thirty-one percent of these populations are under twenty years old (versus 24 percent on average nationwide). Schools, medical facilities, public transportation, and public housing respond inadequately to the demands of parents, tenants, and commuters unable to afford private services. Half the population (52 percent) say they are victims of vandalism and damages (versus 26 percent elsewhere). Drug dealing and other illicit activity in the underground economy make whole families meet both ends. The appropriation of specific public spaces by youth groups dealing drugs is very visible.

Subtle hierarchies are revealed by paths of mutual avoidance among groups, but on the whole, the existence of these zones has an impact on all the residents, who are reluctant to give their address when searching for a job, or in their personal lives.[1] The general rejection of such neighborhoods comes from two sources: their neglect by the rest of society, which generates feelings of resentment and frustration among the most disadvantaged, and the development of "counterworlds," closed communities, the representations of which frighten the general population.

As for the catalyst for urban violence, in the United States as in France, it is almost always a result of a clash between youth gangs and the police, or of a miscarriage of justice, but is born of a history of accumulated grievances. Despite hundreds of editorials written or pronounced after the French events (with a lot of sympathy for the rioters expressed by many members of the elite), what occurred gave an impression of "déjà vu" as if urban threats from marginalized places and residents inevitably resurface periodically in society.[2] After two youths were accidentally electrocuted while purportedly fleeing the police in Clichy-sous-Bois, a problem area in the Parisian region, around ten percent of youths revolted emotionally and torched cars to make a statement of distress and anger. (By contrast, in the United States, according to the Kerner Commission report,[3] many of the 10 percent or so who mobilized in hundreds of riots that took place between 1963 and 1971 in the States were young blacks, who had just lost their jobs; see Body-Gendrot 1993). Torching cars is not usual, it is one resource in the limited repertoire these youths have. Another resource they have is their cell phones, either to communicate with other youths about actions to take and maybe to challenge them or to watch the news and check whether their specific action has been covered. Journalists report that they are abandoned as soon as the news starts, because the youths gather around their cell phones. A jubilant competition that I observed in Strasbourg, where cars are traditionally burned on New Year's Eve or Bastille Day, occurs among youths from poor areas, stimulated by the presence of television cameras and by the potential attention they can get. The pressure these peer groups exert on individual youths to mobilize cannot be underestimated.

In the French disorders, as elsewhere, two sources of violence were in evidence. One is acting out on the part of frustrated teenagers, who are strongly influenced by consumption images and immediate satisfaction (they frequently burned primary schools because they were closer to their housing projects than high schools and had to watch their own turfs). Second, violence was used to create chaos for secondary motivations such as revenge (a bus depot was set on fire by a fired employee), a desire to destroy the status quo (radical groups), or because of a mental disorder (as several mayors remarked).

It must also be emphasized once more that place mattered and that the forms the disorders took from one locality to the other and from one region to the other differed. Paris was not burning. It seems that the minister of the interior was carefully monitoring the youths' blogs; when an allusion to carrying the disorders to the Champs Élysées was made, three thousand policemen were immediately deployed. The torched cars or phone booths that attracted the television crews were frequently in just one or two streets (as in Toulouse). Unrest would start in the evening, so youths could avoid being seen and because fire is more dramatic against a dark background. In 60 percent of the "banlieues" (suburbs) there were no disturbances whatsoever, because mayors, religious leaders, public housing managers, and parents were smart enough to calm things down. The mayors' reluctance to resort to curfews and the restraint with which most of them as well as policemen, educators, and other social actors acted after a national emergency law was passed is a proof in point.

But there are also other deep divergences from the U.S. situation. The centrality of race, the unique history of African Americans imported as slaves, the denial of their full citizenship with the complacence of national and local authorities for centuries, then the civil rights movement, the efforts launched by institutions in the 1960s to redress this situation and the impatience with their slow pace are major aspects of the American context of the riots of the 1960s (Katznelson 2005). The Kerner Commission, pointing to "two societies, one black, one white, separate and unequal" in 1968, encapsulated the American dilemma. In the French problem areas, thirty to forty different nationalities live together, frequently in massive housing projects, together with poor old-stock French families, but multiculturalism is not acknowledged because the second and third generations of children born to immigrants are officially French.

Then, subsidized housing in the United States represents less than 2 percent of the housing stock and it carries a negative stereotype for those who live there. If they can, Americans (about 67 percent) try to move out of public housing and to own their homes (Roberts 2004, 178). Currently, half the population of the historical ghetto of Chicago has moved out. The infamous Robert Taylor Homes have disappeared, vouchers help families willing to do so to leave blighted areas. By contrast, in France, only half the population owns their home, and in the sensitive zones, 61 percent are tenants in public housing. There, 86 percent of housing is collective public housing (Délégation Interministérielle à la Ville 2004, 3). The state spends 1.9 percent of the gross domestic product on subsidized housing, one of the highest rates in Europe, and the quality is considered high (Bennhold 2005). The waiting lists for public housing being huge and the turnover slow, it takes about eight years to get an apartment. Legitimacy is given to tenancy in public housing, which is viewed a desirable good. This points to the specific relationship the French have to the state. It is not accidental that, besides the 10.346 vehicles burned, 255 schools, 233 public buildings, and 51 post offices were also vandalized and 140 public-transport vehicles were stoned.

The human cost of the disorders is also different than in the United States. "Only" two other deaths occurred in November 2005, and in one, the motivation seems to have been personal revenge rather than general rioting. In the United States during the bloody summers of the 1960s rioting led to many fatalities (the American policing style differed from that of the French during the uprisings; on the differences, see Body-Gendrot 2006). Between 1967 and 1968, the number of deaths from the riots fell from 87 to 19, according to the attorney general's data. The rioters found that they had little to gain by destroying their own neighborhoods and had more to gain by organizing politically and developing strategies and defined goals and avoiding confrontations with the police.

Three weeks of disorders in France are estimated to have cost €200 million (Bronner and Ceaux 2005; Rutten 1992); three days of rioting in Los Angeles in 1992 carried a cost of about $750 million dollars. After the November incidents in France, 4,400 people were detained and 800 were incarcerated. Out of the 498 juveniles sent to a juvenile court judge, 108 were locked up (Arteta 2005, 100; Rivayrand 2006). Most high school students with clean records were freed after their arrest for lack of convincing evidence.

Finally, the length of the French outbreaks, the way they spread from city to city, and the severe damage they caused revealed the depth of the social malaise in a centralized country like France. The disorders seem to be the tip of an iceberg. Many residents, although they did not participate, said that they "understood" this revolt because, since the beginning of the 1980s, government policy has failed to stem the social and economic deterioration that these areas experience or create better institutions (many emphasized the failure of public education), or deal with the contempt, discrimination, and racism that residents experience and resent, and has not solicited their participation in urban renewal policies. Student unrest in the spring of 2006 is another expression of this malaise. It reveals a loss of bearings and anxiety regarding a precarious future, a deep disenchantment with and distrust of political elites, and a resentment at the state, which formerly used to act as a buffer against change but now seems to be standing aside passively.

This chapter examines the phenomenon of urban violence that has developed in France over a quarter of century, generated by clashes between some youths and some policemen. Who are these adversaries?

On the one hand, the French police. France has a centralized police and gendarmerie system of 220,000 men in various units, who see themselves as the strong arm of the state. The country is the most policed in Europe after Spain and Italy, but the ratio of police officers to inhabitants is uneven throughout the country. Paris has one policeman per 120 residents and on average, the suburbs have one per 160. Police officers are accountable to the Interior Ministry or, in the case of gendarmes, to the Army Ministry. Traditionally, the gendarmes—90,000 men—operate in the hinterland (3600 brigades) with multiple functions and participate in police investigations. They live among the population in caserns. Their anti-riot corps is the Compagnie Republicaine de Sécurité (CRS). The police forces—130,000 men—are meant to maintain public order, mostly in cities (the police control 15 percent of the territory) to prevent disorders and protect the state. Sections of the police, such as the Brigades Anti-Criminalité (BAC), operate undercover (30 percent of policemen do not wear a uniform).

Policies coming from the top regarding police priorities have changed frequently in recent decades, from maintaining law and order, protecting the state, and fighting against organized crime to a tougher posture against petty crimes and more communication of crime statistics.[4] Experiments in community policing were undertaken in the mid-1980s but the gap between theory and practice has never been filled. "Government control over the police has transformed city police forces into local detachments of a state police, socially and functionally cut off from the city," Dominique Monjardet remarks (1996, 21). Neighborhood police represent less than 3 percent of all police officers and they are looked down upon by numerous policemen and their unions (Body-Gendrot 2000, 86). Indeed the idea of a police officer having ties to the place where he works is inimitable to the system (Zauberman and Levy 2003, 1067):

> Concern with the proximity between the police and population is only meaningful within a conception in which the police are not only serving the state but are answerable for the services they deliver to the public, and this requires cooperation from the public. When controlling disorders is the main concern, such proximity is a handicap. . . . Police officials [in France]

are not accountable to anyone but the central administration and are evaluated on the basis of their ability to act in conformity with the expectations of the latter and to implement the directions specified uniformly for the entire country. . . . There is no tie between officers and the place where they work. . . . They are recruited throughout the country and assigned according to needs; many end up in a city they are generally ignorant of and spend the better part of their career attempting to return to their own region through a series of transfers.

On the other hand, a minority of second or third male generations from formerly colonized countries who are French contend with the police.[5] France has the largest Muslim community in Europe (see table 14.1); Muslims are an important component of the immigrant populations.[6]

It is estimated that there are between 1.5 million and 2 million second-generation citizens of North African origin (but they may be third or fourth generations). Tolerance for diversity is not a feature of French culture. Though racist attitudes continue to diminish in French society, xenophobia is still pronounced, as elsewhere in Europe, and in 2005, 30 percent of the French admitted to sharing Le Pen's ideas.[7] Because France had a long and tormented political past, rife with religious strife, the 1905 law of separation between church and state is viewed by numerous French as protecting the state from religious infringements. This situation explains why French culture is currently not ready to "step down" to accommodate particular demands from Islam that would bring religion into the public space, as shown by the controversy over the head scarf (see Diana Pinto, "The Long, Bloody Path That Led to French Secularism," *International Herald Tribune,* January 8, 2004; Body-Gendrot 2007a).

A few words of explanation: There is no doubt that for a Muslim outsider, the 2004 law banning head scarves (hidjabs) in public schools is astonishing. Who would have thought that a piece of cloth could threaten the stability of French society? How could the birthplace of human rights be so intolerant? One cannot understand this law without taking into account the specific historical and current context, the sacralization of secularism that is the legacy of a history of religious wars; the painful relationship of religion, schools and politics; the status of Islam; and the dysfunctional attempts to integrate post-colonial populations into French society. The law was passed for petty political motivations, but it should be recalled that the ban concerned twelve hundred girls out of probably two hundred thousand Muslim girls. The motivations of the former group were varied (cultural, militant, meant to avoid conflict and harassment, and so forth), whereas the vast majority of the latter group did not want to be essentialized as Muslims. They defended their individual rights (our bodies, ourselves) to be enforced by the Republican law, demanding legal protection against the violence of older brothers and fundamentalists if they did not veil themselves. It is difficult to evaluate how many cases occurred and the hearings held by an ad hoc commission (chaired by

TABLE 14.1   MUSLIMS IN SIX EUROPEAN COUNTRIES

	Number of Muslims (1982 Estimate) (Millions)	Number of Muslims (Most Recent Estimate) (Millions)	Percentage of Population (Most Recent Estimate)
France	2.50	5 (1998)	7
Germany	1.80	3 (2004)	3.6
Italy	0.12	0.825 (2003)	1.4
Netherlands	0.40	0.945 (2004)	5.3
Spain	0.12	0.485 (2003)	1.1
United Kingdom	1.25	1.6	2.8

Source: Dialogues: The Islamic World—U.S.—The West. Conference Report. Salzburg, Austria, May 15–17, 2007, 11.

Bernard Stasi, a Parliament member) are not representative of the whole country. Many French share the idea that public schools should help young minds to detach themselves from primary identities in order to help them find their own political identity and exercise their rights of citizenship. If their beliefs cause some students to protest taking certain courses or school programs—such as refusing to learn about the Holocaust, take biology, or do sports—and some teachers (girls refusing to be taught by male teachers), compromises will be hard to find (see Terray 2004). Because of these continuous controversies, 75 percent of teachers and supervisors in public schools required that a line be drawn against any further special requests relating to religious beliefs. This demand also reflected a more general exhaustion on the part of public servants working in sensitive urban areas. Politicians chose to support them rather than launch a genuine public debate about tolerating diversity, the dysfunctions of the French model of social integration, gender in public schools, imaginary fears, the amplifying role of the media, and so forth. Had they done so, they might have avoided further unrest. But it was easier for a short-sighted political class to opt instead for a narrowly focused law, one that led to international misunderstandings.

This chapter documents twenty-five years of urban violence in disadvantaged neighborhoods.[8] Second, it examines the forms of violence these male youths express in the banlieues, such as clashes among "bandes" (gangs), widespread domestic violence against women, "collective" (gang) rapes, and attacks against symbols and agents of the state, not to mention arson. Third, it looks at allegations of racial profiling and at arrests for rioting. Despite the absence of statistics, despite the evidence of racial profiling and of abuse collected from the toll-free number 114 testimonies, the convictions of those condemned for rioting and attacks against policemen, and the condemnation of France by the European Commission on the prevention of torture are set against French policemen and their viewpoints in public academies.

This essay is based on data, field work, and personal interviews with youths, police officials, residents, organizations, managers of public housing projects, and city officials in Paris and its banlieues, London, and New York in recent years concerning the resources cities have at their disposal to confront violent offenders. It is also grounded in research from two European networks relative to cultures and dynamics of violence (Body-Gendrot and Spierenburg 2007).

A YOUTH AND POLICE HISTORY OF LOW-INTENSITY VIOLENCE

The association of male youths and urban threat is not a new phenomenon in France. Since the 1830s, society has labeled its urban, working-class youngsters "dangerous classes," in contrast with the rural hinterland, where closed societies were perceived as more easily exerting control over young people. Proudhon, in 1851, connected crime with the desperate condition of the working class: "When the hand worker . . . has no more bread, nor pie, no more money, no more stitch, no fire, nor place, then he begs, he thieves, he cheats, he steals, he kills" (quoted in Chevalier 1984, 445). The police were asked to control youthful petty criminals who took over a particular street or neighborhood, but then as now, the police hesitated to venture into really rough neighborhoods. As for justice, the Criminal Code of 1791 ordered that minors under sixteen who had committed a serious crime be locked up and educated until they seemed fit for being returned to society. The Criminal Code of 1810 does not mention a specific treatment for juvenile delinquents. But two institutions, an educational facility, at La Roquette, in 1836, and an agricultural colony, in 1839, were established to house these young people. The first juvenile courts are created in 1912, a formal recognition of the phenomenon of juvenile delinquency (Galliac 1971). At the beginning of the twentieth century, gangs of boys became visible to the public when journalists and novelists started to apply the epithet "Apaches" to bad boys who seemed to threaten the bourgeois order (Perrot 1979).[9]

After World War II, those who transgressed the mainstream order were labeled "zazous." In the 1950s, "blousons noirs" (black-leather jackets), the counterpart of the Mods and the Rockers in United Kingdom, provoked the same fears in established society. They were also marginalized working-class youngsters whose existence was precarious as the country became more urbanized and socially emancipated. The only feature of the current situation that is new is the intense interest of the media in the ethnicization and criminalization of some youths as well as the institutional responses required by an aging and fearful society.

Events in France during the 1980s and 1990 were indeed related to the appearance of juvenile delinquency as a independent issue, one that was formerly linked to immigration (the following discussion draws on Body-Gendrot 2005b). In 1981, the media and politicians interpreted the phenomenon of youths out joyriding with stolen cars in Les Minguettes, a suburb of Lyon, as resulting from immigrant families' poor social integration. But one of the actual joyriders stated: "Chases with stolen cars were for the youths how to find a way to cope with all the humiliations they and their parents had experienced. . . . Their aim was to get back at the cops who kept them from living quietly in their own world and to fight with them, one on one" (quoted in Jazouli 1992, 22). During those years, when dozens of immigrant youths were killed by the police or by homeowners, marches started in the Lyon region whose participants denounced police brutality and racism; this reinforced the links in the public mind of banlieues–immigration–youths–violence. This early civil rights movement collapsed after three years, because of internal divisions, parochialism, and the co-optation of the issue by the left via the creation of the organization SOS Racism. During this period, many French probably realized that immigrant families were not going to be returning to their home countries and that assimilating them in the mainstream would take longer than with previous immigrant groups. These new groups were not Catholic, and a strong association of violence with Islam in the imagination of an old Roman Catholic country had prevailed for centuries.

Large public housing projects became also associated with youth violence and immigrant families in the public mind in 1990, after rioting and arson shook Vaulx en Velin, a suburb of Lyon; one youth was killed during a police chase. The French media latched on to and broadcast the idea that rampant violence on the part of idle, very visible males threatened the peace of local communities and of French society in general. The media also drew many comparisons with the American ghettos and emphasized the dangers of the Americanization of French society (no-go areas, drugs, gangs, communitarianism). They certainly were not being objective; the fears expressed by French citizens was less grounded in objective reality, in terms of documented offenses and social disintegration, than they would have been in the large cities of Africa, Latin America, Asia, and the United States.[10]

That many immigrants come from North Africa undeniably contributes to the idea that they are culturally different and cannot be integrated. But the enduring power of the French nation-state, manifested in its ability to provide continuous symbols of national citizenship, is also seen in its ignorance of immigrants' special needs and in a Republican discourse in which those needs are presented as illegitimate. Numerous French are socialized into the beliefs that a unitary and indivisible nation is a precious good, and multiculturalism and communitarianism are consequently demonized. An older French female resident living side by side with an Algerian family at the periphery of Paris explains: "We cannot get along. We do not have the same tastes, the same behaviors. . . . We do not see things the same way. We cannot agree, we agree on . . . nothing" (Sayad 1993, 45–46). To avoid being labeled as racists, such residents displace their ire on noisy cats, smells, the thinness of walls, and so on. Most of all, they deny the legitimacy of immigrants' right to be in France and to benefit from the same rights as the French—indeed, many "immigrants" are in fact French. The "native" French also say that their own status as French citizens is endangered by "others" who are devalued symbolically and physically. The elderly Frenchwoman also remarked that Arabic children "are coarse, they are full of hatred, they look at you nastily, they always stare at you, with spite. You always feel that they would like to thrash you . . . and you get scared" (Sayad 1993, 45).

YOUTH VIOLENCE IN THE SUBURBS

Official data concerning young offenders is ambiguous and controversial, as in all European countries (the following discussion draws on Body-Gendrot 2005a). Detailed statistics about violent juvenile offenders have been available since 1974. Once the statistics are given to the media, all the constructed discourses are overloaded with political and professional stakes. The statistics from the Observatoire National de la Violence Urbaine (the National Observatory of Urban Violence) are not the only available statistics, but they are the ones that inform public opinion. They reflect police actions taken in response to citizens' complaints, police goals, and the way offences are categorized and tabulated and all of these may vary over time (see figure 4.1). Ironically, one could say that the intensity of the debate is inversely proportional to the scarcity of data. Statistics are hard to get and harder to interpret. Factual errors do occur and the recategorization or decategorization of types of offenses are a continuous problem.

Such statistics have over the years reinforced the same message: delinquents are becoming ever younger and ever more violent. Between 1972 and 2002, the numbers of crimes committed by juvenile offenders compiled by the Interior Ministry has tripled. Assault and intentional injuries have increased by 77 percent since 1996, sexual violence by 68 percent, threats by 58 percent, and thefts with violence but without arms by 26 percent (Réju 2005, 3–4).

However, such statistics refer to individual cases on which judicial decisions were reached. When the types of crimes committed are examined, a different picture is revealed. Violations of drug and immigration laws, rioting, and attacks on law enforcement officers are well documented by the police. By contrast, only 9 percent of burglaries, 7 percent of car or motorcycle thefts, and 3 percent of other thefts go to the courts (Mucchielli 2004). Yet these latter crimes are the most common, the ones that most affect citizens' quality of life. Consequently, the perception of high rates of juvenile delinquency is traceable to the incidence of crimes that are the most easily detected by the police because they are the most visible and also are the most frequently transmitted to prosecutors (a result of new legal requirements). For example, the number of youths arrested for using narcotics increased by 155 percent from 1993 to 1995, and those committing violent acts and attacking law enforcement officer increased by 76 percent at the same time (Aubusson et al. 2002).

FIGURE 14.1   NUMBER OF MINORS TEN- TO SEVENTEEN-YEARS-OLD PLACED
UNDER SUSPICION BY POLICE, 1988 TO 2001
(PER 10,000 RESIDENTS)

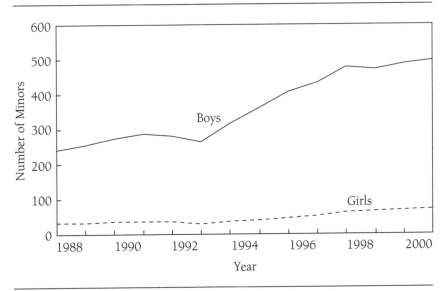

Source: Mucchielli (2004).

According to a Senate report of 2002 (Carle and Schosteck 2002), 5 percent of repeat juvenile offenders are accountable for 60 to 85 percent of offenses. Moreover, crimes are unequally distributed spatially. The heavily urbanized and industrialized regions of Paris, Lyon, and Marseille regions—fourteen of ninety-six departments in France—account for more offenses than the rest of the country combined. The victims of these crimes are more often youths than senior citizens.

What statistics do not record is the collective character of urban violence. Only by means of ethnographic studies such as those carried out by Hughes Lagrange (2000) and François Sicot (2000) can these collective modes of violence be examined. Their typologies distinguish four groups: teenagers who are not offenders; those who are light offenders and occasionally steal and get into fights; "rebels" who plan to break the law: burn cars and mail boxes, commit acts of vandalism, attack police officers with baseball bats, and so forth; and predators, including sexual ones, who make a career of crime.

Violence springs from several motivations. Besides the fun coming from transgressing and taking advantage of disorder, acting out in a context of frustration and of deprivation is exciting. Another motivation comes from having the power to intimidate and to be respected and it is meaningful for those with few resources ("violence is power in a life without power," a prison inmate told me). The youths defend their local turf like a bounty, especially against the police, whom they see as a hostile and cruel gang.

My young interviewees also mentioned that territories are more important than religious, racial, or ethnic differences between gangs. Such ethnic differences are reconstituted here and now, meaning that white boys may be part of a multicultural gang or vice versa. It follows from this that ethnicity doesn't exist in a vacuum and the importance of location, age, gender, socioeconomic disparities and inequalities in the production of social and political cleavages cannot be ignored. Ethnicity thus cannot be studied in isolation. The analysis must include other broader dimensions.

Just as youth is a fuzzy, elusive term that hides more than it reveals (Bourdieu 1984), what, then, is really behind the term "ethnic"? This word is rarely used in France because of its association with the Jews' fate before and during World War II.[11] However, under the influence of Anglo-American and northern European research, for the last ten years, French researchers have referred more and more to a phenomenon of ethnicization of social relations in French society, leading to the emergence of new ethnic identities. The conceptual obscurity of this concept, however, cannot be denied. It is located between race (but the country is supposed to be race-blind) and culture (but the Republican model of social integration does not take into account communities in the public space) (Taguieff 1991). The constant process of transaction between majority and minority groups explains why the concept of ethnicity is no more fixed than the situations in which it is produced and reproduced.

A few studies, however, do allow French researchers to assert that even if the role of ethnicity is modest, it does play a role in the emergence of male collective violence. For instance, parental supervision appears to be more relaxed in families of immigrant origin when male children become teenagers. North African mothers—confined in the home, often unable to speak French, and lacking economic skills—are perceived as having double standards regarding their sons' and daughters' freedoms. Most often, however, it is family crises and dislocations that seem to have the greatest impact on youths who experience violence in their early childhood. School is another predictor of violence. Young males of North African and poor backgrounds experience difficulties in school that lead to frustration and anxiety, since education is the only access to upward social mobility. A majority of teenagers in sensitive urban zones are at least one year behind in school, boys more than girls (Délégation Interministérielle à la Ville 2004, 6). School violence is explosive in 10 percent of high schools and this violence accounts for 50 percent of acts of violence committed in France, in part for such reasons and also because the culture in these areas is violent.

The perception of these youth as violent also comes from diverse groups of victims. The youths who are the most victimized do not come forward as victims. But it is symbolic violence against young women of Muslim culture in these relegated areas that has received wide coverage in the media. A report in 2004 from the

French intelligence agency, which surveyed 630 communities with a heavy concentration of Muslims, pointed out that half of them were "ghettoized" along religious lines. The signs of fundamentalist Islam were on the rise and the second- and third-generation Muslims were the most radical (Johnson and Carreyrou 2005, 20). This statement may or not may be accurate, the intelligence agency having its own bias. But no one will deny that within the last twenty years, the control exerted by young males on Muslim girls' behavior and on their appearance in the name of religion has become marked. Karima Benalli, the chair of a women's movement in Marseilles that has received numerous awards, said she launched it because she could not register her daughters in any leisure activity at the neighborhood level. Boys would not tolerate their presence. "In all the neighborhoods when girls do not have an older brother to protect them, it is very hard for them to dress as they want. I am continuously harassed and insulted" (Nashi 2005). Beyond this symbolic violence intended to pressure girls to behave as certain males desire, a few cases of extreme violence have shocked public opinion. In 2001, a young woman of North African origin, Sofrane, was burned to death after a discarded boyfriend transformed her into a torch. This terrible event generated a march led by eight young Muslim women around France, calling themselves Ni Putes ni Soumises (Neither Whores nor Submissive Women). Their organization, which counts thousands of women as members, can be interpreted as a form of identity politics.[12]

The question of gang rapes committed against girls "who do not behave" properly according to traditional families have been closely linked by the Western media to forms of closely-knit control structuring Muslim families in large public housing projects. Laurent Mucchielli rejects this interpretation, pointing out that, on average, juveniles commit 30 percent of rapes and adults 70 percent.[13] Sexual violence by young men toward young women has nothing to do with their ethnic origin, he says. Gang rapes occur more frequently in these immigrant and impoverished neighborhoods than elsewhere, because the function of machismo is to compensate these male youths' social marginalization and because mechanisms contributing to gang formation are stronger in relegated areas (Mucchielli 2005). Two social scenarios are frequently put forward to explain the phenomenon of gang rape: such rapes reinforce the cohesion of the gang; masculinity rites function to reinforce male solidarity. Male violence directed toward female teenagers in front of group audience is one such rite (Sanday 1990). Gang rapes are also perceived as taking revenge on a victim for the exclusion and devaluation the perpetrators feel society has inflicted on them (Sykes and Marcia 1957, 664–70).

Finally, what distinguishes these forms of collective violence in France from those in other Western countries is that their targets are frequently symbols or agents of the state. According to a director of the National Police heard by the Senate commission in 2002, "Juvenile delinquents are involved in arson against public goods (59 percent) and against private ones (51 percent)" (Carle and Schosteck 2002, volume 2, 439). When these youths act out, they express their resentment relative to deferred dreams, to mainstream society, its symbols, and its representatives and to their poor prospects within the society. Attacks on policemen, bus drivers, firemen, and teachers as well as arson and vandalism against schools, gyms, and bars demonstrate a collective distrust of society and its norms (sometimes of the country itself), and the wish to be left alone in a counterworld largely deserted by adults. They resent the abuse of force and the lack of respect with which service providers treat them. Not surprisingly, the more serious the offenses are, the more negative the offenders' perceptions of social and state institutions (see Roché 2000 and chapter 17, this volume). Forms of machismo and codes of honor oppose male youngsters and young policemen. The tiniest incidents may ignite a neighborhood.

A widespread perception shared by those youths is that acting out is always a response to police abuse or a miscarriage of justice. But the disorders might have been started by the youths themselves, sometimes to protect their drug deals (an explanation that cropped up in the recent disturbances); sometimes as a rite of passage; sometimes to attract the police or the firemen "just for fun," to get some action going or to settle scores.

Youth violence also targets residences. Setting cars or mail boxes ablaze is a common form of delinquency in French problem areas, partly because these items make easy targets. Nine thousand acts of urban violence were registered in the first eight months of 2005, and more than twenty thousand cars were burned; ten thousand vehicles were set on fire during the riots of fall 2005—1,408 of them in one night (Leclerc 2005, 8; Reuters, "France Back to Normal, Police Say," November 18, 2005). As remarked by Dominique Duprez (Body-Gendrot and Duprez 2002), car burning frequently takes place in May and June as a way for intimidating youths to negotiate directly with City Hall and obtain subsidized vacations. Sometimes car burning may also be a purely theatrical gesture, when there is nothing to negotiate. It should also be pointed out that many cars end up burning because they catch on fire through contact with another burning vehicle.

POLICE PROFILING, DISCRIMINATION, AND ABUSE IN THE BANLIEUES

Since the 1980s, urban unrest has stirred a wide-ranging debate in France. The police have frequently been accused of being too soft on youths who intimidate residents or vandalize property. But the revulsion that was felt when a young man named Malik Oussekine died after a chase convinced policemen that public opinion—usually supportive of them—can change one hundred eighty degrees if a young person is killed.

Policemen's Viewpoints

The numerous interviews we carried out with policemen reveal a broad spectrum of opinions, attitudes, and values (Body-Gendrot and de Wenden 2003). Their varied functions and the diversity of their missions lead them to be defined more by competition and opposition than by a common culture. In one cohort of rank-and-file policemen, differences are observed between motivated community policemen engaged in preventive actions and antiviolence squads resorting to intimidation and force, not to mention the intelligence service sent into sensitive areas. Some police officers dismiss all immigrant residents as trouble makers, drug users, and fundamentalists; others have more understanding for youths whose lives are chaotic, and they refuse a zero-tolerance approach. Some who reluctantly admit having racist biases will never engage in discriminatory behaviors, whereas others who make a point of supporting multicultural diversity now and then "blow a fuse" and overreact. On the whole, many rank-and-file police officers say that they have the feeling of doing the "dirty work" that society refuses to do. When sent to problem areas, they feel despised by populations spitting on them, stoning their cars, and insulting them and they lose their own self-esteem. Then, too, they often experience fear, either of being hurt or of hurting someone else and igniting the neighborhood. They are scared of being "taken out" by a rapidly growing crowd of youngsters armed with iron bars and sometimes guns. They all complain of a lack of proper basic and ongoing training and of the absence of support from their mid-level supervisors.

According to opinion polls, two thirds of the French have a positive image of the public services in general (*The Economist,* May 26, 2001, 38). A 2001 survey of 11,919 individuals by the National Institute of Statistics and Studies (INSEE) shows that 83.5 percent of the French had no contact with the police in their neighborhoods (Pottier 2003; Zauberman, Robert, and Potter 2000). For those who did (representing 7,867,000 people), there were important differences according to the respondents' age. Of those twenty to forty-five years old, only one out of five had contact with police officer in their neighborhood. Fifty-four percent of these contacts were initiated by the police. Seventy-three percent of the victims of burglaries and 21 percent of the victims of attacks—mostly verbal—go to the police for revenge, help, insurance. (By contrast, 66 percent of them contact the police if their incapacitation exceeds a week.) The higher their class and the older the victims are, the more likely they are to go to the police. The presence of the police is positively appreciated by 58.3 percent of the sample, whereas 28.9 percent complain about the lack of police presence. The only group to complain that policemen are too present are some of those fifteen to nineteen years of age, but even they represent a small minority in their cohort (5.1 percent vs. 61.1 percent of satisfied youths).

Ethnic Profiling

Some studies have shown that in France and abroad, some policemen gradually resort to ethnic profiling and prejudice during their professional socialization. Ethnic classifications are as useful as age and gender factors for spotting certain individuals. "A certain type of population should fit in a certain space at a certain time," is what the police think. If there is a gap among the three parameters, police suspicion grows and it triggers action on their part. Racism is constructed on the job, it is not ideological, it is a work norm for the rank-and-file police officers, part of their culture and distinct from other forms of racism expressed by society at large (see Zauberman and Levy 2003, 1076).

As elsewhere, the socialization of the police is grounded on a binary vision: law-abiding citizens on one hand and trouble makers on the other. A survey conducted in 1982 among police officers showed that their major suspect categories were immigrants (45 percent), youths (22 percent), and car drivers (6 percent). It also revealed that immigrants were a suspected and (thus) suspicious category because "they are different." The police would say that "they are very touchy . . . they jabber on behind your back, but you are not supposed to get upset . . ." (Ministère de l'Intérieur et de la Décentralisation 1983).

The tensions between youths and the police are acknowledged and institutionalized in the police work as shown by the scale of offenses elaborated in 1988 by a section of the French intelligence agency in charge of banlieues. It defined urban violence as "weakly-organized actions, from youth acting collectively against goods and persons linked to institutions in neighborhoods regarded as 'sensitive' by authorities" (Bui Trong 1993). This definition did not include adults also acting collectively and resorting to violence to express their discontent in cities (farmers or union members vandalizing public buildings). Youth was a euphemism referring to youths of immigrant background. As the self-serving methodology used by the police was dubious—the neighborhoods were not homogeneous, their populations fluctuated over the years, interpretations of incidents were subjective, statistics depended on the number of policemen on the field, and so forth—a new scale for urban violence has been substituted for the previous one and its comprehensive method of recording is supposed to help policemen with preventative work.

On the field, rank-and-file policemen have broad discretion sometimes labeled as a "hierarchical inversion" (Monjardet 1996, 88). Their professional culture leads them to see idle male youths as "hostile" even if their potential of violence is low. As more police officers are sent to poor immigrant areas, the greater the risk of discriminatory actions: young, inexperienced, insufficiently trained policemen are uncomfortable with the populations of public housing projects. They are confronted with territorialized subcultures and norms that they do not share. They have been required to instill a social discipline in groups of youngsters who live in a world of their own, in a vacuum, largely deserted by adults.

Disorder is a matter of interpretation "filtered through a reasoning based on stigmatized groups in disreputable areas" (Sampson and Raudenbush 2004). Due to expectations triggered by specific local situations and accumulated grievances, some policemen may then either overreact in difficult situations in which they are outnumbered or be tempted to misuse their discretionary force in spaces where they know no witnesses will go to the police station to complain. When they are sent to these areas, some of them have the feeling of doing the "dirty work" that society does not want to do. Despite the fact that these rank-and-file policemen know the youths by name, in controlling them they find a way to compensate for their own loss of status and to demonstrate that they are in power, invested with the function of maintaining order. Police abuse or overreaction may be due to the drive that policemen have to mark their territory and their difference from the populations they have to control.

This is understandable. But what is the extent of the phenomenon? How many French belonging to visible minorities are stopped and searched? How many are imprisoned?[14] Have these questions any value? That more than half of the prison population in the United States is made of African American males (7 percent) allows antidiscrimination organizations to build a case, a situation impossible in France for lack of data. Why is it so difficult for the institution to tackle this question? Why is the role played by ethnicity combined with age, gender, poverty ignored? Several explanations have been put forward. In the survey we conducted on the training future policemen receive and on the lack of empirical sessions on racial and ethnic relations, typical comments made by those in charge of the training were as follows (Body-Gendrot and Wihtol de Wenden 2003):

> The French system is so immersed in an egalitarian and universalist ideology that it cannot perceive the problem of discrimination [see Haut Conseil à l'Intégration 1991]. Political parties, trends, movements, and people are blamed but no one admits that the way French institutions function produces discrimination.
>
> In France, the issue of discrimination has not emerged at the political level because no one was eager for this to happen, and for too long it has been thought that having an egalitarian and republican system was enough.
>
> What is never said on this issue probably has a link with the colonial past of France, which explains how difficult it is to recognize discrimination and to act on it.

That accountability, transparency, and responsibility toward citizens do not belong to the French administrative vocabulary is another type of explanation. In general, citizens' grievances appear illegitimate in the eyes of heavily centralized institutions and a culture of denial characterizes French administration, all the more so, in practice, if these citizens are poor, young, and of foreign origin and if the national police are concerned.

The obstacles placed in the way of convicting guilty policemen also explain a widespread feeling of impunity: cases drag on because documents are not forwarded to the justice system and judges close the cases for lack of evidence. Convictions for racial discrimination remain unusual in France: one each in 1992, in 1993, in 1994, in 1997, in 1998; three in 1999; and seven in 2000 (Lanquetin 2000, 79–81). Whereas in the United States, justice has been instrumental in redressing harms experienced by minorities in a context of racism, in France, the conviction of racist policemen is unusual. In 1995, only 21 of 253 complaints led to the conviction of police officers, and in 1996, only 12 of 166 (Jobard 2002). If internal sanctions occur (two hundred fifty to three hundred fifty each year), this information is covered up. The civil service, which employs one fourth of the French, shields policemen from the legal sanctions that would apply to ordinary citizens.

Ethnic Discrimination

Several sources allow researchers to find out about police discriminatory treatment. One of them was provided by 113 anonymous files on grievances against the police, recorded by a toll-free number between May 2000 and May 2002 to which we had access. They had never been made public before then.[15] This number was installed by the left in 2001 to help redress ethnic discriminations by listening to the victims' stories. The grievances were recorded on files which were transferred to decentralized state services, supposed to act on the cases. Although this toll-free number is now discontinued, these calls are very instructive. However one should not draw hasty conclusions from them relative to police discriminatory treatment. The logic of situations structuring the shape and the goal of interactions must be taken into account.[16] Fifty-six percent of the callers say they received an unequal treatment from the police due to their real or assumed origins and 10 percent due to their biological race (Africans are usually better treated by the police in Paris than North Africans). Racially motivated insults, threats, ethnic slurs, and physical harm refer to the Algerian war, to the stigmatization of the Arabic origin and of the Muslim religion.

The follow-up to the complaints by the decentralized commissions having received the most important number of cases to be monitored is instructive. No action has ever been taken when the police were involved and in half of the cases, no explanation was given. When civil servants called the toll-free number to denounce ethnic discrimination in their service, they were sanctioned by their superiors for having spoken to a third party (Body-Gendrot and Wihtol de Wenden 2003).[17]

Besides investigations from the League of Human Rights documenting ethnic discriminations by the police in 2001 and field surveys carried out by community organizations in various cities, our own in-depth interviews with youths and street educators in marginalized urban areas tend to confirm that police misconduct is not exceptional. One of the interviewees said (Body-Gendrot and Wihtol de Wenden 2003):

> What shocked me is the lack of respect. I was shamed by them. We are nothing. I respect the law, why don't they? It is as if I were not like them, they "killed" me with the fact that I am dark-skinned. I was like a war prisoner before he is shot.

They harmed my parents' dignity. Here, we are born a victim and we remain a victim until death. Humiliation is on my mind and nobody can take it away until justice is done.

Youths who have been stopped and frisked based on profiling often know that they have been singled out because of "ethnic-making situations" (Fagan 2002, 150, n.47). This profiling not only hurts them emotionally and is perceived as unfair, it can also escalate into hostile attitudes to the police. The French system of policing differs from those of other northern European countries in the fact that outrage or rebellion are systematically used by numerous policemen to mask discriminatory treatment. A director of the general inspection corps of the National Police acknowledged to us that police abuse can always be shielded by a report of outrage, rebellion, or assault against the police and that those who are the victims are those who are the least able to bring a contradictory statement for lack of guarantees. Between police and the youths, the weight of words is asymmetric.

Outrage and Rebellion

Fabien Jobard, with the help of Marta Zimolag, has studied court decisions between 1965 and 2003 in cases involving offences against policemen holding public authority in a court district of the Parisian region (Jobard and Zimolag 2006). The interest of this analysis is three-fold. First, it confirms that ethnic discrimination does exist: sentences are more or less severe, depending on an offender's profile. A very large proportion of youthful defendants are of North African origin. They are strikingly young: for the period as a whole, 50 percent were under twenty-two and 25 percent were under eighteen. They are less often charged for contempt alone than defendants from the other groups, and more often for assaulting a police officer or "contempt and obstruction."[18] Twenty-four percent of the North Africans, judged immediately in real-time case processing as repeat offenders, are given unsuspended imprisonment as compared to 7 percent of the other categories. It should also be specified that half of the youths of North African origin are unemployed. Jobard and Zimolag observe that "court decisions pitilessly echo and multiply the singularities of a population which differs both in its origins and in its relations with the criminal justice system, in that it is more wont than any other group to be in contact with the judicial system" (10).

Second, the researchers observed an increase in cases of outrage and rebellion between 1965 and 2003, which was not just due to a population or a delinquency increase. The explanation did not come from a growing "roughness" of social relations from the mid-eighties onward in French society, but in changes in criminal law that encouraged the police to classify a whole series of acts as misdemeanors requiring that the person be placed in custody. This change led to significant alterations in the contacts of youths and the police. Between 1960 and 1980, policemen only transmitted to courts cases they felt were particularly serious. Currently, quite the opposite has occurred: all cases are sent to the courts. Policemen add the charge of obstruction to their contempt cases and make sure that the offenders will be prosecuted, a proof of their discretionary power.

Thirdly, these policemen want revenge. When reporting offences, they have gradually added their own civil complaints as private parties associated to the public prosecution, for which the administration provides counsel.[19] In eighty-seven out of one hundred cases between 2000 and 2003, the police officer claimed to have been hurt as a person by the offender. Civil damages, in general, require a North African youth to pay over €300 to the policeman who allegedly or actually mistreated him.

Aside from 12 percent of defendants sentenced to symbolic payment of damage (€1), the average amount of damages per defendant was €307. Over and beyond the problem of solvency for those sentenced, this monetary compensation obviously feeds the suspicion that the police officers are taking advantage of the offence to make money.

Abuse Followed by Impunity

That the public system shields policemen from the legal sanctions that would apply to an ordinary citizen is again proved by an episode documented in detail (Jobard 2002, 3).

The European Court of Human Rights (ECHR) charged France with the use of torture by the French police. Article 3 of the European Convention for the Protection of Human Rights, passed in 1950, states, "No one may be subjected to torture or to inhuman or degrading punishment or treatment." To ensure the enforcement of this article, the ECHR has created a European committee for the prevention of torture (CPT), an independent organization allowed to visit prisons, police stations, and psychiatric institutions, at any time and without warning, anywhere there is a suspicion of mistreatment. France was convicted twice in 1999 (Selmouni case) and in 2002 (Mouisel case).

After seven visits to France, the CPT noted that there was "a nonneglectible risk of being mistreated" in police stations, a mistreatment amounting to "punching and slaps, hitting on the head with a phone book; psychological pressure, insults, deprivation of food and medication." The European conviction of a police perceived as brutal and cynical came as no surprise. The surprise came from elsewhere: the government mobilized, requiring the CPT to provide proofs, and making a distinction between a well-grounded accusation and an allegation. The government asserted that guarantees surrounding the use of force by the police in France and the code of ethics of the National Police were sufficient to reduce the risk of mistreatment. They emphasized the low number of allegations of violence recorded by internal disciplinary and control commissions. In other words, the government played down the charge: police transgressions were unusual and allegations were not proofs.

The same "anomaly" is found in the administrative review boards or other commissions on infringements from security corps. Whereas in Canada, the United States, and the United Kingdom, for instance, citizens' grievances relative to police misbehaviors are handled by civilian review boards, in France the Commission Nationale de Déontologie de la Sécurité (National Commission on Ethics and Security in France) can only be appealed to by citizens via a member of parliament. The first year, 2001, only thirteen complaints against the police were transmitted. Between 2001 and 2004, a total of one hundred cases was sent to the commission. Out of seventy-eight cases, half of them proved to be discriminatory acts, and this number increased year after year. They involved the national police in general and 64 percent of the victims were French (Commission Nationale de Déontologie de la Sécurité 2005). Visibility given to these cases by the media is the only weapon this fragile commission has.

The political scientist Eric Bleich (2004) has compared police standards in the United Kingdom, Germany, and France. Of the three countries, he says, Britain does the most intensive recording of racist incidents, reflecting the pressure put on the police to recognize the seriousness of the phenomenon. Britain tallied 47,814 "racist incidents" in 2000, while that same year, France counted "30 racist and xenophobic actions." The same gap would be reflected in the numbers of policemen being sanctioned for abusing their force or misbehaving. In 2002, only 2 percent of French policemen were sanctioned by police inspectors, while police violence was on the increase (more than 6 percent in 2003), according to official reports of the General Inspection of Services.[20]

Racism is an issue that immigrant populations talk about in the discotheques, in the city, at work, and during leisure time. The symbolic violence of racial discrimination is exhausting, exasperating the victims. Although it is against the law to do so, administrative or police discriminatory practices hurt their victims as much as—if not more than—the violent behaviors of some youths in the neighborhoods.

CRIMINOGENIC AREAS AS BREEDING GROUNDS OF HOMEGROWN TERRORISM

Is it legitimate to link crime and violence, youth, and terrorism, or is this too politically incorrect? This question brings to mind remarks by R. Ballard. Concerning the study of racism in the United Kingdom, he observes that upwardly mobile professionals "have long since learned that breaking cover on such issues invariably causes chaos, most of which falls straight back onto whomsoever [sic] has been foolish enough to raise the issue in the first place. Hence in the interests of one's future survival it is far wiser to keep one's head down" (Ballard 1998). It is obviously risky for research to point at convergences between young rioters (much beloved of left intellectuals) and potential terrorists, since so often far right propaganda, sensationalist media, and governing elites have thrived on such amalgamation due to the fuzziness of the term "Muslim." The nuisance and violence that a minority of young male offenders inflict periodically on their neighborhoods are indeed of a low-intensity nature. By contrast, violent jihadists aim at causing numerous deaths as well as symbolic and material destruction in the West. However, in both cases law enforcers and states in charge of public safety have to face confrontational identities, counterworlds, or what Milton Gordon calls "an adversarial assimilation" (Gordon 1963) which may lead marginalized young men to act out collectively or to instrumentalize violence and cause chaos. In both cases, social exclusion and failed integration are wellsprings of violence in the public space.

The comparison has obvious limits: the recent trauma felt in the Netherlands after the assassination of Theo van Gogh, the political consequences of the Madrid and London terrorist attacks, and new forms of threat force political elites to intervene not just at the local and national levels but at the international as well with coordinated efforts. Antiterrorist policies have to be changed, since, unlike crime policies, few of them have dealt specifically with the lethal violence of Islamist terrorism until now.

Most criminologists are aware that a continuum rarely exists between young violent delinquents, organized criminals, and terrorists. But they also know that frequently, converts to radical Islamism ready to die as martyrs were former delinquents from marginalized neighborhoods or that the goal of some organized criminal organizations is to accumulate funds for the jihad. Such were the cases of the Safé Bourada gang caught in September 2005 or of the Ouassini Cherifi gang, arrested in Paris on December 12, 2005. Recruiting their members in French prisons, they attacked banks and transferred money to networks organizing jihad abroad.

Although with young violent offenders, the task is to apprehend individuals or groups of individuals who must answer for their acts to the criminal courts, the goal with homegrown terrorism is to stop groups of individuals from becoming lethal risks to democratic societies. The issue is not to deal with people who have broken the law and must be indicted and judged but to identify a threat and the target to be destroyed. Internal and external notions of security are blurred.

Yet other dimensions justify a joint study of violent delinquents and potential terrorist "backpackers." First, elusive terms as "Muslim" and "terrorism" rely upon flexible definitions as in the case of youths and violence (one man's terrorist is another's resistor, a mujahid fighter, a crusader; the hard-core juvenile delinquents disrupting the community where they live are a small number). Because only 5 to 10 percent of young Muslims in France are active practitioners of "their" faith, only a minority of these, in deep malaise and in search of bearings, are ready to die for a higher cause (Kepel 2005).

Second, terrorist acts involve Muslims who instrumentalize violence to undermine the values of the Western societies where they live, a motivation already found among disenfranchised delinquent youths (Richardson 2006, 14). Third, the new policies of identification, surveillance, and repression look very similar to policies used in connection with violent young offenders. They involve specialized intelligence services, swat teams, and also rank-and-file policemen doing their routine work.

Fourth, investigations have shown that marginalized urban areas which were already hot spots on police maps are a fishing pond for radical recruiters ("inspirers"). Out of approximately sixty French from marginalized urban areas involved in the insurgency in Iraq, twelve have died, a dozen are still in Iraq, and around forty are currently incarcerated in French prisons for their connections with terrorist networks, specifically Algerian salafists linked to Al Qaeda, not to mention Zacarias Moussaoui, indicted after 9/11.[21] Khaled Kelkal, an ordinary young man who joined Islamist terrorist networks in 1995 and was subsequently killed by the police, offered a profile of that type.

A leaked report of the French Intelligence Service (Renseignements Généraux, or R.G.) in June 2005 provides links between the profiles of violent youths already discussed and those of potential terrorists. It should be read with a critical distance.[22] This report examines the case of 1,610 converts to Salafism or other forms of radical Islam known because of their proselytizing, their delinquency, or their relations with radicals (Le Monde, July 13). One third of them had already been spotted by police. Males make up 83 percent of the cohort, and they live in urban zones within Muslim communities. In 44 percent of the cases, the social environment and the relations they have led them to study salafist Islam (23 percent) or join the Muslim missionary and revival group called Tabligh (28 percent). Marriage or a relationship rank as a second cause (27 percent), for salafism in particular, followed by proselytism (17 percent), which characterizes the Tabligh and its radical preachers. In 4 percent of the cases, prison was the location of their conversion to radical Islam. Half of the cohort is officially jobless. One third of them have low-skill occupations, in airport security jobs, for instance. They are the backpacker types carrying bombs, like the terrorists in Leeds and Madrid. Those who are involved with Al Qaeda are not urban poor and school dropouts but more "the privileged children of an unlikely marriage between Wahhabism and Silicon Valley . . . the heirs not only to jihad and the umma but also to the electronic revolution and American-style globalization" (Kepel 2005).

The number of these invisible and infiltrated enemies is minuscule—an estimated two hundred in France, and one thousand in the United Kingdom. The reasons for their conversion is a point of debate. For Olivier Roy (2004), they find their cause "in the utopia of a universal umma, in an abstract and pure Islam, in the same way as the left radicals in the 1970s—the Baader-Meinhof group or the Red Brigades—opted for terrorism in the name of the 'world proletariat' or of the 'revolution,' without worrying about its consequences." But another motivation is related to specific French domestic and foreign policies such as the French presence in Afghanistan. Another called the autumn threat, revealed in the spring of 2006, linked suicidal attacks against a unidentified European country between September 2006 and April 2007 and terrorist Algerian networks. The maintenance of law and order by police forces may be interpreted as a genuine clash of culture, of civilization and of religion among the most radical Muslims, according to various reports. The November 2005 events may "encourage some decultured delinquent youths, without bearings, to turn to radical Islam and to jihad that they would not hesitate to launch against a [country] that they accuse of rejecting them" (Smolar 2005, 3).

These assumptions may be questioned. Mentioning threats can indeed be interpreted as an instrumentalization of risks by authorities eager to reinforce law and order for electoral purposes. But no one will deny that the fantastical fears that such threats trigger are the hardest to combat. The danger comes from the trend of punitive populism that is now becoming a major component of political choices, from the call to revenge, grounded in popular emotions to the general rhetoric and the dramatization of the media. Promises made by political leaders are radical, opinion is indifferent to their efficacy, and criminal laws are legitimized by everyone's alleged need of security.

According to Bleich, the treatment of new risks of violence relies on a three-stage strategy that is found in all European countries heavily influenced by France (Bleich 2005). The first one tends to confront the threat with the neutralization of the ethnic dimension, ignoring its influence. Such is the case with the Vigipirate program in France and with all the recent steps taken by Germany, Italy, and the United Kingdom to secure public space.

A second trend is to harden surveillance and repression, and resort to the deportation of Islamists hostile to democracy. In France, the domestic intelligence agency has for years monitored problem areas and Muslim activity, as already said. It has infiltrated mosques, bars, restaurants, koranic bookstores, hallal butchers, long-distance telephone shops, day-care centers, and clothes stores suspected of harboring or being used by extremist Islamists. When suspicion moves beyond reasonable doubt, raids take place covertly under the pretext of health and safety checks or of a tax audit. In 2004, eighty-eight raids were carried out, involving 1,180 people, of whom 185 were taken into custody. Some were prosecuted and a dozen radical clerics were expelled from the country. One million euros were seized. Field information gathered by the intelligence agency is transmitted to a unit of command, for instance in Paris, to the police prefect, who heads the regional defense zone and thus coordinating the army, the firefighter units, the territorial security branches, medical services, the judicial police and all the antiterrorist branches in symbiosis with political authorities.

Countries such as the United Kingdom and the Netherlands, which had been very tolerant of expressions of hatred of the West by some Muslim preachers, are moving in the same direction of public order maintenance. A year before 9/11, British policy had been reoriented toward dealing with transnational terrorism. Those frequently targeted for scrutiny were Muslims, either British nationals or immigrants (see Schain 2008). This attitude was denounced in the House of Lords in 2002 and again in 2005 as a breach of fundamental human rights. The most recent legislation on the prevention of terrorism in 2005 and 2006, however, creates new police powers, such as banning some Islamist organizations from Britain, closing troublesome places of worship, and organizing pretrial hearings in "secret" courts, thus making Muslim communities as "racial minorities" subject to special scrutiny. Regularly the British press discloses that thousands of Islamic militants are under surveillance, that terrorist plots threaten the country, and that the boundaries between domestic security and terrorism are becoming less clear. It is difficult to know whether one approach is more efficient that another in France and in the United Kingdom. The links established between some divisions of the British antiterrorist units and circles of moderate Muslims seem promising, but other units, as in France, heavily infiltrate these communities. The lack of coherence is glaring. In the long term, the consequences of antiterrorist measures may hurt Muslim communities which, at the same time, are asked to cooperate with the police. Supposing they cooperate, will police forces believe the clues that they bring them (Stroobants 2005)? It is likely that the widening of executive branches' powers in the name of security will be made at the expense of civil liberties in Europe. After each new attack, it becomes more difficult to avoid hasty arrests and to resist the hypertrophied surveillance systems that control the public space, even in France, which had resisted CCTVs but is now implementing them.

A third strategy consists in increasing measures of social inclusion within societies, encouraging forums and dialogues between Muslim communities' lay and religious leaders. The problem is that Islam, unlike other religions, has no organized leadership. The training of imams emanating from Western countries rather than their import from home countries is under study. The controversial Tarik Ramadan has been asked by Tony Blair to join a circle of advisers. French officials have taken a calculated risk in dealing with the radical Union of French Islamic Organizations, which is also close to the Muslim Brotherhood, in hopes of co-opting the organization so that it softens its line. These moves recall those of the Boston police allying with the Ten Point Program of Eugene Rivers and with forty black churches to restore order to troubled neighborhoods in the 1990s (Body-Gendrot 2001, 108).

CONCLUSION

It would be wrong to think that Islamic terrorism is the only real threat and that with low-intensity violence, democracies have little to fear. Any incident of violence carries unanticipated effects; it generates political processes of repression, which sooner or later foster frustrations and more cycles of violence. Of the types of policies just described, those based on repression receive strong support from politicians, the media, and a large number of voters. The rise of an ill-defined, enigmatic otherness feeds their fears. A courageous political option would be to enlighten the masses on the genesis of their fears, on the dangers of catastrophism, enclosure, intolerance, and punitive populism. The optimal way to fight violence and fears would indeed be for a democracy to be as inclusive of its different components as possible, and this is what the French social contract asserts and succeeds at in many ways.

But at the same time, the French centralized state has a long history of surveillance of groups seen as dangerous and it grants few rights to those it sees as enemies of liberty. The direct identification, surveillance, and repression of marginalized Others perceived as suspicious categories then require that the state receives the full cooperation of the police. The institution makes the choice to praise policemen globally but not to address their malaise, their lack of training, their fortress mentality and their recourse to functional racism. The French police are not a monolithic, corrupt and racist institution and the vast majority of policemen perform their work with ethics. Their image in the population is positive. During the recent unrest, 217 policemen and gendarmes were injured by snipers or by statues, machines, metal balls thrown from the public housing projects' roofs (see Bronner and Ceaux 2005).

Facing dozens of youths throwing smoke bombs at them, police avoided an escalation of violence and were praised for it. But no one will deny that better initial and continuous police training, different hiring practices, an open ear, a more rigorous implementation of the code of ethics and the denunciation of institutional racism might eliminate antagonisms with the youths, bring more consent with the populations, and give police work in problem areas more legitimacy.

Steps have been taken to redress this situation but, compared with neighboring countries, police reforms are overdue in France. The catalyst to the recent disturbances in the Parisian region was the poor relationship the police had with some youths. "You cannot constantly stop people for no reason to check their papers without consequences," a mediator of Clichy-sous-Bois told a journalist (Crampton 2005, 3). The policemen in the field are left to their own devices and they tend to abuse their power, a police union official remarked (Toscer 2005, 78). In a few police academies, sessions focus on good police-civilian relationships, but such innovations remain unusual, as if the centralized institution feared to lose control if it let policemen express their fears and resentments too openly.

Few major policies have been overhauled since the recent disturbances. Anti-discrimination efforts should be mentioned, for example, the statistics can include parents' and grandparents' birthplaces to favor covert affirmative programs on the part of the administration. But will innovations be enforced in the long term, when the debt of France has reached colossal proportions and the state is almost bankrupt? Will members of parliament be courageous enough to open their ranks to more diversified representatives? A law was necessary to promote the political representation of women, but currently political parties preferred to pay heavy fines rather than put them in eligible places on their lists.

Is Jürgen Habermas's prediction correct? "The absence of any enlightening diagnosis of our time lets catastrophes be the only way for us to learn" (quoted in Delacroix 2005).

NOTES

1. In a national survey on households' life stories published in February 2004, 50 percent of those age eighteen to twenty-four and 40 percent of those age twenty-five to thirty-four say they experienced a negative treatment due to their first name, appearance, skin color, or home address. Thirty-nine percent of immigrants or their children say they were the victims of racist attitudes in French society. Most of them indicate that they were hurt by them, and 37 percent said that the pain they felt had serious consequences in their lives.

2. Three months after the disorders, 86 percent of the French and 89 percent of those thirty to forty-nine years old expect more disorders; 82 percent of the French and 90 percent of the cohort under thirty years old do not believe that solutions have been brought to the problems (CSA 2006). This view was confirmed a year later.

3. The Kerner Commission (officially known as the National Advisory Commission on Civil Disorders) was appointed by President Lyndon B. Johnson on July 28, 1967. Ten men and one woman formed a panel chaired by Otto Kerner, Governor of Illinois, and for seven months investigated the racial disorders which had severely disrupted American cities in recent years (578 riots took place between 1967 and 1971, those in Detroit, Michigan, and Newark, New Jersey, having been the most lethal; 87 people were killed and 1897 injured in 1967, with 82 percent of the casualties occurring in those cities). The 426 page report was released on March 1, 1968, and became an immediate best seller, with over two million copies sold. It was meant to answer three basic questions: what happened, why did it happen, and what can be done to prevent it from happening again? The members of the Commission visited riot sites and heard numerous witnesses. They found white racism to be the major cause of the ghetto riots and warned in its pessimistic conclusion that the United States was moving "toward two societies, one white, one black, separate and unequal."

4. One of policemen's complaints concerns constant reforms and the instrumentalization of their work by the political sphere for electoral gains.

5. France's colonial past, the issues of belonging and of racism, had not been dealt with before the recent upheavals. The conservative parties in power have passed a law requiring school textbooks to "recognize in particular the positive role of the French

presence overseas, notably in North Africa." The law was initiated to please pieds-noirs (former French settlers in Algeria) and harkis (Algerians who fought for France), a lot of whom live in the South of France. Although the law was passed without controversy, after the disorders, the left tried to repeal the law and a controversy emerged, not unlike those of the 1960s in the United States, when Black Power advocates demanded a rewriting of textbooks to give a better picture of African Americans and their history.

6. Recently and deliberately, these second and third generations have been labeled Muslims by politicians and the media, but according to surveys, only 5 to 10 percent of them practice their religion actively, a figure similar to that of Roman Catholics (8 percent).

7. The 2000 Eurobarometer (SORA 2001, 40) revealed that 58 percent of European Union citizens surveyed "tend to agree" with the statement that immigrants were "more often involved in criminality than the average." This was the majority opinion in twelve of the fifteen member states, and on average only 30 percent of Europeans surveyed "tend to disagree" with the statement.

8. These so-called riots have little to do with riots experienced in the cities of the south or even in Los Angeles or Miami, and they cannot be defined in terms of the number of deaths or extent of damage. The violence we are talking about here is a low intensity, a crumbly violence, very disturbing for neighborhoods of working people. The socially constructed issue of violence blows out of proportion words of intimidation and isolated incidents, out of which the media construct a narrative that progressively makes sense to the public. But no one should forget that words are words and bullets are bullets and that places where the youths live are not the former Robert Taylor Homes in Chicago nor South American favelas nor South African townships (on caution about the use of words, see Body-Gendrot 2007b).

9. French researchers, the media, and politicians avoid the term "gang" to differentiate the phenomenon from the American one.

10. Unlike in the United States, the number of homicides in France is fairly small and has not increased much since 1991 (1.1 per 100,000), with the exception of 2002, which registered an unexplained 25 percent increase. Homicides by juveniles are unusual. In 2000, fights among youngsters caused 9 deaths in France (43 in 1998). Youth homicides are not, as in the United States, a "black-on-black" crime syndrome. More youths of North African origin are killed by French than vice versa.

11. French Jews were required to wear a yellow star and this signal allowed their persecution, leading to the murder of one third (70,000) of French Jews by the Nazis.

12. Families from the area sided with the offender. Historians point out that in the past, families with a traditional religious background have required young men to act as guardians of young women's virtue in their community. Retaliation occurs when young women leave their neighborhoods alone, dress improperly, or date a boy outside their community. Young men suffer from this type of social control as well.

13. In 2000, 1,044 youths were tried for rapes (with no specification about the collective or individual dimension). A judge from the Parisian region evoked an "epidemic," with seventy cases a year involving 250 offenders. In 2001, nationwide 142 were convicted of collective rapes.

14. Farhad Khosrokhavar (2004, 280) estimates that among the incarcerated who are eighteen to twenty-four and twenty-five to twenty-nine years of age, those with a

North African father are nine times as numerous as the others. The decision to incarcerate them may result from the absence of residential guarantees and stable family references and unemployment, not just from judges' bias.

15. In October 1999, a national commission to study and combat discrimination was created in France (C. Wihtol de Wenden and I were members). The left-wing government, however, never intended it to become a commission on racial equality and it had few resources. A new authority, the Haute Autorité de Lutte contre les Discriminations et pour l'Égalité (HALDE), has been created as an antidiscrimination agency.

16. Only 14 percent of the French were aware of the existence of this number and not all victims used it. Calls to complain about police abuse were not numerous (8 percent of eight hundred calls), few youths called (21 percent, 1.2 percent of those under eighteen), but their parents did.

17. The same silence is observed in schools, where principals are reluctant to report violence, most of all, violence against teachers, in order to communicate to their hierarchy a positive image both of their institution and of their leadership. Only 20 percent of crimes are reported, according to an unpublished victimization survey from the Institute of Higher Studies on Security in 1999.

18. According to the French Criminal Code, "Contempt is punished by a six-month prison term and a €7,500 fine. It consists of any words, gestures or threats . . . addressed to a person discharging a public service mission, acting in the discharge or on the occasion of his office, and liable to undermine his dignity or the respect owed to the office that he holds" (article 433-5). Obstruction is defined as violent resistance to a person holding public authority (article 433-6 of the criminal code). It receives the same punishment as contempt. The third offence, "assault on an officer," is a misdemeanor.

19. Only lawsuits for moral transgressions are included here.

20. Most of the sanctions are summonses. Fewer than two hundred policemen were fired in 1999.

21. Sometimes the nationality is not clear-cut. Ahmed Ressam (the millennium bomber) traveled from Algeria for France via Corsica. He was involved with a terrorist gang, left for Canada, where he became involved in terrorism through an Arab-Afghan veteran network that he met at the local mosque. Djamel Beghal, a key European lieutenant for Al Qaeda, was naturalized French via marriage (Leiken and Brooke 2006). Salafism emphasizes the need of a total rupture with Western society and its corrupted morals.

22. Researchers should be skeptical regarding this information. It is indeed not unusual for intelligence services to fabricate ad hoc enemies and to increase the potential of threats in the eyes of the public, emphasizing, in the words of the French prime minister, that "there is a real continuity between a fundamentalist discourse and terrorist acts" (Smolar 2004). In the past, it has been observed that the French intelligence service, the R.G., then a political police, focused on banlieues after various scandals had tarnished their reputation in the 1980s. It could well be that jihadism has allowed the 3,500 members of the French intelligence service to find a way to carve their niche in a very competitive professional environment. Jihadism is perceived as a widespread threat that alarms the governing elites, fascinates the media, and fuels a diffuse fear in the population, including 73 percent of the Muslims in France (Knowlton 2005, 1). Piotr Smolar labels the R.G. "a box for fantasies. . . . The less one knows them, the worst one fancies their practices"

(Smolar 2007, 2). We share Robert Leiken and Steven Brooke's concerns when they state that the inaccessibility of data on terrorism for research means that much terrorism analysis merely clusters media reports rather than building and analyzing a data set. "Most of the researchers [are] not producing substantively new data or knowledge. They [are] primarily reworking old material. . . . The majority of researchers' . . . writings and analyses [are] based entirely on data produced by others. This lack of individual data generation and research [is] a profound concern (Silke 2004, 3–4). The paucity of verifiable data often has indeed limited terrorism studies to informed opinion rather than data, except for Mark Sageman (2004) and a handful of other scholars (see della Porta 1992, Merkl 1986, Kepel 2004), Roy's (2004) studies, and Khosrokhavar's in-depth interviews of foreign and French Islamists in prisons (2006)).

REFERENCES

Arteta, Stéphane. 2005. "Pluie de condamnations" ["Outpouring of Judgments"]. *Le Nouvel Observateur,* November 17–23, 2005: 100.

Aubusson, Bruno, Nacer Lalam, René Padieu, and Philippe Zamora. 2002. "Les statistiques de la délinquance." ["Statistics on Delinquency."] In *France, portrait social* (Journal of Public Statistics). Paris: INSEE.

Ballard, Robert. 1998. "Asking Ethnic Questions: Some Hows, Whys and Wherefores." *Patterns of Prejudice* 32: 15–37.

Bennhold, Katrin. 2005. "In Egalitarian Europe, a Not-So-Hidden World of Squalor." *International Herald Tribune,* October 17, 2005.

Bleich, Eric. 2004. "Making It Hard to Hate: Responses to Racist Violence in Britain, Germany and France." Unpublished paper. Middlebury College.

———. 2005. "Religion, Violence and the State in 21st Century Europe." Paper presented at the 14th International Conference of Europeanists, Palmer House Hotel, Chicago, Ill., March 11–13, 2005.

Body-Gendrot, Sophie. 1993. *Ville et violence. L'irruption de nouveaux acteurs [City and Violence: The Eruption of New Actors].* Paris: Presses Universitaires de France.

———. 2000. *The Social Control of Cities? A Comparative Perspective.* Oxford: Blackwell.

———. 2001. *Les villes: la fin de la violence? [Cities: The End of Violence?].* Paris: Presses des Sciences-po.

———. 2005a. "France: The Politicization of Youth Justice." In *Contemporary Youth Justice,* edited by John Muncie and Barry Goldson. Thousand Oaks, Calif.: Sage.

———. 2005b. "Deconstructing Youth Violence." *European Journal on Crime, Criminal Law and Criminal Justice* 13(1): 4–26.

———. 2006. "Safe Neighborhoods." In *Policy, People, and the New Professional,* edited by Jan Willem Duyvendak, Trudie Knijin, and Monique Kremer. Amsterdam: Amsterdam University Press.

———. 2007a. "France Upside Down over a Headscarf." *Sociology of Religion.* 68(3): 289–304.

———. 2007b. "Order, Disorder and the Urban Landscape." In *The Urban Age,* edited by Ricky Burdett and Deyan Sudjik. London: Phaedon.

Body-Gendrot, Sophie, and C. Wihtol de Wenden. 2003. *Police et discriminations raciales. Le tabou français [Police and Racial Discrimination: The French Taboo].* Paris: Éditions de l'Atelier.

Body-Gendrot, Sophie, and Dominique Duprez. 2002. "The Politics of Prevention and Security in France." In *The Politics of Prevention and Security in Europe,* edited by Dominique Duprez and Patrick Hebberecht. Brussels: UCV University Press.

Body-Gendrot, Sophie, and Pieter Spierenburg, editors. 2007. *Violence in Europe: Historical and Contemporary Perspectives.* New York: Springer.

Bourdieu, Pierre. 1984. *"La jeunesse n'est qu'un mot": Questions de sociologie ["Youth Is Only a Word": Questions of Sociology].* Paris: Éditions de Minuit.

Bronner, Luc, and Pascal Ceaux. 2005. "Le bilan chiffré de la crise des banlieues" ["The Final Cost of the Banlieue Crisis"]. *Le Monde,* December 2, 2005.

Bui Trong, Lucienne. 1993. "L'insécurité dans les quartiers sensibles. Une échelle d'évaluation" ["Insecurity in Sensitive Neighborhoods: An Evaluation Scale"]. *Cahiers de la Sécurité Intérieure* 14: 235–56.

Carle, Jean-Claude, and Jean-Pierre Schosteck. 2002. *Délinquance des mineurs, la République en quête de respect [Deliquency of Minors: The Republic in Search of Respect].* Report to the Commission of Inquiry on the Deliquency of Minors, 2001–2002. Paris: Sénat. Accessed at http://www.senat.fr/rap/r01-340-1/r01-340-1_mono.html.

Chevalier, Louis. 1984. *Classes laborieuses et classes dangereuses [Working Classes and Dangerous Classes].* Paris: Hachette.

Commission Nationale de Déontologie de la Sécurité [National Commission on Ethics and Security]. 2005. *Rapport 2004 [Report 2004].* Paris: La Documentation Française.

Crampton, Thomas. 2005. "Chance Encounter Set Off Disturbances." *International Herald Tribune,* November 7, 2005: 3.

CSA. 2006. "Aujourd'hui en France Poll." Survey undertaken for *Le Parisien* and i-télé, January 25–26, 2006. *Le Parisien,* January 3, 2006: 1.

Delacroix, Xavier. 2005. "Le capitalisme face à la stratégie de l'émotion" ["Capitalism Must Deal with Strategy and Emotion"]. *Le Monde,* September 10, 2005.

Délégation interministérielle à la ville. 2004. *Zones urbaines sensibles: un enjeu territorial de la cohésion sociale [Sensitive Urban Zones: A Territorial Stake for Social Cohesion].* September: 1–8.

Della Porta, Donatella. 1992. "Political Socialization in Left-Wing Underground Organizations: Biographies of Italian and German Militants." *International Social Movement Research* 4: 259–90.

Eckholm, Eric. 2006. "Life Keeps Getting Worse for Black Men in the U.S." *International Herald Tribune,* March 21, 2006: 2.

Fagan, Jeffrey. 2002. "Policing Guns and Youth Violence." *Future of Children* 12(2): 133–51.

Galliac, Henri. 1971. *Les maisons de correction [Houses of Correction].* Paris: Cujas.

Gordon, Milton. 1963. *Assimilation in American Life.* New York: Oxford University Press.

Haut Conseil à l'Intégration. 1991. *Pour un modèle français d'intégration: premier rapport annuel [Towards a French Model of Integration: First Annual Report].* Paris: La Documentation Française.

Hobsbawm, Eric. 1959. *Primitive Rebels in Modern Europe.* Manchester, England: Manchester University Press.

Jazouli, Adil. 1992. *Les années banlieue [The Banlieue Years].* Paris: Le Seuil.

Jobard, Fabien. 2002. *Compter les violences policières, faits bruts et mises en récit [Counting the Police's Violent Acts: Facts and Narrations].* *Questions Pénales* 15(June): 3.

Jobard, Fabien, and Marta Zimolag. 2006. "When the Police Go to Court: A Study of Contempt, Obstruction, and Assault on Police Officers." *Penal Issues* 17(March): 7–10.

Johnson, Keith, and John Carreyrou. 2005. "Islam and Europe: A Volatile Mix." *Wall Street Journal,* July 11, 2005: 20.

Katznelson, Ira. 2005. *When Affirmative Action Was White: An Untold History of Racial Inequality in the 20th Century.* New York: Norton.

Kepel, Gilles. 2004. *The War for Muslim Minds: Islam and the West.* Cambridge, Mass.: Harvard University Press.

———. 2005. "Le quitte ou double d'Al Qaida" ["Quit or Double for Al Qaeda"]. *Le Monde,* July 26, 2005.

Khosrokhavar, Farhad. 2004. *L'islam dans les prisons* [*Islam in prisons*]. Paris: Balland.

———. 2006. *Quand parle Al Qaida* [*When Al Qaeda speaks*]. Paris: Balland.

Knowlton, Brian. 2005. "Muslim Doubts on Extremism." *International Herald Tribune,* July 15, 2005: 1.

Lagrange, Hughes. 2000. "Sociabilité et délinquance des jeunes" ["Sociability and Delinquency in Youth"]. *Cahiers de la Sécurité Intérieure* 42(2): 63–86.

Lanquetin, Marie Thérèse. 2000. "Le recours au droit dans la lutte contre les discriminations: La question de la preuve" ["Resorting to Law for Antidiscrimination Struggles: The Issue Relative to Evidence"]. *Geld* 2(October): 79–81.

Leclerc, Jean-Marc. 2005. "Sarkozy mobilise contre les violences urbaines" ["Sarkozy Mobilizes Against Urban Violence"]. *Le Figaro,* September 9, 2005: 8.

Leiken, Robert, and Steven Brooke. 2006. *A Quantitative Analysis of Terrorism and Immigration.* Washington: Nixon Center.

Merkl, Peter, editor. 1986. *Political Violence and Terror: Motifs and Motivations.* Berkeley, Calif.: University of California Press.

Mincy, Ronald. 2004. *Black Males Left Behind.* Washington: Urban Institute Press.

Ministère de l'Intérieur et de la Décentralisation [Interior Ministry]. 1983. *Les policiers, leurs métiers, leur formation.* [*The Police, Their Methods, Their Training*] Paris: La Documentation Française.

Monjardet, Dominique 1996. *Ce que fait la police* [*What the Police Do*]. Paris: Editions La Découverté.

Mucchielli, Laurent. 2004. "L'évolution de la délinquance" ["The Evolution of Delinquency"]. *Sociétés Contemporaines* 53(37): 101–34.

———. 2005. *Le scandale des "tournantes." Dérives médiatiques, contre-enquête sociologique* [*The Scandal of Collective Rapes: Media Excesses, Sociological Counter-investigation*]. Paris: La Découverte.

Nashi, Alexandre. 2005. "La Fondation de France distingue les femmes d'une cité" ["The Foundation of France Celebrates Women from the City"]. *Le Figaro,* December 29, 2005.

Orfield, Gary, editor. 2004. *Dropouts in America: Confronting the Graduation Rate Crisis.* Cambridge, Mass.: Harvard Education Press.

Perrot, Michèle. 1979. "Dans la France de la Belle Époque, les apaches, premières bandes de jeunes" ["In France During la Belle Époque, The Apachians, the First Youth Gang"]. In *Les marginaux et les exclus dans l'histoire* [*A Historical View of Marginals and Outsiders*], edited by Michèle Perrot. Paris: UGE.

Pottier, Marie-Lys. 2003. "Cadre de vie, victimisation et relation de citoyens avec les services de police" ["Living Environment, Victimization, and Citizens-Police Relationship"]. *Cahiers de la Sécurité Intérieure* 51(first term): 241–58.

Réju, Emmanuelle. 2005. "La délinquance des jeunes, miroir d'une société en crise" ["Juvenile Delinquency, A Reflection of a Society in Crisis"]. *La Croix,* September 12, 2005: 3–4.

Richardson, Louise. 2006. *What Terrorists Want: Understanding the Terrorist Threat.* London: John Murray.

Rivayrand, Serge. 2006. "L'action de la police nationale dans la lutte contre les violences urbaines" ["The Action of National Police in the Struggle Against Urban Violence"]. *Regards sur l'Actualité* 319(March): 56–57.

Roberts, Sam. 2004. *Who We Are.* New York: Henry Holt.

Roché, Sébastian. 2000. *La délinquance des jeunes. Les jeunes de 13–19 ans racontent leurs délits* [*Juvenile Delinquency: 13–19 Year Olds Recount their Offenses*]. Paris: Le Seuil.

Roy, Olivier. 2004. *Globalized Islam: The Search for a New Ummah.* New York: Columbia University Press.

Rutten, Tim. "A New Kind of Riot." *New York Review of Books,* June 11, 1992: 53.

Sageman, Marc. 2004. *Understanding Terror Networks.* Philadelphia, Pa.: University of Pennsylvania Press.

Sampson, Robert, and Stephen Raudenbush. 2004. "Seeing Disorder: Neighborhood Stigma and the Social Construction of Broken Windows." *Social Psychology Quarterly* 67(4): 319–42.

Sanday, Peter. 1990. *Fraternity Gang Rape: Sex, Brotherhood and Privilege on Campus.* New York: New York University Press.

Sayad, Abdelhmayed. 1993. "Le mode de génération des générations immigrées" ["The Way of Life Across Immigrant Generations"]. *L'Homme et la Société* 111–12: 155–74.

Schain, Martin. 2008. "Reactions to Terrorism After September 11: New Rules on Immigration in US and Europe." In *The Illusion of Change,* edited by A. Chebel d'Appolonia and S. Reich. Forthcoming.

Sicot, François. 2000. "Enfants d'immigrés maghrébins. Rapport au quartier et engagement dans la délinquance" ["North African Immigrant Children: Their Link with the Neighborhood and their Delinquent Career"]. *Cahiers de la Sécurité Intérieure* 42: 87–108.

Silke, Andrew, editor. 2004. *Research on Terrorism: Trends, Achievements, and Failures.* London: Frank Cass.

Smith, Craig. 2005. "A French Underclass Familiar to the U.S." *New York Times,* November 12, 2005.

Smolar, Piotr. 2004. "Les RG s'alarment d'un 'repli communautaire' dans les banlieues" ["Intelligence Service Gets Nervous about Communitarian Enclosures in the Banlieues"]. *Le Monde,* July 6, 2004.

———. 2005. "L'argument islamiste contre la France" ["The Islamist Argument Against France"]. *Le Monde,* December 23, 2005: 3.

———. 2007. "Nicolas Sarkozy dans le piège des RG" ["Nicolas Sarkozy in the RG's Trap."]. *Le Monde,* February 7, 2007: 2.

SORA. 2001. *Attitudes Towards Minority Groups in the European Union.* Vienna: European Monitoring Center on Racism and Xenophobia.

Stroobants, Jean-Pierre. 2005. "Le jeune fils du cinéaste Theo Van Gogh brutalisé par deux jeunes Marocains" ["The Son of Filmmaker Theo Van Gogh Attacked by Two Young Moroccans"]. *Le Monde,* August 1, 2005.

Sykes, Gresham, and Daniel Marcia. 1957. "Techniques of Neutralization: A Theory of Delinquency." *American Sociological Review* 22: 664–70.

Taguieff, Pierre-André. 1991. *Face au racisme* [*Facing Racism*]. Paris: La Découverte.

Terray, Emmanuel. 2004. "L'hystérie politique" ["Political Hysteria"]. In *Le foulard islamique en questions* [*Questioning the Islamic Headscarf*], edited by C. Nordmann. Paris: Éditions Amsterdam.

Toscer, Olivier. "La police aussi porte une part de responsabilité" ["The Police Also Carry Some Responsibility"]. *Le Nouvel Observateur,* June 12, 2005: 78.

Zauberman, Renée, and René Levy. 2003. "Police, Minorities and the French Republican Ideal." *Criminology* 41(4): 1065–1100.

Zauberman, Renée, Philippe Robert, and Marie-Lys Pottier. 2000. "Risque de proximité ou risque lié au style de vie. Enquêtes et évaluation de la sécurité urbaine" ["Risk of Proximity or Risk of Lifestyle: Surveys and Evaluation of Urban Security"]. *Cahiers de la Sécurité Intérieure* 42: 193–220.

CHAPTER 15

Ethnic Minorities and Confidence in the Dutch Criminal-Justice System

Catrien Bijleveld, Heike Goudriaan, and Marijke Malsch

Amsterdam has witnessed a number of incidents of unrest in recent years, centered on large groups of young migrants from North Africa, whom the police accuse of obstructing their work and attacking them for no reason, and who, conversely, accused the police of discriminating against them. Recently, Dutch newspapers have published interviews with municipal officials from Amsterdam and Rotterdam who claimed that they were "desperate" and stated that a small nucleus of troublesome ethnic youths should simply be incarcerated, because "nothing helps." Public remarks by some high-ranking police officers and politicians have not exactly helped to lighten up the atmosphere: one police officer declared in 2001, "Every Moroccan on a scooter is a suspect to me." The Amsterdam town council member Rob Oudkerk of the Labor Party coined the term "kutmarokkanen" (translated best as "[expletive] Moroccans"). The murder of Theo van Gogh by a Moroccan migrant who denounced the Dutch criminal-justice system and refused to defend himself is generally seen as representative of the extreme, fundamentalist end of the spectrum of denunciation of Western norms and values by, especially, Muslim migrants.

The Netherlands, a small, flat, densely populated country situated in the west of continental Europe, is historically perceived as a tolerant and in some ways permissive society. Many dissident writers printed their books in the Netherlands in the late Middle Ages and thereafter (Luther, Spinoza). The Dutch have always been known for their pragmatism and mercantile spirit. They are reputed to be down to earth and frugal (sometimes to the point of meanness) and dislike show-off behavior ("Als je gewoon doet doe je al gek genoeg"—You're nuts enough if you just behave as you normally do). Over the centuries, numerous migrants and refugees fleeing persecution settled in the Netherlands, such as the Jews, the Huguenots in the seventeenth and eighteenth centuries, and many (mainly of mixed descent) from the former Dutch East Indies. The Dutch drugs policy is (in)famous for its pragmatism and permissiveness, as well as for its internal contradictions, such as that users may buy a small amount of soft drugs legally in designated shops but the owners of these shops cannot buy these drugs in a legal retail market. Same-sex partners may marry and adopt children, prostitution is legalized, and euthanasia is legal under certain conditions. Sentencing practices, at least until the mid 1980s, were comparatively mild. The prison population has since grown from a European low to a high position, growing at the fastest rate in Europe.

Although many bigger cities have concentrations of minorities and indigenous Dutch with lower incomes, no real ghettos exist such as in the United States or as the banlieues in Paris. Firearms are prohibited. Wim Kok, the former prime minister, often rode his bike to his office in The Hague. Recently, however, terrorism laws have been passed and the country has changed in the sense that closed-circuit television (CCTV) is operational in many places, security alerts occur regularly, and politicians such as the Somali-born liberal Ayaan Hirsi Ali and the extreme right-wing Geert Wilders have been threatened for their radical views. The relaxed and tolerant atmosphere of bygone days has thus changed.

In this paper, we will investigate to what extent the growing proportion of the population that is of non-Dutch ethnicity perceive the Dutch criminal-justice system in the same way that ethnic Dutch members of the population do. In particular, we will investigate to what extent ethnic minorities perceive the Dutch criminal-justice system as legitimate, and whether they put trust and confidence in the operation of this system as exemplified by the operations of the police and the judiciary. For doing so, we will first briefly describe the Netherlands and its ethnic make-up in more detail. Next, we will describe the pertinent characteristics of the Dutch criminal-justice system. Then, surveying the available literature and performing a number of secondary analyses on existing databases, we will assess to what extent ethnic minorities and ethnic Dutch perceive the Dutch criminal justice system as legitimate. We end with a number of recommendations.

ETHNIC MINORITIES IN THE NETHERLANDS

Dutch society has become ethnically more diverse during recent decades. In the 1960s the Netherlands saw a large influx of labor migrants from mainly Turkey and Morocco. Although their stay was intended to be temporary, most of these migrants have settled with their families, and their descendants now make up a growing part of the population. Almost all migrants from Turkey and Morocco are Muslims. The Moroccans come mainly from the poor rural area called the Rif, and most are not ethnic Arabs but are Berbers. Their communities in their homeland for many years withstood and felt discriminated against by the maghzen, the central, Arab, urban, rulers. They speak Tamazight, a Berber language, and Arabic as a second language. For many years they had their own traditional justice system, which used collective oaths and a lay court. Turkish migrants came mainly from the eastern and central rural areas of Turkey. Many of them are ethnic Kurds.

Migrants from the Dutch colony of Surinam (Dutch Guyana) came to the Netherlands in large numbers around 1975, just before Surinam became independent and its inhabitants had the choice to remain in Surinam or settle in the Netherlands. The ethnic makeup of the population of Surinam is quite diverse. Four main ethnic groups stand out: the often inaptly named "Hindustans," who are originally from India and are either Hindu or Muslim; the "Creoles," who are Africans originally transported to the plantations as slaves; and the Javanese and Chinese, who were later brought as laborers to Surinam. Most Surinamese speak Dutch. The Netherlands Antilles still are part of the Kingdom of the Netherlands, and while travel is not unrestricted, many (mostly young male) Antilleans have also settled, more or less permanently, in the Netherlands; they do not speak Dutch, but Papiamento. Just after the Second World War, migrants from the former Dutch East Indies settled in the Netherlands, as well as a small group of migrants from one of the islands that now belong to Indonesia but that strived for independence, the Moluccans.

In addition, asylum seekers from various countries (most prominently Iraq, China, Iran, Afghanistan, and Somalia) have been added to the non-indigenous population in recent years. This influx has been sizable; in European perspective, the Netherlands received for instance in 2001 the one but highest number of new asylum requests per capita (2.7 per 1,000). In addition, many of those who obtain status apply for family reunification or family formation and their relatives eventually also emigrate to the Netherlands. This regular so-called "volg-migratie" (follow-up migration) is about double the volume of the asylum influx. However, with the tightening of asylum laws, the asylum influx has recently become considerably lower than in previous years, the number of people obtaining a permanent residence permit has also decreased, and the number of rejected asylum seekers who have really been deported has increased. Table 15.1 gives an overview of the sizes of the respective newer and older migrant groups, as well as the size of the Dutch-born population.

In the Netherlands, people have a general dislike of racial connotations, perhaps to do with the persecution and deportation of the Jews in the Netherlands: under the occupation by the Germans in the Second World War approximately 70 percent of the Jewish inhabitants were deported and killed, including 90 percent of all Jews living in Amsterdam. Perhaps for this reason, race is not registered in the Netherlands, and residents are generally counted in statistics as non-ethnic Dutch when either they or their father or mother have been born outside of the Netherlands. Thus, ethnicity is generally registered as to people's or their parents' country of birth. For instance, an ethnic Chinese born in Indonesia is in this manner registered as Indonesian; an ethnic Chinese born in Malaysia appears in the

TABLE 15.1   SIZE OF MIGRANT GROUPS PER THOUSAND, TOTAL OF FIRST
AND SECOND GENERATION

Migrant Group	Size (percent)	Migrant Group	Size (percent)
Non-Western		*Western*	
Turkish	358 (2.2)	EU countries	822 (5.0)
Surinamese	328 (2.0)	Former Dutch East Indies	395 (2.4)
Moroccan	314 (1.9)	Other European countries	135 (0.8)
Antillean/Aruban	130 (0.8)	Other Western Countries	69 (0.4)
Asian[a]	302 (1.9)	outside Europe[d]	
African[b]	194 (1.2)	*Total Western*	*1,422 (8.7)*
Latin American[c]	68 (0.4)		
Total Non-Western	*1,696 (10.4)*	*Dutch*	*13,195 (80.9)*

Source: Statistics Netherlands (2004).
[a] Excluding Indonesian and Japanese.
[b] Excluding Moroccan.
[c] Excluding Surinamese and Antillean and Aruban.
[d] Including Japanese, North American and Oceanian.

statistics as Malaysian. Only those actually born in China (or one of their parents) are labeled Chinese. According to the same logic, children whose parents are second-generation migrants and who themselves were born in the Netherlands are counted as Dutch. The so-called third generation thus disappears in the statistics. That generation is still fairly small, but is rapidly increasing.

Most of the research in the Netherlands on ethnic minorities has traditionally focused on the so-called "G4," the largest groups of recent migrants: the Turks, the Moroccans, the Surinamese, and the Antilleans. Asylum seekers form an even more heterogeneous group, and the respective groups' sizes are often too small to make research—using interpreters—feasible. Thus, also in this chapter, much of the information given centers on ethnic Dutch and these traditional four migrant groups. Only limited information is available on asylum seekers and other recent non-Western migrants and it is much more scattered. It should be noted that for almost all groups—traditional as well as recent non-Western groups—notable language and cultural barriers exist. Surinamese ethnic minorities as a rule speak Dutch; first-generation migrants from other countries as a rule don't. In addition, there is a large segment of non-Western migrants who are not Christian but Muslim: not only Moroccans and Turks but also Iraqis, Afghans, and other asylum migrants.

Although many non-indigenous Dutch, such as migrants from the former Dutch East Indies, are completely integrated, for many of the more recent migrants this is not the case. Many of the non-Western immigrants live in the big cities (for instance, about a third of the populations of Amsterdam and Rotterdam in 2002 are of non-Western descent). A sizable proportion of them are classified in the lower socioeconomic categories of society; and particularly those with refugee status and families of Moroccan origin are found in the lowest income categories. Whereas the overall unemployment rate among indigenous Dutch is 1.9 percent, the rate for non-Western migrants is 2.7 percent; among asylum migrants it is 23 to 40 percent for males and 38 to 70 percent for females (Bijl et al. 2005). Sizable proportions of Turkish and Moroccan (adult) women are illiterate. Two thirds of marriages by Turkish and Moroccan migrants are so-called migration-marriages by which is meant that a resident migrant marries someone brought in fresh from the homeland; even among the second generation the percentage is over 50 percent. Children from ethnic minorities finish school less often and with lower degrees than do children from indigenous families, and the gap is not decreasing notably, although overall, females do better than males (Bijl et al. 2005). Unemployment among non-Western juveniles is twice the rate of that among ethnic Dutch juveniles (40 percent and 20 percent, respectively); particularly recent migrants from the Netherlands Antilles appear increasingly marginalized. The socioeconomic position of ethnic minorities is thus on average distinctly worse than that of ethnic Dutch inhabitants of the Netherlands, and that is particularly the case for some groups such as Moroccans and young first-generation Antilleans.

Ethnic minorities are overrepresented in Dutch crime statistics. In 2002, 62.5 percent of all registered suspects were ethnically Dutch, so 37.5 percent were thus ethnic minorities. Overall, 1.8 percent of all indigenous Dutch have a record in the automated police system as a suspect of an offense; for non-ethnic Dutch males this figure is 4.6 percent; the corresponding figures for females are 0.3 percent and 0.9 percent (Blom et al. 2005). The overrepresentation is higher for juveniles: first-generation Antillean and Moroccan juveniles' representation in police statistics is three times higher than that for Dutch juveniles (Blom et al. 2005); this figure has been calculated correcting for important predictors such as the proportion of males. Erik Snel et al. (2000) pointed to the overrepresentation of Yugoslav and Soviet immigrants. For second-generation migrants, Yugoslavs have a fourfold increased risk, Moroccans' risk is increased by a factor 3.5, and the risk of Antilleans by a factor 2.3 (Blom et al. 2005). Somali youngsters are often mentioned as a "newly emerging" group of problematic youths. Mariska Kromhout and Marion van San (2003) showed how—only counting first-generation migrants and thus counting second-generation migrants as Dutch—recent migrants constitute a larger proportion of suspects than migrants from the traditional immigrants countries of Surinam, the Netherlands Antilles, Turkey, and Morocco. Recent—mostly asylum—migrants thus outnumber migrants from these traditional migrant communities in the Dutch police statistics. In Dutch penal institutions, 74 percent of detainees have Dutch nationality; however, 50 percent were born outside the Netherlands (DJI 2005).

We thus see that the overrepresentation of non-ethnic Dutch increases from the police level to the level of penal institutions. We do not know to what this increasing overrepresentation (nor the initial overrepresentation at the police level) is attributable, and answering that question lies outside of the scope of this chapter. Marianne Junger (1988) and Ben Rovers (1999) argue that although no conclusive proof has been found of ethnic bias in the Dutch criminal-justice system, it cannot be ruled out that some exists. For a long time, the overrepresentation of ethnic minorities at the police and higher levels in the criminal-justice system was a taboo subject in the Netherlands; Ed Leuw (1997), who presented one of the first criminological analyses in this area, was severely criticized for his putative political incorrectness.

Although much of the public debate focuses on perpetrators, it should not be forgotten that ethnic minorities may be overrepresented as victims as well. Remarkably, victimization is not disaggregated for ethnicity in the Dutch victim surveys. We therefore reanalyzed the 2001 wave of the Politiemonitor Bevolking (Police Population Monitor) by ourselves, disaggregating by ethnicity, using the six different ethnicities that are provided in the dataset. It should be noted that in this study, interviewees are asked to self-determine to what ethnic group they belong. As table 15.2 shows, migrants are more often victimized than ethnic Dutch. The pattern is consistent for all non-Western immigrant groups. Although the risk of being the victim of a violent crime is elevated for non-Dutch, this difference is not significant. In total, the risk for victimization is clearly elevated. It should be noted, however, that these differences disappear after correcting for urbanization, gender, and age. From qualitative information it appears as if especially women from minority groups may be victims of domestic violence more often than indigenous Dutch women, for women's shelters have a large overrepresentation of women from minority groups. Although the evidence sometimes appeared conflicting (Van Dijk and Oppenhuis 2002), this has now been corroborated (Wittebrood and Veldheer 2005). Overall, most of the differences as measured by victim surveys in victimization may be attributable to differences in background variables related to victimization risk, but some migrants may be at risk of particular offenses.

All in all, given the marginalized position of several migrant groups in the Netherlands, their overrepresentation at police and further levels of the criminal-justice system, and the language and cultural gaps between the more recent and less-integrated migrants and the general Dutch population, it seems relevant to ask whether immigrant groups in the Netherlands perceive the Dutch criminal-justice system in the same light as indigenous Dutch do, and whether they perceive its operation as legitimate. Such questions are important because immigrant groups will form a permanent and growing segment of Dutch society in the future, and their acceptance of Dutch institutions is both a relevant aspect of integration and contributes to an efficient and fair operation of the criminal-justice system.

TABLE 15.2 CRIMINAL VICTIMIZATION OF INDIGENOUS DUTCH AND NON-INDIGENOUS DUTCH

Ethnic Group	N	Percentage Who Were Property Crime Victims[a]	Percentage Who Were Violent Crime Victims[b]	Percentage Who Were Property or Violent Crime Victims	Percentage Who Were Victims of Any Crime[c]
Ethnicity (dich.)					
Dutch	1,500	34.1	2.3	36.3	42.1
Non-Dutch	3,587	40.8***	2.9	43.4***	49.8***
Ethnicity					
Dutch (reference group)	1,500	34.1	2.3	36.3	42.1
Indonesian	812	32.0	3.3	35.1	39.8
Moluccan	121	38.8	2.5	41.3	43.8
Antillean	288	42.7	1.4	44.1	47.9
Moroccan	286	46.2	3.8	49.7	56.3
Surinamese	1,419	41.2	3.0	44.0	51.0
Turkish	661	48.0***	2.3	49.6***	59.0***
Total	5,087	38.8	2.7	41.3	47.6

Source: Politiemonitor Bevolking (2001).

[a] Includes theft of bike, car, from car, damage of goods, (attempted) burglary, theft of purse without violence, theft from house, other theft.

[b] Includes purse snatching, threats, assault.

[c] Includes theft of bike, car, from car, damage of goods, (attempted) burglary, theft of purse without violence, theft from house, other theft, purse snatching, threats, assault traffic victimizations, other forms of victimization.

***$p < .001$ (two-tailed)

LEGITIMACY

For any legal system to function adequately, it needs to be able to depend on citizens' compliance with the law and cooperation with the police and the courts. Research has suggested that perceptions of legitimacy have a strong association with compliance to both judicial decisions and legal norms (Tyler 1990, 2003; Sherman 1993; Paternoster et al. 1997). When citizens perceive the legal system as legitimate, they will probably follow legal rules to a greater extent, accept judicial decisions, assist the police when they have knowledge of crimes, report crimes to the police, be prepared to cooperate as witnesses in criminal trials when summoned to do so, and, last but not least, not take the law into their own hands.

Legitimacy, located originally in the principle of legality, implying that all or most law can be found in the written codes which the judge as "bouche de la loi" (the mouthpiece of the law) applies, is, however, not self-evident. Additional factors, such as procedural justice, participation, transparency, and fair treatment are important for citizens to perceive a legal system as legitimate. Legitimacy can as such be expected to partly ensue from characteristics of the procedures as well as from the psychological collateral of procedures. In general, confidence in public institutions, including the criminal-justice system, has decreased since the 1980s, not only in the Netherlands but also in other Western European countries (Van der Meer 2004). Confidence in the judiciary appears to be related to confidence in the police and in other state institutions (Van der Meer 2004).

Two aspects are generally deemed to be of special relevance to legitimacy: participation of citizens in criminal trials, and the fair treatment of participants.

Participation

Opportunities for citizens to participate in criminal trials may range from taking part in the decision as a member of a jury or as a lay judge, to, in case of being a party to a civil conflict or being a defendant in a criminal trial, voicing an opinion about the case at the actual trial. According to the theory of procedural justice (Tyler and Lind 1992; Tyler 1990, 2003) defendants who have been offered the opportunity to put forward their opinion about a case will accept the outcome better than defendants who did not have that opportunity. Being able to call witnesses and experts appears to have a similar effect on acceptance of the outcome (Crombag and Van Koppen 2002; Tyler 2003). Research shows that witnesses and victims, on their part, appear to desire some form of participation that goes further than just making a statement. They want to be able to put questions to the legal authority and to make clear certain wishes concerning the procedure (Wemmers 1996; Van der Leij 2002). The processing of information by the legal system to the participants is an important precondition to participation: defendants, witnesses, and victims should know where, when, and how they may have input. On top of that, information is needed for them to assess the fairness of a procedure, the presence or absence of bias, and the neutrality of the decisionmaker.

In other respects, the processing of information is of relevance for the legitimacy of the legal system as well. Views held by the public on the criminal-justice system are, to a great extent, dependent on the information citizens receive. Adequate processing of information concerning the operation of the criminal-justice system, the punishments that are imposed, and general knowledge about the system, all increase confidence in the system. Becca Chapman, Catriona Mirrlees-Black, and Claire Brawn (2002) found that after receiving objective, factual information about the operation of the criminal-justice system, citizens adopted a less "punitive" attitude: they were less often of the opinion that courts sentence too leniently.

Fair Treatment

The aspect of "fair treatment" is central not only in legal writings but also in the psychological literature about Procedural justice. Procedures in which the participants have been treated with respect are known to lead to greater satisfaction (Tyler and Lind 1992; Tyler 1990, 2003). Participants are more cooperative in new contacts with the criminal-justice system when they feel they were treated fairly in previous contacts (Wemmers 1996). The degree of friendliness of the judicial officer is also relevant for future cooperation in the legal system (Van der Leij 2002). Such associations are found not only in criminal law but also in civil, in tax, and health law (Makkai and Braithwaite 1994; Paternoster et al. 1997; Tyler 2003).

Research supplies evidence that recidivism may be affected by fair treatment as well. Lawrence W. Sherman (1993) has contended that the way suspects are treated, as well as the perceived fairness of sentences, contribute to the level of shame an offender feels for his acts, which is a necessary condition for taking responsibility for what he has done. Such feelings of responsibility are needed for preventing relapse.

The question may be posed whether ethnic minorities are affected by the tendencies described here to the same degree as ethnic Dutch: Do they wish to participate as much as others, and do they value being treated fairly? Or do they expect a top-down treatment, i.e. a treatment by judicial officers where the focus is placed primarily on decision making by the authority and not on informing and exchange of arguments with the process participants? In a later section to this chapter, we will pay attention to these questions. We now briefly discuss pertinent aspects of the Dutch criminal-justice system, with the aim of answering the questions: To what extent are participants offered opportunities to participate in legal procedures? And how are they treated by the criminal-justice system?

THE DUTCH CRIMINAL-JUSTICE SYSTEM

Criminal suspects are first processed through the police system. For some offenses, for juveniles who meet certain criteria, the police may impose a so-called "HALT" order, entailing a more or less symbolic sanction tailored to the offense (for example, cleaning up graffiti for a graffiti offense). In such cases, the juvenile perpetrator does not receive a rap sheet. In other situations, after the police have become convinced that the suspect has indeed committed a crime, the case is transferred to the public prosecutor's office. If the prosecutor decides to proceed with a case, he or she may either bring the case to court or deal with the case him- or herself (called a "transactie"). When the case is brought before a court, a punishment may be imposed. This punishment can assume various forms: it can vary from a fine to community service to a treatment kind of sanction "leerstraf" to incarceration.

The Dutch criminal-justice system is highly professional by nature. No use of juries is made for the trial of cases and lay judges are almost absent as well. This is in contrast to most countries surrounding the Netherlands, which use either juries or lay-judges without a professional background, or both. Dutch judges are independent and cannot be discharged because of the sentences they impose. Direct public influence on the appointment of the members of the judiciary is absent. Public prosecutors are also not voted into office.

All three major actors in the Dutch criminal-justice system—police, prosecution, and judiciary—have wide discretionary powers. The police and the prosecution are allowed to deal with cases in the stage before the actual trial by proposing transactions or other conditions to the dismissal of the case. The judiciary has wide discretional powers when sentencing: the criteria for the length of punishments are not very strict in the Netherlands, and neither are the demands for justifying sentences.

Owing to ever-increasing caseloads, the use of these discretional powers by the police and the prosecution have grown substantially during the twentieth century. An ever-increasing proportion of cases is dealt with by the police or the prosecution before an actual trial session takes place. Opportunities for checks and balances are largely absent in these procedures in which police and prosecution deal with cases.

In the Netherlands, guidelines exist for both the police and the prosecution to provide information to victims (Wemmers 1996), encouraging these officials to inform the victims of the developments in the case and to treat them fairly. Also, in the Code of Criminal Procedure, a number of provisions can be found that request the prosecutor to inform the victim of any developments in the case.

In Dutch criminal cases, most investigation is done by the police in the pre-trial stage. Findings are reported in the case file, and at the actual trial there is, most of the time, no interrogation of witnesses and experts. Judges base their decisions primarily on the written reports in the case files (Malsch and Nijboer 1999). Quite serious cases may thus be tried in very little time. The language used by the professional process participants may not be easily comprehensible for the lay public. Because of the absence of lay involvement, the professionals in the system do not have an explicit incentive to use more colloquial language, and legal terms are generally not "translated" for the audience. Research has shown that, indeed, most Dutch citizens have trouble understanding what is going on in court (Malsch and Nijboer 2005). Also, trials are not very clearly visible and audible from the public gallery.

The Dutch criminal justice system provides free interpreters for defendants who have not mastered the Dutch language, during the trial session and during interrogations by various law enforcement officials. Brochures are available in court buildings about, among other things, the rights of defendants and victims, and the operation of the criminal-justice system. These brochures are available in Dutch and in a number of foreign languages, including Turkish and Arabic.

The media have access to criminal trials, but the use of cameras is restricted. Media coverage of criminal trials is limited to the reading of the sentence or the start of a trial; most other parts of trials are not broadcast. In general, Dutch media, when compared to the media of other countries, are relatively restricted in their reporting on criminal trials.

We were unable to obtain recent data on the participation of members of minority groups as professionals in the Dutch criminal-justice system; the general impression is that their involvement is low, and increasingly low as one proceeds up from the police level to the prosecution service to the judiciary. No figures exist as to the participation of minority groups in the Dutch judiciary, nor their representation among the bar (Böcker and De Groot-van Leeuwen 2005).

The Dutch criminal system, like all such systems in the Western world, is nondiscriminatory in design. There are no procedures or material laws that disproportionately put members from ethnic minorities at a disadvantage. At the same time, as outlined previously, ethnic minorities are overrepresented in police statistics as suspects and as offenders. Relatively new sanctions, such as the SOV measure (semi-compulsory treatment for chronically offending drug addicts) and the new ISD measure (selective incapacitation for chronic offenders), do not disproportionately affect ethnic minorities. Recent measures in the field of drug crime for cocaine mules ("bolletjesslikkers"), however, disproportionately affect citizens from the Netherlands Antilles and Latin American countries. Relatively many drug traffickers enter the Netherlands from these countries, and their prison sentences often are much harsher than those handed down for other types of crime.

LEGITIMACY AND ETHNIC MINORITIES

We will now discuss to what extent some properties of the Dutch criminal justice system may affect ethnic minorities' perceptions of the criminal justice system. Most of our assessment will not be based on empirical material, but on our own review of aspects that may in particular bear consequences for ethnic minorities—for instance, language barriers that affect those who have not mastered the Dutch language.

As suggested, the Dutch criminal-justice system provides fewer opportunities for citizens to participate in criminal trials than legal systems in other countries do, either as members of a jury or as lay judges or in the sense of having a substantial input in the process. As a consequence, the gap between the public (ethnic as well as non-ethnic Dutch) and the legal system may be expected to be wider than in countries where more opportunities for participation exist. In addition, few members of ethnic minorities are employed in the police force or prosecution agencies and even fewer are in the judiciary. Thus, absent also lay participation, ethnic minorities are observers rather than participants in the administration of justice.

In court, technical language is avoided to a high degree. However, when legal terms are used, they are generally not explained to the defendant and the public. The reliance on a written dossier does not increase comprehensibility of the treatment of the case in court either. As the media have rather limited access to criminal trials, media coverage does not provide sufficient explanation to the public not in attendance at a criminal trial (Malsch and Nijboer 2005). The distant evaluation of evidence at trials, caused by the absence of witnesses and experts, must also affect comprehensibility for the public. These factors do undermine the principle of open justice to a great extent (Hoekstra and Malsch 2003), for native Dutch speakers but even more so for those whose Dutch isn't that good and who come from different (legal) cultures.

Factors mentioned can be expected to result in reduced confidence in the criminal justice system among minority groups. They probably perceive the justice as less legitimate than do ethnic Dutch.

LITERATURE REVIEW

Studies of minorities and the criminal-justice system in the Netherlands are scarce. A literature search revealed only a limited number of mostly small-scale and qualitative studies in which occasionally some scattered quantitative information can be found. Most studies provide only qualitative information, often even as side remarks to other research questions. To supplement findings from the literature survey, we therefore interviewed a number of specialists: two with specialized knowledge in the area of Muslim minorities, and one clinician with extensive experience in the treatment of juvenile minority offenders.

Eric Bervoets and Wouter Stol (2002) studied perceptions of Dutch (N = 587) and Moroccan (N = 310) residents of neighborhoods in a number of Dutch cities. They found that Moroccans and Dutch identified the same problems in their neighborhoods; they report a striking similarity in the views of the two groups. Moroccans are somewhat more positive about the police; Dutch respondents judge the police to be less approachable, although they notify the police more often; they report offenses as frequently as Moroccans. Bervoets and Stol further report that some Moroccans may have a language problem in their contact with the police. Cécile Nijsten et al. (2002) interviewed key informants as well as sixty-six Antillean, Surinamese, Moroccan, and Turkish parents of youngsters who had committed offenses and had received some kind of sanction (ranging from a community-service order to incarceration) for that offense. They report that parents are relatively unaware of the way the Dutch criminal-justice system works, and of the pedagogical principles underlying some interventions. Although each of the parents had actually been through the motions of each of the criminal-justice institutions they were interviewed about, and so had "hands-on" knowledge, it appeared that with the exception of the police, in each instance more than two-thirds of parents did not understand the role and functioning of the institution. Parents favor authoritarian control of the youngster. Although many parents report that they would like to be involved more in the interventions meted out by the system, key informants point to a low response to invitations for such involvement, particularly among Moroccan parents. Between 37 and 50 percent of parents reported they did not trust the criminal-justice system. More than 40 percent of parents report that members of their own ethnic group are either discriminated against or viewed with prejudices, more than 70 percent report that there are notable cultural differences between themselves and officials of the Dutch criminal-justice system. Key informants in this study reported that particularly low-educated Turkish and Moroccan parents with little mastery of the Dutch language do not understand the criminal-justice system and feel disrespected by that system. E. M. Klooster, A. J. E. van Hoek, and C. A. van't Hoff (1999) conducted interviews among key informants and a small number of juveniles; the aim of their study was to identify how Antilleans, Surinamese, Moroccans, and Turks perceived the sanctions they had experienced. Both key informants as well as the interviewed juveniles reported that juveniles from ethnic minorities are punished more severely than indigenous Dutch juveniles. Some of the interviewed juveniles in fact see the punishment they received as a continuation of the adverse circumstances in which they live in the Netherlands. In addition, some juveniles from ethnic minorities do not understand the Dutch disapproval of violence, coming as they do from a street culture in which violence is normal and for many acceptable behavior. Particularly recent illegal migrants from Morocco and the Netherlands Antilles judge Dutch sentencing as lenient. Many juveniles feel that Dutch judges do not understand them. Their "macho culture" may make it hard for them to admit regret or show feelings.

Frans M. H. M. Driessen et al. (2002), using a small and in all likelihood select sample of twenty-one criminal juveniles, reports how most of the interviewed youngsters are not at all impressed by the Dutch criminal-justice system. The youngsters in this sample regarded incarceration as "no problem," found sentences to be generally light, and mentioned that behavior such as systematic denial under interrogation is profitable. Frank van Gemert (1998) as well reports how many of his Moroccan respondents (again a select, problematic group) consider the Dutch criminal-justice system a "joke." Police officers are viewed as "softies," authorities who can be manipulated easily and who are bound hands and feet by rules and regulations. A. G. M. Hijlkema and E. Otte (1998) report on a sample of nine juveniles undergoing an alternative sentence. From their qualitative interviews one notices a remarkable culture and knowledge gap: for example, one youngster states that of course the employee of the "HALT" bureau has embezzled his fine. Other studies have also provided evidence of a knowledge, or "culture," gap between minorities and the criminal-justice system. It is reported that parents—even when they speak relatively good Dutch—tend to view the Child Welfare Council as "the enemy": this is the institution that "takes away your children." The therapist whom we interviewed reports that many parents, especially Moroccans, see the world as divided into spheres. Inside the home the family assumes responsibility; outside of the family other socializers must do so. When the youngster behaves badly outside the home while he or she behaves well inside the home—and often children are moving in and out of the traditional home and modern Western sphere—it is reportedly hard for them to comprehend that they are held responsible and in a sense punished.

One way to understand this is to realize that many non-Western migrants come, many very recently, from countries where the government is viewed as an entity to distrust a priori. As one of our interviewed specialists put it: "The people are used to the government robbing them. Police, the judiciary, all are viewed as inherently corrupt." In addition, as our other respondent stated, "Many a migrant's recent contact with the aliens police will not have helped to turn around that image." And as the first respondent again put it, "You are used to cheat and bribe your way into getting a passport, getting a birth certificate, and the like. You have been brought up to think the police are there to harass you, not to maintain public order. And then, many asylum migrants have also given false stories to get into the Netherlands, or were told to do so, so this is their first acquainting with the system."

Guillaume Beijers et al. (2003) in a study on reporting behavior in an area of Amsterdam where many migrants live, reports that many migrants find the police pretty hopeless when it comes to helping them, and so they are more inclined to solve problems themselves. The Dutch police is seen, according to some respondents, as just no different from the French or Moroccan police. Again, different conceptions can be found in Ö. Faruk Akınbingöl (1998), who described how many Turkish drugs dealers—given their image of the Turkish government, given their experiences with Dutch confection ateliers, given the incomprehensibilities of the Dutch drugs policy—think that the Dutch government essentially agrees with the drugs trade, and may even benefit from it. Akınbingöl in addition points to a clear "us and them" feeling among these Turkish men: when we deal in drugs, we are not arming our Turkish fellow citizens, we are only disadvantaging Dutch society. In addition he describes how some younger men bitterly complain about the fate that their fathers suffered: they came full of dreams and ended their lives in relative poverty with disabilities from hard work. The younger men reportedly state defiantly that they will not fall into this trap. The Commission on Moroccan Youth (Commissie Marokkaanse Jeugd 1998) describe fundamental mistrust of Moroccan youth toward, particularly, the Dutch police. Moroccans who went to work for the police are in fact known to have been labeled as "traitors."

All in all, summarizing the literature and the information from our specialists, we conclude that there are no indications from the quantitative studies that have been carried out of greater distrust of the criminal-justice system by minorities. Qualitative findings point to a number of issues that are suggestive: quite a number of migrants may have a language problem, which may make it more difficult for them to have confidence in the criminal-justice system and its various representatives. Problems seem to be concentrated in particular groups of young migrants (overrepresented in qualitative small-scale studies focusing on these particular groups), and among older migrants who have not mastered Dutch. A second suggestive finding is that there may be a culture gap between the Dutch government and migrants who come from societies where they are inclined to have as little to do as possible with the government. Problems are traditionally solved within the community, which also maintains public order, and often the law of the strongest applies. For these people it is a stretch to view the secular Dutch criminal-justice system with its fairly technical and sterile procedures (particularly trials) as a priori fair and its actors as a priori there for the betterment of the lives of the citizens.

Secondary Analysis of Existing Survey Data

For this chapter we reanalyzed two survey data sets. The first is the Netherlands Survey on Crime and Law Enforcement (Nederland Survey Criminaliteit en Rechtshandhaving, or NSCR), carried out in 1996 (Wittebrood, Michon, and ter Voert 1997). The second is the Politiemonitor Bevolking, a telephone self-report survey that is conducted every two years among approximately seventy thousand respondents. Both surveys probably suffer from selective nonresponse by members of minority groups, as do many general surveys in the Netherlands.

The NSCR. The NSCR, in 1996, was done with a sample of about three thousand respondents. Interviewing was face to face (using Computer Assisted Personal Interviewing, or CAPI), and respondents could fill in sensitive questions themselves on a laptop. Karin Wittebrood (1997) concludes that the actual sample probably differs little from the representative sample that was originally drawn. The questionnaire drew heavily on regular surveys such as the Statistics Netherlands (2003) victims survey, the police victim survey Politiemonitor Bevolking, and other regular surveys. Ethnicity was defined by self-reported country of birth, so that we are essentially talking about first-generation migrants only. The eventual data set we could analyze came from 2,798 respondents who reported being born in the Netherlands, and 153 born abroad, of whom 64 can be considered non-western first-generation migrants. This number is lower than would be expected with proportionate representation. One explanation for this could be that the response rate among migrants was selectively lower. Findings should thus be interpreted with caution.

We compared the answers of respondents from minority groups with those given by members from nonminority groups, on a number of questions pertaining to general views on compliance with the law, respondents' satisfaction with the police, as well as respondents' views on crime and law enforcement. The results are presented in Table 15.3; the first column, headed "Overall Mean" gives the overall mean on this variable, the second column headed "Within All Respondents" indicates what

Table 15.3 Comparison of Minority Groups' and Indigenous Dutch Views on Law, Police and Judiciary

	Overall Mean[a]	Within All Respondents	Victim of Any Offense in Lifetime	Victim of Violent Offense Within Lifetime	Victim of Property Offense Within Lifetime
General views on compliance with the law					
People should abide by the law.	3.56	—	—	—	—
Only comply with laws that are reasonable.	2.10	mn	—	—	—
Difficult to break the law and keep self-respect.	3.25	mn	mn	—	mn
Breaking the law is no big deal.	2.02	mn	mn	—	—
People breaking the law are a problem for society.	3.93	—	mn	—	mn
Obedience and respect for law are most important values.	3.72	mn	mn	—	mn
You can break a law if it doesn't harm anyone else.	2.58	—	—	—	—
Police satisfaction					
The police are not taking tough enough action.	3.45	—	—	—	—
I have a great deal of respect for the police.	3.42	—	—	—	—
The police are doing a good job.	3.17	mn	mn	—	mn
The police are doing too little.	3.14	—	—	—	—
The police are contributing to crime reduction.	3.46	—	—	—	—
The police are trying their best.	3.66	—	mn	—	—
The police give too few spot fines.	2.81	—	—	—	—
Scale: Satisfaction with police	3.43	—	—	—	—

Views on crime and law enforcement

Crime in the Netherlands is a huge problem.	4.17	—	—	—	—
The government does too little to combat crime.	3.52	in	in	—	—
Crime is adopting more serious forms.	4.09	in	in	—	—
The Dutch police are honest and trustworthy.	3.38	—	—	—	—
The extent of crime is exaggerated.	2.50	—	—	—	—
There is too little money for the fight against crime.	3.51	in	in	—	—
Dutch judges are honest and trustworthy.	3.58	—	—	—	—
The government ensures the safety of its citizens.	3.00	mn	mn	—	—
Citizens are justified in taking the law into their own hands.	2.43	—	—	—	—
Crimes are too lightly punished.	4.02	—	—	—	—
View on responsibility for protection against crime.	3.19	—	—	M: gov I: cit	—
View on type of punishment for property offense.	3.71	—	—	—	—

Source: Netherlands Survey of Crime and Law Enforcement (1997).
Note: mn = minority groups score significantly higher; in = indigenous Dutch score significantly higher.
a Rating scales ranging from 1 = strongly disagree to 5 = strongly agree.

group scored significantly higher on this item, with "mn" indicating minorities, and "in" indicating indigenous Dutch.

Summarizing these results, we conclude that, overall, not many differences between minority and nonminority respondents emerge. On the whole, minorities are somewhat more content with the police, and indigenous Dutch respondents consider crime to be a bigger problem.

In addition to plain tests of means, we also tested whether there were differences not just between respondents of different ethnic groups but between victims from minority and nonminority groups. We looked at differences between lifetime victims of any offense (significant differences are indicated in the table in the column headed "Victims of Any Offense in Lifetime"), between lifetime victims of a violent offense (significant differences are indicated in the table in the column headed "Victim of Violent Offense Within Lifetime") and lifetime victims of a property offense (significant differences are indicated in the table in the column headed "Victim of Property Offense Within Lifetime"). Again, when there is a significant difference, this is indicated with "mn" when minorities score higher, and with "in" when indigenous Dutch score higher. The pattern of differences remains more or less the same compared to overall differences between minorities and ethnic Dutch; some differences disappear, possibly because of dwindling numbers.

The Politiemonitor Bevolking. The Politiemonitor Bevolking is carried out by telephone every two years among a representative sample of all households having a regular KPN (the former state-owned Dutch telephone company) listed telephone connection. We here analyze the 1995, 1997, 1999, and 2001 waves. The samples are huge: every year about seventy thousand respondents are interviewed. Our file has 317,954 respondents. Respondents are asked to self-define as to whether they are a member of an ethnic group. We selected respondents who had defined themselves as Antillean, Dutch, Indonesian, Moluccan, Moroccan, Surinamese, and Turkish. Given the sampling frame, there are serious doubts whether minorities are sufficiently and a-selectly represented. Fewer minorities have a regular telephone service in their homes, and if they do, their numbers are more often unlisted (see Politiemonitor Bevolking 2001 [in Dutch]). To reduce the vastly different sample size for the Dutch respondents, we randomly selected a subsample of Dutch respondents. The resulting file comprised 5,087 respondents, of whom 1,500 were Dutch, 288 Antillean, 812 Indonesian, 121 Moluccan, 286 Moroccan, 1,419 Surinamese, and 661 Turkish.

For our analysis of the respondents' attitudes toward the police, we used a scale of twelve items on the availability, visibility, functioning, and acting of the police, according to the respondent (= .83). The scale minimum is 0 (negative attitude), the scale maximum is 10 (positive attitude). Table 15.4 shows the attitudes toward the police of our seven ethnic groups for the whole sample and also for the respondents who had been victimized in the year preceding the survey.

TABLE 15.4   OVERALL ATTITUDE TOWARD THE POLICE BY ETHNIC GROUP

Ethnicity	Mean Attitude Toward the Police (Respondents)	Mean Attitude Toward the Police (Victims)
Dutch (reference group)	5.38	5.04
Antillean	5.72*	5.42
Indonesian	5.61*	5.11
Moluccan	5.08	4.57
Moroccan	5.41	4.94
Surinamese	5.60*	5.18
Turkish	5.44	5.25
Total	5.50	5.13

Source: Politiemonitor Bevolking (2001).
*$p < .05$ (two-tailed)

As can be seen from the table, minority and Dutch respondents hold fairly similar attitudes to the police. Where differences emerge, minorities score more positively: Antillean, Indonesian, and Surinamese respondents have a slightly more positive attitude toward the police than Dutch respondents. Correction for gender, urbanization, and age does not alter these conclusions. For victims, none of the scale scores differ significantly. In general, respondents who have been victimized over the past year are less positive about the police than people who were not victimized. This holds for all groups (see table 15.4).

In the Politiemonitor Bevolking, respondents are also asked about their experiences with twelve types of violent and property crime. If respondents say they have experienced one or more of these types of crime in their own town, next they are asked about the most recent incident and whether the crime was reported to the police or not. In our sample over 40 percent of the respondents were victimized at least once in their own town in the twelve months preceding the survey. On average, almost 45 percent of these incidents were reported to the police (see table 15.5). Table 15.5 shows the overall reporting percentages of the seven ethnic groups in our sample. None of the reporting percentages from the minorities is significantly different from the Dutch group. Of course, if we had larger sample sizes, some figures would have differed significantly. For instance, there were only forty-four Moluccan victims of a property crime in our sample.

All in all, no evidence emerges from the quantitative surveys we reanalyzed that ethnic minorities perceive the criminal-justice system in a systematically less favorable light than indigenous Dutch do. As we pointed out, the surveys are likely to contain responses from a select, non-random part of the population, possibly the better integrated and law-abiding part.

TABLE 15.5   OVERALL REPORTING PERCENTAGE BY ETHNIC GROUP

Ethnicity	Percentage of Property Crimes Reported[a]	Percentage of All Crimes Reported
Dutch (reference group)	45.4	46.3
Antillean	40.2	38.9
Indonesian	42.2	42.4
Moluccan	38.6	40.4
Moroccan	45.3	50.1
Surinamese	42.2	42.7
Turkish	47.3	47.9
Total	44.0	44.5

Source: Politiemonitor Bevolking (2001).
[a]Sample sizes are too small to test for differences in the reporting of violent crimes.

GENERAL CONCLUSIONS

Our review and analyses have produced mixed results. On the one hand, we showed how the Dutch criminal-justice system is not very transparent in its operations. Trials are performed in legalistic, juridical language that is even hard for ethnic Dutch to understand, not to mention non-ethnic Dutch. The situation is hardly improved by the fact that trials are mostly "paper trials"—making it hard for members of the public to see and verify what goes on during trials. The judge reads from written statements and the whole procedure for that matter assumes an almost ritual nature. In spite of flyers informing the public of prosecution and sentencing matters, it must be doubted whether the steps in a criminal case are clear, particularly, for migrants. Also, the almost total absence of lay participation, and very limited media coverage decrease the amount of information and the participation of the public in the operations of the Dutch criminal-justice system, factors that bolster a sense of legitimacy. Some of the surveys we reviewed corroborated this. They showed that migrant parents hardly know what the institution they are dealing with is actually for and what its mandate is. In addition, some of the literature showed that quite a few immigrant residents believe that the police and the criminal-justice system discriminate against them. A number of qualitative studies among trouble-prone youths further elaborated on this. They showed how ethnic-minority juveniles perceive the system as biased against them, and the police as discriminatory. However, these studies also paint a picture of a cohort of mostly second-generation, often Moroccan youth, who know the system very well (unlike their parents) and who are not daunted by the prospect of interrogation or prosecution, but instead slip seemingly deftly through the maze of the system. In all likelihood, while these qualitative studies yield a wealth of insight for some troublesome and other particular groups, they are not representative for all non-ethnic Dutch youths.

The larger-scale quantitative studies that we reanalyzed, on the other hand, painted a somewhat different picture: for the most part, respondents from minority groups were more satisfied with the police and judiciary institutions than were Dutch respondents. A part of the seeming contradiction in these results is, we believe, due to the different sampling methods of qualitative and quantitative studies. Whereas most of the qualitative studies we reviewed focus on problematic, high-profile groups, the larger-scale surveys are directed toward the general public. In principle, the different results thus need not conflict. However, we do believe that the victimization surveys have more problems establishing contact and ensuring cooperation with non-ethnic Dutch respondents than with Dutch respondents. Minority groups more often live in towns, and urban respondents are harder to contact, and they more often do not have a regular telephone connection. In addition, little is known about differential refusal. We therefore believe that the surveys may have targeted the relatively better-off segment of the migrant population in the Netherlands, and that the proportionally larger segment of the ethnic groups that performs less well (and may be more dissatisfied with the criminal-justice system) may be underrepresented in the final samples. Lastly, differential response styles may have affected the answers.

All in all, our conclusion from our analyses and review is that there is no proof that migrant groups in the Netherlands, as a whole, view the criminal justice system as inherently less legitimate than ethnic Dutch. The criminal-justice system could, however, do with more openness, we believe, not only for legitimacy as perceived by ethnic minorities but also for ethnic Dutch. There are clear indications that minority parents have little understanding of the workings of the criminal-justice system, and one may ask whether the same doesn't apply to Dutch parents.

It does appear from the studies that particular juvenile migrant groups, such as juvenile Moroccans who have been in contact with the police often, may feel more discriminated against by the police. For older Moroccan and Turkish first-generation migrants a striking cultural gap emerged from the studies. In that sense, it is important for the reader to realize that the migrant population in the Netherlands is fundamentally different from the minority population in the United States. Many migrants in the Netherlands have emigrated from countries where Dutch is not a first or even a second language, and many have a different religion than the main religion in the Netherlands, Christianity. Many migrants have arrived fairly recently. Many Turkish and Moroccan migrants marry partners from their home countries, bringing in new unacculturated first-generation migrants. In addition, until recently, there was hardly any pressure for migrants to acculturate, or "integrate," as it is nowadays euphemistically called in the Netherlands. It was not necessary to speak or write Dutch to obtain a Dutch passport, and politicians could be heard praising the joys of multiculturalism (more often than not equated to the possibility of eating exotic food in cozy restaurants). Those days are gone now in the Netherlands.

For an unknown number of juvenile migrants, it appears that there may be huge distrust and a fundamental and perhaps unsolvable breach of confidence between police and "youth," mainly in the larger cities. Such relations may lead to incidents and in fact do so regularly. This distrust and feeling of being discriminated against may be directed not only toward the police but toward society at large; for instance, it is well known that particularly ethnic minority males have trouble getting access to discotheques. On the other hand, some of the research suggests that a number of these juveniles may think their treatment by the police and the judicial authorities not at all unfair but in fact lenient, and no big deal to suffer, and may even accept it as a small price to pay.

Most of the limited information we found dealt with the general public, suspects, and defendants. In general, it was striking how little information at all was available, and how little research interest there appears to have been in ethnic minorities and the criminal-justice system and its institutions. In general, little is known about sampling and interviewing ethnic minorities in the Netherlands. Most of the available knowledge centers on the traditional migrant groups (Turks, Moroccans, Surinamese, and Antilleans). Given the huge influx of asylum seekers during the past decade, surveys that include this group as well are urgently needed. We believe that a large-scale survey, geared toward the questions we have tried to answer here (on levels of confidence in the criminal-justice system, victimization, and offending) would provide knowledge that is badly needed to gauge integration and full socioeconomic participation of migrants in the Netherlands and to gear interventions to groups whom some politicians now label "hopeless" and propose to simply lock up for an indefinite period.

REFERENCES

Akınbingöl, Ö. Faruk. 1998. *Verleiding en rechtvaardiging. Neutraliseringstechnieken van Turkse Delinquenten in Nederland* [*Seduction and Justification: Neutralization Techniques of Turkish Delinquents in the Netherlands*]. Amsterdam: Stadsuitgeverij Amsterdam.

Beijers, Guillaume, Hans Boutellier, Asmaa Ghonedale, and Maartje Vinke. 2003. *Opsporing Verzocht. Bewoners over Criminaliteit en Aangifte doen in Politiedistrict 8 in Amsterdam* [*Crime Watch. Inhabitants on Crime and Reporting to the Police in Police District 8 in Amsterdam*]. Amsterdam: Free University.

Bervoets, Eric, and Wouter Stol. 2002. "Marokkanen en Nederlanders over hun Wijk— Gedeelde Problemen als Mogelijkheid voor Buurtactivisme" ["Moroccans and Dutch on their Neighborhood—Shared Problems as a Basis for Neighborhood Activism"]. *Tijdschrift voor Criminologie* 44(2): 247–61.

Bijl, Rob V., Aslan Zorlu, Annet S. van Rijn, Roel P. W. Jennissen, and Martine Blom. 2005. *Integratiekaart 2005. De Maatschappelijke Integratie van Migranten in de Tijd Gevolgd: Trend- en Cohortanalyses* [*Integration Map 2005. The Societal Integration of Migrants*

Followed over Time: Trend and Cohort Analyses]. Cahiers 2005-16. The Hague: Research and Documentation Centre. Accessed at http://www.wodc.nl/Onderzoeken/Onderzoek_1314.asp.

Blom, Martine, Ko Oudhof, Rob V. Bijl, and Bart F. M. Bakker. 2005. "Verdacht van Criminaliteit: Allochtonen en Autochtonen Nader Bekeken" ["Suspected of an Offense: Indigenous and Non-indigenous Dutch Scrutinized"]. Cahiers 2005-2. The Hague: WODC, CBS.

Böcker, Anita G. M., and Leny E. De Groot-van Leeuwen. 2005. "Meer van Minder in de Rechtspraak: Over Toetredingskansen van Etnische Minderheden" ["More of Less in Court: On Admission Chances of Ethnic Minorities"]. *Rechtstreeks* 4(1): 1–40.

Chapman, Becca, Catriona Mirrlees-Black, and Claire Brawn. 2002. *Improving Public Attitudes to the Criminal Justice System: The Impact of Information.* London: Home Office Research, Development and Statistics Directorate.

Commissie Marokkaanse Jeugd. 1998. *Samen vol Vertouwen de Toekomst Tegemoet* [*Together Confidently Facing the Future*]. Utrecht: Ministerie van Justitie.

Crombag, Hans F. M., and Peter J. Van Koppen. 2002. "Rechtvaardigheid" ["Fairness"]. In *Het Recht van Binnen: Psychologie van het Recht* [*The Law from Within: Psychology of the Law*], edited by Peter J. van Koppen, Dick J. Hessing, Harald L. G. J. Merckelbach, and Hans F. M. Crombag. Deventer, Netherlands: Kluwer.

Dienst Justitiële Inrichtingen. 2005. *Feiten in Cijfers* [*Facts in Figures*]. Accessed at http://www.dji.nl/main.asp?pid=40&sectorid=2&catid=3.

Driessen, Frans M. H. M., Beate G. M. Völker, Helen M. Op den Kamp, Annette M. C. Roest, and Rachel J. M. Molenaar. 2002. *Zeg me wie je Vrienden zijn. Allochtone jongeren en Criminaliteit* [*Tell Me Who Your Friends Are: Ethnic Minority Youngsters and Crime*]. Utrecht and Apeldoorn, Netherlands: Bureau Driessen and Politie en Wetenschap.

Hijlkema, A. G. M., and E. Otte. 1998. *Werken in je Vrije Tijd. Marokkaanse Jongeren en Alternatieve Straf* [*Work in Your Leisure Time: Moroccan Youngsters and Alternative Sanctions*]. Utrecht: Wetenschapswinkel.

Hoekstra, Ruth, and Marijke Malsch. 2003. "The Principle of Open Justice in the Netherlands." In *Adversarial Versus Inquisitorial Justice,* edited by Peter J. van Koppen and Steven D. Penrod. New York: Kluwer Academic and Plenum Press.

Junger, Marianne. 1988. "Racial Discrimination in the Netherlands." *Sociology and Social Research* 72: 211–6.

Klooster, E. M., A. J. E. van Hoek, and C. A. van't Hoff. 1999. *Allochtonen en Strafbeleving. Een Onderzoek naar de Strafbeleving van Antilliaanse, Surinaamse, Marokkaanse en Turkse Jongens* [*Ethnic Minorities and Their Perceptions of Punishment. A Study on the Perceptions of Punishment by Antillean, Surinamese, Moroccan, and Turkish Boys*]. The Hague: Directie Preventie, Jeugd en Sanctiebeleid.

Kromhout, Mariska, and Marion van San. 2003. *Schimmige Werelden: Nieuwe Etnische Groepen en Jeugdcriminaliteit* [*Dim Worlds: New Ethnic Groups and Crime Among Juveniles*]. Series Onderzoek en Beleid 206. The Hague: Boom.

Leuw, Ed. 1997. *Criminaliteit en Etnische Minderheden. Een Criminologische Analyse* [*Crime and Ethnic Minorities. A Criminological Analysis*]. Series K51. The Hague: Research and Documentation Center.

Makkai, Toni, and John Braithwaite. 1994. "Reintegrative Shaming and Compliance with Regulatory Standards." *Criminology* 32(3): 361–85.

Malsch, Marijke, and Johannes F. Nijboer, editors. 1999. *Complex Cases: Perspectives on the Netherlands Criminal Justice System*. Amsterdam: Thela Thesis.

———. 2005. *De Zichtbaarheid van het Recht. Openbaarheid van de Strafrechtspleging* [*The Visibility of Justice. The Open Nature of the Practice of Criminal Law*]. Deventer, Netherlands: Kluwer.

Nijsten, Cécile, Paul Geense, Trees Pels, and Wilma Vollebergh. 2002. *Allochtone Ouders en Justitie. Vragen en Behoeften van Antilliaanse, Marokkaanse, Surinaamse en Turske Ouders van Jeugdigen die in Aanraking komen met Politie en Justitie* [*Minority Parents and the Criminal Justice System. Questions and Needs of Antillean, Moroccan, Surinamese and Turkish Parents of Juveniles Who Come into Contact with Police and Judiciary*]. Rotterdam: Erasmus University, Instituut voor Sociologisch-Economisch Onderzoek.

Paternoster, Raymond, Robert Brame, Ronet Bachman, and Lawrence W. Sherman. 1997. "Do Fair Procedures Matter? The Effect of Procedural Justice on Spouse Assault." *Law and Society Review* 31(1): 163–204.

Politiemonitor Bevolking. 2001. *Politiemonitor Bevolking 2001. Landelijke Rapportage* [*Police Population Monitor 2001 National Report*]. The Hague and Hilversum, Netherlands: Ministry of Interior and Kingdom Relations, Ministry of Justice and Intomart BV.

Rovers, Ben. 1999. *Klassejustitie: Overzicht van Onderzoek naar Selectiviteit in de Nederlandse Strafrechtsketen* [*Class Justice: An Overview of Studies into the Selectivity of the Dutch Criminal Justice System*]. Rotterdam: Erasmus University, Section Criminology.

Sherman, Lawrence W. 1993. "Defiance, Deterrence, and Irrelevance: A Theory of the Criminal Sanction." *Journal of Research in Crime and Delinquency* 30(4): 445–73.

Snel, Erik, Jan de Boom, Jack Burgers, and Godfried Engbersen. 2000. *Migratie, Integratie en Criminaliteit. Migranten uit Voormalig Joegoslavie en de Voormalige Soviet Unie in Nederland* [*Migration, Integration and Crime. Migrants from Former Yugoslavia and Former Soviet Union in the Netherlands*]. Rotterdam: Rotterdams Instituut voor Sociaal-wetenschappelijk BeleidsOnderzoek.

Statistics Netherlands. 2003. *Allochtonen in Nederland 2003* [*Minorities in the Netherlands 2003*]. Voorburg and Heerlen, Netherlands: Statistics Netherlands.

———. 2004. *Statistisch Jaarboek 2004* [*Statistical Yearbook 2004*]. Voorburg and Heerlen, Netherlands: Statistics Netherlands.

Tyler, Tom R. 1990. *Why People Obey the Law*. New Haven, Conn.: Yale University Press.

———. 2003. "Procedural Justice, Legitimacy and the Effective Rule of Law." In *Crime and Justice: A Review of Research,* edited by Michael Tonry. Chicago, Ill.: University of Chicago Press.

Tyler, Tom R., and E. Allan Lind. 1992. "A Relational Model of Authority in Groups." *Advances in Experimental Psychology* 25: 115–91.

Van der Meer, Tom. 2004. "Vertrouwen in de Rechtspraak: Empirische Bevindingen" ["Trust in the Court: Empirical Findings"]. *Rechtstreeks* 1: 9–55.

Van Dijk, Tom, and Erik Oppenhuis. 2002. *Huiselijk Geweld onder Surinamers, Antillianen en Arubanen, Marokkanen en Turken in Nederland. Aard, Omvang en Hulpverlening* [*Domestic Violence Among Surinamese, Antilleans, and Arubans, Moroccans and Turks in the Netherlands. Nature, Extent, and Aid*]. The Hague and Hilversum, Netherlands: Research and Documentation Centre and Intomart BV.

Van Gemert, Frank. 1998. *Ieder voor Zich. Kansen, Cultuur en Criminaliteit van Marokkaanse Jongens* [*Each for Oneself: Opportunities, Culture, and Crime of Moroccan Youngsters*]. Amsterdam: Het Spinhuis.

Van der Leij, Jan B. J. 2002. *Bejegening op Maat: De Behandeling van Getuigen in Strafzaken* [*Tailored Treatment: The Treatment of Witnesses in Criminal Cases*]. Deventer, Netherlands: Gouda Quint.

Wemmers, Jo-Anne M. 1996. *Victims in the Criminal Justice System.* The Hague, Amsterdam, and New York: Research and Documentation Center and Kugler Publications.

Wittebrood, Karin. 1997. "Nederlandse Survey Criminaliteit en Rechtshandhaving" ["The Dutch Survey of Crime and Law Enforcement"]. In *Nederlanders over Criminaliteit en Rechtshandhaving* [*The Dutch on Crime and Law Enforcement*], edited by Karin Wittebrood, John A. Michon, and Marijke J. ter Voert. Deventer, Netherlands: Gouda Quint.

Wittebrood, Karin, and Vic Veldheer. 2005. "Partnergeweld in Nederland: Een Secundaire Analyse van de Intomart-Onderzoeken naar Huiselijk Geweld" ["Partner Violence in the Netherlands: A Secondary Analysis of the Intomart-Surveys on Domestic Violence"]. *Tijdschrift voor Criminologie* 47(1): 3–22.

Wittebrood, Karin, John A. Michon, and Marijke J. ter Voert, editors. 1997. *Nederlanders over Criminaliteit en Rechtshandhaving* [*The Dutch on Crime and Law Enforcement*]. Deventer, Netherlands: Gouda Quint.

CHAPTER 16

Legitimacy and Criminal Justice: Inequality and Discrimination in the German Criminal-Justice System

Hans-Jörg Albrecht

Legitimacy is strongly linked to impartiality, fairness, and neutrality in procedure and proceedings, as the late German sociologist Niklas Luhmann pointed out (Luhmann 1978).

LEGITIMACY, CRIMINAL JUSTICE, AND DISCRIMINATION

Of course, decisionmaking in the criminal justice system at various points provides for substantial risks to fairness and impartiality. Policing in general and for the purpose of law enforcement, stop-and-search activities, arrest of suspects, detention prior to trial, decisions on prosecution and indictment, trial and sentencing, and the process of criminal corrections carry a risk of discriminatory treatment, in terms of both individual and group discrimination. Decisionmaking to the disadvantage of particular groups may be grounded in hostile attitudes of individual decision-makers or in institutional and legal structures that systematically expose marginal groups to discriminatory acts and decisions. Legitimacy, then, is strongly associated with trust and confidence (Coleman 1988). If mistrust is generated by disorder, threats, suspicion, scarce resources, and feelings of powerlessness (Ross, Mirowsky, and Probesh 2001), trust is generated by the opposite of these: faith in others, feelings of security, a feeling of order, and with order a system of social control that is operating in a predictable and impartial way. The basis of trust resides in the state, in particular, the state that creates norms and guarantees the normative structure of a society, the market and the exchange structures that are able to emerge as well as wealth is produced in a functioning economy, and, finally, civil society and its institutions (Braithwaite 1998).

Policing and the process of criminal justice are particularly exposed to problems of legitimacy because of the specific nature of criminal punishment, that is, its potential to inflicting pain, exert power, and serve as a regulatory instrument in the moral economy of a society. Law enforcement, criminal justice, and criminal punishment are the most significant expressions of the state, Thomas Hobbes's Leviathan, which on the one hand has effectively monopolized violence and on the other legitimately uses violence to maintain social, political, and economic order. Legitimacy and the monopoly of power thus are tightly linked and institutionalized. In particular, police, but also criminal justice at large, thus symbolize a specific order (Gesemann 2003, 204). Moreover, penal sanctions are of particular value for symbolic policymaking in times when levels of fear of crime and feelings of insecurity are running high. This particular value is due to the most important aspect of criminal sanctions, that is: conveying messages about values and identity to offenders, victims, and the public at large. Such messages may be conveyed by public debates on sanctions and sentencing; by the legislature, by means of law making; and ultimately, also, through sentencing practices and enforcement of criminal penalties (Garland 1991). These messages are crucially important because they represent a response to the most basic feelings of individuals in societies: fear and anger. Moreover, criminal justice itself may stir up these basic feelings of fear and anger. Criminal sanctions may on the one hand channel and control anger and accommodate fear, and on the other, provoke fear and anger. Ultimately, *pace* Durkheim and his elaborations on the relationship between punishment and society, messages conveyed through punishment provide the glue that holds society together. But punishment also contains a huge potential for conflict when applied unfairly or in discriminatory ways. Such conflicts may be expressed in low rates of acceptance of institutions of order and criminal justice, and may also result in an increase in violence (Groenemeyer and Mansel 2003), the delegitimation of criminal justice, and ultimately the delegitimation of the state's monopoly of power (von Trotha 1995).

Problems of legitimacy in the German criminal justice system during the nineteenth and much of the twentieth century have been predominantly studied as problems linked to the class nature of criminal law, to police and criminal justice institutions, as well as to discrimination and repression of the working class and economically marginal social groups. Political science and criminology in the early twentieth century described the role of criminal law and criminal justice as the implementation of political repression and the maintenance of political power to the advantage of the upper classes. These theoretical concepts were derived mainly from Marxist theory and made use of Marxist analytical categories such as class and class conflict.

Inequality as expressed in criminal law and criminal justice practice, in particular in sentencing, received political scientists' attention again in the late 1960s (Lautmann 1972). At this time alternative theoretical concepts of crime and deviance started to attract attention in German criminology. Criminal justice institutions such as the police, public prosecutors, and the courts became the subjects of studies that assumed bias-laden decisionmaking, again to the disadvantage of powerless and marginal groups. The basic reason for this renewed interest in the study of social control, especially the institutions that implement criminal law, lies in the advent of labeling theory. This theoretical concept led to the idea that crime and deviance are not natural social or behavioral phenomena but are socially created concepts and ascriptions varying over time and space and guided also by criteria that reflect legal and legitimate criteria but also a social order based on inequality. The introduction of an interactionist dimension to the study of crime and deviance into criminology research on criminal law–based social control and the selection process organized through police, public prosecution, and the courts gained momentum. The criteria thought to be most important in this selection and filtering process was class. The institutions that were assumed to contribute most to these distortions were the police, public prosecutors, and the courts. This development coincided with the societal and political unrest of the late sixties and early seventies. Political concern for equal opportunity emerged, and this contributed to an upsurge of research on inequality and discrimination in criminal justice.

The 1960s also saw an increase in research on the police and policing, starting with studies on how criminal suspicion is construed and what guides police practices in stop-and-search and arrests. Research at the end of the 1960s dealt with police activities in patrolling the streets and finding suspects. These studies focused specifically on the structure of situations where police decide on all sorts of interventions based on criminal suspicion (Blankenburg and Feest 1969; Feest and Lautmann 1971). The prevailing assumption was that patterns of policing depend on everyday theories whereby criminal suspicion falls on members of marginal groups who are visible and powerless and thus become easy targets for legal actions such as stop-and-search procedures as well as arrest.

Developments in criminal law doctrine paralleled developments in criminological research, as findings of selection in the criminal justice system revealed by research guided by the interactionist and labeling perspective led to revisions in traditional legal doctrine. Basic assumptions of traditional criminal law grounded on a theory of punishment that was justified with the principle of legality in processing offenders through the system had been affected by the evidence of widespread selection occurring on all levels of penal decisionmaking. But gradual withdrawal from a theory of criminal law and criminal penalties explained solely through individual guilt and adoption of alternative explanations based upon (so-called positive) general prevention and system theory allowed for adjustments of legal and dogmatic theories. Selection and choice have been incorporated into the legal theory of criminal law and into the legal theory on criminal procedure. Criminal penalties are explained by the goal of maintaining legal norms, not by the obligation to respond to individual guilt. This provides a rationale for the flexible handling of punishment and the diversion of suspects from criminal courts as being consistent with legal theory.

In the course of the second half of the twentieth century the focus slowly shifted from discriminatory treatment of members of the lower (working) classes to discrimination against immigrants and ethnic minorities in general. Massive immigration from the 1960s on resulted in an ethnically and culturally heterogeneous society and in ongoing political discourse as to whether Germany should see itself as an "immigration country" (Albrecht 2002). In the 1990s, discrimination in the criminal justice system became an important political issue and the subject of research, not only because the status of immigrants was added to the range of variables that may explain discriminatory and biased treatment, but also because of the internationalization of processes of legitimation and legitimacy. "Internationalization" here refers to the emergence of transnational communities as a result of migrants' and immigrants' links with both sending and host societies. It is also grounded in international and (European) institutions as well as various NGOs, which, adhering to international law and various treaties, monitor discrimination and racism and report cases of ethnically or racially biased law enforcement. As a consequence of these developments, legitimacy can no longer be conceived as a problem inherent to a national territory but has become an international and transnational issue.

Immigration brings other changes in the social structure: the blurring of distinct social classes and the emergence of social milieus, as well as individualization as a major element of advanced modernity point also to significant changes in the mechanisms of social integration (Heitmeyer 1995, 2005).

Finally, it seems that the strong relationship between effectiveness and legitimacy is weakening as a consequence of processes and sometimes also campaigns of delegitimation. The state is increasingly faced with choices between legitimate responses and effective responses, and it appears that effective solutions are seen as the priority.

IMMIGRATION, MIGRATION, AND ETHNIC MINORITIES

Post–Second World War Germany has experienced a rather short history of immigration, which started around 1960; significant changes in immigration patterns occurred in the subsequent decades. Whereas the debate in the 1960s and 1970s emphasized the concept of "guest-workers" (Gastarbeiter: migrant workers who, it was assumed, would return to their home countries after a more or less extended period of work in the German economy), the 1990s saw a growing recognition that in fact immigration had taken place. The ethnic composition of immigrants and motivations for migration have changed significantly over the last forty years. First, the countries where the migrant work force originates have changed, as southeastern European countries (former Yugoslavia and Turkey) have replaced Italy, Spain, and Portugal. At the beginning of the 1960s approximately two-thirds of the foreign population came from countries of the European Community. In the 1990s, their share has dropped to less than 30 percent. People from Turkey and former Yugoslavia today account for almost half of the resident immigrant population in Germany. Furthermore, since the second half of the 1980s, immigrants from developing countries in Africa and Asia have made up a substantial proportion of the immigrant population. The ethnic and cultural diversity of the immigrant population increased at the end of the 1980s after the breakdown of Socialist regimes in central and eastern Europe led to more immigration from these areas. A shift in the motives for migration and changes in its legal aspects have been associated with the change in the ethnic composition of the immigrant community. The status of foreign nationals in Germany differs because different legal standards apply to citizens of European Community countries, Turkish citizens (who currently occupy an in-between status vis-à-vis the European Community), and citizens of non–European Community states. With respect to reasons for entering German territory, the law distinguishes among tourists (or short-term visitors); foreign nationals joining the labor force or enrolling at schools or universities; and asylum seekers and refugees (covered by the Geneva Convention). The total abolition of schemes for hiring workers abroad and severe restrictions on granting permission for non-EU foreigners to work in Germany led in the 1990s to larger numbers of foreigners applying for asylum; until recent amendments of the German constitution and the immigration law this had the effect of granting a preliminary permission to stay on German territory awaiting the final decision on asylum. A rather unique phenomenon with respect to immigration concerns the population of ethnic Germans whose ancestors emigrated to Poland, Russia, and Romania and who are entitled to be renaturalized if they can provide evidence of their German origins. Between the early 1950s and 2003, 4.3 million ethnic Germans were renaturalized (Sachverständigenrat für Zuwanderung und Integration 2004, 62), the majority of whom immigrated to Germany after the second half of the 1980s (Statistisches Bundesamt 1993, 92). They are the most important immigrant and ethnic minority, in quantitative terms.

Another significant change was in the length of the stay of immigrants in Germany. The share of immigrants staying for shorter periods of time has increased over the last two decades. What should be noted then are the apparent differences in the demographic structure found in various immigrant populations. Finally, regional differences in the percentage of immigrants in the population have to be addressed; metropolitan areas and the western part of Germany attract the most immigrants. In the 1990s approximately 2 percent of immigrants in Germany lived in the "new Bundesländer" in the eastern part of Germany, where they made up approximately 20 percent of the population (Statistisches Bundesamt 1993, 72).

Foreign nationals are disproportionately affected by unemployment: unemployment rates are approximately 20 percent among foreign nationals and 10 percent among the German-born labor force (Statistisches Bundesamt 2004). In many respects—housing, social security dependency (three time as high among foreign nationals as among the German-born), education, and income levels—their profile is similar to that of the working class (Statistisches Bundesamt 2004).

Another characteristic of ethnic and foreign minorities in Germany may be found in the structure of historical relationships between countries of origin of immigrant minorities and Germany. Unlike other European countries, Germany has had no history of colonialism since the end of World War I; this may represent for countries who did have colonies an important pull-factor for migration and shape in significant ways the relationship between immigrant minorities and the society at large. Immigration to Germany is explained primarily by labor immigration.

The history of ethnic and racial minorities in twentieth-century Germany as well as research on minorities are under the enormous shadow of German fascism's murderous actions toward ethnic and other minorities in Europe during the 1930s and 1940s. One result of this was the elimination of all variables referring to race and ethnicity from all official data and from most questionnaires and interview forms used in criminological research. Consequently, there are no official statistics on crime or the judiciary or general population characteristics that can be used to study the racial or ethnic composition of the German population. Only estimates are available, such as on the number of black or Afro-Germans, which ranges from forty thousand to fifty thousand (Forbes and Mead 1992, 39). According to research on the size of the population of foreign-born residents, about 10 percent of the population belong to immigrant groups; meanwhile, though, according to official statistics foreign nationals make up 7 percent of the population (Sachverständigenrat für Zuwanderung und Integration 2004, 68). However, the foreign-born group does not include second- or third-generation immigrants, among whom a substantial share has been naturalized. According to a change in the law in 1998, under certain conditions children born to immigrant foreign nationals automatically get German citizenship, and until the beginning of the twenty-first century ethnic Germans immigrating from countries of the former Soviet Union automatically received German citizenship after arriving in Germany. The variable "nationality" or "citizenship" therefore may be used only as a rather crude proxy in analyzing racial or ethnic segments of German society.

The problems that arise from the lack of valid data when interpreting official—in particular, crime-related—statistics become apparent when we look at changes of inmate-population structures in German juvenile prisons. Data from the state of Baden-Württemberg demonstrate that over a period of some twenty-five years this changed completely. Whereas in the mid-1970s virtually all inmates were German citizens, in 1999 young German nationals accounted only for less than 40 percent of prison inmates (see figure 16.1). If one relied only on the variable nationality, it would go unnoticed that immigrant youths in fact represent the majority of prison inmates today.

FIGURE 16.1   ETHNICITY OF INMATES IN GERMAN YOUTH PRISONS,
1974, 1987, 1999

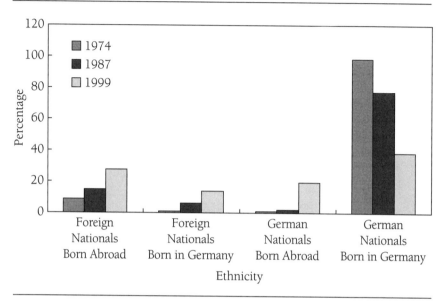

Source: Baden-Württemberg Prison Administration (2004).

To summarize significant developments in immigration and migration as related to Germany:

- Social and economic changes in the last twenty years in general have worked to the disadvantage of immigrants. The success stories of immigration from the nineteenth and even the twentieth century concern immigrant groups that managed to work their way up and to integrate (economically and culturally) into mainstream society. Thus, several waves of Polish labor immigrants settled at the end of the nineteenth and the beginning of the twentieth century in the western area of Germany, especially in coal-mining areas; they integrated rather rapidly into mainstream society and became invisible as a distinct group within half of a century (Albrecht 1997).

- The traditional concept of immigration—that immigrants should gradually lose connections to their native countries—does not fit the immigration pattern in Germany. Immigrants come from European countries (including Turkey) or neighboring areas such as Eastern Europe or the Maghreb countries; this creates networks of migration and a number of "transnational communities."

- The disappearance of low-skilled work has changed labor prospects drastically and this has changed the basic framework of traditional mechanisms of social integration, which used to be labor and employment. The traditional labor market, shadow economies, and black markets, in particular in urban areas, now offer precarious employment opportunities (Kraemer and Speidel 2005) to newly arriving immigrants (Albrecht et al. 2003).

- Political and legal changes have significantly affected the legal status of immigrants through changing the statutory framework of immigration as well as enforcement policies. Between 1960 and 1990 most immigrants entered Germany legally (as labor immigrants or on the basis of family reunification schemes). Today, the legal status of new arrivals points either to illegality or to the precarious status of asylum seekers, refugees, and merely tolerated immigrants who are subject to strict administrative controls and threatened by serious risk of criminalization (Albrecht 2006).

- Immigrants are affected disproportionately by unemployment and are also disproportionately dependent on social security. This means that assumed precursors of crime and deviance such as domestic problems, unemployment, and lack of education and professional training assume paramount importance in determining the potential of immigrant populations to experience problems.

- Immigrants tend to be concentrated in inner-city ghettos in urban areas, which are increasingly plagued by all sorts of social problems.

- In the 1960s, labor migrants came predominantly from rural areas. Today's immigrants are from urban areas, where resources for migration are more readily available than in more disadvantaged rural areas of developing countries.

IMMIGRANTS AND CRIME

Information on crime participation rates of immigrants and criminal justice responses to immigrants are found almost exclusively in official crime and criminal justice data provided by police and justice information systems. Over the last decade, however, self-report surveys increasingly cover also ethnic and immigrant variables. The main limitations of police statistics concerns the category "foreign nationality," which does not fit with the concept of the immigrant. Police statistics in this respect are rather crude, for official data do not allow disaggregating different age groups, citizenship, and differences in legal status. Most research dealing with ethnic minorities and crime merely refers to the general category "foreign citizens." That's why research on ethnic minorities, crime, and justice in recent decades has been limited to questions that, on the basis of available data, cannot be answered, that is, whether immigrant minorities are disproportionately involved in crime or are discriminated against by law enforcement and the criminal justice system.

FIGURE 16.2   FOREIGN NATIONALS IN POPULATION AND CRIME STATISTICS

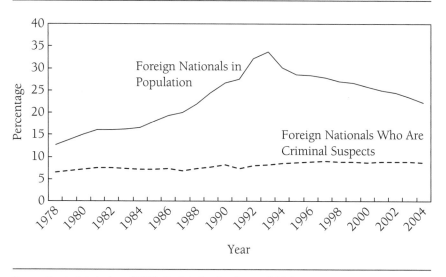

Sources: Bundeskriminalamt (2006); Statistisches Bundesamt (2005).

In Germany, increases in the rates of police-recorded foreign suspects have mirrored fairly well the increasing number of immigrants. In 1953, when police statistics were published for the first time after World War II, the rate of foreign suspects was as low as 1.7 percent (Albrecht 1997). Figure 16.2 contains data on the resident foreign population in Germany and on the rates of foreign national suspects from 1978 to 2004. It is evident that foreign nationals are disproportionately represented in police statistics. However, it is also clear that the significant changes in rates of foreign-national suspects are independent of the rate of the resident foreign population. Although the proportion of foreign nationals in the resident population at large did not change significantly between the beginning of the 1990s and 2004, the rate of foreign suspects dropped in the same period by approximately one third. This drop reflects the drastic decrease in the number of asylum seekers from 1993 on. In that year there was an amendment to the German constitution concerning the right of asylum that resulted in far greater hurdles for asylum seekers. However, the decrease is especially marked in the area of petty property crimes, including shoplifting, which provides insight as to the types of crimes most often perpetrated by asylum seekers.

Police data on young immigrants point to significant differences in crime involvement of young German nationals and immigrants (figure 16.3). A cohort study carried out at the Max Planck Institute for Foreign and International Criminal Law, in Freiburg, reveals that before reaching adulthood, of the members of 1978 birth

FIGURE 16.3   Police Contacts in Four Birth Cohorts of Germans, Ethnic Germans, and Foreign Nationals, at the Age of Seventeen

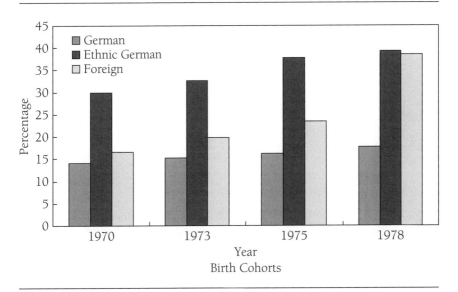

Source: Max Planck Institute for Foreign and International Criminal Law (2004).

cohort approximately 40 percent of ethnic Germans (from regions of the former Soviet Union) and foreign nationals had had at least one contact with police, whereas only 15 percent of young German nationals (born in Germany) were suspected of committing a criminal offense (Grundies 2002).

Over the last decade various self-report studies have been carried out with the aim of testing hypotheses concerning disproportionate crime involvement of young immigrants. It was found that general crime participation rates do not differ significantly between young Germans and various groups of young immigrants (Naplava 2002); but all the studies carried out so far have confirmed a disproportionate involvement in violent activities, in particular by young immigrants from Turkey and southeastern Europe (Heitmeyer 1995; Tillmann et al. 1999; Enzmann and Wetzels 2000; Oberwittler et al. 2001).

To summarize the so far established links between immigration and crime and deviance:

• Some immigrant groups exhibit much higher proportions of criminal activity than do majority groups.

- However, some immigrant groups display the same or a lower degree of criminal involvement than observed in the majority group.

- First-generation immigrants of the fifties and sixties show evidence of less criminal activity than second- or third-generation immigrants and immigrants who arrived in the eighties and nineties.

- A common feature of most immigrant groups is a socially and economically disadvantaged and precarious position, which puts them at risk of becoming involved in shadow economies, the drug trade, and other economic crime.

- Cultural differences between socially similarly situated groups can result in rather different crime patterns, in terms of both the structure and magnitude of criminal activity.

- Relevant cultural differences between immigrant groups are the capacity for community building and for the preservation of the cultural and ethnic homogeneity of the immigrant group.

- Such cultural differences are evidently important in explaining different levels of creation of and access to social and economic opportunities be they legal or illegal in different ethnic or immigrant communities and social groups.

- Immigrants are certainly as much at risk as they pose risks in terms of deviance and crime. In this they do not differ from the marginal groups within the majority group.

DISCRIMINATION AND CRIMINAL JUSTICE

Discrimination and partial treatment have always played a role in research on criminal law and the criminal justice system. Until the 1980s the debates have focused on social class as the major cause of discrimination, but the influx of immigrants has added ethnicity and minority status as important sources of discrimination.

Inter-Ethnic Conflicts and Reporting Patterns

Theoretical approaches to the issue of discrimination and biased law enforcement must distinguish between assumptions related to immigrant minorities' crime involvement as a significant social problem and hypotheses concerning decisionmaking in policing and in the administrative and criminal justice system. Hypotheses concerning the problem of foreign nationals' contribution to crime can be divided roughly into the theory of scapegoating and the theory of conflicts over resources (employment, housing). Furthermore, administrative agencies' search for "new" social problems has been named as well as possible function of immigrant crime as a factor in stabilizing political power and galvanizing political support within majority groups (Kubink 1993, 143).

Although, research efforts designed to analyze selective and discriminatory law enforcement among ethnic minorities should concentrate on reporting behavior first, little evidence can be provided with respect to the role of ethnic variables for reporting behavior by the public or the victims of crime. The studies that have covered variables such as perceptions of the nationality or race of the offender have produced ambiguous results (Donner 1986; Kubink 1993, 56). Some studies claiming evidence of overreporting of ethnic minorities by the public are based upon misinterpretation of police data. Thus, Olaf Donner (1986) and Michael Kubink (1993) use sample of cases drawn from police files of juvenile criminal suspects in Berlin. Since approximately 20 percent of minority suspects and 28 percent of German suspects were reported by the police themselves and not by victims, the researchers conclude that ethnic minorities are subjected to more rigorous reporting than their German counterparts. However, the difference is easily explained by the much heavier involvement of young foreigners in acts of shoplifting and fare dodging. If controlling for these types of offenses (which are reported exclusively by private police in warehouses and public transportation), proportions of suspects brought to the attention of police by private complainants turn out to be the same for young foreigners and young Germans. Minority victims of crime seem to be slightly more reluctant to report an offense if the offender had the same national or ethnic background (Pitsela 1986, 340). This would support the hypothesis of underreporting of ethnic minorities' crimes, especially when it is taken into account that substantial proportions of crimes committed by members of ethnic minorities are within-group crimes, such as personal crimes (Sessar 1981). But ethnic-minority offenders seem to run a somewhat higher risk of being reported in case of shoplifting or workplace (Blankenburg 1973; Kaiser and Metzger-Pregizer 1976). Multivariate analysis of crime reporting came to the conclusion that also in cases of inter-ethnic crime reporting behavior is best explained by conventional crime and seriousness of crime-related variables, whereas ethnicity or the immigration status does not contribute substantially (Mansel 2003).

Police, Policing, and Discrimination

When it comes to allegations of discrimination, police play a particular role. Police are confronted on a routine basis with immigrants and minorities as a consequence of making arrests and interrogating suspects.

Police and Discrimination

With respect to the role of police in initiating criminal investigations it should be noted that German police do not make formal decisions on arrest. German police, when notified about some criminal event, investigate the case. The investigation may lead to the case being sent to the public prosecutor's office, where the actual decision about bringing the case to court or arresting the suspect for pretrial detention is made. Consensus seems to exist that if a person has committed a certain number of offenses, the probability of being treated like a criminal suspect is more or less the same for minority and majority offenders. The probability of being suspected of a criminal offence is extremely low in the case of most offenses anyway, and police investigations seem to be guided by characteristics of the offense, especially the seriousness of the offense (Steffen 1977). It has been hypothesized that higher rates of suspects among ethnic minorities could be the consequence of ethnic minority members' confronting police more negatively during encounters than majority members do. But preliminary research based upon an experimental design does not lend support to this assumption. In fact, ethnic-minority suspects in general seem to be more cooperative while being questioned. Going further in the criminal process, the findings do not support a hypothesis that minority suspects run a higher risk of being formally charged and indicted with a criminal offense (Kubink 1993, 60).

However, there is some merit to criticism that foreign nationals are discriminated against in the criminal justice system. In some areas, such as drug law enforcement, selected ethnic minorities are targeted. In shadow economies police allegedly use excessive force and discriminatory practices (Lederer and Busch 2000, 29). Some critics even characterize law enforcement as racist and brutal (Antirassismusbüro Bremen 1997, 199). It has been charged that such criticism encourages stigmatization of the police as racist and is voiced only by those sympathizing with extremist political parties with an agenda of provoking conflict based on allegations of racist behavior (Franzke 1993, 616).

A number of studies have dealt with attitudes and perceptions of the police toward ethnic and immigrant minorities. Questions have been raised concerning whether discrimination and racism reflect systematic patterns, or whether such attitudes are isolated, the result of bad apples, with state authorities claiming that abusive behavior is restricted to exceptional cases only (Jaschke 1997, 191).

However, insofar as most of the studies of these questions have been based on observations of police or interviews of police officers, it can be assumed that the bulk of this research does not amount to more than descriptions delivered by police themselves.

A number of reports by NGOs have alleged discriminatory police practices toward ethnic minorities. A 1999 report of the NGO Aktion Courage listed seventy-one cases of police maltreatment, ranging from simple insulting behavior to murder (Aktion Courage—SOS Rassismus 1999). Amnesty International regularly reports acts of violence committed by police (see, for example, Amnesty International, Report 2001 Germany, at http://www.amnesty.org). Furthermore, the UN Special Rapporteur on Human Rights documented in his 1997 report several cases of serious violence against immigrants. Either these cases were not prosecuted or the accused were acquitted (Bericht 1997). In its 1997 report, the Committee on the Elimination of Racial Discrimination (CERD) expressed its concern about the treatment of immigrant minorities by the police and called for strict disciplinary measures against offenders as well as implementation of special training programs for police (CERD 1997). The second report of the Council of Europe's Commission Against Racism and Intolerance (Länderbericht 2001) voices concerns arising from allegations of physical abuse of immigrants by police and immigration officials. The report in particular stresses the discrepancy between the large number of allegations of police misbehavior on the one hand and the small number of cases that result in investigations and subsequent criminal proceedings against those responsible on the other hand (ECRI 2001). However, it is difficult to reach any solid conclusions concerning the reliability of statements alleging discriminatory or racist treatment by police or immigration authorities, since most of them result from conflicts between complainants and police in the shadow economy (drug trade) or when entering Germany or being deported. Allegations of abuse may be used to gain tactical or strategic advantage.

The relationship between immigrant minorities and the police has been studied in terms of law enforcement and crime. Discriminatory treatment and inequality have been raised as issues in the context of explaining the high proportion of criminal offenders who are foreign nationals or immigrants.

At the beginning of the 1990s a survey of police officers revealed that a majority felt that there were differences between average citizens and immigrants that justify different treatment. The reasons why they felt immigrants could legitimately be treated differently were based on immigration status and exploitative behavior of immigrants, different values, and behavior patterns. The data convey the general view that police perceive immigrants as different (Franzke 1993, 616). A survey covering metropolitan Frankfurt came to the conclusion that a majority of Frankfurt police felt that there were too many immigrants in Frankfurt and that immigrant youths contribute heavily to the workload of the police (Jaschke 1997, 130). The majority of the police expressed strong support for a repressive approach toward immigrants. A survey of police forces of the neighboring state of Rheinland-Pfalz (Jaschke 1997, 131) produced similar results. Research has targeted the question of what factors explain hostile, racist attitudes on the part of police. Some studies have emphasized the significance of inner-city beats, where the probability of confrontation between police and immigrants is high because of a concentration of immigrants in urban areas and the multiproblem nature of the inner city (Bornewasser, Eckert, and Willems 1996). Drug markets, red light zones, and youth gangs may all contribute to stereotyping and ethnic profiling (Ebel 1987) and to a general view that inner-city problems are strongly linked to immigration. Another study dealt with the question of whether police officers knew about discriminatory, racist, or abusive behavior toward immigrants and how such behavior is interpreted by the police themselves. Virtually all interviewees reported abuse of immigrants; this fact was interpreted as indicating that marginal and powerless social groups are at risk of serving as scapegoats and outlets for feelings of frustration (Maibach 1996, 191). In 1996 a report by the Hamburg Parliament on state police forces that had been triggered by serious allegations of racism (Hamburger Landesparlament 1996) came to the conclusion that deficits in police training and organization and, finally, individual shortcomings explain why police target immigrants in a discriminatory and racist way.

Particular attention has been devoted to the analysis of risk configurations involving police and immigrants. It has been argued that in particular types of interactions between police and immigrants, prejudice and hostile attitudes may be activated by stress. However, general professional cynicism may be the result of such stress (Backes, Dollase, and Heitmeyer 1997, 85). According to this view, immigrants are just another stressor among many that are felt by police. Other surveys confirm that hostility toward immigrants and racist attitudes found among police can also be found among the public at large (Ohlemacher 1999, 31).

Interpretation of the studies presented so far points to structural problems in the relationship between immigrants and police. Immigrants, especially those who have arrived since the 1990s, are placed in disadvantageous conditions. High unemployment rates and the problem of access to the labor market are associated with high participation rates in shadow economies, especially by illegal immigrants (Albrecht 2006). High participation rates in drug dealing or other informal economies expose immigrants to a high rate of encounters with law enforcement.

However, the research designs used in the studies have been criticized. For example, most of the studies were geared toward police self-presentation—how police feel and respond when faced with allegations that they have discriminated against immigrants. Here three discourses can be identified: police racism or hostility is the result of individual cases; police are under general stress; and police react with hostility when confronted with the intractable problems of urban areas (Proske 1998). Another explanation of violent encounters between police and immigrants has been sought in the specific "cop culture" that has emerged as a second code of the "monopoly of power" and the laws regulating policing. This code is described as containing a self-image of standing in the frontline in a war against deviance, a feeling of belonging to a close community of professionals engaged in dangerous activities and the acceptance of violence as an option of action (Pütter 2000). This allows police to adopt a view that presents them as victims—of the "reality" of inner-city problems, of politicians who do not recognize that reality, of strategically operating immigrant offenders who belong to organized-crime groups.

Abandoning individualized theories of discrimination and adopting instead a theory of institutional discrimination has been suggested. Testing this would of course require aggregate data that demonstrate that normally functioning police, or other administrative staff institutions such as courts, generate decision patterns to the disadvantage of immigrant minorities (Proske 1998, 182). In other words this is a group-discrimination perspective. Four decades' worth of research into the reasons for the high crime participation rates of immigrants have led to no solid conclusion. The question corresponds to the one that has been addressed over decades under the assumption of a class bias of policing and criminal law based control.

Prejudices and discrimination against immigrants reflect rationalization which aim at simplifying the complex field of ethnic-cultural relationships into stereotypes of deviant groups of immigrants which legitimately may be excluded (Jaschke 1997, 210).

The data described so far concern attitudes and perceptions of police. Although data on the use of force in general or police practices as regards stop-and-search procedures are not available, deadly and other use of firearms is accounted for by information collected by the Interior Ministry. These data do not, however, distinguish between immigrants and other groups regarding the recipients of police force. Longitudinal data on the use of deadly force by police reveal that the number of persons killed or injured by police firearms is stable and possibly declining, as is the use of guns against persons in general (Pütter 1999; Innenministerium Baden-Württemberg 2005); the numbers are significantly lower than those recorded for France (see Jobard 1998). During the last two decades, police have used firearms on average sixty to seventy times a year against individuals. On average about ten persons are killed and about thirty are injured as a result of police use of firearms. Although in-depth studies on these cases have not been carried out, it seems that virtually all of the cases of lethal use of firearms occurred in situations that had little potential to fueling ethnic tensions.

Immigrants' Views of Police and Discrimination   Research on how immigrants experience encounters with police has been carried out since the 1970s. Complaints about police harassment and discrimination of minority juveniles have been documented in various studies based on interviews with foreign or immigrant youths (Hamburger, Seus, and Wolter 1981, 145–47; Bielefeld and Kreissl 1982; Heitmeyer, Schröder, and Müller 1997 report that one third of Turkish juveniles interviewed complained about being discriminated against by police). In a small-scale comparative study on attitudes of German, Turkish, and Italian male juveniles toward the police, it was found that German juveniles who were matched to minority juveniles on the basis of socioeconomic status felt more strongly that they and the areas where they live are controlled intensively by police than did the Turkish and Italian boys (Staudt 1983). Furthermore, a somewhat larger proportion of German boys complained about police behavior. On the other hand, a smaller proportion of Turkish juveniles complained of police behavior but these complaints were based on the view that police discriminated against Turkish juveniles because of their being Turkish (Bielefeld and Kreissl 1982, 161). According to this study, differences in perceptions can be traced to the assignment of different motives to police activities, not to differential strategies adopted by police in controlling minority and other youths.

Studies on trust in the police as an institution reveal no marked differences between German youth and various immigrant groups. Approximately 25 percent of West German, Italian, and Greek youths state that they distrust police in general, about 37 percent of Turkish youths and 33 percent of East German youths express this view (Gesemann 2003, 210). Trust and mistrust in the police thus might be explained not by immigrant status but by the general feeling of belonging to a marginalized and deprived group in society. The differences, however, are not particularly strong. Differences become more pronounced when variables such as gender, education, and place of residence are introduced. Mistrust in police is particularly strong in metropolitan Berlin, where some 84 percent of Turkish interviewees declare that they have no or only limited trust in police (Gesemann 2003, 211). Approximately 30 percent of German youths said this, indicating a deep ethnic divide. One reason may be spatial segregation and the emergence of inner-city ghettos and ethnic communities, which—also due to the substantial population of immigrants of Turkish origin—have gained significant momentum in Berlin (Groenemeyer and Mansel 2003). Mistrust in police in urban areas may be fueled also by the frequency of arrest-related contacts between police and immigrant youths, which according to the data of the Freiburg cohort study is especially marked in large cities.

Studies of attitudes toward crime and criminal justice indicate that immigrant minorities are less tolerant of crime and criminal offenders than the indigenous/domestic population. In the population surveyed, evidence was found for a stronger commitment to severe penalties as well as to deterrence as a primary aim of sentencing and corrections (Pitsela 1986). A substantial proportion of the minority group felt that criminal courts were putting too many limitations on police to control criminals and investigate crime. In Turkish groups of male youths prevalent authoritarian attitudes approach those found in nationalistic and right-wing conservative groups (Heitmeyer, Schröder, and Müller 1997, 107).

So far, however, in Germany there have been no inner-city riots like those that erupted since the 1980s in France and England.

Responding to Discrimination   Approaches to dealing with conflicts between police and immigrant minorities and to preventing discrimination and racism presented here have emphasized three perspectives:

- Awareness programs aiming at changing ideas, attitudes, and the behavior of police in education and training

- Integration of immigrants into police forces

- Identification of policing strategies that are associated with elevated risk of discrimination

Integration of immigrants into police forces is a relatively new, controversial strategy in Germany. In 1989 high-placed government officials argued that systematic recruiting of police among immigrant minorities should not be pursued (Franzke

1995). Also, surveys of police officers revealed that support for recruiting police among immigrants was weak among them (Jaschke 1997, 132). The main obstacle seemed to be laws mandating German citizenship as a fundamental requirement for civil servants. But the idea gained momentum in the 1990s when the state of Baden-Württemberg declared that it would make use of a clause in the law on civil servants that says that foreign nationals may be hired in case of an urgent need. Serious deficits in crime prevention and law enforcement were such a need, it was argued, one that could not be overcome without integrating immigrants into police forces. Shortly afterward the Standing Conference of Ministers of Interior of German States adopted this view and crafted a common approach which has been implemented in all states of Germany since 2000. However, recruitment has been slow and the number of foreign nationals in the police forces is still low. In the year 1994 some 141 foreign nationals were hired by police forces in Germany (Franzke 1995). Despite new recruitment policies immigrants still do not constitute a significant element in Germany police forces (Duprez et al. 2001).

Public Prosecution and Discrimination

Significant criteria for bringing suspects to criminal courts are their prior records, the seriousness of the offence, and the presence of a guilty plea (Blankenburg, Sessar, and Steffen 1978). There is considerable evidence that minority offenders are brought to court in Germany less often than their native German counterparts (Villmow 1993; Reichertz 1994). This has been explained by assuming that charges were dropped because of the petty nature of crimes and a large proportion of cases with weak evidence, which then are parceled out finally by the public prosecutor, who thus acts as a counterweight and compensatory power against a trend toward overreporting among police. Similar findings have been made for rape cases (Steinhilper 1986). Another hypothesis is that specific problems of evidence lead to higher rates of nonprosecution in criminal procedures against foreign suspects (Donk 1994, 38). The trail followed in this hypothesis starts with an assumption of the structural "dominance" of foreign suspects (Reichertz and Schröer 1993) in interactions with police and public prosecutors (Donk 1994, 38). The opportunity to establish a criminal case through police interrogations of suspects basically is seen as being dependent on the information the suspect gives during interrogations. Actually, this type of interaction is not possible in those cases where a translator must serve as a mediator. But the data obtained so far to test this hypothesis are rather inconclusive. The preliminary data support the view that in some cases translators actually function as "deputies" to police officers. This in turn should preclude a significant impact of "structural dominance" in police interrogations as translators obviously may restore the balance.

However, research could demonstrate that the rates of adjudicated juvenile offenders are rather similar in the groups of foreign and German juvenile suspects if illegal immigrants, tourists, and asylum seekers are excluded from analysis (Karger and Sutterer 1993, 23). These findings clearly point to rather consistent prosecution patterns not distorted by variables such as race, ethnicity, or citizenship. The finding of consistency in decisionmaking by the public prosecutor is not invalidated through a higher rate of dismissals in case of foreign nationals such as tourists and illegal immigrants. As most of these suspects are difficult to trace after conviction, it can be expected that dismissals due to economic considerations occur more frequently here.

Discrimination and Pretrial Detention

A higher risk of being held in pretrial detention has been observed with respect to foreign suspects. Elevated rates of pretrial detention indeed can be expected as the normative framework found in the procedural criminal law considers first of all the type and intensity of incentives for absconding. Besides the possible size of the criminal penalty, variables like the nature and the intensity of bonds to society and the territory of the jurisdiction where the criminal trial will be held guide decisionmaking in this field. So, in case of foreign suspects legal conditions of pretrial detention are more likely to be established than in other offender populations.

While routine decisionmaking in the criminal justice system may account for higher rates of pretrial detention in general, it should not be neglected that regional characteristics may account for particularly high rates of certain nationalities in pretrial detention.

A 1992 study on pretrial detainees in the Frankfurt region came to the not unexpected conclusion that the sharp increase in pretrial detention figures is due to an increasing number of foreigners being held in pretrial detention (Gebauer 1993). Among the group of pretrial detainees, Moroccans had the biggest share, at 15 percent (although Moroccans represent a rather small group in the state of Hessen, accounting for just 0.4 percent of the population). The data have been interpreted as giving evidence of a side function of pretrial detention in case of foreign suspects: keeping foreigners in secure facilities to allow for administrative decisionmaking and action with respect to deportation. This might be one plausible explanation for the heavy share of foreigners in pretrial detention facilities. But there are other explanations for the high proportion of Moroccans serving time in detention centers. During the period when the research on pretrial detention was carried out, Frankfurt police had established a special task force ("Arbeitsgruppe Marokko") to crack down on Moroccan drug trafficking groups that since the beginning of the nineties had managed to establish a large drug distribution network in the Frankfurt area, involving mainly cannabis (Kriminalabteilung Frankfurt am Main 1991, 10; Kriminalabteilung Frankfurt am Main 1993, 7). This task force followed up those Moroccan groups closely over an extended period of time monitoring selling and buying operations and busted the networks after enough evidence was available. It could be shown that among Moroccan drug suspects the rate of pretrial detention was relatively high, approximately 50 percent of all Moroccan suspects (Kriminalabteilung Frankfurt am Main 1993, 9). Furthermore, there is evidence that pretrial detention is used as a deterrent in order to discourage particular offender groups. In 1989, when Senegalese still were involved heavily in the small-scale distribution of heroin in the city of Frankfurt, virtually every Senegalese drug suspect was brought to pretrial detention (independent of the amount of drugs found on him or her) which led to snapshots of the number of Senegalese being detained in the Frankfurt pretrial detention facility during certain periods (up to 150, Kriminalabteilung Frankfurt am Main 1991, 41).

Probation Services and Young Foreign Offenders
The activities of probation services and the juvenile court aide have been made subjects of research into the pretrial stages of law enforcement. The juvenile court aide is assumed to influence the disposition of juvenile offenders by providing a presentence report on the offender as well as on his or her social and educational background; the different cultural, ethnic, or national background of offenders could make a difference at this stage. Social workers sometimes experience specific problems when preparing pre-sentence reports on foreign juveniles, including language and understanding, lack of knowledge about the cultural backgrounds of juvenile offenders, and culturally patterned reactions by parents. These factors can lead to pre-sentence reports that differ significantly from those prepared for majority youths (Savelsberg 1982). This finding is especially troubling because in some urban areas today the majority of suspects processed through the juvenile justice system are foreign youths. In recent years foreign youth entering Germany illegally or as tourists have created particular problems for the juvenile court aide. Some of these youths (Romanian, Polish, Yugoslavian, South Americans) are part of criminal theft or drug trafficking networks (South American, Lebanese, Algerian, Moroccan, and Turkish youths) representing main fields of criminal activities (Johne 1995, 41). Here, professional social work activities are limited to attempting to provide a safe return to the home country (Johne 1995), as illegal foreign youths are not entitled to benefit from services provided by the law on Support for Children and Juveniles (§6 Kinder- und Jugendhilfegesetz; see Huber 1995, 45).

Foreign Offenders and Sentencing
Only small effects of immigration status on sentencing can be found. Minority defendants run a somewhat higher risk of receiving prison or custodial sentences and are somewhat less likely to receive suspended sentences or probation (Steinhilper 1986). But in general, ethnic and minority variables add very little to understanding of variations in sentencing for both juveniles and adults (Greger 1987; Albrecht 1994; Albrecht and Pfeiffer 1979; Geißler and Marißen 1990, 683; Oppermann 1987). The

slight difference with respect to juvenile imprisonment between young German offenders and young foreigners (2.4 percent versus 3.4 percent of all offenders convicted and sentenced) found by Rainer Geißler and Norbert Marißen (1990) is mostly accounted for by drug trafficking convictions. When this offense is controlled for the difference fades away. It is especially noteworthy that differences in dispositions are virtually nonexistent in the case of violent crimes and sexual offenses; similar results have been obtained by Antje Oppermann (1987). As ethnicity is a diffuse status variable, it can be assumed that its impact on sentencing is less pronounced or is even nonexistent in cases of a consistent set of offense and offender-related characteristics (such as seriousness of the offence, prior record) or an obvious need for adopting tariffs in sentencing (petty crimes) or administrative convenience point to rather obvious dispositional strategies (Unever and Hembroff 1988). Therefore, only an inconsistent particular set of characteristics can be assumed to trigger effects of ethnicity or nationality on sentencing. It has been hypothesized that the relatively small effects of ethnic variables on sentencing outcomes might be due to the fact that a substantial portion of serious crimes against the person committed by minority offenders involve a minority victim, too, and that effects might turn out to be larger if crimes were included where the perpetrator is from the minority group and the victim, from the majority group. Up to now this question has not been dealt with adequately.

Superior court rulings have dealt with the legal question of whether ethnicity and the status of a foreigner may legitimately be used in justifying harsher penalties in case of minority offenders. Obviously, criminal courts sometimes refer to such status variables as indicators of the need for more severe punishment. The Federal Supreme Court (Bundesgerichtshof) has underlined that these status variables may not be used to justify increases in the severity of sentences as the constitution precludes differential treatment based on citizenship or ethnicity alone (Bundesgerichtshof, decision on November 29, 1990, 1 StR 618/90). The Supreme Court regularly sets aside verdicts that seem to reflect the point of view that asylum seekers or other foreigners are more obligated than natives to comply with the laws of the country providing shelter (Bundesgerichtshof, Strafverteidiger 1987, 20; Bundesgerichtshof Strafverteidiger 1991, 557; Bundesgerichtshof, decision of January 28, 1992, 4 StR 99/92; Oberlandesgerichtshof (state superior court) Bremen Strafverteidiger 1994, 130). But voices have been raised in favor of adapting sentencing to reflect the sanctions in the countries the foreign offenders come from (Schroeder 1983; Grundmann 1985). Here, the argument has been put forward that certain minority offenders might perceive sentencing in German criminal courts as rather lenient as compared to harsher sentencing strategies favored in their home countries, with negative consequences for general prevention and deterrence (Nestler-Tremel 1986). Although such considerations do not find support in criminal court practice, the Supreme Court has accepted that a need for deterrence may be established in case of a sharp increase of violent acts associated with inter-ethnic or national conflicts (Bundesgerichtshof, decision of November 29, 1990, 1 StR 618/90) or if drug traffickers relocate their business because of milder penalties meted out in Germany (Bundesgerichtshof 1982, 112; Wolfslast 1982). Meanwhile, superior courts have ruled that ethnicity or a foreigner's status may be a legitimate reason to mitigate punishment as certain minority offenders might be especially vulnerable to criminal penalties (Bundesgerichtshof 1992, 106); other legal problems related to differences in values and social norms concern the defense of error as to the prohibited nature of an act as well as characteristics establishing first-degree murder. Such considerations are well founded as criminal penalties can lead to further formal and informal consequences for foreign offenders.

Thus, discrimination against ethnic minorities within the criminal justice system must be discussed also in terms of equal protection under the law. Assumptions of discriminatory treatment of foreign victims of crime (especially when committed by member of the majority group) were raised after the first criminal trials following a wave of violence against immigrants and asylum seekers after the German Reunification of 1990. Controversy ensued over the question of whether a juvenile or young adult arsonist who attacked homes of refugees or asylum seekers with Molotov cocktails should be charged with intent to commit murder (Frommel 1993).

Although discrimination in prosecution and sentencing doesn't seem to be marked, an evaluation of the justice system from the viewpoint of possible discrimination has to take into account overall trends in criminal sanctions. An explanation should be offered that puts discrimination into a general perspective on the development of sentencing patterns and the structure of criminal sanctions imposed. In recent decades there has been a considerable reduction in the severity of sentences and especially a significant reduction in the use of imprisonment. This has been accompanied by a dramatic reduction in the variation of criminal punishment, which is easily demonstrated by the distribution of criminal penalties in the Federal Republic of Germany. In Germany just approximately 2 percent of all criminal sentences exceed two years of incarceration. Within the remainder, primarily offense seriousness is decisive in determining the choice of sentence according to guidelines that have been developed for both petty offenses and more serious crimes (Albrecht 1994). So, it seems quite plausible that discrimination, should it occur, is no longer traceable by means of quantitative approaches; in the study of sentencing disparity there are only minor variations in sentences.

Another trend in criminal justice that seems to contradict hypotheses of discriminatory treatment concerns simplification and streamlining of criminal procedures, which have become prominent topics in German reform of procedural law since the 1960s. The first important change in German criminal procedural law occurred very early in the 1960s when paragraph 153 of the German Procedural Code was introduced, which says that the public prosecutor may dismiss a case if the guilt of the suspect is marginal only. In 1975 the discretionary powers of the public prosecutor were extended considerably. Paragraph 153a of the German Procedural Code went into force, which empowered the public prosecutor to dismiss a case of minor guilt (felonies excluded) if the offender complied with certain conditions, determined by the public prosecutor. A simplified procedure may be initiated by the public prosecutor which consists of mere written proceedings. If the public prosecutor concludes that the case is not complicated in terms of proving guilt and that a fine is a sufficient punishment, a penal order may be suggested to the judge, where, besides the indictment, the public prosecutor proposes a fine (according to the day fine system). If the court agrees with the proposal, a penal order is mailed to the suspect, who has two weeks to appeal the order. If an appeal is filed, ordinary proceedings take place.

In the case of ordinary crimes that in principle could be brought before the court (approximately 1.3 million cases per year), 30 percent are dismissed, half of them by way of fulfillment of conditions imposed by the public prosecutor; another 40 percent are dealt with by means of simplified procedures, and the rest (30 percent) get a full trial. These data demonstrate that most offenders do not go through a full-blown criminal procedure but are dealt with in simplified proceedings that preempt the need for a suspect or accused person to appear before a judge or prosecutor.

Immigration Authorities and the Foreign Offender

A foreign minority offender who has been convicted and sentenced may be deported to his or her home country (Otte 1994). The recently amended immigration law (Ausländergesetz) differentiates between the different groups of foreigners: those from EU countries, those from non-EU countries, and those from countries with undecided EU status. Furthermore, the German constitution as well as the European Convention on the Protection of Human Rights require further differentiation (Otte 1994, 73; Gusy 1993). Prison sentences received by a foreign offender are among the most important legal grounds justifying or even necessitating deportation of a foreigner. Therefore, decisionmaking within administrative bodies implementing immigration laws becomes of paramount importance in cases where the legal status of an immigrant minority offender corresponds to that of an "alien." German statutes regulating deportation and expulsion grant wide discretionary power, so it is not surprising that research has demonstrated large variations in both, criteria adopted in administrative decisionmaking and in decision outcomes (see Otte 1994, 68, for a summary of the debate as to whether a sentence of juvenile imprisonment can be used to establish the legal requirement of deportation). There is a lack of research into the role of immigration authorities in responding to criminal activities of immigrant populations, despite the obviously relevant links between criminal justice and administrative authorities in framing policies toward immigrant groups. Criminal justice objectives may be pursued in administrative law because mainstream legal thinking accepts that deterrence is a legitimate aim when deciding upon deportation because of criminal offenses.

Data from Baden-Württemberg show that in the early nineties, the rate of foreign minority offenders deported after adjudication or having served part or all of the sentence was 2 to 3 percent of all offenders found guilty and sentenced, and the trend has been upward since 1992. Detailed information on decisions made by immigration authorities is available for foreign offenders released from youth correctional facilities in Baden-Württemberg. Of those released during 1993, 25 percent were deported immediately after release, another 25 percent were ordered to leave German territory, and 20 percent were warned by immigration authorities. Of the remainder the administrative procedure was incomplete (15 percent) or no administrative action was taken (15 percent).

The Corrections System and Foreign Prisoners

Adult and juvenile corrections have been neglected as a field of research, although pragmatic approaches to the integration of immigrant minority juvenile offenders into the correctional system have been established. Multi-ethnic social training courses have been developed and implemented in some jurisdictions (Informationsdienst zur Ausländerarbeit 1992). But the potential of the prison system to cope with the ethnic diversity in the population of offenders seems limited. Moreover, the general character of a prison regime designed for foreign nationals who are likely to be expelled after serving a prison sentence must be different from one for German prisoners. The goal of reintegration and the support and help provided within the prison to further reintegration do not represent useful guidelines and investments for those who, according to immigration laws, will not be reintegrated to society but will be repatriated into an environment where the prison system cannot provide any reintegration support (Müller-Dietz 1993, 26).

The correctional system and the way immigrant offenders are treated within this system also have not attracted much attention from researchers. The proportion of immigrant prisoners in Germany did rise considerably in the last decade, amounting now to approximately 25 percent of the prison population, including pretrial detainees and sentenced prisoners, youths and adults. There are significant differences in imprisonment rates between various foreign minorities. Data suggest that the trend is to decreasing rates of imprisonment of German offenders. The increase in the number of prisoners at large is exclusively due to immigrants. Clearly, drug offenses play a significant role in the sharp increase in imprisonment of foreign offenders since the second half of the 1980s.

Criminological research focusing on immigrant populations and their treatment in the correctional system is virtually nonexistent. A study of some characteristics of prison regimes revealed that certain ethnic minorities experience a different prison regime than German inmates. The data show that foreign prisoners participate disproportionately less in furlough and prison-leave programs (Albrecht 1989; Janetzky 1993, 114). But differences in treatment emerge also within the group of foreign prisoners. Prisoners from South America are subjected to extreme isolation. Generally these prisoners are serving sentences for drug trafficking (acting as couriers) and have received long prison sentences. These prisoners cannot connect with a group of countrymen outside the prison.

Foreign offenders also create challenges within prison facilities for providing equal treatment, in terms of access to television, newspapers, and books (Janetzky 1993, 112; Schütze 1993). Furthermore, the potential for inter-ethnic conflict between various groups, such as from former Yugoslavia or from Turkey points to the need of reliable information on such conflicts in order to reduce the risk of inter- and intra-ethnic violence within prison facilities (Janetzky 1993, 116).

Parole can be granted to foreign nationals sentenced to imprisonment after they have served half of their prison sentence, according to paragraph 456a of the German Procedural Code, under the condition that deportation takes place immediately upon release. Otherwise, parole may be granted regularly after two-thirds of a prison term has been served. Available data indicate that drug couriers usually are paroled and deported to their home country some three to four months before two-thirds of the prison sentence has been served (Kraushaar 1992). There is some reluctance to reduce prison sentences by half, although in the nineties some German state governments have expressed great interest in reducing the time foreign offenders spend in the prison system in order to reduce costs. This policy may explain why the average sentences served by young German and young foreign offenders differs significantly. Information from Baden-Württemberg on youth prison inmates indicates that foreign inmates serve less than half of their original prison sentence whereas German inmates serve approximately 60 percent.

CONCLUSIONS

Germany has experienced large-scale immigration in recent decades. Substantial numbers of immigrants live in precarious economic and social conditions that expose them to high unemployment rates and other problems. Immigrant populations are concentrated in large cities.

High crime rates have been observed, especially among groups of young immigrants, independent of nationality.

Perceptions of discrimination are prevalent among Turkish youths. Trust in police and other institutions in general is similar to that of other immigrant youths and German youths. An exception to this is in Berlin, where segregation is most visible.

Although violence rates among Turkish male youths are higher than those of German youths or other immigrants, large-scale violence and riots have not been observed in recent decades.

The police have come under close scrutiny as a result of the internationalization of problems of discrimination and racism. Although discrimination is recognized as a problem in the relationship between immigrant minorities and police, until now most serious acts of violence, such as lethal use of firearms, neither exhibit an upward trend nor point to a potential of triggering ethnic tensions or widespread violence. Explanations of discriminatory or abusive police behavior refer to stress and a special police culture. There has been little effort to respond to discrimination by recruiting immigrants as police officers.

Developments in other areas of criminal justice point to group discrimination, especially in the detention of foreign nationals prior to trial. However, prosecution and sentencing policies do not reflect a significant role of immigration or ethnic-minority status in explaining variations in these decisions.

REFERENCES

Aktion Courage – SOS Rassismus. 1999. *Polizeiübergriffe gegen Ausländerinnen und Ausländer.* Bonn: Aktion Courage - SOS Rassismus e. V.

Albrecht, Hans-Jörg. 1989. "Ethnic Minorities, Crime and Public Policy." In *Crime and Public Policy in Europe,* edited by R. Hood. Oxford.

———. 1994. "Sentencing and Disparity: A Comparative Study." *European Journal on Criminal Policy and Research* 2: 98–104.

———. 1997. "Minorities, Crime and Criminal Justice in the Federal Republic of Germany." In *Minorities, Migrants, and Crime: Diversity and Similarity Across Europe and the United States,* edited by Ineke Haen Marshall. London and New Delhi: Sage.

———. 2002. "Ausländerkriminalität und die Entwicklung behördlicher Reaktionen." In *"Fremder, kommst Du nach Deutschland . . . ". Zum institutionellen Umgang mit Fremden in Staat und Gesellschaft,* edited by Jörg Graduszewski and Jörg Vettermann. Münster, Germany: LIT Verlag.

———. 2006. "Illegalität, Kriminalität und Sicherheit." In *Illegalität. Grenzen und Möglichkeiten der Migrationspolitik,* edited by Jörg Alt and Michael Bommes. Wiesbaden, Germany: VS Verlag für Sozialwissenschaften.

Albrecht, Hans-Jörg, and Pfeiffer. 1979. *Die Kriminalisierung junger Ausländer: Befunde und Reaktionen Sozialer Kontrollinstanzen.* München, Germany: Juventa Verlag.

Albrecht, Hans-Jörg, Joanna Shapland, Jason Ditton, and Thierry Godefroy. 2003. "Informal Economy: A Summary and Perspectives." In *The Informal Economy: Threat and Opportunity in the City,* edited by Hans-Jörg Albrecht, Joanna Shapland, Jason Ditton, and Thierry Godefroy. Freiburg im Breisgau, Germany: edition iuscrim.

Antirassismusbüro Bremen. 1997. "'Sie behandeln uns wie Tiere': Rassismus bei Polizei und Justiz in Deutschland." Berlin, Göttingen: Verlag der Buchläden Schwarze Risse – Rote Straßen. Accessed at http://www.antirassismus-buero.de/polizeipraxis/material/FFMHeft4.pdf.

Backes, Otto, Rainer Dollase, and Wilhelm Heitmeyer. 1997. *Die Krise der Städte.* Suhrkamp-Verlag.

Bericht. 1997. Reporter of the Special Rapporteur to the Human Rights Commission, 1997CE/CN.4/1997/7/Add.1.

Bielefeld, Uli, and Reinhard Kreissl. 1982. *Junge Auslander im Konflikt.* [*Young Immigrants in Conflict.*] München, Germany: Juventa.

Blankenburg, Erhard. 1973. "Die Selektivität rechtlicher Sanktionen. Eine empirische Untersuchung von Landendiebstählen." In *Teilnehmende Beobachtung abweichenden Verhaltens,*
edited by Jürgen Friedrichs. Stuttgart, Germany: Enke.

Blankenburg, Erhard, and Johannes Feest 1969. "Selektive Strafverfolgung durch die Polizei."
Kriminologisches Journal 1969(2): 30–35

Blankenburg, Erhard, Klaus Sessar, and Wiebke Steffen. 1978. *Die Staatsanwaltschaft im
Prozess strafrechtlicher Sozialkontrolle.* Berlin: Duncker und Humblot.

Bornewasser, M., R. Eckert, and H. Willems. 1996. "Die Polizei im Umgang mit Fremden:
Problemlagen, Belastungssituationen und Übergriffe." In *Schriftenreihe der Polizeilichen
Führungsakademie, Fremdenfeindlichkeit in der Polizei? Ergebnisse einer wissenschaftlichen
Studie.* Lübeck/Münster-Hiltrup, Germany.

Braithwaite, John. 1998. "Reducing the Crime Problem: A Not So Dismal Criminology." In
The New Criminology Revisited, edited by Paul Walton and Jock Young. London and New
York: Palgrave Macmillan.

Bundesgerichtshof [German Supreme Court]. 1982. 112.

——. 1987. Strafverteidiger 1987, 20.

——. 1990. Beschluß vom 29.11.1990 [Decision of November 29, 1990], 1 StR 618/90

——. 1991. Strafverteidiger [Defense Counsel] 1991, 557.

——. 1992. Beschluß vom 28.1.1992 [Decision of January 28, 1992], 4 StR 99/92.

Bundeskriminalamt [German Federal Office of Criminal Investigation]. 1979–2005.
Polizeiliche Kriminalstatistik 1978–2004 (Police Statistics 1978–2004). Wiesbaden,
Germany.

Coleman, James S. 1988. "Social Capital in the Creation of Human Capital." *American Journal
of Sociology* 94(Supplement): 95–120

Committee on the Elimination of Racial Discrimination (CERD). 1997. "Stellungnahme zum
13./14. Länderbericht Deutschlands gemäß dem Internationalen Übereinkommen zur
Beseitigung jeder Form von Rassendiskriminierung vom 20.03.1997." (CERD/C/304/
Add.24).

Donk, Ute. 1994. "Der Dolmetscher als Hilfspolizist - Zwischenergebnis einer Feldstudie."
Zeitschrift für Rechtssoziologie 15(1): 37–57.

Donner, Olaf. 1986. "Junge Ausländer im polizeilichen Ermittlungsverfahren." *Recht der
Jugend und des Bildungswesens* 1998: 128–36.

Duprez, Dominique, Michel Pinet, Damien Cassan, Virginies Dillies, and Philis Maguer.
2001. *Policiers et médiateurs sur le recrutement et les appartenances.* Lille, France: rapport
CLERSÉ-IHÉSI.

Ebel, Friedrich. 1987. "Von der Gleichheit der Menschen." *Jura* 9: 302–4.

European Commission against Racism and Intolerance (ECRI). 2001. "Co-operation with the
European Monitoring Centre on Racism and Xenophobia: 33." Joint meeting between
European Monitoring Centre on Racism and Xenophobia and ECRI, Vienna, Austria, June
8, 2001.

Enzmann, Dirk, and Peter Wetzels. 2000. "Gewaltkriminalität junger Deutscher und Ausländer: Brisante Befunde, die irritieren: Eine Erwiderung auf Ulrich Mueller." *Kölner
Zeitschrift für Soziologie und Sozialpsychologie* 2000: 142–56.

Feest, Johannes, and Rüdiger Lautmann. 1971. *Die Polizei. Soziologische Studien und Forschungsberichte.* Opladen, Germany: Westdeutscher Verlag.

Forbes, Ian, and Geoffrey Mead. 1992. *Measure for Measure: A Comparative Analysis of Measures to Combat Racial Discrimination in the Member States of the European Community.* Southampton, England: University of Southampton.

Franzke, Bettina. 1993. "Polizei und Ausländer: Beschreibung, Erklärung und Abbau gegenseitiger Vorbehalte." *Kriminalistik* 1993(October): 615–9.

————. 1995. "Menschen ausländischer Herkunft im Polizeivollzugsdienst – Zur Situation in der Bundesrepublik Deutschland." In *Schriftenreihe der Polizei-Führungsakademie, Thema heute: Polizei und ethnische Minderheiten - ethnische Minderheiten in der Polizei.* 1995 Heft 2: 9–46

Frommel, Monika. 1993. "Alles nur ein Vollzugsdefizit? Warum die Strafjustiz nicht Angemessen auf die Gewaltverbrechen gegen Ausländer reagiert." *DVJJ-Journal* 1993: 67–68.

Garland, D. 1991. "Sociological perspectives in punishment." In *Crime and Justice: A Review of Research,* Volume 14, edited by Michael Tonry. Chicago, Ill.: University of Chicago Press.

Gebauer, Michael. 1993. "Untersuchungshaft - 'Verlegenheitslösung' für nichtdeutsche Straftäter." *Kriminalpädagogische Praxis* 21(34): 20–26.

Geißler, Rainer, and Norbert Marißen. 1990. "Kriminalität und Kriminalisierung junger Ausländer: Die tickende soziale Zeitbombe – ein Artefakt der Kriminalstatistik." *Kölner Zeitschrift für Soziologie und Sozialpsychologie* 42(4): 663–87.

Gesemann, Frank. 2003. "'Ist egal ob man Ausländer ist oder so – jeder Mensch braucht die Polizei': Die Polizei in der Wahrnehmung junger Migranten." In *Die Ethnisierung von Alltagskonflikte,* edited by Axel Groenemeyer and Jürgen Mansel. Obladen, Germany: Leske + Budrich.

Greger, Reinhard. 1987. "Strafzumessung bei Vergewaltigung." *Monatsschrift für Kriminologie und Strafrechtsreform* 1987: 261–77

Groenemeyer, Axel and Jürgen Mansel. 2003. *Die Ethnisierung von Alltagskonflikten.* Opladen, Germany: Leske + Budrich.

Grundies, Volker. 2002. *Basisdaten der Freiburger Kohortenstudie.* Freiburg im Breisgau, Germany: edition iuscrim.

Grundmann, Stefan. 1985. "Berücksichtigung Ausländischer Rechtsvorstellungen im Strafrecht: zur Datumstheorie im internationalen Strafrecht." *Neue Juristische Wochenschrift* 38: 1251–5.

Gusy, Christoph. 1993. "Zur Bedeutung von Art. 3 EMRK im Ausländerrecht." *Zeitschrift für Ausländerrecht und Ausländerpolitik* 1993: 63–77.

Hamburger, Franz, Lydia Seus, and Otto Wolter. 1981. *Zur Delinquenz ausländischer Jugendlicher: Bedingungen der Entstehung und Prozesse der Verfestigung.* Wiesbaden, Germany: Sonderband der BKA-Forschungsreihe.

Hamburger Landesparlament. 1996. PUA "Hamburger Polizei": Bericht des Parlamentarischen Untersuchungsausschusses vom 13.11.1996 (Vorsitzender: Prof. Dr. Ulrich Karpen, Schriftführer: Dr. Holger Christier). Drucksache 15/6200 der Hamburger Bürgerschaft, 1996.

Heitmeyer, Wilhelm. 1995. *Gewalt: Schattenseiten der Individualisierung bei Jugendlichen aus unterschiedlichen Milieus.* Weinheim and München, Gremany: Juventa-Verlag.

————. 2005. "Die zerstörte Gesellschaft." *Die Zeit* 51(15): December 2005.

Heitmeyer, Wilhelm, Helmut Schröder, and Joachim Müller. 1997. "Desintegration und islamischer Fundamentalismus. Über Lebenssituation, Alltagserfahrungen und ihre

Verarbeitungsformen bei türkischen Jugendlichen in Deutschland." *Aus Politik und Zeitgeschichte* B 7-8: 17–31.

Huber, Bertold. 1995. "Flüchtlinge, Asylbewerber, Durchreisende: Was kann die Jugendgerichtshilfe tun." *DVJJ-Journal* 6(1): 44–45.

Informationsdienst zur Ausländerarbeit [News Service for Foreign Workers]. 1992. Institut für Sozialarbeit und Sozialpädagogik e.V. (ISS e.V.), Direktor: Hans-Georg Weigel (Hrsg.) Migration und soziale Arbeit (ehemals Informationsdienst zur Ausländerarbeit). Juventa Verlag, Ausgabe 1/1992.

Innenministerium Baden-Württemberg. 2005. *Schusswaffengebrauch der Polizei.* Stuttgart, Germany: Pressestelle Innenministerium.

Interim Report on the Elimination of All Forms of Religious Intolerance. 1997. Report prepared by the Special Rapporteur of the Commission on Human Rights in accordance with General Assembly resolution 51/93, Distr. General A/52/477, 16 October 1997.

Janetzky. 1993. "Ausländer im Strafvollzug." In *Gewalt gegen Ausländer-Gewalt von Ausländern,* edited by Der Generalstaatsanwalt von Schleswig-Holstein. Kiel.

Jaschke, Hans-Gerd. 1997. *Öffentliche Sicherheit im Kulturkonflikt: zur Entwicklung der städtischen Schutzpolizei in der multikulturellen Gesellschaft.* Frankfurt/Main, Germany, and New York: Campus Verlag.

Jobard, Fabien. 1998. "Polizeilicher Schusswaffengebrauch in Frankreich". *Bürgerrechte & Polizei* (CILIP) 61(3/98).

Johne, Rainer. 1995. "Flüchtlinge - Asylbewerber - Durchreisende. Was kann die Jugendgerichtshilfe tun? Erfahrungsbericht der JGH Frankfurt." *DVJJ-Journal* 6(1): 41–43

Kaiser, Gunther, and Gerhard Metzger-Pregizer, editors. 1976. *Betriebsjustiz: Untersuchungen über die soziale Kontrolle abweichenden Verhaltens in Industriebetrieben.* Auflage and Berlin, Germany: Duncker und Humblot.

Karger, Thomas, and Peter Sutterer. 1993. "Legalbiographische Implikationen verschiedener Sanktionsstrategien bei Jugendlichen am Beispiel des einfachen Diebstahls." In *Kriminologische Forschung in den 90er Jahren* [*Criminological Research in the 1990's*], edited by Günther Kaiser. Kriminologische Forschungsberichte aus dem Max-Planck-Institute Series Strafrecht. Band 66/1. Freiburg im Breisgau, Germany.

Kraemer, Klaus, and Frederic Speidel. 2005. "Prekarisierung von Erwerbsarbeit. Zum Wandel eines arbeitsweltlichen Integrationsmodus." In *Integrationspotenziale einer modernen Gesellschaft. Analysen zu gesellschaftlicher Integration und Desintegration,* edited by Wilhelm Heitmeyer and P. Imbusch. Wiesbaden, Gremany: VS-Verlag.

Kraushaar, Horst. 1992. *Der Körperschmuggel von Kokain.* Giessen, Germany: University of Giessen.

Kriminalabteilung Frankfurt am Main. 1991. *Lagebericht Rauschgift 1990.* Frankfurt, Germany: Polizeipräsidium.

———. 1993. *Lagebericht Rauschgift 1992.* Frankfurt, Germany: Polizeipräsidium.

Kubink, Michael. 1993. *Verständnis und Bedeutung von Ausländerkriminalität. Eine Analyse der Konstitution sozialer Probleme.* Pfaffenweiler, Germany: Centaurus-Verlagsgesellschaft.

Länderbericht. 2001. European Commission against Racism and Intolerance (ECRI), Second Report on Germany. Accessed at http://www.ecri.coe.int/en/08/01/13/CBC%202%20 Germany.pdf.

Lautmann, Rüdiger. 1972. "Abbau von Vorurteilen durch Gesetze." *Jahrbuch für Rechtssoziologie und Rechtstheorie* 3(JbRSoz): 187–204.

Lederer, Anja, and Heiner Busch. 2000. "Polizeiübergriffe auf AusländerInnen. Kaum Chancen vor Gericht." *Bürgerrechte & Polizei* (CILIP), 2000(3): 28–33.

Luhmann, Niklas. 1978. *Legitimation durch Verfahren,* 3rd edition. Darmstadt, Luchterhand, Germany: Suhrkamp.

Maibach, Gerda. 1996. *Polizisten und Gewalt: Innenansichten aus dem Polizeialltag.* Reinbeck, Germany: Rowohlt-Verlag.

Mansel, Jürgen. 2003. "Konfliktregulierung bei Straftaten. Variation des Anzeigeverhaltens nach der Ethnie des Täters." In *Die Ethnisierung von Alltagskonflikten,* edited by Axel Groenemeyer and Jürgen Mansel. Opladen, Germany: Leske + Budrich.

Ministry of Justice, Prison Administration, Baden-Württemberg. 2004. "Sachverständigenrat für Zuwanderung und Integration" ["Expert Commission for Immigration and Integration"]. 2004: Migration und Integration – Erfahrungen nutzen, Neues wagen; Jahresgutachten 2004 des Sachverständigenrates für Zuwanderung und Integration. Berlin.

Müller-Dietz, Heinz. 1993. "Lagebeurteilung und Neuere Entwicklungen im Strafvollzug." In *Caritas Schweiz: Die Reform in Gang bringen (Pushing towards reform).* Bericht 1/93. Luzern, Switzerland: Caritas Schweiz.

Naplava, Thomas. 2002. "Delinquenz bei einheimischen und immigrierten Jugendlichen im Vergleich: Sekundäranalyse von Schülerbefragungen der Jahre 1995–2000." MPI-Freiburg.

Nestler-Tremel. 1986. "Auch für Ausländer gilt allein das deutsche Strafrecht." *Straverteidiger* 1986: 83–87

Oberwittler, Dietrich, Tom Blank, Tilmann Köllisch, and Thomas Naplava. 2001. *Soziale Lebenslagen und Delinquenz von Jugendlichen. Ergebnisse der MPI-Schulbefragung 1999 in Köln und Freiburg (Arbeitsberichte aus dem Max-Planck-Institut für ausländisches und internationales Strafrecht).* Freiburg im Breisgau, Germany: Edition iuscrim.

Ohlemacher, Thomas. 1999. *Empirische Polizeiforschung in der Bundesrepublik Deutschland - Versuch einer Bestandsaufnahme.* Hannover, Germany: Kriminologisches Forschungsinst, Niedersachsen.

Oppermann, Antje. 1987. "Straffällige junge Ausländer: Kriminalitätsbelastung und soziale Bedingungen." *Bewährungshilfe* 34: 83–95

Otte, Wolfgang. 1994. "Die Ausweisung nach dem Ausländergesetz." *Zeitschrift für Ausländerrecht* 1994(2): 67–76

Pitsela, Angelika. 1986. "Straffälligkeit und Viktimisierung ausländischer Minderheiten in der Bundesrepublik Deutschland – Dargestellt am Beispiel der griechischen Bevölkerungsgruppe." Kriminologische Forschungsberichte aus dem Max-Planck-Institut für Ausländisches und Internationales Strafrecht, Freiburg im Breisgau, Germany: Bd. 15.

Proske, Matthias. 1998. "Ethnische Diskriminierung durch die Polizei. Eine kritische Relektüre geläufiger Selbstbeschreibungen." *Kriminologisches Journal* 30(3): 162–88.

Pütter, Norbert. 1999. "Polizeilicher Schusswaffengebrauch: Eine statistische Übersicht." *Bürgerrechte und Polizei* 1999(1): 41–51.

———. 2000. "Polizeiübergriffe als Ausnahme und Regel." *Bürgerrechte und Polizei* 2000(3): 6–19.

Reichertz, Jo. 1994. "Zur Definitionsmacht der Polizei: Reduktion des Tatvorwurfs als Folge polizeilicher Ermittlungspraxis." *Kriminalistik* 48: 610–6

Reichertz, Jo, and Norbert Schröer. 1993. "Beschuldigtennationalität und polizeiliche Ermittlungspraxis. Plädoyer für eine qualitative Sozialforschung." *Kölner Zeitschrift für Soziologie und Sozialpsychologie* 45(4): 755–71.

Ross, Catherine E., John Mirowsky, and Shana Probesh. 2001. "Powerlessness and the Amplification of Threat: Neighborhood Disadvantage, Disorder, and Mistrust." *American Sociological Review* 66(4): 568–91.

Savelsberg, Joachim Josef. 1982. *Ausländische Jugendliche: assimilative Integration, Kriminalität und Kriminalisierung u. die Rolle der Jugendhilfe.* München, Germany: Minerva.

Schroeder, Friedrich Christian. 1983. "Strafen zum Heimattarif? – Probleme der Strafzumessung bei Ausländern." *Frankfurter Allgemeine Zeitung,* October 13, 1983: 12.

Schütze, Hans. 1993. "Junge Ausländer im Vollzug der Straf- und Untersuchungshaft. In *Freiheitsentzug bei Jungen Straffälligen,* edited by Thomas Trenczek. Bonn, Germany: Forum Verlag.

Sessar, Klaus. 1981. "Rechtliche und soziale Prozesse einer Definition der Tötungskriminalität." Kriminologische Forschungsberichte aus dem Max-Planck-Institut für Ausländisches und Internationales Strafrecht, Freiburg im Breisgau, Germany.

Statistisches Bundesamt [Federal Statistical Office]. 1993. "Statistisches Jahrbuch 1993 für die Bundesrepublik Deutschland." Statistisches Bundesamt.

———. 2004. "Statistisches Jahrbuch 2004 für die Bundesrepublik Deutschland." Statistisches Bundesamt.

Statistisches Bundesamt: Wohnbevölkerung [Federal Statistical Office: Population Data]. 2005. "Gebiet und Bevölkerung – Fläche und Bevölkerung." Accessed at http://www.statistik-portal.de/Statistik-Portal/de_jb01_jahrtab1.asp.

Staudt, Gerhard. 1983. "Analyse der Kriminalitätsbelastung von 14- bis 20jährigen männlichen jugendlichen Deutschen und Ausländern gemäß der Verurteilungsstatistik im Saarland in den Jahren 1975 – 1979." Arbeiten aus dem Institut für Rechts- und Sozialphilosophie.

Steffen, Wiebke. 1977. "Analyse polizeilicher Ermittlungstätigkeit aus der Sicht des späteren Strafverfahrens." Mit einem Geleitwort von Günther Kaiser und einer Einführung von Erhard Blankenburg. Band 4, 1976 (390 Seiten).

Steinhilper, Udo. 1986. "Definitions- und Entscheidungsprozesse bei sexuell motivierten Gewaltdelikten : eine empirische Untersuchung der Strafverfolgung bei Vergewaltigung und sexueller Nötigung" Auflage Konstanz, Konzstanzer Schriften zur Rechtstatsachenforschung.

Tillmann, Klaus-Jürgen, Birgit Holler-Nowitzki, Heinz Günther Holtappels, Ulrich Meier, and Ulrike Popp. 1999. *Schülergewalt als Schulproblem: Verursachende Bedingungen, Erscheinungsformen und pädagogische Handlungsperspektiven.* Weinheim and München, Germany: Juventa-Verlag.

Unever, James D., and Larry A. Hembroff. 1988. "The Prediction of Racial/Ethnic Sentencing Disparities: An Expectation States Approach." *Journal of Research and Crime and Delinquency* 25: 53–82

Villmow, Bernhard. 1993. "Ausländerkriminalität." In: *Kleines Kriminologisches Wörterbuch, 3. Auflage,* edited by Günther Kaiser. Heidelberg, Germany: C.F. Müller Verlag.

von Trotha, Trutz. 1995. "One for Kaiser: Beobachtungen zur politischen Soziologie der Prügelstrafe am Beispiel des Schutzgebietes Togo." In *Festschrift für Peter Sebald;* Pfaffenweiler, Germany: Centaurus.

Wolfslast, Gabriele. 1982. "Anmerkung zu BGH Urteil vom 16.9.1981." *Neue Zeitschrift für Strafrecht* 2: 112–3.

CHAPTER 17

Minorities, Fairness, and the Legitimacy of the Criminal-Justice System in France

Sebastian Roché

Tackling the problem of the legitimacy and fairness of the criminal-justice system in France is very complex, especially when the treatment of minorities within the system is the issue. In fact, minority groups themselves have no official existence within the French institutional system. Ethnicity-defined policies are not permitted in the color-blind French republican model. Communities and "communitarianism" (in other words, identified ethnic communities and minorities) are described by top officials as a threat to the unity of the nation-state.[1] Consequently, it is not "politically correct" to question the legitimacy of the criminal-justice system or the state from the point of view of minority citizens.

As in numerous other continental European countries, the notion of race or ethnicity has no legal basis. On the contrary, it is illegal for official statistics units of the government even to gather data on the basis of these criteria. Most academics avert their eyes from the existence of minorities. However, the political issue of migration and the durable presence of minority groups on French soil has contributed to shaking this postwar consensus, embedded in a long-term vision of the state and the nation.

Ethnic discrimination is an important issue that has brought criticism regarding the reassertion of formal equality, which could obscure problems more than contributing to solving them. The perception that migrants and their children contribute disproportionately to street crime has also placed the notion of ethnicity at the center of the political arena. Ethnic minorities pose a legitimacy crisis for the

French state, which is unable to protect either the rights of minority members or those of the "white" majority from minority street criminals. Although the leaders of the national parties have had trouble dealing with this issue at the central level, locally elected political leaders as well as the press have not. The national newspapers and TV channels have produced a large number of articles and broadcasts that examine conditions on the blighted outskirts of large cities (where the less affluent families tend to live, among them a large share of immigrant families and their French-born children) and the malfunctioning of the criminal-justice system (where numerous youths of foreign origins are involved). Because the North African minority is confused with the Muslim minority in France, ethnicity together with religion, supposedly long consigned to the dustbin of history, are forcing their way back into the secular political arena and also into debate surrounding criminal-justice issues.

The legitimacy of the criminal-justice system is caught in a cross-fire: one side charges it with too much leniency (juvenile courts being blamed for their lack of toughness) and the other side with its undue harshness (children of migrants are punished too severely and are overrepresented in prisons and other institutions; discrimination against them explains their higher crime rate). At the same time, no "official" data were available to shed light on this political dispute. National authorities regularly assert that being a united nation implies not having this information.

Since the notion of minority itself is not legitimate, discussing legitimacy and fairness of the criminal-justice system vis-à-vis minorities in France becomes a very peculiar exercise. Very little information is available from government sources or large public social science institutions, such as the Institut National de la Statistique et des Études Économiques (INSEE), the National Institute of Statistics and Economic Studies. This chapter relies mainly on local or regional data and a few national surveys that have provided information on the perception of criminal-justice organizations.

THE ILLEGITIMACY OF THE NOTION OF MINORITY

The core values encapsulated in the French constitution insist that differences in status be ignored and proclaim equality among humans ("Tous les hommes naissent et demeurent libres et égaux en droit"). Citizenship is made the basis of political legitimacy and of social bounds. And in principle each citizen can access institutions and every other citizen without paying attention to any personal characteristics: the state refuses to admit that any group is closed to any other, regardless of reality. Other countries declare the same principles, but the special feature of the French idea concerns the status of intermediate groupings, be they geographical, racial, religious or otherwise: the state is "allergic" to any subgroup of citizens or resident members that can be perceived as minorities. The fusion of the nation and the state in one concept, the nation-state, explains why minorities do not have a natural place in the political imagination in France. Their nature is not political, and only political links authentically bind human beings together in an acceptable way.

To citizens of countries where the census or other comparable governmental surveys require that they select their ethnic or racial identity, France and similar nations might look weird. The historical nation-building process probably explains the differences, at least some of them, in the use of the notion of race and ethnicity, but also in the notion of what a nation should be and what its legitimate components ought to be. All governments insist on being unitary, even those made of communities. Can't we read "E Pluribus Unum" (Out of many, one) on American coins? But some governments insist on the individual adherence to the state while others insist on the coexistence of various socially organized and to a large extent impermeable groups. The basic political unit seems to be different in different countries.

The French model is adamant on the integration of migrants. They cannot remain what they were, members surfacing from a deeper community. I will use the phrase "French model" (although it is by no means fixed in stone and not subject to variation). One of its key characteristics lies in its insistence on the permanent unitary nature of the French people. To comprehend why we as a nation are so ignorant of our minorities and the penal system one must explain how the issue of minority groups is framed. In short, minorities are anti-republican by definition (even if they adhere to no anti-republican ideology), for they embody the opposite of the Republic: a particular identity or interest and the fragmentation of the formal unity of the state. Their presence represents a disruption of the republican model.

Unity Against Minorities and "Particular Interests"

The process that leads to emphasizing unity is a secular one. We will highlight some of the key historical features of France. French historians insist on the long-term state-building process, the monarchy's conquest of the land from the region of Paris expanding out to the "remote" peripheral countries of Burgundy, Brittany, the Basque country, and the city of Nice. The king as well as the French Republic established after the French Revolution of 1789 had to fight against the regional parliaments and their desire for autonomy. Language unity was very early targeted by the central powers. King Francois I (1494–1547) made French compulsory for any administrative documents, replacing Latin and especially all local languages, used by three-quarters of the population. The Villers-Cotterêts ordinance in 1539 (articles 110 and 111) forbade all other languages. Later on, the French revolutionary leaders fought against regional languages (such as Occitan, in Provence) that were called "patois," a very pejorative term stigmatizing an "under-language" (Degrève 2003). Religious unity was also sought after. The Catholic church gained ground along with the state and labeled the peasants' beliefs superstitions. French homogeneity was won through violence and constraints. For example, Louis the XIV intended to impose the Catholic faith to the southern regions of France in the

Cévennes from the 1660s onward. To achieve this he had a thousand "refractories" (people resistant to Catholicism) deported to the Americas between 1686 and 1688. He instituted "dragonades" (named for soldiers of the king, the "Dragons"), who were placed in non-Catholic homes to monitor them. Peasant families had to house the Dragons and feed them from their own pockets.

As shown by the historian Christian Goudineau (2001), the notion that the kingdom of France had its origins in one territory (a land stretching from the Atlantic ocean to the river Rhine) and one people (the Gauls) was proclaimed by the authorities during the sixteenth century. Later on, the Republicans also favored the idea that the Gauls were the ancestors of the people of France; members of the elite, however, were supposed to have descended from the Franks, themselves descendants of the Romans. The Romans were not deeply grounded in what was the French soil, and were "foreigners" in a way. The "true" root of France was seen to be unitarian in its nature. Of course, Goudineau finds little historical reality to back up this representation: the Gauls never existed as a people and never called themselves with this name. Instead, Julius Caesar found more than sixty tribes when he conquered the territory (the Eduens, the Arverns, and others).

The American historian Eugen Weber (1976) synthesized the late phase of this process under the Third Republic after 1870 in the name of his book: *Peasants into Frenchmen*. Weber describes the generations-long effort to transform members of isolated peasant communities into citizens of a nation. France had been a cluster of many separate societies, speaking many languages, using different measurement systems, with various legal and even architectural traditions. Let's recall that in the 1860s, a fifth of the citizens still couldn't speak French. Laws and regulations were not easily enforced on the entire country and the corresponding creation of new crimes not welcome. Weber also describes the government's efforts. The trend toward centralization and unification was not welcomed by all the peasants: experience had taught them to defy Paris and its civil servants, be they tax collector or recruiting sergeants. The centralization trend also applied to the judicial system that progressively replaced the local influential elite. Well into the twentieth century the peasants had a maxim: "Beware of all evils and the courts" ("Méfies-toi de tous les maux et de la justice").

In sum, historically, reluctant minorities were perceived as an obstacle to the creation of a unified, centralized nation by central governments. Minorities were a disruption to the establishment of the central powers and the national ideal. The territorial minorities were to be brought enlightenment by the national educational system, be transported by the national railway system, be arrested by the national police (although this last aspect happened only recently, in 1942), and be sanctioned by the national courts. The minorities are the hidden pieces of what would become the kingdom of France and then the Republic. Today, the notion of minorities is still a synonym for division and archaism, harking back to a premodern era.

Defiance Toward Intermediate Groups

Another feature of the French model is the defiance vis-à-vis intermediary groups. The political organizations, political parties and trade unions, are acknowledged as essential features of the good functioning of the Republic. The role of the political parties is asserted within the French constitution: they contribute to democracy. But other groups (religious, ethnic, an so forth) are not viewed as contributing to democracy.

For example, religious matters are considered private matters. On December 9, 1905, the act that separates the state and the churches was passed. This electoral pledge has been part of all Republican (left-wing) programs since 1869 and was the subject of six articles in the act. The separation of church and state is meant to respect liberty of conscience, as the first and second article declare: "The Republic warrants the freedom of conscience"; "The Republic acknowledges . . . no cult." The state aims to stand apart from, not be hostile or indifferent to, religion. The rationale is that this is a precondition for the central government to be able to pursue the general interest: the state must be apart from any particular group.

Interestingly, although it was passed by the French parliament on August 21, 1790, the 1789 Declaration of the Rights of Man failed to guarantee the right of free association and the right to create organizations to do so. June 17, 1791, saw the passage of an extremely famous act, named after its author, Le Chapellier, that prohibited any intermediate group from interceding between the citizen and the nation, abolished corporations, and, notably, forbade collective bargaining and trade unions because they were seen to be the backbone of the prerevolutionary Ancien Régime. It was only a century later, in 1901, that the freedom of association was fully acknowledged, provided that the society is made known to the state. Of course, things have changed today. However, influential large-scale associations avoid representing specific groups in France: their names do not refer to a particular community and they are supposed to be run as "mini-states" that are universal. And they are inclined to do so because these important associations are heavily state-funded. Elected leaders tend to work with "their" associations that insert the administration deeper into civil society, and this may well be a French peculiarity. Only very recently, in November 2005, did a national umbrella organization called the Conseil Representif des Associations Noires (National Representative Council of Black Associations) surface that explicitly referred to a specific minority group. CRAN claims to tackle "ethnic and racial discrimination." In 2001, for the centennial of the 1901 act, when signing a charter with the largest national umbrella organization, the French state acknowledged that the nonprofit sector contributes to public debate and defines the general interest, which as a consequence is no longer represented as a state-monopolized faculty. But, again, the sociologist Roger Sue (2003) sees it as an important symbol, but not as something that has changed the way of interacting on a daily basis. General interest still equates with state and not civil society groups, even if they are large or are gathered into an umbrella association.

As the historian Pierre Rosanvallon (2004) has summarized, since the revolution, the French state has been seen as the cornerstone of society and the indispensable unifier of a nation of individuals. In this model, any association or corporation is perceived as an expression of special interests (egoism, to put it bluntly). The general interest can only be expressed by the central state. It is not only a question of public versus private, but also a matter of central versus local: locally elected leaders regularly are suspected of not being able to embody and protect the general interest. And this is why responsibilities such as ruling the judiciary or the police remain in the hands of the central powers, not the mayors or the heads of the administrative regions (departments) of France. The Germans and the English can see the quest for the general interest as a compromise between special local interests and the state, the result of discussion and negotiation. This is not the case in France, where the secular state seems to have a religious feature, a sense of transcendence over society. This is one reason why the state would be so often referred to in France: it could do it if only it decided to. In this context, any expression of pluralism is perceived as the greatest of evils. Because it is accepted that freedom of the individual is essential, it cannot be forbidden to them to organize and form societies. But these associations have no virtue. They are not in themselves constructive. They are denied the capability to represent the population (only the elected leaders at the national level can do this). Only citizenship is a noble link.

Curiously, this vision is as distant from Tocqueville (who has no strong intellectual legacy in France, even if he is regularly "rediscovered" and then forgotten again) and his interest in the function of intermediate groups as remedies for pathologies threatening democracy (despotism, individualism) than it is from Durkheim (revered in the French academic world). The founder of French sociology also grandly insisted on the importance of the various groups that would structure society and protect individuals (for example, from suicide). But sociologists are less influential in France than philosophers, probably because the latter have a perception of the state more coherent with the mission still ascribed to it by its top civil servants and political leaders. The roots of the French system can be found in Jean-Jacques Rousseau's philosophy, not in sociology. The author of *Le contrat social* perceived the law of men as legitimate if voted by individuals freed from any belonging, any allegiance to a group. This is probably why, coherent with this vision of things, the political parties are considered legitimate and are not seen as associations that could represent private interests. The individual chooses his or her political party. It is not a corporation, a "natural" community, not an identity group. It results from the voluntary gathering of free men (and, today, women). The fact that France has one of the lowest trade-union membership rates as well as political parties in Europe and that these numbers have steadily declined since 1945 (Labbé and Andolfato 2000) is not interpreted as a disavowal of the Republican model.[2] However, it should lead them to question their vision of political unity and the coherence of citizens without other intermediate groups than political ones.

Massive Migration and the Homogeneous Nation

The French paradox regarding minorities is that the myth of homogeneity and unity, of corresponding culture, nation, and state, was elaborated in a country that always was a mosaic of peoples and one where migration has been a constant.

The reluctance to fully account for the impact of migrations can be found not only among historians. The demographer Michèle Tribalat (2004) insisted that despite strong immigration currents, the French demographers paid little attention to the impact of migration on the total population, the French nation. Only three times in French history has the state endeavored to estimate the segment of the population with foreign origins (born outside France, or born in France from at least one foreign parent): in 1927, 1942, and 1986. She has established that in 1999, 14 million of the residents of France (almost a fourth of France's 60 million inhabitants) were immigrants or had foreign origins (have at least one non-French parent or grandparent born in another country). Tribalat reminds us (2004, 51):

> In France, immigration has been a massive and structural phenomenon for one and a half centuries that has displayed two periods of particular intensity: between the two [world] wars and after the Second [World] War. At the end of the nineteenth century and during the early twentieth century, the migrants were mostly Belgians and Italians. Then came the Poles and the Spaniards. . . . After the Second World War, the Spanish and Italian waves have risen again, while the "Muslim French" from Algeria came for work. . . . The Italian population peaked again in 1962 (629,000 individuals), the Portuguese in 1975 (759,000) and the Algerian in 1982 (805,000).

Ignoring the reality of immigration, some thinkers today, like the historian Dominique Schnapper (2005), have kept alive the traditional vision of a unitary France and recently asserted that "the democratic idea and the ideal imply that the concrete diversities of historic individuals be transcended by the community of equal citizens; it ensues that these diversities must fade away and that concrete individuals should constitute a unique and unified society" (6). Dominique Schnapper and other historians working in a prestigious academic community, the EHESS (École des Hautes Études en Sciences Sociales—Advanced School of Social Sciences) in Paris are not marginal. Their discourse echoes the recurrent discourse of the ministers, prime ministers, and president of the Republic.

Dominique Schnapper (1994) already occupied the same territory in the mid-nineties, when her book *The Community of Citizens* appeared. It is emblematic of the use of the term "community" in France: it only can be used among republicans (in the French sense of an intellectual elite member favorable to a centralized political system) to designate the nation itself, or the state that is its equivalent in the nation-state vision of France. She claimed that integration into their ethnic community of the youths born in France of foreign parents would threaten national cohesion. Reactions to this vision are recent. Other left-wing researchers (who could not be accused of intending to stigmatize the communities when emphasizing the need to take them into account) such as Michel Wieviorka (1997) and his colleagues indicted this view as "abstract universalism" of the French model and blamed it for the lack of success of the republican integration process. The historian Suzanne Citron also criticized the construction of the mythology of the French nation-state, "the faking" of the historiography (2003, 346). She claims that systematic suppression of the violence against minorities was organized and perpetuated (for example, in the textbooks that are the basis of what is taught in schools), whether during the French Revolution by its soldiers in the Catholic department of the Vendée, during the Vichy regime, or the colonization of Algeria. Official historians of the Third Republic (1870 to 1940) even tried to ground the homogeneous and indivisible nation in a mythic Gallic country where France is supposed to have its roots, as if no blend of cultures and peoples had ever taken place. Amédée Thierry and later Jules Michelet and Henri Martin rendered this version official in *Le petit Lavisse,* the flagship history textbook of the Third Republic. Suzanne Citron explains how republican mythology has integrated the monarchist official history and "the saga of kings," dating back to the thirteenth century, originally written to legitimize the then-new Capetian dynasty. This myth was henceforth used by the Republicans. She shows how the republican elite (the top civil servants and politicians) of the Third Republic was educated in ignorance of the deeply multicultural roots of the kingdom of Saint Louis and other major kings. In sum, the historiography of France has converged during many centuries to forge a collective myth that is still strong today. It is so because major French historians and philosophers still defend the vision of a unified nation that cannot contain any components other than individuals.

Historians such as Dominique Schnapper or Gérard Noiriel, members of the faculty of the EHESS, still dream of a future based on a past that never existed except in the indoctrination of pupils and in the eyes of the Parisian elite of the Republic. In *Les politiques d'integration des jeunes issues de l'immigration* [*Integration Policies of Children Born from Foreign Parents*], Gérard Noiriel, in a chapter entitled "Young people with foreign origins do not exist" (1988) went as far as to accuse social workers and the few organizations established to better address migrants' needs of inventing the issue of minorities: "There are today thousands of people that examine, diagnose, study and sometimes solve the 'problems of the young people with foreign origins' "; he concluded that "this way a social 'reality' . . . has turned into an obviousness, mainly because today there are people to designate it, people that make a life from this designation" (18). The philosopher Blandine Kriegel, who was an adviser on social issues to the president of the Republic Jacques Chirac and the president of the Haut Conseil de l'intégration (High Council on Integration), a body attached to the prime minister's office, is also opposed to acknowledgment of minorities because it could lead to ethnic quotas. As a political philosopher, she also shares a vision of Rousseau's Social Contract, where the State embodies the general interest and has a "contract" with the citizen—not with groups.[3]

Minority Policies: Assimilation or Integration Versus Recognition

Since the end of the Second World War, the official national policy has been one of assimilation of foreigners and minorities. During the nineties, its name changed and it was labeled integration. Later, the term "assimilation" resurfaced after the republican logic of integration was strongly challenged by facts (for example, the unemployment rates of qualified and educated young persons with foreign passports) and by left-wing intellectuals.[4] At the ministerial level the expression "equality of opportunities" is now preferred (an "under secretary of state for the promotion of equal opportunities" existed from 2004 to 2007). However, the notion of integration still is very much in use in public policy goals. What is called the "integration policy" is largely encompassed in the "urban regeneration policy" (called "politique de la ville," or "urban policy"). Even the integration policy make no explicit reference to minorities defined as human groups: it is organized along geographical lines (municipal or submunicipal units).

Many examples of the policies for assimilation can be found, and it is important to notice that these do not date back to the economic crisis years of the seventies. Even before the first oil shock, in 1973, the 1971 Trintignac report appeared, written after an interministerial committee instructed social workers to break up the large-family model of migrants. The families should be taught how to be independent, "how to do without one another," and "operate as nuclear families" (quoted in Barou 2002, 78). The community connections of the households had to be wiped out through the actions of publicly funded social workers.

This vision of the role of the state combines with the painful memories from the Second World War. In 1946 a new constitution was prepared, including a preamble, whose first article insisted on the absence of "distinction of race." In many European countries, the bureaucratic knowledge of origins or religious beliefs was used as an extermination tool. Recent history reinforces the proscription of identifying minorities, and especially the collaboration of the French police depending on Vichy officials with the Nazi regime during the occupation of the country. The files that mentioned denomination were used by the collaborationists and the police to deport the Jews—the number of those deported is estimated to be as high as 75,000. The eradication of Gypsies also put a black mark on the risks of stigmatizing minorities inherent in labeling them as such. Only very recently have the archives of the prefecture of Paris on this subject been opened to the public (see Georges Abou, "La police ouvre les archives de l'occupation" ["The police allow access to their archives during German occupation"], June 17, 2005, accessed at http://rfi/actufr/articles/066/article_3692.asp.).

Today, the centralized French state still claims that its mission is to organize the French people's social life through legislation and to promote a social "blending" ("la mixité sociale"). For example, the Housing Act, passed in 2000, claims that its aim is "to be successful in implementing urban blending" and that a major tool is "to build public housing estates in municipalities that do not have any or have too few." This social blending implicitly refers to religious, ethnic characteristics and explicitly to socioeconomic and geographical blending.

Of course, there are differences between minorities in France and in the United States or the United Kingdom. But when the notion of minority is prohibited, systematic observation and comparisons are not easy to establish. As the sociologist Véronique De Rudder wrote in 1994, the French Arab quarters or the Chinatowns are very distant from their American counterparts. The communities are not structured as such, they are not micro-societies organized for defending their interests and identities, with leaders, media outlets, and political and fraternal organizations (1994, 96). Ethnicization seems rather to operate at very small geographical scale, at the subneighborhood level. And these "small ghettos" are multi-ethnic, not mono-ethnic.

It is not obvious that lack of structuring of minorities is due to French public action. Comparative research by the sociologist Jacques Barou found that the French situation was comparable to that in many other European nations: in all the countries that have received a large number of migrants, no political organization of foreigners exists, the internal mobilization of members is weak, and Barou found no strong attempt to be organized as an independent community (Barou 1997, summarized in 2002, 23). The political mobilization of young Arabs has always failed. In 1984, there was a demonstration that started as a protest procession from the South of France. The politicized young people were riding motorcycles under the banner that said "Convergence 84 for equality," but whenever they reach a city they were unable to make contact with the population in deprived neighborhoods (Jazouli 1992, 107; for a theoretical approach see Lapeyronnie 1987). Because they had very few activists, antiracist organizations such as France Plus and SOS Racisme, often headed by persons of northern African Origins, engaged in media activity where they could capture more attention. Lately, they have tried to use a legal approach, prosecuting discriminatory behaviors, for example, when minority members were refused entry to a disco. At the local level, a study in Marseille confirms that the various small Maghrebian grassroots associations never succeeded in transforming themselves into a larger coalition-like organization, in part because the locally elected politicians favored the balkanization of the political representation of this ethnic group (Cesari 1988, 131). (The Maghreb is the region of North Africa bordering the Mediterranean.) Jacques Barou reached the conclusion that an efficient machinery to assimilate foreigners, diminish differences with the French population, and turn them into citizens—an exceptional case in France—was in fact very similar to what he could observe in countries where ethnic communities were acknowledged or even valorized. Ethnicity doesn't vanish when the sons of migrants become French citizens. Simultaneously, French citizens born of French parents in France also tend to emphasize their ethnicity, their foreign national roots (Barou 2002, 23–24). Being workers or employees did not produce a sense of solidarity between the immigrants from northern Africa and those residing in France.

Ethnic tensions resurfaced in France, perhaps also in conjunction with the durable problems in Middle East because of the confrontation of Arabs and Jews: identification to a cross-national community was more important to the young Maghrebians at this time than it was for the previous waves of migrants, such as the Italians, after the Second World War. The issue of Islam gained importance, and major political debate occurred when girls wore scarves on their hair at school. In France, Islam is the religion of people who were born in North Africa or are the sons and daughters of these migrants. Therefore the two issues, ethnic and religious identities, are one. On March 15, 2004, legislation was passed to protect the principle of secularism, prohibiting the use of any religious sign at school if it was "very visible," including the head scarf. In December 2003, 57 percent of the general population agreed with restricting the use of religious signs at school, versus only 42 percent among the Muslim population one month later (see CSA 2003, 2004). A majority of the population shares the vision of a secularized society where religion remains strictly a private matter, but a large minority among French citizens departs from it.

Identifying Minority Members: A Bad Idea?

The politicization of the rise in juvenile crime often involving minority members, rampant discrimination, and international tensions have led to a renewed discussion in the academy of the importance and legitimacy of studying ethnicity. The turmoil has been dramatic in some of the major research bodies in France, and in the Institut National des Etudes Demographiques (National Institute of Demography), where researchers had serious clashes on this issue, to the point that it was widely publicized in the major weekly newspapers.

One hypothesis regarding the effects of having visible minorities is that public opinion is less favorable to them today than in the past. On the contrary, as Guillaume Roux (2004) has demonstrated, on all indicators available, the idea that foreigners and Frenchmen should be treated equality has gained ground. The notion that when unemployment rises foreigners should be laid off first declined from 84 to 61 percent in 1971 and rose to 65 percent in 1975 (after the oil crisis). The question regularly asked since 1991 about giving nationals priority for jobs shows a decline to 25 percent in 2003. In terms of social welfare, giving priority to nationals followed the same trend downward, from 43 percent in 1991 to 26 percent in 2003. The acceptance of inter-ethnic marriages has increased, as has the idea that immigration could have positive consequences. Arabs, which are the most-represented non-European migrants, are perceived as "too numerous," more often than other groups, but the level is unchanged since 1992, when the questions were asked for the first time. Other surveys have even uncovered an increase in positive perceptions between 1990 and 2003: the percentage of people with sympathy to Maghrebians rose from 53 percent to 76 percent (CSA 2003). If any cause can explain the demand for more visibility of various groups, it is not linked with a rising stigmatization or a desire to deprive them of social rights.

The once-dominant view among the intellectual elite, that minorities cannot be described because they don't exist, has been contended by some of them, among right-wing intellectuals or CIOs with a role in public debate—for example, Claude Bebear, CIO of AXA, has created the Montaigne Institute, a think tank that addresses this issue—and even among academics close to the French Socialist Party, such as Rachel Wievorka. It also has been practically challenged by the realization of a large national survey notably by Michèle Tribalat (1995), and more modestly by local surveys on crime and ethnicity that I will present later. Most of the indictment of the republican model came from intellectuals who spoke of a "racist social order" toward which the response to discrimination consists in the reassessment of the legal and formal equality among citizens (De Rudder, Poiret, and Vourch 2000). These persons argue that color blindness is counterproductive for fighting discrimination. But they remain attached to universalism and opposed to affirmative action. The issue of crime and minorities is not tackled by academics, probably because they are frightened to be caught in discussing the extreme right thesis that equates immigration with crime in the political rhetoric in France as in other countries in Europe (Ivaldi 2003).

The social blending is part of the normative framework of the central state: it is meant to legitimately organize daily social life. It implies that all social groups meld into one political people. There is something common to various regimes in the notion that politics is about making unity from diversity, as the philosopher Hannah Arendt explained a long time ago (1954/1972). However, regimes differ in the way the elements to be melded are defined and the ways themselves contribute to building a political society. This is very obvious when one simply compares how nationally elected leaders present their own society. The Canadian minister of multiculturalism (a label simply impossible in France), Jean Augustine, presented the annual report on multiculturalism in February 2004 and said that, as a minister, he was happy to play a major role in realizing the values related to inclusion and respect of diversity, that Canada was a multicultural nation, that diversity has always been an essential characteristics of this society. The acknowledgment of diversity is presented as an aspect of the fight for a society "exempt of racism and discrimination." Maintaining order must, in this framework, strengthen the relations between the police and the communities (see speaking notes for the Honorable Jean Augustine, Secretary of State (Multiculturalism, status of women) on the occasion of the opening of the Minister's Forum on Diversity and Culture. April 22, 2003, Gatineau,

Quebec. Accessed at http://www.pch.gc.ca/special/dcforum/sec/1_f.cfm). Through Statistics Canada the government has conducted a survey on multiculturalism and the way the Canadians perceive of their ethnicity.

Today, the current French legal context is chaotic. The political debate focuses on the Maghrebian ethnic group because of its place at the crossroads of community issues (Can the French Republic tolerate an ethnic group? And what must be done with it, protect it from discrimination or assimilate it?), religious issues (the acknowledgment that Islam has a right to existence in the public sphere), and crime problem (the involvement of second-or third-generation minorities in street crime). From 2002 through 2007, the minister of the interior insistently spoke about positive discrimination when the prime minister didn't want to hear about this idea, in line with president Jacques Chirac. The latter is backed up by the most recent positions about collecting data on ethnicity. The Commission Nationale D'informatique et des Libertés (CNIL—National Commission on Computing and Liberties), an administrative authority in charge of the deontology of all types of computerized information, has rendered a negative opinion for large-scale operations such as the census or employers' data banks: ethnicity per se cannot be included as a variable in the questionnaires. Only in 2005 was this position made public—after it had been an important public issue for more than twenty-five years. The recommendation is as follows:

> The CNIL considers that the following data can be gathered and treated in the framework of establishing tools in order to measure the diversity of origins: family name, first name, nationality, nationality of birth, place of birth, nationality of place of birth of his parents, his address. Regarding the data relative to the racial or ethnic origins of individuals, the CNIL observers the absence of any definition of a national framework of "ethnic-racial" typologies.[5]

In sum, in France it is not possible for an official administrative body to ask people to define themselves by race or ethnicity. And it has been ruled out that the individual surveyed can select one or many such identities by himself from a list. But it is allowed to use the place of birth of the parents. In doing this, the CNIL simply takes into account the current practices of researchers, mainly demographers and sociologists, and remains faithful to the principle that individuals cannot have such thing as an ethnic identity.

National left-wing activist groups against racism take the same position. At the local level, however, there are some noteworthy initiatives. For example, a group of associations has produced a survey (whose scientific rigor is contestable) that takes into account ethnicity when recording the sentences given in courts. At the national level, attempts have been made to understand better the meaning of ethnic belonging in the French context. They are cautiously labeled "exploratory," like the study by the demographers Patrick Simon and Martin Clement (2006). The researchers found that minority members (persons with one or two parents who were immigrants) are twice as uncomfortable with "ethnic and racial" categorization (black, white, Arab) as French nationals with two parents born in France (21 percent versus 8 percent). The same phenomenon occurs when world regions are used, but this method is better accepted. Reluctance to grant the right to record ethnic information to employers or public administration is much greater—for example, 52 percent of Arabs—than for a poll.

It appears that minority identification is much more debated today in France than it was twenty-five years ago. But no clear evolution toward a statistical use of ethnic or racial categories can be found. The government, the administrative authorities, and a large proportion of some minorities themselves seem to be reluctant to see any rapid change.

MINORITIES, NATIONALITIES, AND THE PENAL SYSTEM: SOME STATISTICAL VISIBILITY

As we have seen, the discussion of taking or not taking into account ethnicity is far from being settled. In parallel with other policy sectors, the debate still is quite vehement regarding the police and the judiciary. Two main issues are debated: minority members' representation within the police force and relations between minorities and the police; and the representation of minority members as perpetrators of crimes, behind bars, among convicted persons, or as victims of police violence. Provided that one particular ethnic group can have offending rates completely different from one country to another, as Michael Tonry (1997) has noted, the explanation of the nature and role of ethnicity is not self-evident. This constitutes a central issue also for democracies, as it is consistently found that ethnic and racial minorities are overrepresented all over the world, and that despite vast cultural differences, "there is a troubling relationship between race and ethnicity, and punishment" (Bosworth 2000, 114). In France, young people whose families came from the former colonies of North Africa (Algeria) or the region under French influence (Tunisia, Morocco) are more likely to end up in the criminal-justice system. So the fairness and legitimacy of the criminal-justice system has to be questioned. But on what empirical grounds?

Police and Discrimination

There is a vast lack of knowledge about the representation of minorities in France within the police force due to the circumstances that we have previously enumerated. A high-ranking police official working for the central government at the Ministry of the Interior summarizes the dominant view: "In the French police [national police], there are only Frenchmen. Origin doesn't attract any attention. And is not the business of the administration." This could explain why there would be no more than a dozen nonwhite police executives (chiefs and commissioners), according to an unofficial estimate made by another police official (Maschino 2003, 10). No systematic survey of police officers' origins has been ever demanded by the minister of the interior. The most recent attempt to tackle the issue while not naming it was by Minister of the Interior Jean-Pierre Chevènement (1977 to 2000), during the premiership of the Socialist Lionel Jospin. Two objectives were attributed to his "security policy": make the public police more like the population (nonwhite), and bring the police closer to the deprived neighborhoods where a large number of immigrant families live as well as their descendants who could not move up the socioeconomic ladder. A new police status was created: adjoint de sécurité, or security aide. These aides were to have lower status than police officers. The candidates could be recruited without their having to take the normally qualifying national examination. Local recruiting units were set up. This was meant to allow individuals with a poor education to find a job, a situation that is more frequent with second- or third-generation families. However, this experiment was not evaluated, for the targeted communities were never identified, and it is impossible to form a judgment about the possible impact of the program on the perceptions of the various communities in France. Since 2004 a scheme has been set up to help underprivileged students pass national exams required to be a civil servant and to enter the national police force: the "cadets of the Republic" (one thousand in 2005) have one year to upgrade their knowledge in a special police school. The scheme has been extended to police chief schools and in 2006 to the commissioner school of Lyon (which provides training to all commissioners). It is expected to contribute to forging an elite with foreign origins. But no data related to ethnic origins are gathered: it will not be easy to evaluate.

Police and minority relations have been clarified by means of national surveys focused on minority and politics by the political scientists Sylvain Brouard and Vincent Tiberj (2005). A poll was taken in May 2005; first a representative sample of the adult population of France was designed and then a second representative sample of "new Frenchmen" was added so that a comparison could be made. The level of confidence in the two samples is very similar for schools (82 percent of the adult population has quite or much confidence versus 85 percent of the adult "new Frenchmen"), media, and even the judiciary (respectively 61 and 62 percent). When it comes to the police, the level of trust is quite distinct in the two populations: 77 percent among all adults versus 58 percent among "new Frenchmen." The percentage of those who do not at all trust the police is 8 percent versus 20 percent. This difference remains true after controlling for SES, age, education and political orientation.

There is a little more information available about the second issue: the overrepresentation of minority members as perpetrators of crimes, behind bars, among convicted persons, or as victims of police violence. However, the last aspect, police violence against minority members, even if frequently denounced, is very poorly documented. Not only can the police be biased, but because the police investigates their agents' behavior, cases of discrimination tend to be closed by the inspectorate. Sophie Body-Gendrot and Catherine Wihtol de Wenden (2003) have gathered testimonies from people who say they were victims of discrimination and called a toll-free number, where minority people are overrepresented. Moreover, the authors claim that very few formal complaints lead to administrative or penal sanctions against the police agents. A yearly report is produced by the National Committee on Deontology of Security (CNDS). However, this document has a very shallow empirical foundation for studying discrimination by the police against minority members (called "visible populations"). The CNDS, headed by Judge Pierre Truche, relies on the thirty-six cases that were transferred by national elected politicians (from the National Assembly and the Senate) in 2004. Twenty-five out of thirty-six cases are conveyed to the CNDS by opposition members of parliament (Socialists and Communists) and the rest by majority members (right-wing parties). Under these conditions and due to the limited size of the sample, any variation can be a product of a more active parliamentary opposition as much as a change in police practices.[6] No research has been published in any academic journal on the frequency and intensity of police violence against minorities that is based on solid empirical evidence.

Minorities and Crime, Minorities and the Judicial System: Data Sets

To document fairness and legitimacy of the criminal-justice system in France, data from five different surveys that I have directed since 1999 will be used.[7] The ethnic identification of individuals was included in each of them. The fact that state officials want to ignore ethnic background and also fund almost all social science research in France doesn't imply that they prohibit data collection on this issue. Therefore, it was possible to do field work. This research cannot match that done in the more advanced European countries where comprehensive critical analysis of racism and the criminal-justice process from crime and victimization to policing, punishment, prison, and probation has been carried out (Bowling and Phillips 2002).

The first set of research is based on self-reports. Two self-reported delinquency surveys took place in two large cities in 1999 (Grenoble and Saint-Étienne, N = 2,300) and 2003 (Grenoble, N = 1,600). Those are representative random samples from all types of schools present within the perimeter of the cities for teenagers aged thirteen to nineteen. Another self-reported survey took place from 2003 to 2004 among institutionalized juveniles only. Teenagers thirteen to nineteen years old were interviewed if they lived in the department of Isère, in the southeast of France (N = 93, or half the youths in these centers).

The second set of surveys is based on juvenile-justice files for minors who were put on trial. One data set is made of all available files from the juvenile court of Grenoble from 1985 to 2000, which is the department of Isère minus the juvenile court of Vienne (the territories of the various public entities, whether administrative, educational, or judicial, all are different). Only serious crimes files were recorded. In this research, serious crimes are more serious than in the self-reports: they comprise homicide (2.2 percent of the cases), physical violence (with incapacity to work for more than eight days, 41.8 percent), theft with a weapon (17.5 percent) or violence (with incapacity to work for more than eight days, 6.2 percent), rape (7.1 percent), sexual assaults (25.2 percent). The data collection form was modeled on that of the National Science Foundation (adapted because it was primarily meant to analyze homicides, which are extremely rare among juveniles in France). Three hundred twenty-five perpetrators of crime and a high number of deeds were computerized. The other data set is constituted of all the juvenile files for the juvenile courts of Grenoble and Vienne (again in the department of Isère), for a total of 1,645 perpetrators. One subset consists of the cases that are closed by judges or other personnel working for the juvenile-justice system (not sent to court) (N = 1,240). The other is made up of juveniles who have been tried (N = 405).

Nationality and Ethnicity:
What Percentage of the Population?

One technical difficulty that relates to the more global perspective discussed is inability to compare ethnicity in our studies to any systematic national or regional study. Because census and such surveys do not record ethnicity, the simple comparison of our results with anything else can be a problem. However, it is still possible to compare nationality and ethnicity within our studies: the proportions of nationals and minorities in each survey; the proportion of nationals and minorities in the representative polls compared to the juvenile-justice youth (whether derived from the judicial statistics or the self-reported survey of institutionalized youths). The distinction between nationality and ethnicity can be crucial. A small group of foreign-born persons can hide a large group of people born in France but sharing the same ethnic background.

This first overview of all data enabled us to say that the proportion of foreigners seems to be increasing as one continues through the juvenile-justice system: 3.9 percent in the representative sample; 5.6 percent among perpetrators of a minor crime; 6.5 to 8.6 if brought to trial (which means that the juvenile has repeated minor crimes or committed a more serious offense); 12 percent if tried for one serious offence or more. Detailed tables are presented in appendix 1.

Ethnicity has been defined using parents' country of birth combined with their nationality. This is the most common way to proceed (although some researchers have tried other measures, such as using the first names as a proxy for ethnicity). For example, a young person will be assigned to the North Africa minority group if at least one parent was born in a North African country or if the child declares that he is a citizen of one country in North Africa. This technique for defining ethnicity is based on questions asked to the respondents during the self-reported surveys. It is identical for the three surveys (1999, 2003, and 2003 to 2004) (Roché 2004).

Clearly, the proportion of juveniles with foreign origins from the self-reports doesn't match the census data based on nationality (in appendix 1, compare tables 1A.1 and 1A.3, and tables 1A.2 and 1A.4). The proportion of minority juveniles is higher than the proportion of foreigners, even including "new" Frenchmen in the general population. For example, although 7.6 percent of the juveniles are not French, 39.2 percent have foreign origins in the representative sample of 2003. Among the institutionalized youth, 6.5 percent are not French and 62.2 percent have foreign origins.

We can now compare our baseline figures of 39.2 percent of youths from foreign descent in the representative sample with the proportion found the juvenile court files (see appendix 1, table 1A.4). The three studies based on the judicial files indicate that young people with foreign origins represent between 31.1 percent (cases closed) and 73.4 percent (cases for serious offenses) of the total number of perpetrators. Northern Africans account for 20.6 to 57.1 percent when we focus on serious offenders (see table 17.4). The youths with French origins tend to be overrepresented by eight to nine percentage points for misdemeanors (case closed) versus the representative sample. But kids on trial are more often from non-French-born families (approximately 15 percent) and kids on trial for serious offenses even more (approximately 32 percent).

The detailed geographical origins are available from the longest survey (1985 to 2000), notably for the largest group, North African minors. Those whose families originated in Algeria account for two-thirds of African children brought to court for a serious crime (see figure 17.1). Compared to the baseline numbers in 2003 which indicate that 46 to 50 percent of Africans have Algerian origins (depending on inter-marriage classification within Maghreb countries), an overrepresentation seems likely.

The survey of the post-sentencing stage confirms this overrepresentation: 62.2 percent of young people housed in closed centers are of foreign origin, based on our self-report (2003 to 2004) (Roché 2004). In the department of Isère, among the juveniles aged thirteen to nineteen who had been assigned by a judge to a center (either closed or open) where they live full-time, 40 percent have African origin and 56 percent are of foreign origin (N = 34). This percentage is six times higher than the 6.5 percent of foreigners when the nationality variable is used in the same sample. It is twenty-three points higher than our baseline figures of 38 to 39 percent.

It could be claimed that our study is valid for the department of Isère only. We happened to have at our disposal one of the rare studies carried out by a team of psychologists and epidemiologists from Inserm (Institut National de la Sauté et la Récherche Medicale, the national center for medical studies), which can be used as a comparison, although the sample is not strictly analogous. In a 1998 survey of 917 youths fourteen to twenty-one years old, depending on the PJJ (Protection Judiciaire de la Jeunesse), our probation service for juveniles in seven regions of France (fifteen of France's hundred departments), not restricted to those assigned to a detention center (some are in foster homes or in individual apartments) in

FIGURE 17.1   NATIONALITY AND ETHNIC ORIGIN OF JUVENILE PERPETRATORS
SENTENCED BY A COURT IN GRENOBLE, DEPARTEMENT OF ISÈRE,
FRANCE, 1985 TO 2000

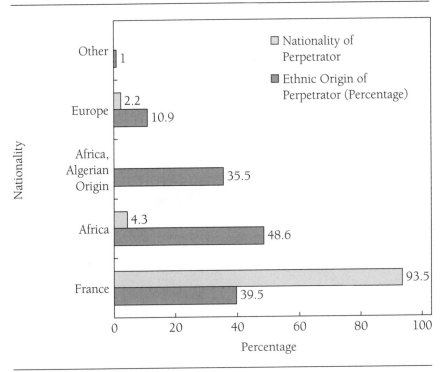

Source: Roché (2006a).

1995 found that 43 percent (Choquet et al. 1998, 25) were of foreign origins and
15 percent were foreigners (Choquet et al. 1998). The even higher percentage of
foreigners might be explained by the fact that very urban regions (Paris, Lyon,
Marseille) were taken included in the Inserm study. Figure 17.2 summarizes the
findings from the Isère and national studies.

    Provided that each survey allows us to compare the percentage of young peo-
ple with a foreign passport and with foreign origins and that the penal surveys can
be compared to the representative self-reports we have been able to draw a general
picture. In sum, in all types of surveys, self-reported for institutionalized kids or
through completion of forms based on juvenile-justice files, the minority groups
are well represented and even overrepresented when compared to the general population. Finally, the overrepresentation is important for Maghrebian children, and
among them for those of Algerian origins.

FIGURE 17.2   PLACEMENT OF JUVENILES IN AN OPEN OR CLOSED STRUCTURE BY A JUDGE

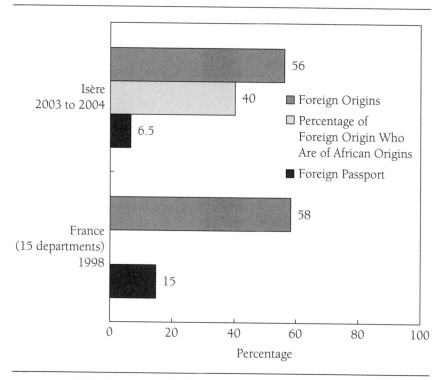

Source: Roché (2004); Choquet et al. (1998).

FAIRNESS AND THE PENAL SYSTEM: POLICING AND SENTENCING

The reasons for overrepresentation of minority groups in the criminal-justice system have been much debated in countries where these groups are acknowledged. Organizations representing minorities and activists say that they receive unfair treatment either because the society at large is racist or because the police officers are biased against minority people. The reason for discrimination can also be located within the judicial process, which is not favorable to underprivileged and less-educated people. Other hypotheses are that members of minority groups simply commit more numerous and more violent crimes, or that they are more hostile to the police—perhaps because most minorities come from the post-colonial countries. It can also be suggested that penal discrimination occurs because they suffer lower socioeconomic status in the first place, so the incarceration rates reflect an accumulation of effects.

It is not possible here to answer the questions linked to discrimination (Where? How? Why?). We only have at our disposal fragments of information. Some light can be shed with our data at two levels. First, the self-reported delinquency surveys are a good basis for determining whether the juveniles with foreign parents are more delinquent by passing the police filter and their alleged bias. They also provide a way to determine whether the French police focuses on members of minority groups, especially the Arabs. Second, sentencing data can be used to determine whether ethnicity is a factor influencing the types of decisions handed down, whether pre-trial measures or sentencing after a judgment.

Self-Reported Delinquency and Ethnicity

We used a questionnaire slightly adapted from the International Self-Reported Delinquency (ISRD). The questions asked regarding delinquent acts committed are similar to the original ISRD; we merely added some questions about throwing rocks or setting cars on fire, crimes that were supposed to be more common in France. This questionnaire allows us to compute a variable for the number of types of crimes committed by one individual (we did this for minor and more serious crimes), but also the number of crimes (provided that each individual can declare none, one, or more crimes in each category). The diversity of the types of crimes by one individual are acknowledged as a good proxy of level of involvement in delinquency (Aebi 1999).

Self-reports are one way to estimate the prevalence of crime among juveniles ("all types" is a category that includes vandalism, thefts, assaults). Based on them, the proportion of perpetrators of crimes appears to be higher among young people with foreign origins, specifically those from North Africa. Of minors who commit seven or more different crimes, minority juveniles are almost twice as involved as French-origin juveniles (13.2 to 14 percent versus 7.5 percent (see appendix 2, figure 2A.1)). The number of serious crimes is also higher among minority juveniles, even for children from a comparable socioeconomic status: 3.1 percent of the sons and daughters of employees and workers declared at least two different types of serious crimes, as opposed to 7.2 and 8.2 percent for the minority groups. A serious crime can be vandalism (setting a car or building on fire), assault (so that the victim needs medical attention), theft with a weapon or violence, burglary, and car theft. The results for those with low-socioeconomic-status parents show a clear difference in the number of types of serious crimes listed when broken down by ethnic origin (see appendix 2, figure 2A.2).

These results are different from those in other countries. For example, in the United Kingdom, David Smith (1994) presented some of the results in the 1992-to-1993 self-report by the Home Office and commented, "There were no significant differences in patterns of self-reported offending between black and white respondents [in a sample of 2,500 youth aged fourteen to twenty-five], either in terms of life-time participation [in crime] . . . or in terms of frequency over the past twelve months" (Smith 1997, 134).

The Risk of Being Caught by the Police—Grenoble-St. Étienne

Is the police biased when it comes to minority juveniles? The French police are accused of having developed a peculiar style of policing to North Africans by Roy A. Carr-Hill (1987). Literature on "stop-and-search" has indicated a differential in some European countries (Marshall 1997; Tonry 1997; Smith 1994) that could be linked to "combativeness" of juveniles, use of public spaces, ethnic composition of the area where the police action took place (as opposed to characteristics of the supposed offender) or because officers anticipate "that this is more effective for getting results" (Antonopoulos 2003, 226–8). Police identification and arrests of offenders per type of crime is another situation where discrimination can be identified, in the United States as in the United Kingdom (Smith and Gray 1985). Sentencing, penal measures, or incarceration is the final stage of the process.

Again, there is little data on France. One study includes analysis of identification checks by the police; individuals are required on demand to present to police officers a national photo ID, which can be a national identification card, a passport, or an immigration card called "carte de séjour." A poll carried out in May 2006 in the disadvantaged neighborhoods of France (called "Zones Urbaines Sensibles"— ZUS for short—or Sensitive Urban Zones) found that during the previous year 30 percent of French Africans and 33 percent of Maghrebians had had their identity checked by the police, as opposed to 16 percent of persons of French descent. On average, the number of ID checks is 3.6 per person for those of French descent versus 8 per person for those of foreign descent. Finally, 12 percent of the former feel they are not treated respectfully by the police versus 25 percent for the latter (unpublished results of Brouard and Tiberj, cited in Roché 2006a, 104–5). However, no local or national study on police arrests can be found where ethnicity is taken into account. We will rely on our surveys to give some indications about young people that are detected (or not) by the police after committing a crime (which constitutes a condition for being arrested).

Aggregating responses from the two waves of self-reports, we find: minority juveniles are not stopped more often by the police in the two French urban areas, neither for all crimes nor for serious crimes only (burglary, car theft, aggravated assault, theft with a weapon, setting a building or a car on fire). Table 17.1 presents the risk of being identified by the police for a serious crime (calculated by dividing the number of times a respondent was detained by the police by the total number of all crimes committed (the sum for declarations in each subcategory).

We lack a measure of the risk of being caught by the police and brought to a police station in the 1999 survey; a question about this was added in the 2003 questionnaire. Because the 2003 survey is smaller and also because serious crimes are relatively rare, we cannot give a more precise estimate of police risks broken down by ethnicity.

To summarize the information we have on the prevalence of delinquency prevalence and police contact, we can state that ethnicity is a factor related with more

TABLE 17.1   THE RISK OF THIRTEEN- TO NINETEEN-YEAR-OLDS BEING IDENTIFIED BY POLICE FOR A SERIOUS CRIME IN GRENOBLE AND SAINT-ETIENNE, 1999 TO 2003

Ethnic Origin	Perpetrators of Serious Crimes (Last Two Years)			
	Number of Juveniles	Number of Crimes Declared	Number of Crimes Detected by Police	Percentage of Crimes Detected by Police
Both parents born in France	205	778	52	6.7
African origin (at least one parent)	136	978	41	4.2
Other origins	68	532	33	6.2
Total (known origin)	409	2,287	126	5.5
Total (including unknown origin)	427	2,341	136	5.8

Source: Author's compilation.

crimes, and especially more serious crime, than less serious crime. The probability of minorities' being caught by the police is proportional to their high rate of delinquency, and not higher than for children of French parents. In fact, the police seem to have more difficulty finding and catching foreign-origin juveniles who commit serious crimes.

The overrepresentation of juveniles caught by the police while committing a violent crime thus seems to be a consequence of the delinquent activities of these youths. If this is true, the hypothesis that minority people are subject to disproportionate police attention, whether because police officers focus on street crime or because they take discriminatory actions, cannot be confirmed. Police hostility toward minorities has not been measured in France but constitutes a sound hypothesis on the basis of studies in other countries; nevertheless it does not seem to be necessary to explain police attention to minorities in France.

Sentencing: Pre- and Post-Trial Data

Juvenile justice in France has evolved a great deal during the last twenty years. Prompted by politicians to respond appropriately to the increasing number of juvenile crimes recorded by the police, ministers of justice have developed a new program

TABLE 17.2   PERCENTAGE OF CASES WHERE POLICE CHARGES ARE DISMISSED BY JUDGES IN ISÈRE, 2002

Ethnicity	Theft (n = 306)	Vandalism (n = 208)	Physical Violence (n = 105)	Drug-related Offense (n = 96)
French origins	15.5	32.7	5.9	3.7
African origins	26.8	55.8	16.2	6.7
Phi /p	.12/.04	.20/.003	.17/.08	.05/.60

Source: Roché (2006a).

that neither simply closes more cases nor puts more juveniles on trial. It is called "third way," or "conditional case closing." It consists mainly of issuing a warning and giving the juvenile a more or less compulsory program to carry out. This may consist of writing a letter of excuse to the victim, repairing something, not missing school, keeping a curfew. When the youth has fulfilled the mandated activities, the case is closed, often without any strict control (for penalties in the community). If the youths were to be brought before a juvenile court and put on trial, they could be sentenced. Usually, they will receive a simple warning—Don't do it again—before being handed back to their parents; a prison warning (if you go on like this you will go to prison); or a suspended prison sentence (so that they don't have to go to jail immediately). Sometimes a youth is sent to another family or a juvenile center, and a few are sent to prison. The latter figure varies between six hundred and eight hundred, depending on the years considered and with no continuous increase or decrease since 1995.

There are two basic judicial steps when a file arrives at the court to the office of the public prosecutor's delegate in charge of juveniles. The first step is that under certain conditions the case is closed. The crimes are dealt with at the first step if perceived as "not serious" by police and judicial authorities. In principle, serious crimes have to be dealt with in courts (be it the juvenile court or the "cour d'assises"). In the latter case the second step is that the young person goes to court and gets a simple warning or a constraining sentence.

An examination of closed cases, the first step, allows us to see whether ethnicity makes a difference at this stage: the charges can be dismissed, or the case will be closed, but it can be done "without any demand" or "under some conditions." The results only take into account the young people with French origins as opposed to those with African origins because these are the two largest groups. We have chosen to look at the most frequent offenses: theft, vandalism, physical violence but excluding sex-related crimes, and drug-related offenses involving cannabis.

Judicial authorities cull the cases at the first stage and a decision is made to dismiss or not to dismiss police charges. All four types of charges presented in table 17.2 tend to be dismissed by the judge more often if the young person has foreign origins.

TABLE 17.3   PERCENTAGE OF CASES CLOSED WITHOUT CONDITIONS ("DRY")
BY JUDGES VERSUS CLOSED UNDER CONDITIONS IN ISÈRE, 2002

Ethnicity	Theft (n = 306)	Vandalism (n = 208)	Physical Violence (n = 105)	Drug-related Offense (n = 96)
French origins	20.9	34.3	25	6.4
African origins	14.6	30.4	22.6	21.4
Phi /p	.06/.36	.03/.72	.03/.80	.34/.01

Source: Roché (2006a).

However, the difference between the two groups is only statistically significant for theft and vandalism (with $p < .05$) and physical violence (with $p < .05$). Recall that this study is based not on a sampling procedure but on the entire juvenile population of the court during the reference period of half a year. This allows us to regard $p < .10$ as significant (Hosmer and Lemeshow 2000; Cohen 1988).

When police charges are dismissed, the files are closed. We can now consider the rest of the juvenile population: those whom the judge considers possibly guilty but nevertheless have their file closed for another reason, under some conditions. Table 17.3 presents, for each type of crime that a juvenile acknowledges he has committed, the likelihood of a judge simply closing the case, or closing it after imposing a condition or punishment such as doing or asking to comply with a decision (appear before a judge to get a warning, repairing something, being punished by school authorities, and so forth).

For three types of offenses—theft, vandalism, and assault—cases tend to be closed by judges without any conditions on the juvenile more often in the case of French youths, but the difference is never statistically significant. For drug-related offenses, however, the opposite is true and significant if the juvenile has African origins: judges are less likely to close the case without warning the juvenile or taking some step against his or her behavior.

In sum up, French judges whose decisions we have studied tend to dismiss police charges for members of minority groups more often. But in the case of the not dismissed charges, when they are certain that the young person is the perpetrator of a minor crime or of many crimes, they tend to put a little more pressure on these minority youths. They don't close cases without asking something from them for three types of offenses. However, the reverse is true with drug-related crimes.

When judges consider the crimes serious enough, the files are sent to a court—step 2. The aim of our study is to determine whether minority and majority youths are sentenced in a similar way for a defined type of offense. Racial disparity in sentencing has been given a great deal of attention in the United States because of the

TABLE 17.4   PERCENTAGE OF TYPES OF SENTENCE IN ISÈRE, 2002

Type of Crime	No Constraint or a Fine	Community Service and Probation	Prison or Housed in Center
Theft (n = 135)			
French origins	51.6	14.5	33.9
African origins	33.9	27.4	38.7
Phi: .20/p.08			
Violence (n = 39)			
French origins	45.5	40.9	13.6
African origins	23.5	23.5	52.9
Phi: .42/p.03			

Source: Roché (2006a).

extreme difference in sentencing outcomes along racial lines. A recent review of research concluded that "race still exerts an undeniable presence in the sentencing process" (Kansal 2005, 1). There are many dimensions of this influence, for example, the ethnic character of the perpetrator and the victim, in interaction with other socioeconomic status; the race of the offender may interact with the race of the victim, such that the perpetrator is sanctioned more harshly if the victim is not black.

Here we look at cases where a sentence is given to the defendant, breaking down his personal characteristics and not those of the victim. The first survey is based on Isère for all crimes (2002) and the second on the fifteen-years study of the court of Grenoble for serious crimes only (1985 to 2000) (Roché 2006b).

The cases are divided into three groups, according to penalty meted out: "no constraint" (absence of any conditions, including fine, which in any case neither juveniles nor their parents need to pay, under French law); the community penalty or probation; and, finally, prison sentences (most often a suspended sentence) or a period of time in a juvenile center. Table 17.4 shows that being a member of the North African minority group is associated with getting a sentence of community service (in case of theft) more often than no constraint or a fine, and more often a prison or juvenile center sentence that anything else. Including sex-related offenses (N = 13) doesn't change the results, but the rate of juveniles sent to prison or to a center is 25.8, versus 57.1 percent (p < .07).

The 1985-to-2000 juvenile court of Grenoble study presents similar results. This study graded the crimes and only serious offenses were selected. The comparison for violent thefts between the two groups of youths shows that the minority-group members are more often imprisoned or sent to a center, whereas 50 percent of French-born juveniles have a "no constraint" penalty. For acts of violence other than theft and stealing, the same applies but to a lesser, not statistically significant, extent.

TABLE 17.5   PERCENTAGE OF TYPES OF SENTENCE HANDED DOWN
             BY GRENOBLE COURT, 1985 TO 2000

Type of Crime	No Constraint or a Fine	Community Service and Probation	Prison or Housed in Center
Theft with violence or weapon (n = 50)			
French origins	50	0	50
African origins	11.4	4.5	84.1
Phi: .34/p.05			
Violence[a] (n = 175)			
French origins	40.0	9.2	50.8
African origins	28.2	9.1	62.7
Phi: .12/p.25			

Source: Roché (2006a).
[a] Blows with wounds eligible for sick leave of more than eight days, rapes, sexual offenses with violence.

The prison stage has not been studied in relation with ethnicity. Data on nationality are available (Tournier 1997) and have been used in cross-national analysis. A study by James P. Lynch and Rita J. Simon (1999) that compared criminal involvement among natives and immigrants in seven nations on the basis of nationality found France to be much harsher with minorities that the United States or any other country studied. France stands out in the crowd, with immigrants being 6.01 times as likely as natives to be incarcerated (versus 1.13 for the United States and 1.9 for Germany) (Lynch and Simon 1999, 10, table 2) and this relationship remains valid for all types of offenses; for example, the immigrant incarceration rate for drug trafficking is 11.06 in France versus 1.48 in the States (11, table 3). The most likely explanation is that pretrial detention of foreigners is very often used in continental Europe. This is probably because the migrants are undocumented and have very weak ties to society and therefore are remanded before trial. But these detention rates do not apply to minorities settled in the country for one, two, and now often three generations. The demographers Pierre Tournier and Mary France-Lise (1996) have calculated that the chance of a foreigner's being sentenced to prison is 1.8 to 2.4 times that for a Frenchman, depending on the charges. These results are without regard to prior records and, again, are based on nationality, not ethnicity.

CRIMINAL-JUSTICE AGENCIES AND MINORITIES: NEGATIVE PERCEPTIONS AND CIVIL UNREST

The perception of the criminal-justice system in a population is very important. As the arm of the state, its functioning embodies justice and fairness or injustice and unfairness. If people obey the law because they respect institutions and are satisfied with the outcome, in terms of education, housing, or personal safety, or because they are satisfied with procedural justice more than outcomes (Tyler 1990), it is important in both cases to integrate these aspects when intending to better understand the legitimacy of the criminal-justice system. Respect for the law is related to respect for the agencies in charge of law enforcement.

The riots in France in October and November 2005 occurred after a police patrol was called to check an alleged violation of property by juveniles. It initially took place in a poor municipality with a high proportion of minorities, before the unrest spread across the country. This major event, the largest case of unrest in recent French history, raises questions as to the relationship between the police and minorities.

Negative Perceptions in Self-Reported Surveys

Can we confirm that when authority is viewed as legitimate or behaving fairly, compliance to the law increases? From the two self-reported delinquency surveys, we obtained the perception by youths of the penal institutions and also asked question about some police behavior. The tensions are highest among minority youths, even controlling for socioeconomic status of the parents.

From the 1999 survey we could get information about the facets of the police that were most criticized by the youths. Two aspects are important. Firstly, the North African minority has a worse image of the judiciary than the rest of the population and an even more negative perception of the police. There appears to be more difference between this minority and the average opinion of other minorities than between other minorities and the French-born children. Second, the criticism is in part of police racism, but far less than of police violence. The correlations between ethnicity and the perceptions are higher when the general image and violence of penal organization is at stake than with racism and its opposite, the protection of juveniles are estimated by respondents. This is noticeable in the sense that the minority doesn't mainly suspect police of an ethnic bias, but criticizes the way police operate. The notion of procedural justice theorized by Tom Tyler (1990) could contribute to understanding the relation between police and minorities. Police behavior, or perception of it, would be a source of resentment.

When the North African minority is isolated, the following regressions show that ethnicity always plays a small but significant role in explaining the perception of authorities (see appendix 3, tables 3A.1 to 3A.4). All of these variables together do not explain a large share of the total variance.

One of the best predictors of the perception of public authorities is the number of types of crimes listed by the respondent during the self-report. As indicated and documented by research, the most delinquent boys and girls have the most negative perception of authorities and of the police. However, the perceptions that minorities have of the police are not entirely predicted by the number of types of crimes that they have perpetrated. In a previous book based on the 1999 survey (Roché 2001), we found that 88 percent of juveniles who had committed no crimes

FIGURE 17.3   PERCEPTION OF POLICE AND JUDICIARY BY ETHNIC ORIGINS,
GRENOBLE AND SAINT ETIENNE, 1999

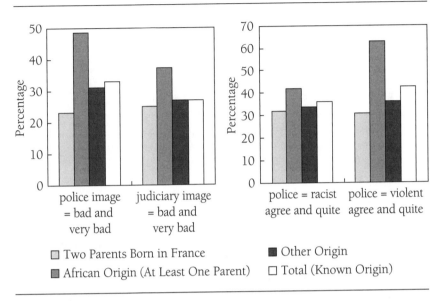

Source: Roché (2001).

have a good or very good image of the police and only 35 percent have this image when they have committed five types of crimes or more (245). Even when they declare no offences, 61 percent of young people of North African origins perceive the police as violent versus 25 percent of those with French origins. The difference is less important for the judgment of racism (37 and 29 percent, respectively) (225).

Clearly, if ethnicity contributes to the formation of a negative police image, this contribution is moderate and the problem is not interpreted as essentially racist by the juveniles themselves.

The 2005 Civil Unrest: Ethnic Riots and the Crisis of Legitimacy

I summarize here elements detailed in a recent book, *Le frisson de l'émeute: violences urbaines et banlieues* (The excitement of the riot: urban violence and suburbs) (Roché 2006a). On October 27, 2005, a special police unit called brigades anticriminalité, or BAC, specialized in dealing with violent street crime, was sent to check a violation of a building in Clichy-sous-Bois, in the department of Seine Saint-Denis, by juveniles after getting a telephone complaint from residents of the building. As soon as the police arrived, the youths fled, and three took refuge in a power plant. The French Electricity Company detected an incident in the Clichy-sous-Bois substation and received an anonymous emergency call to rescue three wounded people. Two juveniles were found dead and one was injured; as soon as the three bodies were found, the news spread to the entire neighborhood and to the city. The police are alleged to have chased the youths therefore were held responsible for the deaths. Public authorities denied this at that time, but a police investigation released one year later confirmed it. People started gathering spontaneously. In two of the poor neighborhoods of the municipality of Clichy cars were set ablaze, window shops were broken, and public buildings were looted. Antipolice behavior was also identified, notably throwing rocks and other missiles ("caillassage," from "cailloux" meaning rock).

After this initial burst of violence, the civil unrest engulfed some of the other impoverished suburbs of Paris and later, other large cities throughout the country. More than five hundred municipalities out of 36,000 were affected by the riots, mainly in deprived sections of large cities. Somewhat similar events took place in the summer of 1981, in the outskirts of Lyon, two months after the first election of a Socialist leader, François Mitterrand, as president of the Republic. Nevertheless, the 2005 rioting was the first of its kind. Never before had we seen rioting spread at the national level. In all, the country was affected for twenty-one days, though separate municipalities were affected for five days on average. As many as fifteen hundred cars could be burned in a single night, and the total count was approximately twenty thousand burned vehicles, along with dozen of buses and some public buildings. No one was killed by the police but one person died in a fracas with rioters. Three thousand people were arrested by the police, of whom 92 percent were French, but 65 percent were of African descent, according to police statistics from departments in the environs of Paris. There was no racial rioting in the sense of one community attacking another, as in Los Angeles in 1992; rather it was a multi-ethnic coalition against the police of residents committed to destroying the neighborhoods where they lived. Rioters were mainly boys from modest-socioeconomic-status backgrounds; half of them were juveniles under eighteen and the other half were young men under twenty-five. Most of them had a police record and approximately half, a judicial file. When it looked as though the situation was getting out of hand, the government declared a state of emergency and decided to use an old piece of legislation dating back to 1955, when France occupied Algeria and was facing an insurrection, to allow prefects, the central state representative at the local level, to organize curfews. Seven out of one hundred prefectures did use this tool. As rioting by disaffected youths spread across France, officials were accused by the opposition parties of neglect of the country's impoverished suburbs and of cutting back funds for non-profit groups working with those populations.

Although rioting can have political consequences, it doesn't have the features of a civil protest. No ethnic- or community leaders surfaced, the protests were not directed toward mainstream institutions such as upper-class neighborhoods or government buildings such as the city hall, the prefecture, the National Assembly. Fights with the police were roughly organized with at most a few dozen youths involved in any one confrontation. Religious leaders publicly appealed to the rioters to bring the unrest to an end. (None of them compared the riots with an intifada.)

These events are called urban violence ("violence urbaine"). This expression is used by the police for violent collective anti-institutional actions; rare is the government official who would use the word "émeute"—riot). Despite the special term, the reality looks very much like riots in other nations or cities. Most of the elements involved in the French context are to be found elsewhere or have been identified in the riots that plagued American inner cities in the sixties (Myers 1997, 2000). First, in poor neighborhoods with a high proportion of migrants and minorities, relations with the police are strained; very often a police action or a judicial decision is a catalyst in triggering the riot. Second, poor social and economic conditions create an environment facilitating the initial outburst of violence.

A difference between France and other nations is that poorer neighborhoods are in the suburbs, called "banlieues" (literally, "beyond the limits"), not in the inner cities, as in Britain and the United States. In France, the socioeconomic conditions in Seine Saint-Denis compared to the average for entire France speak volumes. In 2004, the unemployment rate was 13.9, compared to 9.8 percent for the whole country; the percentage of households eligible for the minimum income allowance (called RMI) was 7.1, as opposed to the nationwide average of 3.6 percent.

In France, some 750 areas on the outskirts of larger French cities are classified as ZUS (sensitive urban zones). These are the typical loci of unrest. In the ZUS, unemployment hovers at 20.7 percent, twice the national average for cities with a ZUS, and unemployment among those fifteen to twenty-five years of age is 38 percent. According to government statistics, the parents of 12.1 percent of elementary school children in the ZUS are foreigners, compared to a 4.2 percent average elsewhere.[8] The percentage of minority youths in these cities is unknown, but it is presumably high. When one walks these neighborhoods the contrast with the center of Paris is striking: the rents are cheaper, and the proportion of nonwhite population is very large. Local surveys have quantified the presence of minority youths in schools in the poorer neighborhoods of large cities; in Bordeaux, for example, 40 percent of the students from Africa and Turkey are in just 10 percent of the high schools, those in the ZUS (Felouzis, Liot, and Perroton 2005, 40).

Before this first national-scale of unrest no studies were done on how such impulses spread from one location to another. So far, no in-depth data collection or analysis has taken place concerning the events of 2005. Anecdotal evidence, however, suggests that the explanation of diffusion elaborated by Daniel Myers (2000) developed for the American situation could apply to France. The location where the initial riot started is very blighted. First, the unrest spread to nearby cities in the region of Paris. Then it spread to locations farther away, possibly as a result of media coverage rather than the characteristics of secondary rioting cities. Neighboring countries (Belgium, Switzerland, Germany) were hardly affected: in these countries media coverage existed, but presumably it was less important than in France. There, TF1, the largest TV network, devoted 40 percent of the 8 P.M. evening news to the unrest during the peak days. Large French cities with very poor neighborhoods, such as Marseille, were not affected, but more rural locales experienced secondary unrest, as did quite upper-class satellite cities of Lyon.

A noticeable contrast between France and the United States concerns the relative social status of the minority of African descent and Muslims. In France, Maghrebians constitute the core of the Muslim population and are largely workers residing in deprived sections of cities. In the United States, American Muslims make up only 13 percent of the population with an annual income under $25,000 (versus 29 percent in the entire American population). Forty-three percent of American Muslims have advanced degrees (versus 9 percent of all Americans) (Cornell University 2002). In sum, Muslims are not less well off than the average citizen in America, which is distinct from the French context.

In France most Maghrebians have low social status. Local surveys of Grenoble and Saint-Étienne show that more than 80 percent of the parents of Maghrebian students are employees or workers. Maghrebian students are more likely to be kept back a year in school and are three times as likely as the average to be more than two years older than they should be before the end of secondary school. People with African origins do not primarily define themselves through religion. Western Europe is a very secularized continent. As Sylvain Brouard and Vincent Tiberj have demonstrated (2005), among Maghrebians, 14 percent of immigrants, 22 percent of the first generation born in France, and 35 percent of the second generation profess no religion. Three-quarters of the second generation are born to mixed couples (one French-born and one not). Only 28 percent of those born to mixed couples declare themselves to be Muslim, as opposed to 78 percent for those born to two Maghrebian parents. Eighty percent of Maghrebians see the notion of secularism ("laïcité") as positive and only 5 percent would like for their children to attend a religious school. For 75 percent of Muslims in France, mosque attendance is limited to celebrations such as weddings and births, a percentage comparable to that among French Catholics (2005, 23–34).

We already have presented minority youths' perception of the police. The strained relations have been rarely analyzed (Zauberman and Levy 2003) and even less subjected to systematic observation. The tension between the police and minority youths is poorly documented but very often referred to. Even police officers sometimes publicly acknowledge that identity checks are disproportionately used against these persons. Many successful immigrants such as TV or radio personalities—even the last minister for Integration, the Algerian-born Azouz Begag—have publicly complained about discrimination. Among minority youths, the frustration is possibly fueled by their high expectations: unlike their parents when they were young, they are French citizens and are here to stay—they have no plans of "going back." It is unacceptable to them to receive second-class treatment or be subjected to repeated identity checks.

This source of conflict is also found in other countries where riots have taken place, and has been well documented in the United States by Seymour Spilerman

(1970). This points to the fact that another difference between France and other countries is the failure, in France, to study the relationship between the police and minorities both before and after civil unrest. In the United States, in August 1967 President Lyndon Johnson created the Kerner Commission to study the disorders that had occurred, and attracted attention to the divide between white and black America. In the early eighties in the United Kingdom, a report also looked into police practices toward minorities in London. There was a public inquiry into the riot headed by Leslie Scarman, and the Scarman report was published on November 25, 1981. In 1999, the MacPherson report, following the Stephen Lawrence Inquiry, concluded that "the need to reestablish trust between minority ethnic communities and the police is paramount." Nothing of the sort happened in France (see Kerner 1968; MacPherson 1999; Scarman 1982). Ignoring the spontaneous character of the initial rioting in Clichy-sous-Bois, the minister of the interior, Nicolas Sarkozy, blamed the riots on criminal organizations, recidivists, and Muslim fundamentalists. Any notion of confronting the underlying problem of the relationship of the police to minority populations was absent.

The government doesn't perceive the riots as a sign of a crisis of legitimacy, and even less as a crisis of police legitimacy. After the riots Prime Minister Dominique de Villepin pledged to fight against discrimination and cancel the cuts in subsidies to nonprofit organizations operating in blighted areas. Minister Sarkozy made no announcement other than vowing to deport foreigners convicted of participating in the violence and increasing penalties for recidivists. Not on his agenda: the issue of police violence, police discrimination, or any initiatives toward community policing or building ways to reaching out to minority and other deprived communities.

CONCLUSION: MINORITY GROUPS, DELINQUENCY, POLICING, AND SENTENCING

At the end of the day, a number of key features appear from these descriptions and analyses. Looking at nationality, we find that more children with foreign passports than from the general population are involved in various stages of the criminal-justice system. Foreign children are more often the perpetrators of crimes and serious crimes that go to trial than of misdemeanors dealt with by the public prosecutor's delegate.

Looking at ethnicity rather than nationality: First, according to self-reports, young people of foreign origins tend to commit more crimes per capita, and specifically more violent crimes. This holds true even controlling for socioeconomic status. Second, the police apprehend more offenders from minority groups, but the risk of being apprehended per crime committed, including serious crimes, is slightly less. It probably is because more crimes are committed by them that the police identify more often with minority youths. This point is very sensitive because the police play the role of a gatekeeper into the criminal-justice system, and any differential treatment of minorities at this stage would probably have cumulative effects later on. If the unit that has to be used to measure police attention is not the individual but the frequency of offending, it cannot be claimed that minority members are the beneficiaries or the victims of disproportionate attention.

This absence of targeting of minority members is quite surprising in the sense that the literature abounds with examples of police bias toward certain ethnic groups. And also because of the mutual hostility that is usually diagnosed between police officers and minority juveniles, of which we could confirm one side in France: North Africans youths are more critical of the police. However, it is not impossible that the police are mainly driven by catching criminals (not minority members), and that the ones with a more active practice (minority members according to our survey) also are better aware of how to escape from the police net. Finally, if police work is oriented by the public and if public opinion tends to be more accepting of minorities, which seems to be the case in France, no indirect incentive in police discrimination should be more present these days.

As David Smith has suggested, ensuring that equal proportions of different social groups are punished has never been a goal of the criminal-justice system (Smith 1994). At the judicial stage, the prosecutor's delegate (personnel in charge of the misdemeanors) tends to reject more often the evidence gathered by the police as unconvincing (cases are closed because identification is not certain) for minority-group members than for the youths with French origins. This is a very interesting aspect because it constitutes the starting point into the juvenile-justice system. If we later on can find some racial disparity in sentencing (and we do), we cannot say that there is racial disparity all along the process against the same ethnic groups. In fact, the prosecutor's delegate seems to be more lenient with minority members than with those that have French origins. That could indicate a sign of police bias that the judges correct when inspecting the evidence gathered by the police into the files to allow prosecution to go on. But we have no real explanation for these findings: it cannot be a general favorable bias of judges against the ethnic groups because they receive "harsher" sanctions at the next step, and it cannot be an unfavorable bias because they benefit from the fact that their cases are closed.

Among the files that are made of youths supposed to be the authors of crimes on the basis of police evidence that are accepted by a magistrate as convincing, ethnicity seems to play a role in sentencing. More often the judge requires some sort of community penalty or response rather than "no constraint" for minority-group members, but this result lacks statistical significance (and is contrary to the exception of drug-related offenses). The next step of the judicial ladder is juvenile court trials. The 2002 Isère court study shows that members of minority groups tend more often to be sentenced to prison or to be housed in a juvenile center as a response to identical crimes (theft, violence). The 1985-to-2000 Grenoble court study provides the same types of result for violent acts (violent theft).

Based on these observations, it can be asserted that there is a higher proportion of juveniles with foreign origins in the criminal-justice system than in the general population. Their share is simply massive. This should prompt reflection on ethnicity in France. The reasons for this overrepresentation are not well established here. However, it seems there is a contribution of lower SES, police perception, and ethnicity that combine into higher criminal activity by these youths. The contribution of the criminal-justice system to discrimination doesn't appear to be blatant. Police work seems to be targeted to perpetrators rather than to minority groups, according to self-reports. But when a police investigation is transferred to the prosecutor, the latter tends to find the evidence often unsatisfying for members of minority groups. Finally, prosecutor's office and judges tend to give stricter penalties to these youths once they have sifted those files that contain solid police evidence. Some of these factors are beneficial while others are detrimental to minority groups in the criminal-justice system. We have determined the sentencing process for defined crimes (serious crimes, and then violent crimes), but not controlled for other crimes or the prison record of youths. It is therefore not possible to conclude that the penal system is biased, but this hypothesis cannot be ruled out.

The legitimacy of the police and the judiciary is less well established among minority juveniles. However, the fact that even those that never committed an offense have a more negative image of the police and the judiciary implies that their perceptions are not grounded only in their personal direct experience or contacts with the personnel of these organizations. Of course, the image of the police could be derived from what youths see: identification checks, police crackdowns on poor neighborhoods and illegal business, the importance of minority groups in the courts and in the juvenile centers.

Is the legitimacy and the fairness of the criminal-justice system different here than in other countries? On the basis of the very fragmented information that we have it is not possible to say whether the French system is better or worse than any other. In the central-state ideology the formation of a social group equates with the closure of this group to the rest of society and is therefore attributed a negative value. This representation doesn't seem to produce specific effects in France: a large number of features found in this country can be seen in others too. The indifference of French historians, philosophers, and state officials to some facts, their ideology of a state made of individuals, is irritating, but does it make a difference in practical terms? Symmetrically, the passion of other nations for facts and statistics combined with their ideology of relying on communities doesn't appear to offer a racial bias–free society. The French model doesn't seem to imply any peculiarity and may not be a different model. The fact that a government has consciousness of existence of minorities and communities or that it hasn't, that they are given or not a status in the public sphere, the political ideology in sum, seems to operate on a different level than the criminal-justice system. Communities are an institutional reality in the United Kingdom, but minorities are almost absent from the police force, where they represent 3.3 percent (Home Office (U.K.) 2006, 101) and resent the police more often. Communities do not exist in France and minorities are absent from the police force (and from the statistics about the force) and resent the police more often. The differences between these systems, if there are any, seem to be more of degree than of essence. It is even unclear whether the comparative legitimacy of the criminal-justice system is related to its fairness. We know from the International Crime Victim Surveys that the public's confidence in the police cannot be derived from the crime rate in the country. Would it be so surprising that perceptions of the legitimacy of the police and the judiciary among minority groups also bear no clear relation to the behavior of its personnel?

APPENDIX 1: SIZE OF MINORITY GROUPS AND SIZE OF NATIONALITY GROUPS

There is no census of the general population that takes foreign origins into account, but nationality is documented. In 1999 there were 1.1 million residents in Isère, of which 68,000, 6.2 percent, were foreigners. Thirty-four percent of the foreigners, or 2 percent of the total population, were from Algeria, Tunisia, or Morocco, which represents.[9]

The first column of table 1A.1 shows the geographical distribution of nationalities among juveniles in the surveys that we have conducted. In 2003, the young people with a French passport represent 96.1 percent of the entire sample. Juveniles with two passports are 116: when one of their passports is French they have been included in the category "French." Other nationalities are mainly from Africa (2.2 percent) and Europe (1.4 percent). In total, only 3.9 percent of young people are foreigners according to our poll.

Of course, the socioeconomic status, the family context, or any other variable might influence this global presentation of results. And it must be recalled that the geographical territories are not strictly identical (cities and their periphery are only used for the representative self-reported surveys, and a larger part of the department of Isère for the rest of the studies, which implies a slightly more rural recruitment of juveniles, although the vast majority come from urban settings). Therefore, the percentage of young foreigners might vary from one geographical area to another and explain in part the different percentages. This last explanation is not the most convincing, for migrants tend to be concentrated in or around the large cities: taking the department (or a large part of it) into account should lower the proportion of foreigners, whereas our results show an increase.

Let's now observe the content of the juvenile files. Young people who have entered the juvenile-justice system are very often French. The 2002 data in the department of Isère present the following results (see table 1A.2): Among juveniles whose cases have been closed, 5.6 percent are foreigners. Among those who were put on trial 8.6 percent were foreigners. This is corroborated by the self-reported delinquency survey among institutionalized children: the second column of table 1A.1 shows that 6.5 percent of the juveniles housed by the decision of a judge do

TABLE 1A.1   NATIONALITY ACCORDING TO SELF-REPORTED DELINQUENCY
SURVEYS (THIRTEEN TO NINETEEN), GRENOBLE AND
SAINT-ETIENNE (1999), GRENOBLE (2003),
AND ISÈRE (2003 TO 2004)

Nationality (area)	SRDS 1999 Representative, Two Cities' Schools		SRDS 2003 Representative, One City's Schools		SRDS 2003 to 2004 Departement of Isère, Institutionalized	
	N	Percentage	N	Percentage	N	Percentage
French	2,114	92.4	1,548	96.1	87	93.5
Africa	118	5.2	35	2.2	4	4.3
Europe	44	1.9	23	1.4	2	2.2
Other	12	0.5	5	0.3	0	0.0
Total	2,288	100.0	1,611	100.0	93	100.0

Source: Author's compilation.
Note: In the self-report, 116 young students and 2 institutionalized children have two passports. Among them respectively 113 and 2 juveniles have a French passport.

TABLE 1A.2   NATIONALITY OF JUVENILES ACCORDING TO JUDICIAL FILES,
GRENOBLE AND VIENNE

Nationality (Area)	Case Closed, Departement of Isère 2002*		On Trial, Departement of Isère 2002[a]		On Trial, Isère[b] 1985 to 2000	
	N	Percentage	N	Percentage	N	Percentage
French	1,170	94.4	370	91.4	286	88.0
Africa	32	2.6	13	3.2	9	2.8
Europe	37	3.0	21	5.2	28	8.6
Other	1	0.1	1	0.2	2	0.6
Total	1,240	100.0	405	100.0	325	100.0

Source: Roché (2006a).
Note: In the self-report, 116 young students and 2 institutionalized children have two passports. Among them respectively 113 and 2 juveniles have a French passport.
[a] Juvenile courts of Grenoble and Vienne (entire departement).
[b] Without the juvenile court of Vienne.

TABLE 1A.3   ETHNIC ORIGINS OF JUVENILES THIRTEEN- TO NINETEEN-YEARS-OLD ACCORDING TO SELF-REPORTED SURVEYS, GRENOBLE AND SAINT-ETIENNE

Ethnic Origin	SRDS 1999 Representative, Two Cities' Schools		SRDS 2003 Representative, One City's Schools		SRDS 2003 to 2004 Departement of Isère, Institutionalized[a]	
	N	Percentage	N	Percentage	N	Percentage
French	1,338	61.2	952	60.8	28	37.8
African	537	24.6	350	22.4	35	47.3
European	260	11.9	220	14.1	9	12.2
Other	50	2.3	43	2.7	2	2.7
Total	2,185	100.0	1,565	100.0	74	100.0

Source: Author's compilation.
[a] Institutionalized adolescents.

not have a French passport. The 1985-to-2000 study restricted to files of serious offenders gives the value of 12 percent of foreigners.

For 1999, data from a representative self-report show a higher rate of foreigners (7.6 percent) than the 2003 data (3.9 percent). Because the region of the study was even more diverse in 1999 and includes Saint-Étienne, which is not in the department of Isère, these figures are not taken as comparison points.

Clearly, the proportion of juveniles with foreign origins from the self-reports doesn't match the census data based on nationality (compare tables 1A.1 and 1A.3, and tables 1A.2 and 1A.4). The proportion of minority juveniles is higher than the proportion of foreigners, even including "new" Frenchmen in the general population. For example, while 7.6 percent of the juveniles are not French, 38.2 percent have foreign origins in the representative sample of 2003. Among the institutionalized youths, 6.5 percent are not French and 2.2 percent have foreign origins. This gap is certainly partly explained by the difference in the number of young people: families with foreign origins have more children per household than people with French origins. But that cannot entirely explain the gap.[10] Moreover, among foreigners, the proportion of people from North Africa is smaller than the proportion of juveniles from North Africa sentenced in a court of justice, where they form the majority group.

We have applied the same methodology to circumscribe ethnicity in the juvenile court files. However, the information is gathered from the documents that constitute each file. Between 11 percent (on trial, 2002) and 18 percent (case closed, 2002) of

TABLE 1A.4   NATIONALITY OF JUVENILES ACCORDING TO JUDICIAL FILES IN GRENOBLE AND VIENNE

Nationality (Area)	Case Closed, Departement of Isère 2002*		On Trial, Departement of Isère 2002[a]		On Trial, Isère[b] 1985 to 2000	
	N	Percentage	N	Percentage	N	Percentage
French	712	68.9	143	45.7	75	26.6
Africa	213	20.6	137	43.8	161	57.1
Europe	94	9.1	32	10.2	44	15.6
Other	14	1.4	1	0.3	2	0.7
Total	1,033	100.0	313	100.0	282	100.0

Source: Roché (2006a).
Note: In the self-report, 116 young students and 2 institutionalized children have two passports. Among them, respectively, 113 and 2 juveniles have a French passport.
[a] The juvenile courts of Grenoble and Vienne (entire department).
[b] Excludes the juvenile court of Vienne.

the cases could not be determined because of lack of all relevant information for one individual. The closed files generally speaking are thinner and far less detailed than the trailed files. By comparison, the percentage of undetermined ethnic group in the representative self-reports was 4.5 percent in 1999 and 3 percent in 2003.

Notwithstanding these difficulties, it is possible to compare the rates after excluding the undetermined cases. It doesn't constitute a perfect solution to the puzzle, but the only possibility. Arguably, subtracting those individuals with uncompleted files tends to take away young people who are less often of French origin. The representative survey can be used as a baseline: minorities represent 38.2 percent of juveniles in 1999 (two cities: Grenoble and Saint-Étienne) and 39.2 percent in 2003 (Grenoble only). The number of households whose head has foreign origins would be less than that, for these families have more children on average. But, in terms of the young population, its presence is massive.

The three studies based on the judicial files indicate that young people with foreign origins represent between 31.1 percent (cases closed) and 73.4 (cases for serious offences) of the total number of perpetrators. Northern Africans account for 20.6 to 57.1 percent when we focus on serious offenders (see table 1A.4). The youths with French origins tend to be overrepresented by eight to nine percentage points for misdemeanors (case closed) compared to the representative sample. But juveniles on trial are more often from non-French-born families (over fifteen percentage points) and juveniles on trial for serious offenses even more (more than thirty-two percentage points).

APPENDIX 2: PREVALENCE OF CRIME AMONG MINORITY GROUPS

FIGURE 2A.1   PERCENTAGE OF PERPETRATORS OF SELF-REPORTED TYPES OF CRIME DURING THE LAST TWO YEARS, BY ETHNIC ORIGINS, GRENOBLE AND SAINT-ETIENNE, 1999

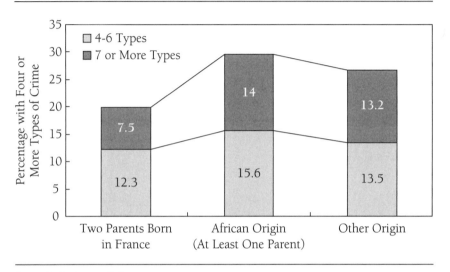

Source: Author's compilation.

FIGURE 2A.2   PERCENTAGE OF PERPETRATORS OF SELF-REPORTED SERIOUS
CRIMES DURING THE LAST TWO YEARS, BY ETHNIC ORIGINS
(CHILDREN OF WORKERS AND EMPLOYEES ONLY),
GRENOBLE AND SAINT-ETIENNE, 1999

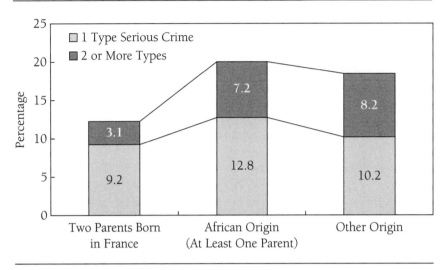

Source: Author's compilation.

APPENDIX 3: ETHNIC ORIGINS AS A FACTOR EXPLAINING THE PERCEPTION OF THE POLICE IN FRANCE (GRENOBLE AND SAINT-ÉTIENNE, 1999, AND GRENOBLE 2003)

TABLE 3A.1   PERCEPTION OF POLICE AMONG A REPRESENTATIVE SAMPLE OF THIRTEEN- TO NINETEEN-YEAR-OLDS, GRENOBLE AND SAINT-ETIENNE, 1999

	(R)	β	t	Significance of T
Gender	−.06	−.06	−2.4	.016
Age	.14	.13	5.5	.000
SES	.04	−.02	−0.8	.435
Ethnic origin	.21	.21	8.8	.000
R^2=.064—F=30.6; 4/1802 df; p= .0000				

Source: Author's compilation.
Note: Question asked: "What image of the police do you have?" (very good, fairly good, fairly bad, very bad).

TABLE 3A.2   PERCEPTIONS AMONG THIRTEEN- TO NINETEEN-YEAR-OLDS THAT THE POLICE ARE RACIST, GRENOBLE AND SAINT-ETIENNE, 1999[a]

	(R)	β	t	Significance of T
Gender	.000	.001	0.04	.96
Age	−.10	−.10	−4.02	.000
SES	.004	.02	1.0	.33
Ethnic origin	.10	.10	−4.0	.000
R^2= .02—F=8.5; 4/1679 df; p= .0000				

Source: Author's compilation.
Note: Question asked: "When it comes to your neighborhood, do you agree or not with this sentence: 'The police are racist'?"
[a] Representative sample.

TABLE 3A.3   PERCEPTIONS OF A REPRESENTATIVE SAMPLE OF THIRTEEN- TO NINETEEN-YEAR-OLDS OF FRENCH AND MAGHREBIAN ORIGIN THAT THE POLICE PROTECT THE YOUTH, GRENOBLE 2003

	(R)	β	t	Significance of T
Gender	.03	−.03	1.0	.323
Age	.13	.13	4.84	.000
SES	.067	.04	1.47	.142
Ethnic Origins	.11	.10	3.68	.000
R2= .033—F=10.8; 4/1275 df; p= .0000				

Source: Author's compilation.
Note: Question asked: "When it comes to your neighborhood, do you agree or not with the sentence: 'The police protect the youth'?"

TABLE 3A.4   PERCEPTIONS OF A REPRESENTATIVE SAMPLE OF THIRTEEN- TO NINETEEN-YEAR-OLDS OF FRENCH AND MAGHREBIAN ORIGIN THAT THE POLICE ARE VIOLENT WITH YOUTH, GRENOBLE 2003

	(R)	β	t	Significance of T
Gender	−.02	−.02	0.53	.59
Age	−.07	.07	−2.65	.008
SES	.17	.12	−4.51	.000
Ethnic Origins	.23	.21	−7.46	.000
R2= .074—F=15; 4/1252 df; p= .0000				

Source: Author's compilation.
Note: Question asked: "When it comes to your neighborhood, do you agree or not with the sentence: 'The police are violent with youth'?"

NOTES

1. For example, President of the Republic Jacques Chirac reiterated that view during his speech of December 31, 2006, his annual presidential new year's address.
2. Twenty-eight and a half percent of workers still join a trade union, 5 percent in the private sector, less than 1 percent a political party (see Labbé and Andolfatto 2000).
3. For further information, see Jacqueline Remy, "L'heure des comptés," *L'Express,* September 15, 2005, http://Pexpress.fr/info/societe/dossier/immigration/dossier.asp?ida=434933.
4. It must be explained that left-wing parties were in power at the national level most of the time during the period from 1981 to 1995.

5. See CNIL, "Lutte contre les discriminations: les recommandations de la CNIL pour mésurer la diversité des origines" [Struggle against discrimination: recommendations for measuring cultural diversity], meeting of September 7, 2005, at http://www.cnil.fr/index.php?id=1844.
6. See Commission Nationale de Déontologie de la Sécurité, "Rapport annuel au Président de la République, 2004" (http://www.cnds.fr/ra_pdf/ra_2004/CNDS_rapport_2004.pdf), chapter 3, "Étude sur la part de la discrimination dans les manquements à la déontologie."
7. These studies were funded by the Caisse Nationale d'Allocation Familiale (CNAF), the MAIF foundation, the Interior Ministry (National Institute of Studies on Domestic Security, IHESI), the National Defense Ministry (National Gendarmerie), the Justice Ministry (Mission of Modernization and Juvenile Justice Directorate), and the Public Transportation Ministry, Department of Isère, France 5 (France Television Group). Without their support the research would not have been possible.
8. These data are compiled by the Observatoire National des Zones Urbaines Sensibles (ZUS) [National Observatory of Sensitive Urban Zones] from INSEE (Institut National de la Statistique et des Études Économiques, National Institute of Statistics and Economic Studies) data; see http://www.ville.gouv.fr/infos/dossiers/observatoire-des-zus.html.
9. See Tribalat 2004; Institut National de la Statistique et des Études Économiques (INSEE) (Census of 1999). Sixty-six thousand are French citizens who were not born French. When added to the 68,000 foreigners, they represent a total of 11.6 percent of the population.
10. We asked those thirteen to nineteen years old how many siblings they had. The average number including the respondent is 2.7 when both parents have French origins, 2.9 if one or more has European origins, 4.7 if they have African origins, and 3.1 percent if they are of other origins. This is not the average number of children per family, but the average number of children per family that had at least one child who could be interviewed.

REFERENCES

Aebi, Marcello. 1999. "La validité des indicateurs de la criminalité" ["The Validity of Indicators of Criminality"]. Ph.D. dissertation, University of Lausanne.

Antonopoulos, Georgios A. 2003. "Ethnic and Radical Minorities and the Police: A Review of the Literature." *Polio Journal* 76(3): 222–46.

Arendt, Hannah. 1954/1972. *Between Past and Future.* 1954; French ed., Paris: Folio.

Barou, Jacques. 1997. *Aspects spécicifiques des politiques d'intégration des populations immigrées dans quelques pays européens* [*Specific Aspects of the Politics of Integration Among Immigration Populations in Several European Countries*]. Report on research for the Ministry of Social Affairs. 2 volumes. Grenoble, France: Cerat.

———. 2002. *Immigration, ethnicité, territoire. Rapport d'habilitation à diriger les recherches* [*Immigration, Ethnicity, Territory: Report to Direct Research*]. Grenoble, France: Université Pierre-Mendès France.

Body-Gendrot, Sophie, and Catherine Wihtol de Wenden. 2003. *Police et discriminations raciales. Le tabou français* [*Police and Racial Discrimination: The French Taboo*]. Paris: Éditions de l'Atelier.

Bosworth, Mary. 2000. "Race and Punishment." *Punishment and Society* 2(1): 114–8.

Bowling, Ben, and Coretta Phillips. 2002. *Racism, Crime and Justice*. London: Longman.

Brouard, Sylvain, and Vincent Tiberj. 2005. *Français comme les autres?* [*Are the French Like Others?*]. Paris: Les Presses de Sciences-Politiques.

Carr-Hill, Roy A. 1987. "O Bring Me Your Poor: Immigrants in the French System of Criminal Justice." *Howard Journal of Criminal Justice* 26(4): 287–99.

Cesari, Jocelyne. 1988. "Les Musulmans à Marseille: enjeux d'une reconnaissance politique" ["The Muslims of Marseille: The Stakes of Political Recognition"]. *Pouvoirs* 47: 123–32.

Choquet, Marie, Sylvie Ledoux, Christine Hassler, and Catherine Paré. 1998. *Adolescents (14–21 ans) de la protection judiciaire de la jeunesse et santé. Rapport pour la direction de la PJJ et la MILDT* [Mission Interministerielle de la lutte contre la drogue et la toxicomanie]. [*Adolescents (14–21 Years Old) Under Judicial Protection for Youth and Health. Report Under the Direction of the PJJ and the MILDT*]. Paris: INSERM.

Citron, Suzanne. 2003. *Mes lignes de démarcation—croyances, utopies, engagements* [*My Lines of Demarcation: Beliefs, Utopias, Engagements*]. Paris: Syllepse.

Cohen, J. 1988. *Statistical Power Analysis for the Behavioral Sciences*. 2nd edition. Hillsdale, N.J.: Erlbaum.

Cornell University. 2002. "Market Analysis of American Muslims." Report prepared for the U.S. Census Bureau. Ithaca, N.Y.: Cornell University.

CSA. 2003. "Le suivi du racisme et de l'anti-sémitisme en France" ["The Return of Racism and Anti-Semitism in France"]. Survey prepared for *Le Figaro*. Accessed at http://www.csa-tmo.fr/dataset/data2003/opi20030402b.htm.

———. 2004. *Les français et la rentreé scolaire* [*The French and Reentry to School*]. Survey prepared for the Ministry of Education. Accessed at http://www.csa.fr.com/dataset/data2004/opi20040915b.htm.

De Rudder, Véronique. 1994. "Le logement des immigrés" ["Housing for Immigrants"]. In *L'immigration entre loi et vie quotidienne* [*Immigration Between Law and Daily Life*], edited by Jacques Barou and Khoa Le Huu. Paris: L'Harmattan.

De Rudder, Véronique, Christian Poiret, and Françoise Vourch. 2000. *L'inégalité raciste. L'universalité républicaine à l'épreuve* [*Racist Inequality: Republican Universality Put to the Test*]. Paris: Presse Universitaire de France.

Degrève, Renaud. 2003. "Langage et société" ["Language and Society"]. In *Ecarts d'identités*, no. 102. Grenoble, France: Adate Édition.

Felouzis, Georges, Françoise Liot, and Joelle Perroton. 2005. *L'apartheid scolaire* [*Academic Apartheid*]. Paris: Le Seuil.

Goudineau, Christian. 2001. *Le dossier Vercingétorix* [*The Vercingétorix Dossier*]. Paris: Actes-Sud.

Home Office (U.K.). 2000. *Statistics on Race and the Criminal Justice System*. London: Home Office.

———. 2006. "Race Equality." The Home Secretary's Employment Targets, Report 2005: 20. Accessed at http://www.homeoffice.gov.uk/documents/race-equality-targets-2005.

Hosmer, D. W., and S. Lemeshow. 2000. *Applied Logistic Regression*. 2nd edition. New York: Wiley.

Ivaldi, Gilles. 2003. "Enjeux sécuritaires et droites populistes en Europe" ["Security Risks and Populist Rights in Europe"]. In *En quête de sécurité* [*In Search of Security*], edited by Sebastian Roché. Paris: Armand Colin: 199–212.

Jazouli, Adil. 1992. *Les années banlieues* [*The Suburban Years*]. Paris: Le Seuil.

Kansal, Tushar. 2005. *Racial Disparity in Sentencing: A Review of the Literature*. The Sentencing Project, Washington.

Kerner, Otto. 1968. *US Riot Commission Report*. *Report of the National Advisory Commission on Civil Disorders*. New York: The New York Times/Bantam.

Labbé, Dominique, and Dominique Andolfatto. 2000. *Sociologie des syndicates* [*Sociology of the Syndicates*]. Paris: La Découverte.

Lapeyronnie, Didier. 1987. "Assimilation, mobilisation et action collective chez les jeunes de la deuxième génération de l'immigration maghrébine" ["Assimilation, Mobilizations, and Collective Action Among a Second Generation of North African Immigrant Youth"]. *Revue Française de Sociologie* 28(2): 287–318.

Lynch, James P., and Rita J. Simon. 1999. "A Comparative Assessment of Criminal Involvement Among Immigrants and Natives Across Seven Nations." *International Criminal Justice Review* 9(1): 1–17.

MacPherson, Sir William. 1999. *The Stephen Lawrence Inquiry, presented to the Parliament by the Secretary of State for the Home Department*. London: The Stationery Office.

Marshall, Ineke Haen. 1997. *Minorities, Migrants, and Crime*. London: Sage.

Maschino, Maurice. 2003. "La république et ses étrangers. Vers une police Black-Blanc-Beur" ["The Republic and its Outcasts: Towards a 'Black-Blanc-Beur' Police"]. *Le Monde Diplomatique* October: 10.

Myers, Daniel J. 1997. "Racial Rioting in the 1960s: An Event History Analysis of Local Conditions." *American Sociological Review* 62(1): 94–112.

———. 2000. "The Diffusion of Collective Violence: Infectiousness, Susceptibility and Mass Media Networks." *American Journal of Sociology* 106(1): 173–208.

Noiriel, Gérard. 1988. "Les jeunes d'origine immigrée n'existent pas" ["Young People with Foreign Origins Do Not Exist"]. In *Les politiques d'intégration des jeunes issues de l'immigration* [*The Politics of Integration Among Immigrant Youth*], edited by Bernard Lorreytte. Paris: L'Harmattan.

Roché, Sebastian. 2001. *La délinquance des jeunes. Les 13–19 ans racontent leurs délits* [*Juvenile Delinquency: 13–19 Year Olds Recount Their Offenses*] Paris: Le Seuil.

———. 2004. "La délinquencé auto-déclaré des jeunes judiciarises et d'un échautillon représentif des 13–19 ans, rapport final pour le Ministaire de la Justice" ["Self-Declared Delinquency of Youths and a Representative Sample of 13–19 Year Olds: Final Report for the Minister of Justice"]. Grenoble, France: Pacte-Université de Grenoble.

———. 2006a. *Le frisson de l'émeute: violences urbaines et banlieues* [*The Chill of Outbreak: Urban Violence and the Suburbs*]. Paris: Le Seuil.

———. 2006b. "Les reponse judiciaries locales á la délinquance des mineurs. Rapport pour le ministère de la Justice et le Conseil Général de l'Isère" ["Local Judiciary Responses to Delinquency in Minors. Report for the Minister of Justice and the General Council of Isère"]. Grenoble, France: Pacte-Université de Grenoble.

Rosanvallon. Pierre. 2004. *Le modèle politique français: la société civile contre le jacobinisme de 1789 à nos jours* [*The French Political Model: Civil Society Against Jacobinism from 1789 to Our Time*]. Paris: Seuil.

Roux, Guillaume. 2004. "Quelle évolution de la xénophobie en France?" ["What Evolution of Xenophobia in France?"]. Paper presented at a seminar of the Security and Society Department, Institut d'Études Politiques, University of Grenoble. Grenoble.

Scarman, Leslie George. 1982. *Report of an inquiry presented to the Parliament by the Secretary of State for the Home Department.* Harmondsworth, England: Penguin.

Schnapper, Dominique. 1994. *La communauté des citoyens: sur l'idée moderne de nation* [*The Community of Citizens: The Modern Idea of the Nation*]. Paris: Gallimard.

———. 2005. "Ideal et limites de la mixité sociale" ["The Ideal and Limits of Social Blending"]. *Informations Sociales* 125: 6–15.

Simon, Patrick, and Martin Clement. 2006. "Comment décrire la diversité des origines en France? Une enquête exploratoire sur les perceptions des salaries et étudiants" ["How to Describe the Diversity of Origins in France? An Exploratory Search for the Perceptions of Salaries and Students"]. *Population et Société* 425: 1–4.

Smith, David J. 1994. "Race, Crime and Criminal Justice." In *The Oxford Handbook of Criminology,* edited by M. Maguire, R. Morgan, and R. Reiner. Oxford: Clarendon Press.

———. 1997. "Ethnic Origins, Crime and Criminal Justice in England and Wales." In *Ethnicity, Crime and Immigration: Comparative and Cross National Perspectives,* edited by Michael Tonry. Chicago, Ill.: University of Chicago Press.

Smith, David J., and J. Gray. 1985. *Police and People in London.* The PSI Report, Aldershot, Gower, England.

Spilerman, Seymour. 1970. "The Causes of Racial Disturbances: A Comparison of Alternative Explanations." *American Sociological Review* 35(4): 627–49.

Sue, Roger. 2003. *La société civile face au pouvoir* [*Civil Society Faces Power*]. Paris: Éditions Presses de Sciences-Po.

Tonry, Michael, editor. 1997. *Ethnicity, Crime, and Immigration: Comparative and Cross National Perspectives.* Chicago, Ill.: University of Chicago Press.

Tournier, Pierre. 1997. "Nationality, Crime and Criminal Justice in France." In *Ethnicity, Crime, and Immigration: Comparative and Cross National Perspectives,* edited by Michael Tonry. Chicago, Ill.: University of Chicago Press.

Tournier, Pierre, and Mary France-Lise. 1996. La répression pénale des étrangers en France" ["Penal Repression of Foreigners in France"]. *Le Croquant* 22: 133–39.

Tribalat, Michèle. 1995. *Faire France.* Paris: La Découverte.

———. 2004. "Une estimation des populations d'origine étrangère en France en 1999" ["An Estimation of the Foreign-Born Population of France in 1999"]. *Population* 59(1): 51–82.

Tyler, Tom R. 1990. *Why People Obey the Law.* New Haven, Conn.: Yale University Press.

Weber, Eugen. 1976. *Peasants into Frenchmen: The Modernization of Rural France, 1880–1914.* Palo Alto: Stanford University Press.

Wieviorka, Michel, ed. 1997. *Une société fragmentée: le multiculturalisme en débat* [*A Fragmented Society: Multiculturalism Debated*]. Paris: La Découverte.

Zauberman, Renée, and René Levy. 2003. "Police, Minorities and the French Republican Ideal." *Criminology* 41(4): 1065–1100.

INDEX

Boldface numbers refer to figures and tables.

accountability of the police: in Chile, 126; disciplinary systems in Latin America, 118; in Slovenia, 102–7
ACPO. *See* Association of Chief Police Officers
African National Congress, 230, 233
Akinbingöl, Ö. Faruk, 290
Aktion Courage, 314
Albrecht, Hans Jörg, 13, 39, 48–49, 241
Allende, Salvador, 119
Alliance of Concerned Men, 157
Al Qaeda, 265
alternative policing, 19, 44–47, 165–6; in Brazil (*see* Grupamento Policial em Areas Especiais); in Mexico (*see* Community System for Security, Justice Administration, and Reeducation); in South Africa, 215–7 (*see also* Mapogo a Mathamaga). *See also* community policing
American Association of Retired Persons, 151
Amnesty International, 103, 314
Anderson, Elijah, 155–56
Angelo, Ubiratan, 204
Arendt, Hannah, 344
Argentina, 118, 127–8, 131
Armandi, Barry R., 110n3
Arslanián, León, 127

Assaneng, Patrick, 219
Association of Chief Police Officers (ACPO), 72, 75
Augustine, Jean, 344
Augusto de Oliveira, José, 200–202
Australia, 105, 152–54
Australian Capital Territory Restorative Justice Act of 2004, 152
authority/"authorization," legitimacy and, 10–11, 14
Aylwin, Patricio, 120

Ballard, R., 263
Barou, Jacques, 342
Baywatch, 224–5
Bebear,Claude, 344
Beckley, Alan, 79
Begag, Azouz, 364
Beghal, Djamel, 271n21
Beijers, Guillaume, 290
Benalli, Karima, 255
Berkes, Leslie J., 93
Bervoets, Eric, 288
Bijleveld, Catrien, 13, 36, 38, 48–49, 241
Bittner, Egon, 34
Blair, Tony, 66, 81n6, 267
Bleich, Eric, 263, 266
Body-Gendrot, Sophie, 13, 37–38, 42, 49–50, 242, 348

Boston Ceasefire project, 196
Bottoms, Anthony E., 65
Braithwaite, John, 12, 19, 40, 46–47, 61–62, 150–1
Braithwaite, Valerie, 150–51
Brawn, Claire, 285
Brazil: class divisions in, 39, 187–8; confrontations with police, persons killed and injured in, **189**; Grupamento Policial em Areas Especiais (*see* Grupamento Policial em Areas Especiais); police and community cooperation in, 19; police legitimacy in, 18; police organizations and their roles, **188**; police violence in, 187–9, 193; racial composition of the population of, 210*n*2; Rio de Janeiro (*see* Rio de Janeiro); violent crime in, 187, 189–91
Brigades Anti-Criminalité, 247
Britain: citizen involvement in oversight of the police, 105; community policing in, 64, 76; courts, perceptions of, 6–7; crime, trends in and perceptions of trends in, 69–71; ethnic minorities, biased treatment of and racial prejudice within the police, 48, 50; instrumentalism, populism, and the retreat from ideas of consent, 64–66; MacPherson report, 365; Morgan report on police practices toward minorities, 365; myth of legitimation in, 38; National Intelligence Model, 69; Neighbourhood Policing Programme, 76; New Public Management (*see* New Public Management); organization of police in, 67–68; partisanship in the legal system of, 7–8; police and the law, public views of, 16; police legitimacy, struggle to establish, 34–35, 37–38, 64; police ratings, trends in, **71**, 71–73; police standards and administrative review boards in, 263; policing, crime, and public perceptions, questions regarding, 63, 77–78; Policing for London Study (PFLS), 73–75; procedural justice, lack of concern regarding, 65, 78–79; race and perceptions of

police legitimacy, 6, 64; the "reassurance gap" between crime statistics and public perceptions, 72–73, 75; Reassurance Policing, 63, 75–77; reconceptualization of performance management, need for, 78–80; restorative justice in, 151–52; terrorism in, 264, 267; TOGETHER campaign, 76–77
British Broadcasting Corporation, 73
British High Commission, 223
Brogden, Mike, 110*n*.5
Brooke, Steven, 272
Brouard, Sylvain, 347, 364
Business Shield. *See* Mapogo a Mathamaga
Business Watch, 224–5

Cabezas, José Luis, 127
Caesar, Julius, 336
Canada: citizen involvement in oversight of the police, 105; multiculturalism in, 242, 344–5; police standards and administrative review boards in, 263; restorative justice in, 149
Cano, Ignacio, 12, 165, 210*n*9
Carabineros de Chile, 115, 120–1, 124–6, 128–36, 138–42
Carballo Blanco, Antonio, 196–202, 204–6
cargo system, 182*n*2
Carr-Hill, Roy A., 354
Cerqueira, Carlos Nazareth, 195
Chapman, Becca, 285
Chevènement, Jean-Pierre, 347
Chevigny, Paul, 210*n*9
Chiapas Media Project, 179
Child Welfare Council, 290
Chile: Carabineros, actions by, **139, 140–1**; Carabineros, public perceptions of, **134, 136, 137**; class divisions and public perceptions of the police, 40, 130, 133–7, 142; confidence in and legitimacy of the police, public perception of, 129–32; crime, rise in, 115, 121–4; crimes of greater social significance, changes in the rate of, **123**; legitimacy of the police, reasons for perceptions of, 139, 141–2; order *vs.*

freedom, public opinion regarding, 126–7; the police forces, changes in, 125–7; the police forces in, 120–1 (*see also* Carabineros de Chile; Investigative Police (Policía de Investigaciones de Chile)); police reform, comparison with Argentina regarding, 127–8; police reform and public opinion in Latin America, 117–9; police role in crime control, public perception of, 128–9; police service, public perceptions of the quality of, 132–5; political background in, 119–20; problems and Carabineros' response, ranking of, **138**; public insecurity, new actors in the response to, 124–5; public perception of crime and the police in, 16, 115–8, 128–39; the public's demands of the police, 135–39; Quadrant Plan, 126, 131–2; Quadrant Plan, percentage of people who know about by socioeconomic group, **132**

China, 20–21

Chirac, Jacques, 345, 375n1

Citizens for Better Care in Michigan, 151

Citron, Suzanne, 340

class and class divisions: in Brazil, 39, 187–8, 191, 193; in Chile, 40, 130, 133–7, 142; criminal justice systems and, 38–40; extralegal criminal-justice system in Mexico and (*see* Community System for Security, Justice Administration, and Reeducation); as generational struggle in South Africa, 231–33; German criminal law/justice and, 303–4; in Mexico, 39–40, 180–1; in South Africa, 216–7; vigilantism and, 169–70. *See also* neoliberalism; poverty

Clement, Martin, 345–6

code of silence, 95–96

Coetzee, John, 232

Colombia, 118

Comando de Policiamento em Áreas Especiais (CPAE), 204

Comaroff, Jean, 12, 36–37, 44, 52, 165

Comaroff, John, 12, 36–37, 44, 52, 165

Commission Against Racism and Intolerance, 315

Commission Nationale D'informatique et des Libertés (CNIL—National Commission on Computing Liberties), 345

Commission on Moroccan Youth, 290

Committee on the Elimination of Racial Discrimination, 314–5

communities: ethnically diverse (*see* diversity in societies); favelas in Rio de Janeiro, 191–4 (*see also* Rio de Janeiro); perceived police legitimacy and cooperation/support of, 15–16; policing in minority, 16–17 (*see also* minority groups); policing in poor, 199, 208 (*see also* Community System for Security, Justice Administration, and Reeducation; Grupamento Policial em Areas Especiais); "sensitive urban zones," 244; "the community" as governmental panacea, 218; transnational, emergence of, 305

community police forums (CPFs), 218–9

community policing, 35; American roots of, 110n5; in Brazil, 195–6, 211n15 (*see also* Grupamento Policial em Areas Especiais); in Britain, 64, 76 (*see also* Reassurance Policing); extralegal in Mexico, 173–5 (*see also* Community System for Security, Justice Administration, and Reeducation); in France, 247; in Slovenia, 97–101; in South Africa, 217–9 (*see also* Mapogo a Mathamaga). *See also* alternative policing

Community System for Security, Justice Administration, and Reeducation (CSSJAR), 44–46, 167–70; alliances with regional, national, and international rights organizations, 178–9; as alternative policing, 19; class divisions as background to, 39–40; legitimacy of, 37, 51–52, 175–81; origins of, 171–5; penal philosophy and sentencing practices of, 177; state campaign against, 178–80

Compagnie Républicaine de Sécurité, 247

Concerned Residents Association (Pretoria, South Africa), 222

Conquest for Life, 223

Conseil Representif des Associations Noires (National Representative Council of Black Associations), 337

Council of Europe: Commission Against Racism and Intolerance, 315; Slovenia and, 86, 89

courts: American and European procedures in, contrasting, 8; Constitutional in Slovenia, 89; deliberative democracy, as a site for, 155; discrimination in German, 319–20; fairness of procedures and perceptions of legitimacy, 31 (*see also* procedural justice); hypotheses regarding minority groups' perceptions of legitimacy of, 5; minority groups' perceptions of legitimacy of, 6–7, 16; mistrust of in Latin America, 118; partisanship in (*see* partisanship)

CPFs. *See* community police forums

criminal-justice systems: courts (*see* courts); extralegal in Mexico (*see* Community System for Security, Justice Administration, and Reeducation); fairness of legal authorities' actions, elements of public judgments regarding, 24–25; fairness *vs.* class as basis for legitimacy of, 38–40; in France (*see* French criminal-justice system); in Germany (*see* German criminal-justice system); "informal justice" and competing centers of legitimacy, 37; legal systems (*see* legal systems); legitimacy of, using restorative justice to increase, 157–8 (*see also* restorative justice); in the Netherlands (*see* Dutch criminal-justice system); police (*see* police and policing); politics of in Britain, 67–69 (*see also* Britain); publicization and professionalization of, 146–7; punishment, problems of legitimacy and, 303; restorative justice, 19 (*see also* restorative justice); in Slovenia, reform of, 88–90 (*see also* Slovenia)

CSSJAR. *See* Community System for Security, Justice Administration, and Reeducation

Daly, Kathleen, 150

da Silva, Graziella Moraes, 12, 39, 52–53, 165

Davis, Diane E., 169

Declaration of the Rights of Man, 337

deference-based legitimacy, 14–15

Delattre, Edwin J., 93

democracy: policing in, common traits of, 107; restorative justice and, 153–5 (*see also* restorative justice)

Derby-Lewis, Gaye, 235n18

De Rudder, Véronique, 342

deterrence-based approaches to order maintenance, 13–15, 21

Dirty Harry, 42

diversity in societies: French denial of, 18, 25, 245–6, 248, 333–46; pluralism as an approach to/conceptualization of, 18–19, 23, 25; policing strategies and managing, 18–19, 242; shared values *vs.* pluralism in response to, 23, 46–47; social order and, the problem of, 17, 242 (*see also* social-order maintenance); variation in causes, forms, and impact of, 17–18. *See also* ethnicity; immigrants; minority groups

Dominican Republic, 117–8

Donner, Olaf, 313

Driessen, Frans M. H. M., 289

Duhalde, Eduardo, 127

Duprez, Dominique, 256

Durkheim, Emile, 26, 38–39, 303, 338

Dutch criminal-justice system: attitudes towards the police by ethnic group, **295**; comparison of indigenous Dutch and ethnic minority groups' views on, 291–7; confidence of minorities in, 287–8; crime statistics, overrepresentation of ethnic minorities in, 281–2; criminal victimization of indigenous and non-indigenous Dutch, **283**; experiences of minorities in, 6; institutions and procedures of, 285–7, 296; the judiciary, perceptions of and trust in, 7; juvenile migrants' views on and experiences with, 297–8; legitimacy of, questions regarding, 284–5; literature on confidence of minorities in, 288–91; percentage of crimes reported by ethnic group, **296**; police legitimacy, minority groups' perceptions of, 18; procedural justice in, 20, 285

Economy and Society (Weber), 11, 23
El Salvador, 117–8, 118
England. *See* Britain
ethnicity: discriminatory practices in Germany based on (*see* German criminal-justice system); ethnic communities, negotiation of norms and values for police enforcement in, 19; the French criminal-justice system and (*see* French criminal-justice system); of German immigrants, changes in, 305–6; legitimacy and, 47–51; the Netherlands, ethnic minorities in, 278–3; sentencing in German courts and, 322–3; youth violence in France, as an element of, 254. *See also* diversity in societies; minority groups; race
ethnic profiling, 257–61
European Commission Against Racism and Intolerance, 37, 101, 103
European Committee for the Prevention of Torture, 37, 89, 103–4, 262
European Convention on Human Rights, 86, 89, 104, 324
European Court of Human Rights, 4, 37, 89, 104–6, 262
European Declaration of Human Rights, 4

failed states, emergence of alternative policing due to, 166
Fielding, Nigel, 41–42, 75
Fivaz, George, 234n11
Foucault, Michel, 218
Fox, Vicente, 168

France: assimilation/integration as minority policy, 341–3; colonial past as an issue in, 270n5; Commission Nationale D'informatique et des Libertés (CNIL—National Commission on Computing Liberties), 345; Conseil Representif des Associations Noires (National Representative Council of Black Associations), 337; criminal-justice system of (*see* French criminal-justice system); criminogenic areas and homegrown terrorism, 263–7; ethnic diversity, official refusal to recognize, 18, 25, 245–6, 248, 333–46; ethnic identities in, 254; head scarves banned in, 42, 248–9, 343; homicides in, 270n10; immigrants and crime in, 17–18; Institut National des Etudes Demographiques (National Institute of Demography), 343; intermediary groups, historical disavowal of, 337–8; minority, illegitimacy of the notion of in, 334–5; minority/racial identification, debate over, 343–6; myth of legitimation in, 38; National Committee on Deontology of Security (CNDS), 348; police in (*see* French police); republican mythology over immigration reality, the homogeneous nation and, 339–41; riots in, ethnic diversity and the crisis of legitimacy, 17, 25, 360–5; social malaise in, 246–7; Trintignac report, 341; unity emphasized over minorities, historical reasons for, 335–36; urban violence in the United States and, comparison of, 243–6, 363–5; xenophobia in, 248–9; youth/immigrants, perceived threat posed by, 250–2 (*see also* youth violence in France)
France-Lise, Mary, 359
France Plus, 342
Francis I (King of France), 335
French criminal-justice system: cases closed without conditions *vs.* under conditions, **357**; cases where police charges are dismissed by judges, percentage of, **356**; ethnicity according to

French criminal-justice system (*continued*) self-reported delinquency surveys, **370**; ethnic minorities and the fairness/ legitimacy of, 333–4, 346, 365–8; juveniles placed in an open or closed structure by a judge, **352**; minorities' experiences in, 6, 261–2; nationality according to self-reported delinquency surveys, **369**; nationality and ethnicity, comparing in a study of, 349–51; nationality and ethnicity, size of respective groups, 368–71; nationality and ethnic origin of juveniles sentenced in Grenoble, **351**; nationality of juveniles according to judicial files, **369, 371**; negative perceptions in self-reported surveys, 360–1; negative perceptions of, significance of, 359–60; perception of police and judiciary by ethnic origins, **361**; perpetrators of self-reported serious crimes by ethnic origins, percentage of, **373**; perpetrators of self-reported types of crime by ethnic origins, percentage of, **372**; self-reported delinquency and ethnicity, 353; sentences, percentage of types of, **358**; sentences handed down, percentage of types of, **359**; sentencing data, uses of, 352–3; sentencing of juveniles, ethnicity and, 355–9; survey data regarding, 348–9. *See also* French police

French police, 247–48; administrative review boards and professional standards for, 263; attitudes and values of, 256; ethnic discrimination/misconduct by, 260–1, 347–8; ethnic profiling by/racism of, 257–61; European charges of mistreatment by, 37–38, 262–3; judicial actions against defendants, ethnic discrimination and, 261–2; legitimacy, minority groups' perceptions of, 18; minorities, relations with, 6; minority juveniles, question of bias regarding, 354–5; minority representation within, 346–7; perceptions of by juveniles, **374–5**; public opinions of, 256; reforms, need for, 268–9; risk of juve-

niles being identified for a serious crime, **355**; trust in, difference between all adults and "new Frenchmen" regarding, 347

Freud, Sigmund, 26

Frühling, Hugo, 12, 40, 61–62

Fry, Louis W., 93

Fuentes, Claudio A., 126

Gaebler, Ted, 67

GAPE. *See* Grupo de Aplicaçao Prático-Escolar

Garland, David, 39

Geißler, Rainer, 322

German criminal-justice system: the corrections system and foreign prisoners, 325–6; crime participation rates of immigrants, 309–12; immigrants' views of police and discrimination, 317–8; legitimacy and discrimination in, problems of, 302–5, 326–7; police attitudes toward immigrants, 315–6; police contacts in birth cohorts of Germans, ethnic Germans, and foreign nationals, **311**; police discrimination and racism, strategies for preventing, 318–19; police discrimination and racism, 313–17, 326–7; pretrial detention, discrimination in, 320–1; probation services and juvenile court aides as potential source of discrimination, 321; public prosecution, discrimination in, 319–20; reporting of crimes, discrimination in, 312–3; sentencing, immigration status and, 321–4

Germany: the criminal-justice system in (*see* German criminal-justice system); criminology and criminological research in, theoretical concepts of, 302–5; data on ethnic and racial minorities, lack of, 307; deportation of foreign offenders by administrative authorities, 324–5; ethnicity of inmates in youth prisons, **308**; foreign nationals in population and crime statistics, **310**; immigrants and crime, 17–18, 309–12; immigration, developments in and questions raised

by, 305–9, 326; judicial system experiences of minorities in, 6; procedural considerations and perceptions of legitimacy in, 20; professionalization of justice, management of, 147; sociology of law in, shifting between traditions of, 39; Standing Conference of Ministers of Interior of German States, 319
Gordon, Milton, 264
Goudineau, Christian, 336
GPAE. *See* Grupamento Policial em Areas Especiais
Gramsci, Antonio, 38
Graterford State Penitentiary, 156
Graves, Wallace, 110*n*4
Great Britain. *See* Britain
Grupamento Policial em Areas Especiais (GPAE), 187, 208–9; Comando de Policiamento em Áreas Especiais (CPAE), 204; criticism and evaluations of, 205–8, 212*n*25; implementation and early performance of, 196–200; legitimacy and the effectiveness of, 52–53; limitations and expansion of, 202–4; origins of, 194–6; police "productivity," pressure to increase, 201; resistance to, 198, 204, 207–8; weak institutionalization, impact of and changes in command, 200–202
Grupo de Aplicaçao Prático-Escolar (GAPE), 195–8
Guatemala, 117

Habermas, Jürgen, 269
Hahn, Paul H., 93
Hamilton, V. Lee, 14
Haute Autorité de Lutte contre les Discriminations et pour l'Egalité (HALDE), 271*n*15
Hay, Will, 65
hegemony, 38–39
Hijlkema, A. G. M., 289
Hirsi Ali, Ayaan, 278
Hobbes, Thomas, 303
Honduras, 117, 127
Hood, Christopher, 81*n*8

Hood, Roger, 6
Hope, Tim, 110*n*5
Hopkins, Belinda, 151–52
Horman, Herbert, 110*n*3
Horton, Christine, 79
Hough, Mike, 12, 41, 53, 61
housing: large public projects, youth violence and, 251; public in the United States and France, 246; as a tool for social blending in France, 342
Houston, James, 93
human rights: Community System for Security, Justice Administration, and Reeducation and the indigenous peoples of Mexico, 178–9; Slovenia, violations in, 102–6

immigrants: assimilation *vs.* multicultural models in policing and social control policies, 18–19; attitudes of German police regarding, 315–6; crime rates and, 17–18; discriminatory practices in Germany against (*see* German criminal-justice system); in France, attitudes of "natives" regarding, 251–2; in Germany, 305–12; Muslims in France, 248–9, 254–5 (*see also* youth violence in France); Muslims in six European countries, **249**; in the Netherlands, 278–83, 288–90; perceptions of legitimacy and expectations brought from the home country, 36; as suspect category for French police, 258. *See also* diversity in societies; ethnicity; minority groups
Innes, Martin, 41–42, 75
Institut National des Etudes Demographiques (National Institute of Demography), 343
international law and organizations: influence on the process of legitimation by, 37–38; Slovenia, influence on, 37, 89, 103–4; transnational communities, emergence of and the internationalization of legitimacy, 305
International Self-Reported Delinquency (ISRD), 353

Investigative Police (Policía de Investiga-
    ciones de Chile), 115, 120–1, 125, 130,
    133
Ithutheng Trust, 224

Japan, 20
Jobard, Fabien, 261
Johnson, Jennifer, 12, 19, 36–37, 39, 44,
    51–52, 165
Johnson, Lyndon B., 269n3, 365
Jospin, Lionel, 347
Joutsen, Matti, 85
judicial systems. *See* courts
Junger, Marianne, 282

Kali, Sarah, 220
de Keijser, Jan, 7
Kelkal, Khaled, 265
Kelling, George L., 42, 79
Kelman, Herbert C., 14
Kerner, Otto, 269n3
Kerner Commission, 269n3, 365
Khosrokhavar, Farhad, 271n14
Klemenčič, Goran, 12, 35, 37, 61–62
Klockars, Carl B., 42–43
Klooster, E. M., 289
Kok, Wim, 278
Kriegel, Blandine, 340–41
Kriek, Hannie, 229
Kromhout, Mariska, 281
Kubink, Michael, 313

LaFree, Gary, 155
Lagrange, Hughes, 253
Langan, Sophie, 75
Latin America: honesty of the police in,
    118–9; police reform in, 117–8; vigilan-
    tism in, 169–70, 172, 178
law: common *vs.* civil (*see* legal systems);
    sociology of, 38–39
League of Human Rights, 260
Lefenyo, Irene, 218
*Le frisson de l'emeute: violences urbaines et
    banlieues* (Roché), 361
legal systems: courts (*see* courts); delibera-
    tive democracy, as a site for, 155; legiti-

macy based on European civil *vs.* Anglo-
    Saxon common, 5, 7; legitimacy of pro-
    cedures in civil and common,
    hypotheses regarding perceptions of, 8;
    oversight of police and, 105; partisan-
    ship in (*see* partisanship)
legitimacy: conceptions of, 4, 10–11,
    13–14, 23, 26, 116; data regarding, lack
    of, 23; ethnic identity and, 47–51 (*see
    also* ethnicity); hypotheses regarding,
    4–5; internalization of processes of,
    305; international perspectives on,
    11–13; myths of, 38; power, as alterna-
    tive to ruling based on, 25–27; privatiza-
    tion of, 36–37; procedural justice as
    basis for belief in (*see* procedural jus-
    tice); questions regarding, 3–4, 20–22,
    26, 33–34; social-order maintenance, as
    basis for, 9–11, 13–15, 30–31 (*see also*
    social-order maintenance); stories,
    drama, and symbols as sources of social
    knowledge required for, 40–42; working
    rules and formal rules, meeting public
    expectations through distinguishing,
    43–44
Leiken, Robert, 272
Le Pen, Jean-Marie, 248
Leteane, Joe, 218–19
Leuw, Ed, 282
LIFERS Public Safety Initiative Steering
    Committee, 156–7
Lins, Paulo, 210n7
Lobnikar, Branko, 110n4
Lopes, Tim, 211n22
López Obrador, Manuel, 168
Louis XIV (King of France), 335–6
Low, Antoinette, 218
Luhman, Niklas, 302
Lynch, James P., 359

Maarohanye, Jackie, 224, 234n10
MacCoun, Robert J., 54
MacPherson report, 365
Mafikeng Development Forum, 222
Mafisa, Motlatsi, 235n18

Magolego, Monhle John, 44, 216–7, 225–32, 235n13–18, 235n21
Makkai, Toni, 150–51
Malsch, Marijke, 13, 36, 38, 48–49, 241
Mandela, Nelson, 153, 234n10
Mao Tse-Tung, 30
Mapogo a Mathamaga: as alternative policing, 44–46, 217; backlash and political ambivalence regarding, 229–30; effectiveness as source of legitimacy for, 52; generational conflict in South Africa and, 231–32; Magolego, as creation of, 225–7; meaning of the name of, 227; modus operandi of, 227–9; police, relations with, 230–31
Marco Aurelio Santos, 201, 203, 206
Marißen, Norbert, 322
Martin, Henri, 340
Maruna, Shadd, 156
Marx, Karl, 38–39
Mashiyane, Mduduzi, 234n9
Matko v. Slovenia, 104
Mayne, Richard, 80n3
Mbatha, Shalo, 221
Meares, Tracy L., 109
media, the: politics of policing in Britain, impact on, 73, 77–78; riots in France and the U.S., representation of, 243; youths and youth violence, ethnicization and criminalization of, 250–51
Meško, Gorazd, 12, 35, 37, 55–56, 61–62, 93
Mexican Health Foundation, 168
Mexico: class divisions in, 39–40, 180–1; extralegal criminal-justice system in (*see* Community System for Security, Justice Administration, and Reeducation); Guerrero, militarization of, 172–3; Guerrero, origins of community policing in, 173–5; Guerrero, poverty and crime in, 171–2; honesty of the police, public beliefs regarding, 118; indigenous autonomy, activism supporting, 178; international organizations and informal justice in, 37; nonreporting of crimes in, 168; police legitimacy in, 18; public perceptions of law enforcement and judicial system in, 168–69; vigilantism and lynching in, 169–70, 172, 178
Mgulwa, Tutu, 219–20
Michelet, Jules, 340
Mincy, Ronald, 244
minority groups: courts, perceptions of legitimacy of, 6–7; the French criminal-justice system and (*see* French criminal-justice system); French refusal to recognize, 18, 25, 245–6, 248, 333–46; as a historical obstacle to creating unified nations, 335–6; hypotheses regarding perceptions of, 5; identification of in France, debate over, 343–6; immigrants (*see* immigrants); police, perceptions of/lack of confidence in, 5–6, 16–17, 25; policing and order maintenance in communities of, 16–17; policing approaches and, 18–19; race and poverty, linkage of and the law-enforcement experience, 25 (*see also* poverty; race); in Slovenia, policing and, 101–2; United States, relations with legal authorities in, 241 (*see also* United States). *See also* diversity in societies; ethnicity
Mirrlees-Black, Catriona, 285
Mittérrand, François, 362
modernization: New Public Management (*see* New Public Management); of the police in Britain, 67–69, 73–75
Molefe, Popo, 222
Monjardet, Dominique, 247
Montaigne Institute, 344
Moussaoui, Zacarias, 265
Mucchielli, Laurent, 255
Muslim Brotherhood, 267
Muslims, 248–9, 254–55; in France, 343; in the Netherlands, 278–9, 288–90; terrorism and violent delinquents, 264–7
Myers, Tom, 363

National Association of State Long Term Care Ombudsman Programs, 151
National Children's Service (Chile), 130

National Citizens' Coalition for Nursing Home Reform, 151
National Committee on Deontology of Security (CNDS), 348
National Human Rights Commission (Mexico), 168
National Intelligence Model (NIM), 69
national-level policing, 18–19
National Practice Guidelines on Restorative Justice in Schools, 152
National Women's Service (Chile), 130
Neighbourhood Policing Programme, 76
neoliberalism: class divisions and elevated crime rates associated with, 216–7; generational impact of, 233; the political economy of law and order in South Africa, role in, 231–3. *See also* class and class divisions
Netherlands, the: Child Welfare Council, 290; Commission on Moroccan Youth, 290; the criminal-justice system (*see* Dutch criminal-justice system); ethnic minorities in, 278–3; government, minority groups' perceptions of, 36; myth of legitimation in, 38; size of migrant groups in, **280**; terrorism in, 264; tolerance as a bygone era in, 277–8, 297–8
Netherlands Survey on Crime and Law Enforcement (Nederlands Survey Criminaliteit en Rechtshandhaving), 291–4
New Public Management (NPM): conceptualizing policing in Britain under, crudity of, 78; critique of as approach to modernizing the police, 73, 79–80; legitimacy eroded by approach of, 53; modernizing government through, 66–67; policing in Britain and, 67–69; Reassurance Policing, impact on, 76; unintended effects of target setting, 73–75
Newton, L. H., 94
Neyroud, Peter., 79
NGOs. *See* nongovernmental organizations
Nijsten, Cécile, 288
NIM. *See* National Intelligence Model

Ni Putes ni Soumises (Neither Whores nor Submissive Women), 249, 255
Noiriel, Gérard, 340
nongovernmental organizations (NGOs): discriminatory practices by German police against ethnic minorities alleged by, 314–5; in South Africa, 223–4
Novaes, Regina, 205
NPM. *See* New Public Management
Nthai, Seth, 228–29

Observatoire Nationale de la Violence Urbaine (National Observatory of Urban Violence), 252
O'Connell, Brian, 110n3
Oosthuizen, Pieter, 235n13
Open Society Foundation, 223
Oppermann, Antje, 322
order maintenance. *See* social-order maintenance
Orfield, Gary, 244
Osborne, David, 67
Otte, E., 289
Oudkerk, Rob, 277
Oussekine, Malik, 256
oversight of the police. *See* accountability of the police

PAGAD. *See* People Against Gangsterism and Drugs
Pagon, Milan, 95, 100–101, 110n3–4
Panama, 117
Paraguay, 118
Parker, Christine, 150
Parker, Tyrone, 157
partisanship: in Guerrero, Mexico, 177; hypotheses regarding perceived legitimacy of courts and, 5; professionalism *vs.*, perceptions of legitimacy and, 7–8
Peace and Development Project Western Cape, 223–4
Peace Brigades International, 179
Peace Corps (Gauteng, South Africa), 223–24
Peel, Robert, 146

People Against Gangsterism and Drugs (PAGAD), 222–3

performance management: new approach to in Britain, need for, 79–80; New Public Management (*see* New Public Management)

PFLS. *See* Policing for London Study

Phosa, Matthews, 230

Pinochet, Augusto, 119–20

police accountability. *See* accountability of the police

Police Act of 1996 (Britain), 68

Police Act of 1998 (Slovenia), 87, 89–90, 92

Police and People in London: A Survey of Londoners, 74

police and policing: alternative and informal forms of (*see* alternative policing); behavior and procedures, fairness of and perceptions of legitimacy, 16, 20, 24–25, 31 (*see also* procedural justice); the code of silence, 95–96; community cooperation and perceived legitimacy of, 15–16; community policing (*see* community policing); definitional problems bedeviling, 110n.5; democratic, common traits of, 107; the Dirty Harry problem, 42–44; honesty of in Latin America, 118–9; hypotheses regarding legitimacy of, 4–5; hypotheses regarding minority groups' perceptions of, 5; immigrants/ethnic minorities and approaches to, 18–19; injury risk and perceived legitimacy of, 14–15; institutional and political framework of, 34–38; minority groups' perceptions of/lack of confidence in, 5–6, 47–51; political and institutional framework, as situated in a, 34; process *vs.* results in the legitimacy of, 51–54; racial profiling as undermining legitimacy of, 16. *See also* names of countries for specific police forces

police cynicism: definition of, 109–10n3; in Germany, 316; police leadership as antidote for, 110n4; in Slovenia, 96–97

police ethics, in Slovenia, 92, 94–95

Policing for London Study (PFLS), 73–75

Politics of the Police, The (Reiner), 34–35

Politiemonitor Bevolking, 291, 294–6

Popper, Karl, 57n2

poverty: in Brazil, 39; in the favelas of Rio de Janeiro, 191–2; as a predictor of violence in Brazil, 188; race, linkage with and the law-enforcement experience, 25; urban violence and, relationship of, 244. *See also* class and class divisions

power: influence/control over others based on, 25–27; legitimacy and the monopoly on, linkage of, 303

private security industry, 124, 224–5

privatization: alternative policing (*see* alternative policing); of the criminal justice system, legitimacy and, 36–37; of governance in South Africa, neoliberalism and, 216–7; "market testing" in Britain and, 81n7; of policing in Mexico (*see* Community System for Security, Justice Administration, and Reeducation)

procedural justice: alternative justice/policing and, 46; American literature on, 3–4, 31–33, 36; British lack of concern regarding the American literature on, 65, 78–79; civil *vs.* common law systems and perceptions of, 8; the decision to trust law enforcement authorities, as a factor in, 54–56; the Dirty Harry problem, 42–44; Durkheimian tradition of research regarding, 38–39; ethnic minorities and legitimacy based on perceptions of fairness, 47–51; fair procedures and perceived legitimacy of police and courts, 24–25, 31, 35–36, 108–9; in the Netherlands, 285; police actions/behavior and legitimacy, 16, 20, 24–25; process *vs.* results in police legitimacy, 51–54. *See also* legitimacy

professionalism of the police: characteristics of, 94; in Slovenia, 93–97, 102–7

professionalization of justice, 146–7

Proudhon, Pierre-Joseph, 250

Quadrant Plan, 126

race: the Brixton riots and police legitimacy among black Londoners, 64; centrality of for urban violence in the United States, 245; civilian review boards and grievances against the police for racism, 263; ethnic profiling by/racism of the police in France, 257–61; German law enforcement, charges of racism in, 314; in the Netherlands, official non-registration of, 279–80; poverty, linkage with and the law-enforcement experience, 25. *See also* diversity in societies; ethnicity; minority groups
racial/ethnic profiling, 16, 257–60
Ramadan, Tarik, 267
rationality, in deterrence-based models of order maintenance, 14
Reassurance Policing, 63, 75–77
Rede Globo, 199, 211n22
Rehbock v. Slovenia, 104
Reiner, Robert, 34–35, 37–38, 43, 65
Ressam, Ahmed, 271n21
restorative justice, 62; building legitimacy through higher-quality justice, 157–8; declining legitimacy and the development of, 19; early-release restorative justice conferences, benefits of, 155–8; justice in many rooms, working out of, 154–5; legitimacy, bubbling up and filtering down of, 149–54; as reempowering victims while rebuilding legitimacy, 148–9; social order through using street legitimacy, building, 155–7; storytelling and, 150–3; truth and reconciliation commissions, 153. *See also* victims
Riebe, Steffan, 215, 218
Rio de Janeiro: crimes per 100,000 residents in, **191**; evolution of homicide rate in, **190**; favelas in, 191–4; police violence in, 193, 210–11n13; policing favelas in, 186–7, 194 (*see also* Grupamento Policial em Areas Especiais);

trends in the city and its favelas, **192**; violence in, 188–91
Rivers, Eugene, 267
Roche, Declan, 150
Roché, Sebastian, 13, 49–50, 242
Roma family, 100
Rosanvallon, Pierre, 338
Rousseau, Jean-Jacques, 338, 341
Roux, Guillaume, 343
Rovers, Ben, 282
Rowan, Charles, 80n3
Roy, Olivier, 266
Ruckauf, Carlos, 127–28
Rushdie, Salman, 48

sanction-based approaches to order maintenance, 13–15, 21
Sandoval, Luis, 124
SAPS. *See* South African Police Services
Sarkozy, Nicola, 365
Scarman, Lord Leslie, 64, 365
Schnapper, Dominique, 339–40
Seleko, Josephine, 221–2
self-regulation: legitimacy and, 11, 14–15; Weber on the development of, 26–27
Setumo, Chief, 221, 234n7
Sherman, Lawrence W., 285
Shute, Stephen, 6
Sicot, François, 253
Signal Crimes Perspective (SCP), 75
Simon, Patrick, 345–6
Simon, Rita J., 359
Sistema Communitario de Seguridad Impartición de Justicia y Reducación. *See* Community System for Security, Justice Administration, and Reeducation
Skogan, Wesley, 54, 109
Slovenia, Republic of: accountability of the police for mistreatment of citizens, 102–7; "approval ratings" of the police, 86–87; attitudes and values of police officers, impact of reforms on, 92–93; background information on country and police, 86–87; community policing in, 35, 97–101; the Constitutional Court, 89; democratic policing, impediments

to, 107–8; human rights violations, police accountability for, 102–7; institutional framework of the police, reform of, 87–88; international influences on, 37, 89, 103–4; legal framework, reform of, 88–90; minority groups and policing in, 6, 101–2; police legitimacy in, 18; police recruitment and training, reform of, 90–92; policing in a transitional society, 84–86, 107–9; procedural justice and legitimacy of policing in, 108–9; professionalism of the police in, 92–97; the Prosecution Service, 89–90

Slovenian Security and Intelligence Agency (SOVA), 87

Small, Stephen, 40–41

Smith, David J., 42, 61, 79, 353, 366

Smolar, Piotr, 272n22

Snel, Erik, 281

Soares, Luiz Eduardo, 196, 211n16, 211n21

social control model of social regulation, 14

social-order maintenance: alternative policing as a means for (see alternative policing); deterrence-based sanctions vs. legitimacy-based deference to authority, 13–15, 21; legitimacy as basis for, 9–11, 13–15, 30–31 (see also legitimacy); in minority communities, 16–17 (see also minority groups); power and legitimacy in, 25–27; the public and, 15–16; questions regarding, 20–21; shared values vs. pluralism and, 23; social diversity as a challenge to (see diversity in societies); strategies of, 9, 13–15, 18–19

sociology of law, 38–39

SOS Racism, 251

SOS Racisme, 342

South Africa: alternative policing in, 19, 215–7; community policing in, 217–9; generational conflict in, 231–3; kangaroo courts and tribal police dispensing justice in, 221–2; lone rangers dispensing justice in, 219–20; Mapogo a Mathamaga (see Mapogo a Mathamaga);

neoliberalism's impact on, 216–7; non-governmental organizations dispensing justice in, 223–24; police legitimacy, questions raised regarding, 231; the political economy of law and order in, 216–7, 231–3; private justice in, types of, 219–25; the private security industry in, 224–5; procedural considerations and perceptions of legitimacy in, 20; religion's role in dispensing justice in, 222–3, 226–7; restorative justice in, 153; women's groups dispensing justice in, 220–1

South African National Civics Organization, 220, 234n6

South African Police Services (SAPS), 217–20, 222

South African Stop Child Abuse organization, 220

Soviet Union, 20–22

Sparks, Richard, 65

Spileman, Seymour, 364

Staggie, Rashaad, 222

Standing Conference of Ministers of Interior of German States, 319

Stasi, Bernard, 248

state, the, failed and the emergence of alternative policing, 166

Steinberg, Jonny, 228

Stol, Wouter, 288

Sue, Roger, 337

Teodoro, Sebastião, 201

terrorism, criminogenic areas as breeding grounds of, 263–7

Thibaut, John, 65

Thierry, Amédée, 340

3-M, 152

Tiberj, Vincent, 347, 364

Tocqueville, Alexis de, 338

TOGETHER campaign, 76–77

Tonry, Michael, 346

top-down policing, 18

Tournier, Pierre, 359

Tribalat, Michèle, 339, 344

Trintignac report, 341

Truche, Pierre, 348
truth and reconciliation commissions, 153
Tyler, Tom R., 30–31, 55, 65

Umek, Peter, 93
Union of French Islamic Organizations, 267
Union of Soviet Socialist Republics, 20–22
United Democratic Movement, 229
United Kingdom. *See* Britain
United Nations (UN): Committee Against Torture, 37, 101, 103; International Crime Victimization Survey, 168; Special Rapporteur on Human Rights, 314
United States: citizen involvement in oversight of the police, 105; city-level approach to law enforcement in, 9; community policing rooted in the culture of, 110n5; confrontations with police, persons killed and injured in, **189**; criminal court procedures of contrasted with European notions of procedural justice, 8; group differences and law enforcement in, 25; immigrants and crime in, 17; immigrants and ethnic diversity, official policy regarding, 18, 242; importance of legitimacy in, 10; the judicial system as a tool against racism in, 260; Kerner Commission, investigation and report of, 269n3; myth of legitimation in, 38; partisanship in the legal system of, 7–8; police and the law, public views of, 16; police behavior as procedural justice, legitimacy and, 20; police legitimacy, gap between minority and white perceptions of, 6, 16, 18, 25, 241; police standards and administrative review boards in, 263; procedural justice, reasons for concern with, 65; racial disparities in sentencing, 357–8; restorative justice in, 150–1; urban violence in France and, comparison of, 243–6, 363–5
urban violence, by youths. *See* youth violence
Uruguay, 127

Valenzuela, Arturo, 119
van Gemert, Frank, 289
van Gogh, Theo, 48, 264, 277
van Hoek, A. J. E., 289
van San, Marion, 281
van t' Hoff, C. A., 289
Vicchio, Stephen J., 93
Victim Offender Conference Pilot Project, 223
victims: restorative justice as effort to empower victims (*see* restorative justice); retributive just-deserts movement as effort to empower victims, 147–8; sanitizing and disempowering of, 146–7
victim's rights movement, 19, 149
vigilantism, 169–70, 172, 178; in South Africa, 216, 219–25, 234n1 (*see also* South Africa). *See also* Community System for Security, Justice Administration, and Reeducation
Villepin, Dominque de, 365
violence, by youths in France. *See* youth violence in France
Viva Rio, 196, 199, 212n25
voluntary cooperation: legitimacy and, 9–11, 14–15; level of need for, 21

Waddington, Tank, 43
Walker, Lawrens, 65
Weber, Eugen, 336
Weber, Max: classical organizational principles detailed by, 104; on legitimacy, 11, 23; legitimacy as a positive concept, 35; power, authority, and compliance, analysis of, 63–64; self-regulation, development of, 26–27; the state's monopoly on the legitimate use of force, 36
Why People Obey the Law (Tyler), 30
Wieviorka, Michel, 340
Wievorka, Rachel, 344
Wihtol de Wenden, Catherine, 348
Wilders, Geert, 278
Wilson, James Q., 42
Wittebrood, Karin, 291

women, as victims of youth violence in France, 254–5

Women of Vision, 220

World Congress of Criminology, 2005, 157

Young, Iris, 152

Youngsters for Peace (Jovens pela Paz), 199

youth violence in France: ethnicity as a factor in, 254; gang rapes, 255; low-intensity and the appearance of juvenile delinquency, 251; minors placed under suspicion by the police, number of, **253**; police response and contribution to, 256–3; sources of/motivations for, 245, 253–4, 255–6; statistics regarding, 252–3; terrorism and, 263–67; and the United States, comparison of, 243–6; victims of, 254–6

Yugoslavia, Socialist Federal Republic of, 84–86. *See also* Slovenia

Zapatistas, 178

Ziembo-Vogl, Joanne, 93

Zimolag, Marta, 261